"I am so proud to have been part of this wonderful world of soap operas over the years. And I can never say enough about the fans. They have always been there to welcome me 'home' whenever I've come back to a show. (And if you want to know how many times I've done that – this book will tell you.)"

Kim Zimmer
Reva, *Guiding Light*

"When I came back to Days of Our Lives *it was like coming home to a family. And I include the fans, who are like an extended family. And if Hope has any problems remembering everything about her past, all she'd have to do is read all about herself in this book."*

Kristian Alfonso
Hope, *Days of Our Lives*

Seli Knows Soaps!

A well-known journalist in the soap opera world for more than 20 years, **Seli Groves** is eminently qualified to give you the inside soap scoop. She has been a contributing editor at *Soap Opera Digest* since the early 1980s, and is author of its monthly "Person to Person" feature. In addition, she writes the soap opera summary page and the news column "Soap Scraps" for King Features Weekly Service and contributes four syndicated soap opera columns for Hearst Daily Newspapers. Groves is a member of the Academy of Television Arts and Sciences Blue Ribbon Panel (which judges Emmy Award nominees).

A frequent television guest and a popular lecturer, Groves specializes in the topic, "The 60-Minute Sudsing of America: How Soaps Affect Our Lives." Even though she has never *personally* suffered from amnesia or multiple personality disorder, nor has she unwittingly fallen in love with her long-lost half brother, Groves *intimately* knows all the soap characters who have! She makes her home in New York City.

Foreword from a "Daytime Diva"

R obin Strasser has been a star of daytime television since the mid–1960s, when she created the role of Rachel Davis on *Another World*. In 1979, after a two-year stint on *All My Children* as Christina Karras, she metamorphosed (within two days) into Dorian Lord on *One Life to Live*. She won the Emmy for Best Actress in a Daytime Series in 1981. With impressive theater credits on Broadway and off, she has also made numerous prime-time appearances, which include movies of the week, *Coach*, and *Murphy Brown*. An AIDS activist, she also heads up a company that produces videos on women's health care issues.

Cover photographs:
Eileen Fulton
courtesy of Jan Goldstoff;

Thom Christopher
courtesy of Robert Milazzo;

Sonia Satra
courtesy of Bridget Petrella.

The *Ultimate* Soap Opera Guide

To Freddy, Dorothy, and Julie

SELI GROVES

The

Ultimate

Soap

Opera

Guide

Foreword by Robin Strasser

A Stearn Publishers Ltd. Book

The Ultimate Soap Opera Guide

Published by Visible Ink Press™
a division of Gale Research Inc.
835 Penobscot Building
645 Griswold Street
Detroit, MI 48226-4094

Visible Ink Press™ is a trademark of Gale Research Inc.

Most Visible Ink Press books are available at special quantity discounts when purchased in bulk by corporations, organizations, or groups. Customized printings, special imprints, messages, and excerpts can be produced to meet your needs. For more information, contact Special Markets Manager at the above address. Or call 1-800-877-4253.

Design: Tracey Rowens

Library of Congress Cataloging-in-Publication Data

Groves, Seli.
    The ultimate soap opera guide / Seli Groves.
          p. cm.
    "A Stearn Publishers Ltd. book."
    Includes bibliographical references and index.
    ISBN 0-7876-0508-5
    1. Soap operas—United States—Miscellanea.   I. Title.
PN1992.8.S4G76 1995
791.45'6—dc20   95-31831
                        CIP

Contents

Foreword by Robin Strasser	ix
Introduction	xi
Acknowledgments	xvii
A History of Soap Operas	1
All My Children	29
Another World	66
As the World Turns	106
The Bold and the Beautiful	143
Days of Our Lives	164
General Hospital	206
Guiding Light	258
Loving	304
One Life to Live	318
The Young and the Restless	356
Bibliography	401
Cast Lists	403
Fan Clubs	409
Daytime Emmy Awards	413
Soap Opera Digest Awards	421
Photo Credits	427
Index	429

Foreword

BY ROBIN
STRASSER

What an *ultimate* honor it is to be asked to write the foreword to *The Ultimate Soap Opera Guide*. What an ultimate opportunity to say a few words about something I feel very passionate about. For the past thirty years, I have been involved in three different "soaps," and I have seen many changes in daytime television and the way that it is perceived by the "industry," media, and the public at large. Justifiably, daytime television and its loyal fans have been allowed to "come out of the closet" and throw off the shroud of misconceived prejudices.

I can remember a time during an audition when a well-known movie director, whom I told I was working on a soap, said, "If you stand in s--- long enough, you begin to smell like it." Another time my manager told me to leave the soap material off my audition reel because it would destroy my credibility. I did not get the part and I fired my manager.

I can say with ultimate pride that my training, the mainstay of my creative growth and my financial well-being has come from daytime television, and I am grateful for all the years I have been privileged to be a part of it. The dedication of the producers, writers, production staff, crew, design staff — the hundred or more people it takes to create an hour of programming — is *awesome*! And, as far as I am concerned, the quality just keeps getting better.

Absent a subsidized national theater in every great American city, or a studio system like Hollywood of the 1930s and '40s, there is *no other* training ground for the young American actor *but* daytime television. *No one* can work faster, improvise quicker, and adjust to change on a dime better than a seasoned daytime actor, and the best of them, at all times, incorporate a sense of style and humor into their work. Soaps allow an actor to practice their craft, develop a character, get a regular paycheck, and acquire an extended family of discerning, vocal, and loyal fans.

And what about the fans? Haven't they been maligned, made fun of, and stereotyped, too? While the initial target audience of the original radio soaps was housewives, that audience has evolved to include college students, professional hockey players, the young, the old, the rich, and the poor — soap opera fans defy the demographics that attempt to define them. Soap fans are passionate and loyal, and their power to influence has helped raise and maintain the level of quality of their favorite "stories."

And talk about abundance! Five days each week, the viewer can get romance, fantasy, glamour, and delicious escapism. When soaps present issue-oriented stories, they help educate and raise the consciousness of the country. Like its origin, the Greek drama, daytime television is bigger than life, and at its best it reflects our culture and the times in which we live.

Soaps subsidize the New York theater scene. Broadway would not, *could not* exist without daytime television. Because soaps provide a financial foundation, actors are able to do theater, which pays marginally. It is always a joy for a daytime actor to "moonlight" in a play and delighted fans have shown up at theaters in New York, Los Angeles, and the Strawhat circuit to see their favorite actors.

Preeminent among journalists covering daytime television, Seli Groves has always been at the ramparts, defending the soaps against the slings and arrows of negative stereotypes and second class status. Seli knows her "stuff," and with *The Ultimate Soap Opera Guide,* so will you! Win bets! Never lose sleep wondering, "What *was* that actor's name?" Let *The Ultimate Soap Opera Guide* take you on a stroll down memory lane. I did, and loved every minute of it.

Introduction

Seeding the Family Tree

The first soap opera, at least in format, was *The Arabian Nights*. These were stories said to have been told by a woman named Scheherezade who was married off to a Pasha from Samarkand who had a penchant for beheading his wives on the morning after the wedding.

To avoid the fate of her predecessors, Scheherezade became a storyteller — but a storyteller with a difference. For 1,001 nights, she spun one tantalizing tale after another, stopping each story just before the denouement. Of course, her husband realized that he couldn't have her killed until the next evening when he learned how the story turned out. But Scheherezade managed to start another story just as she was finishing the last one. (The technique is familiar to soap fans who know that as one storyline winds up, another has already been skillfully woven in so that the audience won't fail to "tune in tomorrow.") So, again, the Pasha had to delay her execution.

This went on for almost three years. By this time, the couple had two children, and the Pasha, in true soap tradition, had fallen in love with Scheherezade. So, what might have been just another 1,001-night stand turned into a happily-ever-after love story.

The serial format achieved its peak in print form in the nineteenth century. Journal editors knew they could attract a continuing readership by featuring popular novels in installments. Charles Dickens and Sir Arthur Conan Doyle, two literary giants, gained fame both from and for the format. Dickens's American fans waited at seaports and train stations every week to pick up the new installment and read how last week's episodes turned out, and to learn what was in store for the characters this week.

At one point, Conan Doyle decided he had had enough of Holmes and killed him off during a fight with his arch enemy, Professor Moriarity, in Switzerland. But when Holmes's fans protested, Doyle brought him back, using a ploy that would later become a common device in returning "dead" soap opera characters to life. Holmes simply explained that he took another identity and allowed everyone except his brother, Mycroft (who had to send him money), to believe he was dead until he felt it was time to return to London.

Silent films, too, featured popular serial stars who were caught up in deadly dilemmas every week. A classic example was *The Perils of Pauline,* starring Pearl White. Each weekly episode would end with the heroine in mortal danger; sometimes lashed to a railroad track or grasping a crumbling ledge (which gave rise to the term "cliffhanger") or facing some other deadly peril. With each new episode, she was able to free herself, only to find new danger waiting before the next fade-out.

The First Real Soap Operas

The serial form reached radio in the 1920s. At first, the radio dramas were self-contained stories directed at housewives who listened while they worked in their kitchens. By the late 1920s and early 1930s, soap product manufacturers, such as Procter and Gamble, Palmolive, and Lever Bros., realized they could reach this important consumer group by producing their own daytime radio dramas, which, by 1932, had evolved into the serial format. Because these dramas were replete with all the elements of grand opera — joy, sorrow, love, hate, goodness, revenge, heroism, cowardice, pathos (and sometimes even bathos) — they were dubbed soap operas.

Although the genre began as a marketing mechanism to sell soap products to housewives, it soon became a unique dramatic art form, attracting some of the best actors in theater. Most of Orson Welles's Mercury Theatre group, including Agnes Moorehead, Joseph Cotten, and Everett Sloane, took roles on soaps. (Ruth Warrick, whom Welles cast to play the beautiful and dignified Mrs. Kane in *Citizen Kane,* later enjoyed a successful career in soaps.)

Irna Phillips, a Chicago-born University of Wisconsin graduate, writer and actor, became the Doyenne of Daytime Dramas. She introduced powerful, sometimes controversial themes into her scripts, and established the format for all subsequent soaps, both on radio and television. Phillips also established the conventional soap practice of taking story themes from the news of the day.

In 1933, Phillips created and starred in her first series, *Today's Children.* In 1937, she created *Guiding Light,* which made a successful transition to television in 1952, and is still on the air — the longest-running daytime drama. Other Phillips soaps that are still broadcasting are *Another World,* *As the World Turns,* and *Days of Our Lives.*

Two of Irna's protégés, Agnes Nixon and William J. Bell, created five soaps currently on the air: Nixon gave us *All My Children, One Life to Live,* and *Loving.* Bell created *The Young and the Restless* and *The Bold and the Beautiful.*

The "Soap Test"

Although daytime dramas are the most recognized form of soap operas, some prime-time shows have qualified for entry into the soap genre. Among them are the now-canceled *Dallas, Knots Landing, Falcon Crest,* and *Dynasty,* as well as the current series *Sisters, Beverly Hills 90210,* and *Melrose Place.*

For some mavens of the medium, the litmus test to determine whether a nighttime series qualifies as a soap opera is the series' story-telling approach. If it uses a device called an "arc," which carries a story-line over several episodes, it can be considered a soap or soap-like. Marnie Winston-Macauley, author and former writer for *As the World Turns,* suggests several criteria for determining whether a nighttime production is a soap or not a soap. First, Ms. Winston-Macauley points out that the show should have an ensemble cast. Relationships should exist among the characters portrayed by that ensemble cast. There should also be a trajectory (or arc) in which a storyline is carried over several episodes.

Another element in determining a show's qualification for the soap genre, according to Winston-Macauley, is concentration on heightened emotions. Melodrama must be involved. Winston-Macauley adds, "The show should have what we call in the business a DPU for each character: That stands for Direct Pick-Up." This means that, in a daytime drama, what happens to a character in the last episode is directly picked up for the next day's show. If it's a nighttime soap, the pick-up for each character is directly linked to the last week's episode.

For some people who ponder such cosmic considerations, the determining factor is much simpler: Does the audience care enough about the characters and their problems to discuss them with other fans at any great length, or at all?

Finally, we seem to be blessed with a gene that helps us recognize a soap when we see it, and recognize when it's not.

Or, as Gertrude Stein might have said, "A soap is a soap is a soap..."

xiii

Soaps and Society

The radio soaps of the 1930s and 1940s were populated by strong, independent female characters, many of whom held jobs outside the home. They were nurses, lawyers, doctors, and reporters. Although the women who listened to these shows spent their lives cooking, cleaning, and caring for their families, many a schoolgirl who came home for lunch listened to the shows. Who can tell how many of them began to think about making choices in life that their mothers couldn't?

Over the years, soaps have tackled some of society's most vexing problems: Spousal abuse, alcoholism, teenage pregnancy, rape, impotency, abortion, and, more recently, racial bias, childhood sexual abuse, sexual harassment, incest, homosexuality, and AIDS.

Soaps became the first medium to deal with AIDS and sexual responsibility. While some groups were railing against the use of condoms, the soaps began doing stories in which prospective lovers discussed ways in which AIDS might be prevented. In some of the storylines, the lovers took tests for HIV. Condoms were not only talked about, but shown.

An AIDS activist told me that when the soaps began writing dialogue for their characters about safe sex and the use of condoms before getting into bed with each other (or bedding down in a stable — a favorite soap trysting place), the message got out, and was received, by more people than could have been reached by any other medium.

Soaps manage to get a lot of important information out to an audience, while not losing sight of their prime directive: To Entertain.

Soaps and the American Family

Family is the common theme in all soaps. Relationships within the family ultimately affect all relationships.

Most soaps, especially those created by Irna Phillips or her protégés, Agnes Nixon and William J. Bell, feature two core families: the rich and powerful clan that lives high on the hill, and the strivers who live below. (Although families may be written out over the years, they are always replaced by other families.)

Unlike the British soap opera *Upstairs, Downstairs,* in which the two groups always travel in parallel lines, never to meet, most American soap operas have stressed the basic American concepts of equality and opportunity. This means the two groups not only get to meet, mingle, mate and marry one another, but sometimes wind up living next door to each other up on that hill.

Often, the older blue collar characters remain pretty much in place. But they'll see their children move up the economic and social ladders, sometimes by marrying into the upper stratum, but more often than not, making it on their own, frequently as doctors or lawyers. In real life, poor depression-era families idealized these two professions for their children, as did immigrant parents for their American-born offspring.

Soap Stuff

While the only absolute may be that there are no absolutes, we can be sure of one thing: on any given soap, at any given time, you can find any number of the following situations.

- *A character's hitherto unknown illegitimate offspring will come to town.*
- *A woman will fall in love with a charming young man, only to discover he's her half-brother.*
- *A twin will turn up (a) to assume the identity of the twin already in residence or (b) to allow an actor to return to the soap after his character has absolutely, irrevocably, died.*
- *A woman will have a child whose father is not her husband, and, sometimes, not even her lover.*
- *A character will be raped, but won't report it.*
- *At least one character will be a doctor or a lawyer.*
- *Someone will have a split personality.*
- *A character will have amnesia.*
- *Someone will be kidnapped.*
- *A marriage of long-standing will fall apart, but the couple will reconcile.*
- *A woman will be raped, but if the rapist has "audience appeal," the incident will be downplayed and the rapist redeemed.*
- *Someone will be unjustly accused of a crime.*
- *A character will marry someone she/he doesn't love.*
- *Someone will plot to break up another relationship.*
- *A character will be being blackmailed.*
- *Someone will be using an assumed identity.*
- *A character will have plastic surgery to change, completely, his/her identity.*
- *Someone will run the town's favorite bar, fast-food place, beauty salon, or disco.*
- *A woman doesn't want the baby she's carrying.*
- *A character will sue for a child's custody and expect to win because he/she is powerful and rich.*

- *Someone will marry someone else because he/she believes (erroneously) his/her previous mate is dead.*
- *An older woman will have a difficult time admitting her love for a younger man.*
- *A character is a virgin, and wants to change the status quo.*
- *Someone is a crooked business person or politician.*
- *A character is being threatened by the mob, a foreign power, or a CIA clone.*
- *A new woman in town is a reformed prostitute.*
- *A woman is a reformed prostitute whose former pimp arrives to unsettle her newly respectable life.*
- *Someone will kill the pimp.*
- *A character will return from the dead to find life has passed him/her by.*
- *Someone is named Jennifer, Hope, Victoria, Nikki, Jack, John, Amanda, Samantha, Lisa, Kim, Julia, Paul, Bob, Connor.*
- *A character will commit adultery because his/her spouse is cold, unkind, or unfeeling.*
- *Someone overhears part of a conversation.*

Acknowledgments

The Ultimate Soap Opera Guide was helped into print by many fine professionals, including but not limited to the following.

At the Academy of Television Arts & Sciences, thanks go to Tony Angelotti, Mark Rosch, and Murray Weissman. Thanks Marcia Lien of Associated Press and Liza Anderson at Baker Winokur Ryder. At Cap Cities/ABC, thank you Stacy Balter, Scott Barton, Amy Bordy, Robyn Cavalieri, Sheryl Fuchs, Carmen E. Gonzales, and Salli Schoneboom. Thank you Nancy Sherman of CBS; at D'Arcy Masius Benton & Bowles, Inc., thanks go to director of publicity Janet Storm, Nancy Liebowitz, Liz Susman-Karp, and Gillian Strum. I am grateful to Ed Geller; Globe Photos; John Goudas; and David Granoff Associates. Thank you very much Sylvia Gold at ICM. I appreciate the contributions of Diane Eckert at King Features Syndicate; Mike Casey and Selma Gore at The Lee Solters Company; L.S. Communications; Robert Milazzo; and The Museum of Television and Radio, New York. At NBC, thank you Paulette Cohn, Kim Grabowski, and Charles Riley; thanks to the New York Public Library of the Performing Arts. I am grateful to Thomas O'Neil; Bridget Petrella Public Relations; *Soap Opera Digest;* and *Soap Opera Magazine.* At Frank Tobin Public Relations, thank you Charles Sherman, Frank Tobin, and Jonathan Zaleski. Thanks Marnie Winston-McCauley and thanks Tom Trott. I am very grateful to Tony Rizzo for combing his copious backfiles and providing so many lovely photographs, for the story of soaps cannot be told without pictures.

Editorial fine-tuning came from editor Julie Winklepleck, Marie J. MacNee, Kathleen Dauphinais, Sharon Remington, Dean D. Dauphinais, and Kevin Hillstrom and Laurie Collier Hillstrom of the Northern Lights Writers Group. Marco Di Vita of The Graphix Group supplied his usual faster-than-the-speed-of-light typesetting. Finally, special thanks to Christine Tomassini and Kathleen Marcaccio, two super soap fans.

A History of Soap Operas

In the beginning was the word ... and the word was radio! America in the 1920s wasn't just a society of flappers, bathtub gin drinkers and coupon-clipping Wall Street speculators. It was also a time when radio became a part of most American's lives and when the only indigenous dramatic art form, which was midwifed by radio, namely, the soap opera, was born.

Daytime radio had, by this time, become an important companion for millions of women who worked at home cooking, cleaning, scrubbing, and laundering. Short, self-contained dramatized stories were beginning to air and soon gained popularity. The actors, or at least their voices, were welcome "guests" for women who spent long hours alone or in the company of small children. Listening to the stories was like sharing gossip with a friend or neighbor. Even better. Sure, maybe a wicked woman was out to get her sweet friend's husband, or that no-good son was spending his widowed mother's money in the pool hall, or the nasty landlord was about to evict the blind man whose son had (presumably) died in the Great War, but fifteen minutes after each story began, it would all come together with the good, indeed, inheriting the happy ending.

Most media mavens agree that the first radio drama that could qualify as a proto-soap was a program called *The Smith Family,* which was introduced in 1925. It starred a pair of former vaudeville troupers, Jim and Marion Jordan, who would later become famous as *Fibber McGee and Molly.* Each show ran for seventeen minutes. Although not yet a soap, *The Smith*

1

Family took on some rather daring story lines (which would become staples of the soaps later on) including one in which an obviously Anglo-Saxon Protestant Smith daughter dates a Jewish boy. The program also foreshadowed the soap format by linking many of its stories over several episodes.

In 1926, two white men named Charles Correll and Freeman Gosden created a comedy series called *Sam 'n' Henry,* which would later be called *Amos 'n' Andy.* It was a continuing story about two young black men from Alabama who come to Chicago and find themselves caught up in one humorous adventure after another. (*Amos 'n' Andy* would later be translated into a television serial starring black actors.)

As the show and its characters gained listeners, some astute advertising executives in New York saw the potential in having their clients sponsor an entire program. The Pepsodent people agreed that *Amos 'n' Andy* would be an effective show for them, and persuaded NBC to sell time in chunks of fifteen minutes, rather than in hour or half-hour segments. This resulted in the first national network presentation of a fully-sponsored daily serial. It was only a matter of time before other sponsors followed suit.

The first really "soapy" soap, *Clare, Lu 'n' Em* (somehow, back then, dropping "and" was the 'n' thing to do) debuted on NBC nighttime in 1932. It was soon followed by *Myrt and Marge* (which was to have been called the more folksy *Myrt 'n' Marge"* but someone obviously realized the announcer would have a problem repeating it). Both shows soon moved to daytime.

Clare quickly showed its early soap roots. For one thing, it was sponsored by a soap company, Colgate. For another, it introduced the husband with wanderlust: that is, his eyes wandered and the rest of him lusted. So now, we had two parts of the soap opera formula in place: sponsorship and the betraying (and, by inference, the betrayed) spouse. (And if spice were the plural of spouse, it would certainly describe most once and future soap relationships.)

Several months after *Clare,* et. al., debuted, happy NBC executives learned their daytime audiences were responding favorably to the show. They quickly introduced *Vic and Sade,* considered by many historians of early radio to have the most vivid, fascinating, fully fleshed-out serial characters, many of whom never appeared, but were simply spoken of by Vic and Sade.

That same year, another daytime drama was introduced that would mark the continuing evolution from proto-soap *(The Smith Family)* to pre-soap *(Clare, Lu 'N' Em)* to early soap opera. This was *Betty and Bob,* created by Anne and Frank Hummert, who would go on to create several more serials that were, in every respect, bona fide soap operas.

Betty and Bob dealt with the darker sides of domestic life. Although Betty and Bob Drake loved each other, it was obvious to the listeners that love does not always immunize a marriage against problems. After a while, the darker side tended to dominate the series; it became less mellow and more melodramatic, fitting more and more into the opening epigraph, — "[They] ... surmounted everything: divorce, misunderstandings, the interference of other people and, sometimes the worst of all foes, the passage of time." Most, if not all, radio soaps and, later, many television soaps, were introduced with a few lines that set up the premise of the serial. Called epigraphs, perhaps the most famous of which still opens each episode of *Days of Our Lives*: "Like sands through the hourglass, so are the days of our lives."

It may or may not be significant that when the increasingly doleful *Betty and Bob* ended their run on radio in 1940, they were replaced by a series called *Light of the World,* which was not a soap as such: the show featured dramatized stories from the Bible.

In 1933, with the Great Depression raging, and war clouds gathering in Europe, Irna Phillips, the prolific writer some call the Mother of Soap Operas (she would later become the mentor of two brilliant protégés, Agnes Nixon and William J. Bell) created and starred in her first serial on NBC. Called *Today's Children,* its epigraph gives us a definite impression of how much radio soaps were beginning to close in on the more modern effort, to wit — "And today's children with their hopes and dreams, their laughter and tears, shall be the builders of a brighter world tomorrow." (This epigraph is loaded with future buzz words that would become part of soapdom's glossary: "brighter world ..." "tomorrow ..." "hopes ...." "children ...")

On October 10, 1933, CBS introduced the concept of block broadcasting. Previously, shows could appear anywhere, any time. CBS decided to air all of its daytime talk shows, soaps or otherwise, one after the other in a continuing block format.

The first show that debuted that day was *Marie, The Little French Princess.* (She was dethroned in less than two years.) The next series on the schedule was *Easy Aces,* starring writer Goodman Ace and his wife, Jane. Their easy patter and Jane's delightful malaprops ("you could have knocked me over with a fender") made for easy listening. But it wasn't quite what the daytime audience wanted. It moved to NBC nighttime where it became a big hit.

The next show in the block format was another one of Irna Phillips's soaps, *Painted Dreams*. Irna had written it three years earlier for Chicago's station WGN. (Most of the early soaps were produced in and aired from Chicago.) Her *Today's Children* was taken from this original premise. *Painted Dreams* faded relatively quickly.

On October 16, 1933, CBS presented *Just Plain Bill,* which was originally a nighttime soap. The epigraph tells us that it's "The .... story of people we all know...." The show stayed on CBS for two years, then moved to NBC where it ended its run in 1955.

3

Ma Perkins first aired in Cincinnati: Cincinnati, of course, being home base for P&G. A silhouette of the city's skyline always appeared in the opening credits of the late and still lamented P&G television soap, *Edge of Night*.

On October 30, 1933, CBS introduced the soap opera that really shook up the genre. Rather than tell a story about folks like us, with their day-to-day sometimes wonderful, sometimes woeful experiences, *The Romance of Helen Trent* took its listeners into a world of fantasy and excitement. Although she wasn't quite like that latter-day libertine of soapdom, Alexis Carrington of *Dynasty,* Helen did quite well for herself. She was a widow with a mysterious past. The audience was told she had been a seamstress who quickly rose to become a famous Hollyood designer.

Helen enjoyed life even if it sometimes meant flirting with danger or even death. And, speaking of flirting, she had admirers — twenty-seven years worth of same — who obviously adored her although she was (and would remain for a quarter of a century) thirty-five years old! Most of her listeners couldn't help but be fascinated by that, since most of them had been told that thirty-five for a woman is the cut-off point between youth and desirability and encroaching old age and ultimate rejection as a sexual being. Helen Trent proved that living and loving can go on even though she might be approaching the onset of her "changes." (For today's reader, that word was a common euphemism for menopause.)

Meanwhile, over at NBC, a classic soap opera made its nationwide debut on December 4, 1933. Although its title was, technically, *Ma Perkins,* the proprietary factor stuck fast when the announcer introduced it as — "*Oxydol's own* Ma Perkins...." It was the first of the many-more-to-come Procter and Gamble owned, sponsored and supervised serials.

Ma Perkins was a bit of a "Mary Worth" comic strip character: full of advice and emotional pats on the back. She was a comforting soul who survived on air until 1960. (She might even have gone on to television but by then the country had become more than a mite cynical about those who posed easy answers to complicated questions. Someone like John Fitzgerald Kennedy had come on the scene and showed the country that platitudes don't solve problems, and that in time of trouble, one needed to search out solutions, not reach out for solace.)

In 1934 P&G introduced three serials: *Dreams Come True,* sponsored by Camay Soap, featured music, a singer, and his novelist woman friend (one of a number of women with careers who would populate the radio soaps for almost three decades well before Betty Friedan wrote *The Feminine Mystique*).

Home Sweet Home starred the movies' *Dead End Kid,* Billy Halop, whose sister, Florence, would become a regular on the nighttime series, *Night Court* some fifty years later; and *Song of the City.* Although *Song* lasted barely a year, it introduced the concept of the romantic doctor which

4

would be increasingly picked up on radio soaps, and become a standard on daytime TV later on when a physician's bedside manners could be seen instead of just being imagined.

In 1934 CBS aired *The Gumps,* based on a popular comic strip. Today most media historians remember it mainly for two people: writer Irwin Shaw and star Agnes Moorehead.

By the mid 1930s, the Mutual Network had become a successful competitor with CBS as well as with NBC's Red and Blue Networks. (In the 1940s, the FCC required NBC to divest itself of one of its two networks. NBC kept the Red Network; the Blue became the new American Broadcasting Company.) They were airing several popular late day shows, including *The Lone Ranger.* In 1934 they introduced their first soap, *Life of Mary Sothern.*

> When asked to name the first soap to be televised, most people will say *Search for Tomorrow.* But they would be off by at least five years. The correct answer is *Big Sister.* It aired on the old coaxial cable system in 1946. Although it had a total tenure of just fifteen minutes on the tube — not exactly a record for longevity — it was on long enough to qualify as the first televised soap opera.

In 1935 Mutual introduced *Backstage Wife.* The series went on to NBC where it ran until 1959. The epigraph ran almost as long as a first act — "The story of Mary Noble, a little Iowa girl, who married Larry Noble, handsome matinee idol, dream sweetheart of a million other women, and her struggle to keep his love in the complicated atmosphere of backstage life...." Years later, it would provide the basis of a brilliant classic satire of the soap medium by the comic team of Bob and Ray, which they called, *Mary Backstage, Noble Wife.*

Another 1935 soap, *The Story of Mary Marlin,* aired on the NBC Red Network until 1945; then was picked up by ABC in 1951. The series earns its asterisk in soap history because it ended ABC's long hold-out against a genre it believed had nowhere to go but down and out of public favor.

1935 also saw the daytime debut of CBS's *Mrs. Wiggs of the Cabbage Patch* whence cometh the inspiration for the Cabbage Patch Dolls that were all the rage some years ago. In the series, the desperately poor Mrs. Wiggs fights to keep her children from being taken by the state. She makes it clear that poor women give birth the same way rich women do, and that they don't find their babies in cabbage patches to be turned over to anyone who has the price of adoption.

1936 saw an explosion of soaps on the air: *The Goldbergs,* written by and starring the great Gertrude Berg, had been on nighttime since 1929. The show moved to NBC for Pepsodent in 1931 and then went on daytime in 1936 where it remained until 1945. Among its graduates were Van Heflin, Joseph Cotten, Marjorie Main, Keenan Wynn, Alfred Ryder, Everett Sloane and Metropolitan Opera stars, Mme. Schumann-Heink,

5

A school girl from Brooklyn named Beverly Silverman — nickname, Bubbles — sang the soap opera's theme song: "Rinso white, Rinso bright, Happy little wash day song." She would later sing in "real" opera as the great diva, Beverly Sills.

who played a lullaby-singing social worker, and Jan Peerce, who sang the cantorial prayers for religious holidays.

The serial was not so much a story about a Bronx Jewish family as it was a story about an American family who lived in the Bronx, in New York and whose religion was Jewish. Listeners all over the country responded to it. When the Goldbergs's son, Sammy, went off to war, Gertrude Berg's Molly received sympathetic and encouraging letters from mothers around the country whose children were also in the service.

Another famous writer, Elaine Carrington, came onto the daytime air with *Pepper Young's Family*. Mason Adams (later the hard-boiled editor on the television series *Lou Grant*) played Pepper. The show lasted until 1959.

Anne and Frank Hummert were represented in other 1936 soaps including: *David Harum* on NBC; *Rich Man's Darling* on CBS; *Love Song* on Mutual, and *John's Other Wife*. John was not a bigamist. The woman of the title was what used to be called an "office wife;" a devoted employee who put her boss's interests and needs above hers. In this soap, John's "other wife" was his adoring secretary who sometimes thought about trying to find a life for herself without John. But she would invariably go back to dutifully dusting his desk every morning and straightening his papers, even if it seemed unlikely that she would ever clean up after him in their very own little love nest.

The other major radio soap to debut in 1936 was *Big Sister,* sponsored by Lever Bros. The CBS serial started each episode with the sound of a clock tolling the hour. A voice would then intone: "Yes, there's the clock in Glen Falls' town hall telling us it's time for Rinso's story of Big Sister."

The show, which starred Alice Frost as Big Sister, and Haila Stoddard and, later, Dorothy McGuire, as her Little Sister, soon became a big hit. And, thanks to the popularity of the series, so did Rinso, which went to the top in sales.

1936 saw the introduction of three other soaps: *Modern Cinderella, Girl Alone,* and *Bachelor's Children.* In 1937, several soaps debuted. *Myrt and Marge*, which originally debuted on nighttime in 1931, was moved to daytime. Most of the year's entries faded quickly. Some lingered a while longer. One of them is still going strong. Out of the pack that aired that year, four are accorded more respect by chroniclers of the genre:

Hill Top House was considered one of the better written series. Those who have heard old wire transcriptions (Some shows were recorded on wire during a performance. Wire recording, or wire transcription, was a forerunner of today's tape technology.) say it was probably ahead of its time. The public was not yet ready to accept how it dealt with controversial issues, especially involving children. Its theme song was Brahms's "Lullabye." Its epigraph was: "A child crying in the night, a child crying for light."

The Road of Life, which was written by Irna Phillips, starred Don McLaughlin as Dr. Jim Brent (he would later star in Phillips's *As the World Turns*) and Virgina Dwyer (who later starred in Irna's *Another World*). Both shows were created by Phillips for P&G's continuing soap presence on television.

Our Gal Sunday is probably remembered most for its epigraph: "The story of an orphan girl named Sunday from the little mining town of Silver Creek, Colorado, who in young womanhood married England's richest, most handsome lord, Lord Henry Brinthrope. The story asks the question: Can this girl from a mining town in the West find happiness as the wife of a wealthy and titled Englishman?" And did anyone care if she did? Apparently, so. Many young women who were struggling through the Depression of the 1930s dreamed of marrying a handsome, titled Englishman who would rescue them from behind their counters in their local five-and- ten-cent stores. *Sunday*'s success made the dreams of her fans even sweeter. (One Baltimore belle named Wallis Simpson married the ultimate English Lord, King Edward VIII, around this time. The two would later party around the world as the Duke and Duchess of Windsor.)

As for *The Guiding Light,* this 1937 series remains the only soap that was created for radio that would make a successul transition to television. Irna Phillips's inspiration for the series came out of her meeting with a nondenominational Protestant minister in Chicago named Dr. Preston Bradley. Although Irna was Jewish, she had become an admirer of Dr. Bradley because she felt he expressed the same beliefs she held about peace and brotherhood. The hero of her serial, the Reverend Rutledge, was based on Dr. Bradley. He was the guiding light who showed the way for all who struggled to find their way out of the darkness of their lives. Reverend Rutledge's message — inspired by Dr. Bradley's philosophy — became the soap's early epigraph: "There is a destiny that makes us brothers / None goes his way alone. / All that we send into the lives of others / Comes back into our own."

The Rutledges, like Moses who didn't enter the Promised Land, didn't cross over into television in 1952. The Bauers, did, however. This family, whose patriarch had emigrated from Europe, continues to be represented on the series, although other "core" families — such as the urbane, sophisticated industrial-complexed Spauldings and the Lewises, whose rough edges have been oiled smooth by years of pumping an ocean of sweet petroleum out of the earth — have come on scene to represent the late twentieth century wealth and power base of American society.

Family relationships lie at the base of every successful soap. Although *Guiding Light* has moved between some of the brightest and

7

darkest extremes of the human condition, its focus on family remains as fixed as it was during the Reverend Rutledge's time.

Trouble Threatens the Soaps

In the late 1930s, a movement began to "clean up" the soaps. The country had already gone through a period when Shakespeare was being "censored" and Mae West had been arrested for daring to suggest that women can find sex a fun thing to do, and the movies had to meet certain "decency" requirements as dictated by the Hays Office. Now, the Auntie Septics (most of them were members of women's groups — some had ties to temperance societies who were still trying to restore Prohibition) attacked the radio soaps with their story lines about independent women and divorce, etc., which they said threatened the American family. Some male doctors said the soaps made men look weak in comparison to women, and *as everyone knows,* men are physically, mentally, and maybe even morally stronger than women.

The soaps survived the crusaders, largely because both the networks and the sponsors refused to let these money-making, soap-selling enterprises be flushed down the drain. But the Big Lie — about women's inferiority — really hurt the image of daytime drama. Since the soaps were considered a woman's medium, by inference, the soaps, therefore, had to be an inferior art form. Never mind that many of them were written by some of the best writers in the country — some would eventually win Pulitzers and Oscars — and performed by some of the best actors in the theater, the stigma stuck for years. It's only within the last twenty years that actors, producers, writers, and novelists, move freely among the various media — theater, literature, film, prime time, and soaps. Much of the credit has to be given to writers such as Agnes Nixon and William J. Bell, who wrote story lines that appealed to young people.

These young people responded and formed a new audience. Their numbers would also provide the next generation of new actors, writers, and producers who saw soaps as a co-equal in the panoply of the dramatic arts. College students formed soap-watching groups and wrote papers on soaps as part of their American culture classes. Even Broadway actors were competing for soap work between plays, and proudly listed their soap credits in the *Playbill* bios. Film and prime-time actors no longer saw soaps as a sort of elephants' graveyard where they might spend the last gasps of a dying career.

From a once-downplayed and unfairly downgraded medium, soaps have come into their own.

In 1938 Johnson Wax sponsored *Terry Regan: Attorney At Law* starring Jim Ameche, film star Don Ameche's amazingly sound-alike brother. Macdonald Carey, who would later go on to a successful film career, starred in the 1938 radio soap, *Woman in White.* Some thirty years later, Carey would debut in *Days of Our Lives* as the strong, sensitive Dr. Tom Horton, a role he would play until his death in 1994.

1938 was a good year for introducing several other new soaps. *Stepmother* starred one of the greatest actors in silent films, Francis X. Bushman. *Your Family and Mine* featured Lucille Wall, who would later become the first "mature" bride on television to wear white to her wedding because, as her friend and coworker, Jessie Brewer (played by the late Emily McLaughlin) made clear to her, unlike many women, she was actually qualified.

Stella Dallas, based on the book and film (the Barbara Stanwyk flick, not the latter-day interpretation by Bette Midler) debuted with Macdonald Carey in the cast. *Central City* featured four of the theater's finest: Arlene Fancis, Van Heflin (brother of the late Fra Heflin, who played Mona Kane Tyler on *All My Children*), Shirley Booth and Kent Smith.

The super hits of 1939 were: Elaine Carrington's *When A Girl Marries,* and *Young Dr. Malone,* which stayed on radio until 1960. The soap also had a television version which went on in 1958, but never caught on with the viewing audience. The biggest star of 1939 was *The Right to Happiness* created by Irna Phillips and cowritten with John M. Young. This was a spinoff from her successful *Guiding Light* series. Cast members included Gary Merrill and John Larkin. The show continued on radio until 1960. Unlike its older sister, however, it never made a successful TV transition.

The 1940s began with a long list of new soaps, including *Portia Faces Life,* also starring Lucille Wall as a bright young lawyer.

Film star Richard Widmark appeared on two soaps in 1941. (Actors sometimes not only played several characters on a soap, but appeared in several, especially if they all aired from the same studio.) He starred in *Home of the Brave,* which reflected the strong patriotic feelings of Americans as the country faced the growing threat of war, and *Front Page Farrell.*

Bright Horizon reintroduced characters from *Big Sister,* and in 1942, Irna Phillips reworked her series, *Today's Children,* and reintroduced it as *Lonely Women.*

> In some quarters, soaps are considered a lesser form of entertainment life. For that, we can probably blame those actors who still refer to it as a "training ground" for newcomers, when the genre is a well-established format whose casts include many seasoned veterans. We can also blame actors who let themselves be called "hunks" or "bitches" — and then wonder why they're not taken seriously. *ATWT* stars Margaret Reed (formerly Shannon) and Patrick Tovatt (Cal) have started a movement to bring soaps into full recognition as a dramatic form that deserves the respect and dignity given to the other media.

Years after his role on *The Right to Happiness,* Gary Merrill's then-wife, Bette Davis, would say, "The best acting in America is done on the soaps."

In 1943, with America fully engaged in World War II, NBC introduced a new P&G series called *Woman of America.* The serial began as a wagon train rolled westward. It then moved into the present. Its heroine, a descendant of that courageous pioneer, had her own challenges which she, too, faced with courage and conviction. The audience tuned out quickly. The listeners felt that if they wanted patriotism with their entertainment, they could get it at the movies with Betty Grable dancing on the deck of an aircraft carrier, or Errol Flynn single-handedly destroying a Japanese machine gun nest.

The success story of 1944 was *Rosemary,* an Elaine Carrington series starring such acting stalwarts as Betty Winkler, Virginia Kay, and George Keane, who would go on to take Broadway by storm in *Brigadoon* (and for whom the author later worked and got to meet many of his colleagues, all of them great performers, including E. G. Marshall and John Randolph).

By the mid-1940s, the output of new soaps slowed. Many folded within a year. Even Irna Phillips's much heralded *Masquerade* faded quickly. One major success was Jello's *Wendy Warren (Girl Reporter),* which featured real-life CBS newcaster Douglas Edwards playing a newscaster.

In 1948, the specter of television was haunting actors on the radio soaps. The prospect of converting to the new live, and increasingly popular visual medium wasn't a welcome one. Although live television was being done for weekly prime-time shows, the possibility of going on live every day was considered unworkable. No one, it was suggested, could memorize a new script every day. Televised daily dramas, they said back in 1948, was as unlikely a prospect as going to the moon before Buck Rogers did it in the twenty-first century.

Meanwhile, the ever prolific Irna Phillips had produced *The Brighter Day.* Six years later, in 1954, it moved into television. But as with all other radio soaps, except *The Guiding Light,* it too, failed to make a successsful crossover.

The next year, CBS introduced what was being touted as a sure winner. *King's Row* was based on the successful book and film which starred Ronald Reagan as a hapless football player who has his legs amputated by the jealous and incestuous doctor whose daughter Reagan's character loved. Reagan's classic line in that film after he came out of surgery was "Where's the rest of me?" Poor ratings forced CBS to amputate it from its schedule within a year.

By the mid-1950s, several soaps were already on television, among them *Search for Tomorrow, Guiding Light, Love of Life, As the World Turns,* and *Edge of Night.*

The networks were conceding the playing field to television. Radio soaps were fading and by 1960, most of them were gone. That same year, only one new radio drama debuted, CBS's *Best Seller,* which dramatized novels in serialized form. It had a brief tenure on the tube before the No Sale sign was hung up.

TV or Not TV? — No Longer a Question

Andy Warhol said that everyone of us will have our fifteen minutes of fame in our lifetimes. For *Big Sister,* in 1946, it was fifteen minutes that would go down in media history as the first bonafide televised airing of a soap opera. The next year, another radio soap, *A Woman to Remember,* also went on television for a brief run.

Despite the lack of audience response (most television set owners were still watching only prime-time shows), network television hadn't given up on the possibility of mounting successful daytime dramas. Soap companies, the traditional sponsors of the serials, were beginning to see consumers responding to television commercials more than they were to print ads. For them, (copy) writing potential was on the wall. TV was the future. And at one time or another, more than seventy-five daytime dramas have been on television since 1950. Ten daytime dramas are airing on network television today.

In 1950, NBC introduced the first soap made for television, *The First Hundred Years.* (NBC's parent company, RCA, had been experimenting with televised shows in the 1930s and resumed after World War II. This is probably why the network was better equipped for the role of TV soap pioneer.)

Although it didn't get much of an audience, *The First Hundred Years* proved the process could work. The next year, NBC moved *Hawkins Falls,* from nighttime to daytime. The series, considered a *Peyton Place* prototype with its large cast of interrelating characters, stayed on the air until 1955. NBC also introduced the much less successful series *Miss Susan* in 1951.

That same year, CBS and Procter and Gamble introduced that network's first three soap offerings: *The Egg and I,* based on a successful novel and film, *Love of Life,* and Agnes Nixon's *Search for Tomorrow.* Of the three, everyone bet on *The Egg...* to survive. But within months of its premiere, it had a great fall in the ratings, and never recovered. Both *Love...* and *Search...* went on for several decades.

11

Notable *Love of Life* Moments

Love of Life and *Search for Tomorrow* were first produced in a television facility CBS set up in the marble-walled nether regions of New York's Grand

When one of the young *Storm* actors, Christina Crawford (later to write *Mommy Dearest*), needed emergency surgery, her mother, Joan Crawford, stepped in to play her role for four episodes. Producer Gloria Monty was delighted. The publicity helped push the soap's ratings to new highs. Also, the appearance of a major film star on a soap helped raise the image of the medium.

Central Station. Mary Stuart, who starred as the oft-tempest-tossed Joanne Barron, was late for her first day's shooting because she got lost in that vast underground city beneath a city.

Christopher Reeve had a role on *Love of Life* where he was seen by Katharine Hepburn, who asked him to join her on a theatrical tour. After the tour ended, Reeve returned to the soap. His agent submitted him for the role of Superman and his alter ego Clark Kent in an upcoming film based on the comic book hero.

Reeve got the role and, in one of those coincidences that soaps dote on, as Superman scoured the lower levels of Grand Central Station in search of his nemesis, Lex Luthor, who had turned the marble-columned expanse into a resplendent retreat.

Love of Life was also the first soap to introduce a virile male character, Charles Lamont, who becomes temporarily impotent. This topic would later become a standard "shtick" on most soaps whenever a writer needed a reason to ease an otherwise almost boringly faithful wife into an affair. Soap writers, apparently, feel being in love with your husband doesn't have to include hearing him say 'I'm sorry' night after night.

Soaps Gone But Not Forgotten

From 1952 to 1955, CBS and NBC introduced twenty-one soaps, both original and radio crossovers, such as *The Brighter Day, Portia Faces Life, Road of Life,* and *One Man's Family.* Except for *The Guiding Light,* only one other series introduced in this three year period was successful: *The Secret Storm,* which went on the air in 1955 and lasted through 1974. One of *Storm's* producers was Gloria Monty, who would later move to *General Hospital,* where she created, among other memorable stories, the Luke and Laura phenomenon and the character of Helena Cassadine, "tailored" (as promised) for her friend, Elizabeth Taylor's guest stint. (Elizabeth wanted, and got, a role that would allow her to wear some of her jewelry.)

The Secret Storm was once called "the compleat" soap opera. It had drama, pathos, and humor, and was the first television soap to be produced with the same production values provided for prime-time shows.

In 1956, Procter and Gamble introduced two more soaps on CBS. *As the World Turns,* created by Irna Phillips, is still earning high ratings on the air. *ATWT*'s sister P&G soap *The Edge of Night,* a mystery melodrama whose cast included, over the years, Kim Hunter, Larry Hagman, Lori Loughlin, and Holland Taylor, lasted into the mid-1980s.

In 1960, ABC, which had been the lone long-time hold-out on radio soaps, finally aired one on television the same year, ironically, that radio was producing its last daytime drama. It was a short-run venture called *The Road to Reality.*

John Beradino, who plays Dr. Steve Hardy on *General Hospital,* and is a member of the original cast, told the author on the show's 30th anniversary in 1993, "We went on the air on April 1. No one expected us to last very long. But every year, on April 1, I tell myself, 'Well, we fooled them again.'"

But while ABC may have been playing the tortoise to its twin Energizer bunny competitors all these years, it surged into soap production three years later, in 1963, with the introduction of two soaps, *Ben Jerrod: Attorney at Law* and *General Hospital.*

Just as CBS guessed wrong on which of its three 1951 TV entries would succeed, ABC guessed wrong on its 1963 series, giving the nod to *Ben...* and not holding out much hope for its other show. Ben lost. *General Hospital* went on to make soap opera history.

In 1963 *The Doctors* debuted on NBC. It was a well-written show, over the years populated by some fine actors, including Kathleen Turner, Meg Mundy, and Alec Baldwin. It was the first show to deal with the pregnancy of an unmarried teenager and the first to feature an amneoscentisis for a mature woman.

In 1964 *The Young Marrieds* went on ABC, and Irna Phillips's newest series for Procter and Gamble, *Another World,* went on NBC. Only *Another World* is still on the air. Irna had hoped her new soap would complement her CBS series, *As the World Turns.* She wanted *AW*'s Bay City setting to be next to *ATWT*'s Oakdale site, and planned to have members of the dominant families on each show visit with one another. But CBS and NBC were not only rival networks, they had become fierce competitors for the daytime audience, with each hoping to stake out as much territory as possible to fend off any potential encroachment from ABC now that the youngest network made clear that it wanted a share of the daytime drama market.

The last half of the 1960s was marked by ABC's growing influence on the daytime scene. The network introduced six new soaps. Two of them, *Dark Shadows* (1966), and Agnes Nixon's *One Life to Live* (1968), became instant hits. (*Shadows* faded in 1971; *OLTL* is still on the air.)

Nixon's previous work had been with Procter and Gamble, which has always shown a more conservative approach to the way their daytime dramas are structured. With ABC, Agnes Nixon would be able to expand on her approach to dramatizing the human condition. Both ABC and the soap medium benefitted by Nixon's growing influence on daytime drama.

13

Dark Shadows was a Gothic mystery centering around a curious family named Collins, and their even more curious vampire cousin named Barnaby, who was played by Canadian actor, Jonathan Frid, and the increasingly curiouser and curiouser story lines which took the characters all over the space-time continuum.

The famous film star Joan Bennett played the mistress of Collinswood, the family domain. *Dark Shadows* also starred David Selby, Kate Jackson, Abe Vigoda, and Marsha Mason. The show, which lasted until 1971, became a cult favorite and eventually spawned two movies, a series of novels, and a nighttime version with British actor Ben Cross as Barnaby.

In 1965, NBC brought forth four new soaps: *Days of Our Lives, Moment of Truth, Morning Star,* and *Paradise Bay.* None of the shows did well. The latter three were cancelled quickly. *Days* was given a reprieve because Screen Gems (later, Columbia Pictures Television) believed in the people who created the series: Irna Phillips, Ted Corday, and Allan Chase. Irna also brought in her fellow Chicagoan, William J. Bell, as head writer. Screen Gems took a chance and within a short time, the soap's ratings began to rise, and it remains a high-ratings series to this day.

This was the first time a Hollywood film maker would get involved in producing soaps. It marked a change in production values, camera work, costuming, etc. The lesson would not be lost on Bill Bell when he created his own series, *The Young and the Restless,* for Screen Gems later on.

The 1970s marked several important events in the history of daytime drama:

Agnes Nixon's second soap, *All My Children,* debuted on ABC. The Nixonian passion for social relevance (the soap took a stand on the Vietnam War) and human relationships were given even fuller expression in this series. It set standards against which other soaps would be measured.

NBC's *Another World* produced its first "companion show" (the term the producers used instead of "spinoff") called *Another World: Somerset.* Three characters from the "mother" soap moved into *Somerset.* All the other characters were originals. Among the actors who appeared in these roles were JoBeth Williams, Ted Danson, Sigourney Weaver, Jameson Parker, and Ann Wedgeworth. The series earned its asterisk in soap history as the first daytime drama to go to an hour-length format. It should also have won recognition for one of the more intriguing murder-mystery story lines involving a character who disguises herself as a clown to poison someone's drink. The idea was to make sure any witness would be so impressed by the disguise, he or she wouldn't be able to remember any really relevant details.

(One can imagine the story conference where the dialogue writers considered how a witness might say... "Yes, detective, I saw a clown go into that room with a small bottle of green liquid, and later come out with the same bottle. Was it full or empty? I'm not sure. But I am sure the person was a clown. I'll never forget that red nose, that chalk white face, and those huge shoes flapping around, and most of all, how skillfully he got into that toy car that was already packed with other people dressed just like him.... Yes, I'm sure he was a clown. (Camera closes in on speaker's face) I couldn't have been mistaken about that..." (beat) "or could I?" (Camera pulls away slowly).)

In 1972, NBC premiered *Return to Peyton Place,* which the Peacock network expected would put another feather in its proud tail. Instead, the series laid an egg! If the networks learned anything from the *Peyton Place* experience, it was that daytime audiences prefer shows that are original to the daytime genre; not reworked versions of a nighttime series. As this is being written, *Return to Peyton Place* would be the last such derivative.

In 1973, CBS premiered *The Young and the Restless.* The soap was created by Bill Bell for Screen Gems. The company liked the way he handled the headwriting chores for their *Days of Our Lives* series and asked him to come up with a series of his own for them to produce. Bell and his wife, Lee Phillip Bell, who co-created the series with him, populated his new soap with characters drawn so vividly, as one reviewer said, "[They] seem to jump out of the screen at you...." *Y&R* has been among the top-rated series for over twenty years.

The Many Firsts of *Ryan's Hope*

The next important move on the daytime game board was made in 1975 by ABC with the introduction of *Ryan's Hope,* created by Claire Labine and Paul Avila Mayer. This series went on air with a slew of "firsts" to its credit:

It was the first soap to be set in New York City.

It was the first soap to have an Irish-Catholic core family.

It was the first soap to feature French-Canadian characters, the Beaulacs. (Claire's husband, publisher Clem Labine, is of French-Canadian origin.)

The young heroine, Mary Ryan Fenelli, was based on one of the show's writers, Mary Ryan Muniestieri.

The first actor to play Mary Ryan was Kate Mulgrew, who went on to a prolific career in prime time. In 1995, she debuted as Captain Kathryn Janeway on *Star Trek: Voyager.*

One of the Ryan sons, Frank, was a police officer before he earned his law degree and entered politics. He was described in the show's "bible" (the long-term story projection) as a "John F. Kennedy look-alike." Apparently, he was to have been assassinated by a Lee Harvey Oswald type after winning a major election, but the story line was dropped and Frank Ryan could get on with the business of being a New York City politician.

Maeve Ryan, the show's matriarch, was played by Broadway musical star Helen Gallagher, who had only one disappointment with her role in the ten years the soap was on the air: "I tried to persuade them to put more music and dancing into the show...I explained the Irish love to sing and especially love to dance and I would have enjoyed letting the audience see some examples of the wonderfully wild Celtic dances." But except for one short story line where Maeve gets involved in a ballroom dancing contest, she never did get to "stompin' out" the banshees.

Unsuccessful Spinoffs

In 1977, *Another World* spun off its second satellite (or "companion show"), *Lovers and Friends.* The series fell to the bottom of the ratings scale almost as soon as it was set free from its parent soap. It was taken off the schedule for a few months and reworked, and then retitled and resubmitted as *For Richer, For Poorer.* Alas, for NBC, the ratings continued to get poorer, and it was finally removed altogether. But the producers of *Another World* refused to be daunted by previous spinoff failures, and when 1980 dawned, they were sure they now had a winner with their new *AW* offshoot, *Texas.*

The success of the prime-time soap, *Dallas,* set off a country wide indulgence in anything that looked, felt, and even smelled Texan, including Stetsons, snakeskin boots, and fortunes based on cattle and oil. Texas had all that, and *Texas,* the soap, would also have all that, plus enough sex scenes in boudoirs and barns to inspire some people to consider selling Texas tapwater as an aphrodisiac.

In less than two years, this saddle soap was washed out of the schedule. The series forgot an essential element of daytime drama: while prime-time can do stories about people who like to make love, but love to make money even more — daytime needs to emphasize relationships as primary. Everything else is secondary.

In 1982, John Conboy, the former executive producer of *The Young and the Restless* (he applied Screen Gems' film making techniques to the soap) went on CBS with his own series, *Capitol.* It was a sleek, chic, beautifully produced and wittily written show about Washington D.C.'s movers and shakers, with some of the best actors in the business, including Constance Towers and the late Carolyn Jones in the talented cast. The deceptively down-home Carters (who were more sophisticated than many people suspected) left Washington to be replaced by the more glamorous Reagans, and *Capitol* reflected the shift from grits to glitz. The series even created a short term role for President Reagan's elder son, Michael. (It was said Michael hoped his mother, Jane Wyman, would be so impressed by his work, she'd give him a role on her series, *Falcon Crest*. She didn't.)

Bold New Directions

Meanwhile, Bill and Lee Phillip Bell had created a sister soap to *The Young and the Restless,* which they called *The Bold and the Beautiful.* CBS wanted the series as soon as it was air-worthy. But its afternoon schedule was filled up so, something had to give; that something was *Capitol.* The show ended with its plucky heroine, Sloane Denning, facing a firing squad, with the nasty Abdullah yelling, "Ready, Aim, ..."(FADE OUT)

By the early 1980s, ABC, the slow starter in the soaps race, and the baby of the then three major networks, saw its daytime dramas drawing increasingly larger shares of the viewing audience. *General Hospital* was rescued from almost certain cancellation by executive producer Gloria Monty and had become a top-rated series among college students as well the general audience. *One Life to Live* and *All My Children* continued to broaden their appeal. Most networks would have been content to just lean back and enjoy the lucrative sponsorship that comes with high-rated shows. But ABC always showed a sporting bent, and knew well that even if the score is heavily in your favor, you never stop trying to get another hit. (I should say, instead, score another goal, since most members of the New York Rangers and the New York Islanders were avid *AMC* fans — something actor Michael Tylo appreciated when he was on the soap as Matt Connolly. As a dedicated hockey fan (albeit for the Detroit Red Wings) Tylo enjoyed swapping rink-talk with team members who sometimes visited the set. For him, this was the "icing" of an already top role assignment.)

ABC wanted another soap on the network and turned to two of the most talented people in the medium, Agnes Nixon and Douglas Marland for product. And they produced. In 1983 their show *Loving* debuted. However, it didn't start on daytime as one would expect. Instead, the soap — which had a pre-debut party at Gracie Mansion, the home of New York City's mayors — premiered the night before with a two-hour movie starring Lloyd Bridges and Geraldine Fitzgerald, neither of whom went on to do the soap.

NBC moved to fill the slot left vacant when *Texas* was cancelled. The network turned to Jerome and Bridget Dobson, who had done well as writers for *General Hospital* several years earlier (her parents, Doris and Frank Hursley, created GH) to come up with a show. They did. And in 1981, NBC went on the air with *Santa Barbara*.

There were some who suggested the Dobsons set their soap in that city because it was the site of the Reagans' ranch. Maybe so. But unlike the way *Dynasty* made people see Denver as a power center, and *Dallas* did ditto for that city, *Santa Barbara* told stories about all its people: the rich and privileged, the poor and striving; the families of Anglo and Spanish

17

> Lloyd Bridges, who starred in *Loving*'s prime-time pilot, told the author, "I'm fascinated by the whole process (of daytime television) but I'm afraid it's just too much work...."

origins; and the Native American descendants of the area's original inhabitants.

The series was the first to feature a marriage between two people who might have walked in parallel lines if love hadn't created a bridge between them. Eden Capwell, played by Marcy Walker, and Cruz Castillo, played by A Martinez, were the most popular couple the soaps had seen in years. The soap also included Robin Wright as Eden's sister, Kelly. She left the role of the Capwell "princess" to star in the film *The Princess Bride,* which set her on the path to continuing film stardom.

Santa Barbara introduced innovative story lines involving people of different economic and ethnic backgrounds. The series boasted a fine cast which included, in the first year, another famous Santa Barbara resident, the eighty-plus-year-old Dame Judith Anderson as matriarch Minx Lockridge. She was the first person who had been given the equivalent of a knighthood by a British monarch (men become Sirs; women become Dames) to do a soap.

In spite of a steadily growing audience in its first year, the soap would soon start to go into a downward spiral caused, primarily, by lots of squabbling between and among writers and producers. As one actor told the author a year after *SB* was cancelled, "People were fired who knew what was going on, and were replaced by people who didn't know what the hell they were doing. So many mistakes in judgment were made, that by the time some knowledgable people were brought in to save it, it was too late."

The show lost stations around the country. This sent its ratings down, and its sponsors fleeing the sinking soap, which went down with all the Lockridges, Capwells, Cruzes who were still aboard.

Once more into the breach ... NBC tried again. And the newest soap to go on the Peacock's roost was, indeed, a soap with a difference. Although black characters and families had been increasingly represented on soap operas, the core clans were always white. In 1989, *Generations,* a new soap set in Chicago (ironically, the birthplace of soap opera) went on the air with an African-American family and a Caucasion family of equal weight and importance who shared links with each other that went back over several generations. The series featured some well-known film and soap actors, including Taurean Blacque, Joan Pringle, Jonelle Allen, Kelly Rutherford, Debbi Morgan, Kristoff St. John, and Richard Roundtree. Many of the stories dealt with important issues such as sickle-cell anemia, wife battering, racism, and interracial romances. The series was cancelled in 1990 because of low ratings attributed, apparently, to network affiliates who either dropped it completely or aired it late at night. BET (The Black Entertainment Network) picked it up for rerun showings.

The story of America's daytime soaps can't be told without at least a mention of the soap created to revolutionize the medium, the Christian Broadcasting Network's *Another Life.*

It's probably not understating the case when one says the media often misread the public's mind. In this case, the people at CBN assumed that most soap watchers were upset at having no daytime alternative to the continuing daily exposure to shows that were becoming more sexplicit all the time. That's when they came up with *Another Life,* which they promised would tell adult stories, but in a way that didn't offend the viewers' sense of decency and morality. Evil doers would be punished or, if possible, redeemed. Homosexuals would discover they could be "cured" of the sinful "lifestyle." Good folks might have problems, but would trust in God to see them through the worst — from sinful lusting to deadly diseases.

Another Life, which included veterans of the soap genre as producers, directors, actors, and writers, went on the air in 1981 and was cancelled less than three years later. That huge "silent majority" of viewers whom CBN presumed was waiting for them never showed up.

Milestones — Soaps As Reflections of Reality

Mary Stuart once told an interviewer that for several years after *Search for Tomorrow*'s debut in 1951, the only time her character could sit on a bed with an adult of the opposite sex was if she were fully dressed, and if that person was either her spouse or obviously ill. By the next decade, American society would witness a sea change in matters of mores and manners. Accompanying the changes in social attitudes was an explosion of medical marvels.

The soaps, perhaps more than any other mass medium, have acted as a giant reflector of milestones in history, including them in their dramatizations. Although the dramas are fictional, they mirror the reality of the events. For example, soaps very early on got out the message about AIDS prevention by incorporating the subject in their story lines. In some parts of the world, soap operas carry messages about family planning, child labor, and wife-beating, for example, to remote areas.

Many important events are noted in individual soaps' chapters; a few are noted here.

Medical Miracles

In the 1970s, Agnes Nixon took on the subject of postpartum depression on *One Life to Live* by having the character of Meredith Lord Wolek develop the debilitating condition after the birth of her son, Danny. Instead of having Meredith receive advice to "snap out of it," or "put your mind on other things," etc., the soap brought in Dr. Joyce Brothers, a real-life psychologist playing a psychologist. Dr. Brothers treated Meredith and helped her recover. Women from around the country who had been victims of post partum depression wrote in to say how much that story line had helped them. For many, it validated the fact that what they had suffered was real and not imaginary and was treatable.

In another important medical breakthrough story on *OLTL,* when the character, Samantha Vernon, was killed during the early part of her pregnancy, her close friend, Delilah Buchanan, had the fetus transplanted into her womb and carried safely to term. (Just a bit of trivia of a more whimsical nature: both Samantha and Delilah were ex-wives of the already much-married, and still more-to-wed Asa Buchanan, played by veteran film actor Phil Carey.)

The first mastectomy on a soap occurred on *The Young and the Restless* during the soap's first years on the air. The story line not only concerned the surgery that Jennifer Brooks (played brilliantly by actor Dorothy Green) would undergo, but also dealt with the post-operative counselling that helped her regain her self-esteem and see herseslf as no less a woman despite the loss of a breast. When asked why he introduced this story in an "entertainment" medium, then Executive Producer John Conboy said: "We knew we were entering a difficult area here. But we also knew that there were many women who have had to face this situation in real life and many people who were either related to these women or were friends who would experience anxiety on their behalf. While it's true we are an entertainment medium, we also recognized the fact that our audiences were becoming more sophisticated and wanted stories of substance."

Both *Loving* and *Guiding Light* introduced pap tests for cervical cancer into their story lines. Both soaps reported letters from hundreds of women who said the stories sent them to a gynecologist for the first time. Many others wrote to say the tests proved positive, but their cancers were caught in time and they would survive.

The Doctors had the first middle age (so-called "change of life") pregnancy and the first discussion of whether the child should be carried to term or aborted. There were discussions about possible birth defects that sometimes occur when the mother is middle aged. There were also discussions of how the child would affect a woman who already had a grown family. However, Maggie Powers (played by Lydia Bruce) miscarried before she could make the decision. The soap was criticized for using miscarriage as a convenient way to settle a potentially troublesome story line. To its credit, however, it did open up the subject of unplanned, possibly inconvenient pregnancies and the options for dealing with them.

Racial and Religious Breakthroughs

The 1960s reflected the country's turnaround on most racial issues and the soaps were among the first television media to follow through.

The first interracial soap romance occurred in 1967 with the debut of Irna Phillips's *Love is A Many Splendored Thing,* based on the film starring Jennifer Jones and William Holden, which was based on the autobiographical book by Dr. Han Suyin, a Eurasian woman, and her love affair with Mark Elliott, a war correspondent.

Irna picked up the story when Han's and Mark's daughter, Mia Elliott, (played by Nancy Hsueh, of Scottish-Irish-Chinese descent) has come to San Francisco from Hong Kong to study medicine. The young woman became involved with two men, Paul Bradley (Nicholas Pryor) and Jim Abbott (Robert Milli). Although Irna expected some objections over Mia's relationships from certain sections of the audience, to her surprise, the objections came mostly from CBS executives who were taking a preemptive strike against negative audience reaction (which, except for the usual claque of naysayers, never happened). When they ordered her to kill the Mia story line, Irna quit. Six months later, Mia Elliott left town.

It would be up to Irna Phillips's talented protégé, Agnes Nixon, to bend the interracial taboo a little more the following year. Agnes Nixon started her new series, *One Life to Live,* in 1968, with two important breakthroughs: This was the first soap to include black actors in the original cast playing "front burner" characters; that is, characters who would regularly be given dominant, not back-up story lines. Up to that point, black actors on soaps were relegated to playing domestics, hospital orderlies, or patients in charity wards. *OLTL* also presented the first "passing" story on soaps, which dealt with the sensitive question about denying one's black family because it's socially more expedient to allow oneself to be accepted as white.

Once the scattering of objections over the racial issue settled down, *OLTL* continued to make breakthroughs with story lines involving religious intermarriages. Victoria Lord (first played by Gillian Spencer, then Joanne Dorian, and, since 1971, Erika Slezak), was the very very WASP daughter of Victor Lord, the most powerful man in Llanview. Much to Daddy's dismay, Viki married an Irish-American Catholic reporter, Joe Riley (played by Lee Patterson), the son of a blue-collar family.

Riley's sister, Eileen (Alice Hirson), married a Jewish lawyer, Dave Siegal (Alan Miller). Former nun Jenny Wolek (Kathy Glass and later, Brynn Thayer) married Tim Siegel (played by Tom Berenger).

By the mid 1970s, the racial taboo on the soaps still hadn't been broken. There were hints on various soaps that an interracial friendship could be something more, but the series would stop short of showing the couple embracing, much less kissing.

21

In 1975, the writers on *Days of Our Lives,* which was owned by a film company, Screen Gems (later to merge with Columbia Pictures), realized the interracial romance taboo had been broken in movies; maybe it was time to do it for the soaps. They chose a likeable young couple named David Banning and Valerie Grant (played at the time by Richard Guthrie and Tina Andrews) for the story line. Banning was the son of one of the serial's major characters, Julie Horton Williams (played by Susan Seaforth Hayes). After an argument with Julie he left Salem to live with the Grants, a middle class black family, where he met their daughter, Valerie. The two fell in love. The relationship was treated with senstivity on screen, but negative viewer mail put a stop to the story before it really got started.

Although the taboo hadn't been broken, the decision by the *Days* people to take it as far as they did weakened it further. The next steps would not only be easier to take, they would take the story further along. By the 1980s, interracial romances were an accepted fact of soap opera life. Many of these romances led to marriage.

One relationship that nearly reached the altar was that of Drs. Cliff Warner (Peter Bergman) and Angie Hubbard (Debbi Morgan) on *All My Children.* (Hubbard had not yet left *AMC* for *Generations,* from which she later moved into *Loving.*) The two looked very much as if they would soon hang up a double-shingle. But Warner's estranged wife, Nina, returned. The couple remarried and left town. (Peter Bergman went to *The Young and the Restless,* while Taylor Miller decided to go home to Chicago to be with her husband and child full time.)

Wedding bells did toll for an interracial marriage on *General Hospital,* courtesy of Drs. Tom Hardy and Simone Labelle. In this case, it was the bride's parents who were initially against the marriage but, in time, came to accept their white son-in-law. However, Tom went off to do relief work in Somalia and when he returned in 1995, he realized he and Simone had grown apart.

Meanwhile, *General Hospital* revealed that during Edward Quartermaine's younger days, when he was a dashing naval officer, he had a relationship with a beautiful black woman who turned out to be Mary Mae Ward, and she bore him a child. When it was revealed that the Quartermaines were now related by blood to a black family, there was hardly a ripple of dissent from the soap's audience.

Times had changed, and people's attitudes had changed as well.

Meanwhile, *Days of Our Lives* had an interesting interreligious story line between Drs. Mike Horton and Robin Jacobs. Viewers were positive about this relationship. Letters from people identifying themselves as both Jewish and Christian were especially pleased about the way Robin was able to explain certain tenets of Judaism.

Much to the disappointment of the audience, the couple didn't marry (Robin felt the marriage might not work out and she married someone else, unaware that she was pregnant with their child). However, for the first time on daytime television, a Jewish wedding was shown and, again, the reaction from the audience was enthusiastic.

One of the most popular interracial/intercultural marriages was between Eden Capwell and Cruz Castillo (Marcy Walker and A Martinez) of *Santa Barbara.* She was the blue-blood, blue-eyed blonde princess from the mansion on top of the hill; he was the Mexican-American man from the *barrio* with a strong sense of identity with his American Indian heritage. John Conboy, who makes a habit of bringing distinction to whatever soap he works with, was executive producer during the evolution of the Eden-Cruz relationship. He said, "Not only are they popular characters, but so is their marriage. The viewers just won't let us break them up. Which pleases me because I also like having them married. They prove that marriage does not mean a couple comes to the end of a passionate relationship when they go from lovers to wife and husband. If anything, this marriage makes them a more exciting couple...."

In 1994, *The Young and the Restless* revealed that Jack Abbott (Peter Bergman) scion of the wealthy and influential Abbotts of Genoa City, had been in love with a beautiful Vietnamese woman during the Vietnam War. They lost track of each other for years. But Luan (Elizabeth Sung) moved to Genoa City. In time, Jack discovered she was his long-lost love; he also discovered that Keemo, her Vietnamese son, was his son as well.

The audience reaction to this story line has been enthusiastic all the way. There was, however, some resistance to the possibility that Chris Blair (played by Bill Bell's daughter, Lauralee Bell) might become involved with Keemo (played by Phillip Moon). However, the resistance was largely based on the audience preferring she either marry Paul Williams (Douglas Davidson) or remarry her ex, Danny Romalotti (Michael Damian).

Incest

Soap writers will tell you that dealing with incest is one of the most difficult things they do. Almost all of the incest stories have been between people who didn't know they were related, and who were stopped short of commiting the act by timely revelations.

The Young and the Restless has several such examples, involving characters such as Lauralee Brooks, Jill Abbott, Christine (Cricket) Blair and, more recently, Victoria Newman and Cole Howard, who was believed to be (but wasn't) her father's illegitimate son.

On *Days of Our Lives,* there was one of those almost-incestual story lines that involved Tom Horton's (the late Macdonald Carey) two children, Marie and his eldest son, Tom, Jr. The young man had been disfigured during the Korean War. He was also left with amnesia and believed he was Dr. Mark Brooks. He met Marie when he came to Salem. Because his face had been completely rebuilt, she didn't recognize him. The two were drawn to each other and fell in love. Through a series of twists in the story line, Marie learned she had been dreaming of a wedding night with her own brother. The shock was too much for her. She left town and entered a convent for several years.

A more recent *Days* story line involved the character of Victor Kiriakis (John Aniston) and a young woman named Isabella who were also drawn to each other. Later, it was revealed that Isabella was Victor's illegitimate daughter. Isabella felt guilty for having had erotic thoughts about the man who turned out to be her father. But Kiriakis reassured her that neither of them had to be ashamed or feel any guilt. They were simply reacting to a natural need to love one another, although at the time they didn't know why.

On *All My Children,* one might question the intense possessiveness of Palmer Cortlandt (James Mitchell) for his daughter, Nina (Taylor Miller) and his need to try to destroy any relationship she had with a man. Was it a form of incest, or just the need of a man whose wife had had an adulterous affair and was desperate to keep his world together? Maybe someday Palmer will say something that will give us an added insight into his psyche.

An actual story line involving a daughter's sexual abuse occurred for the first time on a soap on *Loving.* Soon after its debut in the early 1980s, the story line turned to the character of Lily Slater (Britt Helfer) who suffered a nervous breakdown because her father sexually abused her for much of her life.

The Bold and the Beautiful had the tragic story of a young man who thought he'd been sexually abused by his father, but learned it was his uncle who had committed the outrage.

Victoria Lord Riley Buchanan Buchanan Buchanan Carpenter (Erika Slezak) on *One Life to Live* started splitting off in more than her usual Niki Smith alternate personality in 1995 after learning she'd been sexually abused by her father, Victor Lord, and had suppressed the memory. As this is being written, Viki has split into Niki, Jean, Tori, Tommy, and Princess: the latter came out when Jean looked at a portrait of the Lord of Llanfair.

While some may feel using incest in soap stories is simply a way of getting ratings during sweeps, as one soap writer told the author, "the more these stories come out in the way we tell them, the more comfortable real victims might feel with themselves when they see that we never blame the victims for what happened to them. The villain is always the incestuous parent or relative...."

Vietnam: A Long Time Coming Home

Loving was the pioneer soap to deal with the problems of returning Vietnam veterans. The character of Mike Donovan (James Kiberd) experienced a frightening onset of delayed traumatic stress syndrome, a psycho-logical disorder marked by anger, alienation and depression. One of the most compelling parts of the story was told through Donovan's agonizing journey to the Vietnam War Memorial in Washington, DC. where he was finally able to come to terms with his ghosts. (Ironically, this story came full circle from the one Agnes Nixon first broke on *All My Children* over a decade earlier when she introduced the first anti Vietnam War statement on a soap, using a Mother's March for Peace story line to get the message across to her viewers.)

Another soap that dealt with the realities of post-traumatic stress was *Another World*. This time, however, a real Vietnam-era veteran, David Forsyth, playing a vet, John Hudson, contributed his experiences to the story. As Forsyth told the author: "I didn't want to risk the character of John Hudson turning into something he wasn't and couldn't be." Forsyth explained that most vets with this condition don't become wild, danger-ous, even criminal types. No one has to be afraid of them. As he said. "I wanted the audience to understand that they have problems and they need help and they need understanding."

The Young and Zestful:
Daytime's New Power Group

The audience for the soaps had begun to change in the 1970s when teenagers, who grew up watching television — and thought radio was only for playing music — started watching daytime serials when school broke for the summer. Soaps became aware of this new constituency and its potential for growth. A new season entered the soap medium: School Break Time. Story lines began to be written for those periods when teens would be watching; (between June and September and, again, during Christmas and Easter holidays). Actors were hired with whom the younger people could identify. *Love of Life,* the second series to debut on TV in 1951, introduced the first teenage girl on whom subsequent female teens would be fashioned. Stacey Corby (played by Cindy Grover) and the girls who followed her, showed the pain and confusion of someone hovering between childhood and adulthood. Teens tuned into soaps because for the first time they found characters with whom they could identify.

Douglas Marland created some of the most successful teenage char-acters on a soap when he was doing head writer duties for *Guiding Light*. Among them were were Tim Werner (Kevin Bacon), Kelly Nelson (John Wesley Shipp), and Morgan Richards (KristenVigard). These teenagers played out some remarkably sensitive, yet powerful love stories. Good buddies Tim and Nelson competed for the love of Morgan who was hav-ing a terrible time even thinking about having to make a choice. These

25

were not the kind of teenagers you'd find in Andy Hardy movies or even the *Beach Party Bingo* film collection, or certainly not in *Ozzie and Harriet*. These were young people whose hormones really flowed!

Asked how he was able to make young people so believable, Marland (who had already created the Scotty and Laura Baldwin (Kin Shriner and Genie Francis) romance and marriage on *General Hospital*) said: "I just remembered what it was like to be their age."

In the 1970s, teenage pregnancy was becoming a reality in the real world, It was reflected in the first teen pregnancy story line on *The Doctors*. The expectant teenager, Greta Powers (Jennifer Houlton), the daughter of two of the soap's major medicos, Drs. Maggie and Matt Powers (Lydia Bruce and Jim Pritchett) had her baby and faced the problems of being a single mother — a story line which made clear to any teenager watching that babies are not always cuddly, cooing bundles of joy: they get sick and colicky and they need constant attention.

The Young and the Restless was the first new soap geared for both the traditional viewership and the new audience that was coming out of the baby boomer demographics.

Homosexuality on the Soaps

About ten years ago the author asked a soap writer what story line she predicted would not run any time soon. "Stories about homosexuality," she said. "The audience won't accept them. And I'm sorry about that. We could do a lot with this subject." She explained that there was still too much distortion about the subject for a soap opera to try to deal with it. "We would only be asking for trouble," she said, noting that it would be easy for any religious leader looking for publicity, "to use us...."

Fortunately, progress, even when slow or disguised, doesn't always wait for "the right time." Although the soaps moved slowly on homosexuality, they did at least move.

Another World was the first soap to introduce a story line that suggested male homosexuality. Sandy Alexander (Chris Rich), one of Mackenzie Cory's several out-of-wedlock children turned up in Bay City with a past he wouldn't talk about. He finally admitted to having been a call boy in Las Vegas; in other words, a male prostitute. However, there are sources who have indicated that Sandy was supposed to have been the first homosexual character on a soap, but Procter and Gamble and the network felt the audience would reject the story and the soap.

One might wonder at the logic of having the character become a prostitute instead.

On *All My Children,* a young woman character undergoing therapy becomes attached to her psychologist. When the woman says she's a lesbian, her patient persists in wanting to expand the relationship, insisting that she loves her and wants to be with her sexually. The doctor, played by Donna Pescow, however, shows her that her affection comes out of feeling that someone cares for her and wants to help her. The story was told gently, and with sensitivity, and while some viewers took exception to it, most fans accepted it.

As the World Turns introduced the first male character who openly acknowledged his homosexuality. Hank Eliot (Brian Starcher), experienced both acceptance and rejection. At least one of the young male characters was especially hostile, almost as if he were setting up a deliberate barrier between them. However, as the story line continued, Hank's adversaries began to see him as a human being whose sexual orientation was increasingly less important to them.

Soaps and the Oldest Profession

Prostitution came into soaps with television. There were attempts to sort of "sneak" it in during radio days with comments about girls going wrong, fallen women, etc. But it wasn't until the movies opened up their storytelling that the vamp, or scarlet woman, or lady of the evening became part of the general entertainment culture. Greta Garbo and Jean Harlow played the roles of women with — as the old song said, "Love for Sale." Joan Crawford's *Sadie Thompson* showed us not only a woman who is a prostitute, but also a woman who is a victim of religious hypocrisy.

Perhaps because most soaps are written by women, prostitutes were never judged harshly or treated as if they were pariahs. If the women suffered, it was because of their pimps or johns. If anything, the writers tried to show that the women fell into the life usually because they had to help their families, or care for a child, or were too young to understand the seduction of a pimp.

The soaps also showed that the prostitute can change her life.

All My Children's Donna Beck (Candice Earley) was a prostitute. She tried hard to break out of the life and when she did, she wound up marrying Dr. Chuck Tyler and Palmer Cortlandt.

On *Another World,* the characters of Clarice (Gail Brown) and Blaine (Laura Malone) were introduced as prostitutes. They courageously defied their pimps, left the life, and each found a man who loved her. (As previously noted, there was also a male prostitute story line involving Sandy Cory.) *Another World* has also dealt with prostitution with characters such as Sharlene Frame and her daughter, Josie; both of whom also broke from the life.

On *One Life to Live,* the character of Karen Wolek (Judith Light) gives sexual favors for gifts and is then blackmailed into working for a pimp. She, too, left the profession.

General Hospital's Bobbie Jean Spencer (Jackie Zeman) walked the docksides of Port Charles when she was first introduced to the audience. She later put that life behind her and became a registered nurse and even considered going to medical school.

The audience will criticize any story line at any time. But no soap writer to whom the author has spoken can recall when a prostitution story was singled out for criticism. It's almost as if many women know deep within themselves that in seeing a story line involving a prostitute that there but for the grace of God or any other fortunate happenstance go any of us.

What the soaps have done with prostitution that no other medium has done so well is show these women not as sinners, but as victims of whatever choice they may have made or allowed to be made for them.

The Not-So-Distant Mirror

The historian Barbara Tuchman showed us through her books that our lives today have been shaped by history. In this overview of the history of America's soap operas, we can see the changes in American culture and mores as reflected in the themes and story lines of this popular medium.

Can soaps do more than reflect? Can they actually change things?

Can soaps change bigotry to tolerance?

Can soaps stop spousal abuse?

Can soaps stop racial and religious bigotry?

The answer to each question is probably no. But if we inserted the word "help" before the subject: if we asked, for example, will soaps help stop spousal abuse; help change racial attitudes, etc., then the answer is yes. By helping to make people aware of situations they might not otherwise be concerned with, the soaps do something very important — they shed light in dark corners.

The best of the soap writers — Irna Phillips, Agnes Nixon, William J. and Lee Phillip Bell, John Conboy, Douglas Marland — never promised their work would change the world. But what their work has done is make us look at the world in ways we might not have otherwise.

All My Children

B ob Dylan was singing about the times and how they were "a-changing" back in 1970 when *All My Children* debuted on ABC on January 5, of that year. The ferment of the 1960s had spilled over into the new decade. The war in Vietnam was still raging. Student protests were continuing. Social issues that had exploded in the previous decade were now dominating literature and politics.

It was during this questioning, searching period in our history that *All My Children,* created by Agnes Nixon, one of Irna Phillips's protégés, found its voice.

In its more than twenty-five years on the air, *All My Children* would deal with stories taken from the daily newspapers, the evening news, and medical journals. What was happening in America and what was happening to Americans and American families would happen in Pine Valley, USA, as well.

All My Children almost didn't get on the air. Having begun writing the outline in 1965, Nixon lost a suitcase containing the only copy of the manuscript. A few months later, the suitcase, with the manuscript safely tucked inside, was found and returned to her. Nixon, who had developed a relationship with Procter & Gamble through her association with Irna Phillips, worked on the material until she felt it was ready, and submitted the manuscript to P&G. They took an option on it, but soon after dropped it, explaining there was no available network time for it. Nixon, assuming that P&G didn't think the material was good enough, tucked it away in a file drawer and forgot about it.

Some time later, when *Another World,* one of the last soaps Irna Phillips created for P&G (with the assistance of Bill Bell) ran into ratings problems, Agnes was asked to come in as head writer. Within months, Nixon had the soap back at the top of the ratings scale. ABC, which was a late starter in developing original soaps for television, had been trying to play catch-up with CBS and NBC. Of the seven soaps they produced after 1963, only *General Hospital* and *Dark Shadows,* a late afternoon Gothic series, were successful. The network was impressed by Nixon's success with *Another World,* and asked her to create a soap for them. By that time, Agnes had been working on developing a series she called, *Heaven and Hell;* she submitted the work to ABC. They loved the concept of the new soap, but were wary of the title. In 1968, the series debuted as *One Life to Live,* and became an instant success. When ABC asked her for another soap submission as quickly as possible, Nixon was about to tell them she was fresh out of ideas until her husband reminded her of the manuscript in the file drawer. Nixon took it out, had it retyped on fresh white paper, and sent it to ABC. The network loved it. Less than two years later, *All My Children* went on the air, and with Rosemary Prinz playing one of daytime's first liberated women, Amy Tyler, quickly won a new audience from among a growing number of young women who were coming of age during this turbulent social period, and who felt other soaps had passed them by.

The soap that almost wasn't, became the soap many others would use as a standard for fine dramatic content mixed with socially relevant issues. In short: A soap for our times.

Original Cast

Actor	Character	
Michael Bersell	Bobby Martin	Frances Heflin ....Mona Kane
Mark Dawson	Ted Brent	Larry Keith ....Nick Davis
Paul Dumont	Lincoln Tyler	Susan Lucci ....Erica Kane
Mary Fickett	Ruth Brent	Ray MacDonnell ..Dr. Joseph Martin
Hugh Franklin	Dr. Charles Tyler	Rosemary Prinz ....Amy Tyler
Karen Gorney	Tara Martin	Jack Stauffer ....Chuck Tyler
Richard Hatch	Phillip Brent	Christine Thomas .....Kate Martin
Hilda Haynes	Lois Sloane	Diana deVegh ....Anne Tyler
		Christopher Wines .....Jeff Martin

First Air Date: January 5, 1970 / ABC

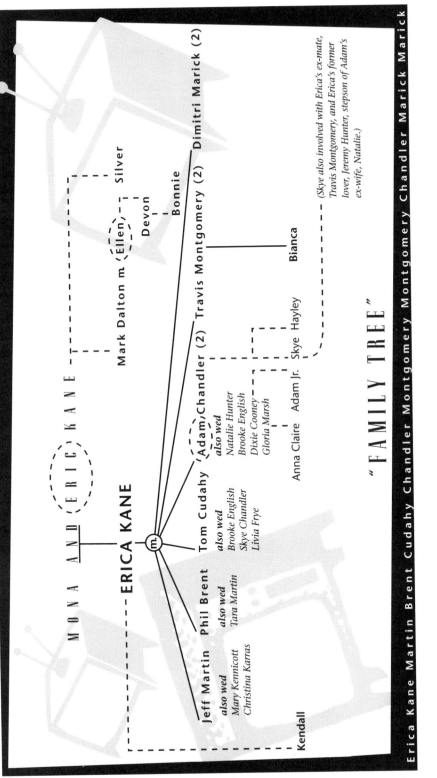

MONA AND (ERIC) KANE

ERIC KANE

Mark Dalton m (Ellen)

Silver

Devon

Bonnie

ERICA KANE

m.

Dimitri Marick (2)

Travis Montgomery (2)

(Adam) Chandler (2)
also wed
Natalie Hunter
Brooke English
Dixie Cooney
Gloria Marsh

Bianca

Skye   Hayley

Anna   Claire   Adam Jr.

Tom Cudahy
also wed
Brooke English
Skye Chandler
Livia Frye

Phil Brent
also wed
Tara Martin

Jeff Martin
also wed
Mary Kennicott
Christina Karras

Kendall

"FAMILY TREE"

(Skye also involved with Erica's ex-mate, Travis Montgomery, and Erica's former lover, Jeremy Hunter, stepson of Adam's ex-wife, Natalie.)

Although everyone who lives or passes through Pine Valley makes some mark on the community, no one person has affected, or been affected by, more of Pine Valley's citizenry than the once and forever Erica Kane Martin Brent Cudahy Chandler Montgomery Montgomery Marick Marick, played by Susan Lucci.

31

Erica Kane Martin Brent Cudahy Chandler Montgomery Montgomery Chandler Marick Marick

The People of Pine Valley

Agnes Nixon wanted Pine Valley to be the sort of community in which most of us would like to live. She had it set close to New York City so that its characters could move back and forth between their homes and whatever awaited them in the metropolis beyond.

In her original bible for the series, Agnes Nixon wrote: "...The Valley will be what everyone thinks of when they think of 'home'...."

Over the past quarter of a century, Pine Valley has been home to some of the most popular soap characters. On the following pages, you'll find some of the actors and characters considered by most *All My Children* fans as representative citizens of Pine Valley.

The Founding Families

There were four "founding families" when *All My Children* debuted in 1970: The Brents, the Martins, the Tylers and the Kanes. Below are descriptions of the characters who set the world of Pine Valley in motion.

The Brents

Ted Brent, played by Mark Dawson; husband of Ruth Brent, a registered nurse; and adoptive father of Phillip Brent. A former football player who felt his best years were behind him, Ted became increasingly difficult to live with. He drank heavily and made Ruth feel guilty for spending time at her demanding job. He began to suspect she was having an affair with one of the doctors, Joe Martin (she wasn't). He was killed in a car accident and, ironically, Ruth turned to Dr. Joe for comfort. Comfort led to love, etc., etc.

Ruth Brent (See Ruth Brent Martin under The Martins.)

Phillip Brent, originally played by Richard Hatch, then by Nick Benedict. Phillip was raised as the son of Ruth and Ted Brent. However, he was actually the son of Ruth's sister, Amy Tyler (Rosemary Prinz) and Nick Davis (Larry Keith).

If ever the term "star-crossed lover" applied to any man, it applied to Phillip Brent. He was in love with Tara Martin, but Erica Kane had set her sights on him. She accidentally overheard the truth about his parentage and told Phil about it. After he confronted Ruth and Ted, who confirmed the story, he was overwhelmed by the sudden torrent of truth and fled. Ted followed him and was killed in an automobile crash. Phil went to New York, had an accident, and developed amnesia. He even forgot

Tara. Tara turned to Chuck Tyler (grandson of Charles and Phoebe), who proposed. She accepted, but Chuck became ill before they could marry. Meanwhile, Nick found Phil and with his memory restored, he returned to Pine Valley. When he received his draft notice, he and Tara decided to marry the day before he shipped out of Pine Valley. Unable to find a minister, they exchanged their own vows (a device that would become popular with soap couples over the years). Phil went to Vietnam unaware that Tara was pregnant. He was listed as missing in action and presumed dead. When he finally returned home, he learned Tara had married Chuck and they had a son.

By this time, Erica had married and divorced Jeff Martin and was feeling lonely. Phil was feeling vulnerable. She seduced him and became pregnant. When he learned she planned to abort the child, Phil insisted he wanted to marry her. In 1974, she became his first wife; he became her second husband. After suffering a miscarriage, Erica had a nervous breakdown. While Erica was away, Phil deduced that he, not Chuck, was actually little Phillip's father. Once again, he confronted Ruth for the truth, and once again, she confirmed it. This time instead of running from it, he ran to Tara and they reaffirmed their love. When Tara's marriage to Chuck ended over his attraction to a former hooker named Donna Beck, Tara and Phil were married in 1976. Young Phillip demanded to be called Charlie. Poor Phil was upset that he couldn't get his own son to even *like* him. Phil and Tara argued about how the boy should be raised. Although their marriage was strained, they stayed together. The family left for Washington, D.C. in 1979 where he was supposed to take on a "mysterious" government assignment.

The Martins

Kate Martin, matriarch of the Martin clan; mother of Dr. Joe and lawyer Paul Martin. She was played by Kay Campbell from 1970 to 1985. (The role was previously played by Kate Harrington and Christine Thomas; both in 1970.) When Ms. Campbell died in 1985, the role was not recast. The soap held a touching memorial for the character. For the actors, it was also a loving tribute to their long-time colleague and friend.

Joe Martin, a doctor. Played by original cast member, Ray MacDonnell. Husband of Ruth Martin; father of Jeff, Bobby, and Tara by his first marriage; father of Joey with Ruth; adoptive father of Phil Brent and Tad Gardner. In a recent talk with the author, MacDonnell said, "Joe Martin is a decent, moral man, who judges no one. He is concerned, always, with doing the right thing himself, and if there were more like him in this world, we'd have fewer problems."

33

Bobby Martin — Dr. Joe Martin's son who disappeared from the soap early on — may be gone, but he's not forgotten by those who "knew him when." Each time there's a sound off stage, someone — either cast or crew — will inevitably ask, "Is that you, Bobby?"

Agnes Nixon created a pioneering storyline involving spousal abuse, which would run through 1982. The story involved the upper-middle-class characters of Curt and Leora Sanders. With Dr. Joe Martin's help, Leora stopped denying that her husband was abusing her; she also stopped blaming herself for any of the emotional or physical abuse he inflicted on her. Eventually, Leora went to a woman's shelter where she learned to stand up for herself. Curt went to Chicago and was not heard from again.

Ruth Brent Martin, a nurse. Played by original cast member, Mary Fickett. Widow of Ted Brent; wife of Joe Martin. Adoptive mother of Phil Brent (who was actually her sister, Amy's child); step-mother of Tara, Jeff, and Bobby Martin; mother of Joey Martin; adoptive mother of Tad Gardner, son of Opal Gardner and the vicious Ray Gardner. Young Tad, who had been brutally mistreated by his father, was left in the care of the Martins, who eventually adopted him. Furious that Tad had been taken from him, Ray vowed revenge. Raped by Gardner, Ruth endured a difficult recovery which was eased largely by the love and support of her husband. Mary Fickett told the author: "What I've always appreciated about Ruth is her strength. Many things have happened to her, and she's buckled a few times, but she's always been able to fight her way back. Her strength gives strength to others. And, if you haven't guessed by now, I like her. She's the sort of woman every woman would love as a friend."

Bobby Martin, played by original cast member Michael Bersell. One of three children of the widowed Dr. Joe Martin; brother of Jeff and Tara. Bobby disappeared from Pine Valley very early in the series. Two stories attempt to account for Bobby's mysterious disappearance: One claims that Bobby went up to the Martin attic to get skis or snowshoes, and is still there. The other speculates that he went off to summer camp, and hasn't written home since. Then again, he may be with his sister, Tara (see below).

Tara Martin, daughter of Dr. Joe Martin; stepdaughter of Ruth Brent Martin; sister of Bobby and Jeff; half-sister of Joey; adoptive sister of Phil Brent and Tad Gardner; mother of Phillip (Charlie) Brent. First played by original cast member, Karen Gorney; later by Stephanie Braxton, Nancy Frangione, and Mary Lynn Blanks. Tara had a checkered love life. She fell in love with Phil Brent, but married Chuck Tyler when she learned that Phil was supposedly killed in Vietnam. Phil later returned to Pine Valley to learn Tara and Chuck had a son, Phillip Charles (later Charlie). Phil Brent eventually learned he was the boy's dad; Tara and Phil were finally married in 1976. When problems arose with young Charlie, the couple argued, and Phil left. Tara turned to her ex-husband, Chuck, for comfort. The two began to fall in love again, but Chuck was now wed to Donna Beck, the woman who first broke up their marriage. Tara and Phil reconciled; even young Charlie began to accept Phil as his mother's husband, and stopped resenting him for keeping him away from his "dad," Chuck.

In the early 1980s, Agnes Nixon wrote both Tara and Phil out of the series. Phil died while Tara and her new husband, Jim Jefferson, left Pine Valley to set up housekeeping in the Northwest. (Tara returned briefly in 1985 for Kate's funeral.)

P.S. There have reportedly been Tara sightings in a city called Twin Peaks, and in Rome, Wisconsin, and Cicely, Alaska. But the All My Children *people deny they sent her to any of those places. There is also no comment on a report she and Bobby run a ski, snowshoe, and dog sled gear shop called* Mush and Slush *in an Edmonton, Alberta mall.*

Jeff Martin, a doctor. Played by original cast member Christopher Wines; then by Charles Frank, Robert Perrault, James O'Sullivan, and, finally, Jeffrey Byron. Son of Joe Martin; stepson of Ruth Brent Martin; brother of Tara and Bobby; half-brother of Joey; adoptive brother of Phil and Tad. Jeff's first major story line involved Pine Valley's resident temptress, Erica Kane, who made him her first husband. The two parted when he learned she had aborted their child. Jeff eventually married his great love, Mary Kennicott, a nurse (played by Susan Blanchard). After Mary's death, Jeff married the beautiful Dr. Christina Karras (Robin Strasser) and went off with her to San Francisco.

Joey Martin, Ruth and Joe's miracle baby. Ruth was in her 40s when she conceived. She considered an abortion because she feared she might bear a child with Down's Syndrome. She underwent amnioscentisis (a relatively new process in 1979) and got the good news: The baby was fine. Joe, Jr. (Joey) was born Christmas Day.

Paul Martin, a lawyer. First played by Ken Rabat, then by William Mooney. Like his brother, Paul was always a strong, moral man, who tried to do the right thing under the most difficult circumstances. Like his nephew, Phil Brent, Paul went off to Vietnam and was reported missing in action. And, like Phil, he was found alive and came home to Pine Valley. Paul's first wife was Anne Tyler, daughter of Dr. Charles Tyler and the very, very social Phoebe English Tyler (Ruth Warrick). When Paul realized Anne was still in love with Nick Davis (Larry Keith), her previous husband, he let her go. Margo Flax (played by Eileen Fletchworth) was so anxious to marry Paul, she had a face-lift to make herself more attractive. Still on the rebound from losing Anne, Paul married Margo. After learning that Margo planned to adopt a baby and pretend it was theirs, Paul ended their marriage. He and Anne remarried. Their child, Beth, was mentally retarded; while Paul tried to accept the situation, Anne denied that their daughter was retarded. Eventually, the child died of SIDS, Sudden Infant Death Syndrome, in the first dramatized "crib death" on daytime. In 1981, Anne was killed by a car bomb meant for Paul, who was running for political office.

In an amusing story line, the reserved Paul Martin was propositioned by the outspoken and outrageous Opal Gardner, Tad's mother (then played by Dorothy Lyman) who was planning to seduce men of increasingly higher stature on Pine Valley's social scale as a way of raising her own social and financial condition. Paul said no.

The Tylers

Charles Tyler, a doctor. Played by Hugh Franklin until his death. Former husband of Phoebe English Tyler; father of the late Charles, Jr., Lincoln, and the late Anne Tyler Davis Martin; grandfather of Chuck Tyler. He married Mona Kane, a woman who worked in his hospital, after ending his unhappy marriage to Phoebe.

Phoebe English Tyler Wallingford, played by Ruth Warrick. Former wife of Charles Tyler; stepmother of the late Charles, Jr.; mother of the late Anne Tyler Davis Martin and Lincoln Tyler; step grandmother of Dr. Chuck Tyler; adoptive great-grandmother of Charlie (Tyler) Brent; sister of Ed English; aunt of Brooke English Cudahy Chandler Martin; wife of Langley Wallingford (actually, Lenny Wlasuk); stepmother of Langley's daughters, Verla Grubbs (played by Carol Burnett) and Hillary Wilson. The doyenne of Pine Valley society, Phoebe has mellowed somewhat since the days when she machinated and manipulated to get things done her way, regardless of who might be hurt in the process. She still meddles even where angels fear to tread, but at last, her intentions are good.

Anne Tyler Davis Martin, played

by original cast member Diane deVegh, then by Joanna Miles, Judith Barcroft, and Gwyn Gillis. Daughter of Charles

> ### RELATIVITY ON THE SOAPS:
>
> Lincoln's second wife, Kitty, was the ex-wife of Nick Davis, who was the first husband of Linc's sister, Anne. Linc's nephew, Chuck, raised Nick's grandson, whose mother was Amy, Linc's first wife. (See Phillip Brent and Tara Martin.)

and Phoebe Tyler; mother of the late Beth Martin; ex-wife of Nick Davis and Paul Martin; sister of Lincoln Tyler, half-sister of Charles, Jr. Anne defied the patrician Phoebe to marry entrepreneur Nick Davis, a man from way beyond the other side of the tracks. Although he loved her, he was afraid he was sterile; rather than condemn her to a childless marriage, he left her. She married Paul Martin, the lawyer who handled her divorce from Nick.

Anne was devoted to her daughter, Beth, and was devastated when the child died of SIDS, Sudden Infant Death Syndrome. Later, Nick came back into her life. Sensing that Anne wanted to go back to Nick, Paul decided to let her go (actually, while she loved Nick, Anne wanted to stay married to Paul). Eventually Anne and Paul remarried and lived happily until her tragic death.

Lincoln Tyler, played originally by Paul Dumont, then James Karen,

Nicholas Pryor and Peter White. Son of Phoebe and Charles Tyler; brother of Anne Tyler; half brother of Charles, Jr.; uncle of Chuck Tyler; ex-husband of Amy Tyler; and widower of Kitty Shea Davis Tyler (Francesca James). A successful lawyer, Lincoln married Kitty, a young woman of humble origins, despite all of Phoebe's efforts to keep them apart. Kitty later died of a terminal illness.

Lincoln's first wife, Amy (sister of Ruth Brent Martin) was an outspoken critic of the Vietnam War, much to the chagrin of her mother-in-law, Phoebe, who thought she was being unpatriotic. But Amy, with the tacit support of Linc, helped Phoebe to see the sense in at least questioning the war.

The Kanes

Mona Kane, played by original cast member, Frances Heflin (whom

everyone called Fra) until her death in 1994. She had one daughter, Erica, by her husband, Hollywood director, Eric Kane, who abandoned his family. Mona was a strong woman who had many problems, including trying to raise a strong-willed daughter. One of her closest friends was Nick Davis,

37

to whom she confided her worries about Erica — little realizing that one day Erica and Nick would become lovers.

Mona was kind to her errant husband's two (known) illegitimate children, his son, Mark Dalton, and his daughter, Silver. (Silver proved to be a fraud, however.) She was also a fierce "mama lion" when it came to her Erica. When Jason Maxwell, head of a modeling agency was killed, and suspicion fell on Jeff Martin, Erica's husband, Mona agreed to be injected with sodium pentothal ("truth serum") and recalled killing him by accident. But was it completely accidental? Jason, after all, had broken up Erica's marriage and was probably about to betray his promises to her as well.

When Erica was raped as a teenager, Mona gave the child (Kendall Hart) up for adoption. Some twenty years later, when Kendall's father returned to Pine Valley, Mona threatened to kill him when she perceived he would be dangerous both to Erica and Erica's daughter, Bianca, whose father was Travis Montgomery.

Mona's employer at the hospital, Dr. Charles Tyler, turned to her for friendship as his marriage to Phoebe — who was manipulating like mad to get Mona out of his life — became more difficult. Mona eventually "blackmailed" Phoebe into giving Charles a divorce after catching her in one of her machinations. Mona confessed to Charles who wasn't at all upset with her. For the first and last time in his life, this good man let the end justify the means.

Fra Heflin was married to the late composer, Sol Kaplan. One of her actor daughters, Mady, appeared on *AMC* at one time. Fra's brother was the late actor Van Heflin.

Erica Kane, played by original cast member Susan Lucci. *She came* (to Pine Valley); *she saw* Phil Brent, Nick Davis, Jeff Martin, Tom Cudahy, Lincoln Tyler, Mike Roy, Jeremy Hunter, Lars Bogard, Adam Chandler, Travis Montgomery, Jackson Montgomery, Dimitri Marick, and many others; and *she conquered.*

Closeups: Current Cast and Characters

Actor: Grant Aleksander

Birthplace: Baltimore, Maryland
Birthdate: August 6

Aleksander planned a sports career until he made his first appearance in a school production. He went on to major in theater at Washington and Lee University in Virginia. He continued to study drama at New York University and Circle in the Square professional theater program. From 1982 to

1991, he played Phillip Spaulding on *Guiding Light.* He also appeared on *Capitol,* His primetime credits include *Dark Shadows* and *Fall Guy.*

Grant and his wife, actor Sherry Ramsey, are active in animal welfare groups, including PETA (People for the Ethical Treatment of Animals).

Character: Alec Mcintyre

McIntyre started as an unscrupulous associate in the publishing business of a worthy mentor, Adam Chandler, and soon seduced his wife, Gloria. Alec also stole *Enchantment* from Erica Kane, one of Adam's ex-wives.

Alec has been somewhat redeemed since learning he's the father of young Jamal by a previous lover. Hayley Vaughan, Adam's daughter, finds him attractive, but marriage may not be in the works for these two people who are still trying to find themselves.

Grant on Alec:

"He's more of a good guy now. But I think he'll always have a need to succeed. Maybe he can focus that need on where it will do some good."

Actor: Julia Barr

Birthplace: Fort Wayne, Indiana
Birthdate: February 5

Julia believes "I was probably always interested in theater. I may have thought about doing other things but I found myself always drawn back to acting." Julia began acting at the Fort Wayne Community Theater. She followed up with Purdue University productions that included *Endgame, Our Town,* and *A Streetcar Named Desire.* Before getting her first big professional break in NBC's *A Gathering of One,* she worked in a New York City telephone service. Her previous soap stint was as Renee Szabo in *Ryan's Hope.* She also appeared in the feature film, *I, the Jury* as the head of a drug cartel. Julia and husband, Dr. Richard Herschlag, an oral surgeon, have a daughter, Allison Jane, born in 1984. They share their home with two cats, Dinah and Goldie. The Emmy-award winning actor (five bids; one win) is a spokesperson for "The Company of Women," a merchandise service catalog that helps fund the Rockland County, N.Y. Family Shelter for battered women and their children. In May, 1995, her character Brooke, became involved with just such a shelter.

Character: Brooke English

The daughter of Ed English, and the niece of Phoebe Tyler, Brooke arrived in Pine Valley in 1976. She was impetuous, spoiled and very much aware of her wealth and position in the community. Over the years, Brooke became a more sympathetic character. She moved from social princess to social awareness, including involvement in a shelter for abused and home-less women and children.

Brooke has had her share of the misfortunes of a soap opera heroine. She was shocked when her mother, Peg, tried to kill her. She later learned Peg was the head of a drug cartel, and was actually her stepmother who always resented having to raise her husband's child. Brooke married several times, but has yet to find happiness with any of her husbands — including Tom Cudahy, Adam Chandler, and Tad Martin. Laura, her daughter with Cudahy, was killed by a drunk driver. Adam sired a baby with Dixie believing Brooke was infertile. Brooke later had a child, Jamie, with Tad; Tad, however, loved, and eventually married, Dixie. Brooke had a nervous breakdown but recuperated. In 1994 Brooke learned she had a tubal pregnancy and fled Pine Valley to avoid having the operation that would save her life, but would take the life of her unborn child. Ultimately, she agreed to have the operation.

Early in 1995, her decision to take Adam's side in his dispute with his wife, Gloria, proved rash. It led to an estrangement (which later healed) between her and Adam's daughter, Hayley. It's a reminder to Brooke that she often trusts well, but not wisely.

Julia on Brooke:

"I love this character, even when I've had to play her in terrible darkness for weeks on end. But while it's wonderful stuff to play, it also means having to go into that part of yourself that, while it will help you do certain things with the portrayal, can also be emotionally draining."

Actor: Teresa Blake

Birthplace: Tuscaloosa, Alabama
Birthdate: December 12

Teresa started as a model. She moved to Miami and began getting roles in various Miami-based productions such as *B.L. Stryker* with Burt Reynolds. She describes Burt as "the kindest, most gentle man I've ever worked with." She also appeared in feature films, including the James Bond flick *A License to Kill*. She is fluent in American Sign Language, which she learned so she could better communicate with several hearing-impaired friends.

Character: Gloria Marsh Chandler

Gloria came to Pine Valley in 1991. She was a nurse who nursed a grudge against a man who did her wrong. She met the disarming Adam Chandler and fell for him, while Stuart, Adam's gentle twin brother, was falling for her, but was unable to compete with his more dashing (if dastardly) sibling. Pursued by Adam's protégé, Alec McIntyre, she bargained for a one-time only seduction so that Alec would leave her alone. But as Gloria was to learn, life with Adam was no Eden, and once his jealousy was aroused, his dark side dominated their relationship. Adam's behavior toward her when she was pregnant was emotionally and physically abusive. Their baby was stillborn. Gloria had a nervous breakdown and tried to poison Adam. Stuart reemerged as a loving friend. She also had an ally in Hayley, Adam's daughter.

Teresa on Gloria:

"She's a gentle, sensitive, vulnerable woman. But deep down there's a reservoir of strength that she'll be able to draw on."

Actor: John Callahan

Birthplace: Brooklyn, New York
Birthdate: December 23

John Callahan has a long list of television credits. His previous soap roles were as Leo Russell, a tactile, if not tactful masseur, on *General Hospital*; and Craig Hunt on *Santa Barbara*. One of his primetime soap roles was as Eric Stavros, Cesar Romero's son on *Falcon Crest*.

Callahan planned to be a lawyer. Earning his tuition at the University of California at Berkley as a manager in a nightclub, he soon found himself turning from torts and courts to scripts and flicks.

Callahan and his wife, Linda, have two sons, Josh and Matthew.

Character: Edmund Grey

Edmund spent most of his life unaware of his true identity. When the truth came out, he learned he was a full-fledged member of the distinguished Marick family. (This, no doubt, may explain his still suppressed subconscious fantasies about doing a czardas (a Hungarian dance) with Zsa Zsa Gabor.)

But wealth, family tradition, and social position couldn't change Edmund's love for journalism. He wasn't about to give up his international correspondent's trench coat for an international correspondence school course in manners for the Manor Born.

Although Edmund has been involved with several Pine Valley women, including Brooke English, he married the lovely Dr. Maria Santos — only to learn that she had a past that he found difficult to accept. The two have gone for marriage counseling with some amusing results.

41

Grey had a chance to attend his own funeral after it was assumed he'd been blown up by a car bomb, most likely set by dastards he was investigating.

Actor: David Canary

Birthplace: Elwood, Indiana
Birthdate: August 25

David went to the University of Cincinnati on a football scholarship. He was graduated with a degree in music, specializing in voice. He made his Broadway debut with the late, great Colleen Dewhurst in *Great Day in the Morning.* Over the years he's appeared in films, theater, and, of course, television. He played Candy in Bonanza, (ironically, replacing Pernell Roberts who played another Adam; Adam Cartwright) and Russ Gehring in *Peyton Place.* Before joining *AMC* in 1983, he played Stephen Frame in *Another World.*. A four-time Emmy winner, David is devoting more time to writing plays these days. He works closely with Robert Lupone's Manhattan Classic Company.

Character: Adam and Stuart Chandler

The name, Adam, means earth in Hebrew, and no one in Pine Valley is better at unearthing long-buried secrets about anyone he considers a real or potential adversary.

Adam's brother, Stuart, is his kinder, gentler twin. Sometimes Adam sees him as his conscience and allows Stuart to pull him back when he's gone too far. But sometimes, even Stuart's quiet strength can't keep his brother from causing pain to others.

Adam came to Pine Valley to avenge himself on Palmer Cortlandt, who left his sister with a child (Ross Chandler), whom he raised as his own. But revenge was not the only emotion that fueled his passions. Adam met and fell for the enchanting Erica Kane. They married but she soon found life in the Chandler mansion spooky. (Adam's then "secret" twin, Stuart, made noises when he moved around the place.) Erica finally decided life in the Gothic mode was not for her, and the two were divorced.

Ironically, Adam and Palmer — who really hate each other — are not only linked by Palmer's son and Adam's nephew, they are also linked by Adam's son who is also Palmer's grandnephew. Eager to have another child, but believing his then wife, Brooke, to be infertile, Adam seduced Palmer's niece, Dixie Cooney; he then divorced Brooke and married Dixie when she became pregnant. After their son, Adam Jr.'s, birth, Adam tried to drive Dixie insane so that he could commit her and take full custody of their baby boy.

In 1987, Stuart Chandler tutored a young boy named Scott Parker in one of his art classes. He met Scott's mother, Cindy, who had become HIV infected through her husband, an IV user, who died of the disease. In a touching story line, Stuart and Cindy were married and lived happily until her death. After Cindy died, Stuart adopted young Scott. The story line had a unique quality. Through skillfully written scenes, the audience was let in on the fact that this marriage was not a union in name only: These were not two celibate souls just marking time. Instead, they were obviously aware of the opportunities available via "Safe Sex."

Stuart fell in love with Gloria Marsh, but was unable to compete with Adam's more aggressive courtship. Adam and Gloria were married, but did not live happily ever after. He was jealous of her friendship with his own protégé, Alec. He tormented her when she was pregnant, and discovered, to his horror, that he may have contributed to the death of their baby daughter. His daughter, Hayley — by former love Arlene Vaughan — was suspected of trying to poison him because of his treatment of Gloria. But it turned out that Gloria was the culprit.

Will Adam ever be redeemed by all this? Well, maybe he'll be tempered a little in his need to dominate everyone around him. Will Stuart ever become cynical and untrusting? Maybe a little wiser, but no less loving.

Actor: William Christian

Birthplace: Washington, D.C.
Birthdate: September 30

William Christian prepared himself for three days' work when he got the call in July, 1990 to report to *All My Children*. Three months later, he was called back on a recurring basis. In May, 1991, he was raised to contract status.

Christian was nominated for an Emmy in 1991, and nominated in 1993 and 1994 for the NAACP Image Award for Featured Male in Daytime. He was graduated from Catholic University and received a Master's in drama from American University (both in Washington, DC). His previous soap role was as Dr. Marshall Reed on *Another World*.

Character: Derek Frye

Detective Derek Frye seems to be proof of that Gilbert and Sullivan song that tells us that "a policeman's lot is not a happy one...." Frye tries do his best as a law enforcement officer in Pine Valley, but he not only has to deal with miscreants and murderers, he also has to deal with the demands his work puts on his personal relationships. More often than not, his mood is bluer than his uniform. So far, Derek has scored an A in police work, but he needs to take a remedial course in how to make room for happiness in his private life.

43

Actor: Mary Fickett

Birthplace: Bronxville, New York
Birthdate: May 2

Long-time AMC *cast members Jill Larson, Gillian Spencer, and James Mitchell.*

Mary Fickett, one of the original cast members of *All My Children*, says she decided to become an actor because she grew up surrounded by actors and writers. (Her dad was radio director, Homer Fickett.) "I could hardly think of anything more exciting than to be part of that world," she says. Mary has children by a former marriage.

Character: Ruth Brent Martin

Ruth means *pity* in Hebrew, but although Ruth Brent Martin has endured much tragedy in her life in Pine Valley, the last thing she would want us to do is pity her. Her first husband was unfaithful; she's been widowed; one of her adopted sons died; another one, Tad, has been in and out of scrapes, and, a few years ago he was all but given up for dead. She's been kidnapped. She's been raped. She's had her house blown down by a tornado. But she's managed to muddle through like the trouper we've all come to admire over the years.

Mary on Ruth:

"I was once asked how it feels to play the same role for twenty-five years. My answer is that as I have grown over these years, so has Ruth. One can never tire of playing someone like her...."

Actor: Keith Hamilton Cobb

Birthplace: North Tarrytown, New York
Birthdate: January 28

Tell Keith Hamilton Cobb that you appreciate Shakespeare, and you will probably have made a friend for life. Much of his professional life has revolved around the great writers of the theater, with the Bard at the center of his classical universe. Cobb's first professional job was in Jean Cocteau's play *The Infernal Machine*. He teaches acting at Youth Theatre Interactions, Inc. He's also involved in a performing arts program for children in South Yonkers, New York. Through the Playwright's Theatre of New Jersey's Special Needs Program, Cobb teaches play writing and performs in works written by young people in the New Jersey correctional system.

Character: Noah Keefer

Noah arrived in Pine Valley in July, 1994 and soon became a hero in spite of himself when he sheltered the scarred, scared Julia Santos. That act of kindness changed his life. Up to then, he had been a young man from the wrong side of town. Suddenly, he had friends among the very people he once thought alien to him — as alien as if they had been dropped from the Planet Mongo.

Noah has been Julia's friend and supporter through many of her recent trials, including a brutal rape. Although there's no doubt he loves her, he may have to deal with a manipulative Taylor.

Actor: Eileen Herlie

Birthplace: Glasgow, Scotland
Birthdate: March 8

Eileen joined *All My Children* in 1976, bringing with her a credits list that included a long career in both the Scottish and English theater. She played Gertrude, Hamlet's mother, in the film that starred Lord Laurence Olivier as the Melancholy Dane. She later played the same role on stage with Richard Burton as Hamlet. Once asked which of the leading men with whom she worked in her long and brilliant career were her favorites, Herlie answered: "Each was my favorite when we worked together...." However, she did admit that both Olivier and Burton were, somehow, special.

Character: Myrtle Lum Fargate

Myrtle came to Pine Valley after working most of her life in a carnival. She opened a boarding house that catered to many of the town's newer arrivals.

There they began to share their hopes, their secrets, and, sometimes, even hinted at their true agendas! (That last phrase would have been accompanied by a swell of ominous sounding organ music back in the early days of TV soaps.) Myrtle knew one big secret that could have had explosive reverberations for the very social Phoebe Tyler Wallingford. Her husband, Professor Langley Wallingford, was really Myrtle's erstwhile carny circuit cohort, Lenny Wlasuk, a small-time con man.

Actor: James Kiberd

Birthplace: Providence, Rhode Island
Birthdate: July 6

If there were just one word to describe James Kiberd, it would be artist. He is a strong, sensitive actor. He is also a gifted painter who creates beautiful things on canvas and, sometimes, on cravats.

45

Kiberd was studying at the Graduate School of Fine Art at the University of Pennsylvania with every intention of filling his life with palettes, paints, and sketching pencils. Then he played Macbeth in a college production and when the curtain fell to rousing applause, he knew he would be making room in his life for another art form: Acting. ("I once read," he said, "that I gave up art for acting. Not so. I just added acting to everything else I love to do.")

As a UNICEF spokesperson, Kiberd has worked hard to tell people how the organization helps children. He also came up with a unique fund raiser: When Trevor Dillon's flamboyant ties caught the attention of the audience, Kiberd told fans he would paint a design on a tie for any viewer who sent one to him along with a donation. As a result, lots of people now own "Trevor Ties" and lots of youngsters served by UNICEF are benefitting from the generosity of Kiberd's fans.

James met his wife, Susan Keith, on *Loving*. He played Mike Donovan, a Vietnam veteran and the first soap character to suffer post traumatic stress disorder.

Character: Trevor Dillon

Trevor Dillon came to Pine Valley in 1989 as a police detective. He was supposed to stay in town for a few days and then move on. However, fan reaction to Kiberd/Dillon was so enthusiastic, the soap was happy to expand his story line and extend his stay and even give him a new job: lawyer.

An old friend of Jeremy Hunter's, Trevor was married to the late Natalie Hunter, and is raising her son, Timothy.

Trevor was also unwittingly involved with Natalie's sister, Janet Green, a lady whose neurons often misfire. Trevor slept with Janet — believing she was Natalie — and Janet later gave birth to a daughter, Amanda. In early 1995, Janet lost her case for custody of the child, prompting her to concoct some bizarre scheme for revenge against Trevor and his most recent love, Laurel.

Actor: Michael E. Knight

Birthplace: Princeton, New Jersey
Birthdate: May 7

Michael is the first member of his academic family to follow an acting career, and his choice has paid off quite well for the talented thespian. Over the years, Knight has won two Emmy Awards for his work in daytime. He's also done considerable work on stage, in features, and on prime time.

Michael has taken several sabbaticals from the series. In 1992, he returned to *AMC* playing his familiar character, Tad Gardner Martin, and a look-alike, Ted Orsini, who also became Tad's rival for the love of Dixie Cooney Chandler.

Michael is married to Catherine Hickland, formerly of *Capitol* and currently playing Tess on *Loving*. Catherine's first husband was actor David Hasselhoff (ex-*The Young and the Restless*) who, coincidentally, played a character named Michael Knight on the series *Knight Rider*.

Character: Tad Gardner Martin

Tad is the adopted son of Joe and Ruth Martin. His biological mother is Opal Gardner, now married to Palmer Cortlandt. His father was the late Ray Gardner. His sister, Jenny Gardner, played by Kim Delaney, died in a jet ski explosion trying to protect Greg Nelson (Larry Lau), the man she loved.

The character was first played by Matthew Anton, then by John F. Dunn. In his early teens, Tad quickly earned the nickname Tad the Cad because of his cavalier attitude towards the women who loved him.

During his last absence from Pine Valley, Tad suffered from amnesia and was taken in by a wealthy California winery owner who believed he was her long-lost kidnapped son. When Tad accompanied her on a business trip to Pine Valley in 1992, he had no memory of anything before he became the heir to the Orsini fortune. But as his memory returned, and as he reentered the lives of those who thought him dead, he realized he'd been given a second chance to live his own life.

Tad's look-alike, the long-missing Ted Orsini, also came to Pine Valley and soon fell in love with Tad's beloved Dixie, whom Tad helped escape being committed to a mental institution by her husband, Adam Chandler. Increasingly jealous over their relationship, Ted persuaded Tad to accompany him on a hunting trip to Canada. Dixie followed. And just when Ted was ready to kill both Tad and Dixie (after she spurned his proposal), he turned and walked into the forest, leaving the lovers to go home and marry.

Almost forgotten in the Tad/Ted/Dixie drama was Brooke, Tad's pre-Dixie wife and the mother of his son, Jamie. (Ironically, Adam seduced Dixie in hopes of fathering a child when he believed his then wife, Brooke, could no longer have children.) Her problems with Tad led to a nervous breakdown. She emerged from it a stronger, more resilient woman, ready for the (inevitable) next blow.

Tad would not have been Palmer's choice of husband for his adored niece, even though Palmer was married to Tad's mother, Opal Gardner. Palmer, who played fast and loose with five of the seven deadly sins (sloth and gluttony were not his style) considered Tad the consummate Cad, and he had plenty of history to back that up.

In his young lifetime, Tad has made more than a few trips to the altar — and the bedroom. He was married to Hillary Wilson, daughter of Langley Wallingford, stepdaughter of Phoebe Wallingford, and half-sister of Verla Grubbs (Carol Burnett). The marriage was not a happy one. He had an affair with the middle-aged Marion Colby whose daughter, Liza, thought she was his one and only. Edna Thornton paid him to date her unhappy, overweight daughter, Dottie, whom he had to marry when she became pregnant. When she miscarried, he asked for a divorce.

Although he seems to have settled down with Dixie and their child, he was strangely sympathetic to the beautiful Janet Green, despite Dixie's reminder that Janet killed her brother, Will.

Michael says that although Tad has grown up a lot and has changed, he'll always be tempted by a challenge.

Actor: Felicity Lafortune

Birthplace: Oak Park, Illinois
Birthdate: December 15

Felicity's lovely mezzo-soprano voice led her to a career in opera long before she accepted her first television role. She sang with the Repertory Opera Theater in Chicago, and with the chorus of the San Francisco Opera, and has been a soloist with the Santa Fe Opera Company.

Felicity has also compiled a theatrical credits list that includes productions directed by Jose Ferrer, Gene Saks and Jerome Robbins. She had a recurring role on *thirtysomething*. Her previous soap role was on *Ryan's Hope*.

Felicity and her husband, Steve Gilbert, share their homes in New York and Los Angeles with their cat, Jacques.

Character: Laurel Banning Montgomery Dillon

Laurel came to Pine Valley on December 15, 1993, and started off on the proverbial wrong foot. She embezzled funds to pay for the care of her autistic daughter, Lily. When she fled arrest by Trevor Dillon, she indirectly caused the death of his wife, Natalie. Jackson Montgomery, Erica's former brother-in-law, and erstwhile lover, fell in love with Laurel, and in the normal-as-possible course of events for a soap couple, they were married.

Laurel saw through the disguise worn by Jane Cox, who was really Janet Green, (Dillon's dead wife Natalie's evil sister), and almost paid with her life for being so observant. While "Jane" was eventually revealed to be Janet, Laurel was still on the lady's hit list: This time for attracting the attention of Trevor Dillon, father of Janet's daughter, Amanda. For Janet, stripping Pine Valley of its Laurel would be an act of kindness in Trevor's behalf, since he would be free of the one impediment keeping him from claiming Janet as his true love.

Can Laurel live with this threat? As far as she's concerned, she'd rather live with it than die by it.

Actor: Jill Larson

Birthplace: Minneapolis, Minnesota
Birthdate: October 7

Jill joined the cast of *All My Children* in 1989, and within two years, won the first of her two Emmy nominations. Jill earned a degree in communications from New York City's Hunter College. She studied drama at the prestigious Circle in the Square Professional Theater Program. Much of her career has been in theater. She's a founding member of GLM Productions, which produces off-Broadway plays and documentaries.

Jill previously appeared on *One Life to Live,* where she played the psychotic Ursula Blackwell, a housekeeper who could give Daphne DuMaurier's Mrs. Danvers (in *Rebecca*) lessons in spookiness.

Jill Larson enjoys carpentry and cooking.

Character: Opal Gardner Purdy Cortlandt

The character of Opal Gardner was first played by Dorothy Lyman who pulled out all the stops to create an outrageously uninhibited woman who did what she felt like doing and said what she felt like saying, just as long as it felt right to her.

The mother of the late Jenny Gardner, and of Tad (Gardner) Martin, she was never overly concerned with her maternal responsibilities. But that has changed in recent years.

After a six-year absence from Pine Valley, Opal returned in 1989 with Jill Larson in the role. She was still wonderfully outspoken, but a mite more tempered. Opal was from so far beyond the other side of the tracks that she would have considered a three-seater outhouse to be home improvement; when she married Palmer Cortlandt, she became the Chatelaine of Cortlandt Manor. Palmer was nonplussed to learn Opal was about to fulfill the Biblical injunction to "multiply." After all, he had had a vasectomy years earlier. But time heals many things, including, apparently, severed body parts (at least on the soaps) and when Opal delivered her son and Palmer learned he was, indeed, the boy's father, he was a very happy man.

In early 1995, Opal found herself interested in Seabone Hunkel, a man from Palmer's hometown, Pigeon Hollow, West Virginia. Will Opal give her heart to the smooth-talking charmer or will she stay true to Palmer? That could depend on the Janet Green factor, to wit: Palmer may think Opal is a real gem — but Opal could seek out a new setting if she learns Palmer let himself be seduced by Janet Green, Pine Valley's equal-opportunity villainess, who doesn't care whom she uses, so long as it's in her behalf.

Actor: Eva LaRue

Birthplace: Long Beach, California

Birthdate: December 27

Eva was six years old when she started doing television commercials. Her adult television career has included roles in *Married...with Children, Nurses, Dallas, Perfect Strangers,* and *Freddy's Nightmares.* Her feature films include *Robocop III, The Barbarians,* and *Crash 'n Burn.* Her previous soap role was as Margo on *Santa Barbara.*

LaRue is also a singer. When she lived in Los Angeles, she often sang the National Anthem at hockey and football games.

Eva stays in shape by working out in the ancient art of Tae Kwon Do.

Character: Maria Santos Grey

Dr. Maria Santos is a neurologist. In the course of her studies, she had to learn the intricacies of the human brain. Too bad her specialty wasn't cardiology: She might have learned something about the human heart — at least in the way it can be broken by the most important human emotion — love.

Since coming to Pine Valley in 1993, Maria fell in love with, and married the dashing Edmund Grey, who she thought might dash away once he learned she had miscarried a child fathered by Del Henry, leaving her unable to have children. The crisis sent them to a marriage counselor, where some of the counseling was more fun than they expected. (They especially liked their homework assignments.)

One of the most painful experiences in her life was having to stitch up the torn face of her lovely sister, Julia, when she was injured in Pine Valley's Tornado of 1994. The resulting scar traumatized Julia, who fled into all kinds of terrible experiences.

Early in 1995, Maria was informed that Edmund had been killed by a car bomb. Fortunately, he survived. But will the same be said of their marriage? Stay tuned.

Actor: Christopher Lawford

Birthplace: Los Angeles, California

Birthdate: March 29

Christopher Lawford would seem to prove that genetics may well dictate life's choices. His father was the late actor, Peter Lawford. His mother is Patricia Kennedy Lawford. Chris grew up in a family that emphasized public service. Several of his first cousins, including Caroline, John, Kathleen, and Joseph, Jr., are lawyers who use their professions to extend the Kennedy family dictum.

Christopher, like his famous kin, was drawn to the Bar and holds a Doctorate in Law from Boston College. But he was also drawn to acting, and ultimately chose that as his profession.

Chris has made several films, including *The Doors, Mr. North, Spellbinder* and *Jack the Bear* with Danny DeVito. He appeared with Danny's erstwhile co-star, Arnold Schwarzenegger (who also happens to be married to his cousin, Maria Shriver) in a television version of *Christmas in Connecticut.*

Although Christopher Lawford seems happy in his chosen career, one wonders if his Kennedy genes sometimes make him think about going into politics one day: Maybe even becoming president. After all, another actor of Irish descent had an address on Pennsylvania Avenue for eight years.

Meanwhile, Chris shares a New York City address with his wife, Jeannie, and their two children, David and Savannah.

Character: Charlie Brent

Charlie has gone through a lot of changes since he returned to Pine Valley in 1992. He was a model, but not your run-of-the-mill runway mannequin who poses and pivots in his Calvins. Instead, Charlie was a cosmetics model known as the Man of Enchantment.

Charlie eventually tossed out his makeup sponge and put on the gumshoes as proprietor of his own detective agency. He worked closely with the lovely Hayley Vaughan, with whom he fell in love, but Hayley was eventually drawn to the more dashing Alec McIntire. For a while, he found comfort with the understanding Cecily. But can understanding ever replace love? That, Charlie Brent, Detective, knows is the biggest mystery of all.

Actor: Susan Lucci

Birthplace: Westchester, New York
Birthdate: December 23

Unlike her soap character, Erica Kane — who has been married so often that commodity traders love what she does for rice futures — Susan Lucci has been happily married to just one man: producer Helmut Huber, with whom she has a son and daughter.

While most people would assume Susan has very little in common with Pine Valley's Princess of Passion, Susan sees Erica in a much more sympathetic light. "Erica wants what many women want," Susan has said. "She wants to be loved; she wants to find the right man and spend the rest of her life with him. And she wants her child to be happy; she would defend her child with her life. And in that, she's like every good mother you know."

Susan has been nominated some fourteen times for a Daytime Emmy, but as of 1994, has yet to win. She's always been a good sport about it — even agreeing to co-host the Emmy Awards when another actor who was ignored by the Academy might have boycotted them. Susan has said she feels honored just by being nominated by her peers.

Lucci has won a slew of other awards: The 1992 People's Choice Award, the 1993 Soap Opera Digest Award for Outstanding Lead Actress, the 1994 Crystal Apple Award, the 1988 Soap Opera Digest Editor's Award for Outstanding Contribution to Daytime Television, and the 1989 Canadian TV Guide People's Choice Award for Best Soap Actress.

Lucci's contract allows her to do work outside the soap. She had a recurring role on Dallas, and has made several television films. She's hosted *Saturday Night Live* and, in 1991, launched the Susan Lucci beauty products collection on the QVC home shopping network. Asked if she ever considers leaving the soap for a career in features and primetime, Lucci has said, "I couldn't imagine not being here (on *AMC*) anymore..."

Character: Erica Kane
Breathes there a fan who hath not said,
How many times hath Erica wed?
And with whom in the Valley known as Pine
Did each of her marriages intertwine?

Then gaze if you will at this special "tree"
Of her numerous weddings, and you will see
How some of Pine Valley's best-known denizens
Were linked through her marriages to various citizens.

Her first altar trek was with Jeff, whose dad,
Dr. Joe Martin, adopted Tad,
Who was once wed to Brooke, now Dixie's his spouse.
(Both are exes of Adam, who has been quite a louse!)

Erica's second husband was gentle Philip Brent,
Whose grandson, Charlie, found Hayley heaven-sent.
Adam is Hayley's out-of-wedlock *pater*
Whom Erica married once, and then again, later.

Tom Cudahy marked Erica's third nuptial tie
He later married Brooke and a lady named Skye,

Who was another of Adam's "forgotten" daughters
(This man does a lot of what he "hadn't oughters")

Adam was Erica's fourth and seventh matrimonial course
Both marriages ended in acrimonial divorce.
With Travis, who was husband five and six, she happily bore
Their daughter Bianca, whom they both joyfully adore.

Before Dimitri became her spouse number eight,
He proposed to Natalie, but it was her sad fate
To learn of Angelique, his then long-comatose wife
So, Natalie, lamentingly, got out of his life.

Natalie, who once had been Jeremy's stepmother
Also married Adam, as she did many another.
Jeremy hoped to wed Erica, for whom he deeply cared,
But a metaphysical vision left him totally scared.

Kendall, the daughter Erica didn't know she had
Had been doing things ranging from beastly to bad.
And Dimitri reacted with an emotional pang
To news that he fathered young Anton Lang.

Anton reacted to this paternal revelation
By turning Kendall into a double relation,
To wit, stepsister and wife,
Until he later divorced her with much *sturm und* strife

With eight treks to the altar in the valley called Pine
One question remains: who will be spouse number nine???

Actor: Ray MacDonnell

Birthplace: Lawrence, Massachusetts
Birthdate: March 5

Ray MacDonnell is one of the original cast members of *All My Children*. His previous soap role was as Philip Capice on *Edge of Night,* a character he played for some eight years. MacDonnell was part of television's so-called "Golden Age." He worked in live television on such programs as *Studio One* and *Armstrong Circle Theater.*

Ray starred on Broadway with Angela Lansbury and Ann Miller, both of whom played the dazzling dame named *Mame.* MacDonnell attended Amherst College before switching to the Royal Academy in London on a Fulbright scholarship. Ray and his wife, Patricia, have three children: Kyle, Daniel, and Sarah.

Character: Dr. Joe Martin
   See Founding Families.

53

Actor: Rudolf Martin

Birthplace: Berlin, Germany
Birthdate: July 31

If anyone could be called a truly "Continental" man, Rudolf Martin would certainly qualify. He was born in Germany, and lived in Italy and France, where he was graduated from the Université de Paris.

He moved to the United States after graduation and lived for a while in New York where he studied acting at the Lee Strasberg Institute. He appeared in an Oscar-nominated short called *The Dutch Master.* Martin speaks several languages, including German, French, Italian, and of course, English. His current marital status is single, but, he says that probably will change in the near future.

Character: Anton Lang

Anton Lang is a medical exchange student from Hungary. Little did he dream when he first set out for America, that love, marriage, divorce, and the father he never knew, all awaited him in Pine Valley, U.S.A. He was sponsored by Dimitri Marick. Later, he learned his mother, Corvina — whom he believed to be his sister — conceived him during a drunken one-night affair with the dashing Dimitri. The revelation drove the impulsive Anton to marry his stepmother, Erica's, naughty daughter, Kendall Hart. Later, after learning of the nasty things Kendall did, he divorced her, and set his sights, once more, on the lovely nursing student, Julia Santos. But whether Julia still wants him, or wants someone else, is something Anton will have to deal with. And if anyone can help Anton learn how to charm a member of the opposite sex, daddy Dimitri has a goulash of tips to offer.

Actor: Robin Mattson

Birthplace: Los Angeles, California
Birthdate: June 1

Robin is one of daytime's favorite stars. She made her soap debut as Heather Webber on *General Hospital,* and also played Gina Timmons on *Santa Barbara.* She started her career at age 6 doing guest shots on episodic television. Her first feature film was *Namu, The Killer Whale.* Some of her leading men in films include Nick Nolte, Rod Steiger, and Don Johnson.

Robin's real-life leading man is Henry Neuman, for whom she enjoys cooking. Her father was a well-known chef, and she is a graduate of the Gastronomique Directives Course at the Los Angeles International Culinary Institute. She has continued her studies in New York, where she also has her own cooking segment on a LIFETIME cable show.

Robin Mattson has three Emmy nominations to date, and three Soap Opera Digest Awards.

Character: Janet Green

If ever a villain lived who was "foiled" more often than she fooled her adversaries, it would have to be Janet Green. The character was first played by Kate Collins, who also played Janet's sister, the late Natalie Hunter. Soon after Janet arrived in Pine Valley, she hid her sister in a well, and assumed her identity. She slept with Natalie's then lover (later, husband), Trevor Dillon, and had a child, Amanda, with him. After killing Dixie's brother, Will Cooney, Janet was committed to an institution. In 1994, she was released after agreeing to undergo experimental facial surgery that was supposed to give her a more benign personality. She returned to Pine Valley disguised as Jane Cox, determined to regain her daughter's custody and to persuade Trevor that what they had was not a one-night stand of mistaken passion, but the real thing. After being unmasked as Janet Green, she continued to concoct plots, even managing to have a look-alike actor pose as the late Will Cooney's ghost in an effort to spook Dixie. With each turn of the screw in her various plots, Janet manages to loosen the bolts in her own brain box.

Robin on Janet:

"Even if a character is absolutely the most evil person imaginable, you have to find something in her to which the audience can relate. If you can find some humor in that, it helps the audience retain interest in her."

Actor: Cady McClain

Birthplace: Burbank, California
Birthdate: October 13

Cady's first professional role was in a Band-Aid commercial. She moved into guest roles on *Cheers, St. Elsewhere, Spenser: For Hire,* and *Lou Grant.* Her feature films include *My Favorite Year* as Peter O'Toole's daughter. She also appeared in *Pennies from Heaven.* Her theatrical credits run all the way from Shakespeare to Sondheim.

Cady won an Emmy in 1990, and an Emmy nomination in 1992. *Soap Opera Digest* gave her their Best Heroine Award in 1994.

Character: Dixie Cooney Chandler Martin

Dixie came to Pine Valley to live with her wealthy uncle, Palmer Cortlandt, who, like her, originally hailed from Pigeon Hollow, West Virginia. She was seduced by Adam Chandler, who hoped she would conceive a child because he believed his then wife, Brooke, was infertile. After marrying Dixie, Adam tried to drive her insane so he could institutionalize her and take full custody of their son, Adam, Jr. With Tad's help, Dixie realized that Adam's concept of commitment was not quite what she had expected to find in a husband.

55

Dixie was involved in a strange triangle with Tad and his look-alike, Ted Orsini. Ted wanted her, and was prepared to kill Tad if necessary; he was also prepared to kill Dixie if he couldn't have her. But just when it looked as if Ted was about to dispatch the lovers, he relented and walked out of their lives.

Dixie's brother, Will Cooney, was killed by Janet Green. Later, In 1994, Dixie's half-brother, Del Henry, came to Pine Valley hoping she would donate one of her kidneys to save him from dying of a degenerative renal condition. Dixie knew this might jeopardize any chance she and Tad could have a baby, but chose to save her brother despite objections from Tad and her Uncle Palmer.

New problems will, no doubt, challenge her, but she's stronger now and it's safe to assume that Dixie will take her stand against anything and anyone, including Janet, who may threaten her and her family in the future.

Actor: James Mitchell

Birthplace: Sacramento, California
Birthdate: February 29

Mitchell created one of the slickest, sleekest, sexiest, smoothest, gentlemen of the soap genre in Palmer Cortlandt.

However, long before Palmer looked down his noble nose at the citizenry of Pine Valley (and long before anyone in Pine Valley knew he had been born Peter Cooney in Pigeon Hollow, West Virginia), Mitchell had marked out a number of memorable milestones in his long and distinguished career as a performing artist.

A brilliant dancer (he was Agnes DeMille's protégé) he played Curly in the dream sequence of the film, *Oklahoma*. He also appeared in *The Bandwagon, Deep In My Heart,* and *Turning Point,* in which he played the artistic director of the ballet company for which Anne Bancroft was principal dancer.

His theatrical career includes the Broadway productions *Brigadoon,* and his favorite theater piece, *Carnival*. He also toured with *Funny Girl, Bloomer Girls,* and *Paint Your Wagon*.

Besides his acting and dancing, Mitchell is also a director and teacher. He has conducted classes in movement for actors at Yale, and also holds an honorary Doctorate in Fine Arts from Drake University.

James Mitchell's previous soap roles were on *Edge of Night* and *Where the Heart Is*.

A seven-time Emmy nominee, Mitchell has described his role as one of the most interesting any actor can hope to play, noting that in a typical five-day week, Palmer is likely to present him with a variety of dramatic textures: domineering, tyrannical, loving, scheming, contrite, possessive, jealous, manipulative — the whole range of emotable challenges.

Character: Palmer Cortlandt —
a.k.a. Peter Cooney

Since his arrival in Pine Valley in 1979, Palmer, an electronics tycoon, has been involved with a number of beautiful women, including the great love of his life, Daisy, the mother of his daughter, Nina.

Palmer married most of the women with whom he fell in love. But for him, marriage was less a matter of social morality than a means of possession: His women belonged to him! But short of locking them up in the top turrets of Cortlandt Manor, Palmer was never able to hold on to his wives for any length of time. Even his most recent wife, Opal, has had those provocative fantasies which are harmless in real life, but are often a prelude to hanky-panky on the soaps.

THE PRINCESS FALLS IN LOVE

The love story of Nina Corlandt and Dr. Cliff Warner lasted through much of the 1980s. At one point, Cliff was accused of murdering his former lover, Sybil Thorne, mother of his son, Bobby. The mysterious Monique Jonvil took the stand to reveal the murderer's true identity: Sean Cudahy. Nina learned that Monique was really her mother, Daisy, whom Palmer sent away when she had an affair; that Palmer's housekeeper, Myra Murdoch, was really Daisy's mother and Nina's grandmother; and that Sean, Sybil, and Palmer were in a plot to have Sybil pressure Nina into ending her marriage to Cliff. Nina (temporarily) walked out on her father, leaving him a (temporarily) broken man.

Palmer Cortlandt's wives include the aforementioned Daisy (Gillian Spencer); Donna Beck (Candice Earley); Cynthia Preston (Jane Elliot); Natalie Hunter (Kate Collins); and Opal Gardner (Jill Larson), who provided him with an instant stepson, Tad Martin (who was never one of Palmer's favorite people) and a biological son.

Palmer also has a son, Ross Chandler (formerly played by Robert Gentry). Ross's mother is Lottie Chandler, Adam Chandler's sister. Adam raised Ross as his own child.

Palmer was a mite unsettled when Opal told him she was pregnant. He had had a vasectomy years earlier, and assumed he could no longer father children. But Palmer's paternity was reaffirmed with tests. (The soaps have a long history of medical miracles.)

Palmer's machinations have landed him in all kinds of trouble. He's been a suspect in at least two murders. He's been in prison. Adam Chandler tapped into his fortune. He's been close to death. But he manages to triumph over his problems and, sometimes, even learns something from his mistakes.

Early in 1995, Palmer allowed himself to be seduced by Janet Green, and soon realized he may have to pay for his indiscretion — and with Janet keeping the accounts, the price may be higher than he imagined.

Some observers have noted that Palmer seems to have lost some of his sharp edge. But don't bet on it. The classic "Cortlandt Manner" may be dormant, but hardly dead.

Actor: Michael Nader

Birthplace: St. Louis, Missouri
Birthdate: February 19

Michael Nader started his film career in a series of *Beach Party* films with Annette Funicello and Frankie Avalon. He then became a regular on the television series, *Gidget,* starring Sally Field.

Nader moved to New York to study at the Actors Studio. He was cast in several well-received off-Broadway productions. He was then cast as Kevin Thompson on *As the World Turns,* and played the role for three years before heading back to the West Coast to take the role of Alexi Theodopolous in the primetime soap, *Bare Essence.*

In November, 1983 he joined *Dynasty* as Dex Dexter, the sometime lover of Alexis Carrington (Joan Collins) who must have referred to him in their private moments as *dextrose* because he was so sweet and stimulating. One of his more recent television roles was opposite his *AMC* costar, Susan Lucci, in *Lady Mobster.*

Nader, his wife, and their dog, live in New York City.

Character: Dimitri Marick

Dimitri came to Pine Valley in September, 1991. He was a mysterious presence who soon became the object of much curiosity. The first Pine Valleyite he encountered was Natalie Hunter whose deranged sister, Janet Green, had thrown her down a well.

After rescuing Natalie, Dimitri was stunned by how much she looked like his wife, Angelique, who had been in a coma for 15 years. Although Angelique was still alive, Dimitri proposed to Natalie; meanwhile, back in Hungary, Angelique miraculously awakened and traveled to Pine Valley to confront her husband on his wedding day. Dimitri and Natalie never married — which was just as well: He soon fell in love with Erica and after his divorce from Angelique, married her and made her the mistress of his sprawling estate, Wildwind.

Helga, Dimitri's maid and Angelique's mother, revealed that the well-known reporter, Edmund Grey, was Dimitri's half-brother. Later, another member of Dimitri's household, Corvina, revealed that Dimitri had fathered her son, Anton.

Anton was so upset to learn the truth about his paternity, he rushed to marry Kendall, Erica's manipulative daughter. But that marriage crashed when she and Corvina admitted to being part of a cabal against Dimitri and Erica.

Poor Dimitri: He comes from a long line of Hungarian aristocrats whose history is punctuated with cabals and conspiracies. He would dearly love to settle down to a calm, content life with the lovely Erica, occasionally nipping over to the Marick vineyards to stomp on a few bushels of grapes with her. But so long as he lives in Pine Valley, the chance for a tranquil life is as unlikely as finding a Magyar gypsy with agoraphobia.

Actor: Sydney Penny

Birthplace: Nashville, Tennessee

Sydney Penny used to travel with her parents, country/western singers Hank and Shari Penny. She made her debut at age three singing her version of "My Little Pony." The audience applauded wildly, and Sydney knew, from that moment, that she was going to be a performer.

A few years later, Sydney was chosen to play Maggie as a child in the classic television miniseries, *The Thorn Birds.* Her several films include *Pale Rider* with Clint Eastwood. She also appeared in *The New Gidget.* Her last soap role was as B. J. Walker in *Santa Barbara.*

Sydney appreciates films, clothes and decorative objects from the 1930s and 1940s.

Character: Julia Santos

Julia Santos arrived in Pine Valley in September, 1993 to join her sister, Dr. Maria Santos. Her first scene for the soap showed the lovely Julia clad only in a towel.

Julia befriended the handsome, gentle, Anton Lang, a medical student. But before romance could bloom, Julia was badly injured in the Tornado from Hell that struck Pine Valley in 1994. Her sister, Maria, was forced to stitch up the gash on her face without any proper equipment, leaving Julia with an ugly scar. Unable to deal with the trauma, she fled her home and wound up on the mean streets of Pine Valley where she was found by one of the neighborhood denizens, Noah. Despite his attempts to protect her, Noah couldn't save her from being raped. They became closer as friends and, at times, seemed on the verge of becoming lovers.

In time, with Noah's help, Julia began to heal emotionally. She had surgery to remove the scar and learned she was HIV negative. She was also accepted as a nursing school student. With Anton divorcing Kendall (whom he married in haste after learning he was Dimitri Marick's son) it looked as if he and Julia could resume the relationship they were trying to build. But what about Noah?

Actor: Kelly Ripa

Birthplace: Stratford, New Jersey
Birthdate: October 2

The story of the *Ugly Duckling* tells us about a sad little waterfowl whose duck pond companions "quacked up" with laughter every time they looked at him because he looked nothing like them. As a matter of fact, they considered him quite ugly. But, in time, he grew into a beautiful swan, and was admired by every waterfowl in the area, including his former tormentors.

For Kelly Ripa, the story has a very special significance. She was appearing in a high school production of the classic fairy tale and, in true fairy-tale fashion, was seen by someone with show business credentials who persuaded her to pursue an acting career. Kelly took that person's advice and went on to study drama and work in local theater groups. She made her daytime debut in *All My Children* in 1990 as Hayley Vaughan, the rebellious out-of-wedlock daughter of Adam Chandler.

Character: Hayley Vaughan

Hayley came to Pine Valley in 1990 to meet her father, Adam Chandler, for the first time. But instead of developing a warm father-daughter relationship with him, Hayley found herself more and more put off by Adam's machinations. Early in 1995, she became even more estranged when she blamed him for the death of his newborn daughter, and for the emotional breakdown of her most recent stepmother, Gloria. Hayley's obvious hatred for Adam made her a suspect when it was discovered that Adam was being poisoned.

Hayley has several secrets in her past, most of them linked to her mother, Arlene. As these secrets are revealed, she's forced to make difficult emotional adjustments. A recovering alcoholic, Hayley has faced her problems with courage, and joined Alcoholics Anonymous; however, she knows she will probably always be one emotional crisis away from her next drink.

She's had to deal with her mixed feelings for her detective agency partner, Charlie, and for the man who wants to marry her, Alec (once her father's protégé). She also has to deal with her unresolved problems with both parents.

Kelly on Hayley:

"What I like about Hayley is that she's not a quitter. She may sometimes feel like giving up, but I have this sense that she never will...."

Actor: Ingrid Rogers

Birthplace: Toronto, Ontario, Canada
Birthdate: April 27

Playing Taylor Cannon on *All My Children* marks Ingrid's professional debut. She had been a business major at the University of Toronto, but became increasingly interested in acting and decided to transfer to the Academy of Dramatic Arts in New York, and joined the school's Theater Company.

In 1992, she became part of the *All My Children* roster in the role of the sharp and somewhat sassy teenager, Taylor Roxbury Cannon, who decides to become a police officer.

Ingrid and her husband, David Fryberger, live in New York City.

Character: Taylor Roxbury Cannon

Taylor arrived in Pine Valley in 1992, and immediately became part of a group of teenagers who got into scrapes — some of them more serious than others.

She could have gone on to be the privileged princess from a well-to-do family, but somewhere along the way, she realized she wanted to find a way to give something back to society. She decided to become a member of the Pine Valley Police Department. In early spring of 1995, Taylor was assigned to protect Noah, whose life had been threatened, and was forced to shoot and kill his attacker. The experience left her shaken, but it may have drawn her closer to Noah.

Actor: Ruth Warrick

Birthplace: St. Joseph, Missouri
Birthdate: June 29

She was one of Hollywood's most beautiful movie stars of the 1940s. And she could also act! Her talent led her to being personally chosen by Orson Welles to join his prestigious New York theater group, The Mercury Theater, which included Agnes Moorehead, Everett Sloan, Joseph Cotten, and other great stars of the stage (many of whom were also doing radio soaps).

Warrick later went to Hollywood when Welles decided that she would be the woman to play his wife in *Citizen Kane.* Welles told Warrick he couldn't think of any other actress who could play Mrs. Kane as he saw her; a woman of intelligence and breeding who had the grace and strength to endure Kane's machinations.

Warrick had a successful film career before becoming a major television star in the role of Hannah Cord (a sort of precursor of Phoebe) on *Peyton Place.* She later joined *As the World Turns,* before moving into Pine Valley as Phoebe English Tyler.

61

In her busy private life, Ruth Warrick is active in social and cultural activities. She supports several programs fostering the inclusion of the arts in the public school systems of the country. She worked in Jimmy Carter's campaign and became a close friend of the former president's family, especially of his late mother, Miss Lillian. She is also active in projects that involve AIDS education and help for AIDS patients.

Ruth Warrick has become a sort of keeper of the Orson Welles flame. She is often asked to address groups who study his films and his influence on American film making.

Character: Phoebe English Tyler Wallingford
Phoebe English Tyler Wallingford had all the prerequisites for the role of social arbiter of Pine Valley. She had the ancestors; the wealth; the social position. In short, she believed she had an unquestionable right to dominate Pine Valley's social life.

But Phoebe's well-ordered life came a cropper when her husband, Dr. Charles Tyler, rejected her rigidity in favor of the warmth and love of his secretary, Mona Kane. Although Phoebe resisted the divorce, she was finally forced into it when Mona used a bit of Phoebe's penchant for manipulation (e.g., blackmail). That divorce made Phoebe aware of the shocking truth: You can't rely on your past to protect your future.

Phoebe eventually met a con man who called himself Professor Langley Wallingford. (He was actually a former carnival performer named Lenny Wlasuk.) He was charming and disarming, and much to her surprise, she let him seduce her. Phoebe's seduction drew thousands of letters from women in their fifties, sixties, and even seventies, who said she proved that older ladies can still star in their own passion plays.

Freeing herself from her hidebound background left Phoebe open to experiences she once thought could never happen to her. She was wooed by a gigolo; she endured the shock of learning who Langley really was; she learned he had two illegitimate daughters (one of whom, Verla Grubbs, was created for Carol Burnett); she almost lost her beloved niece, Brooke. But Phoebe has learned to grow with each event in her life and paraphrasing Mark Antony's description of Cleopatra, age cannot wither her, nor custom stale her infinite ability to get involved in anything life in Pine Valley holds for her.

Actor: Walt Willey

Birthplace: Ottawa, Illinois
Birthdate: January 26

Walt Willey loves to do stand-up comedy; he enjoys science fiction movies; he plays chess; he writes; he paints; he sculpts. And it's not so much that he does so many things, but that he does them all so well.

While still in college, Willey decided to concentrate on drama rather than art. He joined an improvisational tour group. When he came to New York to study and work, his first professional job was as an extra on *AMC*. Later, he was asked to play Joe Novak on *Ryan's Hope*. After he began working in off-Broadway productions, he returned to *All My Children* in 1989 in the newly created role of Jackson Montgomery, and became an instant favorite with the fans.

Character: Jackson Montgomery

Lawyers lament that they aren't well loved in our society. However, if there were more lawyers like Jackson Montgomery, the population might look more kindly on the profession. He's kind. He's sensitive. He's smart. And he's successful.

As far as his private life is concerned, success is a relative thing. He wooed his former sister-in-law, Erica Kane (who was married to his brother, Travis Montgomery, twice) and thought he would be the third Montgomery in her increasingly long list of married surnames. But instead, he married his former client, Laurel Banning. When Erica separated from her most recent husband, Dimitri Marick, she and Jackson shared a tryst or two. But that was as far as it went. Erica resumed with Dimitri. Jackson tried to reestablish his marriage with Laurel, but she had already committed to Trevor.

Love does await Jackson Montgomery, Esquire; of that we have no doubt.

The Creator: Agnes Nixon

Birthplace: Chicago, Illinois
Birthdate: December 10

Agnes Eckhardt Nixon grew up in Nashville, Tennessee. In her early teens, Nixon became a devotee of the novels of Louisa May Alcott — the author of *Little Women* — which, she said, "taught me how to tell stories." Nixon studied drama at Northwestern University. Her classmates included Charlton Heston, Patricia Neal, and Cloris Leachman. While still a student, she sold a radio play. This first success led to her decision to switch from acting to writing. Irna Phillips, dubbed the "Mother of Soap Operas," was impressed with the young writer, and hired her to write dialogue for Phillips's radio soap, *Woman in White*. In the 1950s, Nixon started writing television dramas for shows such as *Playhouse 90* and *Studio One*.

In 1981, Agnes Nixon drew on the experiences of her Irish kin who migrated to America ("crossing the pond," as they're wont to say) to create *The Manions of America,* an ABC miniseries starring Kate Mulgrew and introducing a young Irish-born, English-trained actor, Pierce Brosnan, to an American audience.

Nixon has been both creator and head writer of some of the medium's most successful soap operas. She worked frequently with her mentor, Irna Phillips, and with Phillips' long-time associates, Procter and Gamble. In 1951, Nixon and Roy Winsor co-created *Search for Tomorrow* for P&G; the series ran for some thirty years. In 1956, Agnes and Irna Phillips co-created *As the World Turns* for Procter and Gamble. She later became head writer for *Guiding Light,* which Phillips also created for P&G.

Irna Phillips's life-long interest in timely events influenced her talented protégé. Nixon's daytime dramas have always incorporated current events and topics of social relevance. (Agnes Nixon once wrote a story line about pap-smear tests for the detection of uterine cancer. Women from around the country wrote to say that, thanks to her, they had pap tests — some for the first time in their lives — and because their cancers were found in time, they were able to be treated successfully.)

Agnes Nixon developed *All My Children* while still doing head writing chores for *Guiding Light.* P&G optioned it, but held back production. Meanwhile, they asked her to take over as principal writer for another one of their Phillips-created series, *Another World,* which had gone into a serious ratings decline. When Nixon came on board in 1967, she introduced the character of Rachel Davis who was inspired by the Erica Kane character in her then still unproduced soap, *All My Children.* (Robin Strasser was the first to play the role, which eventually was assumed by Victoria Wyndham.) Nixon also introduced the longest-running love triangle in soaps with Alice Matthews (Jacqueline Courtney), Steve Frame (George Reinholt), and Rachel Davis.

Nixon's success prompted the ABC network to ask her to create a soap for them. In 1968, she obliged with *One Life to Live,* the first soap to feature an ethnically, socially, and racially diverse cast of characters, including Episcopalians, Polish Catholics, Jews, Blacks, factory workers, waitresses, and a powerful press tycoon.

ABC asked for another soap, and two years later, Nixon was able to give them *All My Children.* And everything in Pine Valley flowed from there.

Susan Lucci Talks about "Life" in Pine Valley

The most significant story line for Susan Lucci in the twenty-five years she's played Erica Kane on *All My Children* is one she shared with the late Frances Heflin, whom everyone on *AMC* called "Fra": "I would say it's the mother-daughter relationship between Mona (Fra Heflin) and Erica," the actor explains. "I think it may have been the first such relationship on daytime. It was so innovative of Agnes (Nixon) in her writing, and Fra and I always felt so lucky to be part of that. We both got such tremendous response from the audience. They said it was the only realistic relationship of a mother and a daughter they'd ever seen on television. It had everything: humor and anger and love and search for approval, and all those elements that are mixed into this special and wonderful relationship.

"Also outstanding for me has been Erica's humor. She's shown both her dramatic and humorous sides. I've also enjoyed the modeling stories, which are a lot of fun to play."

Susan feels anyone who puts Erica into the "villain" category limits their perception of this extraordinary character.

"There has always been so much more to Erica," Susan says. "I know Agnes has always seen that as well. Yes, Erica was, and still is, headstrong and willful. She's also energetic and wants a great life. She wants love, acceptance, happiness, and she wants her little girl, Bianca, to be with her. Of course, Erica does have her own way of going about getting what she's after and, sometimes, she can be rather *naughty.*"

The author once referred to Erica Kane as one of television's earliest liberated women.

Susan commented, "At first, I didn't think of her in political terms. But several years ago I received a wonderful letter from *Ms. Magazine* saying they felt she was the first liberated soap character, and they admired her for that. And, of course, that comes out of Agnes's concept and her writing for Erica. I believe there have always been women, such as Jenny Churchill (the American-born mother of Winston Churchill), for example, who never thought of themselves as being unable to do what they want to do. Like those women, Erica has always felt if she wants to do something, she would just do it."

As for what we can expect to find Erica doing over the next twenty-five years, Susan Lucci asserts, "I have no doubt Erica will still be Erica...."

Another World

nother World joined the daytime galaxy on May 4, 1964. When the show premiered, an off-camera announcer solemnly intoned, "We do not live in this world alone, but in a thousand other worlds."

While scientists may have their explanations for how other worlds come into existence, this one was created by Irna Phillips with the assistance of her bright young protégé, William J. Bell, who would later go on to write for another Phillips soap, *Days of Our Lives,* before creating *The Young and the Restless* and *The Bold and the Beautiful.*

The original character list carried nine Matthews, two Baxters, and one Palmer. Irna Phillips's plan was to make the Matthews clan of Bay City an equivalent family grouping to the Hugheses, the dominant family in her other soap, Oakdale's *As the World Turns*; she wanted Bay City to be set close enough to Oakdale for the characters to visit frequently. However, although both shows were Procter and Gamble productions, there was some concern that characters from the new series might, somehow, create confusion for fans of the older P&G soap. Other sources have said the thumbs down was strictly the product of network rivalry: CBS didn't feel it should offer an NBC soap "air time," and the NBC peacock ruffled its feathers just at the thought of lending one of its nestlings to its long-time competitor.

Irna Phillips and Bill Bell populated their new domain with people who wanted to hold on to some of the old, comforting values of family and love, but who were caught up in the changes of the times. One of the characters, Pat Matthews (played by Beverly Penberthy), was involved in an illegal abortion, an illegitimate pregnancy, and murder — and that was just in the first year!

Bay City Chronicles

Soon after the series debuted, William Matthews died, leaving his wife, Liz, his children Susan and Bill, his brother Jim and Jim's wife, Mary, and their children, Pat, Russ, and Alice, to carry on the Matthews legacy.

By 1967, Bill Bell had left the show; Irna was taking a less active role in its production, and it needed help to get through a serious downturn in ratings. (Irna had even imported one of her strongest *Guiding Light* characters, lawyer Mike Bauer — played by Don Stewart — and his daughter, Hope, to add some drama, but the Bay City/Springfield hybrid didn't work. Viewers knew Bauer as a *Guiding Light*-er and never accepted him as anything else.) The show was rumored to be slated for cancellation, but some executives at NBC were persuaded to give the series another chance. Agnes Nixon, another of Irna's protégés,

Another World debuted a year after President John F. Kennedy was assassinated. The country was still in shock over the loss of their young leader, our involvement in Vietnam was expanding, Cuba's Fidel Castro was making threats in Central America: The country had been jolted out of the relative apathy of the post–World War II 1950s into a period of political and social foment. Civil rights leaders were demanding changes in the old Jim Crow laws. Women were being encouraged to demand equality under the law. Even abortion — "the illegal operation" — was coming out of the closet; women were now gathering petitions to have the procedure legalized.

It seemed we were, indeed, living in "*Another World.*"

Original Cast

Vera Allen . . . . .Grandma Matthews
John Beal . . . . .Jim Matthews
Liza Chapman . . . . .Janet Matthews
Jacqueline Courtney . .Alice Matthews
Sarah Cunningham . . .Liz Matthews
Virginia Dwyer . . . . .Mary Matthews
Joe Gallison . . . . .Bill Matthews
William Prince . . . . .Ken Baxter
Nicholas Pryor . . . . .Tom Baxter
Carol Roux . . . . .Melissa Palmer
Joey Trent . . . . .Russ Matthews
Susan Trustman . . . . .Pat Matthews

First Air Date: May 4, 1964 / NBC

67

A 1964 portrait of the Matthews women, counter clockwise from top: Susan Trustman (Pat), Vera Allen (Grandma), Jacquie Courtney (Alice), and Liza Chapman (Janet).

came over from head writing duties at *GL* to assume the *AW* challenge. She took bold action almost from page one of her first script: She had a plane crash kill off most of the characters who had been introduced by her immediate predecessor, James Lipton. She rescued the Matthews family from near oblivion and used two of Jim and Mary Matthews's three children, Russ and Alice, as core characters around whom new characters and stories would be built.

Two of those new characters were Rachel Davis, played by Robin Strasser, and Steve Frame, played by George Reinholt. In juxtaposition with the blue-blooded Matthews, Rachel and Steve had no silver spoons in their background. Steve was a member of the working class Frame family who became successful in the construction business. Rachel was a girl from across the tracks, who was bright, beautiful, and ambitious — and determined to find *"Another World"* of wealth and privilege that was light years from her own humble beginnings.

Rachel took her first step up into that other world by marrying Dr. Russ Matthews. Meanwhile, Steve, who had fallen for Alice Matthews, proposed. Then Rachel seduced Steve and became pregnant. Thus was created the longest-running triangle in soap history. The success of the story line was so phenomenal, *Another World*, which NBC almost put on ice, scored a hat trick with its hot threesome.

Highlights of the 1970s

In 1970, two years after Agnes Nixon rebuilt *AW* into a soap to be reckoned with in the ratings race, she left to put *One Life to Live* on the ABC network. That year, *Another World* became the first soap opera to spin off a new daytime drama. (*As the World Turns* had previously spun off a late-night series called, *Our Private World*,.) *AW's* daughter cell was called *Another World-Somerset* (eventually, the title was shortened to just *Somerset*). It ran for six years. Some of its alumnae and alumni include Ann Wedgeworth, Nicholas Coster, Jameson Parker, Gary Sandy, Holland Taylor, Michael Nouri, Sigourney Weaver, JoBeth Williams, and Ted Danson.

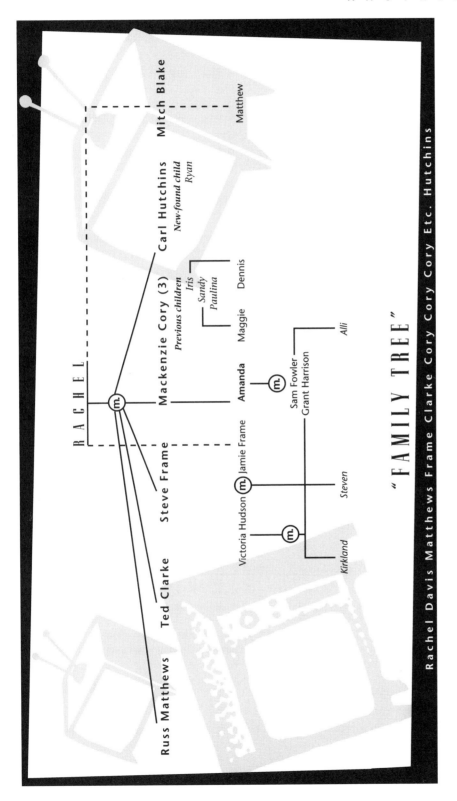

"FAMILY TREE"

RACHEL

Russ Matthews

Ted Clarke

Steve Frame

Mackenzie Cory (3)
Previous children
Iris
Sandy
Paulina
Dennis

Maggie

Amanda — m. — Sam Fowler / Grant Harrison

Alli

Carl Hutchins
New-found child
Ryan

Mitch Blake

Matthew

Victoria Hudson — m. — Jamie Frame

Steven

m.

Kirkland

*F*or a quarter of a century, Rachel Davis Matthews Frame Clarke Cory Cory Cory Hutchins (Victoria Wyndham) has been at the center of just about everything that happens in Bay City. And when she's not stirring things up on her own, someone to whom she's either related or involved with is doing the moving and shaking.

Rachel Davis Matthews Frame Clarke Cory Cory Cory Cory Etc. Hutchins

There's a story about the late Bette Davis, who was a soap opera fan: Remembering one especially interesting story line in *Somerset* involving a murderer putting poison in the victim's tea and avoiding detection by dressing as a clown, Ms. Davis was supposed to have said something like, *What a marvelous dramatic device: you make yourself so obvious to everyone, no one will remember what you did — only how you looked.* ("Yes, officer. I saw it all. I'll never forget that red nose, that chalk white face, those size sixteen shoes flapping around...")

In 1977, with the relative success of *Somerset, Another World* spun off another series called *Lovers and Other Friends.* Taken off the air within a few months, it was returned to the schedule, retuned, and renamed *For Richer, For Poorer.* Alas, the show proved that by any other name, it was still, as the network nabobs in New York said, "a lox." In 1978, it was canceled.

In 1978, *Dallas* debuted, and suddenly the whole country went western. Stockbrokers wore Stetsons on Wall Street; advertising agency executives jangled down Madison Avenue in snakeskin boots and silver-roweled spurs. Out in Hollywood, a starlet posed with a bra top from which the handles of two dainty Texas-type Derringers dangled.

The Lone Star State's appeal was apparent even on the soaps. In 1979, *One Life to Live* introduced the wealthy Buchanans of Texas, Asa Buchanan, and his Buchanan buckaroos, sons, Clint and Bo, played, respectively, by Phil Carey, Clint Ritchie, and Robert S. Woods.

In 1980, *Another World* responded to the growing interest in all things Texan—including Texas tea and grass (oil and money, that is)—with a new spinoff called *Texas.* The migration from Bay City to the Lone Star State was led by Iris Cory Carrington Delaney Bancroft (Beverlee McKinsey). By 1982, however, the saddle soap was flushed down the ratings drain. It was the last spin-off (so far) from *Another World.*

I Am Lion — Hear Me Roar

Although soaps tend to have women dominate the stories — and AW certainly has featured some of soapdom's most fascinating females, including Rachel, Elena de Poulignac (played by both Christina Pickles and Maeve McGuire), her daughter, Cecile de Poulignac (Susan Keith and Nancy Frangione), Felicia Gallant (Linda Dano), etc. — the men of Bay City have been among the strongest male characters in the medium. These stalwart laddies include the two big Daddy Lions, Mackenzie Cory (Douglass Watson) and Carl Hutchins (Charles Keating). These two "main" men were lifelong adversaries; each would not have been sorry to hear the other had been destroyed. Ironically, both would be linked by their love for the same woman, Rachel.

The other members of Bay City's major male category include the Hudson brothers, John (David Forsyth) and Michael (Kale Brown); Cass Winthrop (Steve Schnetzer); the sometimes enigmatic Jake McKinnon (Tom Eplin). Completing the ranks of the manly men were the Harrisons: father Spencer, (David Hedison), and sons, Grant (Mark Pinter), and Ryan (Paul Michael Valley). (Ryan's biological father, by the way, is Carl Hutchins, who had an affair with Ryan's mother, Justine.)

The "Mac Attack"

By 1972, the series began to slide in the ratings. Harding Lemay was brought in as head writer. Having been associated for years with the theater, his only soap credit was with a weird Canadian series called *Strange Paradise,* which starred a fine Broadway actor, Douglass Watson.

Robin Strasser had left the role of Rachel Davis and returned briefly early in 1972; by mid-1972, however, she had left again. Victoria Wyndham took over the role. Lemay felt Rachel needed to change, and Wyndham could help turn her from the Bitch of Bay City into a sympathetic character. It would take some doing, but Lemay felt Wyndham could get the audience to accept the change. He was right.

Beverlee McKinsey in 1976. She later created the role of Alexandra Spaulding on Guiding Light.

Lemay next introduced the character of Mackenzie Cory, a powerful press tycoon (originally played by Robert Emhardt, then by Douglass Watson) and his strong-willed daughter, Iris, played by Beverlee McKinsey.

By this time, Rachel had married and divorced Steve Frame. Mac and Rachel met, fell in love, and married. With worldly and sophisticated Mackenzie Cory to play Professor Higgins to Rachel's Eliza Doolittle, Lemay was able to transform Rachel from man-eater to well-mannered young woman. Although Rachel and Mac loved each other, that didn't prevent them from separating from time to time. Mac was involved with various women — including Elena, Alice, and Steve's sister, Janice — but he always eventually, went back to Rachel.

Meanwhile, *Another World* ran into problems when Lemay decided to drop the character of Steve Frame by having him die in a helicopter

71

·Film stars who appeared on Another World include:

Eric Roberts · Ted Shackleford · Susan Sullivan · Jackee Harry · Ray Liotta · Rue McClanahan · Charles Durning · Audra Lindley · Cleavon Little · Kyra Sedgwick · Howard Rollins · Nicholas Coster · Dorothy Lyman · Nancy Marchand · Morgan Freeman

crash. (There were rumors at the time that the actor, George Reinholt, was "difficult" and that Lemay was becoming increasingly incensed at his behavior.) When Reinholt left in 1975, so did his long-time co-star, Jacquie Courtney (Alice). Both actors went over to *One Life to Live* where it was hoped they'd spark a new reaction with the fans — but their stay in Llanview generally fizzled instead of fizzed.

The 1980s

In 1981, both Steve and Alice returned to the series. Steve was played by former "Bonanza" star, David Canary (see also *All My Children*), while Dr. Alice Matthews Frame was played by Linda Borgeson. Steve explained that he survived his helicopter crash in Australia, but had been wandering around the Outback for years suffering from amnesia. Mac and Rachel had split (again); admitting that they loved each other, she and Steve planned to remarry. But the groom-to-be was killed in a car crash in 1983 and that, presumably, was the last the fans would ever see of Steve Frame.

In 1984, when *Another World* was marking its twentieth anniversary, Courtney returned as Dr. Alice Matthews Frame. The story line turned her into a passive character whose primary role was as a confidante for her adopted daughter, Sally Frame. Courtney left in 1985.

Meanwhile, *AW* writers were developing other themes in the series. One of Mac's illegitimate children, Sandy (Alexander) Cory, came to Bay City. (At last count, Mac Cory had three illegitimate children: Sandy, Iris, and Paulina — and one child, Amanda, with his wife, Rachel. He was also the stepfather of Rachel's two sons, Jamie and Matt.) Sandy had previously lived in Las Vegas as soapdom's first male prostitute; although he called himself a paid "escort," it was obvious to the audience that he offered a full-service operation.

(As startling as it was to the fans to learn about Sandy's previous profession, they would have been even more surprised if Sandy had been presented as the first gay male on soaps. Apparently, the concept had been approved, but was changed at the last minute, when network poobahs decided not to take a leap of faith that relied on the tolerance of the daytime audience.)

The soap then brought on two female prostitutes. Clarice (Gail Brown, sister of film actor, Karen Black) and Blaine (Laura Malone). Both women would eventually be "redeemed." Clarice married Blaine's brother, police officer Larry Ewing (Rick Porter) — later having one of the first amnioscentesis procedures on a soap — and Blaine married both Jamie and Sandy, becoming first Rachel's and then Mac's daughter-in-law.

The Love family — including Marley and her "sister," Donna — came to Bay City and quickly lived up to their name. Eventually, Marley learned that Donna was actually her mother. Donna would also learn that she had given birth to identical twin girls; having been sedated during the delivery, she didn't realize that one of the children had been taken from her. Enter Marley's twin, Victoria, with her beau, Jake McKinnon. The twins competed for Jake, who finally proposed to Marley. In time, Jake and Marley split.

The Hudson brothers — Michael and John — came to Bay City. Donna, who had once been married to Michael, remarried him. During one of Donna and Michael's frequent flareups, Donna sought comfort from brother-in-law, John. Daughter Vicky caught her about to make love to her uncle, and was so upset she crashed her car into a tree.

Rachel and Steve's son, Jamie, was in love with a lovely young woman named Lisa who seemed to have ESP. He was seduced by Vicky, but stayed (otherwise) true to Lisa.

Marley divorced Jake. He and his former lady love, Vicky, slept together. Vicky discovered she was pregnant and although she assumed the child was Jake's, she told Jamie he was going to be a father. Jamie broke his engagement to Lisa and married Vicky. Jake later raped Marley.

Vicky's son became the object of two putative papas: Jake insisted the child was his. Jamie was sure he was little Steven's father. Ultimately, blood tests proved the boy was Steven Frame's and Rachel Cory's grandson.

As time marched on in Bay City, relationships grew ever more complicated: Mitch Blake, Matthew's father, came back to Bay City to get to know his son; John and Russ Matthews became rivals for Russ's former wife, Sharlene Frame; Rachel and Mac's daughter, Amanda, married artist Sam Fowler, and gave birth to Allison (Ally). Mac Cory had a fatal heart attack (Mac's death followed the sudden death of actor Douglass Watson.) Rachel and Iris were devastated by Mac's death. For the first time in their lives, they turned to each other for comfort over their common loss.

Ellen Wheeler created the role's Marley and Victoria.

Later, a young woman named Paulina turned up and proved to be Mac Cory's illegitimate daughter. (Actually, she was his second illegitimate daughter: It seems he never married Iris's mother either.) Meanwhile, Sharlene's daughter, Josie, made love to Matthew, then fled to Los Angeles. Russ was furious when Sharlene told him for the first time that he was Josie's father. (Of course, he was upset: Think of all the Father's Day gifts he missed.)

John married Sharlene after Russ left Bay City; following his divorce from Vicky, Jamie left town — as he's done before — and will no doubt return; when Sharlene — who suffered from multiple-personality syndrome — was presumed to have died in an accident, John married Spencer Harrison's niece, Kelsey (Kaitlin Hopkins), a former flame of Jamie's.

The 1990s

Several years after Sharlene's "death," she returned to Bay City as one of her alter-egos, Kate. After treatment, Sharlene was able to emerge as the strongest of her three personalities and eventually remarried John after his divorce.

Ian Rain (Julian McMahon) came to town seeking revenge against both Carl and the Corys. Meanwhile, Josie came back to Bay City and revealed she'd been a hooker. She got a job as a waitress in the restaurant Ian owned, and they were drawn together. Before making love to Ian, she had an HIV test which proved to be negative. Ian became something of a rebel hero, eventually returning to his native Australia to establish an environmental foundation. Josie wasn't ready to commit, and after several months of attempting a long-distance relationship, Ian told her he had met someone new. Josie then decided to become a police officer and met Gary, one of her instructors, who has an alcohol problem stemming from the death of a partner.

Iris became increasingly angry over Rachel's plan to marry Carl. Although she and Carl had once been "involved," she hated him for at least two reasons: Because he had been her late father's long-time enemy (Carl blamed Mac for the death of his father), and because he might become too influential in Cory Publishing.

Iris proved to be behind a series of events that almost took Carl's life, as well as the lives of her half-sister, Paulina, and Jake, who had been kidnapped by a man Iris hired. (Iris never intended for him to harm the young couple. But her hireling took matters into his own hands.) Ryan rescued Paulina and Jake from the wilderness. Iris was convicted of attempted murder (of Carl), but later realized that she had been manipulated by the returning vengeful Evan Frame.

Paulina and Jake remarried, but Jake got deeply in debt to a loan shark (naturally without telling Paulina), who eventually sent a hit

Ruth Warrick (All My Children), *Coleen Zenk Pinter* (As the World Turns), *Mark Pinter* (Another World), *and Mary Stuart* (Search for Tomorrow).

woman named Bunny Eberhart to collect. Paulina and Jake were trapped by Bunny and her henchman, but outfoiled them. Bunny went to jail, but her partner seemingly escaped, only to turn up in Jake's car. In a horrible accident, Jake was thrown clear of the car while the bad guy perished, and his badly burned body was presumed to be Jake's.

Jake, meanwhile, had amnesia, and almost wandered into his own funeral in Bay City before heading west. (Tom Eplin, who had played Jake since 1985, took a leave of absence.) Jake eventually made his way back to Bay City.

Vicky, who had been in love with the dashing detective, Ryan Harrison, married his half-brother Grant instead. But the marriage to the ambitious young Senator was a disaster, and he vowed to get custody of their child, Kirkland, when they divorced. Vicky, however, pulled a baby switch in an attempt to thwart Grant's efforts.

Grant married Amanda Cory Fowler as a way of establishing himself as a settled family man with a wife and adoring stepdaughter. But the marriage didn't work out. Determined to get custody of his son — and to punish Vicky for what he perceived were her sins (this from a man who tried to keep her incommunicado for months after their marriage) — Grant accused her of shooting him; just when it looked as if she would lose both her child and her freedom, however, Grant admitted he had pulled the trigger.

75

Meanwhile, in the South of France, a titled lady read about Grant and Ryan and made plans to fly to Bay City immediately. The *comtesse* turned out to be the former Justine Harrison, Spencer's "late" wife, and Carl's former mistress, and the mother of both Grant and Ryan.

Justine used her uncanny resemblance to Rachel to take her place, having Rachel dispatched to a Swiss sanitarium. She then gave Spencer pills that caused his high-blood pressure to skyrocket, and he suffered a stroke. Although he couldn't speak, he was finally able to alert Ryan to the fact that his mother was still alive. Meanwhile, Justine, as Rachel, tried to seduce Carl, who realized, to his horror, who she really was.

Marshall Lincoln Kramer III, the first African-American head of Cory Publishing, encouraged Felicia to write books other than romance novels. Felicia was kidnapped by an obsessive fan (echoing Stephen King's *Misery*), who tried to force her to write a romance novel for him. Kramer was one of her rescuers. His concern for her was obviously more than that of a publisher for a star writer, and she started to respond in kind.

Felicia's daughter, Lorna, had once accused young Dr. Morgan Winthrop (Cass's brother) of raping her, although someone else was proven to be the culprit; Lorna knew Dr. Morgan loved her, but she was drawn to Grant. However, Justine was determined to do anything to keep Grant from marrying Lorna.

Meanwhile, Paulina became attracted to Joe Carlino, the private detective looking into Jake's mysterious death. Joe had been smitten from the first time they met. Would he be rejected if Jake came back? As Joe Barbara, the actor who plays Carlino told the author, "If Paulina would decide simply on the basis of food, Joe would win: He's a great Italian cook. You should taste his pasta aglio oglio."

Social Themes

In recent years, *AW*'s writing team has developed several important social themes: The character of John Hudson, for instance, has had to deal with recurring problems stemming from his military service (and actor David Forsyth is himself a Marine veteran who served in Vietnam).

Sharlene Frame Matthews Hudson had also been a prostitute — or, at least, her alter ego, Sharly, did the hooking. It was as Kate, another alter ego, that Sharlene (who was assumed to have died in an accident) returned to Bay City in 1994. Sharlene later recalled having been raped as a child, which was the trauma that created the "alters." Sharlene's rapist was tracked down and found to have a history of abusing young girls.

The first soap to deal with an AIDS storyline, *AW* recently developed two strong story lines that defied the traditional taboos of age: Rachel and her former adversary, Carl Hutchins (Charles Keating) became lovers, then spouses. The characters, though mature, were deeply passionate about each other. Keating told the author, "We're here to prove to the young upstarts that there is nothing they can do that we can't do, and, perhaps, do better."

The mature love story of Rachel Cory and Carl Hutchins became one of soapdom's most popular themes. Asked how she would compare the love stories of Rachel and Mac and Rachel and Carl, Victoria Wyndham told the author: "They are alike in the fact that what Rachel and Mac felt for each other was real; its the same with Rachel and Carl. When Rachel met Mac, she was still someone who didn't care whom she might hurt so long as she got her way. Mac helped bring out the person she really was by persuading her that she didn't have to be manipulative or conniving.... As Rachel was redeemed by the love of a good man, Carl was redeemed by the love of a good woman."

> **Guest Stars Who've Shined Brightly on Another World:**
>
> Anne Sheridan (the first Hollywood film star to do a soap) · Liberace · Jose Ferrer ·Roberta Flack · Crystal Gayle · Dick Cavett

Meanwhile, Rachel's son, Matthew, had fallen in love with Donna Love Hudson, former mother-in-law of his half-brother, Jamie, and grandmother of his nephew, Steven. At one point in their relationship, Donna thought she was having menopausal hot flashes; she wasn't. (At least, not yet.) Despite Rachel's earlier reservations about the couple's age difference, she finally gave the marriage her blessing.

Another World has also dealt with the topic of breast enlargement involving a character, Brett, who believed it would please her boyfriend, Morgan, if her breasts were larger. This story developed concurrently with the news about possible complications from silicone breast implants. The story took a twist when Brett found a lump during a preliminary examination for the surgery, which proved to be benign.

Alcoholism was a major theme in the story of Pat Matthews Randolph (Beverlee Penberthy) in the 1970s. The theme was picked up again with the character of Felicia Gallant (Linda Dano) who started to drink as a way of handling the death of her husband, Lucas. Felicia was introduced to Alcoholics Anonymous and learned how to deal with her addiction. She now counsels newcomer Gary.

The Founding Families

Technically, there was one "founding family" when *Another World* debuted on May 4, 1964, namely, the Matthews. The other original characters, Greg and Tom Baxter, and Melissa (Missy) Palmer, were involved with the Matthews clan, but were soon relegated to oblivion. Below are descriptions of the original characters and the actors who played them:

The Matthews

Grandma Matthews, played by Vera Allen, mother of James and the late William; grandmother of Janet, Alice, Susan, Bill, Russ, Pat Matthews; mother-in-law of William's widow, Liz, and James (Jim's) wife, Mary Matthews. The character was phased out very early in the series.

William Matthews: The series commenced with the death of William Matthews, and dealt with the effect it had on his widow, Liz, and their children, Susan and Bill; and his brother, James (Jim) and his family, including wife, Mary, and children Pat, Russ, and Alice.

Janet Matthews, played by Liza Chapman. The character was written out shortly after the soap debuted.

James Matthews, originally played by John Beal, then Leon Janney, Shepperd Struddwick, and, finally Hugh Marlowe, who played him from 1969 until his death in 1982. Marlowe's death coincided with Matthews's passing.

Like his late brother, William, Jim worked for an accounting firm. But unlike his brother, who had become wealthy, Jim and his family were middle class. Jim was married to Mary, and was the father of Alice, Pat, and Russ. With Alice, he was Steve Frame's father-in-law; with Pat, he was John Randolph's father-in-law, and with Russ, he was Sharlene Frame's father in law.

Liz Matthews, originally played by Sarah Cunningham, then by Audra Lindley, Nancy Wickwire, and Irene Dailey, sister of the film actor, Dan Dailey. Liz is the widow of William Matthews, and the mother of the late Bill Matthews and Susan Douglas Shearer. Liz remained a strong character long after many members of the Matthews clan had been written out of the soap. She dispensed advice to her niece, Alice, especially when it came to dealing with Alice's long-time rival for Steve Frame's love, Rachel Davis.

Rachel was also Liz's sometime rival: Mackenzie Cory's daughter, Iris, had hoped to have Liz as a stepmother, but to the chagrin of both women, the manipulative Rachel Davis won his heart. (Later, Mac was engaged, briefly, to Alice Matthews Frame.)

Susan Matthews, originally played by Fran Sharon, then by Roni Dengel, Lisa Cameron, and Lynn Milgrim. The character was not a member of the original cast, but joined the show later in 1964. Susan married Liz's long-time friend, Fred Douglas, then divorced him and married Dr. Dan Shearer. She left later in 1964 and returned several times for brief stays in Bay City.

Alice Matthews Frame Gordon Frame, originally played by Jacqueline Courtney. Other actors who played her include Susan Harney, Wesley Ann Pfenning, and Linda Borgeson. The daughter of Jim and Mary Matthews, Alice was the sister of Russ and Pat Matthews. She was in love with Steve Frame, but lost him to Rachel Davis, then got him back, then lost him, then ... you get the picture.

Alice had a miscarriage and learned she was unable to have children. While her husband, Steve, was in Australia, Alice, who was then a nurse (she later became a doctor) adopted Sally Spencer, an orphaned accident victim.

Alice left Bay City in 1975, shortly after the death of her beloved mother, Mary, and the presumed death of her husband, Steve Frame, in Australia. (Actually, Virginia Dwyer, who played Mary, and Jacqueline Courtney and George Reinholt, who played Alice and Steve, were all let go by then head writer, Harding Lemay, reportedly over "artistic differences" with the three actors. Courtney and Reinholt were immediately hired by *One Life to Live*.)

The character of Alice returned to Bay City and eventually married Ray Gordon, originally played by Ted Shackleford, who later went on to star in *Knots Landing*. She divorced him after he nearly ruined the Frame family business. Alice then found herself falling for Steve's brother, Willis Frame, but he married Gwen Parrish, who, at one time, was engaged to her brother, Russ.

When Rachel, Alice's long-time rival for Steve Frame, was confused by her feelings for the newly returned Mitch Blake, father of her son, Matthew, she left her husband, Mac Cory, to be with him. Mac turned to Alice for comfort and soon fell in love with her. They announced their engagement. But Steve Frame (now played by David Canary) returned to Bay City and revealed he suffered amnesia after the helicopter crash — having been wandering around Australia, no doubt, absorbing the sounds of digereedos while working for Don King promoting boxing matches with kangaroos. When Steve came to see Alice, all her old feelings for him returned and she left Mac.

Before Steve and Alice could remarry, Steve and Rachel were trapped together in a collapsed construction site; as they waited to be rescued or to die, they admitted they still loved each other. The Alice/Steve/Rachel triangle was broken for good, however, when Steve died in a car crash shortly after he and Rachel renewed their pledge of love. Alice left town. Rachel and Mac eventually reconciled. In 1984, Alice, once again played by Jacqueline Courtney, returned, and left a year later.

79

Russ Matthews, originally played by Joey Trent, then by David Bailey. A doctor, Russ was the son of Mary and Jim Matthews; the brother of Pat and Alice Matthews; first cousin of Susan and the late Bill Matthews. First mar-

ried to Rachel Davis, he divorced her when he realized the child she was carrying was fathered by his sister, Alice's, erstwhile fiancé, Steve Frame.

Russ fell in love with student nurse, Cindy Clark, sister of Rachel's second husband, Ted Clark. She suffered from a terminal illness. Russ married her on her deathbed in the hospital. Later, Russ was engaged to Iris Cory, who had tried to play matchmaker for his mother, Liz, and her father, Mackenzie. But Rachel Davis, Russ's former wife, married him instead. Russ broke his engagement to Iris when he learned she had arranged for Mac to believe (erroneously) that Rachel was having an affair with a younger lover.

Russ married Sharlene Frame, and later learned that her daughter, Josie Watts, was actually his child. He left Bay City in 1981 after Sharlene and Dr. John Hudson announced their engagement.

Pat Matthews, originally played by Susan Trustman, then by Beverly Penberthy, was the daughter of Mary and Jim Matthews; sister of Russ and Alice Matthews. She was married to John Randolph, the father of her twins, Michael and Marianne. Soon after the series debuted, Pat became pregnant by her lover, Tom Baxter, who urged her to have an abortion. After learning (mistakenly) that she could never have children again, she shot Baxter dead. John Randolph (Michael M. Ryan) defended her in court and she was found not guilty. To the disappointment of his daughter, Lee, Randolph proposed to Pat and she accepted.

After Randolph was paralyzed in an accident, Pat was drawn to another handsome lawyer, widower Mike Bauer (a cross-over from *Guiding Light*), played by Don Stewart. But Pat only lusted in her heart, telling Mike she could never betray John. After John recovered from his paralysis, they became parents of twins Marianne and Michael.

John had an affair with another woman, which drove Pat to drink. After they reconciled, she stopped drinking. Later, after learning their daughter, Marianne, had had an abortion after her boyfriend left her, John stormed out and began another affair. This time, when he tried to return home, Pat had found someone else and left to start a new life with him.

Bill Matthews, played by Joe Gallison, was the son of Liz and the late William Matthews, and the brother of Susan Matthews Douglas Shearer. He was a cousin to Alice, Pat, and Russ Matthews. He was a lawyer who successfully defended Melissa (Missy) Palmer when she was accused of killing her husband, Danny Fargo, after he raped her. Bill and Missy were married and moved to California. He was killed in a boating accident soon after.

Melissa (Missy) Palmer Matthews, played by Carol Roux. She was an orphan. Young Bill Matthews fell in love with her, but his mother, Liz,

kept breaking them up, finally telling her she wasn't good enough for Bill. Heartbroken, Missy ran off to Chicago where she married Danny Fargo, a man she didn't love. After he raped her, he was shot dead. Missy was found holding the gun, but insisted she didn't remember if she killed him or not. Bill rushed to defend her, and after she was acquitted, she gave birth to the child conceived during the rape. She and Bill were married and left for California. Tragically, he died soon after.

The Baxters

Tom Baxter, played by Nicholas Pryor, was the lover of Pat Matthews. He urged her to have an abortion. When she mistakenly believed the procedure had left her unable to have children, she shot him. She was acquitted thanks to her lawyer, John Randolph, whom she later married.

Ken Baxter, played by film star William Prince, left the show within a year of its debut.

Closeups: Current Cast and Characters

Actor: Joe Barbara

Birthplace: New York, New York

Joe Barbara came to *Another World* from the hit off-Broadway production *Tina and Tony's Wedding.* "It's my first soap," Barbara said, "and I don't know who's happier about my being on the show; me or my family."

On the show, Barbara expects to do a lot of cooking in the person of Joe Carlino. He told the author, for a piece in *Soap Opera Digest,* "I definitely enjoy cooking, and I had hoped to have an opportunity to do it on the show. They wrote something for me the first time Carlino was supposed to be in the kitchen, and when I read it, I was absolutely blown away. My grandfather used to talk about making a dish called aglio oglio. It means, garlic in oil. He was the only person I ever heard mentioning the dish, and that's probably because I grew up in a relatively non-Italian, non-ethnic neighborhood in Florida. When they gave me the script, as I said, I was blown away when I read I was going to make pasta aglio oglio."

Character: Joe Carlino
Carlino is a former New York City police detective who decides to return home to Bay City where he was born and raised — and even dated Rachel's sister, Nancy, for a while.

81

Carlino traded in his police badge for a private investigator's license and began working with Frankie Winthrop to discover more about Jake's mysterious "death." Joe Carlino's first meeting with the still-grief-stricken Paulina is, for him, love at first sight. Eventually, she begins to return his affection. Then Jake returned! Stay tuned.

Actor: Alice Barrett

Birthplace: New York, New York
Birthdate: December 19

Alice knew she wanted to be an actor when she found herself competing for (and getting) roles in productions in elementary and high school. She earned her Bachelors Degree in Theater from Hunter College, which is part of CUNY, the City University of New York. She's done scads of off-Broadway plays, and starred in *The Catlins* on prime time. Her previous soap roles were on *As the World Turns* and *Ryan's Hope*. She also appeared in a feature film, *Mission Hill*.

Character: Mary Frances "Frankie" Frame Winthrop

One of the sprawling Frame family, Frankie is the niece of Sharlene Frame Matthews Watts Hudson, which makes her also the aunt of Sharlene's daughter, Josie Watts. She is also a cousin of Rachel's son, Jamie, whose father was Steven Frame, Frankie's uncle. Frankie is the wife of lawyer Cass Winthrop (Stephen Schnetzer) and the mother of their daughter, Charlotte (Charlie). She is Dr. Morgan Winthrop's sister-in-law.

Frankie came to Bay City in 1989. She has a high degree of extrasensory perception and is often able to sense things happening far away, both in terms of time and space.

Frankie owns a detective agency, and has begun working with Joe Carlino, a former New York City police detective who grew up in Bay City and once dated Rachel's sister, Nancy.

Actor: Randy Brooks

Birthplace: The Bronx, New York
Birthdate: January 30

Randy who was raised in Harlem, in Manhattan, came to *Another World* from his role as Nathan Hastings in *The Young and the Restless*. Prior to *Y&R*, he appeared in the late soap, *Generations*, and in such prime time productions as *Brothers and Sisters*, *Mork and Mindy*, *The Jeffersons*, *The Renegades*, and *Murder, She Wrote*. His feature films include *Colors* and *Reservoir Dogs*.

Brooks, who studied classical voice, has appeared with opera companies and is also a great blues, rock 'n roll, and pop singer. He plays several instruments including piano, guitar, drums, violin, trumpet, and saxophone.

Character: Marshall Lincoln Kramer III

Marshall came to Bay City to head Cory, the company that published Felicia Gallant's romance novels. He is that company's first African-American CEO.

His relationship with Felicia started on the wrong foot when he refused to publish any more of her romance books, insisting that she put her energies and her obvious talents to work on a "real" book. In time, Felicia agreed, and Kramer's faith in her talent paid off. But romance is not out of the Gallant one's life by any means, nor has Kramer deleted the subject from his personal database: Indeed, Kramer and Felicia are creating a very special story of their own.

Actor: Kale Browne

Birthplace: San Rafael, California
Birthdate: June 16

Kale came to *Another World* with a long list of credits including guest shots on *Hill Street Blues, Dallas, Dynasty, Knots Landing,* and *Webster.* He also appeared on several daytime shows including *As the World Turns, Guiding Light, One Life to Live, Search for Tomorrow* and *General Hospital.* He's married to actress Karen Allen.

Character: Michael Hudson

When Michael Hudson came to Bay City in 1985, he encountered his teenage lover, Donna (Anna Stuart), and learned that they had had twin daughters, Victoria and Marley. The two fell in love again and were remarried. But Donna had also fallen for Michael's brother, John (David Forsyth). Michael divorced her, but decided to remarry her when she said she was pregnant. He kept his word, even though she had miscarried.

Donna had hoped that this time, the Hudsons would stay married. But Michael met Iris, and the next thing Donna knew, Iris was telling everyone that Michael had promised to marry her. Although Michael and Iris never did make it to the altar, he did divorce Donna — yet again — and left town.

In 1995, Michael returned to Bay City just as his perennial former wife, Donna, was preparing to marry her younger lover, Matt Cory. Victoria greeted him with hisses instead of kisses. She resented the way he had walked out on his family before, and resented even more the fact that he brought with him his newly discovered illegitimate son, Nick Terry.

Michael's brother, John, also wondered why the wandering Hudson brother really returned to Bay City when he did. What was his agenda? And would Donna and Victoria and Marley be hurt again? Michael finally revealed he had leukemia. Would a bone marrow transplant from Nick save him?

Actor: Jensen Buchanan

Birthplace: Montgomery, Alabama
Birthdate: July 18

Jensen Buchanan played the twins, Victoria Love and Marley Hudson, from July 1991 to April 1994. Her timing on the show has been keyed to two important personal events in her life. She married Gray O'Brien just a few months after she joined *Another World*, and gave birth to her son, John Conor, on April 24, 1994, the same month she left the series. Buchanan returned to the soap in October, 1994.

Jensen was raised in Neenah, Wisconsin. Her late father, William Buchanan, was involved in the family's paper business; her mother, Mary, writes about animal issues in the local newspaper. Her stepfather is a veterinarian. She has a half-sister, Amy, who attended the University of Wisconsin at Milwaukee.

Jensen began her career as a singer. She appeared with the Young Vocalists Program at Tanglewood, where she studied with Seiji Ozawa, the conductor of the Boston Symphony, and the late Aaron Copeland and Leonard Bernstein. She was a music major, concentrating on opera, at Boston University's School of Fine Arts. Since opera is also a theatrical art form, she studied theater as part of the curriculum.

After several summers touring with stock theater companies, Jensen moved to New York and joined the ABC Network's Talent and Development Program. Buchanan's first soap opera role was as Sarah Gordon on *One Life to Live*. She also appeared briefly on *All My Children*.

Character: Victoria Love Frame Harrison/Marley Hudson McKinnon

Victoria Love came to Bay City with her lover, Jake McKinnon, in 1985. She soon discovered that she had a twin sister named Marley Hudson, and that Michael Hudson and Donna Love Hudson were her father and mother.

When Marley fell in love with Jake, they married and left to start a new life in the real city by the bay, San Francisco. When they divorced, he returned to Bay City and Victoria comforted her former brother-in-law by taking him into her bed. But Victoria had also gone to bed with Jamie Frame, Rachel's son. She became pregnant. Unlike many women who find their lovers fleeing at the sound of a stork's approach, Jake and Jamie both insisted on claiming her, and her child, as their own.

Victoria and Jamie were married, and although she suspected Jake as the father, she named Jamie instead. After a definitive blood test, she was pleased to learn that Jamie was, indeed, the father of baby Steven. Victoria was happy when her parents reconciled, but she was unhappy when she thought her mother was going to make love to her Uncle John. She crashed her car and almost died.

When Victoria and Jamie eventually divorced, he claimed custody of Steven. For a while, he had the boy in his care, but he agreed to return the child to Vicky before he left town. While Marley became involved in good works, Victoria concentrated her energies on finding a man she could live with for the rest of her life. The handsome, honest, earnest, and dedicated police detective, Ryan Harrison, came along, and after some initial sparring, the two found themselves very much in love. But then, along came Ryan's dashing brother, Grant Harrison, who was a businessman and politician. He swept her off her feet and before long, Ryan became her brother-in-law. Vicky's marriage to Grant soon developed cracks that showed a darker side to her husband's nature: His love for her was more one of possession than affection. For a while, he kept her a virtual prisoner. When she tried to tell people about his behavior, no one would believe Victoria's tales about the respectable United States Senator.

Victoria gave birth to her second child, Kirkland Harrison. Since she had also slept with Ryan, she believed he was the father. (Poor Vicky: Is she destined to go through life giving birth to babies and guessing whose genetic codes they inherited?) But it seemed that Grant was, indeed, little Kirkland's daddy, and he wanted sole custody of the child. To thwart her husband, Vicky pulled off a baby switch, which gave her time to work out a way to keep Grant from taking her child. She also proceeded to divorce him. Grant accused Vicky of shooting him. Just when it seemed as if she was going to lose her child, as well as her freedom, Grant confessed that he had done the deed himself.

Vicky and Ryan were reunited, and talked about marriage. But something neither of them expected developed, and it had the power to change the lives of both Ryan and Grant. To wit: Victoria's first mother-in-law was Rachel Cory, Jamie's mother. She had no mother-in-law (or so she thought) when she was Grant's wife. Grant's father, Spencer (David Hedison) said Grant's mother had died years earlier. But in 1995, Justine returned to Bay City. The irony is that she took the identity of Rachel Cory, whom she closely resembled. And if Victoria thought she had a tough fight keeping Kirkland, it was nothing compared to what she might find when Grandma Justine decides to claim her grandson. And, of course, Mother Justine might not appreciate having Vicky marry her baby, Ryan, even though Vicky inherited her grandfather's estate.

Actor: Amy Carlson

Birthplace: Glen Ellyn, Illinois
Birthdate: July 7

Carlson, who traveled the world when she was a youngster, finally "settled down" in Bay City in December, 1993, as Sharlene Frame's troubled daughter, Josie Watts. Amy's previous television credits include *The Untouchables, Missing Persons,* and *Legacy of Lies.* She was also in the feature film, *Babe,* starring John Goodman.

Amy Carlson began acting while still a student in Knox College. After graduation, she worked in Chicago television for a while, and then went out to Hollywood, where she was soon doing guest roles in episodic television. She tried out for the role of Josie, but says "I never expected to get it." She did get it, flying to New York to make her debut as Josie just as Bay City was welcoming in the New Year.

Character: Josie Watts
See Bay City Chronicles — The 1990s

Amy on Josie:
"I really love this character," says Carlson. "She's strong and isn't afraid to face problems and deal with them."

Actor: Robin Christopher

Birthplace: Revere, Massachusetts
Birthdate: June 18

Robin joined the cast of *Another World* in 1994, assuming the role of Felicia's sometimes headstrong daughter, Lorna Devon. Her previous soap was as Skye Christopher, Adam Chandler's daughter on *All My Children.*

Robin's prime time credits include guest roles on *Matlock, Empire City,* and *Vinny and Bobby.* She also appeared in the feature flick, *Bodies of Evidence.*

Character: Lorna Devon
Lorna is the child of Felicia Gallant and Bay City's "mystery man," Lucas, (played by John Aprea) who came with Iris Cory when she returned to Bay City in 1989. Lucas told Felicia he'd learned that the child she believed to have been stillborn had actually been taken from her at birth — giving her hope that they could find their daughter.

After a long search, Felicia, Lucas, and Mitch Blake found Lorna; far from being grateful for having been "rediscovered," she resented her parents.

Later, she warmed up — to her father first — and was devastated when he died.

When Felicia began abusing alcohol as a way of dealing with Lucas's death, Lorna at first rejected her, and then became part of the support group that helped her deal with her alcoholism.

Lorna was raped and blamed Cass Winthrop's newly arrived brother, Dr. Morgan Winthrop. Although she admitted she couldn't see his face clearly, she was sure he was her assailant. When he was able to prove his innocence in court, she took a gun and went after the real rapist: a former friend — and fellow med student — of Morgan's. Lorna's post-trauma reactions became part of a story line that dealt with the problems many women go through after having been raped.

Actor: Matt Crane

Birthplace: Kimberton, Pennsylvania
Birthdate: May 4

Matt says getting the role of Matt Cory had nothing to do with the fact that the two shared the same name. "Someone told me that when they saw my picture, I looked like the character they felt the grown-up Matthew Cory should look like."

Crane attended the University of Honolulu and New York's Academy of Dramatic Arts, and he also worked as a model while studying acting. His television credits include roles in *Gidget, Tour of Duty,* and the miniseries, *War and Rememberance.* He has traveled through Europe, Asia, Africa, and much of the United States.

Like his fictional mother Rachel, and like Victoria Wyndham, who plays her, Crane is also a talented sculptor whose works have been exhibited in New York City galleries.

Character: Matthew Cory

Matthew Cory's life started eventfully. He was conceived when his mother, Rachel Cory, agreed to sleep with the (then) wicked Mitch Blake, so that she could get Mitch to reveal where he and his lover, Janice Frame Cory, had hidden Mac Cory as part of their plot to kill him, leaving her to inherit his publishing empire. (Janice was Steve Frame's sister; Rachel's former sister-in-law; and then wife of Mackenzie Cory.)

Matthew was adopted by Mac Cory and always considered him his real father until Rachel told him that Mitch Blake was his biological dad. Matthew was rocked by the news, but eventually accepted the fact that he was loved by two fathers: Mac and Mitch. Matthew dated Josie Watts, Sharlene's daughter. But they broke up shortly after they made love. Josie felt guilty and ashamed, and ran off to Los Angeles. He also had an affair with Lorna Devon.

Matthew has some of the most interesting familial ties with many of Bay City's most important citizens: Besides being the son of Rachel Davis Matthews Frame Cory, Cory (etc.) Hutchins, and Mitch Blake, he is also the stepson of Carl Hutchins. He was adopted by Mackenzie Cory. He is also the half-brother of Jamie, Rachel's son with Steve Frame, and Amanda Cory, Rachel's daughter with Mac Cory. Amanda's daughter, Allison, was fathered by her first husband, Sam Fowler, Mitch Blake's brother. This makes Sam Fowler not just Matthew's former brother-in-law, but also his nephew. Therefore, Ally is not only his niece, but also his cousin, since she's the daughter of his Uncle Sam.

Want more? Jamie has a son, Steven, with Victoria Love Frame Harrison, former wife of Grant Harrison, who is the former husband of Amanda Cory Fowler Harrison, Jamie and Matt's half-sister. Matt is also the stepbrother of Iris and Paulina Cory, both of whom were Mackenzie Cory's illegitimate children.

In 1994, Matthew Cory fell in love with a woman old enough to be his mother, Donna Love Hudson, mother of his former sister-in-law, Victoria Love Frame Harrison, and Victoria's twin sister, Marley. In 1995, Donna and Matt made plans to marry. If the wedding comes off and Donna doesn't reconcile with her former husband, Michael Hudson, Matthew will become the step grandfather of his nephew, Steven Frame, son of Jamie Frame and his former wife, Vicky.

Actor: Linda Dano

Birthplace: Los Angeles, California
Birthdate: May 12

Linda has a long, distinguished background in daytime dramas. Before joining *Another World*, she appeared in *As the World Turns,* as Cynthia Haines, and in *One Life to Live,* as Gretel Cummings. Her credits include prime time television and feature films, and she also cohosted the popular *Attitudes* talk show on the Lifetime cable network for six years.

In 1984, Linda Dano and her daytime alter ego, romance novelist, Felicia Gallant, were honored by the Romance Writers of America for their co-authorship of a Harlequin novel, "Dreamweaver."

Dano has "dressed" many stars via her "Strictly Personal" fashion consulting business. Among the women who have done well by Linda's fashion sense are her daytime colleagues, Susan Lucci and Robin Strasser, and film and theater star Glenn Close.

Character: Felicia Gallant

Felicia came to Bay City in 1983; so did lawyer Cass Winthrop, and the two soon became lovers. Indeed, what passed between them when they were between the sheets was said to have inspired Felicia's steamy romance novels.

Cass soon two-timed her with Bay City's temptress par excellence, Cecile de Poulignac, erstwhile wife of Jamie Frame and Sandy Cory, and mother of Sandy's daughter, Maggie Cory. Felicia was not, in those days, the forgiving kind. She vowed to get Cass whenever (and however) she could. But time put out the ire. In any event, Felicia had moved on to Mitch Blake, Rachel's former lover and father of Rachel's son, Matthew Cory.

Mitch, by this time, had become a solid citizen. He and Felicia fell in love and were married. They held the nuptials at a racetrack in honor of their late good friend, Wallingford, who loved to go to the races. They also co-own a bookstore called "Wallingford's."

Felicia told Mitch that while working on her autobiography she began to have unpleasant memories of defying her father, falling in love, and giving birth to a stillborn child. Meanwhile, a mysterious man began to watch her, playing music that brought back long supressed memories.

William Gray Espy (Mitch) and Linda Dano (Felicia).

While all this was happening, Jason Frame was pulling all sorts of nasty deals, including blackmailing some of Bay City's citizens. He thought he was doing Felicia a good turn by giving her a gun to protect herself against her stalker. At her fortieth birthday party, she sensed someone following her down a hall of mirrors; wheeling around, she shot at the menacing figure. It turned out to be Jason. Although Felicia was booked for the murder, Cass was able to prove she hadn't fired the fatal shot, thanks to Frankie's revelation that the cocaine-addicted Nicole Love, Donna's sister, did it.

Felicia eventually learned her teenage love, Lucas, had come to Bay City. He told her he'd learned the child they thought was stillborn was alive and living with the family who took her. Together with Mitch, Felicia and Lucas found Lorna.

Mitch and Felicia parted, still friends and vowing always to care for each other. Felicia remarried Lucas, but her happiness was short-lived when he was shot to death. This sent her into a deep depression, made worse by substance abuse: She smoked and drank too much.

89

Wallingford was played by the late actor Brent Collins, who once told the author that, as a "little person," he would play roles that would make the audience forget his height and consider only his performance. He said: "Of course, I'm a little person; it would be dishonest to try to persuade you that I'm not. Unless you were very suggestible, it would also be impossible. But when I have a choice of roles, I want to play one you will remember more for who he is than for how he appears."

Felicia eventually found a way out of her despair with Alcoholics Anonymous. More recently, she's become close to her new publisher, Marshall Lincoln Kramer, III, the publishing company's first African-American CEO. He risked his life to help save her from a crazed fan who, having read that she was giving up romances in favor of serious novels, kidnapped her to force her to write a romance for him. Felicia has become deeply involved with AA and often hosts meetings.

Linda on Felicia:

"I was thrilled when they gave me the story line where Felicia seems to come apart after Lucas' death. So many people, women and men alike, have to face grief in their own way. For Felicia, she found comfort in alcohol, but she didn't realize that she was an alcoholic until she hit bottom. Once she did that, she had a choice: stay there or fight to come back. Felicia decided to fight. And, as she learned through AA, it's a fight that starts fresh every day of her life."

Actor: Tom Eplin

Birthplace: Hayward, California
Birthdate: October 25

Tom Eplin can be called the "once and future" Jake McKinnon. He's taken leaves from his popular role several times, and always returns to find he's not only remembered by the fans, but his reappearances inevitably lead to even higher fan appeal.

Asked once what he thinks he does that makes the viewers like him so much: "I think most of the credit has to go to Jake," he said.

Tom's background includes studying drama with the American Conservatory Threatre in San Francisco, and with Joan Darling and Alan Rich, two of the most distinguished drama teachers in the country.

His prime time television credits include *The Facts of Life, 240 Robert,* and *Private Practice.* He also produced a feature film, *Delta Fever,* and a TV pilot called *Odd Jobs.* When not acting, Eplin likes to drive race cars, and sky and scuba dive.

He left *Another World* most recently in early 1995 to check out the pilot season on the West Coast, but returned in July 1995.

Character: Jake McKinnon

He came to Bay City originally in 1985, and for one year, caused a lot of people a lot of trouble. He arrived with Victoria, Donna Love Hudson's long-lost daughter and the identical twin of Donna's young "sister," Marley. (Marley didn't know she was Donna's daughter until Victoria's presence forced her to reveal the truth.) Jake soon found himself the object of the affections of both Love sisters, Marley and Victoria; their exploits are described earlier in this chapter.

Jake was later accused of raping Paulina, Mac Cory's most recently discovered illegitimate daughter. He was later shot by Paulina, but pulled through. In time, Jake and Paulina became lovers and later married. They had several adventures, including a near-death experience with one of Iris Cory's hired hands, who was determined to kill Carl Hutchins, Rachel's fiancé. Currently he is suffering from traumatic amnesia and is making his way back to Bay City. Will he and Paulina reconcile, or will she have found new love with Joe Carlino?

Actor: Judi Evans Luciano

Birthplace: Montebello, California
Birthdate: July 12

Judi was born to be a performer. She traveled throughout the country with her parents (her father was a trapeze artist and ring master with the circus) and her three siblings. When she was two years old, she made her debut as a baby circus clown. That gig lasted until she was eight.

As a student in Pasadena City College, Judi decided to pursue an acting career. In 1983, she debuted as Beth Raines in *Guiding Light,* giving a consistently brilliant performance that won her the Emmy for Best Supporting Actress in 1984. She also appeared in *Days of Our Lives,* and in the film, *Dreams of Gold.* Judi joined *Another World* in 1991, replacing Cali Timmins in the role of Paulina.

Character: Paulina Cory

After Mackenzie Cory's death, Rachel and the rest of the Cory clan learned he had fathered an illegitimate daughter named Paulina Cantrell, who had arrived in Bay City to claim the right to be acknowledged as one of the Cory children. However, the family welcome she expected was not forthcoming. Iris, for example, who had to deal with the shocking fact that she was illegitimate, was not sympathetic to Paulina's situation. After all, how many out-of-wedlock daughters could there be? And if they acknowledged Paulina, how many more would discover that they, too, were Corys?

91

However, Rachel accepted her late husband's child and insisted she be treated fairly, sharing in the Cory largesse on an equal basis. Except for Iris, who was still either skeptical or jealous (she had a hard enough time dealing with Amanda's birth since she obviously wanted to be daddy's only little girl), everyone else welcomed Paulina into the Cory circle.

Over the years, Paulina has had her share of soap heroine trauma. She was raped. She shot Jake McKinnon, who then blackmailed her into marriage. She almost died of a mysterious tropical illness. And, to her surprise, she began to fall in love with Jake. Although she knew he was like the landscape of Southern California — the really dangerous faults were those you don't see — she felt it was worth risking an occasional earthquake to be with him.

Actor: David Forsyth

Birthplace: Long Beach, California
Birthdate: September 18

David Forsyth's soap opera debut was in *Search for Tomorrow* in which he played Hogan McCleary. (Matthew Ashford, now on *General Hospital*, played his brother, Cagney McCleary.) He also appeared on *Texas, As the World Turns,* and *One Life to Live.*

Forsyth, himself a decorated Marine Corps veteran who saw service both in Vietnam and Central America, grew up as an "army brat," traveling to wherever his father, a Marine Corps colonel, was posted. Before becoming an actor at age thirty, Forsyth worked as a firefighter and paramedic in Florida. He kicked off his acting career performing mostly in local dinner theaters, including Burt Reynolds's theater in Jupiter, Florida.

Forsyth joined *Another World* in 1987 as Dr. John Hudson, brother of Michael Hudson (Kale Brown). He is a certified scuba diver and underwater rescue specialist.

Character: John Hudson

Dr. John Hudson is the former and current husband of Sharlene Frame Matthews Watts Hudson, and the stepfather of Josie Watts. Hudson's rival for Sharlene was her former husband, Dr. Russ Matthews, who, Sharlene later revealed, is Josie's real father. John and Sharlene fell in love and were married. Russ, by that time, had left town, and John felt he now had a chance to enter the residency program at the hospital.

Hudson soon became one of the hospital's best doctors and life looked pretty good (in spite of the occasional flashback to his service in Vietnam). But tragedy struck. He discovered that Sharlene suffered from multiple personality disorder when her alter ego, Sharly, had come back and was starting to take control. In 1991 Sharlene was presumed to have died in an accident, although her body was never found. John was shattered by the loss of the woman he had loved for so long. He tried to pull his life together and eventually had other relationships, including marriage to a medical colleague.

In 1991, the mysterious Kate Baker came to Bay City. Eventually, John learned Kate was one of Sharlene's alternate egos. He wooed her gently until Kate was secure enough to retreat, allowing Sharlene to return. John divorced his wife, and remarried Sharlene.

Actor: David Hedison

Birthplace: Providence, Rhode Island
Birthdate: May 20

Hedison — whom many people still recall as Captain Crane in the series *Voyage to the Bottom of the Sea,* and as the star of the original cult film *The Fly,* brings a wealth of experience to his role as the sophisticated and manipulative Spencer Harrison. "I was fortunate in that I always worked with wonderful people," Hedison told the author. "I was able to learn a great deal from watching them and working with them."

Hedison, who grew up in Boston, Massachusetts, attended Brown University and appeared in a number of college productions. On Broadway, he co-starred with the great actress Uta Hagen in *A Month in the Country,* for which he won the prestigious Theatre World Award.

Of his role as Spencer Harrison, Hedison says, "He's an ambitious man who wants the best for his sons, Grant and Ryan. However, he may have finally learned that what he thinks is the best for them may not be." Hedison's favorite moments as Spencer? He has many to cite, including when he realized his mentally unstable wife, Justine, was still alive and in the same room with him, and there was nothing he could do about it since she had already caused him to have a crippling stroke. For Hedison, "those were the moments when you know, as an actor, that you have a chance to do some very interesting things with your role."

Character: Spencer Harrison

Spencer Harrison came to town in 1991 with his politically ambitious son, Grant. His younger son, Ryan, had come to Bay City a year earlier and had joined the police force. Spencer was ambitious for both of his sons, but only Grant picked up his fervor, doing whatever he had to do to achieve his goals and make his father proud.

Spencer had been married to the lovely Justine Kirkland, mother of Grant and Ryan. Although he knew Ryan had been conceived during her affair with Carl Hutchins, Spencer loved the boy as much as if he were his flesh-and-blood child.

93

While Spencer couldn't light a fire in Ryan's belly to pursue power, he had no problems with Grant. He was so successful that he eventually realized that he had created a Frankenstein's monster in Grant. At one point, he begged Grant to resign his Senate seat when Grant was exposed for falsely accusing his ex-wife, Victoria, of shooting him, although he had done the shooting himself.

For years, Spencer had told his sons that their mother, Justine, was dead. But in mid-1995, Justine returned from France where she had lived for many years, determined to make both Spencer and Carl pay for their sins against her. She threatened to kill Spencer, and drove him into having a stroke. Without the ability to speak or write, Spencer was unable to warn anyone of Justine's presence. Eventually, however, he regained some movement and was able to alert Ryan that his mother was still alive — and still dangerous.

Will Spencer survive the Justinian assault on Bay City's handsome older men, whom she believes have done her wrong? Let's hope so.

David on soaps:

"I was not sure about this medium. But when I knew I was coming to the show, I started watching this series and others, and I was struck by the talent that was there in front of my eyes. I remember saying aloud, 'My God, these are wonderful actors.' And, of course, they are."

Actor: Anna Holbrook

Birthplace: Fairbanks, Alaska
Birthdate: April 18

Anna Holbrook assumed the role of Sharlene Frame Matthews Watts Hudson in 1988. The character had been off the show for some time. Holbrook's performances in the challenging double role of Sharlene and Sharly made her a favorite with the daytime audience.

Holbrook's career includes work in off-Broadway productions and prime time television, including *Law and Order* and *Benji*. She also appeared in *Dallas* and *One Life to Live,* and she made a feature film with Nick Nolte called *I Love Trouble*.

Anna's hobbies include singing, skiing, tennis, and horseback riding.

Character: Sharlene Frame Matthews Watts Hudson

Sharlene is one of Steve Frame's many siblings, which makes her Rachel's former sister-in-law, and Jamie's aunt. She's also the great aunt of

Jamie's and Vicky's son, Steven. The character of Sharlene was first played by Laurie Heineman from 1975 to 1977. She was brought onto the show at the start of the great Frame in-gathering when headwriter, Harding Lemay, peopled the series with a family as large and as close as his own.

Sharlene was a warm, giving person with whom Dr. Russ Matthews soon fell in love. He had been badly hurt when his former wife, Rachel, betrayed him with Steve Frame, Sharlene's brother. Sharlene and Dr. Russ were married, but were later divorced. She left town in 1977.

In 1988 she returned to Bay City (played now by Anna Holbrook). Dr. John Hudson fell in love with her, and so did her former husband, Russ Matthews, who had also returned to town. He was upset to learn that he was the real father of her daughter, Josie Watts. When Sharlene chose to marry John, Russ left again.

Sharlene suffers from multiple personality disorder. One of her alter-egos, Sharly, was a hooker. Sharlene tried to deal with Sharly's increasing strength, but ultimately gave up. In 1991, she was presumed to have died. In 1994, she returned in the alter personality of Kate Baker, a volunteer worker at the community center. Eventually, her true identity was revealed, and with John's loving, patient care, she was able to recall Sharlene, making her the dominant personality.

Sharlene's daughter, Josie, returned to Bay City and after revealing that "like mother, like daughter," she'd been a prostitute, reconciled with Sharlene and formed a close mother-daughter bond with her. Sharlene began having flashbacks to her childhood. The memories grew stronger and she recalled that she had been raped as a child. This trauma, apparently, created the MPD.

With Frankie's help, she was able to trace the rapist and discovered that he was in charge of a runaway center, and still taking advantage of young girls. Helping to bring him to justice was another important closure point for her.

Actor: Charles Keating

Birthplace: London, England
Birthdate: October 22

Charles Keating created one of daytime's classic villains in Carl Hutchins. "It is a role," he once told the author, "that is an actor's joy. He is not an ordinary villain … He is an extraordinarily intelligent man, so the challenge in playing him is much greater…" In other words, it's easier to play the mustache twirling, teeth gnashing, mouth-foaming dastard, than the charmer who thinks his way through a plot.

Keating played Carl from 1983 to 1986, then left the series to do a number of other things. He returned in 1991, then left to star in the series,

Going to Extremes. He returned once more in August 1993, and began the process of conversion from knave to knight in Rachel's life.

Keating's background includes film, television, and theatre. He was featured in two classic television productions, *Brideshead Revisited* and *Edward and Mrs. Simpson*. Most recently, he's teamed with his *Another World* co-star, Victoria Wyndham (Rachel) in the play *Couplets*.

Keating has also appeared with his sons' rock and roll band. "It always gives the youngsters a start to see someone they consider old somehow finish a set without collapsing."

Character: Carl Hutchins

Hutchins came to Bay City in 1983 determined to do in Mackenzie Cory, whom he blamed for killing his father. For three years, his villainy affected Mac as well as all the other Corys. Before he vanished from their lives, he tried to ruin the Corys financially; he apparently had David Thatcher (Lewis Arlt) murdered because he knew too much about his shady activities; he kidnapped Cecile de Poulignac, the woman Cass Winthrop loved, and took her to Majorca; and he was suspected of trying to kill Mac's son, Sandy Cory. Previously, he had been a partner of Reginald Love's and married Donna for her money.

Although Carl left in 1986, no one could really believe the Melancholy Bane of Bay City was gone for good. And with good reason: In 1991, Hutchins returned. Little by little viewers began to see glimpses into the past of this man. Ryan Harrison (Paul Michael Valley), the straight-up, stalwart police officer, learned, to his shock, that Carl was his biological father. (Carl had had an affair with his mother, Justine, while she was still married to Spencer Harrison, who raised Ryan and loved him as much as he did his biological son, Grant.) Their relationship was strained, but in time, Ryan came to love both his fathers.

Carl fell in love with Rachel Cory (Victoria Wyndham), the widow of his long-time adversary, Mac Cory. At first, she rejected him, unable to forget how he had terrorized her, but he persisted and eventually won her over. He encouraged her to find her free artistic spirit again after it had been smothered by years of being the conventional business woman. Their relationship was fought by the Corys — one of whom, Iris Cory (Carmen Duncan), even tried to do him in before he could trade I dos with Rachel.

In 1995, Carl and Rachel were married and might have lived happily ever after except for the return of Justine, who set out to do away with both Carl and Spencer because of wrongs she believed they inflicted upon her. They would soon learn that Justinian justice could be deadly.

Actor: Kevin McClatchy

Birthplace: Philadelphia, Pennsylvania

Kevin joined *Another World* on June 28, 1995, replacing Justin Chambers. Kevin's previous soap role was as the well-received Vinny on *Guiding Light* in the summer of 1993.

McClatchy was graduated from Washington & Lee University in Lexington, Virginia, with a double major in journalism and English. For several years, he worked in a sports marketing firm, but the idea of acting was always in the back of his mind. Finally, he enrolled in an acting class, and was soon convinced that he would make a career change. He auditioned for roles in theater productions and eventually found himself on stage in various productions in New York. He also did a feature film, *This Boy's Life*. In 1995, he wrote and starred in a one-man show in New York City called *Walking in the Shadow of the Big Man*.

Character: Nick Terry

Michael Hudson returned to Bay City in 1995 with a young man named Nick Terry, the son he never knew he had. Judging by the young man's frequent brushes with the law, Michael might well have wished he had never discovered his prodigal son.

Nick's first encounter with Maggie Cory (Jodi O'Keefe) could lead to problems with Tomas Rivera (Diego Serrano). But that may well be just one of the many scrapes Nick will get into as his character faces new challenges.

Actor: Grayson McCouch

Birthplace: New York, New York
Birthdate: October 29

Grayson's theatrical career began in summer theater in Connecticut where he attended the Kent School during the rest of the year. In 1990, he enrolled in the British American Drama Academy in Oxford, England. He returned to the United States and was graduated from Hamilton College with a degree in theater arts. He went on to do four seasons with the Williamstown Theatre Festival. His first prime time series was *Sibs*. He had recurring roles on *Loving* and *As the World Turns*. In 1993, he joined *Another World* in his first contract role as Dr. Morgan Winthrop.

Character: Morgan Winthrop

Had Dr. Morgan Winthrop consulted his psychic sister-in-law, Frankie Frame Winthrop, before he arrived in Bay City in September, 1993, he would have stayed away.

97

Fortunately for the fans of *Another World*, Morgan decided to come to town to get involved in several intriguing stories, including: a) being rejected, at first, by his brother, Cass Winthrop (Steve Schnetzer), who probably felt mother loved him better; b) being falsely accused of raping Lorna Devon and suspended from his duties at the hospital; c) falling in love with a lovely lady named Brett (Colleen Dion), who decided she liked Chicago better than Bay City and that she preferred another man to Morgan; d) falling in love with the lovely Lorna, but (perhaps) losing her to the rascally Grant Harrison.

Actor: Jody O'Keefe

Birthplace: New Jersey
Birthdate: October 19

Jody O'Keefe replaced Robyn Griggs as Maggie Cory in June, 1995. Although the role marks her soap opera debut, she's no stranger to the television cameras: A model since she was nine, Jody has appeared in countless television commercials.

She lives at home in New Jersey with her mother and father and two older sisters. Her favorite off-screen past time is horseback riding.

Character: Maggie Cory

Maggie is the daughter of Cecile de Poulignac (played by both Susan Keith and Nancy Frangione) and Sandy Cory (Chris Rich), Mackenzie Cory's illegitimate son. Although she has dreams of becoming a Broadway star, when she was offered a role in the revival of *Grease,* she chose to stay in Bay City with Tomas rather than move to New York.

The tie-in between the character of Maggie Cory and the Broadway musical came via a former *Another World* character: Dean Frame, played by Ricky Paul Goldin. Goldin (and his character) joined *Grease* in 1994. Dean returned to Bay City for a holiday visit and told Maggie there was a role for her in the musical if she wanted it. Maggie seemed to want it, at first, but then changed her mind.

Maggie's relationship with Tomas Rivera was marked by several problems, including the arrival of his former lover, Angela, who was also the mother of his daughter. Eventually, Angela left town. Maggie had also left Bay City for Europe. (Maggie's trip to the Continent was arranged to allow the soap to change over from Griggs, who had previously played the role, to O'Keefe.) When Maggie returned, she hoped she and Tomas could take up where they left off, but the unexpected appearance of Michael Hudson's previously unknown illegitimate son, Nick Terry, could create complications.

Actor: Mark Pinter

Birthplace: Decorah, Iowa

Birthdate: March 7

Mark is married to Colleen Zenk Pinter who plays Barbara Ryan Stenbeck Munson on *As the World Turns.* The couple met when Pinter was on the series as Brian McColl. They are raising a blended family of six youngsters; his, hers, and theirs. Pinter's soap background also includes *Secrets of Midland Heights, Loving, Guiding Light,* and *Love of Life.*

Mark's first love (professionally speaking, that is) was, and is theater. A graduate of Iowa State University, he helped fund The Old Creamery Theatre Company in Garrison, Iowa. He went on to earn a Masters of Fine Arts degree in the Hilberry Graduate Repertory Program at Wayne State University in Detroit, Michigan.

Mark and Colleen are involved in several charitable causes including Bread and Roses, which supports the only facility between New York City and New Haven, Connecticut providing services for children and families struggling with AIDS.

Character: Grant Harrison

Grant Harrison arrived in Bay City in 1991. The son of Spencer Harrison and the brother of Ryan Harrison, he had the dash of his dad and the determination (if not exactly the moral fiber) of his sibling. Pretty soon, Grant became involved in Bay City's business community and made enough of a favorable impression on the citizenry of the entire state to be elected senator.

Romantically, Grant won the heart of the lovely Victoria Love Frame (Jensen Buchanan), who had also had a romantic relationship with brother Ryan. Grant and Vicky were married and went off on a honeymoon to the beautiful Banff area of Canada where Grant's ardor was supposed to keep Vicky warm, but thoughts of Ryan kept intruding.

As Vicky became disenchanted with Grant (especially over his decision to keep her a virtual prisoner) she decided to divorce him. Grant, however, was determined to claim custody of their son, Kirkland. On the advice of his father, Grant realized that he'd have a better chance of getting custody if he could present a settled domestic image. (It would also be better for his political future.)

Grant romanced Amanda Cory Fowler, daughter of Rachel and the late Mackenzie Cory. Not only was he attracted to Amanda's beauty and her obvious connections to Bay City's movers and shakers, but she had a daughter, Alli Fowler, who would help enhance his image as a confirmed family man. At first, Amanda resisted, but he persisted. She relented when Alli obviously told her mommy she liked the handsome, smiling man who seemed to dote on her.

When Grant learned of Vicky's determination to fight his custody suit for Kirkland, he devised a devious plan. He was found shot outside his home and accused Vicky of pulling the trigger. For a while, he allowed people to think Ryan was also implicated since it was Ryan who found him, and everybody in Bay City knew Ryan never stopped loving Vicky. But, as the investigation wore on, Grant eventually admitted he'd shot himself.

Meanwhile, Grant had begun an affair with Lorna Devon. After the truth about the shooting came out, Amanda divorced him, and he resigned from the senate. Only Lorna stood by him.

When news of his exploits reached the South of France, Grant's mother, Justine, whom he thought was dead, came back to Bay City just in time to learn he proposed to Lorna Devon, his political consultant and right-hand woman.

Learning that your mother is still alive when you thought she was dead should be a great experience. But when your mother is Justine, you might not agree.

Actor: Stephen Schnetzer

Birthplace: Boston, Massachusetts
Birthdate: June 11

Stephen Schnetzer, who was raised in Canton, Massachusetts, was graduated from the University of Massachusetts and studied drama at the Juilliard School and the American Conservatory Theatre. He is married to his former *One Life to Live* co-star, Nancy Snyder (they played Katrina Karr and Marcello Salta on *OLTL*). Nancy returned to soaps on *AW* as the doctor treating Cass's bi-polar illness.

Over the years, Schnetzer has compiled a list of distinguished theatrical credits. One very special production was the national tour of *Shakespeare's People,* in which he co-starred with the great English actor, Sir Michael Redgrave. Stephen also appeared on *Days of Our Lives,* as Steve Olson.

Character: Cass Winthrop

Cass has known love, joy, sorrow, rejection, hate, despair and depression. In 1994 depression overwhelmed him so completely that he faced losing the profession he loved — the law — and, possibly, the people he loved — especially his wife, Frankie Frame Winthrop (Alice Barrett) and their daughter, Charlie.

The story of Cass's fight against this debilitating condition was the first time depression had been shown so vividly on daytime television. All the horror, helplessness, and hopelessness was played out in Cass's story.

Cass Winthrop, brother of Dr. Morgan Winthrop (whom he successfully defended against a false rape charge), considers himself a good lawyer. Stephen Schnetzer, who plays Cass, told the author: "He loves the law and he loves the idea that he can help people find justice through the law."

Cass Winthrop's personal life was not always quite so upright. He came to Bay City in July 1983, the same year Felicia Gallant (Linda Dano) arrived. He was soon involved in a torrid romance with the romance novelist. But as soon as he met the beguiling Cecile de Poulignac (played by both Susan Keith and Nancy Frangione) he began two-timing Felicia, which did not please her. Despite her anger over his indiscretion, she turned to Cass many times for legal advice and relied on him to defend her when she was accused of murdering Jason Frame. Although he lost the case, he continued to believe in Felicia's innocence.

Identical twins are commonplace on soaps, vis-á-vis Marley and Victoria. Cass found he had a doppleganger who was not related to him, one Rex Allingham. Before he died, Rex almost wrecked Cass's life. Nicole Love, Donna's sister and aunt of Marley and Victoria, had been in love with Rex. When he died, she turned to Cass (guess she liked his type) and before Winthrop knew it, he was falling for Nicole.

Meanwhile, he was still trying to find evidence to clear Felicia. As luck (and a soap script) would have it, Frankie Frame, a private investigator, told him Nicole had killed Jason. This ended Cass's plans to marry Nicole, but it left him open to other relationships.

He married the lovely Kathleen McKinnon, and was shattered when she later died in a plane crash. But this being a soap, Kathleen turned up again alive and well, and determined to resume her life with her "widower." One thing led to another, and Kathleen left town, this time destined to be a divorcée.

Cass, who was also involved with Caroline Stafford, found himself dealing with a furious Cecile who had come back to reclaim him. Meanwhile, Frankie Frame had set her sights on Cass Winthrop and thought it would be nice if the private investigator who did so much work for the diligent lawyer started a more personal relationship — beginning with a trip to the altar. Soon, she persuaded Cass to see things her way.

Cass's life with Frankie has been a relatively happy one for a soap opera hero. The illness of their baby daughter, Charlie, propelled him into his bout with depression. But the child recovered and while Cass was not so sure about having another baby, once again, he may find his mind being made up by the gentle persuasion of his loving wife, Frankie.

Incidentally, there was one other "woman" close to Cass: He once borrowed a lot of money from Bay City's resident loanshark, Tony the Tuna (George Pentecost). When he realized the loan was overdue, and Tony was about to turn from Tuna to Barracuda, Cass started wearing a

101

dress, and called himself Krystal Lake. This gave him time to bail out of Bay City for a while until it was safe to return.

Actor: Diego Serrano

Birthdate: February 5

Diego is amused when he's asked how he felt when he made his soap opera debut on *Another World* in 1994. The fact is, Serrano had starred on a Spanish-language soap, *Los Tres Destinos* for several years before coming to *AW*.

Diego's appeared in a Gloria Estefan music video, *Seal Our Fate,* and hosted *Telemusica,* the Latin equivalent of MTV. His other credits include *The New Lassie,* and the film, *The Tender,* with John Travolta.

Serrano is an avid soccer and basketball player, and also enjoys weight-lifting and golf.

Character: Tomas Rivera

Tomas Rivera appeared in Bay City in 1994 in the company of the mysterious Kate Baker and a small child. Kate was later found to be the supposedly dead Sharlene Frame Watts Hudson. The girl, Luisa, turned out to be Tomas's daughter. Tomas fell in love with Maggie Cory, and the two made plans for the future, but the appearance of Angela Corelli, Luisa's mother, changed everything. Eventually, Angela, who was certainly no angel, was found to be a manipulative schemer and she left Bay City.

Maggie and Tomas have since renewed their relationship. But just when Tomas thought all his romantic problems were over, Michael Hudson's newly discovered illegitimate son, Nick Terry, turned up and tried to turn Maggie on to his charms.

Will Maggie choose Nick or Tomas or someone else? The answer lies in the next episode.

Actor: Anna Stuart

Birthdate: November 1

Anna Stuart created the role of Donna Love Hudson in January 1983. Prior to her arrival on *Another World,* she appeared in *The Doctors, General Hospital,* and *Guiding Light.*

If you've heard rumors that the bewitching Ms. Stuart was once part of a coven, they're true. Actually, The Coven was a production company formed by Stuart and other women in daytime television in 1976. They mounted several plays by William Shakespeare, including *As You Like It,* and *A Midsummer Night's Dream.*

Anna Stuart's last feature film was *The Angel Levine,* starring Harry Belafonte.

Character: Donna Love Hudson (and soon Cory?)

Donna Love came to Bay City with her brother, Peter, and her sisters Nicole and Marley — although Marley was actually her daughter. Donna had to tell Marley the truth after learning that Marley had an identical twin named Victoria, who came to Bay City two years later. As a rich young teen, Donna had fallen in love with Michael Hudson, the stablehand on the Love estate. Her father Reginald drove Michael away when Donna became pregnant; when she gave birth, she was so deeply sedated, she never knew she had delivered two baby girls, and that one of them had been taken from her and raised elsewhere. Reginald never accepted Michael, and years later they had a rooftop fight that resulted in Reginald's death. In his will, he disinherited everyone but Vicky (leaving her very rich).

Donna has had an "interesting" life in Bay City. Peter was upset that she doted on her former husband Carl's son, Perry. Rachel's son, Jamie (later to be Donna's son-in-law) fell for Nicole, but Nicole became a cocaine addict, aided and abetted in her habit by Perry. Nicole later killed Jason Frame and was placed in a mental institution.

When her former husband, Michael Hudson, came to Bay City, Donna had just recovered from a nervous breakdown. When it became obvious that there was still something between her and Michael, they remarried. By this time, Michael's brother, Dr. John Hudson (David Forsyth), a Vietnam War veteran, had come to town, and Donna felt drawn to him. She was just about to go to bed with him when her daughter, Victoria, came along; she was so distressed at seeing Mommy and Uncle John in a compromising position just shy of having sex, that she rushed out, got into her car, crashed into a tree and wound up in a coma.

Michael filed for divorce. But then Donna told him she was pregnant. When she miscarried, she thought she had lost him for good, but he insisted on marrying her again. Michael and Donna later adopted a small boy, Mickey (who was later returned to his birth parents), and the Hudsons seemed to have found domestic tranquility at last. But then Michael and Iris found each other, and although Donna put up a good fight, she learned Michael had promised to marry Iris.

Rachel — who shared the grandmotherhood of young Steven Michael Frame with Donna (his parents were Jamie Frame, Rachel's son, and Victoria Love Hudson, Donna's daughter) — teamed up with Donna to prove to Mac Cory that Iris was not a nice person. Mac believed them, and Donna had her revenge when Mac fired his manipulative eldest daughter. But Michael eventually walked out on Donna, again.

More recently, Rachel and Donna found they had something else in common: Matt Cory, Rachel's younger son. Matt and Donna co-own the local TV station, and work soon became pleasure. Although Donna is old enough to be young Matt's mother, she and he insist their love makes them both younger than springtime — or sentiments to that effect.

But just as Donna was imagining married life with someone other than Michael, Michael returned to town with a young man named Nick Terry, who he claimed was the illegitimate son he never knew he had. (Now, was that a warm glance Donna felt from Michael, her many-times once and maybe many-times future husband? Or was it the first menopausal flush she's been dreading?) And in true soap fashion, if Donna does marry Matt, her ex-husband Carl will become her stepfather-in-law.

Actor: Paul Michael Valley

Birthplace: Whitefish Bay, Wisconsin
Birthdate: September 24

Paul Michael Valley came to *Another World* straight from The Juilliard School in New York City. He also attended American University in Washington, D.C. where he performed in college productions.

He's appeared in numerous plays by William Shakespeare, including *Romeo and Juliet, Love's Labor Lost, Macbeth, The Winters Tale,* and *The Tempest.* He took a short leave of absence from *AW* in 1993 to appear in *Beckett,* which was produced for The Mockingbird Theatre, the production company he co-founded in Memphis, Tennessee.

Paul is engaged to marry Christina Tucci, who recently left the role of Amanda Cory on *AW*.

Character: Ryan Harrison

Ryan Harrison came to Bay City to be a good cop. But, every now and then, he bends the rules (in the name of justice, of course), and finds himself suspended or otherwise chastized for his zealousness. In spite of his loose procedures, he was recently promoted to precinct captain.

Harrison grew up believing he was the son of Spencer Harrison (David Hedison) and the brother of Grant Harrison (Mark Pinter), and that his mother, Justine, died in childbirth.

As a police officer, he knew about the churlish Carl Hutchins and was determined to see him brought to justice for all the crimes he believed Carl had committed. But to his astonishment, he learned that Carl was his biological father, and that Justine had had an affair with him when she was married to Spencer. It took a while before Ryan accepted Carl in his life.

Ryan and Victoria Frame, Jamie's former wife, and daughter of Donna and Michael Hudson, met and eventually fell in love. But to Ryan's chagrin, Vicky flipped for his dashing half-sibling, Grant, and married him instead.

Ryan tried to find a new love, but Vicky was always in his heart and his mind. When she divorced Grant, they reconciled and began making plans for the future. But who should turn up in Bay City, but mother Justine. She had been living in Europe, and returned to wreak havoc against both Spencer and Carl, Ryan's two beloved "fathers." Poor Ryan: He had to accept that his biological dad had been on the shady side of the law, and now learns that Mother could turn out to be the most dangerous villain of all.

Actor: Victoria Wyndham

Birthplace: Chicago, Illinois; raised in Westport, Connecticut

Birthdate: May 22

Victoria was born into a showbusiness family and occasionally appeared on soaps as a little girl with her actor parents.

She co-starred with Bette Midler in the Broadway production of *Fiddler on the Roof* and also performed political satire with Lily Tomlin at the New York nightclub, Upstairs at the Downstairs. Victoria was on *Guiding Light* for three years before joining *Another World* in 1972.

Victoria is a painter, and has co-written a libretto entitled *Winter Dreams* which has been performed by the Pennsylvania Ballet. Wyndham is also a sculptor — as is her on-screen character, Rachel. As Rachel, she sculpted a small nude statue of Carl Hutchins (her co-star, Charles Keating's, character) that was, as Wyndham said, "anatomically correct." When asked if she had a life model for her work, Victoria said, "No, but I do have a good imagination."

Character: Rachel Davis Matthews Frame Cory Cory Cory (etc.) Hutchins

See The Mac Attack and Bay City Chronicles, etc.

As the World Turns

On April 2, 1956, Procter & Gamble midwifed the birth of the first two daytime dramas to run a half-hour: *As the World Turns* and *Edge of Night*. Long considered sister soaps, they actually had very little in common except for their length, their ownership (P&G), and their network, CBS. *Edge of Night* was the mystery-theme soap P&G had wanted to do for a long time. Having tried to buy the rights to the *Perry Mason* radio show that ran from 1943 to 1955, P&G was unable to make the deal. So they created their own mystery and hired the actor who played Mason on the radio, John Larkin, to play their Masonic equivalent to a crusading attorney, Mike Karr.

Meanwhile, Irna Phillips had been petitioning P&G to let her put a new kind of daytime drama on the air. She already had the successful *Guiding Light* series on both radio and television, and her long association with P&G had been fruitful for both of them. But her concept for the new series was, as, P&G opined, a mite revolutionary for the daytime medium.

For one thing, Ms. Phillips insisted it would have to run a full half-hour. Up to that time, soaps ran no more than fifteen minutes. The resistance to lengthening the shows seemed logical: Since they were done live, the actors couldn't be expected to memorize longer scripts. Besides, they were already writing lines and cues on everything the actors could see (but the cameras couldn't). With scripts half-again as lengthy, they would probably have to put in more curtains, tablecloths, and chair backs to carry the added prompts.

P&G also objected to Phillips's insistence that her new soap break with the radio format that their television counterparts still followed. Instead of having dialogue fill every on-air moment, Phillips wanted more space between the lines. She wanted the camera to become dialogue, to have it zoom in on an actor to let her or his face take part in telling the story. An actor no longer had to say, for example, "I - I - I'm crushed at John's behavior" — to the beat of three (as was common in radio). Now, the expression in her eyes, the quiver of her lip would say it for her.

With more camera work filling in for dialogue, the actors wouldn't have so much to memorize. Plus: up to now the audience was often referred to as listeners. With Irna's new format, daytime would finally have what primetime already had: viewers.

Procter & Gamble's objection to the new length was not so much technical as it was practical. Everyone knew that most people who watched soaps in the 1950s were housewives who had grown up listening to radio soaps. Also, these housewives had too much work to do to sit down and watch a show for half an hour when they could be listening to it for fifteen minutes. Phillips believed, however, that women took coffee breaks between their tasks. Her new show would give them something to watch while they were sipping.

Procter & Gamble finally agreed to go ahead with Irna's experiment. At least, they reasoned, they would still have *Edge of Night* — a show they were so proud of that they included the skyline of Cincinnati, P&G's home base, in its opening logo — if the other new show, *As the World Turns* turned sour.

In much the same way that Irna Phillips created the daytime format for radio and early television, her innovations with *ATWT* would form the pattern for staging television soaps: She portrayed real people who came to the breakfast table in robes and pajamas instead of looking as if they

Original Cast

Bobby Alford . . . . . . .Bobby Hughes	Don MacLaughlin . . . . .Chris Hughes
Ann Burr . . . . .Claire Lowell	Santos Ortega . . . .Grandpa Hughes
Les Damon . . . . .Jim Lowell, Jr.	Helen Wagner . . . . . .Nancy Hughes
Wendy Drew . . . . .Ellen Lowell	Ruth Warrick . . . . .Edith Hughes
William Johnstone . .Judge James T. Lowell	

107

First Air Date: April 2, 1956 / CBS

In theater, there is something called the "fourth wall" which stands between the audience and the players. Sometimes it dissolves and the audience becomes part of the play. With Phillips's new format, the "fourth wall" between the viewers and the action on screen disappeared, so that the camera became the eyes of the audience.

tumbled out of bed fully clothed and coifed: Included were chats over cups of coffee, close-ups that betrayed what characters were thinking, fade-outs that immediately picked up on action elsewhere, and those pauses much like those made famous in theater by English playwright Harold Pinter (who may or may not be kin to Mark Pinter, an actor who would go on to play one of *ATWT's* classic suave villains, Brian McColl).

Today, *As the World Turns* continues to spin in ether-space, while *Edge* is a fond memory for its many fans.

The Oakdale Chronicles

That all-important cup of coffee became a critical dramatic device in Irna's series. The show debuted with the character of Nancy Hughes (Helen Wagner) suppressing a yawn as she groggily said, "Good morning" to her husband, Chris Hughes (Don MacLaughlin), while she poured him a cup of coffee.

For the first several months, the show went nowhere. No one had become pregnant (maybe); no one died; no one killed anyone; no one came down with an exotic disease; no one gave away (maybe) or kidnapped a new-born infant. Audiences tuned in, and tuned out. But by the second year, word got around that this was a series to watch! The ratings began to climb. Phillips was right: The format fascinated the viewers.

Of course, Oakdale did not remain immune to the toils and troubles that afflict the lives of soap opera characters. As a matter fact, the series — which started with no extraordinary incidents — became famous for a scene I like to call the equivalent of Fred Astaire dancing on the ceiling in *Royal Wedding*. In this example, one of the characters, Elizabeth Talbot Stewart, Betsy's mother, died by falling UP THE STAIRS.

The circumstances that led up to Elizabeth's death were replete with soapish drama: She had had an affair with Dan Stewart, her husband, Paul's brother, who was the real father of her daughter, Betsy. Paul died of a brain tumor; Dan and his wife, Susan, mother of their daughter, Emily, divorced. Of this star-crossed group, the characters of Susan and Emily are still included in the story line; Betsy returns now and then (at one point, she married Steve Andropoulos; they have a daughter, Dani).

Oakdale is a suburb of Chicago, Illinois, Irna Phillips's home state. In the beginning were the Lowells and the Hughes clans. In 1960, the Stewarts

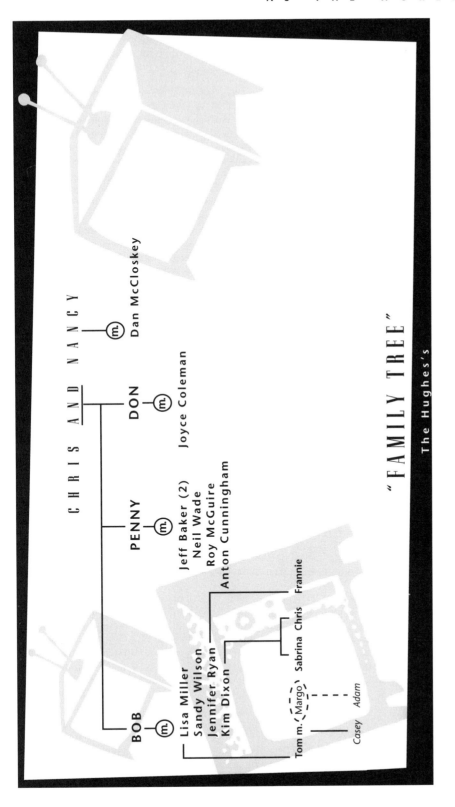

"FAMILY TREE"

The Hughes's

CHRIS AND NANCY

BOB (m.) Lisa Miller / Sandy Wilson / Jennifer Ryan / Kim Dixon

PENNY (m.) Jeff Baker (2) / Neil Wade / Roy McGuire / Anton Cunningham

DON (m.) Joyce Coleman

(m.) Dan McCloskey

Tom m. (Margo) — — — Adam

Casey

Sabrina   Chris   Frannie

Chris and Nancy Hughes started the first show in 1956 with a morning cup of coffee. For the next four decades, a Hughes has been part of the events that make Oakdale a center of intrigue and intriguing people.

109

moved to Oakdale. The patriarch, David Stewart (Henderson Forsyth), was a doctor. He and his wife, Betty (Patricia Benoit) had two sons, Drs. Dan and Paul Stewart. Dan was adopted. And as the elder Stewarts discovered, his mother was Ellen Lowell, who gave her child away after she'd had an affair. After Betty died, David fell in love with Ellen and married her. For years, they kept the truth from Dan. When he finally learned his real mother was Ellen, he rejected her because he felt she had rejected him. In time, however, the two became reconciled.

Since this is an Irna Phillips show, there would have to be strong women with a strong sense of who they were and what they wanted. In the Lowell clan, that woman was Ellen Lowell; in the Hughes family, Edith Hughes, played by Ruth Warrick, was the liberated woman who taught her teenage niece, Penny (Rosemary Prinz) to believe in herself, while Nancy Hughes, the family's matriarch, kept the clan together through its many crises and challenges. She continued to show strength as she coped with her second husband's Alzheimer's disease.

In 1960, one of the most fascinating female characters in daytime drama would make her debut on *ATWT*. Lisa Miller, played by Eileen Fulton, married seven times, attaching names to herself like a chemical polymer or a German noun: to wit, Lisa Miller Hughes Eldridge Shea Colman McColl Mitchell Grimaldi. And at last count, she will have had some fifty-two lovers (Eileen's late father, a minister, used to keep a tally of her character's liaisons). Although Lisa endured a long period of grief following her brief marriage to Eduardo Grimaldi (played by Nicholas Coster, who also played her second husband, John Eldridge, father of her son, Scott), no doubt another man will arrive at the scene determined to "altar-rate" her name.

Although Irna Phillips was no longer writing *As the World Turns* in the 1980s, the creation of the Lucinda Walsh character — and the decision to cast Elizabeth Hubbard in the role — were evidence of the pattern she established for putting women into strong decision-making roles.

Villainy Afoot

Wonderful villains have populated Oakdale from time to time. Anthony Herrerra's James Stenbeck, with blood as cold as the fjords of his Scandinavian home, persuaded his former lover, Barbara Ryan (Colleen Zenk Pinter) the mother of their out-of-wedlock son, Paul, to marry him. He felt this was the only way he could eventually get complete control of the boy.

Stenbeck created problems for everyone before he was supposedly killed when his helicopter was shot down. Stenbeck resurfaced later on and tried to kill his ex-lover Emily (played then by Melanie Smith) because she had slept with his son, Paul. Paul arrived and shot James dead.

> **These Guest Stars Have Turned Our Heads:**
>
> Robert Vaughn · Zsa Zsa Gabor · Phyllis Diller · Tony Bennett · Jermaine Jackson · Robert Horton · Betsy von Furstenberg

Then there was the mysterious Miranda Marlowe (Elaine Princi) who came to Oakdale in the mid 1980s to reveal she had once been married to Bob Hughes. Miranda had been imprisoned in France for selling dope. Although she claimed she was innocent, she was definitely a woman with a "past."

In the early 1980s, Margo and Tom, who were then lovers, became involved with one of soapdom's most fascinating bad guys, "Mr. Big." They pursued Mr. Big — a dwarf who was very big among his miscreant colleagues — throughout France and other far off places before he was brought to justice.

Craig Montgomery (Scott Bryce), Margo's brother, has been a rather nice guy during his more recent appearances on the show. But back around 1982, he was anything but. He had fallen in love with Betsy (then played by Meg Ryan) and was determined not to let anyone have her if he couldn't possess her. He did some nasty things before his mother, Lyla (Anne Sward) and his sister finally forced him to see the light.

Lily (Martha Byrne), Lucinda's adopted daughter, was wooed by and wed the dashing (but dangerous) Derek Mason (Thomas Gibson), who planned to kill her and inherit her fortune. Instead, the villain realized he had fallen in love with his bride, and he wound up being killed.

More recently, viewers have watched as the psychopathic Hans menaced Lily and her erstwhile lover and ex-husband, Holden Snyder (Jon Hensley), before they could be rescued.

The Grimaldis, Orlena (Claire Bloom), Damian (Paolo Seganti), Lily's most recent husband, and Eduardo (Nicholas Coster) introduced mystery, murder, and mayhem that stretched from Malta to Rome to Oakdale and back again. Was Damian ever really a villain? Was Eduardo? Was Orlena ever really a nice lady? Will everyone accept the answers to these questions, or will they spin off a new mystery? Stay tuned.

111

Real Vs. Reel Love

While Cupid has been shafting the denizens of Oakdale for some four decades, the chubby cherub hit the mark off camera as well. Among the

*Colleen Zenk Pinter and
Mark Pinter.*

couples who met on the soap and later married were: Don Hastings (Bob Hughes) and Leslie Denniston (Karen Peters); Larry Bryggman (John Dixon) and Jacqueline Schultz (Dee Stewart Dixon); Mark Pinter (Brian McColl, now on *Another World* as Grant Harrison); and Colleen Zenk Pinter (Barbara Ryan); and Marie Masters (Dr. Susan Stewart) and Robert Lipton (Dr. Jeff Ward).

(The late actor Roy Shuman, who played one of Lisa's husbands, Dr. Michael Shea, fell in love with one of the author's colleagues who had come to interview him. They were later married and were very happy until Roy, tragically, had a heart attack and died much too soon.)

Breakthroughs

Over the four decades the show has been on the air, it posted several break-throughs, among them:

The first marital rape. The character of Dr. John Dixon (Larry Bryggman) forced himself on his wife, Dawn (Dee) Stewart (Jacqueline Schultz), Ellen and David's daughter. Instead of accepting this as his due and her duty, Dee had John Dixon arrested and charged. The case went to court, but Dee decided to withdraw charges before it went to the jury.

The first set of quadruplets born on a soap. The foursome were the children of Dr. Annie Stewart (Lynn Blanks), another one of Ellen and David's children, and her husband, Dr. Jeff Ward (Robert Lipton).

The first openly gay character, Hank Eliot (Brian Starcher), brought into Oakdale in 1989 by the late Douglas Marland after he assumed head writing duties on the show. (Marland had previously played a gynecologist on the series, a fact, he once told the author, "probably pleased my mother since she wanted me to become a doctor and have a secure profession ...")

The first rape by an HIV-positive rapist. This happened to the character of Margo Montgomery Hughes. She underwent several tests and endured a long waiting period before she was pronounced HIV-negative. Her husband, Tom Hughes, son of Lisa and Bob Hughes, was completely supportive throughout her ordeal.

Founding Families

In the beginning there were two founding families; the patrician Lowells and the Hughes clan, who were solid middle class, with middle-class family values that included having one of their sons, Bob, become a doctor.

Today, the Lowells, except for Ellen Lowell Stewart, are gone. And except for Nancy, who had remarried after David's death, the Stewarts, who produced soapdom's first (and so far, only set of quadruplets) are also largely out of the picture. Other families have come and gone as well. However, Bob Hughes remains the one constant that ties the beginning of the series to its ongoing story lines. And his first wife, Lisa, continues to influence and be influenced by events that shape the lives of the people of Oakdale.

The Lowells

Judge James Lowell, played by William Johnstone, the head of a law firm. He is the father of Ellen and Jim Lowell, Jr.

Claire Lowell, played by Ann Burr. The unhappily wed wife of Judge Lowell. She is the mother of Ellen and Jim Lowell, Jr.

Larry Bryggman and Marie Masters.

Jim Lowell, Jr., played by Les Damon; son of Judge James Lowell and Claire Lowell; brother of Ellen Lowell.

Ellen Lowell, daughter of Claire and the Judge; sister of Jim Lowell, Jr. Her parents' unhappiness has deeply affected her. Involved in a love affair that ended when her lover discovered she was pregnant, she gave up her son for adoption. She later learned the boy, Dan, had been adopted by David and Betty Stewart. After Betty's death, Ellen married David, and had two daughters with him, Annie and Dee.

The Hughes

Grandpa Hughes, played by Santos Ortega. He lived with his son and daughter-in-law, and was a strong force within the Hughes family. When Ortega died in 1976, the role was not recast.

113

Chris Hughes, played by Don MacLaughlin. Husband of Nancy Hughes; father of Bob, Penny, and Don; brother of Edith Hughes. A lawyer, he was a member of the law firm founded by Judge James Lowell, father of his best friend, Jim Lowell, Jr. His widow, Nancy, later remarried.

Nancy Hughes, played by Helen Wagner, the only remaining member of the original cast. Nancy was the wife of Chris Hughes, and is the mother of Bob, Penny, and Don. After the death of her husband, Chris, Nancy went into a deep depression. She regained her emotional health and married Mac McClosky who developed Alzheimer's disease.

Bob Hughes, played originally by Bobby Alford. Currently played by Don Hastings. Bob is the son of Chris and Nancy Hughes; the brother of Don and Penny Hughes; the nephew of Edith Hughes. Bob has been married several times: His wives include Lisa Miller (Eileen Fulton) whom he met while he was a medical student. They had a son, Tom (currently played by Scott Holmes). Lisa left him to run off to Chicago. He also married Sandy Wilson, who had a son from a previous marriage, and Jennifer Ryan, mother of Rick and Barbara Ryan (later Barbara Ryan Stenbeck Munson). Bob was unhappy with Jennifer but found comfort with her sister, Kim Reynolds (Kathryn Hays), a widow. Kim became pregnant, but since Bob was still married to Jennifer, she married one of his colleagues, Dr. John Dixon.

After one of their fights, Bob bolted from Jennifer's home and was hit by a car. A very pregnant Kim miscarried on her way to the hospital to see him. Kim later had a son, Andy, with John; Bob had a daughter, Frannie, with Jennifer.

Eventually, Bob and Kim were married, and except for a time when Dr. Susan Stewart, a recovering alcoholic, had become emotionally dependent on Bob, the couple have had a happy marriage. They even learned that they had another daughter, Sabrina, whom they believed to have died at birth; instead, the infant was sold by a hospital worker to a childless couple. They also have a little boy named Chris.

Don Hughes, played by Connard Fowkes, son of Chris and Nancy; brother of Bob and Penny, and nephew of Edith Hughes. Don, a lawyer, and member of the same law firm in which his father, Chris, was a partner, married Joyce Colman, ex-wife of Grant Colman, one of Lisa's husbands. She became almost manic in her desire to have the most beautiful home in Oakdale. She ran up so many bills that Don was forced to take on sensational divorce cases for their huge fees. The publicity jolted the conservative firm and Don found his future in jeopardy. The character, who was never really fully developed, became a recurring role.

Penny Hughes, played by Rosemary Prinz, daughter of Chris and Nancy; sister of Bob and Don, niece of Edith Hughes, and best friend of Ellen Lowell. Penny and Jeff Baker became soapdom's favorite young lovers. Jeff was rich and led what Penny believed to be a glamorous life. She married him, but discovered he was mentally unstable and the marriage was annulled. However, she still loved him, and they remarried. But Jeff was killed soon after.

Penny then turned to Neil Wade, a former doctor. Sadly, Wade was also killed. (Didn't someone warn these men about turning up a bad penny?) She then exchanged vows with Roy McGuire, but that marriage ended in divorce.

Douglas Marland once told the author that he planned to create a soap opera that would center around a farm family who loved and protected each other. They would have, Marland said, "all the values I was taught to believe in by my own family when I was growing up ..." When Marland became head writer of *As the World Turns,* he introduced the Snyders, a family very much like the one he hoped would become the core of the daytime drama he planned to write one day. Douglas Marland, unfortunately, died before he could write that soap opera.

The last time anyone heard from Penny, she was off to Europe with her most recent husband, race driver Anton Cunningham.

Edith Hughes, played by Ruth Warrick, was a liberated woman who believed that life is for living. She often raised eyebrows among the more conservative people of Oakdale, Illinois. Edith left town when Ruth Warrick departed to do films and other television shows, including creating the role of Phoebe Tyler Wallingford on *All My Children.*

He Turned on *As the World Turns*

The late Fred Bartholomew, who as a child actor starred in *Little Lord Fauntleroy and Captains Courageous,* became executive producer of *As the World Turns* in the 1970s.

Current Cast and Characters

Actor: Brooke Alexander
Birthplace: Kailua, Hawaii
Birthdate: December 13

Brooke's career began at age three when she played Mother Mary in a

Nativity scene. A few years later, she played Snow White in the fifth grade production of *Snow White and the Seven Dwarfs*.

Besides her background as a successful commercial actor, Brooke's resume includes recurring roles in *Magnum, P.I., Island Son, P.S. I Luv You, Tattinger's,* and the lead in *The Last Nightmaster.* She also appeared in *One Life to Live.*

Brooke holds the Miss World America 1981 and Miss Hawaii World 1981 titles. She is a qualified scuba diver and played all-star basketball in high school. She also plays the guitar.

Character: Samantha Markham

Lucinda Walsh (Elizabeth Hubbard) believed she had half-siblings, although she couldn't be sure. She set up a search for them, and turned up Neal Alcott, long-lost sister, and Royce Keller (Terry Lester) her long-lost brother. After Neal was murdered and Royce left Oakdale, Lucinda learned that Royce may have had a twin named Sam. Indeed, he did — but Sam turned out to be Samantha.

For a while, Samantha, and Eliot, the man who had adopted her as a child, conned Lucinda. Sam was to paint duplicates of some of Lucinda's art collection and replace the real paintings (which her dad would sell to art collectors) with her fakes. But Sam had become close to Lucinda and couldn't do it.

Later, Lucinda persuaded Sam to accept their relationship, which she did, grudgingly.

One of Sam's most recent cons involved "marrying" Kirk Anderson; to her surprise, who should turn up to try to stop her but her former lover, Scott Eldridge, Lisa's son and Tom Hughes's half-brother.

The history Sam and Scott shared made for some interesting story lines through 1995.

Actor: Claire Bloom

Birthplace: London, England
Birthdate: February 15

Claire Bloom is an actor of international fame. One of her earliest films was *Limelight* with the great Charlie Chaplin, who directed her in the movie and predicted she would be both a great actor and a star. She also appeared in the films, *Crimes and Misdemeanors,* with Woody Allen, and *Richard III,* with Laurence Olivier. Her stage credits include everything from Aeschylus to Shakespeare to Shaw to Tennessee Williams, and so on.

Ms. Bloom joined *As the World Turns* in the role of Orlena Grimaldi in March, 1994.

Character: Orlena Grimaldi

Orlena, the stepmother of Damian Grimaldi (Paolo Seganti) is a manipulative woman with a need for power and control. She pulled many of the strings that involved her daughter-in-law, Lily Walsh Grimaldi (Martha Byrne) in some dangerous situations. She also killed the dashing Eduardo Grimaldi (Nicolas Coster) shortly after his marriage to the lovely Lisa Miller Hughes Eldridge Shea Colman McColl Mitchell (Eileen Fulton), though Dr. John Dixon was blamed for the death.

During the summer of 1995, Orlena began to recall events involving Damian's father and his real mother, Bettina. Will she be unmasked for Eduardo's murder? Will she be unmasked for other murders? No doubt, when Orlena's secrets come to light, they will reveal a veritable torrent of crimes and misdemeanors.

Actor: Patricia Bruder

Birthplace: Brooklyn, New York
Birthdate: April 14

Patricia Bruder was on Broadway in *Gypsy* in 1960 when she was asked to join the cast of *As the World Turns* as Ellen Lowell Stewart: Already a show business veteran, she started her career at age nine as a featured singer on a radio show, *Rainbow House,* and later joined radio's *Juvenile Jury,* accompanying the show when it moved to television.

Bruder's early television work took place during the medium's so-called "Golden Age" when such shows as *Alcoa Presents, Studio One,* and *Kraft Television Theater* were all done live.

Patricia Bruder met her husband, Dr. Charles Debrovner, when they were both students in James Madison High School in Brooklyn. They have two daughters, Diane and Carolyn Joy, who occasionally appear with their mom on stage.

Character: Ellen Lowell Stewart

The character of Ellen — soap opera's first unwed mother — was first played by Wendy Drew who was part of the original cast. Irna Phillips had to buck a lot of resistance from Procter and Gamble who felt daytime audiences would be offended by the theme of unwed motherhood. But she overcame their reluctance, and, as she predicted, the audiences were sympathetic to Ellen's situation. When Ellen's lover left when he learned she was pregnant, the audience saw her not as a loose woman, but as someone who was betrayed for loving well, not wisely.

Ellen's son, Dan, was adopted by David Stewart (played by stage and film actor, Henderson Forsythe). After David's wife, Betty, died, David and Ellen became close friends, fell in love and were married. Ellen became the stepmother of Paul and Dan. (She later told Dan she was his real mother,

117

ATWT castmates (l-r)
Ed Fry, Marie Masters,
Patricia Bruder, and
Don Hastings.

but he rejected her at first because he felt she had rejected him at birth.) David and Ellen had two daughters, Dr. Annie Stewart-Ward, who presented her parents with four grandchildren at once (the only quads to be born on a soap), and Dawn (Dee), who married David's long-time adversary, Dr. John Dixon.

Ellen and David faced a crisis in their marriage when he developed amnesia and fell in love with another woman. Eventually, the situation was straightened out. But the couple had only a few more years of happiness together before David died suddenly.

The character of Ellen was written out of the soap in 1975, but returned in 1976. The role has since become a recurring one.

118

Actor: Larry Bryggman

Birthplace: Concord, California
Birthdate: December 21

Larry joined the cast of *As the World Turns* as Dr. John Dixon in 1969. He later married his former *ATWT* co-star, Jacqueline Schultz, who played one of his wives, Dee Stewart. Larry is the father of three children: His eldest,

Heidi Brennan, is a writer and actor in Los Angeles. His younger two are sons, Michael and Jeffrey.

Bryggman is one of New York's busiest actors. He can be counted on to be on stage somewhere in the city at least three times a year. Among his many credits are *Picnic* (for which he earned a Tony nomination in 1994), *Henry IV, Part I and II, Waiting for Godot, Richard III, The Basic Training of Pavlo Hummel* (the last two with Al Pacino), *Prelude to a Kiss,* and *Ulysses in Nighttown* with the great Zero Mostel.

Larry also has a distinguished list of film credits including *...And Justice for All* with Al Pacino, *Hanky Panky* with Gene Wilder and Gilda Radner, and his most recent, *Die Hard With a Vengence,* with (who else?) *Ryan's Hope* alumnus Bruce Willis.

Character: Dr. John Dixon

Oh, was there ever a soap character so despised, so disposed to tell a lie, and so apparently unregenerate too, who could ever love such a man...could you?

Well, the fact is many women took a chance on Dr. Dixon, even when his reputation preceded him. He had at least five wives we know of: Dee Stewart (who took him to court for the first-ever marital rape charge on a soap); Kim Reynolds Stewart Hughes (Kathryn Hays), mother of their son, Andy; the troubled Ariel, who was once suspected of murder; Karen, who became the guardian of Dustin Donovan (Brian Bloom); and Lucinda Walsh (Elizabeth Hubbard), a businesswoman who never stopped caring for him even after their divorce.

John was also involved with Rosemary Kramer, a woman who became the mother of his illegitimate son, Duke. He also had a love affair with Lyla Montgomery (Anne Sward) and is the father of their daughter, Margo Montgomery Hughes.

John made a great many enemies over the years, including his former father-in-law, David Stewart, and Bob Hughes (Don Hastings), Kim's current husband and father-in-law of Margo. Dr. Larry McDermott (Ed Fry), one of his medical colleagues, also considers him an adversary.

He has, however, been somewhat redeemed in the past several years: A bout with cancer hastened the process. However, he found himself caught up in a malpractice suit brought by Lisa Grimaldi (Eileen Fulton) after the death of her husband, Eduardo Grimaldi (Nicholas Coster). Lucinda made sure to get him the best counsel available, in the person of Jessica Griffin McKechnie.

Of course, as the story progressed, several secrets were revealed that might have helped or hurt Dr. John Dixon.

Brian Bloom and Martha Byrne.

Actor: Martha Byrne

Birthplace: New Jersey
Birthdate: December 23

Martha Byrne started her career in good company, the cast of the Broadway hit, *Annie*. She played July, and also stood by for the lead. In 1985, she joined the cast of *As the World Turns* as Lily Walsh. She became an instant favorite with the viewers and in 1986 won the Daytime Emmy for Outstanding Ingenue in a Drama Series.

Martha left the show in 1989 for a stint in California where she appeared in several nighttime series including *In the Heat of the Night, Murder, She Wrote, Doogie Howser, The Young Riders, Jake and the Fatman* and *Pros and Cons* with James Earl Jones. She also worked on a Bob Hope special with the great comedian. Byrne's feature films include *Drop-Out Father* with Dick Van Dyke and Mariette Hartly, and *She's Hired, He's Fired* with Wayne Rogers and Karen Valentine.

Martha returned to *ATWT* in 1993, and the next year was nominated for a Daytime Emmy for Outstanding Younger Actress in a Daytime Series. Martha is married to New York City police officer Michael McMahon.

Character: Lily Walsh Mason Snyder Grimaldi

Being the daughter of the strong-willed Lucinda Walsh has been a mixed blessing for the sensitive Lily. It took some time before she could stand up to her adoptive mother and be her own woman. Indeed, at one time, she had the adoption legally overturned.

Lily has been close to death several times. She was once being lured into a cottage with her then husband, Derek Mason, who was supposed to have killed her to inherit her fortune; the cottage blew up, but she escaped (of course.) She was also captured on the Caribbean island of Montega where she met the dashing Duncan McKechnie (Michael Swan), who saved her life and helped return her to Oakdale. More recently, Holden and Lily were both held prisoner by a madman named Hans, but managed to escape being blown up.

Lily discovered that Iva Snyder (Lisa Brown) was her real mother and that she had been conceived when Iva was raped. She was furious when she learned that Holden Snyder, whom she had come to love, knew the truth and had kept it from her. She rushed into the willing arms of Dusty Donovan (Brian Bloom).

Eventually, Lily and Holden were married, but they did not live happily ever after. Holden was rushing to return to Lily from New York (they had had a misunderstanding) when he was hit by a car and suffered traumatic amnesia. When he returned to Oakdale, he rejected Lily, having no memory of their love. A heartbroken Lily moved to Italy where she met and married the dashing Damian Grimaldi (Paolo Seganti).

It was obvious that Lily and Holden were still in love, and poor Damian couldn't help but sense that his wife was always just one kiss away from kissing off their marriage. Lily and Holden did have one night together. She later learned she was pregnant, and wondered, was the baby her husband's, or Holden's? In any event, she found herself caught up in one of her mother-in-law's (Orlena) schemes: She woke up in Malta, wondering if Orlena was driving her crazy, or if she was really losing her mind.

Can Lucinda help her? Will Holden turn up as the hero of the piece? Or will Lily lose her mind and wind up as the mentally unbalanced Signora Grimaldi, the Maltese Cuckoo?

Actor: Scott DeFreitas

Birthplace: Boston, Massachusetts
Birthdate: September 9

Scott, who joined *As the World Turns* as Andy Dixon in 1984, spent much of his childhood in Hudson, New York. His family moved to Connecticut where he did his prepatory work at the King School.

Scott began his career doing television commercials. He made his stage debut in New York in the Albert Innaurato play, *Coming of Age in Soho*. As Andy, he's had three Emmy nominations in 1988, 1992, and 1994 for Outstanding Younger Lead Actor in a Daytime Drama.

He enjoys hockey, baseball, golf and rollerblading. He also loves acting but says he would like to direct and produce as well.

Character: Andy Dixon

Andy is the son of Dr. John Dixon (Larry Bryggman) and Kim Reynolds Stewart Dixon Hughes (Kathryn Hays). His stepfather is Dr. Bob Hughes (Don Hastings), and his half-sisters are Sabrina (daughter of Kim and Bob), and Margo Montgomery Hughes (John's daughter), who is married to Bob's son, Tom Hughes; Tom is thus his stepbrother as well as brother-in-law. He also has a half-brother, Duke, John's illegitimate son. Frannie Hughes, Bob's daughter with the late Jennifer Hughes, is his stepsister as well as his cousin, since Kim and Jennifer were sisters.

121

Andy began drinking in his early teens. He initially rejected the possibility that he could be an alcoholic, but eventually had to accept the fact and find help. He finally managed to deal with his drinking problem, but realizes that he is not cured; everything is a one-day-at-a-time process for him. His AA sponsor is Dr. Susan Stewart McDermott.

Andy has had problems with relationships. He loved Julie, who loved Duke Kramer. He then fell for Lien Truong Hughes. His marriage to Courtney Baxter ended because she tired of competing for his attention with his work as a photographer. Later, Andy was smitten with the manipulative Janice Maxwell (Holly Cate), and was devastated when he discovered that she had tried to poison Kim.

Will love ever find Andy Dixon? Of course it will. Stay tuned.

Scott on Andy:

"I know a lot of young people see Andy as someone they can understand. He has problems, and sometimes they're more than he thinks he can handle. But he doesn't give up, and that's what they like about him."

Actor: Ellen Dolan

Birthplace: Monticello, Iowa
Birthdate: October 16

Ellen was raised in Decorah, Iowa, where she began acting in elementary school. Later, she earned her M.A. and M.F.A. at the University of Iowa in Iowa City. She also studied at the Webber Douglass Academy in London.

Ellen's stage career began in 1980 with the Milwaukee Repertory Theatre. In 1982, Ellen created the role of Maureen Bauer on *Guiding Light,* staying four years before moving to Los Angeles. The late Douglas Marland, who created Maureen Bauer when he was head writer for *GL,* had become head writer of *ATWT* and called her in L.A. to ask if she'd consider coming back to the Big Apple to play the pivotal role of Margo Montgomery Hughes. Ellen agreed to return (as she told the author once, "Who could ever say no to Doug Marland?") and in 1989, she assumed the role of the intrepid policewoman, Margo Hughes.

In 1993, Ellen went back to Los Angeles to pursue several projects. A year later (and not only because of the earthquake scare) Ellen returned to New York — and to Oakdale — much to the delight of her fans and coworkers.

Character: Margo Montgomery Hughes

Margo is the daughter of Lyla Montgomery and Dr. John Dixon. She has three half-brothers — Duke Kramer, Craig Montgomery, and Andy Dixon. She is married to Tom Hughes, son of Dr. Bob Hughes and Lisa Grimaldi. Margo is the mother of Adam Hughes, whom she conceived with fellow police officer, Hal Munson. Tom adopted Adam. Margo is the stepmother of Lien Truong, whom Tom fathered when he was in Vietnam; she and Tom also have a son, Casey.

Margo Hughes was raped by a man who was suspected of being HIV-positive, although he resisted having his blood tested. Margo had several tests before she was finally found to be HIV-negative.

In 1995, Margo and Tom found themselves taking sides in the lawsuit Lisa Grimaldi brought against John Dixon for malpractice in the death of her husband, Eduardo. But then, everyone in Oakdale was taking sides — and once the full truth came out, there were plenty of sheepish grins to go around.

Actor: Eileen Fulton

Birthplace: Asheville, North Carolina
Birthdate: September 13

Eileen comes from a long line of clergymen, including her father, a Methodist minister. Asked once if he ever spoke to her about her character, Lisa, and all her husbands and lovers, Eileen said, "Yes. He has. Many times. He thinks I'm doing a wonderful job with the role. And he keeps count of her lovers."

Eileen is active on behalf of many good causes. She worked hard to help call attention to the Equal Rights Amendment. She also provides a scholarship to the Neighborhood Playhouse School of the Theatre in New York. "As My World Still Turns," the sequel to her book, "As My World Turns," was published in 1995 by Carol Publishing.

Eileen first came to New York in 1956, the same year *As the World Turns* debuted. She had no idea, at that time, that in a few years she would join the show and become one of soapdom's great stars. She studied at the Neighborhood Playhouse, and appeared on Broadway in *Abe Lincoln in Illinois, Sabrina Fair, Any Wednesday, Cat on a Hot Tin Roof,* and others. For a while, she worked in the mornings on the soap, then dashed out to do matinees on Broadway in *Who's Afraid of Virginia Woolf?,* and appeared at night in the long-running off-Broadway musical, *The Fantastiks.*

Eileen loves to sing and is one of New York's favorite cabaret stars. She's been married several times ("I have a long way to go before I catch up to Lisa") but despite her divorces, the ever-optimistic Eileen hasn't given up on love, certainly, or even on marriage.

123

Character: Lisa Miller Hughes Eldridge Shea Colman McColl Mitchell Grimaldi

The Wife of Bath in Chaucer's *The Canterbury Tales* had several husbands and lovers, but Lisa Miller, etc., of *As the World Turns* probably outscored her on both counts. At last reckoning, Lisa had been married seven times and had some fifty-two lovers.

Among Lisa's mates were Dr. Bob Hughes, the father of her son, Tom Hughes; John Eldridge, father of her son, Scott; Dr. Michael Shea, father of her late son, Chuckie; Grant Colman; Whit McColl; Earl Mitchell (played by Farley Granger); and most recently, Eduardo Grimaldi, played by Nicolas Coster, who had previously played John Eldridge.

A brief rundown of Lisa's life in Oakdale follows:

She arrived in town in 1960 with the young medical student, Bob Hughes, whom she trapped into marrying her. The couple moved in with her in-laws, Nancy and Chris Hughes and, in time, Tom Hughes was born. In 1965, Lisa was bored with life as the wife of a young doctor and mother of a small child. She fell in love with the wealthy Bruce Elliott and divorced Bob. But Bruce wouldn't marry her, so Lisa left her son with his father and grandmother and headed off to the bright lights of Chicago. (And to the first, and so far, only, prime-time spin-off of a daytime soap, called *Our Private World*.)

In Chicago Lisa met, and eventually married, the wealthy John Eldridge, who fathered her son, Scott. Lisa later returned to Oakdale a very rich woman. Just as she had left Tom with his grandparents when she took off for the big city, she left Scott with his grandparents when she returned to try to rekindle something with Bob. But his life had moved on by then.

Lisa met the socially prominent Dr. Michael Shea, and had an affair with him. However, he rejected her when she became pregnant. Later, when his wife divorced him, Shea proposed to Lisa, but this time she rejected him.

Lisa's older son, Tom, had returned from Vietnam and started taking drugs to forget the war. When Shea caught him trying to steal his drug supplies, he blackmailed Lisa into marrying him, using the confession he forced Tom to sign. When the marriage collapsed, Shea threatened to take Chuck away. Lisa fled.

Lisa returned to learn that Tom had been arrested for killing Shea. The shock gave her amnesia, which was cleared up when the real culprit was found.

Lisa tried, again, to reconcile with Bob, but to no avail. She had an affair with Bob's brother, Don (Connard Fowkes). Several men became loyal admirers, but she married Grant Colman, who won her heart with his gentleness and honesty. After their marriage, Grant's ex-wife, Joyce, kept badgering him with her problems. An exasperated Lisa left Grant. They reconciled. Then he left her for another woman.

Lisa later met Whit McColl, a newspaper publisher. They were married, and again, a former wife appeared — only this time, the lady named Charmane was able to prove that she was still legally Mrs. McColl.

Lisa's next marriage was to the charming Earl Mitchell. Theirs seemed to be a happy one, but, alas, he didn't tell her that he was involved in dangerous government work overseas. He was killed by being smothered with a pillow.

Lisa devoted much of her time after Mitchell's death looking after her dress shop. She was delighted when her son Scott came to Oakdale, and was especially pleased when she had to tell him that the woman he was flirting with was his mother. Scott left soon after and Lisa wondered where he had gone.

Lisa met the handsome Eduardo Grimaldi, Damian's uncle, and felt the two of them were meant for each other like pesto and pasta. She was delighted when she won him away from the equally smitten Lucinda Walsh. They were married, but Eduardo was murdered soon after. Lisa felt Dr. John Dixon, father of her daughter-in-law, Margo Hughes, had somehow botched things in the hospital, and sued him for malpractice.

Scott returned to Oakdale but Lisa wasn't sure he would stay. Little did Lisa know that the woman Scott loved, and thought he had lost, was Lucinda's long-lost sister, Samantha Markham.

Eileen on Lisa and thirty-five years on As the World Turns*:*
"I'm really just getting started ..."

Don Hastings (r) with brother Bob Hastings, formerly of General Hospital.

Actor: Don Hastings

Birthplace: Brooklyn, New York
Birthdate: April 1

Don started his career as a singer on the radio at the age of six. "My older brother, Bob (an ex-*General Hospital* regular), was singing on a children's radio program. While I was waiting for him one day, the producer heard that I could also sing and put me on the program, which was called *Coast to Coast on A Bus,* as well."

Don then went into the national company of *Life With Father.* He did several more plays over the years and also started working in television. He

125

became part of *Captain Video,* a show that would become a classic in early TV sci-fi productions.

On April 2, 1956, the same day *As the World Turns* debuted, Don joined the cast of its sister soap, *The Edge of Night* in the role of Jack Lane. Four years later, in 1960, he joined *ATWT* and has been in residence in Oakdale ever since.

Don married his co-star, Leslie Denniston, who played Karen Peters. They have a daughter, Katherine Scott Hastings. Don also has two daughters and a son from his previous marriage.

A member of the Writers Guild, Don Hastings has written scripts for *ATWT* and *Guiding Light.* In 1993, the National Academy of Television Arts and Sciences (NATAS) honored him with its coveted Silver Circle Award.

Character: Dr. Robert (Bob) Hughes
See Founding Families.

Actor: Kathryn Hays

Birthplace: Princeton, Illinois
Birthdate: July 26

Kathryn Hays studied at Northwestern University in Evanston, Illinois, an institution famous for turning out fine actors. Hays has appeared on Broadway in *Mary, Mary* with Barbara Bel Geddes (who would later go on to star in *Dallas*) and *The Irregular Verb to Love,* with Claudette Colbert. Her feature films include *Counterpoint* with fellow Northwestern graduate Charlton Heston. She also co-starred with George C. Scott in *The Savage Land* and with Clint Walker in *Yuma.*

On television, she accumulated over fifty prime-time appearances, including two Emmy-nominated roles in *High Chapparral* and *Star Trek.*

Hays, who has a married daughter, Sherri, is an accomplished singer and has made appearances in musicals on Broadway as well as with the Pittsburgh Civic Light Opera. She joined *As the World Turns* as Kim Reynolds in 1972.

Character: Kim Reynolds Stewart Dixon Andropoulous Hughes
Kim was a young widow when she first met Bob Hughes. He was married to her sister, Jennifer, mother of two children, Rick and Barbara Ryan. The couple bickered often over her son, Rick, who was determined to break up his mother's marriage.

Bob and Kim spent a night together, and she became pregnant. Unwilling to give up the child, Kim married Dr. John Dixon, one of Bob's adversaries at the hospital. Dixon was not in love with Kim (not yet, that is), but he did have his eyes on the money that she would bring into the marriage. He soon fell in love with her, but she didn't share his ardor.

After Bob and Jennifer had another dispute, he walked out and was hit by a car. In his delirium, he confessed to being the father of Kim's expected child. Jennifer forgave him. Meanwhile, Kim had a miscarriage on her way to see Bob.

Later, with Bob and Jennifer reconciled, Kim turned to Dan Stewart and decided to leave John for him. But she was caught in a tornado and fell unconscious. When she awoke, she had amnesia. John took advantage of her condition to woo her and try to win her back. Flattered by his attentiveness, Kim resumed their relationship as husband and wife. But when she regained her memory, she left him again. She was also pregnant again, but this time the father of her child was John Dixon.

Kim gave birth to Andy Dixon. She then divorced John and married Dr. Don Stewart, who died after a lingering illness. She took over parenting of Don's daughter, Betsy.

Kim later fell in love with Nick Andropoulos. Their plans to marry were postponed when his supposedly dead wife, Andrea, turned up. But eventually, love cleared a path for them, and they were wed.

After Nick's death, Kim and Bob found each other again, and were married. To their joy, they learned that the child Kim thought she had lost, was alive and had been sold by a hospital employee to a wealthy couple. That child was Sabrina.

In recent years, Kim has had to deal with Andy's alcoholism, Betsy's ill-fated marriage to Craig Montgomery, Susan Stewart's infatuation and dependency on Bob, and, more recently, the lawsuit her best friend, Lisa Grimaldi, brought against her former husband, John Dixon. But, as with everything in her life, Kim manages to overcome the bad to find the good.

Actor: Benjamin Hendrickson

Birthplace: Huntington, New York
Birthdate: August 26

Hendrickson's introduction to acting came with a role in a high school production of *Bye, Bye Birdie*. Soon after he was graduated, he was accepted into the newly created drama section of the prestigious Juilliard School of Music, and Benjamin eventually went on to tour in classics and contemporary works. His Broadway credits include *The Elephant Man, Awake and Sing,* and *Strider.* Hendrickson has also guested on several prime-time shows, and has had roles on *Texas, Guiding Light,* and *Another World.* He is single and has homes in Manhattan, in New York City, and in Stowe, Vermont.

Character: Hal Munson

Police detective Hal Munson arrived in Oakdale in 1985. Shortly after Barbara Ryan Stenbeck was cleared of all charges in the death of her husband, James Stenbeck, Hal married her. He later learned he was the father of Adam Hughes, the child his partner on the police force, Margo Hughes, gave birth to in Greece. Tom Hughes, Margo's husband, adopted the boy. Hal is also the father of Nikki Graves.

Hal's marriage to Barbara has had many rocky moments. She has always been jealous of his relationship with Margo. In 1994, she became involved with another man. Hal, meanwhile, had sustained a head injury while on a case, and began having violent reactions. After he learned of Barbara's infidelity, the two separated. For a while, he tried to gain custody of their children, but at last report, Barbara and Hal seemed ready to make some compromises. Whether that leads to a reconciliation remains to be seen.

Actor: Jon Hensley

Birthplace: Browns Mills, New Jersey
Birthdate: August 26

Jon grew up in Bucks County in Pennsylvania where his parents have been in the restaurant business for years. Hensley originally planned to major in journalism in New York University. But after a year in college, he began to study acting, and still does.

Jon's acting career began with productions at Bucks County Playhouse. His soap career began with the role of Brody Price on *One Life to Live*. He joined *As the World Turns* in October 1985, playing the newly created role of Holden Snyder. He left in September 1988, and returned in June 1990. While Hensley was away from Oakdale, he studied Shakespeare at the London Academy of Music, Drama, and Art (LAMDA). His favorite off-screen activities include sports and writing music.

Character: Holden Snyder

Holden Snyder may have loved many women, but he's been in love only once, with the beautiful Lily Walsh Grimaldi (Martha Byrne). Long before Holden and Lily were married, they were drawn to each other. He was Lucinda Walsh's stable hand; she was Lucinda's daughter. Lily was also attracted to Dustin Donovan (Brian Bloom), but Holden eventually won her heart.

For Holden, life would be a series of "Just whens...." For example — Just when he thought he and Lily would eventually marry, his mother,

Emma Snyder (Kathleen Widdoes), learned her daughter, Iva (Lisa Brown), was returning to the Snyder farm after an absence of fifteen years. To Holden's dismay, Lily learned that Iva was her real mother, and that she'd been conceived when Iva was raped. When Lily learned that Holden knew that he'd been romancing his mother's granddaughter, she fled back into the arms of Dusty Donovan. (Iva is adopted, so she is not Holden's biological sister. Thus, Holden and Lily are not related.)

Holden married Emily Stewart, the pregnant former mistress of the then-supposedly dead James Stenbeck. Just when Holden had hoped to settle down in happy domesticity with Emily and the baby, she miscarried the child, and turned to the handsome Tonio Reyes, Holden's brother-in-law, for love.

Holden, who had been in business with Tonio, pulled out of the partnership when he learned of his affair with Emily. He started a business with Craig Montgomery (Scott Bryce) instead. But, to Holden's chagrin, Emily also turned to Craig (but for other reasons, of course) when she broke up with Tonio.

Martha Byrne and Jon Hensley.

Meanwhile, John Dixon's illegitimate son, Duke, turned up and tried to turn Lily on to his charms, but realized she was Caleb Snyder's love interest. Caleb, however, soon learned that Lily was still in love with his brother, Holden.

Eventually, the oft-star-crossed lovers, Lily and Holden, were married. And just when life seemed to be going smoothly for him, he had an accident in New York and lost much of his memory. He could not remember his relationship with Lily, and they broke up; she and went to Italy, where she met and married Damian Grimaldi.

While Holden's memory never completely returned, he became increasingly aware of how important Lily had been to him. He found her in Italy, but she rejected him. She was, after all, another man's wife now.

Holden and Lily began an international pursuit — much of it platonic. He would follow leads on the Grimaldis that inevitably had him catching up with her in Malta and Rome. At one point, they shared one night together. Lily, in good time, learned she was pregnant. To Damian's chagrin, Holden helped Lily give birth to her son.

129

Will Holden and Lily ever reunite? One thing is sure: For Holden Snyder, just when things seem to be working out, something — or someone — will be working against him.

Actor: Scott Holmes

Birthplace: West Grove, Pennsylvania
Birthdate: May 30

Scott Holmes grew up in Oxford, Pennsylvania. When he was five, he began to play the piano, and later added the trumpet to his musical skills. He has continued his interest in music since then.

Holmes's interest in acting began in high school with an "influential" drama and English teacher. He took a B.A. degree in Music and Drama from Catawba College in Salisbury, North Carolina, where he met his future wife, Pamela. She went on to choreograph the touring production of *Godspell* in which he starred for almost two years. Scott then spent a season with the Pittsburgh Civic Light Opera Company, during which time he was in a production of *Shenandoah,* starring Howard Keel.

He's done a slew of productions on Broadway, including Tommy Tune's *Best Little Whorehouse Goes Texas.* (Henderson Forsythe, who played David Stewart on *All My Children,* starred in the original Broadway production of *Best Little Whorehouse in Texas.*)

Holmes previously appeared in *Ryan's Hope.* He assumed the role of Tom Hughes in 1987. Scott and his wife, Pamela, are the parents of a son, Taylor Nicholas.

Character: Tom Hughes

Tom Hughes is the son of Dr. Bob Hughes (Don Hastings) and Bob's first wife, Lisa (Eileen Fulton). He is a lawyer, following in the professional footsteps of his grandfather, Chris Hughes, and his uncle, Donald. Tom is currently married to Margo Montgomery, and is the adoptive father of Adam Hughes, Margo's son; they also have a boy, Casey. Tom is the father of Lien Truong (later, Lien Hughes) who was born of a relationship he had while he served in Vietnam. He is the half-brother of Lisa's sons, Scott Eldridge, and the late Chuckie Shea. His half-sisters are Bob's daughters, Frannie (by the late Jennifer Ryan) and Sabrina (with Bob's current wife, Kim).

Tom's Vietnam service left him with memories he tried to shake by taking drugs. He eventually learned to deal both with his post-service stress and his addiction.

Tom was previously married to Carol Demming, who became restless because he spent so much time working; she turned to a man named Jay

Stalling, who, ironically, had once courted Tom's mother, Lisa (as did almost every male in Oakdale).

Tom married his client, Natalie Bannon, who also found Jay attractive. Tom divorced Natalie, who was pregnant with Jay's child, but she left town before Jay and the very forgiving Carol could adopt the youngsters. Later, Tom and his teenage half-brother, Chuck Shea, were hurt in a car accident. Tom survived, Chuck didn't.

Tom became Dawn (Dee) Stewart Dixon's lawyer in her marital rape case against John Dixon. He found himself attracted to Maggie, the sister of Lyla Montgomery, who is the mother of John's daughter, Margo.

Margo had a fling with James Stenbeck before deciding she really liked Tom Hughes. By this time, Maggie realized Tom was in love with her niece, Margo, and withdrew from the relationship. Tom and Margo became a team for law and order: He was the lawyer who upheld the law; she was the police officer who enforced it.

Tom learned that his son, Adam Hughes, was actually the son of Hal Munson, but he adopted the child and loves the boy as much as if he were his own.

Tom's devotion to Margo helped both of them through a difficult period. She had been raped by a man who was HIV-positive. Margo had to take tests and wait out the results over a long period of time. Tom insisted he would stay with her and be supportive whatever happened. Ultimately, the couple got the good news: Margo was HIV-negative.

Tom's relationship with his half-brother, Scott, is a distant one. He resented Scott's first appearance in Oakdale two years ago, and hasn't warmed up to him since he returned in the spring of 1995. But Tom is a generous soul and no doubt he'll finally warm up to his mother's other son.

Actor: Elizabeth Hubbard

Birthplace: New York, New York
Birthdate: December 22

Elizabeth Hubbard was graduated from Radcliffe and pursued her theatrical training at the Royal Academy of Dramatic Arts in London, where she received their coveted Silver Medal Award. She has also studied drama with Lee Strasberg and Harold Clurman, and continues to study singing.

Hubbard has a slew of Broadway and off-Broadway credits, including Noel Coward's *Present Laughter* with George C. Scott, and the musical version of *I Remember Mama* with Liv Ullmann. Among her feature films are *Ordinary People* with Mary Tyler Moore, and *The Bell Jar.*

Elizabeth Hubbard's first soap role was as Dr. Althea Davis in *The Doctors,* for which she won one of her two Emmys. The second award was for her role as Edith Wilson in NBC's special, *First Ladies' Diaries*. Since creating the role of Lucinda Walsh on *As the World Turns* in 1984, Hubbard has earned seven Emmy nominations for Outstanding Lead Actress.

Off-screen, she enjoys writing and traveling. She's a spokesperson for the Women's Commission on Women and Children Refugees, and has traveled to Bosnia on their behalf. She has one son, Jeremy Bennett.

Character: Lucinda Walsh Dixon

She's a powerful woman, this Lucinda. She heads up business enterprises. She makes decisions that can determine the fate of many people. She's tough. But over the years, Lucinda has revealed that she's vulnerable where many people often are: She needs to be loved by those whom she loves, and she needs to have her family around her.

Lucinda is the adoptive mother of Lily and biological mother of Sierra. She adores her daughters, although there have been times when they were not as loving to her.

It was Lucinda's stable hand, Holden Snyder, who eventually won Lily's heart. But Lucinda was opposed, and their marriage didn't last. Lily went on to marry Damian Grimaldi. At one point, Lily sued successfully to have her adoption overturned. Lucinda was crushed, but never stopped loving her child. Lily eventually reconciled with her mother. Lucinda was shattered by news of Sierra's assassination in Montega, but later was overjoyed to learn Sierra had survived. More recently, she played Cupid in an effort to reconcile Sierra with her estranged husband, Craig Montgomery.

Lucinda was married to John Dixon. She resented the attention he lavished on his newly found illegitimate son, Duke, especially when Duke showed interest in Lily. Eventually, too many problems forced the Walsh-Dixon union to dissolve. Although they were divorced, Lucinda never really stopped loving John, standing by him in times of trouble, and paying big legal fees to Jessica McKechnie for defending Dixon in the malpractice suit brought by Lisa Grimaldi over the death of her husband, Eduardo.

Ironically, Lucinda fell for the handsome Eduardo, Lily's uncle-in-law, when he first came to Oakdale. But Lisa won his heart.

With all her power and all her money, Lucinda Walsh felt she was poorer for not having a family of her own. Somewhere, she believed, she might have a brother or a sister. She set her private detectives to work, and to her delight, she learned she had a half-sister named Neal and a half-brother named Royce (played by Terry Lester), both of whom came to Oakdale. To Lucinda's horror, however, Neal was killed and later, Royce — who had a split personality — turned out to be the killer. Or, rather, one of Royce's alter egos did the killing, which allowed Royce to go free. Lucinda also learned that her mother had been abusive to Royce, which may have accounted for his developing multiple personality disorder.

After Royce left town, Lucinda learned he may have had a twin. He did: The twin's name was Sam. But Sam turned out to be Samantha Markham, the adoptive daughter of a man who was not above conning others, including Lucinda.

Lucinda was crushed when she learned Sam planned to replace her priceless paintings with her own forgeries, sending them to her father in South America. But Sam changed her mind.

Later, when Sam questioned her relationship to Lucinda, Lucinda took it upon herself to prove they were sisters. More than anything, she wanted to keep her sibling.

More recently, Lucinda went up against the Grimaldis when Lily called her from Malta, convinced that her in-laws were trying to drive her insane. The Grimaldis may be an old and distinguished family, but they soon learned that if Lucinda felt they were harming her Lily, they would face better odds in the arena of the Colosseum with starving Komodo Dragons than if they came up against this protective Mama Lion.

Actor: Marie Masters
Birthplace: Cincinnati, Ohio
Birthdate: February 4

Being born in Cincinnati — the home base of Procter & Gamble, which produces *As the World Turns* — is just a happy coincidence for Marie Masters, who first joined the show in 1968. She won an art scholarship to Marian College in Indianapolis. However, she started spending her summer vacations doing summer stock, and after graduation, instead of pursuing her art career, she headed to New York to study with Uta Hagen, among others. Her Broadway debut was in *There's A Girl in My Soup*. Marie continues to do theater both on- and off-Broadway, as well as in regional playhouses.

133

Marie's soap debut was in *Love of Life*. She also appeared in *The Secrets of Midland Heights* and in a cable series, *Our Group*, as well as several prime-time shows.

Ms. Masters has twins, Jenny and Jesse, who are both Cornell University graduates. Jenny made an appearance on *ATWT* as a youngster, playing Emily, the daughter of Marie's character, Dr. Susan Stewart.

Character: Dr. Susan Burke Stewart McDermott

Of all the experiences that have marked the life of Dr. Susan Stewart McDermott, probably nothing compares with the one in which her sometimes willful daughter, Emily, donated an egg for implantation in Susan's womb so that she could have a child with her current (and younger) husband, Dr. Larry McDermott.

While Emily certainly did a good deed helping her mother give birth to a child who was both her half-sister and her daughter (at least in terms of DNA), Susan had problems keeping Emily out of her marriage. Apparently, Susan felt because Emily provided the egg that Larry's sperm fertilized, she felt a proprietary interest in him.

More recently, Susan has been preoccupied with some of Larry's personal problems, including his feud with John Dixon, and the real reason he didn't get the job he hoped for in Texas: John knew Susan didn't want to move, and in trying to help her out, cost Larry the new job.

A brief rundown of Susan's past reveals some of the woes with which this classic soap opera character has dealt: Susan Burke was a medical student when she met another medical student, Dan Stewart. They were married. He wanted children; she didn't. Meanwhile, Dan had also fallen for Elizabeth Talbott, who married his brother, Paul. Dan later learned that Elizabeth's baby was his child. Meanwhile, Susan conceived, but after baby Emmy was born, the couple split up. Dan got custody of Emmy after Susan married (and later divorced) another man.

Susan turned to drinking when she lost custody of the child. She also became jealous of Dan's romance with Kim Reynolds and tried to break them up. In time, she learned to deal with her alcohol problems, but her dependency on others remained with her.

A few years ago, she asked Dr. Bob Hughes to help her deal with an emotional problem. Bob's wife, Kim, perhaps remembering how she tried to break up her relationship with Dan, warned Bob not to get involved. But good old Bob felt it was his duty to come to the aid of a human being in need — only later to realize that he had narrowly escaped being sucked in emotionally by Susan.

Susan was instrumental in breaking up the marriage of John Dixon and Lucinda Walsh. Lucinda tried to get John's son, Duke, involved with Julie. Julie told Duke she was pregnant (but not with his child). Meanwhile, Lucinda was paying Julie to stay in Oakdale, while John was hoping she'd leave. Susan told him about Lucinda's scheme. John walked out after an argument with his wife, and spent the night in Susan's comforting arms.

Will Susan and Larry make it through their problems, or will Larry's PROBLEM be too much to deal with?

One thing is sure, Susan will look for someone to help her get through her next emotional crisis.

Actor: Kelly Menighan

Birthplace: Glenview, Illinois
Birthdate: February 15

Kelley has two sisters, Kathleen and Karoline, who are also actors. She had a rather interesting ecumenical education: She attended Regina Dominican High School, an all-girls Catholic institution in Wilmette, Illinois, and then went on to Southern Methodist University in Dallas, where she majored in Theater and English, and minored in Art. She also studied dance and the business of theater, from budgeting to casting, etc.

Kelley, who assumed the role of Emily Stewart in July 1992, has done several films, including *Charlie Chaplin*. Her previous soap was *Santa Barbara*. She lives in New York City and loves to shop for antique furniture, quilts and jewelry. She's famous among her friends and castmates for her oatmeal cookies.

Character: Emily Stewart

If you're ever asked to come up with a synonym for the word manipulative, repeat the name Emily Stewart; if your inquisitor is a fan of *As the World Turns*, she or he will understand.

Emily, who was first known as baby Emmy on the soap, came into the world practically unwanted by her mother, Susan, who didn't intend to get pregnant, but did. She was later taken by her father, Dr. Dan Stewart, who refused to return her even when Susan had a change of heart. Eventually, Dr. Dan died, and although Emily rejoined her mother, their relationship was always strained.

Over the years, Emily has not shrunk from causing trouble if she sees something in it for her. She was about to tell Tom Hughes that his son, Adam, was actually Hal Munson's son, but Margo Hughes beat her to the punch.

She became the mistress of the evil James Stenbeck, former husband of Barbara Ryan Stenbeck, and after his presumed death, married Holden Snyder. Emily was pregnant with Stenbeck's child, but miscarried after the marriage.

She then broke with Holden and picked up with Tonio Reyes. She broke with him when she learned Tonio's wife, Meg (Holden's sister), was pregnant.

Emily then went after Craig Montgomery. After learning that he was interested in Ellie Snyder (another of Holden's sisters), Emily got someone to dig up Ellie's past. She confronted Craig with revelations about Ellie's former marriage and an affair with a married man. Craig told her Ellie had already told him everything, and he blasted her for her tactics.

Emily also turned to Paul Stenbeck, the son of her former lover, for comfort after she'd been spurned by another man. As it turned out, James was not dead after all. He came with a plan to kidnap his son. When he found love letters from Paul to Emily, he was so angry about her daring to sleep with Paul that he started to strangle her. Paul arrived and saved her by shooting his father. More recently, Emily fell in love with Lucinda's long-lost brother, Royce. They were about to exchange "I dos" when his dangerous alter-ego emerged. Royce left town.

Emily's old interest in Craig resurfaced when he returned to Oakdale after separating from his wife, Sierra. But again, poor Emily was twice trumped by Cupid: The first time was when Craig became involved with Royce's sister, Samantha. Then, with Lucinda filling in for the winged arrow-shooter, Craig returned to Sierra courtesy of a ploy Lucinda used to reunite them.

Whom will Emily turn to next? Will Royce come back and will he still want her? Or will there finally be a man with whom she can find love and happiness, minimizing her manipulations so that they become irritations at most?

Actor: Joanna Rhinehart

Birthplace: Springfield, Massachusetts
Birthdate: November 14

Joanna, who assumed the role of Jessica McKechnie in April 1995, has four brothers: Marc is a PBS producer; Karl is a produce inspector with a national supermarket chain; Arthur owns a record store; and Roy is a retired air force sergeant.

Joanna doesn't say if her taste in sports is related to having four brothers, but she's said to be very good at both basketball and billiards. She began dancing fifteen years ago, which led to her taking theater courses in college. She later worked in regional theater in everything from Shakespeare to Lorraine Hansberry. She's also done several films, including *The Trial of Bernhard Goetz*, and *Taabu*.

Joanna's previous soap role was on *One Life to Live*.

Character: Jessica Griffin McKechnie
Jessica Griffin McKechnie is a brilliant lawyer who has stood up in court for many of Oakdale's citizens when they were *in* legal *extremis*.

She met the handsome Scotsman, Duncan McKechnie, who had been married to the beautiful but psychopathic Lilith. He was also married to Lisa's niece, Shannon O'Hara (Margaret Reed). While Shannon was presumed dead (she was actually a political prisoner in Africa), Duncan courted Jessica. The relationship between Duncan and Jessica, who is African-American, brought out the best and the worst in people. While many of Oakdale's citizens supported the couple's plan to marry, Lisa voiced disapproval. She insisted she was not bigoted — just concerned that society wouldn't give them or any child they might have a decent break.

Jessica's parents were also against the marriage. But the couple went ahead and got hitched and, in time, had a daughter, Bonnie. But Shannon returned and Jessica sensed Duncan was still in love with her. She gave him a divorce and left town for a while.

Shannon and Duncan remarried, but separated again. Shannon left Oakdale in mid-1995. Jessica had already returned. Although she and Duncan still have feelings for each other, and it makes Bonnie happy to see Mommy and Daddy together, Jessica has not forgiven him for leaving them for Shannon.

Jessica is currently keeping busy defending Dr. John Dixon in the medical malpractice suit brought by Lisa Grimaldi. But as the year winds down, McKechnie faces events that would change his life before the New Year rang in, signaling such an important holiday for the Scots.

Actor: Paolo Seganti
Birthplace: Italy
Birthdate: May 20

Paolo has lived all over Italy: Rome, Naples, Florence, Bologna, and Oblia in Sardinia. Since joining *As the World Turns* on April 30, 1993, he's become, as he says, "very much a New Yorker as well...It was amazing how quickly I found myself at home in this city...." He adds, "Of course, it helps that there are so many people of Italian background living here, and so many wonderful Italian restaurants from the different regions... But I still enjoy cooking for myself and my friends when they visit .."

Seganti's idol is the late, great Welsh actor, Richard Burton, who once played the noblest Roman of them all, Marc Antony. Paolo enjoys doing theater whenever he has the time. He also enjoyed flying around the world to prepare for his narrating role in *Earthquest*, an MTV-style documentary for The Discovery Channel.

Before becoming a star of theater, film, and television in Italy, he worked as a gas station attendant, farmer, tinman, iron and construction worker, auto mechanic, painter, seaman on a container ship, bus boy, model, and was in business with his brother, Elia, in a steel cable company.

The author once asked him what advice he would give Damian Grimaldi, his *ATWT* character. His response: "I would tell him not to be so intense and to enjoy his good fortune in having such a beautiful wife as Lily."

P.S. Paolo's nickname is Pillo. Does that mean chatting with him is "Pillo talk?"

137

Character: Damian Grimaldi

International businessman Damian Grimaldi met the lovely Lily Snyder in Italy where she sang in a club owned by his family. He fell in love with her at a time when she was most vulnerable and needed comforting. She believed the great love of her life, Holden Snyder, was dead.

Damian married Lily and returned with her to Oakdale. His family was interested in establishing their business interests in this most cosmopolitan of small towns. However, there were some who wondered if the Grimaldis — who included Damian's dashing uncle Eduardo (Nicolas Coster) — were everything they said they were. Damian realized even his wife occasionally questioned his moves and motives.

When Holden returned and threatened to become a strong factor in Lily's life again, Damian's jealousy grew. He became especially angry when he missed being with Lily when she went into labor, and Holden delivered her son, Luciano (Luke). There was even some suggestion that Holden fathered the baby.

Damian had been under the influence of his stepmother, Orlena (Claire Bloom) who killed his Uncle Eduardo — a fact he was unaware of when he agreed to have Lily drugged and taken to Malta, where Damian was determined to provide his son with Maltese citizenship.

As the summer of 1995 heated up, so did the affairs of the Grimaldis. Will Orlena be unmasked as a killer? Will Damian lose Lily if she discovers that he may have been involved in the plots hatched by this latter-day Lucretia Borgia? And what about Holden? And speaking of men named Mark, as we did in the last paragraph about Paolo Seganti, a man named Mark does turn up in Malta just when Lily is, again, vulnerable, and in need of someone to care for her.

Stay tuned.

Actor: Helen Wagner

Birthplace: Lubbock, Texas

Helen, the only remaining member of the original cast of *As the World Turns,* started acting in Monmouth College in Illinois where she earned degrees in dramatics and music. She went to New York to continue voice and piano training and sang with various choirs. She went on to do musical theater, including Sigmund Romberg and Oscar Hammerstein's *Sunny River* and, later, Richard Rodgers and Oscar Hammerstein's *Oklahoma.* She also starred in the drama, *The Bad Seed* on Broadway, and toured as Blanche in *A Streetcar Named Desire,* which starred Lee Marvin.

In 1988, Ms. Wagner was awarded an Honorary Degree of Doctor of Humane Letters from her alma mater. After helping to raise funds to replace the school's little theater, she opened the new theater in 1990 in a role she had become famous for, Eleanor, in *The Lion in Winter.* The production was directed by her husband, Broadway producer, Robert Willey.

Character: Nancy Hughes McClosky
See Founding Families.

Actor: Alexander Walters

Alexander Walters joined *As the World Turns* in July, 1995 as the mysterious "Mark," who turns up in Malta when Lily Grimaldi is there.

Prior to being cast in the soap, Walters had a role on *The Young and the Restless* and also appeared in the Fox series, *Married...With Children.* On Canadian television, he starred in *He Shoots, He Scores.*

Walters has been in several films including *Men Are from Pluto* and *Dunston Checks In,* which starred Jason Alexander of *Seinfeld.*

Character: Mark
Just when Lily Grimaldi was so vulnerable there in Malta, surrounded by a scheming mother-in-law, Orlena, and a husband, Damian, whose motives she questioned, along came a handsome man named Mark. Her life changed with his arrival, and so did the lives of many of the people Lily loved, feared, or both.

Helen Wagner.

Actor: Kathleen Widdoes
Birthplace: Wilmington, Delaware
Birthdate: March 21

Kathleen started her stage career with the legendary Luther Adler in Arthur Miller's powerful play, *A View from the Bridge.* She has since gone on to do plays by Shakespeare, Neil Simon, Oscar Wilde, and others. Her films include *Petulia, The Group, The Mephisto Waltz, I'm Dancing as Fast as I Can* and *The End of August.*

She's done a slew of prime-time series including *The Secrets of Midland Heights, Kojak,* and *Nurse.* She starred in the PBS special, *Edith Whar-*

ton, and co-starred with Tony Curtis and *All My Children's* Susan Lucci in the TV film *Mafia Princess.*

Character: Emma Snyder

Emma Snyder came to the farm outside Oakdale in November 1985. Emma is not only the matriarch of the Snyder clan, she's its heart and its backbone. Whenever things look bad for any of her children — Holden, Caleb, Ellie, Iva, Meg, and Seth — Emma is there to love, protect, and advise.

In her personal life, Emma had the attentions of at least three handsome swains, the oilman, Cal Stricklyn; the doctor, John Dixon; and her publisher, Jarred Carpenter. It was Cal, however, who finally persuaded Emma to let him slip in under one of her country quilts with him.

Emma didn't marry Cal. She didn't feel he was quite the "Mr. Right" she was looking for. But, don't worry; she hasn't given up looking.

Actor: Douglas Wert

Douglas Wert joined *As the World Turns* in June, 1995, assuming the role of Scott Eldridge, who had originally been played by Joe Breen.

Wert's background includes recurring roles in *Star Trek: The Next Generation,* and *The Trials of Rosie O'Neill.* His soap background includes roles on *One Life to Live* and *The Young and the Restless.* He also had roles in several features including *Dracula Rising* and *Caroline at Midnight.* He also won rave reviews for his performances in *Passover* at the American Jewish Theater.

Character: Scott Eldridge

Lisa Miller Hughes (Eileen Fulton) divorced her husband, Dr. Bob Hughes (Don Hastings), and left their small son, Tommy, to be raised by his grandparents. She arrived in Chicago, and fell in love with a man named John Eldridge, with whom she had a son, Scott. Their divorce left Lisa a wealthy woman. She decided to return to Oakdale, and again left her son behind. Two years ago, to her surprise, Scott turned up in Oakdale. He didn't know her at first, and even flirted with her. When he learned who she was, he at first rejected her, and gradually reconciled with her.

Scott abruptly left Oakdale after the death of the woman he loved, Neal Alcott, Lucinda Walsh's long-lost half sister. He returned once more in June, 1995 and, to his surprise, found Samantha Markham about to marry (albeit in a phony ceremony) Kirk Anderson.

It turned out that Scott hadn't been very far from home after all, even though Lisa had followed a lead to Mexico to try to find him. It also turned out that Scott and Samantha had been lovers. The irony is that Sam was also one of Lucinda's half-sisters.

Scott's reemergence in his mother, Lisa's, life will have an effect on her, on his brother, Tom, and on many other people, including, of course, Samantha.

Actor: Colleen Zenk Pinter

Birthplace: Barrington, Illinois
Birthdate: January 20

Colleen planned to become a dancer, but switched to acting after sustaining a knee injury. She has worked in plays and musicals around the country and in Europe via the Army Special Services. She made her Broadway debut in 1981 in *Bring Back Birdie* opposite Chita Rivera and Donald O'Connor. Her first film was in John Huston's *Annie.*

Colleen is active on behalf of many good causes, including Bread and Roses, which runs an AIDS hospice in the Connecticut area where she and her husband, Mark Pinter (Grant, *Another World*), live.

Colleen and Mark met when he was playing Brian McColl on *ATWT*. When they married, they combined children from both his and her previous marriages, and they added one of their own, for a total of six.

Character: Barbara Ryan Stenbeck Munson

Barbara and her brother, Rick, were the children of Jennifer Ryan, who would later marry Bob Hughes. Their aunt is Jennifer's sister, Kim Reynold Stewart Dixon Hughes, mother of her cousins, Andy Dixon and Sabrina Hughes.

Barbara was an easygoing young woman when she was wooed by the dashing James Stenbeck. After she gave birth to their son, Paul, James Stenbeck persuaded her to marry him to ensure Paul's rights to inherit the Stenbeck fortune. James proved to be anything but a devoted husband, having affairs with other women. He also tried to make her believe she was going crazy: He had her drugged and made her believe she had attempted suicide.

Fortunately, for Barbara, James's good-guy cousin, Gunnar (a real straight-shooter) helped get her out of James's clutches.

Later, after Paul killed James — who had been strangling Paul's mistress at the time — Barbara donated the late villain's fortune to charity.

Barbara went on to involve herself with various men. She eventually married police detective Hal Munson, who she later learned was the father of Margo Hughes's son, Adam.

Barbara developed her own fashion business and became one of Oakdale's women of note. She also developed a passion for young Evan Walsh. Poor Hal felt left out of the loop and decided to leave her. He also

141

decided to sue for custody of their children. But the two realized they still cared for each other.

Guest Star: Robert Vaughn

The internationally famous film and television star Robert Vaughn, who created the role of Napoleon Solo in *The Man From Uncle* series, guest stars as Rick Hamlin, a high-powered lawyer representing Lisa Grimaldi in her malpractice suit against John Dixon, who she believes is responsible for her husband's death.

Vaughn, who holds a Ph.D., makes his soap opera debut in *As the World Turns* opposite another international star, Claire Bloom (Orlena Grimaldi).

The Bold and the Beautiful

O n March 23, 1987, Bill and Lee Phillip Bell brought forth their new daytime drama, *The Bold and the Beautiful,* conceived in Los Angeles, California, and dedicated to the principle that mixing passion and fashion can produce an entertaining daily half-hour soap that oozes chic and chicanery.

The soap debuted with two major families: the wealthy Forresters, who run a self-named *haute couture* fashion house, and the working-class Logans. True to the principle that America is the land of opportunity (first laid down in soaps by Bill Bell's mentor, Irna Phillips), the Logans occupied a lower economic rung. Nevertheless, their son, Storm (Ethan Wayne), became a lawyer, and their daughter, Brooke (Katherine Kelly Lang), a chemist.

The Forresters' sprigs — Thorne, (Jeff Trachta); Ridge (Ronn Moss); and their other now-you-see-them-now-you-don't offspring, Kristen and Felicia — all have something in common: They all went into the "rag" business. As a matter of fact, the Bells' original title for the show was *Rags.*

The original cast featured two young actors from two famous Hollywood families: Ethan Wayne is one of the late John Wayne's children, and Carrie Mitchum is the granddaughter of Robert Mitchum.

The Bold and the Beautiful marked the final lap of the Bells' trek from Chicago to L.A. For years, they had written the scripts for their premiere soap, The Young and the Restless, in Chicago, and commuted to Hollywood to oversee the production of the series, which itself is set in the Midwest. Once all the Bells — Bill, Lee, daughter Lauralee (who plays Chris on Y&R), and sons Bradley and Bill, Jr. — were relocated to the West Coast, the new L.A.-based series, which had originally been set in Chicago, was born under the palms of Southern California.

Love, Lust and the Rag Business

Made to order or off the rack — few soaps have packed as much power and passion into their story lines — and in less than ten years — as The Bold and the Beautiful. An overview of some of those stories follows:

If Dr. James Warwick, a psychiatrist played by Ian Buchanan, could help Stephanie Forrester (Susan Flannery), the aristocratic matriarch of the family, he would diagnose her as being self-esteem challenged. In spite of her wealth and social position, Stephanie never seems to believe that she can be loved for herself. She always seems to feel that whatever happiness she has can be taken from her at a moment's notice. She is also extremely loyal and protective of her family, and can become nasty if she feels threatened.

Viewers realized from the start: Stephanie learned that the woman she hired to cater one of her parties, Beth Logan (Judith Baldwin), had been husband Eric's (John McCook) great love. Stephanie still recalled how she had coerced Eric into marrying her by becoming pregnant with

Original Cast

Judith Baldwin	. . . . .Beth Logan	Carrie Mitchum	. . . . .Donna Logan
Susan Flannery	. .Stephanie Forrester	Ronn Moss	. . . . .Ridge Forrester
Bryan Genesse	. . . . . . .Rocco Carner	Clayton Norcross	. . .Thorne Forrester
Joanna Johnson	. . .Caroline Spencer	Stephen Shortridge	. . . . .David Reed
Lauren Koslow	. . . . . . .Margo Lynley	Nancy Sloan	. . . . .Katie Logan
Katherine Kelly Lang	. . .Brooke Logan	Jim Storm	. . . . .William Spencer
Teri Ann Linn	. . . . . .Kristen Forrester	Ethan Wayne	. . . . .Storm Logan
John McCook	. . . . .Eric Forrester		

144

Premier Date: March 23, 1987 / CBS

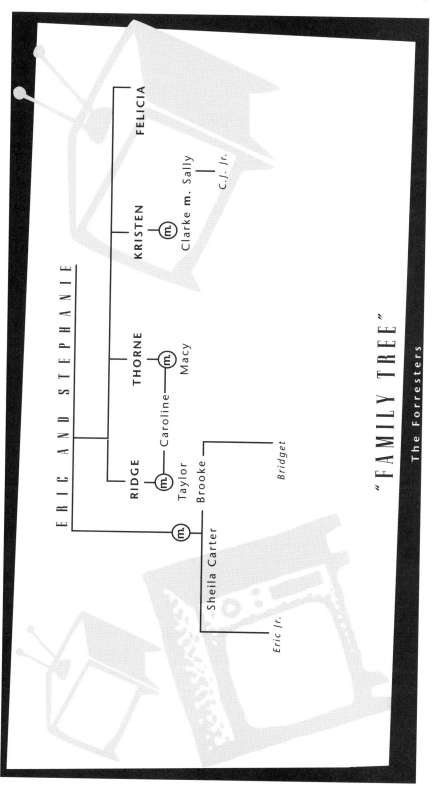

"FAMILY TREE"

The Forresters

ERIC AND STEPHANIE

RIDGE — Caroline — **THORNE** — **KRISTEN** — **FELICIA**

RIDGE (m.) Taylor

Caroline

THORNE (m.) Macy

KRISTEN (m.) Clarke m. Sally

C.J. Jr.

Brooke (m.) Eric Jr.

Sheila Carter

Bridget

E ric and Stephanie Forrester's four children have, like their parents, loved well, if not always wisely. Keeping it in the family, Caroline married Thorne, and then Ridge; Brooke married Eric but never got over Ridge. But even when Cupid carves a big X through their hearts, they won't give up on love.

Bold and Beautiful Guest Stars

Charlton Heston made his daytime debut playing himself as host of a fund-raising fashion show; Tippi Hedren played the role of Helen MacClaine. Phyllis Diller and Fabio have also graced *B&B*.

their first child, and she dreaded the day when he might leave her and return to Beth. And now, here was Beth, setting out hors d'oeuvres right on her Hepplewhite table top.

The tension between the two families continued well after Stephanie found Steven, Beth's long-missing husband, just before he could be declared legally dead. And even when Stephanie arranged for the Logans to be transferred to Paris, she had to contend with Beth's daughter, Brooke, as her rival.

But never mind Stephanie: Beth, who never stopped loving Eric, and, like him, hoped their meeting after so many years might spark a renewed relationship, was stunned to learn she would have to compete with her daughter for her former lover.

Also in the mix were the Spencers, represented by magazine publisher, Bill Spencer (Jim Storm), and his beautiful daughter, Caroline (Joanna Johnson). Ridge Forrester fell for Caroline, who had become best friends with Brooke. Ridge's brother, Thorne, also fell for the lovely Ms. Spencer.

The innocent Caroline was brutally raped, but the stoic soap heroine took her attacker to court. While both Forrester brothers stood by her, it was Thorne, the quieter, gentler brother — and not rambunctious Ridge — whom she married. An angry Ridge turned to Brooke, who saw her opportunity and moved in with him.

Ridge, however, still pined for Caroline. One night when Caroline had drunk too much, Ridge got into bed with her and pretended to be Thorne. They made love. Thorne learned about it and shot his brother. But momma Stephanie took the blame, saying she thought Ridge was a prowler.

Caroline told Ridge she loved him. Ridge told Caroline he loved her, but Brooke was pregnant so he had to marry her. The day before her wedding to Ridge, Brooke miscarried, and the wedding was canceled.

By this time, Caroline had divorced Thorne and eventually married Ridge. Brooke turned to Eric, and became pregnant with their son, Eric, Jr. Eric told Stephanie he wanted a divorce. After a while, Stephanie gave him his freedom and Eric married Brooke. Caroline, meanwhile, became ill, and, before dying of leukemia, told Brooke to marry Ridge.

Well, eventually, Brooke did, but only years later, after the presumed death of another of Ridge's wives, Dr. Taylor Hayes (Hunter Tylo). But that's another story to be told later in this chapter. Except for Brooke, the

B&B creator Lee Phillip Bell, Susan Flannery, Charlton Heston, Darlene Conley, and designer Diane von Furstenberg.

Logan clan — comprised of Steve, Beth, son Storm, daughters Donna and Katie (Carrie Mitchum and Nancy Sloan) — faded from the soap. Ditto the Spencers, with one relatively short period when Joanna Johnson returned as Caroline's long-lost kidnapped identical twin, Karen. The Forresters were also pruned: Both Felicia (Colleen Dion) and Kristen (Teri Ann Linn) moved away.

In came Sally Spectra, the flamboyant knock-off artist played by the magnificent Darlene Conley. Her daughter, Macy Alexander (Bobbie Eakes) would join her mother later on and, eventually, win the heart of Thorne Forrester — much to the distress of momma Stephanie, who considered her son much too good for the likes of Sally's daughter.

Several important story lines were developed. Sally, a middle-aged woman, married a younger man, Clarke Garrison (Daniel McVicar), and tried to believe he loved her for herself, and not for the opportunity to take over her business. She even had a child with him. (Clarke was not only virile, but fertile: he also fathered a child with Bill's former wife, Margo Spencer (Lauren Koslow).) Although crushed by the collapse of her marriage after Clarke's motives were revealed, Sally rebounded and waited for love to strike again.

Meanwhile, Stephanie was keeping a mysterious rendezvous. Did she have a lover? No. Years earlier, Stephanie had delivered a stillborn

147

The Bold and the Beautiful was the first soap to feature a mentally disabled actor, Keith Jones, in a recurring role (Kevin Anderson).

daughter. Two scamsters learned about the baby and schemed to get money by persuading her that the little girl had survived, albeit brain damaged. Stephanie visited her now grown "daughter" to care for her, although the young woman seemed to be completely unresponsive to Stephanie's loving touches.

Later, the scam was revealed. Angela, the imposter, was cruelly burned in a car accident and disappeared. She returned to Los Angeles to wreak vengeance on the Forresters. Good-hearted Thorne, who didn't know who she was, arranged for Angela to have surgery done by the best plastic surgeon in the world, who happened to live in Switzerland. Angela went off to the Alps, and hasn't been seen since. Perhaps, in time, she'll return to Los Angeles with her new face.

Because the series has the polished patina of a sleek nighttime series, it's easy to overlook some of the more socially relevant story lines.

One example is Stephanie's encounter with homelessness. After an emotional confrontation with Eric, Stephanie rushed out and somehow hit her head. She lost her memory and wandered around in unfamiliar areas. The expensively dressed and obviously confused woman was easy prey for the street people. She was saved from injury by a homeless woman, Ruth, who shared what she had with her. In time, Stephanie regained her memory and, fortunately, remembered the kindnesses done for her by her homeless friends.

In another important story line, a young man named Jake MacLaine (played by Todd McKee) came to Los Angeles to work as a tennis instructor. Felicia, one of the Forrester daughters fell for him, but he was strangely unresponsive to her seductiveness. He's not gay; he's just not able to deal with — let's say the word — SEX!

Later, Jake recalled having been molested as a child by a man who would come into his bedroom at night. Jake believed it was his father. Later, he learned it was his uncle who had filled his childhood with fear and hate.

The incest story would have stood on its own. But the Bells added an important factor — the enabling adult. In this case, it was Jake's mother who refused to believe her son had been sexually abused, adding to Jake's feelings that he, somehow, was to blame for causing trouble in the family.

148

The Founding Families

The Forresters

A Forrester family portrait: Jeff Trachta, John McCook, Susan Flannery, Ronn Moss.

Eric Forrester, played by John McCook, the patriarch of the Forrester family, and the head of the fashion business that carries his name. He's the former husband of Stephanie, Brooke, and Sheila; he's the father of Ridge, Thorne, Kristen, and Felicia with Stephanie, and Eric, Jr. with Brooke. He is also the grandfather of Brooke and Ridge's daughter.

Stephanie Forrester, played by Susan Flannery. The matriarch of the Forrester family, she helped make Eric Forrester a business success. Too bad she couldn't make their marriage work. Although they've been divorced for years, and he's been married twice more — once to Brooke, with whom he had a child, and once to Sheila Carter Grainger, his former company nurse with a talent for murder — Stephanie still believes they'll remarry.

　　She's the mother of Ridge, Thorne, Felicia and Kristen, and the grandmother of Ridge and Brooke's daughter.

Ridge Forrester, played by Ronn Moss. He's the eldest Forrester of his generation. A Beverly Hills Casanova, circumstances have changed him from playboy to settled husband and father. He's been married three times: His first wife was the late Caroline Spencer; his second wife, the beautiful psychiatrist, Dr. Taylor Hayes. He married Brooke, the mother of their daughter (and his former stepmother) after learning of Taylor's death

149

in a plane crash. Later, Taylor turned up on his doorstep alive, and eager to renew their relationship.

Kristen Forrester (Teri Ann Linn). The eldest daughter, she and Stephanie had been at odds for years. Kristen was married to Clarke Garrison (Daniel McVicar) who later married Sally Spectra. Kristen moved to New York with an old flame, Mick Savage.

Felicia Forrester (Colleen Dion). A talented designer, Felicia has had to struggle to get her father's approval. She fell in love with Jake MacClaine and Zack Hamilton, who would later become her brother-in-law courtesy of Ridge's marriage to Zack's sister, Taylor.

Thorne Forrester (originally played by Clayton Norcross; now played by Jeff Trachta.) Thorne is the youngest of the Forrester kids. He had once been married to Caroline Spencer, but they were divorced when she decided she really liked his brother better. After learning Ridge tricked Caroline into making love to him, he has no memory of having shot Ridge. His second wife is Macy, Sally Spectra's daughter. Thorne was once framed by one of Spectra's designers, Anthony, for the murder of a model.

The Logans

Beth Logan (originally played by Judith Baldwin, later by Nancy Burnett and Marla Adams). Beth is Eric Forrester's first love. She lost him to Stephanie. Her marriage to Stephen Logan produced four children: Brooke, Donna, Katie, and Storm (Stephen, Jr.) She later moved with her husband and two younger daughters to Paris.

Brooke Logan Forrester (Katherine Kelly Lang), former wife of Eric Forrester, with whom she had her son, Eric, Jr. Former lover and then wife of Ridge Forrester, father of their daughter, Bridget.

Brooke is a brilliant chemist who invented a cloth process, "Belief" (wrinkle-free fabric) that enabled her to gain a controlling interest in the company. A glitch with the application gave the patent to Brooke, and not Forrester's.

Brooke and Ridge were married after the "death" of his second wife, Taylor. The marriage, ironically, fulfilled Caroline's deathbed message to Brooke to marry Ridge, the man for whom both vied at one time. Taylor's return from the dead caused Brooke to fight hard to save her marriage, no matter what it took. Note: Is Ridge really Bridget's father? Or did Sheila manipulate the paternity test vials so that Eric — who might be Bridget's dad — would feel free to marry Sheila?

Storm (Stephen, Jr.) Logan, originally played by Ethan Wayne, then by Brian Patrick Clarke. Storm, a lawyer, can be as hot-headed as his nickname implies, especially if he thinks his sisters are in need of his protec-

tiveness. (Most of the time, they wished he would just take his legal briefs and stay out of their love lives.) Storm has been involved with both Kristen Forrester and Dr. Taylor Hayes.

Donna Logan (Carrie Mitchum). The middle Logan child, Donna is the free spirit in the family. Donna was briefly involved with Bill Spencer, for whose adult magazine she once posed. Donna's unfulfilled love life has been a product of bad timing at least twice: She fell in love with Thorne Forrester who just happened to be in love with Macy Alexander at the time. Her romantic overtures to Jake MacClaine went unanswered: How could she have known that Jake was having problems with sexually troublesome memories?

Katie Logan (Nancy Sloan) is the baby of the Logan family. She suffered with acne and because of her skin problem was shy and quiet.

The Spencers

Bill Spencer (Jim Storm) is a publisher.
He is the father of the late Caroline Spencer, and Caroline's long-lost kidnapped twin, Karen, whom he found and brought back to Los Angeles.

Katherine Kelly Lang.

Bill's second wife was Margo Lynley, who had a child with Clark Garrison before they were married. He later developed a romantic interest in Stephanie Forrester, the mother of his former sons-in-law, Thorne and Ridge Forrester, both of whom had once been married to his daughter, Caroline. Bill was also romantically interested in Darla, Sally Spectra's assistant.

Caroline Spencer Forrester Forrester (Joanna Johnson). The young debutante married Thorne Forrester, who had been especially comforting after she was raped. She later divorced him and married the man she really loved, Ridge Forrester. Caroline died of leukemia less than a year after she and Ridge were married.

Faith Roberts / Karen Spencer (Joanna Johnson). Caroline's identical twin was kidnapped at birth and raised by a woman named Bonnie Roberts as her daughter, Faith. Blake Hayes, Taylor Hayes's former hus-

151

The assembled B&B cast celebrates the show's 2,000th episode.

band, found her in Starlight, Texas, waiting tables. He brought her back to Los Angeles, hoping Ridge would fall in love with his dead wife's identical sister, leaving him room to maneuver a reconciliation with *his* ex-wife, Taylor.

Although briefly attracted to Ridge, Faith, who resumed using her real name, Karen Forrester, eventually left town after her affair with lawyer Connor Davis ended.

More Originals

Rocco Carner, played by Brian Genesse. He made Katie Logan's heart beat faster, but he had eyes only for Donna.

Margo Lynley, played by Laura Koslow. Forrester's top designer, she had designs on Eric, but he didn't reciprocate. Margo had an affair with Ridge Forrester. She later became involved with Clarke Garrison, with whom she had a son; she planned to marry him, but he had fallen for Kristen Forrester. She later married Bill Spencer.

Margo is the sister of Jake MacClaine, and eventually helped him to stand up to their mother in his desperate fight to learn the truth about his childhood sexual abuse.

Dave Reed, played by Stephen Shortridge. A policeman, he was in love with Brooke, but couldn't compete with Ridge.

Closeups: Current Cast and Characters

Actor: Kabir Bedi

Birthplace: India
Birthdate: January 16

Kabir Bedi is an international film and television actor who has played opposite stars such as Roger Moore, Michael Caine, Peter Ustinov, Omar Sharif, Timothy Dalton, Rutger Hauer, Stacy Keach and, most recently, Hunter Tylo in the miniseries, *The Maharaja's Daughter.*

Bedi's mother, an Englishwoman, is an ordained Tibetan Buddhist nun; his father was a famous philosopher in Italy. Kabir met his wife, Nikki, when they co-starred in a production of *Othello.*

Character: Prince Omar Rashid

Although the character of Prince Omar Rashid was never intended to be a long-running role on the series, he became an instant fan favorite.

Rashid is a romantic character whose love for his late first wife was so deep that he couldn't imagine giving his heart to anyone again. But then he took in the mysterious unconscious stranger he called Leila — who proved to be Dr. Taylor Hayes Forrester, assumed by everyone in Beverly Hills to have died in a plane crash — and was smitten.

Taylor, of course, still pined for her husband, Ridge. Could Omar compete with his love for her?

Actor: Kimberlin Brown

Birthplace: Hayward, California
Birthdate: June 29

Kimberlin began her career at the age of nine, combining acting and modeling. Several years later, she moved to Europe. She modeled in the Orient for six months, establishing a reputation as an international star on the fashion circuit. When she returned to the United States, she began to con-

153

centrate on her acting career, making guest appearances on prime-time; she also appeared on *Santa Barbara* and *Capitol.*

Kimberlin started her career as the beautiful but deadly nurse, Sheila Carter, on *The Young and the Restless,* and then went on to repeat the role in *Y&R's* sister soap, *The Bold and the Beautiful.*

Kimberlin, her husband, Gary Pelzer, and their daughter, Alexes Marie, live in Las Vegas.

Character: Sheila Carter Grainger Forrester

Everyone saw Sheila Forrester die when she took a poison potion she whipped up in June 1995, capping a spree that included murder, attempted murder, kidnapping, and blackmail — all of which she rationalized in the name of love. However, Sheila did not die. And why aren't we surprised? Possibly because she's just too wonderfully wicked to lose. After all, if there were no Sheilas in the world, we'd never know how lucky we are that we're not (currently) in her sights.

No doubt, Sheila is on her way back to either *Young and the Restless,* where she stole Lauren's (Tracey Bregman-Recht) son, Scotty, and husband, the late Dr. Scott Grainger. (She also still bears a grudge against Lauren for finding out the truth about her.) Or she may return to *The Bold and the Beautiful,* where she has unfinished business with Dr. James Warwick (Ian Buchanan).

Then again, she may turn up on that oft-rumored third soap the talented Bell-Phillip team may be turning out even as we meet on this page.

Actor: Ian Buchanan

Birthplace: Hamilton, Scotland
Birthdate: June 16

Ian began his American career on the New York stage and then moved into guest shots on prime-time television. His first soap role was as Duke Lavery on *General Hospital.* He left the soap to join the cast of *The Gary Shandling Show* as Gary's next-door neighbor named Ian.

Later, Buchanan was doing a Calvin Klein television commercial with Laura Flynn Boyle, directed by David Lynch. The next thing Ian knew, he had agreed to play the pompous Richard Tremayne in Lynch's unconventional television series, *Twin Peaks.* He then became a member of the Lynch Mob, joining the director in another series, *On the Air.*

Playing Dr. James Warwick is not Ian's first role as a psychiatrist. He previously played Dr. Martin Dysart in a production of *Equus,* for which he won a Drama-Logue Award. Incidentally, for those who like to know these things, Ian wears the Gunn tartan.

Ian Buchanan.

Character: Dr. James Warwick

Physician, heal thyself. That was good advice for James Warwick, a psychiatrist who had a lifetime of buried memories that affected his personal relationships. He first appeared on *The Bold and the Beautiful* as Dr. Taylor Hayes's former mentor. She helped him come to terms with his past by encouraging him to go to Scotland to face his brutal father (played by James Doohan, *Star Trek's* Scotty).

Warwick learned his father's cruelty came out of guilt about his mother. James returned to Los Angeles, where he found himself attracted to his former student. While they were together in a cabin following an earthquake, they made the earth shake in a more metaphorical sense. It was, James admitted, his first time. Apparently, Taylor, who had reversed the student-teacher roles, gave him more than a passing grade.

Warwick was one of the first to deduce that Taylor might not have died in the plane crash. He traveled to Morocco and discovered that she was, indeed, very much alive, but she made him promise to tell no one. She later revealed herself to everyone back home.

James later took on Sheila Forrester (or did she take him on?). In any event, his attempts to probe her convoluted mind about murder, menace, and mayhem landed him in chains in her cellar. (She happened to own a

155

John McCook, Maitland Ward, Barbara Crampton, and Susan Flannery on the set of B&B.

house once occupied by magician Harry Houdini.) He wooed her and won his freedom but in the end, he might have made a lifetime enemy.

Actor: Barbara Crampton

Birthplace: Levittown, Long Island, New York
Birthdate: December 27

Barbara made her acting debut on stage in Vermont and then went to New York where she played Cordelia in *King Lear.* She went west to Los Angeles and soon found herself starring in *Reanimator* and *From Beyond,* two films that would take on cult status.

Crampton made her daytime debut as Tricia Evans on *Days of Our Lives.* She then went on to create the role of Leanna Love, one of Victor Newman's (Eric Braeden) many wives on *The Young and the Restless.*

Barbara was playing Melinda Lewis Spaulding on *Guiding Light* in New York when she decided to return to California to spend more time with her ever-lovin' fiancé, actor/director Kristoffer Tabori. No sooner had she settled in than she got word that the Bells wanted her to create the role of Maggie Forrester on *The Bold and the Beautiful.* Of course, she said yes.

Character: Maggie Forrester

Maggie is the former wife of Eric Forrester's brother and the mother of Jessica Forrester (Maitland Ward). She came to Los Angeles from Iowa to persuade her daughter to give up all this nonsense about going to USC, convincing her instead to come back home and get a job waitressing or whatever.

However, Maggie soon fell under the spell of the Southern California lifestyle — especially the beach at Malibu — and decided to stay a while. Of course, Jessica may have cause to regret being one of those who persuaded Maggie that life among the palms can be idyllic. After all, mother Maggie met Jessica's love, Dylan (Dylan Neal), and Dylan was willin' to see more of Maggie than Jessica might have appreciated.

But Maggie is destined to be more than a one-note character. Whatever happens, her relationship with Dylan will be but a prologue to what Maggie intends to do in la-la-land.

Actor: Darlene Conley

Birthplace: Chicago, Illinois

Darlene Conley's first feature film was *The Birds,* for which she was cast by the great Alfred Hitchcock himself. Darlene's theatrical credits include productions with Richard Chamberlain, Basil Rathbone, Jean Stapleton, and Michael York.

In films, she co-starred with Burt Lancaser, Kirk Douglas, and John Cassavetes. She's also made dozens of prime-time appearances.

Daytime audiences first met Darlene when she played the nasty, nefarious no-good Rose DeVille on *The Young and the Restless*. Rose was the woman who took Nina's (Tricia Cast) first-born child and sold it. She also played Edith Baker on *Days of Our Lives,* Louie on *Capitol,* and Trixi on *General Hospital*.

Darlene Conley.

Darlene has raised one son and two stepsons.

Character: Sally Spectra

She's flashy, flamboyant, funny, but, as Darlene Conley told the author, "Sally Spectra is everything you could ever want in a friend. She is warm and generous. If life kicks her into the gutter, she keeps her eyes on the stars, and gets up and starts all over ..."

Although she is primarily a "knock-off" artist, Sally has worked hard to give her company respectability. She's tried to bridge the gap between herself and Stephanie Forrester, her daughter, Macy's, mother-in-law; despite Stephanie's iciness, she remains confident they'll one day be friends.

Sally has been in love with younger men: Her former husband, Clarke Garrison, is the father of her young son. She also fell for her designer, Anthony Armando (Michael Sabatino) and was crushed when she learned he was in love with Macy. Sally has lived through misfortunes.

157

But she's a lucky woman because she's never let herself stay down so long that she can't find her way back up.

Actor: Bobbie Eakes

Birthplace: Atlanta, Georgia
Birthdate: July 25

A former Miss Georgia, Bobbie placed in the top ten of the Miss America contest. Blessed with a beautiful voice, she went to Los Angeles to continue her musical training and found work as a studio-sessions artist. She later joined an all-woman group called "Big Trouble."

Between musical gigs, Bobbie did guest roles on *Cheers, Full House, Jake and the Fatman, Falcon Crest, Werewolf, The Wonder Years,* and *21 Jump Street.* Bobbie, who joined *Bold and the Beautiful* in 1989 as Macy Alexander Forrester, has recorded an album with castmate Jeff Trachta, who plays her husband, Thorne Forrester. She, Jeff, and John McCook appeared in a sell-out concert in Holland last year.

Bobbie is married to writer David Steen.

Character: Macy Alexander Forrester

Macy has been described as the daughter every mother wishes she had. Even when Sally Spectra "disowned" her because she thought Macy had come between her and Sally's perceived admirer, Anthony Armando, everyone knew Sally could never turn her back on this wonderful child.

Macy is loyal. She's smart. She's generous. She loves her husband, Thorne, and always believed he was innocent of the murder of the beautiful Forrester model, Ivana. Macy put her life on the line to get the real killer, Anthony, to admit he set Thorne up for the crime.

This wasn't the first time Macy risked her life for her husband. Although she knew she had a cancerous growth in her throat, she refused to cancel her appearance in Holland because she knew it would disappoint Thorne (who didn't know about the cancer).

Macy has also battled alcoholism. She knows life for her is a one-day-at-a-time proposition, but she's a courageous woman who intends to stay sober. Indeed, if there is any soap character who deserves to be happy, it's Macy. And you can tell Gimbel's I said so.

Actor: Susan Flannery

Birthplace: New York City
Birthdate: July 31

Emmy and Golden Globe award winner Flannery has starred in both television and film productions almost from the day she arrived in Hollywood

Susan Flannery and Macdonald Carey with the Emmys they won as costars on Days of Our Lives, *1975.*

fresh from graduate school at Arizona State University. She was cast by producer Irwin Allen in *Voyage to the Bottom of the Sea,* which starred David Hedison (who played Spencer Harrison on *Another World*) and the late Richard Basehart.

Susan went into *Days of Our Lives* as Dr. Laura Horton. She stayed with the show for eight years, managing in the meantime to do several films, including Irwin Allen's epic disaster flick, *The Towering Inferno.* Her other credits include *Dallas, Women in White,* and the Arthur Hailey miniseries, *The Moneychangers.*

Susan is a licensed pilot and gourmet cook. She produced the cable soap opera *New Day in Eden* with Michael Jaffe.

Character: Stephanie Forrester
See The Founding Families.

Actor: Katherine Kelly Lang
Birthplace: Hollywood, California
Birthdate: July 25

Katherine Kelly Lang was born into a show business family. Her father, former Olympic long-jump skier, Keith Wegeman, played television's "Jolly Green Giant." Her mother, Judith Lang, is an actor. She's also the granddaughter of the famous cinematographer Charles Lang.

Katherine made her acting debut in the feature film *Skate Town USA.* She went on to do guest shorts on *Happy Days, Magnum, P.I.* and *Last Precinct.* Lang's first daytime role was as Gretchen on *The Young and the Restless.* She starred in *Discovery Bay,* which was produced by erstwhile daytime stars, Ellen Wheeler (ex-Vikki Marley from *Another World)* and Tom Eplin (who played Jake on *AW).*

Katherine and her husband, director Scott Snider, have two sons, Jeremy and Julian. Jeremy has played her character Brooke's son, Eric, on the show.

Character: Brooke Logan Forrester Forrester
See The Founding Families.

Actor: John McCook

Birthplace: Ventura, California
Birthdate: June 20

John McCook had a long career on stage and screen as a romantic leading man before he became the patriarch of the Forrester clan on *The Bold and the Beautiful.* He was just a youngster when he worked on stage with Betty Grable and Hugh O'Brian. The great Jack Warner himself discovered John's film potential after seeing him as Tony in the New York City Center revival of *West Side Story.* John joined Warner Bros. studio system and talent development program and then went to Universal before the United States Army decided to assign him to a two-year stint.

After service, John returned to the stage and worked with stars such as Ann Miller and Virginia Mayo. He landed his first daytime role as Lance Prentiss in *The Young and the Restless.* The role provided him with national prominence, and he found himself working in one musical after another. He also guested on prime-time series. John and his wife, television actor Laurette Spang, have three children; Jake, Becky, and Molly. John also has a son, Seth, from a previous marriage.

McCook's album of romantic love songs, entitled, "John McCook Sings Bold and Beautiful Love Songs" was a top seller.

Character: Eric Forrester
See The Founding Families.

Actor: Ronn Moss

Birthplace: Los Angeles, California

Birthdate: March 4

Ronn began his career as a rock-and-roll musician, performing on drums, guitar, and electric bass. In 1976, he joined with three other musicians to form the group, Player. They were signed to do albums with RSO Records and later joined Casablanca Records. In 1978, their single, "Baby Come Back," was No. 1 on the charts.

Ronn began to pursue an acting career in 1981. He worked in various films before joining *The Bold and the Beautiful* as Ridge Forrester in 1987.

Ronn and his wife, actor Shari Shattuck, have a daughter.

Character: Ridge Forrester
See The Founding Families.

Actor: Jeff Trachta

Birthplace: Staten Island, New York

Birthdate: October 6

Jeff's introduction to daytime was as Hunter Belden in *Loving*. He then played Boyce McDonald on *One Life to Live*. Jeff has a degree in Psychology and Theatre Arts from St. John's University in New York. He studied at the American Academy of Dramatic Arts.

Some of his pre *Bold and Beautiful* credits include the feature film, *Do It Up* and the HBO special, *Robert Klein on Broadway*. He also appeared with the Los Angeles Civic Light Opera opposite Bobbie Eakes, who plays his wife, Macy, on the show.

Character: Thorne Forrester
See The Founding Families.

Actor: Hunter Tylo

Birthplace: Fort Worth, Texas

Birthdate: July 3

She's not a doctor, but she plays one on TV — namely, Dr. Taylor Hamilton Hayes Forrester "Rashid." In real life, Hunter Tylo was previously enrolled in a pre-med program at Fordham University in New York; she is considered to be on leave from that institution. "Someday," she told the author, "I hope to go back and eventually go to medical school."

Hunter and Michael Tylo.

Meanwhile, she's busy with her work on the soap. She did take time out to do a miniseries, *The Maharajah's Daughter* with her soap castmate, Kabir Bedi, which was shot in India.

Hunter was introduced to daytime audiences as Robin McCall in *All My Children*. She met her future husband, Michael Tylo (who plays Blade on *The Young and the Restless*), on the show. She went on to play Marina Toscano in *Days of Our Lives*, and then into the feature film, *Zorro*.

Hunter, Michael, their children Christopher and Micky, and their assorted cats, dogs, and other pets live in Las Vegas, Nevada.

Character:
Dr. Taylor Hamilton Hayes Forrester

Dr. Hayes arrived in Los Angeles in 1989. She's the sister of the (then) troubled Zak Hamilton and the daughter of Jack Hamilton (Chris Robinson, formerly Dr. Rick Webber on *General Hospital*), Stephanie Forrester's and Sally Spectra's erstwhile gentleman friend.

Taylor was pursued by her former husband, who hoped to reconcile with her. However, he couldn't compete with Ridge Forrester. Ridge was a widower — his wife, Caroline, had died of leukemia only a year after they were married. Brooke, his father's wife, was in love with him, but it was Taylor who got him.

Taylor's life with Ridge has been marked by anxiety over his lingering feelings for Brooke, which were reinforced by the birth of their daughter, Bridget, and Taylor's difficulty conceiving. Following an earthquake, she had a one-night affair with her mentor, Dr. James Warwick (Ian Buchanan), but never wavered in her resolve to stay married to Ridge.

Taylor went off to a convention of psychiatrists in the Middle East. Her plane went down and she was presumed to have died in the crash. However, during a stopover in Morocco, Taylor went sight-seeing and was hit on the head and robbed of her plane tickets. The thief took her place and died in the accident.

Taylor was taken to the palace of Prince Omar Rashid, where she hovered between life and death for weeks. Omar, who fell in love with his mysterious guest, had refused to allow the life support system to be turned off until he was finally persuaded that she would never recover consciousness. Just moments before the plug was to be pulled, Taylor woke up but had no memory of who she was.

She was named Leila. When her identity was discovered, Omar tried to keep her from finding out who she really was. Finally, he manipulated the newlyweds, Brooke and Ridge, to dine at his palace, and let Taylor watch the happy couple from a secret window.

Heartbroken, Taylor decided not to return to Los Angeles, even when James Warwick turned up to try to persuade her to come back. Believing her situation was hopeless, trying to protect Ridge, she agreed to marry Omar, but insisted they were not to sleep together.

When she got word that her father, Jack, had had a heart attack, she returned to Los Angeles and disguised herself (with the help of a beautician played by Phyllis Diller) so that no one would recognize her. She later became friendly with the then-temporarily blinded Ridge, who was in a hospital room down the hall from Jack's. (Brooke had left a pot of chemicals brewing in the microwave while she and Ridge made love in the laboratory. It exploded.) Stephanie uncovered her secret and Taylor told her the full story.

Taylor rebuffed Omar's attempts to get her to come back to him. Still in love with Ridge, she believed Ridge would choose to remarry her if he had the chance. Brooke, however, did not agree. And waiting in the wings is Dr. James Warwick, who still remembers that special night in the cabin when they made love for the first time.

Days of Our Lives

Like sands through the hour glass, so are the days of our lives."

That epigraph has been part of the daytime drama *Days of Our Lives* ever since it debuted as a half-hour daily serial on NBC on November 8, 1965. (It expanded to a full hour on April 21, 1975.)

In 1965, seven soaps debuted: three on ABC — *Never Too Young, The Nurses,* and *A Time for Us,* also known as *Flame in the Wind;* and four on NBC — *Moment of Truth, Morning Star, Paradise Bay,* and *Days of Our Lives.* The latter was a production of Columbia Pictures' new television division, Screen Gems, now called, appropriately, Columbia Pictures Television. In less than two years, all the soaps except *Days* had become a footnote in the daytime chronicles.

Despite early low ratings, NBC decided to stick with *Days of Our Lives* largely because of its troika of creators — Ted Corday, Allan Chase, and Irna Phillips — each of whom brought excellent references to the job. Corday, who came up with the idea for the soap during a summer afternoon spent with Chase and Phillips at his Southampton, Long Island home, had produced two of Phillips's other soaps, *As the World Turns* and *The Guiding Light.* Allan Chase had created *Valiant Lady,* which starred the wonderful Margaret Hamilton, who played the Wicked Witch of the West in *The Wizard of Oz;* James Kirkwood, who would later go on to win a Pulitzer Prize for *A Chorus Line;* and character actor Martin Balsam. Corday shared directing duties with two other helmsmen for *Lady.* Irna was the undisputed Doyenne of Daytime, who, over some three decades on radio and television, had given Procter & Gamble an equally undisputed place as daytime's premier producer. With *Days,* Phillips would give Screen Gems a chance to put itself on the daytime map.

Ted Corday died a year after *Days of Our Lives* debuted. His wife, Betty, took over as executive producer and head of Corday Productions. Today, their son, Ken Corday, is executive producer.

One of Betty's first moves was to bring in Irna's talented protégé, William J. Bell, who took the soap from a low but slowly climbing position on the ratings roster. He immediately introduced story lines that presented several bold new concepts in daytime storytelling, much of which he would later introduce into *Young and the Restless,* a daytime series he would create for Screen Gems. With Bell's arrival in Salem, the site of *Days of Our Lives,* its popularity zoomed. Although the series has had occasional ratings losses over the years, it has always bounced back, and remains one of the most popular soaps on the air.

Original Cast

Macdonald Carey . .*Dr. Tom Horton	*Robert Knapp* . . . . .Ben Olson
Dick Colla . . . . .Tony Merrill	*Flip Mark* . . . . .Steve Olson
Carla Doherty . . . . .Julie Olson	*Dick McLean* . . . . .Craig Merrill
Burt Douglas . . . . .Jim Fisk	*Frances Reid* . . . .**Alice Horton
Pat Huston . . . . .Addie Olson	*Robert J. Stevenson* . . . .A Detective

First Air Date: November 8, 1965 / NBC

* The late Macdonald Carey was a theater and film star before joining *Days of Our Lives.* Prior to that he was a popular radio soap actor, appearing in such daytime serials as *Stella Dallas, John's Other Wife, Just Plain Bill, Ellen Randolph, Woman in White* and *Young Hickory.* He was a distant cousin of Phil Carey (Asa Buchanan, *One Life to Live).*

** Frances Reid is the only member of the original cast who is still with the series.

Sin-tillating Salem

Long before the demonic possession line of 1994–95 — which involved the lovely Marlena Evans Brady (Deidre Hall), her erstwhile lover,

Macdonald Carey and Frances Reid.

John Black (Drake Hogestyn); Black's long-time nemesis, Count Stefano DiMera (Joseph Mascolo), and the Arch Villain of Villainy, Satan himself — Salem was full of sexual situations and sin-tillating characters. As Susan Seaforth Hayes, who played Julie Olson Banning Anderson Williams Williams, said, "We are a bunch of horny devils."

Time magazine put Susan and her husband co-star, Bill Hayes (Douglas Williams) on its cover in 1976. Inside, the magazine called the soap daytime's "most daring drama, encompassing every trend from artificial insemination to interracial romance...."

Although Ms. Seaforth Hayes's remarks raised some eyebrows, there was no denying the fact that all this hell-raising was also raising the ratings.

The Hebrew word, *sholem,* meaning peace, is the origin of the town, Salem, in Massachusetts. However, the Salem of *Days of Our Lives* has been anything but peaceful over the last thirty-plus years, much to the delight of the soap's devoted fans.

The series began with two core families: The Hortons and the Olsons. Dr. Tom Horton (Macdonald Carey) and his wife, Alice (Frances Reid) had five children: twins Tommy and Addie; Marie; Mickey; and Bill. (The characters of Alice and Mickey are still on the soap; Bill appeared in 1994 when Laura — Jaime Lyn Bauer — returned home.)

When the soap debuted, Tommy had been reported missing in action in Korea years earlier, and presumed dead. Addie soon moved to Europe with her rich husband, Ben Olson. Their daughter, Julie, was left to be raised by her grandparents.

Young Mickey had become a lawyer while his brother, Bill, became a surgeon. Marie, originally played by Marie Cheatham, who went on to star in *Search for Tomorrow* and *General Hospital,* was married to Tony Merrill.

Julie, who felt rejected by her mother, turned to a man named David Martin for love. But she learned her best friend, Susan, played by Denise Alexander, who later went to *General Hospital* as Laura Spencer's mother, was also in love with him and was carrying their child. (The *GH* character coincidentally would have the same name as another *Days* character

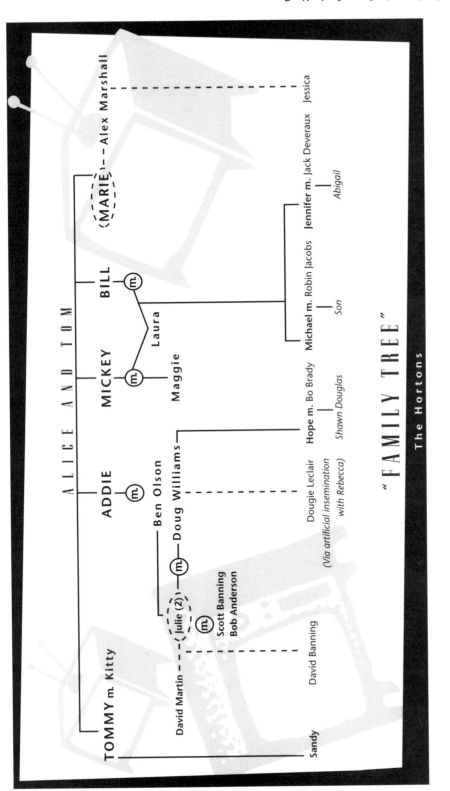

"FAMILY TREE"

The Hortons

A lice and Tom Horton practically "seeded" the town of Salem courtesy of their children, Tommy, Addie, Mickey, Bill, and Marie. Hortons have been married to, or involved with, just about every Salemite of note since the show began back in 1965.

noted in the next paragraph). Susan and David were married. Later, their son, Richard, died after falling from a swing while David was supposed to be watching him. In her grief, Susan shot David dead.

Bill, meanwhile, fell for another doctor, Laura Spencer (the character returned to the soap last year and is currently played by Jaime Lyn Bauer, formerly Lauralee Brooks of *The Young and the Restless*). When he developed problems with his hands, the brilliant young surgeon abruptly left Salem. Meanwhile, Susan had become Laura's patient. Mickey defended her at the trial, and got her off on a plea of temporary insanity. He and Laura fell in love and were married. But soon after the wedding, Bill returned to find his beloved was now his brother's bride. One night, he drank too much and his passion got the better of him. He raped Laura, and she became pregnant. Tom, her father-in-law, had recently learned that Mickey was sterile. Laura told him what had happened, and both agreed to keep the rape a secret.

Meanwhile, Marie had divorced Merrill and was now attracted to Bill's new friend, Dr. Mark Brooks. Bill was happy to see his sister interested in another man, but there was something about Mark that troubled him. And, as it turned out, there was much that should have troubled Bill. Mark's secret would evolve into a powerful line involving incest.

Oh, Brother!

Mark Brooks proved to be Tom Horton, Jr. He had been brutally tortured by his captors during the Korean War, and horribly disfigured. He developed amnesia and believed himself to be Mark Brooks, who was actually one of his dead comrades. Plastic surgeons removed his scars and rebuilt his face. But he emerged from the surgery looking unlike the Tommy Horton his family and friends would have recognized when he came to Salem — to which he was drawn, he would later say, by some inexplicable inner drive.

Marie, like the other Hortons, believed Tommy was dead. But as her sexual attraction to Mark Brooks became stronger, she began to have unnerving dreams about a wedding night with her own brother. Although the Hortons were overjoyed when Mark proved to be Tommy, Marie found it difficult to deal with the realization that her dreams had been so uncannily close to the truth and that she had these passionate feelings for her brother. She turned to the Church for comfort and later entered a convent — but not before becoming involved with Alex Marshall (Quinn Redker, who would go on to play four roles on Bill Bell's *The Young and the Restless*) and giving birth to a daughter, Jessica, whom she placed in an orphanage, but later tried to find again.

Once Tommy learned who he really was, he had to adjust to his true identity, including getting to know his wife, Kitty, and their daughter, Sandy, who would grow up to be a doctor.

The half-brother incest phenomenon became part of Bill Bell's repertoire: it occurred on *The Young and the Restless* at least four times. On *Days of Our Lives,* it would involve one character twice: the suave Count Antony DiMera (Thaao Penghlis). In the first instance, the glamorous Renee Dumonde (Philece Sampler) had fallen in love with Tony, and was later dismayed to learn they could never be bed mates since he was her half-sibling.

Some ten years later, Tony DiMera would resurface in Salem, this time engaged to marry his sister, Kristen (Eileen Davidson, ex-Ashley Abbott, one of the characters on *Y&R* who had fallen for a man later revealed to be her half-brother). Both their father, Count Stefano DiMera, and Kristen's "other" brother, Peter (Jason Brooks) encouraged the union. However, just when it seemed to the fans that they were about to see a line unfold that would spell Decadent with a capital D (as in DiMera), it was revealed that Stefano was Kristen and Peter's foster-father. This left Tony and Kristen free to wed in a magnificent church ceremony.

Another "incestuous" line involved the character of Victor Kiriakis (John Aniston) and a young woman named Isabella who were also drawn to each other. Later, it was revealed that Isabella was Victor's illegitimate daughter. Isabella felt guilty for having had erotic thoughts about the man who turned out be her father. But Kiriakis reassured her that neither of them had reason to be ashamed or to feel any guilt for how they felt about each other. It was a natural reaction to the love they shared, although at the time they didn't understand it.

Salem's Passion Ploys And Players

Laura and Tom didn't know their conversation about Mickey's infertility and Bill's rape had been accidentally recorded. Kitty found the tape and intended to use it for her own ends. When she and Bill fought over it, her weak heart gave out and she died. Rather than expose his brother, Mickey, to the truth, Bill accepted blame for her death and served time for manslaughter.

In jail, he met a con man named Doug Williams, who would later become a major player in the lives of several Hortons, including Bill's sister, Addie, and Addie's daughter, Bill's niece, Julie.

Meanwhile, Julie, who had also borne a child fathered by the late David Martin, gave her son up for adoption to Scott and Janet Banning. Janet had a brain tumor and was not long for this world. The Bannings' neighbor, Susan Martin, babysat for them frequently, and found herself drawn to the child, perhaps because she saw the little boy as a substitute for her own dead son.

After Janet's death, Susan hoped to marry Scott Banning. But Julie sued to reclaim her son and was awarded custody of the boy. Julie then

169

persuaded Scott to marry her so they could raise the child they both loved together. Scott agreed. Julie then changed the boy's name to David, after his father.

Released from jail, Doug Williams came to Salem to jump the broom with the Widow Martin — unless he could get a chunk of her inheritance by wooing without wedding her. Susan, however, offered to pay him to charm Julie Olson Banning in order to break up her marriage to Scott Banning. Doug agreed — and this led to the start of a love between Doug and Julie that would play itself out over several years and through many obstacles before they were finally able to face a happy future together.

Their first problem involved Julie's mother, Addie, who had returned from Europe after Ben Olson's death. Julie felt remote from the mother who had left her behind. Meanwhile, Addie had a private detective confirm that Julie and Doug were lovers.

Doug asked Julie to go to Portofino with him, but insisted she leave young David behind. Julie couldn't reject her child as Addie had rejected her. They quarreled. That night, Addie — who had been attracted to Doug from the moment they met — proposed to him, and he accepted. They eloped with the tickets he had bought for himself and Julie.

Doug, who had been Julie's lover, was now Julie's stepfather, and wasn't one bit abashed about taking advantage of Addie's generosity. She bought him a nightclub, which was called Doug's Place. The setting gave Bill Hayes, who had starred in musical theater as well as on the television classic, *Your Show of Shows,* many opportunities to sing on the soap.

While Addie and Doug were becoming closer, Scott Banning died, leaving Julie with a sense of guilt for not having given their marriage a real chance.

Addie had become pregnant. Although she had been diagnosed with leukemia, she refused chemotherapy because she was afraid it would harm her unborn baby. She believed her faith in God would see her through. To her and Doug's delight, she went into remission and delivered a beautiful baby girl they named Hope. The baby's birth, and Addie's illness, brought Julie closer to her mother.

Believing she could never have Doug, Julie married Bob Anderson. Addie died when she was hit by a speeding car while rushing to push her baby daughter out of the way. Doug was shattered by grief.

About this time, Bill got out of prison. When Laura learned that he had chosen jail rather than let Mickey find out he was Mike's real father, she testified for him at a Medical Boards meeting so he could regain his license to practice medicine.

Mickey suspected Laura and Bill were having an affair — so he had one with his secretary, Linda, who later married Bob Anderson. She became pregnant. However, Mickey's fertility hadn't miraculously been restored. Laura got her to admit the baby was another man's. The affair led to Laura and Bill admitting their love for each other. Young Michael overheard them

The Days *cast celebrates the show's 5,000th episode.*

and was so upset by what Mommy and Uncle Bill were saying to each other he ran into the street and was hit by a car. The near-fatal accident made Laura and Mickey decide to stay together. But this time, Michael learned about Daddy's lapse from marital grace, which led to an argument between Mike and Mickey, whose weak heart gave out. He collapsed, and was saved by Bill's surgical skills. But he later suffered a stroke and walked out of the hospital to find himself at a farm, unaware of who he was. He called himself Marty Hansen because it went with the initials on his belt. He met the beautiful Maggie Simmons, who had been handicapped in an accident. They fell in love. By the time they married, Maggie knew who he was, but didn't reveal it because she feared she'd lose him to the wife he already had. Eventually, Bill and Laura found Mickey and told him the whole truth. Laura divorced Mickey and married Bill; Mickey and Maggie remarried. She came to Salem and had the surgery that allowed her to walk again.

Just when the Horton brothers could hope to find happiness in their new marriages, once again, young Mike Horton became the catalyst that forced another secret out into the open. He had been injured on the farm and needed blood. Mickey's blood didn't match; neither did Laura's. That meant he couldn't be Mike's father. Mickey's search through Bill's files revealed that his blood type matched Mike's. He accused Bill of taking everything from him that he loved and shot at him. The bullet hit Bill's arm. Mickey was committed to a sanitarium.

171

Meanwhile, Bill and Laura's daughter, Jennifer Rose Horton, was born on their way to visit Mickey. (Jennifer is currently played by Melissa Reeves, whose husband, Scott Reeves, plays Ryan McNeil on *The Young and the Restless*.)

By this time (1976), the beautiful psychiatrist, Dr. Marlena Evans (Deidre Hall) had come to Salem. Along with Laura, she persuaded Mickey not to tell young Mike who his real father was. He agreed, but blurted it out in an irrational moment. It took some time for Mike to forgive Laura and Bill, but he finally did. Mickey eventually regained his health and returned home to Maggie.

The "Buss" Stop

Young David Banning, Julie's son, also came home to Salem to claim his inheritance so that he could marry a young woman named Brooke Hamilton, who turned out to be a troublemaker par excellence. She caused a fight between David and Julie. He rushed out and had a car accident, and was taken in by the Grants, a black family. The Hortons, meanwhile, believed he'd been killed and held a memorial service for him. When Paul Grant learned who the young man was, he told Julie the truth.

Soon after, Brooke learned her real father was Bob Anderson. She also had an abortion when she realized David would marry her, but only out of duty. He had already fallen in love with the Grants' beautiful daughter, Valerie, which would lead to an interracial love affair that would become a daytime cause célèbre.

Agnes Nixon introduced an interracial relationship on *One Life to Live*. However, David and Valerie (played at that time by Richard Guthrie and Tina Andrews) would show their feelings — not just talk about them.

The relationship was treated very carefully on screen. The producers and writers felt that if given enough time, the viewers would come to accept it. However, negative mail poured in from the start, and didn't let up throughout the story's run.

Ms. Andrews reportedly says she wished the writers would let David and Valerie have their first kiss as soon as possible. Viewers anticipated the kiss, and most expressed hostility to the idea. But Tina believed that once it was over and done with, the could move along.

The writers agreed with her. They planned to have it happen during the first of what would be several weddings between David's mother, Julie, and Doug Williams. But when word leaked out, viewer reaction was so strong that Pat Falken-Smith, the head writer, had to stop the *buss* (kiss), and reroute the line.

Before Doug Williams married Julie, or anyone else, he wanted to give his little girl, Hope, a sister or brother. Meanwhile, his housekeeper, Rebecca (played by Brooke Bundy), who lost her husband and child in an accident, wanted to have a baby. Doug arranged for artificial insemination, but had no idea that the woman who carried his child was Rebecca. She told her boyfriend in Paris that she was having their baby. Doug's nightclub manager, Robert LeClair, (played by stage actor Robert Clary, a French-born Holocaust survivor) was in love with Rebecca and married her after Johnny left her. By that time, Rebecca learned who the real father was. However, Doug had grown closer to Julie again and had given up his rights to the child carried by the surrogate mother (who was still unknown to him). Robert's happiness with Rebecca ended when Johnny returned, and she took the baby and went away with her erstwhile lover. After Rebecca's death in a car accident, Doug learned that her son, Dougie, was really his child. Father and son were reunited, but were parted again when Robert returned to France and took the boy with him.

> In the late 1980s, Joseph Gallison, who played Dr. Neil Curtis, was rumored to be the star of the first spin-off from *Days of Our Lives*. There was also talk that Deidre Hall (Marlena Evans Craig Brady) would also head up the new soap. The spin-off never materialized — but the idea was never completely shelved, either.

Tea And Lots Of Sympathy

Mike had fallen in love with the beautiful Trish Clayton. But each time he tried to make love to her, he failed. He was sure this was a sign that he was homosexual. However, in a sort of *Tea and Sympathy* replay, another woman took him to bed, and he performed very well, indeed.

Meanwhile, David Banning was seeing Trish and had better luck between the sheets than did his cousin, Mike — at least, for one night. Trish's cruel stepfather learned about it and held her prisoner in her apartment, threatening and terrorizing her. By the time Michael arrived she was shaking, and when Jack and Mike fought, she killed her stepfather with an iron. The trauma caused her to split into two other personalities, Cynthia and a little girl named Lisa.

Trish later married David, with whom she had their son, Scotty, but her heart was with Michael. However, Michael was now married to Margo. Trish left Salem, but later returned and reconciled with David.

173

Salem's Wicked "Witches"

Long before Marlena Evans Craig Brady's demonic possession in 1994, she would be the victim of one of Salem's three most deviously wicked and witchy women, to wit:

Deidre and Andrea Hall.

Wicked Witch No. 1 — In 1977, Marlena's identical twin sister Samantha (played by Deidre's actual identical sibling, Andrea Hall-Lovell) arrived in Salem unexpectedly. She was a medical school dropout who blamed Marlena for all her problems. She managed to have Marlena committed to an institution, and passed herself off as the respected psychiatrist. She even managed to fool Marlena's fiancé, Don Craig (Jed Allan). Eventually, Samantha's wicked scheme was discovered and the real Marlena was free to marry Don and resume her practice. However, she and Don broke up after the death of their newborn child.

Wicked Witch No. 2 — Julie had been terribly burned in a kitchen fire, and was afraid Doug would stay with her only out of pity. She got a divorce in Mexico, and then had plastic surgery done. By the time her scars had been removed, she returned to Doug only to learn he had married Lee Dumonde. However Lee was aware that Doug still loved Julie, and to keep herself in his life, she mixed up a batch of her medications and induced paralysis. Julie realized Lee had done this wicked thing deliberately, but she could not prove it to Doug, who felt a sense of duty to his poor, paralyzed wife.

Eventually, Doug and Julie were reunited and life promised to be happy, at last.

Wicked Witch No. 3 — Despite Marie's and Alex's attempt to keep their daughter, Jessica Blake, from learning they were her parents, Alex's former wife, Mary, was jealous of his love for another woman — especially when that other woman was a nun. She probed Marie's past and discovered Jessica's parentage, and passed the information to Jessica. This helped to trigger the girl's mental breakdown into three separate personalities: her own; Angelique, a convent school girl; and Angel, a prostitute.

New Brooms Can Make Bad "Sweeps"

It took Dr. Laura Horton some fourteen years to sweep the cobwebs from her mind and return to Salem. Bill had had her committed to a sanitarium in 1980 when she tried to kill herself on orders from her dead mother.

At the risk of sounding as paranoid as poor Laura was, one still needs to point out that her breakdown was part of a greater plan. Some cast members would later call it The Valentine's Day Massacre, although it actually took place over six months. Al Rabin, who had been one of the soap's directors, replaced H. Wesley Kennedy, who had been the show's long-time Executive Producer. There were rumors of a feud between Susan Seaforth Hayes and the relatively new arrival, Brenda Benet, who played Lee Dumonde, a new love interest for Doug Williams. Apparently, Rabin felt a housecleaning was required to weed out those off-camera personnel who he believed were contributing to a negative atmosphere on the show. He also felt it was time to do away with some of the characters.

No sooner suggested, than done: Fourteen characters were either sent into exile or killed off. Among the latter were Bob Anderson (heart attack), Brooke Hamilton (car crash), and Margo Horton (leukemia). As for the exiles, Laura was sent to a sanitarium, and Bill was so overwhelmed that he left town. (Ed Mallory had played Bill for fourteen years when he was given his pink slip.) Robert LeClair was sent back to Paris. Other characters were written off in various ways.

By 1983 (three years after the big change), of nine new characters, only one — Liz Chandler, played by Gloria Loring — remained. She left the show in 1986.

Days' audience rebelled against the loss of so many favorite actors and characters. *Days,* which usually swept up a pile of high ratings during the sweeps periods (those quarterly events in which the shows try for high ratings so the network can charge more for advertising) was being left in the dust by several other soaps.

In 1982, the talented Pat Falken-Smith, who had helped propel *General Hospital* back to the top of the ratings roster, returned to *Days* after a five-year absence and brought back some of the exiles. She wrote dialogue that allowed actors to refer to other characters from the past from to time, which restored a much-needed sense of continuity.

Pat Falken-Smith also created the Salem Strangler line, and set in motion another long-running love — this one between the newly arrived Roman Brady (played by *Dynasty's* Wayne Northrop) and the increasingly popular Marlena Evans Craig (Deidre Hall), who would soon become Salem's most fascinating character.

After Pat left the show, her associate, Maggie DePriest, continued the Salem Strangler story line, and gave it something extra. Marlena began getting strange calls. Detective Roman Brady was assigned to guard her. They were instantly attracted to each other. Meanwhile, the Strangler, who the audience later learned was Jake Kositchek, played by Jack Coleman, saw Marlena in her home, and broke in and strangled her. Later, a distraught Roman held Marlena's lifeless body in his arms and vowed to get the killer. But it wasn't Marlena who died. It was her oft-scheming twin sister, Samantha.

Before the victim's real identity was revealed, the switchboards at NBC on both coasts lit up for hours. It was said that even the president of the United States couldn't have broken through because every line was a-buzz with anger over the death of Marlena. There was even a picket line set up in front of NBC's Burbank offices. In New York, the site of the Peacock Throne, executives could see people moving through the Channel Gardens at Rockefeller Center intent on raising something of a ruckus in front of "30 Rock," — the RCA (now GE) Building. Ratings skyrocketed. For years, soap producers wondered which twosome could possibly replace Luke and Laura (Anthony Geary and Genie Francis) of *General Hospital*. Indeed, what duo could replace Doug and Julie, who were finding themselves with less and less to do on the soap? The answer was obvious: Marlena and Roman.

Just before Marlena and Roman could say their I dos, his supposedly dead wife, Anna Brady (Leann Hunley) returned with their daughter, Carrie (Christie Clark). When Roman chose to stay with his new beloved, Anna turned to the infamous DiMeras for help in destroying Roman's career. The DiMeras, father and son, never met a nefarious task they could refuse, and they were happy to supply a hit man to shoot Roman at the altar. But the shooter was thwarted and Roman and Marlena were married.

Soon after the wedding, Marlena was kidnapped by Stefano. (And not for the last time would he carry off the lovely Dr. Brady.) Marlena was rescued. Stefano died of a stroke in prison. (And not the for last time did he die, either.)

Later accused of stabbing a woman, Roman was arrested. With the help of his brother, Bo, Roman escaped and set out to prove his innocence. Meanwhile, Doug and Addie's daughter, Hope Williams, had returned to Salem and had fallen in love with Bo. This was the start of another long-running romance that, like Marlena's and Roman's, would come up against every imaginable obstacle — most of them placed there by Stefano DiMera, who was still very much alive.

During a struggle with Stefano, Roman was killed in a fall. Stefano took his body away. Marlena, already angry over Roman's death, became a furious Mama Lion when Stefano kidnapped her twins, Samantha (Sami) and Eric. She and Bo found Stefano in an ice arena and when she struggled with him, she shot him.

Meanwhile, Anna's new love, Prince Nicholas, was killed by someone called the Dragon. Bo Brady and his sister, Kimberly — along with I.S.A. agent Shane Donovan (Charles Shaughnessy), and Hope Williams (Kristian Alfonso) — went to England to find Prince Nick's killer. In Blighty, Bo and Hope blighted the Dragon's murderous career and were

Peter Reckell, Kristian
Alfonso, and Stephen
Nichols.

rewarded with a lavish wedding that may have set the standard for Charles and Diana's big 'do.

Did Bo and Hope live happily ever after? Not if Count Stefano DiMera could help it. And since whatever Stefano wanted, Stefano got, you can guess the rest.

Kimberly Brady (Patsy Pease), who had become blind during the Dragon affair, moved in with the newly arrived tycoon Victor Kiriakis who turned out to be an associate of some drug smugglers. Kimberly's mom, Caroline (Peggy McCay) was not pleased that her daughter was living in Victor's home, albeit (for a while, at least) platonically. Caroline had had an affair with Victor years earlier and, as the Bradys and Victor would later learn, Bo Brady was actually his son.

Kimberly slept with Victor to save Shane's life. She later gave birth to baby Andrew who, if he was Victor's child, was also the half-brother, as well as the nephew, of her half-brother, Bo.

Hope and Bo had a child they named Shawn-Douglas for both their fathers. (Bo rejected Victor as a father, preferring to be Shawn Brady's son.) The couple left town. Later, everyone in Salem heard the terrible news that Hope had died in an explosion. Her body was not recovered. Did Stefano kill her? Was Stefano himself still alive?

177

*Patsy Pease and
Charles Shaughnessy.*

Meanwhile, the other Brady sister, Kayla, a nurse, (Catherine Mary Stewart) became involved with one of Kiriakis's henchmen, Steve Johnson (played by Stephen Nichols), nicknamed Patch for the eye patch he wore. However, Kayla was wooed by an old friend, Jack Deveraux, son of Senator Harper Devereaux. When Patch learned he was actually Jack's brother, he pushed Kayla towards Jack. Kayla married him, but couldn't stop loving Patch. Furious that she'd been seeing Patch secretly, Jack raped Kayla, who then divorced him.

The Salem Strangler was caught, but a new killer was abroad stalking prostitutes. Known as the Riverfront Knifer, he almost killed Shane's daughter, Eve, as well as her mother, his former I.S.A. colleague, Gabrielle Pascal. Eve had been a prostitute but gave up the streets when she met Frankie Brady, who had become part of the Brady Bunch via adoption. Kayla was also attacked and lost her hearing and speech. Senator Harper Devereaux turned out to be the Knifer. Jack learned he was Patch's brother and would soon become his brother-in-law. Surgery restored Kayla's hearing. Her speech returned during her wedding ceremony to Patch.

Meanwhile, the mysterious stranger named John Black turned up in Salem and was later identified as Roman Brady. He had survived imprisonment by Stefano.

A joyous Marlena reunited with Roman. But later, she was abducted by someone called Orpheus, who had a grudge against Roman. She was taken to his island to raise his children. On the way, the plane crashed and they died. (Yeah, sure, they did.) Roman went wild with grief. A beautiful woman named Diane Colville (Genie Francis) came into his life, but her former husband, Cal, interfered with their relationship. Cal later turned his attentions to Kimberly and almost won her for good after Shane supposedly died in an explosion. But Shane returned. After enduring more Cal-culated machinations, Shane and Kimberly eventually reunited.

In Salem, Roman Brady proved not to be Roman Brady after all, but John Black (Drake Hogestyn), who had also served a sentence in Stefano's hellish dungeons. Apparently, Stefano had given Roman's memories to John, deleting his own in the process.

The real John Black had fallen in love with Isabella Toscano, who had previously been attracted to Victor Kiriakis until they learned they were father and daughter. Isabella died soon after she and John were married, leaving behind their son, Brady. Marlena returned once again from the dead. She, too, had apparently been held prisoner by Stefano. But she couldn't remember if that were so.

The real Roman (Wayne Northrop) and the newly returned Marlena reunited. But Marlena found she still had lingering feelings for John. However, she put that down to the fact that she was so happy to have Roman back when she thought he was Roman, that she poured so much love into those months together. Some of it had to stick.

However Dr. Brady rationalized her feelings for John Black, she slept with him and later became pregnant, although she was sure that Roman had fathered her child. She gave birth in the Horton mountain cabin assisted by Kristen and John, who had found her going into labor. She named the baby Isabella (Belle) after John's late wife, Isabella Toscano Kiriakis Black. Even Roman had to agree it was a lovely gesture. Roman and Marlena's daughter, Samantha (Sami) later discovered proof that Roman was not her little sister's father and tried to kidnap Belle to keep the secret from Roman. Marlena revealed Belle's paternity at Belle's baptism. Roman felt he'd been betrayed (and who can blame him?), and he and Marlena divorced; when the chance came to take an undercover assignment out of town, he bid bye-bye to Marlena and the Bradys and left. (Incidentally, for those who may wonder where Sami's twin brother, Eric, is: he chose to go to school in Colorado where Marlena's parents live. No doubt he'll return to Salem one day.)

Meanwhile, Lawrence Alamain (Michael Sabatino), who had a penchant for pitching tents in the desert, came to Salem with his son, Nicholas, and his Aunt Vivian (Louise Sorel), a beautiful and imposing woman with a dutiful servant named Ivan (Ivan G'Vera). Alamain was used to getting what he wanted, and he wanted Jennifer. To prove he wasn't used to rejection, he raped her. Later, Jack helped her escape. The two eventually married, much to the distress of grandmother Alice Horton who remembered when Jack was a dastard who raped his then wife, Kayla Brady.

Victor Kiriakis's nephew, Justin, and his bride, Adrienne, honeymooned on Tahiti where they met Dr. Carly Manning, an outspoken feminist. Manning moved to Salem where she and Bo (Peter Reckell) found each other and fell in love. She enjoyed being with his son, Shawn-Douglas. Her own son had died in infancy.

Vivian desperately wanted to keep Carly away from Nicholas. She feared Carly might recover the lost parts of her memory and realize Nicky is the child she was told had died. Vivian bought a drug from a Chinese herbalist that creates an illusion of death: Those who take it have no discernible heartbeat and show no other sign of life. Vivian gave it to Carly — and to Bo's utter devastation, Carly died.

After the last shovel of earth had been thrown over Carly's coffin, Vivian sent down a message through a device she'd installed in the casket, reminding the inert, but still living Carly that she had been buried alive.

Of course, Carly was rescued. But just when Bo thought they had a future together, Carly began to recall her past. She realized Nicholas was her son and left for Europe with Lawrence and their child. Only two Alamains remained in Salem: Vivian and John Black, who learned he was a rich man by virtue of being Lawrence's half brother, Forrest Alamain, and heir to half the Alamain fortune. But there was much, much more for John to learn about himself....

In the meantime, Kate Roberts came to Salem with her son, Lucas (Bryan Datillo). Two young people, Billie and Austin Reed (Lisa Rinna and Patrick Muldoon) also turned up, as did their no-good father, Curtis, who worked for Peter Blake (Jason Brooks), a mystery man who seemed to have targeted John Black for death.

John, meanwhile, had fallen for Peter's sister, Kristen, a social worker (played by Eileen Davidson). Peter was under orders by Count Stefano DiMera to keep John and Kristen apart by any means necessary since Kristen was to marry her adoptive brother, Tony DiMera (the newly returned Thaao Penghlis). Stefano raised the Blake children after they were orphaned. They considered him their father, and never knew he was to blame for the deaths of their real parents.

Kate learned Billie and Austin were the two children she had lost years earlier after fleeing her abusive husband, Curtis Reed. Austin responded quickly to his newfound mother; Billie was less enthusiastic. Lucas plain flat out didn't like the idea of sharing mom with two half-siblings.

Curtis was killed and everyone seemed to be a suspect: Victor, because Curtis tormented Kate whom Victor had married; Billie, because of Curtis's threat to sexually abuse her again; Austin, because of his protectiveness of Billie; Kate Roberts Kiriakis, because of Curtis's blackmail and threats; and Lucas Roberts because of his protectiveness of his mother. The killer was none of the above, and Stefano was suspected of being involved in the murder.

Meanwhile, Billie and Bo fell in love; ditto Austin and Carrie. Sami, however, intended to take Austin away from her half-sister, while Lucas intended to take Carrie away from his half-brother. Jack left Jennifer after he realized he almost caused the death of their daughter, Abigail. Peter quickly moved in to try to fill the empty space in Jennifer's heart.

Kate wanted to have a child with Victor and arranged for an *in vitro* procedure. Vivian, who still hoped to replace Kate in Victor's life, maneuvered to have Kate's fertilized egg implanted in her womb. Although the Kiriakises were furious, they realized there was nothing they could do except allow Vivian to carry their baby to term.

Fourteen years earlier, Laura Spencer Horton was institutionalized. Vivian had herself put into the same institution to make sure that Laura remained in a drug-induced catatonic state. But Vivian ran afoul of the women who ran the place. She and Laura were to be punished for misbehaving by having part of their brain lobes removed. But just after Vivian's head was shaved, Vivian and Laura accidentally set a fire which gave them a chance to escape.

Laura went home and was happily received by her children, Jennifer and Mike, and her former mother-in-law, Alice. Even her ex-husbands, Mickey and Bill, were there to welcome her home. Marlena promised to help her regain her medical license. Everyone was pleased except Peter, who feared Laura might influence Jennifer against him. Peter arranged for Laura to have "spells" that would send her back to the institution. But Laura's son, Dr. Michael Horton, suspected that something other than Laura's mind was causing the problems. Peter stopped the "gaslighting" before suspicion fell on him.

Deidre Hall and Drake Hogestyn.

Laura went off to a retreat where she met the newly returned Jack (previously played by Matthew Ashford; now played by Mark Valley). They each used assumed names, and when Jack spoke hopefully of reconciling with his former wife, Laura encouraged him, although she was falling for him.

Ruining any chance that Kristen and John might marry, Stefano DiMera let John discover that in part of his forgotten past he had been an ordained Catholic priest. DiMera left John with the knowledge that he could never again hold either Kristen or Marlena in his arms.

Kristen and Tony were married. Stefano turned up for the wedding and when he tried to escape arrest, his car blew up. But Stefano DiMera,

181

who has more lives than the chorus line of *Cats,* survived to do more villainy, starting with the kidnapping of Marlena and John Black.

Both Marlena and John Black were kidnapped by Stefano and taken to the dungeons beneath his mansion in New Orleans. Stefano's passion for Marlena grew stronger, but she resisted him until she realized she could use him to help free herself and John. John, meanwhile, tried to charm Stefano's assistant, Celeste.

While all of this was going on in New Orleans, back in Salem, the newlywed Kristen told her husband, Tony, she wanted to have a party in the DiMera's New Orleans digs. Stefano tried to get Tony to dissuade her from her plans, but Kristen persisted.

Once the festivities began, other events fell into place — eventually Marlena and John escaped (we knew they would). But the big surprise was the appearance of a young woman named Gina who was a *doppelganger* for the presumed-dead Hope Williams Brady. Bo was shaken by seeing her. Billie was shaken by Bo's reaction.

Gina returned to Salem with Bo and Billie. Alice was sure she was seeing her beloved granddaughter again. But Bo was skeptical, especially when he learned that Celeste was "feeding" selected memories of his and Hope's past into the hypnotically conditioned Gina's subconscious. Although Stefano obviously knew the truth about Gina, all he would say is that he had found her wandering and had taken her in as a charitable gesture.

By mid 1995, after running down clue after clue, it seemed more and more obvious that Hope had, indeed come home. Billie prepared to leave Salem — and Bo prepared to learn how to be Hope's husband all over again.

Or was she really Hope? After all, Salem's the place where a guy named Mark turns out to be Thomas, and where Roman turns out to be John and John turns out to be Roman. (With all those names, one can almost see them inspiring Dana Carvey's *Saturday Night Live* Church Lady to preach a Sunday morning sermon straight out of the New Testament. But, if she's watched the show, she's more than likely to ask the writers if they were inspired by … Satan?????)

The major line that broke in 1994 and ran through mid-1995 was the Devil's assault on Salem starting with terrible storms (the hail you say) and other horrible happenings, including the demonic possession of Dr. Marlena Evans Craig Brady. Once again, Stefano opened the door for the evil to come in. He had taken an apartment next to hers and worked out a way to enter her bedroom through an opening in an armoire. He hypnotized her at night and took her for glamorous evenings on the town. The good doctor woke groggily every morning and dragged herself through the day, wondering why she was so tired after sleeping so deeply through the night.

Strange things began to happen in Salem. Christmas trees, toys, even St. Luke's Church were set ablaze. Religious objects were desecrated. Who was doing these dastardly things? Marlena, with yellow eyes (the sign of demonic possession) turned to the camera and smiled, as if to say, "The devil makes me do it."

Kristen suspected the worst before anyone else did. But John was unable to believe the woman he had once loved — and still cared for — could be the devil's handmaiden. He rationalized Marlena's attempts to seduce him, although she knew he was a priest, as a need for love.

Finally, Father John Black and Kristen's favorite priest, Father Francis, got permission to perform an exorcism. The bishop had been reluctant to give them the go-ahead until he saw Marlena levitating over her bed.

The devil was not prepared to go back to hell quite as readily as his adversaries hoped: there was still a lot of mischief to stir up. For example, it was easy giving Tony a subliminal vision of Kristen and John making love. Indeed, if it weren't for Celeste talking him out of it, Tony might have killed John in a jealous rage.

Realizing he was to blame for Marlena's demonic possession, Stefano tried to save her by giving her his mother's Bible. But the demon in her forced him over a patio. Emergency surgery saved his life, but he lost his memory. Celeste, incidentally, turned out to be Lexie Carver's (Renee Jones) long-lost aunt, with a family secret she's loathe to reveal to her niece.

Marlena died during the exorcism, and was zipped into a body bag and taken to the morgue. While everyone in Salem prepared for her funeral, John was drawn to see her one last time, and when he unzipped the bag, she opened her eyes — her yellow eyes!

What followed on that July day in 1995 was a daylong struggle between the devil and John Black. As the day moved towards night, the devil gloated. He knew that in a few minutes, he would own John Black's soul. But with his last bit of strength, Black called for help from Heaven — and a reinvigorated John Black vanquished the devil, who picked up his spike-tail and hoofed it back to hell.

Marlena was free — and alive — and John Black was happy for her.

Sure, the good guys won. But did they win the war, or just a battle?

And what about Stefano's love for Marlena? Will something good come out of that? And will Tony learn that he hasn't inherited his father's evil side? And what about Father John Black? Will he leave the priesthood now that he's finally remembered how to say a Mass and give absolution?

183

And is the devil gone from Salem for *good?*

Stay tuned.

Points Of Interest

Benjamin Franklin's descendants are represented in every profession and walk of life, including at least one soap star, Jack Coleman, who played Jake Kositchek, the Salem Strangler.

John de Lancie, who played the psychic Eugene Bradford on *Days* (and also played "Q" on *Star Trek: The Next Generation)* is descended from an early colonial family that gave their name to Delancey Street in New York City's lower East Side.

Bradford's friend, Chris Kositchek (Josh Taylor) invented the robot assistant that zoomed through the halls and wards of Salem Hospital. The device was actually produced by a New York company that makes robots for various uses.

Gregg Marx, who was one of several actors to play David Banning, is the grandson of Zeppo Marx, one of the Marx Brothers. His granduncles were Harpo, Chico, Groucho and Gummo Marx. (Zeppo and Gummo turned to the business end of being a Marx Brother, and left the performing to their three siblings.)

Robert Clary, who played Robert LeClair, is a French-born Holocaust survivor who has lectured to high school students — who are about the same age he was when he was sent to a concentration camp — about the horrors of the Nazi period.

When the character Steve Johnson (Stephen Nichols) had surgery on his eye, he was able to remove the eye patch that gave him the nickname, Patch. However, viewers complained that he lost his dashing image without it. Johnson got into a fight, reinjured the eye, and *voila,* the patch was back, and so was Patch.

One of Gloria Loring's (Liz Chandler DiMera) legacies to succeeding *Days* actors was her successful negotiation of the first contract that allowed a Days performer to act on prime-time shows.

Soon after Bill Hayes arrived in Los Angeles, he told the author he had given up touring with musical productions after his divorce because he needed a job that would keep him at home with his children. He hoped the soap job would last at least two years. It lasted fourteen years on the first go-round, and then again another two years.

Bill not only gave his children a stable home life, he also gave them a lovely stepmother, Susan Seaforth Hayes, with whom he has been touring in musical theater for some fifteen years or more.

Brenda Benet (Lee Dumonde) was divorced from the actor Bill Bixby (*My Favorite Martian* and *The Incredible Hulk*). In 1981, their young son died. Brenda was devastated. In 1982, beset by many psychological problems, she committed suicide. All the scenes she had taped before she died were dedicated to her when they aired.

Days of Our Lives is the only soap to have featured surrogate motherhood in two story lines: The first was when the character, Rebecca (Brooke Bundy) was impregnated with Doug Williams's sperm and bore his son, Dougie. The second was when Maggie Horton (Suzanne Rogers) agreed to become a surrogate mother for Dr. Evan Whyland (Lane Davies, who later starred on *Santa Barbara* and more recently, in *The Crew*). Whyland decided not to claim the child. Maggie's husband, Mickey, was happy to become the baby's legal father. Additionally, Vivian had Victor and Kate's baby (Phillip) through a "mixup" she planned at the fertility clinic.

Susan Seaforth and Bill Hayes.

Dr. Whyland's father was played by the late Robert Alda, father of Alan Alda. The elder Alda was a screen star in the 1940s and '50s. He told the author that when he joined the soap, "I figured I'd get mail from kids asking me about Alan (but instead) I'm getting mail from people who saw me in the movies when they were younger, and are seeing me again when the movies are on TV."

Relative–ity

Hope Williams Brady is Doug and Addie Williams's daughter. Julie Olson Williams is Doug's wife and Addie's daughter, which makes Hope her half-sister as well as her stepchild. Hope's son with Bo Brady, Shawn-Douglas, is Doug's grandson; Julie's stepgrandson; and also, Julie's nephew. David Banning, Julie's son, is Hope's half-brother. Dougie LeClair, the child of Rebecca LeClair, who was impregnated with Doug's sperm, is

Doug's natural son and the legal son of Robert LeClair and the half-brother of Hope, and is Shawn-Douglas's uncle.

Finally, Shawn-Douglas, although a Brady by name, is actually Victor Kiriakis's grandson. S-D's father, Bo, is Victor's son by a brief affair with Caroline Brady. This means if Kimberly Brady's son, Andrew, is Victor's and not Shane Donovan's, Shawn-Douglas and Andrew are nephew and uncle; not just cousins.

The Founding Families

Two major family groups, the Hortons and the Olsons, were introduced on *Days of Our Lives* on November 8, 1965. Over the years, the Olsons have moved out of the soap and are represented now only by descendants of Ben and Addie Olson, many of whom have ties to other families. The Hortons remain an important family with ties to other families — mostly the Bradys — in Salem.

The Hortons

Tom Horton, played by the late Macdonald Carey from day one of the soap until his death in 1994. Tom was the husband of Alice Horton (Frances Reid) and the father of five Horton offspring: Tom, Jr., Addie, Mickey, Bill, and Marie. His grandchildren include Julie Olson Williams, Dr. Michael Horton, Jennifer Rose Horton Devereaux, Jessica Blake, Dr. Sandy Horton, Sarah Horton, and Hope Williams Brady. His great-grandchildren include David Banning, Abigail Devereaux, Shawn-Douglas Brady, and Michael's son with Dr. Robin Jacobs. Scotty Banning, David's son, was Horton's great-great grandchild

Carey's own large family of children gave him the inspiration for his portrayal of the Horton patriarch. In the early 1980s, he told the author that raising children is a craft that has to be adapted to each child. The major constant, he said, is teaching them the difference between right and wrong. Everything else grows out of that basic concept.

Alice Horton, played by Frances Reid from day 1 to the present. The matriarch of the Horton family, she remains actively involved in the lives of her family and her community. (See family members above.) Someone once described Alice as the mother and mother-in-law no one is lucky enough to have. She's devoted without being domineering, and loving

Frances Reid, Ed Mallory, producer Betty Corday, John Clarke, Macdonald Carey.

without demanding love in return. (She doesn't have to demand; it comes to her naturally.)

Addie Horton Olson Williams, played originally by Pat Huston, then by Patricia Barry. Addie was the twin sister of Tom, Jr., and sister of Mickey, Marie, and Bill Horton. She and her late husband, Ben Olson, were the parents of Julie Olson. Had they lived long enough, they would have been the grandparents of Julie's son, David Banning, and great-grandparents of David's son, Scotty. Addie married Doug Williams and gave birth to their daughter, Hope, before she died in a car accident while in remission with leukemia.

Dr. Tommy Horton, played by Tom Lupton. He was Addie's twin brother, and brother of Mickey, Bill, and Marie. He was lost in Korea and assumed dead. He returned to Salem as Dr. Mark Brooks, and he had no memory of his real identity. With his face rebuilt after extensive burns and injuries, he entered a romantic relationship with Marie Horton, without either of them knowing they were brother and sister. Dr. Bill Horton learned the truth before Marie and Mark could marry. Tom, Jr. learned he had a wife, Kitty, and a daughter, Sandy.

187

Sandy Horton, (last played by Pamela Roylance) is the daughter of Tommy and Kitty, and the first (and so far, only) female Horton to become a doctor.

Bill Horton, (played first by Paul Carr, then for fourteen years by Edward Mallory) is the son of Alice and Tom; brother of Mickey, Marie, Addie, and Tommy. He's a brilliant surgeon. He is the real father of Mickey's son, Mike, who was born to Dr. Laura Spencer Horton (currently played by Jaime Lyn Bauer) after he had raped her in a drunken rage. Bill is also the father of Jennifer Rose Horton Devereaux and Lucas Roberts. His affair with Lucas's mother, Kate, was a prime reason Laura had to be institutionalized. Of course, he is the grandfather of Mike's son and Jennifer's daughter.

Mickey Horton, played by John Clarke since 1965. He's the son of Tom and Alice; brother of Bill, Marie, Addie, and Tommy. He's the legal father of Dr. Michael Horton and Sarah Horton, the child his wife, Maggie, conceived as surrogate mother for a colleague. The biological father gave custody to Maggie and Mickey. Mickey is a lawyer.

Marie Horton, originally played by Marie Cheatham and last played by Lanna Saunders. She is the daughter of Tom and Alice, and sister of Tommy, Mickey, Bill, and Addie. She had a child, Jessica Blake, with her lover, Alex Marshall. Her first husband was original cast character, Tony Merritt. She was romantically attracted to a newly arrived doctor, Mark Brooks, who turned out to be her brother, Tommy, Jr., whom the family assumed had died during the Korean War. The shock was so overwhelming she became a nun. She later left the convent and resumed a relationship with her daughter's father and started a new one with Neil Curtis (Joe Gallison) before leaving Salem in 1985.

Julie Olson Banning Anderson Williams Williams (played by Susan Seaforth Hayes) is the granddaughter of Tom and Alice; the daughter of Addie and Ben Olson, the mother of David Banning, and grandmother of Scotty Banning. Her husband, Doug's daughter, Hope is her half-sister born to Doug and Addie. She is the stepmother of Doug's biological son, Dougie LeClair, who was born to a surrogate mother, Rebecca, and adopted by Deborah's husband, Robert LeClair (Robert Clary).

188

Michael Horton, a doctor, (last played by Michael Weiss; currently played by Roark Critchlow) is the legal son of Mickey and Laura Horton, and the biological son of Bill Horton. He's the brother of Jennifer Rose Horton Devereaux, and uncle of her daughter, Abigail. He went to Israel to be with Dr. Robin Jacobs and their child, and returned to Salem in 1994.

Mike's first wife, Margo, died of leukemia. He was involved with Trish Clayton before she married his cousin, David.

Hope Williams Brady, daughter of Addie Olson and Doug Williams; half-sister and step-daughter of Julie Olson Williams and half-sister of Dougie LeClair; granddaughter of Tom and Alice; wife of Bo Brady and mother of their son, Shawn-Douglas Brady. Played by Kristian Alfonso.

Hope fell in love with Bo Brady (Peter Reckell) as a teenager. She followed him, his sister, Kimberly Brady (Patsy Pease), and Kimberly's main man at the time — international agent, Shane Donovan (Charles Shaughnessy) — to England to help track down the nefarious, notorious killer, The Dragon, who was ultimately caught by Bo and Hope. The Brits were so happy, they gave the couple a lavish wedding.

Hope disappeared and was presumed dead in 1987. She, or her lookalike named Gina — who had no conscious memory of her past — reemerged some seven years later. By mid-1995, it looked as if Grandma Alice's instincts were on the mark. She was sure that Gina was Hope and she had an increasing amount of evidence to back up her accusations.

Jennifer Rose Horton Devereaux, played by Melissa (Brennan) Reeves, is the daughter of Bill and Laura Horton; the sister of Dr. Mike Horton; most recently the ex-wife of Jack Devereaux (currently played by Mark Valley) and mother of their child, Abigail; and fiancée of Peter Blake (Jason Brooks).

Jennifer was raped by Lawrence Alamain, and nearly died when she tried to save her mother, Laura, who had been set up by Peter to "commit suicide" (because he thought she would be an impediment to his courtship of Jennifer).

Jennifer knew her own mind and defied Granny Alice who didn't want her to marry Devereaux, the son of Senator Harper Devereaux, the Riverfront Knifer. Jack had personality problems. He raped his former wife, Kayla Brady, when he thought she was still in love with his brother, Patch Johnson, and he almost killed their daughter who had become a victim of one of his environmentally unsound projects. Jennifer stuck with him, but he left her out of guilt over their child. She eventually divorced him, although she realizes she probably still loves him.

Jennifer and Peter planned to marry in a place called Aremid, which some people believed held dire consequences for them. Stay tuned.

189

Closeups: Current Cast And Characters

Actor: Kristian Alfonso

Birthplace: Brockton, Massachusetts
Birthdate: September 5

Kristian, who at thirteen won a Gold Medal for skating at the Junior Olympics, and at fifteen was one of the world's most sought-after models, made her acting debut opposite Rock Hudson in an NBC film called *Starmaker*. The title proved prophetic. She soon found herself cast in one film and television production after another. She joined *Days of Our Lives* as Hope Williams in 1983. She left the show a few times, but has always returned to a warm welcome from the fans.

Alfonso's recent prime-time credits include roles on *Melrose Place, Falcon Crest, Burke's Law;* the feature film *Joshua Tree* with Dolph Lundgren, and the USA Cable movie *Blindfold* with Shannen Doherty and Judd Nelson. Kristian has a young son, Gino.

Character: Hope Williams Brady
See Founding Famlies.

Kristian on *Days*:

"I was never concerned about coming back after so many years away.... The show had been like a family to me when I was on it earlier. Coming back was just like coming home...."

Actor: John Aniston

Birthplace: Crete, Greece
Birthdate: July 24

John Aniston says he enjoys being introduced these days as the father of Jennifer Aniston, who stars as Rachel on NBC's prime-time series, *Friends*. Fluent in Greek and Spanish, Aniston served as an intelligence officer in the United States Navy. He holds degrees in biology and theater arts. His previous soaps were *Love of Life* and *Search for Tomorrow*. He has also done prime-time guest roles and was featured in the films *Love with the Proper Stranger* and *What a Way to Go*.

Aniston moved to Greece with his wife and young children to study medicine. "Just my luck," he said, "the country was in one of their politi-

cal turmoils; the universities were shut down — and that included their medical schools. After a year waiting for the schools to reopen, I realized it was time to come home and go back to work as an actor. Regrets about missing out on a medical career? No. It didn't work out, but at least I tried."

Character: Victor Kiriakis

Victor came to Salem in 1985; he was a wealthy man. The sources of his wealth were shrouded in suspicion. He soon became involved with people who pushed drugs and did other nefarious things. The viewers were fascinated by this tall, dark, handsome villain who charmed every woman who came into his life. Even Caroline Brady, the wife of Shawn Brady and mother of Roman, Bo, Kayla, Kimberly, and adoptive mother of Frankie, became his lover for a brief time. When Victor vowed to destroy Roman (the police detective who was always on his trail) and Roman's brother, Bo (who worked with him), Caroline told Victor that Bo was his son, whom she had conceived during their affair. Victor's brief marriage to Carly Manning interfered with Bo's desires for Carly.

Victor also had an illegitimate daughter, Isabella Toscano, who married John Black. Their relationship was unknown to them when they first met and were attracted to one another. But they learned they were father and daughter before attraction turned to action.

Victor vowed to destroy I.S.A. agent Shane Donovan, who was involved with Roman's sister, Kimberly. She slept with him to save Shane, and later became pregnant and delivered a son, Andrew, who may be Victor's child.

More recently, Victor married Kate Roberts, mother of Lucas, Billie, and Austin. Their son, Phillip, was conceived through *in vitro* fertilization. Vivian Alamain, who loved Victor, had the embryo implanted in her womb and carried the child to term.

Although Kiriakis started as a thoroughly villainous character — and still retains powers drawn from some mysterious source — he has been somewhat redeemed in recent years.

Actor: Jaime Lyn Bauer

Birthplace: Phoenix, Arizona

Jaime Lyn started her career as a model in Chicago. She moved to Los Angeles to work on prime-time shows. Her first production was *Bronk* starring Tommy Lee Jones. She was then cast as Lauralee Brooks in the new daytime series from William J. and Lee Phillip Bell, *The Young and the Restless*. After leaving the soap in the early 1980s, Jaime Lynn appeared in a slew of nighttime shows including *Bare Essence, Mike Hammer, Love Boat, Fantasy Island, Knots Landing, Hotel,* and *Secrets*. She returned to daytime in

Christie Clark (second from left) with (l.-r.) boyfriend Chris Cade, Bryan Datillo (Lucas) and Allison Sweeney (Sami).

November 1993 in the role of Dr. Laura Horton, who was coming back to *Days of Our Lives* after fourteen years in a sanitarium.

Jaime Lynn and her songwriter husband, Jeremy Swan, have a daughter and two sons.

Character: Dr. Laura Spencer Horton
See Salem's Passion Ploys and Players.

Actor: Tanya Boyd

Birthplace: Detroit, Michigan

Tanya moved to New York at age fifteen to study dramatic arts at the Lee Strasberg Institute. She then moved to Los Angeles where she soon found roles in *A Different World, Parker Lewis Can't Lose,* and *Tricks of the Trade.* Her feature films include *New York, New York, Up the Academy* and *Jo Jo Dancer.* On stage, she starred in *Jelly's Last Jam* and *Indigo Blues.* She has sung on tour with Natalie Cole, Anita Baker, Lou Rawls, and is a director and producer with the Mojo Theatre Ensemble in Hollywood.

Character: Celeste

When *Days of Our Lives* viewers first met Celeste in April, 1994, she seemed to be nothing like her name, which means heavenly. Indeed, this devotee of the infamous Count Stefano DiMera, appeared to be someone who would follow his orders regardless of who might have to pay for his will and whims.

One of Celeste's tasks was to implant memories of Hope and Bo Brady in the hypnotically prepared mystery woman, Gina. But as time went on, Celeste became more of Stefano's conscience. If she couldn't stop him from one of his misguided pursuits, at least she could warn him and make him think about the consequences of his actions.

Celeste's mysterious past began to unfold when Caroline Brady (Peggy McCay) recognized her as her long-missing neighbor and told Lexie Carver (Renee Jones) that her Aunt Frances had returned. Lexie's parents left a note about Celeste. But Celeste didn't think Lexie needed to know what it contained, so she burned it. Will we learn more about Celeste? Stay tuned.

Actor: Jason Brooks

Birthplace: Colorado Springs, Colorado

Jason studied business administration at both the University of Arizona and San Diego University. His first show-business job was in a studio mail room. He left "showbiz" for a while to head up a yogurt distribution company. He decided to give acting a try and got an agent. Before too long he was being cast in films (he played Spa Guy #1 in *Captain America*) and in guest roles on prime-time television. He also racked up a list of theater credits.

Brooks and his wife, Corrine, enjoy quiet evenings at home.

Character: Peter Blake

Peter came to Salem in 1993 and immediately got involved in plots that threatened the life of John Black (Drake Hogestyn). Under orders by his adoptive father, Stefano DiMera, to make sure John didn't woo his sister, Kristen (Eileen Davidson) from her commitment to marry Tony DiMera, Peter was prepared to do anything to please papa.

He fell in love with Jennifer Rose Horton Devereaux and plotted to have her mother, Laura Horton, returned to a mental hospital because he feared she would block his courtship of Jennifer. The return of Jack Devereaux created new problems for Peter, but he was determined to marry Jennifer. He was also determined to have the wedding in Aremid, a place Celeste fears will bring tragedy to the young couple.

193

Actor: Christie Clark

Birthplace: Orange County, California
Birthdate: December 15

Christie first played Carrie Brady from 1986 to 1990. She returned to *Days of Our Lives* in December 1992. Christie's credits include a role on the soap *General Hospital*, and guest stints on *Life Goes On, Hull High,* and *Changes* with Cheryl Ladd. Her feature films include *Children of the Corn II: The Final Sacrifice,* and *A Nightmare on Elm Street, Part II.*

Character: Carrie Brady

Carrie is the daughter of Roman Brady and his first wife, Anna. She's the stepdaughter of Dr. Marlena Brady and the half-sister of twins, Samantha and Eric, and little Isabella.

Carrie fell in love with Austin Reed while recovering from burns she received when she was hit by a bomb meant for Austin, whom her sister, Sami, also loves. Lucas, Austin's half-brother, is also in love with Carrie, and is working to make sure she and Austin never get to the "I do" stage. But many a surprise was waiting for all the principals involved, reminding us that our best-made plans certainly do go awry.

Actor: John Clarke

Birthplace: South Bend, Indiana
Birthdate: April 14

Clarke holds a B.A. and an M.A. in television arts from UCLA. The son of a U.S. Army career officer, he's lived in over twenty states and several countries. He was graduated from a Tokyo high school. When he's not spending time with wife, Faith and their family, John enjoys riding around on his classic Harley Davidson.

Character: Mickey Horton

See Founding Families.

Actor: Roark Critchlow

Birthplace: Calgary, Alberta

Roark Critchlow compiled a long list of credits before assuming the role of Dr. Michael Horton on *Days of Our Lives* in April 1994. Among them are *The Commish, Highlander, The Round Table,* and *Top of the Hill.* He also had a role in the feature film, *Cadence.*

Roark majored in theater at the University of Victoria, in British Columbia, and performed in several stage productions in Canada. He and his wife, Maria, a writer, have two daughters, Jara Shea, and Reign.

Character: Mike Horton
See Founding Families.

Actor: Bryan Datillo

Birthplace: Kankakee, Illinois
Birthdate: July 29

Bryan's career started with the live-action Saturday morning series *California Dreams.* He also appeared on *Doogie Howser, In the Heat of the Night, Class of 96,* and *Charles in Charge.* He played the street-wise teenager, Jeff, in the feature film, *Arcade.*

Bryan calls himself a people person. As he explains, anyone who has grown up with six siblings (three of whom are his half-sisters) learns quickly how to get along in a crowd.

Character: Lucas Roberts
The son of Kate Roberts by her affair with Bill Horton, he is also Victor Kiriakis's stepson. He came to Salem in 1993 fresh from a rigid military school background. To his shock, he learned Mom was also the mother of Billie and Austin Reed, whose father, Curtis, had been a criminal.

Lucas has been in competition with Billie and Austin from the beginning. He is in love with Carrie Brady who is in love with Austin, and he's determined not to lose her to his half-brother. How far will Lucas go to get what he wants? As far as he has to.

Actor: Eileen Davidson

Birthplace: Southern California
Birthdate: June 15

Eileen was a fashion model before she joined *The Young and the Restless* as Ashley Abbott in 1982. She left the soap in 1989. She was cast opposite Jon Voight and Armand Assante (*The Doctors* alum) in the feature film, *Eternity.* She co-starred with Miguel Ferrer in Stephen J. Cannell's prime-time series, *Broken Wings,* and also assumed the daytime role of Kelly Capwell in *Santa Barbara.*

Eileen joined *Days of Our Lives* in the newly created role of social worker Kristen Blake in 1993. She and *General Hospital* star Jon Lindstrom became, as the gossip columnists like to say, an item.

Eileen grew up with four sisters, two brothers, and thirteen nieces and nephews. She is active with an organization called "Para Los Ninos," which benefits inner-city children.

Character: Kristen Blake
See Salem's Passion Ploys and Players.

Actor: Deidre Hall

Birthplace: Milwaukee, Wisconsin; raised in Florida
Birthdate: October 31

Deidre first joined *Days of Our Lives* as Dr. Marlena Evans in 1976. She left the series on several occasions to concentrate on prime-time work. She starred with Wilford Brimley in *Our House,* and guested on *Wiseguy* and other series. Her films, some of which she did while still on *Days,* include *And the Sea Will Tell, Woman on A Ledge,* and *Take My Daughters, Please.*

Deidre and novelist husband, Steve Sohmer *(Favorite Son)* were married in 1991 in England. They are the parents of two children born through a surrogacy arrangement.

Character: Dr. Marlena Evans Craig Brady
See Salem's Passion Ploys And Players.

Actor: Drake Hogestyn

Birthplace: Fort Wayne, Indiana
Birthdate: July 29

Drake Hogestyn originally planned to be a dentist. (How boring!) He attended the University of South Florida in Tampa on a baseball scholarship and majored in pre-dentistry. After graduation he played third base for the New York Yankees farm team until he was injured in 1978. He then decided to try to see if he could move into an acting career. In a nationwide talent search conducted by Columbia Pictures, he was one of thirty prospects culled from some 75,000 aspirants. He was given a starring role in the prime-time series, *Seven Brides for Seven Brothers.* In 1978, he joined *Days of Our Lives,* one of Columbia Pictures Television daytime properties. His role as the mysterious John Black catapulted him into instant soap stardom, where he's been holding forth ever since.

Drake is married to his childhood sweetheart, Victoria. The Hogestyns have three daughters and one son.

Character: John Black / Forrest Alamain
See Salem's Passion Ploys and Players.

Actor: Joseph Mascolo

Birthplace: West Hartford, Connecticut

Days of Our Lives audiences have been chilled and thrilled by Joseph Mascolo's portrayal of that superb international villain, Count Stefano DiMera, since he first appeared on the soap in 1982. He's left several times (with his character usually presumed dead) but his returns have always been welcomed by the fans.

Off camera, Mascolo and DiMera probably have very little in common except for the fact that they each have one son. DiMera does like good music, however, and Joe is an accomplished clarinetist who played with the Metropolitan Opera Company Orchestra in New York for several years; no doubt, the Count probably has a box in every opera house in the world — most likely under an assumed name. Indeed, Mascolo may have gotten some of his inspiration for soap opera's Stefano DiMera from having been exposed to the dastardly deeds of some of Grand Opera's nastiest villains. DiMera, in turn, probably sees these rascals as role models for himself.

When he's not on *Days,* Mascolo often makes guest appearances on prime-time series, and he can also be found making films or doing stage work. For relaxation, he likes to garden, ride horses, and play tennis for charity fund raisers. The citizens of Ocilla, Georgia, named a mile-long street after him in recognition of his work with the Sunnydale School for handicapped persons in Ocilla.

Character: Count Stefano DiMera

The no-account Count has done many nasty things since he first appeared in Salem in 1982. Many of these are re-Counted in *Salem's Passion Ploys and Players,* including the kidnapping of Marlena (several times); the kidnapping of Marlena's twins; the attempted murder of Roman Brady; the imprisonment of both Roman and John Black; the drugging of Marlena that made her vulnerable to demonic possession; and the bomb he sent to blow up Dr. Neil Curtis (Joseph Gallison) when his daughter-in-law, Liz Chandler (Gloria Loring) left Tony DiMera for him.

Actor: Thaao Penghlis

Birthplace: Sydney, Australia
Birthdate: December 15

Thaao Penghlis was a *Days* favorite from his first appearance as the suave Count Antony DiMera. He left the show in 1985. In the years that followed, Thaao kept busy doing films such as Ken Russell's *Altered States, Slow Dancing in the Big City, Memories of Midnight* with Omar Sharif, *The Look-Alike* with Melissa Gilbert and Diana Ladd, *Sadat* with Lou Gossett,

Jr., and *Under Siege* with Peter Strauss and Hal Holbrook. He also starred in the remade television classic series, *Mission: Impossible* which was shot in Australia. One of his co-stars was ex *The Young and the Restless* actor, Phil Morris, who is the son of Greg Morris, who played Barney in the original *Mission: Impossible* cast. Morris told the author that working with a "real Australian was great — Thaao was able to tell us about places to visit my wife and I might have otherwise missed..."

Thaao also appeared in *General Hospital* as the villainous Victor Cassadine, and in *Santa Barbara* as the mysterious Micah DeAngelis.

Penghlis, who is proud of his Greek heritage, visits Greece as often as his schedule will allow. He has a home in Athens.

Character: Count Antony Dimera

When *Days* fans first met this intriguing man, he was a smart, suave, and sexy charmer as well as more than a bit of a knave. In short, he was the perfect villain — and the viewers loved him, especially when he was at his best being his worst.

When Tony returned to Salem after an absence of close to ten years, he was still smart, suave, sexy, and with traces of that old knavery that made viewers anxious to see how, and to whom, he'll apply it this time around.

But, to the surprise of many, Tony also showed a loving, caring side of his nature.

Tony reemerged as the fiancé of his foster sister, Kristen Blake. He had to deal with her romance with John Black, one of his father's adversaries. Sometimes he'd show the darker side of himself. But his love for Kristen — although it inspired deep, raging jealousy — also helped bring out the better part of him. Some of the nasty things he did came out as his way of loving her: He switched her birth control pills with placebos, hoping that a child would bring them closer. He pretended to be blind so that he could check to see if she and John were making him a cuckold.

But there was something within him that was creating a change: Even when the devil in Marlena implanted images of Kristen and John making love, Tony didn't shoot John as the devil had hoped. Not yet, that is.

One of the most intriguing changes Tony DiMera showed was in his relationship to his father. Where he had once followed Stefano blindly, he now questioned his father's activities. He was against Stefano's forays into Marlena's bedroom, from where he whisked her away for glamorous nights on the town. He was suspicious of Stefano's insistence that Kristen not throw a party in their New Orleans mansion. (Stefano was holding Marlena and John Black as unwilling guests, and Gina as a bewildered soul without a memory on the premises.)

When Kristen left Tony after feeling betrayed by what he had done for love of her, Tony went to his father for the first time to ask for help. This proved to be a major turning point for both men.

Tony's conflict between his dark side and the better part of himself is a as classic as those told by the great playwrights whose works were first seen by Thaao Penghlis's ancestors in Athens several thousand years ago.

Actor: Peter Reckell
Birthplace: Elkhart, Indiana

Peter is an accomplished musician and singer. He attended the Boston Conservatory of Music, working as a singing waiter to earn his tuition. ("It was a great time," he said. "Living in such a beautiful place; living the life of a student; singing nights; studying days, sleeping with my head on the desk in the library.")

With his B.F.A. in Theater (he minored in music and dance), Reckell headed to New York where he soon won a role in the longest-running musical in the world, *The Fantasticks*. (This is where Jerry Orbach got his start.) He then moved into television with his first soap role as Eric Hollister on *As the World Turns*. He traveled with a theater group before joining *Days* for the first time in 1983 as Bo Brady — and changing, in one fell swoop, the face of the daytime hero. Brady was a bearded, long-haired, tatooed, earring-wearing motorcyclist. The audiences went wild. And, although the producers were happy about the reaction, they were also a mite surprised — albeit pleasantly surprised. (Remember: This was the period of the Reagan "revolution" when everyone was supposed to jettison their jeans and cut their hair; yesterday's flower children were putting expensive silk floral arrangements in their Lalique vases. So, who could have predicted this wildy successful pursuit of the hirsute Messrs. Reckell and Brady?)

Peter Reckell was at the top of the daytime polls when he left Salem and moved to *Knots Landing,* where he gained a whole new audience, many of whom found themselves sitting next to his loyal daytime fans when he toured the country in musicals and straight dramas.

Reckell's return to *Days of Our Lives* in July 1995 was welcomed by his fans. They, and his nighttime admirers, will see a lot more of Peter in the years ahead: he made a movie in Russia called *Brooklyn Bridges,* and signed to do a syndicated comedy drama called *Heavenly Road* (which, we're assured, will not affect his commitment to *Days*).

199

Character: Bo Brady

It's not that Bo Brady doesn't get the girl on *Days of Our Lives* — he does. The problem is, the girl tends to get away from him.

Bo is the son of Caroline Brady and her one-time lover, Victor Kiriakis. He has learned to acknowledge his true paternity, but considers himself the son of both Caroline and Shawn Brady, who are the parents of his half-siblings, Roman, Kayla, and Kimberly.

Through his biological father, Victor Kiriakis, Bo is half-brother to the late Isabella Toscano Black and Philip Kiriakis, son of Victor and Kate Roberts. And if his half-sister Kimberly's son, Andrew, is actually Victor's, then he's also Andrew's uncle and Andrew's half-brother.

Soap opera history is replete with memorable couples. Luke and Laura of *General Hospital;* Julie and Doug of *Days of Our Lives;* Steve and Alice of *Another World,* etc. Certainly, Bo and Hope (Williams) are more than suited to be part of that pantheon of soap lovers.

Bo fell in love with Hope the moment he saw her. They made love for the first time on the day she turned eighteen. (Actually, it was that night.) Bo's hopes of future happiness with Hope have always been tainted. Even from that very first night. Talk about afterglow — while they were cuddling together, Hope's father, Doug Williams, walked in and promptly had a heart attack.

He survived, and so did the romance. Meanwhile, Bo was building a reputation for himself as a crime fighter; same as big brother, Roman. He loved his big bro' and saw him as a great role model. Imagine, then, how he felt when he learned Stefano had killed him. Imagine how he felt when he also learned that Stefano had taken his body away. He became more determined to be the man his brother would have been proud of.

Bo was the man who rescued Marlena's kidnapped twins from one of Stefano's lairs. He and Hope later snared the nefarious Dragon in London and were given a splendid wedding by the grateful British. He and Hope had a son, Shawn-Douglas. But Bo's happiness with Hope was cut short when she was presumed to have been killed by the Brady's long-time nemesis, Count Stefano DiMera.

Bo (now being played by Robert Kelker-Kelly) then fell in love with Dr. Carly Manning. Again, happiness with Carly seemed just within his grasp, when she "died." But she was only in a death-like state and buried alive by the vindictive Vivian Alamain (Louise Sorel). To Bo's delight, Carly was found and they reunited. But then she learned Nicholas Alamain was her son, and as much as she loved Bo, she chose to go off with Nicholas and his father, Lawrence Alamain. Once more, Cupid's arrow had shafted Bo.

He met and fell in love with Billie Reed. This time, he was sure there would be no impediment to their marriage. But a beautiful young woman named Gina appeared. She was the double of his "dead" wife, Hope. Or was she really Hope?

Bo and Billie's wedding ceremony was interrupted by a fracas caused by the demonic Marlena. That should have been a warning to Bo that the phrase, happily ever after, was not going to be something he could anticipate — at least, not yet.

In the end, Billie accepted the fact that she had lost Bo to both a memory and a reality. Will Bo be able to keep his beloved forever this time around? Stay tuned.

Actor: Melissa Reeves

Birthplace: Eatontown, New Jersey
Birthdate: March 14

Melissa Reeves is married to Scott Reeves, who plays Ryan McNeil on *The Young and the Restless*. The couple are parents of a daughter.

Soap Opera Digest named Melissa one of the most beautiful women on television; *YM Magazine*'s 1992 Reader's Poll cited her as Favorite Soap Siren. She's been nominated for an Emmy and was a winner at the 10th Annual Soap Opera Awards ceremony in 1994.

Melissa's previous soap roles were on *Santa Barbara* and *Another World*. She also appeared in the HBO film, *Somewhere, Tomorrow*. She studied acting at the prestigious Lee Strasberg Studios in New York City.

Character: Jennifer Rose Horton
    See Founding Families.

Actor: Louise Sorel

Birthplace: Los Angeles, California
Birthdate: August 6

Daytime dramas are much the richer for having actors such as Louise Sorel grace their casts. Sorel, who has also been featured on *Santa Barbara* and *One Life to Live*, has a long list of accomplishments that include primetime shows such as *Knots Landing; Star Trek; Bonanza; Ladies' Man; Sunset Limousine;* and *Zorro*.

Her feature films include *Plaza Suite; Airplane II; Where the Boys Are, 1984; Every Little Crook and Nanny;* and Ken Russell's *Crimes of Passion*.

Broadway audiences know her from such productions as *Philadelphia, Here I Come; Man & Boy; Take Her, She's Mine* (with Art Carney and Elizabeth Ashley); *The Dragon, Lorenzo;* and *The Sign in Sydney Brustein's Window*.

Sorel is fluent in French. She enjoys traveling and spends a great deal of her free time in Europe.

201

Character: Vivian Alamain

There has probably been no soap villainess quite like Vivian. Credit the writers for that, of course. And also, credit Louise Sorel who brings a wonderful sense of both the humorous and the absurd to a woman who doesn't think what she does is funny, and certainly doesn't see herself as absurd.

Whatever the villainy — which is often done with the aid of her adoring servant, Ivan Marais — Vivian always comes a cropper, but it's not for want of trying. She buried Carly Manning alive when she thought Carly might discover that she's the mother of her beloved grand nephew, Nicholas Alamain. She tried to keep Laura Horton in a catatonic state in the mental institution, but she also helped herself and Laura escape from being lobotomized. And she managed to have Kate and Victor Kiriakis's fertilized embryo implanted in her womb; but once they accepted what Vivian had done, they were grateful that she gave birth to a healthy little boy for them. Vivian also tried to put Kate into a drugged stupor when she took off for a business trip. How could she be blamed for the fact that the pilot drank the coffee and crashed the plane? And if truth be told, as much as she would like to replace Kate in Victor's life, she was upset, for a while, that Kate might be dead.

Vivian can be troublesome, but she's fun to watch while she plots — and even more fun when her plots go to pot.

Actor: Alison Sweeney

Birthplace: Los Angeles, California

Alison made her show business debut at age five in a Kodak commercial. She soon got roles in prime-time series including *Family Man, I Married Dora, Tales from the Darkside, St. Elsewhere, Webster,* and *Simon & Simon.* She also appeared in the feature films, *The End of Innocence* and *The Price of Life.*

Alison, who made her *Days of Our Lives* debut as Sami Brady on January 22, 1993, says she hopes one day to become a director.

Character: Sami Brady

Sami and her twin brother, Eric, are children of Marlena and Roman Brady. She is the half-sister of Carrie, Roman's daughter by his first marriage, and Isabella, born of Marlena's affair with John Black.

Sami returned to Salem after a long stay with her mother's family in Colorado (where brother Eric still resides). She became a candy striper in the hospital where Marlena practices. She developed a crush on Austin Reed, who was interested in her sister, Carrie.

A serial rapist was loose in Salem. The rapist, Alan, tried to attack Carrie but failed. He continued to be fixated on her, but he was also intrigued by Carrie's younger sister, Sami.

The teenager was dazzled by his attentions and had no qualms about going to his apartment. He raped her and warned her not to tell anyone. Eventually, Carrie got her to speak up and persuaded her to bring charges against Alan. She told her young sister she would support her through the ordeal on the stand.

To Carrie's dismay and Sami's horror, the clever defense attorney got Carrie to say something that made Sami look as if she had taken part in consensual sex. Sami vowed vengeance against Carrie. She arranged to have Austin drugged and, thinking he was with Carrie, he made love to her. After Austin rejected her, Sami ran away, spending some time on the West Coast. She returned just in time to stop Austin and Carrie's wedding with the news that she is carrying Austin's child.

Sami was also the first to suspect that her father was not Isabella's father. Knowing that her mother had slept with John Black created a terrible conflict in Sami: She loved her mother, but she also loved her father.

Sami Brady has had problems, starting from when she and her twin brother were kidnapped as infants by Stefano DiMera and rescued by their uncle Bo. She has caused problems for a lot of people — and probably will continue to do so on *Days* for a long time to come.

Actor: Mark Valley

Birthplace: Ogdensburg, New York

Mark Valley replaced Matt Ashford in the role of Jack Devereaux in October 1994. Valley, whose last soap stint was a short-run role as a priest, Father Pete, on *Another World,* has spent most of his career doing prime-time television, theater, and films.

Valley's life has been rich with activity and experience. He chose to go to West Point "...for two reasons: A good education and the challenge. I felt that if I could make it through the demands of those four years, I would be able to do whatever I wanted in life."

He was graduated with a degree in math and was sent to Germany. Except for his participation in Operation Desert Storm, he spent most of the next five years in Berlin, where he saw the Wall come down. It was in Berlin that Mark was "discovered" by an agent who saw him while he was shopping in Berlin and suggested he might want to go to an audition for a new film. Mark had done some acting in high school, but shelved the idea when he was accepted at West Point. Now the idea seemed more and more like a good one; especially when he found himself in a film with Anthony Hopkins, *The Innocent,* directed by John Schlesinger. His next film was opposite Peter Falk in Wim Wenders's *Far Away, So Close!*

Mark went on to do other films and productions in Europe. He also appeared on stage in Berlin. When he moved back to New York in 1991,

203

his stateside career began with commercials and *Another World*. The NBC peacock is proud of the fact that this talented thespian is still in the network's nest.

Character: Jack Devereaux

If the Jack is the Knave in a deck of cards, this character was well named. Devereaux, the son of Senator Harper Devereaux (who turned out to be the vicious Riverfront Knifer), schemed and scammed his way through Salem for years.

He was married to Kayla Brady, who was first in love with the dashing antihero, Steve (Patch) Johnson. When Jack learned she was still in love with Patch, he raped her. After their divorce, she turned again to Patch who eventually told Jack they were brothers.

Although still a knave at heart, Jack tried to change. He became involved with Jennifer Horton. He helped Jack's former sister-in-law, Isabella escape from a mental hospital where she'd been wrongly committed. (Isabella turned out to be Victor Kiriakis's illegitimate daughter; she later married John Black.) He also helped free Kayla from a kidnapper, and rescued Jennifer when she was abducted and raped by Lawrence Alamain.

After Jack and Jennifer were married, they had a daughter, Abigail. Although Jack had become a nicer guy by now, he still seemed to need to cut corners. He was responsible for an environmental hazard that almost killed his child. Filled with remorse, Jack (then played by Matt Ashford) left Salem. Eventually, Jennifer divorced him.

Jack returned to Salem (now played by Mark Valley) and tried to win back Jennifer's heart, but by then she was involved with Peter Blake. Jack suspected Peter was one of Stefano DiMera's henchman, as well as his foster son. Jack was right, of course, but couldn't prove it.

Meanwhile, Jennifer's mother, Laura Horton, had fallen for Jack, whom she met when both were using assumed names at a resort. Will Jennifer eventually return to Jack? Will Jack turn to Laura? If Laura and Jack make it to the altar, will Jennifer find it difficult to explain to their daughter that daddy is her grandpa?

Stay tuned. It gets better.

Mark on Jack:

"I like this character because he's rich with activity and experience. I'm discovering all sorts of things about him ... I just don't know what he'll do next."

Supporting Cast

Ivan G'vera: Ivan Marais, Vivian Alamain's devoted servant.

Renee Jones: Lexie Carver, Abe's wife; niece of Celeste. A former police officer, she is now a doctor.

Thyme Lewis: Jonah Carver, loves Lexie, but despite temptation, she's loyal to Abe. He was kicked out of medical school as a result of her vigilante activities.

Peggy McCay: Caroline Brady; wife of Shawn Brady; mother of Kayla, Kimberly, Roman, and Bo; adoptive mother of Frankie.

Frank Parker: Shawn Brady; husband of Caroline Brady; father of Kayla, Kimberly, and Roman; legal father of Bo (whose biological father is Victor Kiriakis) and adoptive father of Frankie.

Suzanne Rogers: Maggie Simmons Horton, wife of Mickey Horton; mother of Sarah through a surrogacy agreement with Dr. Evan Whyland, who later gave up rights to the child.

Miriam Parrish: Jamie Caldwell, Sami Brady's best friend. She loves Lucas, who loves Carrie, who loves Austin. She was molested by her father.

James Reynolds: Abe Carver, Jonah's brother and husband of Lexie Carver. Abe is a detective with the Salem Police Department and Roman Brady's best friend.

General Hospital

J ohn Beradino, the only remaining member of the original cast of *General Hospital,* once told the author, "Having our debut date as April 1 is somewhat ironic. We were not expected to last more than a year; two at the most. Now, each year on April 1 — which is April Fool's Day — I tell myself, 'Well, we've fooled them for another year.'"

The ABC network produced its first daytime drama, *Road to Reality,* in 1960. It proved to be a *Road* to nowhere soon after its debut.

The then-newest network on the air tried again with two soaps in 1963. It was a toss-up whether *General Hospital,* with its theme centered on the private lives of its doctors and nurses, or *Ben Jerrod,* with its handsome lawyer hero, would succeed. The common wisdom among the media observers was that *GH* would fail, because there were already doctor-oriented soaps on the air, with *Guiding Light* leading the pack.

Although *Ben Jerrod* lasted barely a year, *General Hospital* had rough going against the competition until ABC brought on Gloria Monty, one of the best people in the business, to take charge of operating the *Hospital* as executive producer.

Monty, who had been one of television's first women directors (she got her training in theater), produced *Secret Storm* and pushed that show's ratings to new heights when she asked Joan Crawford to step in for her ailing daughter, Christine. (Years later, Monty would invite another movie queen, Elizabeth Taylor, to do a guest role specially tailored for her.)

Monty was allowed to make whatever changes she felt were needed. She was innovative from the first day. She told the author, "Television, like film, is a visual medium. The audience expects people to move across the screen, not stand in front of the nurses' station and talk about the action."

Where the action had largely been concerned with making mitered corners on hospital bed sheets, Monty now had her people moving from place to place, including out of the hospital itself. She also changed story lines, introducing controversial themes that were as powerful, in their way, as a Joan Crawford film. Lots of conflict between and among people — and lots of sex!

One of Monty's most successful innovations was the creation of the lovers Luke and Laura (Anthony Geary and Genie Francis), who caught the imagination of millions of soap fans. (Somehow, in the midst of all the romance, the fact that the story began with a rape was conveniently rationalized by emphasizing, whenever the question was raised, that Laura had actually consented. But the last word Laura spoke when the scene went to black was "No.")

In any event, *General Hospital* was saved from cancellation, and has gone to produce some of the best socially relevant story lines over the years. Although *GH* has produced its share of clunkers (the "Ice Princess" story line, for example, was one of the worst despite the presence of Liz Taylor) the show has never been afraid to take chances.

Original Cast

John Beradino . . . . . .Dr. Steve Hardy	Lenore Kingston . . . . .Mrs. Weeks
Tom Brown . . . . .Al Weeks	Ralph Manza . . . . .Mike Costello
Robert Clarke . . . . .Roy Lansing	Emily McLaughlin . . . . . .Jessie Brewer
Carolyn Craig . . . . . . .Cynthia Allison	Hunt Powers . . . . .Dr. Ken Martin
Craig Curtis . . . . .Eddie Weeks	K.T. Stevens . . . . .Petty Mercer
Neil Hamilton . . . .*Philip Mercer	Roy Thinnes . . . . . .***Dr. Phil Brewer
Allison Hayes . . .** Priscilla Longworth	

* Neil Hamilton went on to star in the Batman television series.

** Allison Hayes starred in the cult film classic, Attack of the 50 Foot Woman.

*** Roy Thinnes, who has appeared on other soaps (two roles on One Life to Live, for example) starred in a 1967 television cult classic, The Invaders, which was introduced into France in 1994 and made Thinnes a new star of French TV.

207

Port Charles Chronicles

Port Charles is somewhere in New York. Although you probably won't find it on the map of the Empire State, many of the world's movers and shakers seem to find it easily enough. Over the years, more villains of every stripe, from paranoiac politicians to megalomaniacal mobsters have come to Port Charles to ply their unsavory trades and do their dishonest deeds.

The series began in typical soap opera fashion: The stories centered around a beautiful young nurse, Jessie Brewer (Emily McLaughlin) and her unfaithful husband, Dr. Phil Brewer (Roy Thinnes). She adored her husband, and sacrificed to help him become one of the country's most famous cardiologists. But when he wasn't repairing malfunctioning hearts, he was breaking Jessie's heart with his frequent forays into the bedrooms of other women.

Emily got lots of mail from women who empathized with her character's problems. She once told the author, "So many of these women worked so hard to put their husbands through medical school or law school ... and then were left alone when their husbands found other women.... They write to tell me that they know what Jessie's going through...."

Another romantic situation involved Dr. Steve Hardy (John Beradino) and an ex-flight attendant (in those days they used the term stewardess) Audrey March (Rachel Ames). Steve had been born and raised in China, the son of a missionary family. He married the fun-loving Audrey who felt she was ready to settle down and raise a family. When she couldn't get pregnant, she assumed Steve was sterile and had herself impregnated by artificial insemination. Audrey was sitting beside Steve in their car when he crashed his car. The child died, and Audrey divorced Steve. Still yearning for children, she went to Vietnam to care for the war orphans. She trained as a nurse, and returned to work at the hospital where she met and married Dr. Tom Baldwin — not because she loved him, but to prove to herself she no longer loved Steve. She became pregnant during this loveless marriage and left town after divorcing Tom. She returned saying the baby had died.

She was actually hiding the baby in her home. Tom had the child kidnapped and left town. Eventually, Steve and Audrey remarried and Steve adopted the boy who grew up to become Dr. Thomas Hardy, now played by Matt Ashford. (Tom must have inherited his mother's predisposition for good deeds because he went to Africa for a while to help provide medical service to the victims of the war in Somalia.)

Tom Baldwin's brother, lawyer Lee, was in love with Jessie before she married Phil Brewer. He married a woman named Meg who had a young son named Scotty. Meg had become very ill and was treated by Dr. Lesley Williams (Denise Alexander), a beautiful, independent young woman who

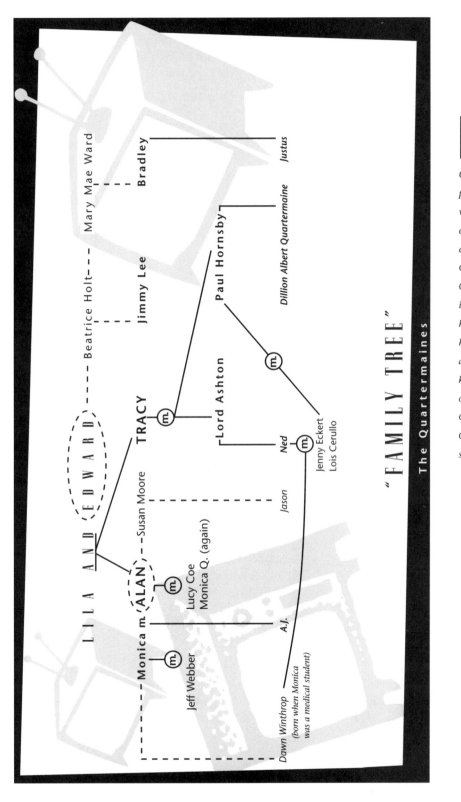

"FAMILY TREE"

The Quartermaines

Machiavelli would have been proud to claim Edward Quartermaine as a prime example of how to wield power by extending his power into every area of Port Charles. Lila Quartermaine's influence over her husband has sometimes helped temper his ambitions. But she knows it's only a matter of time before Port Charles finds the Quartermaine brand on something else.

209

John Beradino and Rachel Ames.

would later become an important part of young Scotty's future. After Meg's death, Lee adopted her son, who was renamed Scotty Baldwin.

Phil Brewer met a violent death. At first, Jessie was suspected when she was found cradling his lifeless body and moaning, "I'm sorry" over and over again. And, indeed, most of the folks at the hospital agreed that if anyone had reason to part Phil's pate with a blunt instrument, it was Jessie. Diana Taylor, who had been raped by Phil, confessed to the murder to protect her husband, Dr. Peter Taylor, Jessie's ex-spouse, whom she suspected of killing her rapist. But the murderer turned out to be another victim of Brewer's savagery, Augusta McLeod, played by Judith McConnell. Augusta claimed Philip threatened her unborn baby, and she struck him to protect her child. She bore the baby in prison, placed it in a foster home, and later left Port Charles.

In the meantime, Lesley — now married to the wealthy Cameron Faulkner — learned that the daughter she thought was dead had been adopted by Barbara Vining (Judy Lewis, daughter of Loretta Young and Clark Gable and, later, producer of *Texas*) and her husband. The couple were determined not to give up their beloved little Laura. It took time, but eventually Laura learned to care for her biological mother.

Later, *General Hospital's* population increased with the addition of some of soapdom's most vibrant young people: Dr. Monica Bard (Leslie Charleson), who had been raised in a foundling home; Dr. Rick Webber (Michael Gregory; then Chris Robinson) and his brother, Dr. Jeff Webber (Richard Dean Anderson — who later starred in *MacGyver* and *Legend*).

After Cameron Faulkner's death, Lesley married Rick — whom Monica wanted for herself. David Hamilton, an old buddy of Rick's, seduced the teenage Laura (Genie Francis). She adored him, but she later overheard him say he had made love to her only to make Lesley jealous. Laura confronted him, and in a fit of anger, threw a statue at him. He fell, hit his head on the hearth, and died. To save her daughter from jail, Lesley confessed to the murder. Laura blocked the incident from her mind and fled to New York City.

Young Scotty Baldwin (Kin Shriner) was in love with Laura. He found her involved in a drug and prostitution ring and brought her back to Port Charles where she confessed she had killed David.

The Webber family was crushed by these events. Laura turned to Scotty, but Scotty had been ensnared by a scheming young prostitute named Barbara Jean (Bobbie) Spencer (Jackie Zeman). Eventually, Scotty broke with Bobbie and returned to Laura.

But Bobbie was determined to get Scotty. She asked her brother, Luke, a small-time hood, to help her break up Scotty and Laura. Luke agreed, and found himself becoming interested in Laura.

Meanwhile, Monica married another doctor, Alan Quartermaine (Stuart Damon), the handsome but insecure scion of the wealthy Quartermaine family. Rick turned to Monica when Lesley proved to be incapable of giving him the love he needed. Later, Monica became pregnant and believed the child was Rick's. While Lesley was willing to divorce Rick, Alan warned Monica he would take her child if she tried to leave him.

Alan's sister, Tracy (Jane Elliot), hoped to see Alan and Monica break up so that her son, Ned, would inherit the Quartermaine fortune without having to share it with a cousin. She played on Alan's insecurity by insisting the newborn Alan, Jr. was not his. Although Alan's mother, Lila (Anna Lee), found a birthmark identical to her son's, Alan remained skeptical until a new type of paternity test (using DNA) proved he was the boy's daddy.

In the meantime, Laura and Scotty were married. But Laura quickly realized she'd become fascinated with Luke Spencer and found him far more interesting than her quiet, conventional husband. Luke was drawn to her as well. But fate took a cruel twist when Luke's mob bosses ordered him to kill Tracy Quartermaine's husband, Mitch Williams (Christopher Pennock) a corrupt assistant district attorney who was running for senator, promising to scour Port Charles of its resident crime bosses. Realizing he would die if he didn't kill Mitch — or would be thrown in jail for life if he did — Luke poured his heart out to Laura and confessed his love for her. He became more passionate, and when she resisted, he raped her.

Laura now knew too much about the mob, and the big boss, Frank Smith, decided she had to die. What's more, his daughter, Jennifer, had a hankering for Luke. Luke and Jennifer were to be wed on Smith's yacht. An angry Scotty boarded and beat him up. Luke fell overboard and was presumed drowned. Instead, that event sparked one of the most popular story lines in soap history: Luke and Laura on the run and having fun, while Smith's mobsters (among others) chased after them to retrieve Smith's coded little black book filled with a record of his crimes.

Eventually, the couple returned to Port Charles. But Laura seemed strangely unwilling to divorce Scotty and marry Luke. However, Luke

Tony Geary and Tristan Rogers in pursuit of the Ice Princess.

didn't have much time to worry about Laura's curious change of heart: The Ice Princess venture would soon focus his mind elsewhere.

The Ice Princess story introduced the character of Robert Scorpio (Tristan Rogers), who came on scene as a scoundrel, but was actually an agent who worked for the World Security Bureau. He and Luke became good friends and, together, worked to capture the notorious Cassadine family and their shrewd aider and abetter, Alexandra Quartermaine.

The Ice Princess was a statue that held a formula that could alter the world's weather. Victor, Mikkos, Tony, and Helena Cassadine (Elizabeth Taylor) wanted the formula. (Taylor wore jewels from her own fabulous collection during her scenes.)

Luke, Scorpio, and Laura (who had to get involved, of course) eventually cornered the three Cassadine men and turned Mikkos's devilish machine on him, freezing him to death along with the calculating Alexandra Quartermaine. Victor was put on ice up the river. (Translation: He was jailed.)

Dr. Noah Drake (Rick Springfield, who was a popular musician) came to town and romanced Bobbie. But Drake ducked making a commitment to Bobbie and soon left town. Meanwhile, Laura divorced Scotty and married

Luke. Scotty turned up at the wedding vowing to cause trouble.

Laura and Luke tiffed over her work as a model. Suddenly, she disappeared. Would she ever return? Luke was mad with worry. He met Jackie Templeton (Demi Moore before her movie star days), an investigative reporter for a New York newspaper. Jackie was seeking another Laura in Port Charles; her sister, Laura Templeton (Janine Turner), who had also disappeared. Jackie and Luke learned the disappearances were engineered by a man named David Gray. Eventually, Laura Templeton was found alive and well. Learning that David had killed his Laura, Luke killed him in a fight.

Luke went hiking and met Holly Sutton (Emma Samms) who claimed to be an orphan with some land she'd inherited in Port Charles. Holly was actually a member of a notorious family that specialized in scams. She and Luke became lovers. They had a fight. He stalked off, was mugged, and left paralyzed. People back in Port Charles believed he was dead. Holly, meanwhile, was pregnant. Scorpio married Holly to save her from being deported. She miscarried. By this time, she had fallen for Robert, who was in love with her, and their marriage of convenience became a marriage of love. When Luke returned to Port Charles, he ended his friendship with Robert because of his marriage to Holly.

Tony Geary and Elizabeth Taylor.

Another scam that didn't work out involved Susan Moore's attempt to blackmail the Quartermaines with "proof" that Edward and Lila weren't legally married. But the scheme ended with the death of one of the blackmailers, Crane Tolliver, who, before he died, gave Jimmy Lee Holt (Steve Bond) papers proving he was Edward's illegitimate son.

Several more people of note came and went in Port Charles: Celia Quartermaine (Sherilyn Wolters) arrived with her fiancé, Dr. Grant Putnam (Brian Patrick Clarke). But Grant was a plant: He was in Port Charles to get hold of an important disc for his Motherland. (The country was never identified, but his colleague in deception was named Natasha.)

Later, Celia exposed Grant Putnam as a psychopathic killer. In England, the real Grant Putnam — i.e., Grant Andrews — came to Port Charles and he and Celia found each other.

Luke and Laura's wedding portrait. This is one of the all-time highest-rated episodes of daytime.

Laura returned after a two-year absence to find Luke was now Mayor of Port Charles. But she was now married to Stavros Cassadine, who had kept her prisoner in Greece. (Remember: Helena Cassadine went to the Luke and Laura wedding and made it clear she was not happy about the way the couple iced her family's plans for power and would probably do something about it. And speaking of ice, Liz wore some of her best on that occasion since she knew it would be a ratings buster — and it was.)

Stavros followed Laura to the United States and was killed when he fell down the stairs of Luke's home. Luke and Laura reunited and left town together.

The Luke and Laura–Less Years

General Hospital prepared for the vacuum that would be left by the eventual departure of Luke and Laura. Writers focused attention on Robert Scorpio and Holly Sutton (Tristan Rogers and Emma Samms). Scotty Baldwin married Susan Moore, the mother of Alan Quartermaine's son, Jason. Bobbie Spencer married the wealthy New York entrepreneur, D.L. Brock (David Groh), who tried to frame Rick Webber after Rick closed down his plant as unsanitary. But Brock's scheme was exposed. After Dr. Leslie Williams Webber died in a car accident, Rick married again and left town.

Meanwhile, Jimmy Lee Holt's mother, Beatrice, came to Port Charles, and together with her son, planned to blackmail the Quartermaines with proof of their illegitimacy. She also managed to get enough material on other Port Charlesians and blackmailed them as well. Beatrice died when she took a sip of Lila's medication which, on top of all the other medications her victims slipped into her drinks, stopped her heart. Jimmy Lee wound up with $20 million from the Quartermaines in exchange for the embarrassing documents. Celia decided she loved Jimmy Lee Holt and not Grant Andrews, and after divorcing Grant, married Jimmy Lee. Their marriage broke up when Jimmy Lee had financial problems after some of his waterfront buildings collapsed. Jake Meyer (Sam Behrens) and Rose

214

Kelly (Loanne Bishop) couldn't bridge their religious differences, and split. Jake turned to Bobbie, who was now single again.

While all of these intertwining relationships had their moments, nothing — not even Scorpio's and Holly's love scenes, in which he expressed passion in a "strine" (Australian) accent, and she murmured sweet nothings in her clipped English speech — could compare with the Luke and Laura epic.

But Cupid, who seemed to be missing his shots, would return to Port Charles with a quiver full of arrows that would hit right on target.

Strong Women, Strong Men, Strong Stories

Spoiled "princesses" were not uncommon in Port Charles: There was Jennifer Smith, mob boss Frank Smith's daughter and former fiancée of Luke Spencer; there were the Quartermaine cousins, Jane and Celia, who believed that money was the "route" to the good life; there was D.L. Brock's daughter, Terri, who knew how to turn a petulant pout into a Hermes pouch from doting daddy; and there was the Ice Princess, of course, whose frigid front hid a really hot property. Finally, there was Elizabeth Taylor's Helena Cassadine, who believed that her rule was everyone's law.

And real royalty came to the city as well: Felicia Cummings (Kristina Malandro), an Aztec princess, came in search of an ancient ring that, when matched with a royal scepter, would lead to a treasure. Joining the search were Luke; Frisco Jones (Jack Wagner), an investigator and brother of Dr. Anthony Jones (Brad Maule); Scorpio; and Sean Donely (John Riley), an ex-agent pal of Scorpio's.

A beautiful woman with a scar on her face came to Port Charles with a little girl. She was Anna Devane (Finola Hughes), Scorpio's former wife and an ex-WSB agent who had earned a reputation for courage in the field. She introduced Robert to Robin (Kimberly McCullough), his daughter.

Anna helped find the treasure, and then got involved in other cases with international overtones. Holly left for Australia. Robert cleared up one more case with the help of Anna and Frisco and the questionable Donely. They freed the people of the city's Asian quarter who had been enslaved by a Chinese gang lord.

Frisco and Felicia were engaged. Monica and Sean started an affair and schemed to get the Quartermaine fortune, but Monica had second thoughts and tried to warn the family that Sean had concocted a scam about a merger that had never happened. No one listened and the Quartermaines lost everything. They even had to move from their mansion into Ruby's (Norma Connolly) diner.

Tiffany Hill (née Elsie May Krumholtz) agreed to help Edward Q. get the goods on Sean. But she found herself falling for the charming rascal

215

Sharon Wyatt and Tristan Rogers.

who could turn on the Irish charm with a wink of an eye. (This time, though, Sean found himself more interested in Tiffany than he expected to be.)

Meanwhile, Alan faked his own murder and made it look as if Donely did the dire deed. Rather than face a trial and possible imprisonment, Sean returned the Quartermaines' fortune.

Tony Jones found happiness with his wife, Tanya (Hilary Edson) and their little daughter, Barbara Jean (B.J.). But a hit and run driver killed Tanya, leaving the grieving widower with a small child to raise. Lucy Coe (Lynn Herring) described as a librarian-turned-nympho-maniac (a sort of librarian with an unbound libido?) moved in to care for B.J. She and Tony fell in love and were married. He divorced her soon after; not for what you might think — she was remarkably faithful during her brief marriage — but for not stopping B.J. from drinking nail polish.

Jake Meyer, who had a brief fling with Lucy before she married Tony, went off to South America. Scotty Baldwin returned to town and never told Bobbie about the messages Jake left for her. Lucy teamed up with Scotty for mirth — which she supplied — and mischief — which they both created in good measure.

Exciting story lines continued to develop with the characters of Duke Lavery (Ian Buchanan) a man with ties to organized crime, and the dashing Colton Shore (Scott Thompson Baker), Lucy Coe's cousin.

By now, Felicia had learned that Frisco was dead. Scorpio learned that Holly had died in a plane crash. Bobbie and Jake were divorced. Cupid was ready to move his chess pieces around to see who gets to "mate" with whom. (The chubby cherub has his own rules of the game.)

Anna and Duke Lavery fell in love and she became his duchess. But their marriage was continually fraught with danger. Duke was on the outs with the mob when he refused to go along with a dubious real estate scheme. Rather than put Anna and Robin at risk, he let everyone believe he was dead, blown to bits in an explosion. He went to Brazil where his face was rebuilt, and later returned to Port Charles. Eventually, Anna learned he was still alive, but by the time the couple were ready to resume their lives together, he was killed — this time for real.

Felicia learned that Frisco died while on assignment. The devastated Widow Jones turned to Colton for comfort. He got a divorce from Arielle Ashton, the former wife of Tracy Quartermaine's former husband, Lord Ashton. Colton and Felicia were married. Frisco, meanwhile, was languishing in a Turkish jail.

Frisco returned to Port Charles and expected to be welcomed by his lovely wife. Instead, Felicia insisted she had married Colton in good faith, and would remain true to her vows to him.

Meanwhile, Monica was having an affair with Ned Ashton, Tracy's son, whom she later found out was her nephew by marriage. Ned and Alan fought bitterly — but not over Monica. Their competition was for control of ELQ Industries.

Monica had a rival for Ned's affections, a lovely young woman named Dawn. Tracy, meanwhile, was upset with her son's fascination with someone no one knew anything about. Tracy discovered that Dawn was the child Monica had borne and given up for adoption.

Kin Shriner and Lynn Herring.

Monica was stunned by the news and by the time she told Dawn who she was, Ned told Dawn he loved her. But Dawn found herself drawn to Decker Moss, Colton's brother, a fun-loving motorcyclist; she was later killed. Decker had provided Felicia with shelter when she developed amnesia after being hurt when Colton cracked up Ned's bike.

Eventually, Colton and Frisco found Felicia with Decker (it was a purely platonic relationship); she decided to return to Frisco. That was probably a good choice for several reasons, not the least of which was the fact that Colton had twice been programmed to kill Frisco by a megalomaniac called Domino, who planned to take over the world.

Dr. Tom Hardy, Steve's adopted son, learned that his wife, Simone, was pregnant. However, Simone had slept with both her husband and Dr. Harrison Davis on the same day. So, who was papa? (It turned out Tom was.)

But Harrison raised some interesting issues. Did Simone really want the baby to be Tom's, or should she think about the fact that she was black

217

Quartermaine family portrait: matriarch Lila (Anna Lee), daughter Tracey (Jane Elliot), her then-husband Paul Hornsby (Paul Satterfield), her son Ned Ashton (Kurt McKinney, who created the role), his then-girlfriend Dawn, Monica (Leslie Charleson), Alan (Stuart Damon), and Rick Webber (Chris Robinson).

218

and the child would be black — even if Tom, a Caucasian, were its father. And shouldn't she consider whether the child would be better off with a black father like Harrison?

Simone had already faced black bigotry: Her parents didn't want her to marry Tom, but she defied them because she loved him. Was she now going to say they were right and she was wrong? Ultimately, Simone chose to stay with Tom, so that they could both raise their son.

But later, Tom would leave to serve in a clinic in Somalia. When he returned (this time played by Matt Ashford, formerly Jack Devereaux of *Days of Our Lives*) he would again find Simone involved with another man. This time it was Justus Ward (Joseph C. Phillips), whose grandmother, Mary Mae Ward (Rosalind Cash) revealed she had had an affair with Edward Quartermaine during World War II. This meant that Justus was a member of the Quartermaine family.

A decade before this story aired, *General Hospital* dealt with a dramatic story line involving baby brokering. Tiffany's sister, Cheryl Stansbury, had an affair with Robert Scorpio and became pregnant. She claimed the child was fathered by one of the mob bosses, Julian Jerome.

Cheryl had a son and was told the child died at birth. The infant actually had been given to a baby broker. Bobbie, who was unable to have children, desperately wanted to be a mother. She was told of an "available" baby and agreed to buy it; Tony helped her with the payment. They were both unaware that the little boy was Cheryl's. Tiffany discovered that her sister's baby was alive. She traced it to the broker and then to Bobbie and Tony, who were now married. Each party was determined to keep Lucas. Tiffany, as the baby's closest relative, was awarded custody.

Where There's a Will

Despite his business acumen — which he would describe as expedient for the greater good (the Quartermaine good that is) — Edward Quartermaine was not a very secure man. He believed his wife, Lila, loved him for himself. She said so many times, and he couldn't imagine that it wasn't so. But his children? His grandchildren? How could he be sure they cared for him and didn't just covet his assets?

Edward came up with a plan. He would pretend to have rewritten his will, switching legacies around. He then accepted Nicholas Van Buren's invitation to visit his estate in the Bahamas. (Van Buren was actually the villain named Domino who set out to kill Frisco in the Turkish jail.) Quartermaine planned to set things right regarding his will when he returned. But his plane crashed and everyone assumed he was dead. And everyone was stunned by their inheritance. Alan was so upset at losing his expected inheritance to Ned that he tried to have Edward declared mentally incompetent — but Lila wouldn't go along with him. Alan turned to Lucy Coe Jones who was more than happy to comfort the distraught (and rich) doctor.

Although Edward was presumed dead, Lila kept in constant touch with him and made decisions based on his advice.

Of course, Edward had not died, and he eventually returned to Port Charles. But in the meantime, the real will was found and everything was put right. And it gave his son, Alan, his daughter, Tracy, and other heirs more reason to bicker over their potential inheritance.

The 1990s — Changes Come to Port Charles

Tracy and her son, Ned, have been involved in a number of romances. But in the same way that Ned seems to have inherited her steely approach to business (which she probably inherited from her father, who insists she's much colder than he could ever be), mother and son also seem to share an inability to be lucky in love. Throughout the 1980s, Ned Ashton couldn't seem to find true and lasting love. His affair with Monica went nowhere.

His romance with her daughter, Dawn, ended when she decided to find another knight. As the '90s got underway, Ned's marriage to the lovely Jenny Eckert ran into problems caused mainly by his mother, Tracy, who left town with her infant son, Dillon Albert Quartermaine Hornsby. Her ex-husband, Paul Hornsby, was sympathetic to Jenny's plight. After all, they had both been lashed emotionally by Tracy. Sympathy turned to passion and, eventually, Jenny and Paul became lovers.

Ned's marriage to the tempestuous Katherine Bell (Mary Beth Evans) wasn't exactly legal, especially since he had already married the Brooklyn bombshell, Lois Cerullo, a rock band manager (played by Rena Sofer) who thought he was Eddie Maine (which comes from his full first name, Edward, and half of his mother's surname, Quartermaine), a pharmaceutical salesman who could sing. Katherine Bell used blackmail to rope him into marriage, and by the time the marriage met its eventual collapse, Katherine couldn't even pawn her engagement ring since it was a genuine fake.

To Lois's relief, "Eddie" signed his real name to their marriage certificate. The union was safe (and legal). The Cerullos, however, wanted a church wedding, and Ned and Lois obliged with a ceremony in her parish church in Bensonhurst, her family's Brooklyn neighborhood. They then left on a honeymoon tour of the world-famous (make that, woild-famous) New York borough.

Has Ned Ashton finally found true and lasting love with Lois? Will he able to say that for the first time Cupid shot him in the heart instead of always making him the butt of his arrows? Any bets one way or the other?

The Eckerts

The Eckert family's arrival in Port Charles was supposed to mark an important turning point in *General Hospital*'s history. For the first time in years, a whole new clan was being introduced. Luke and Laura were gone. But Anthony Geary agreed to accept a bid to return. However, it was decided not to have him come back as widower or divorced.

The last time Luke was Laura-less, the fans never really accepted him with any other woman except Holly (Emma Samms); but that story line was cut short when the Holly-Scorpio combination proved successful. So they brought Tony back as Luke's cousin, Bill Eckert. The family resemblance was amazing — except for the hair — Bill didn't have curls. The soap gave the Eckerts plenty to do. But the family never really caught on with the fans. Perhaps they saw too much of Luke in Geary and couldn't accept him as Bill.

The foreshortened Holly-Luke story of a decade earlier was replayed with a variation. Although Holly was presumed to have died in an airplane crash, she was actually alive. By this time, Robert Scorpio had died, and his brother, Mac Scorpio (John J. York) Robert's long-lost brother, came to Port Charles and took over raising his niece, Robin.

Emma Samms agreed to bring Holly back for a short run, during which time Holly would get involved with Bill, obviously, to remind folks of what could have been with Luke. The Eckert family was phased out — and the long-rumored, long-awaited return of Luke and Laura was slated for October 1993.

Stalking the Stork

The stork doesn't make as many stops in Port Charles as he does in most of the other soaps. But when he does, it's always more than just a biological event.

Scotty Baldwin, the man who loved and lost Laura, and who had become an embittered man, found love with the beautiful but tragic Dominique. She made him feel whole again. But there was something she felt they needed to bless their love: a child. When Dominique fell ill with cancer, which was diagnosed as terminal, she made Scotty promise two things: not to prolong her illness when the time came for her to die, and to have a child with her. Tony Jones said the cancer hadn't affected her ovaries or her eggs, and Scotty agreed to a surrogacy procedure. Dominique, aware that Lucy cared for Scotty, asked her to carry her baby. Lucy agreed. Perhaps she thought Scotty would want to marry her and they could raise the baby together. But she realized she would have done it for Dominique in any event.

After Lucy gave birth, Scotty picked up his child, Serena, and walked out of Port Charles, and out of her life. Will Scott Baldwin come back? He always has in the past. But will Lucy be there for him? Of course, that would depend on whom Lucy is in love with at the moment.

Felicia, who had a daughter, Maxie, with Frisco, became pregnant with her second child on his last home trip. Mac Scorpio, with whom Felicia had become involved, was disappointed to learn he was not the child's father.

Felicia later gave birth to a daughter she named Georgie in a night club owned by Luke Spencer. The child was kidnapped by Dr. Ryan Chamberlain (Jon Lindstrom), the mad-murderer twin of Dr. Kevin Collins (also played by Lindstrom). He took the baby into Canada, and was later found on a carousel, holding the child in his arms.

Grateful that she had her baby back, Felicia, nonetheless, felt more estranged from Frisco because he never seems to be there when she needs him most. Instead, he's out there saving the world through some spy thing. Mac Scorpio heartily agreed.

Two other auspicious births highlighted the first half of the 1990s. Laura and Luke Spencer, who had a son, Lucky, while they were away from Port Charles, had their second child, a daughter, Lesley Lu, when they returned. And the Spencers and Quartermaines would be linked by a blessed event involving Lucky's dog, Foster, and the Q's canine, Annabelle.

Luke and Laura Return

Luke and Laura Spencer didn't come back to Port Charles directly. Instead, they were involved in a confrontation with members of one of the criminal fraternities who always seem to be trying to get Luke out of the crime-busting business. The early episodes, in which the Spencers alternately confront and duck their enemies, were shot in Buffalo, New York, close to where Port Charles is supposed to be located. (Historians refer to this as the "Burned Over" area since it's the site of the start of so many historical movements, including the first women's rights convention and the first gathering of followers of the newly established Mormon church.)

The elder Spencers were accompanied by their ten-year-old son, Lucky (Jonathan Jackson). Eventually, the family got back to Port Charles and moved into a house that seemed to hold some strange sense of mystery, to which Laura was especially sensitive. The place had once been the home of Mary Mae Ward (Rosalind Cash) and her son, Bradley, who disappeared many years earlier. She and Laura became friends.

Laura found items in the old house that seemed to point to clues to the mystery of Bradley's unexplained disappearance. Meanwhile, the Spencers became involved in a community battle against an incinerator. Ned backed it; Alan bucked it. Eventually, Ned agreed to relocate it.

The mystery surrounding Bradley Ward was solved — almost. Mary Mae admitted she'd buried him in the backyard of Laura's house because she didn't want anyone to know he'd committed suicide. But Luke was skeptical. An investigation revealed Bradley's gun was not involved in the shooting. Someone else killed him.

Although suspicion fell on Edward as the killer since the gun came from his collection, he was ultimately exonerated. One of his friends committed the crime.

Mary Mae then dropped another bombshell: Bradley was not her husband's son. When she was younger, she was attracted to a handsome young Naval officer named Edward Quartermaine and they had an affair. The child of that affair was Bradley. Her grandson, Justus, therefore, is

Edward Quartermaine's grandson and a cousin of Jason, A.J., and Ned Quartermaine.

Fortunately for Keesha, Mary Mae's other grandchild, she's not related to the Quartermaines; at least not by blood. But if things develop as expected with Jason, Keesha may become a Quartermaine by marriage.

Young Lovers

Although *General Hospital* respects its veteran characters, the soap has a history of introducing vibrant young people to the series. The early 1990s saw characters such as John "Jagger" Cates (Antonio Sabato, Jr.); Mike "Stone" Cates (Michael Sutton); Sonny Corinthos (Maurice Benard); Brenda Barrett (Vanessa Marcil); and Karen Wexler (Cari Shayne) coming on board.

Jagger and Karen brought their troubled family pasts to their relationship and found their friendship had turned to love. Karen was an excellent student and tried to persuade Jagger to complete his education. At one point, Brenda tampered with Karen's term paper, jeopardizing her educational future. But Brenda eventually confessed all and Karen left Port Charles for an out-of-town college. Jagger went with her. (Actually, Antonio Sabato, Jr. left to take the co-starring role in an NBC series, *Earth 2*. Karen was offered a role as the young Wynonna Judd in NBC's bioflick about Naomi and Wynonna.) Jagger and Karen hinted they might return to Port Charles one day.

Luke and Laura realized many of their problems with the nasties of Port Charles stemmed from Frank Smith, Luke's one-time mob boss employer, and would-be father-in-law. Frank never forgave Luke for running off with Laura instead of his daughter, and never forgave Laura for running off with a book that blew the whistle on him.

L&L traveled to Atlantic City to meet with Jennifer Smith, Frank's daughter. They hoped she could talk sense into her father. Laura wondered how Luke would react at seeing the slim beauty he almost married. She also wondered how Jennifer would react to seeing the man she once claimed she would love forever.

Laura's fears were soon dissolved by a healthy dose of reality. Jennifer was happily married. Playing Jennifer was series star Roseanne, and playing her husband was her then spouse, Tom Arnold. Luke and Laura also made a crossover appearance on *Roseanne*.

After Frank Smith's death, things didn't get much better. Damian Smith (Leigh J. McCloskey), son of Frank Smith, dreamed that his father came to him and gave him control of his enterprises. Sonny, however, seemed to be more involved in those "endeavors" than he liked to let on.

Indeed, Sonny's underworld connections created problems for Luke and Laura. His criminal cronies shot up their home while Laura hovered protectively over her infant.

When the smoke cleared, Laura looked at the rubble and said she'd had enough. She was taking her baby girl and leaving Luke, vowing not to return until things changed.

Was this to be the end of the Luke and Laura story? Would they go out, not with a whimper, but with the bang of semi automatic weapons? Well, let's not keep you in suspense. The two tentatively reconciled.

Lily's father in Puerto Rico had his own shady operation in the Commonwealth and at one time threatened to have Miguel killed (daddy didn't think he was good enough for his daughter) and Sonny rubbed out (the self-proclaimed inheritor of Frank Smith's business was a rival Mr. Rivera could do without). But when he learned he was dying, he wanted Sonny to take over his business.

Sonny had become involved with Brenda and tried to persuade her that he'd given up his mob ties. But when he learned she had been persuaded to wear a wire so that his business links could be traced, he was furious. He decided he would go to Puerto Rico with Lily. Poor Brenda was devastated and turned to Miguel for comfort.

The relationships among Brenda, Miguel, Lily, Ned, Lois, and Sonny were more than matters of friendship. They were all part of a recording business, and romantic complications could therefore affect commitments worth a lot of money. The story line provided an interesting insight into the way concerts and record deals are set.

Lucy Coe has been a dramatist's dream character. She's capable of creating mirth and mischief. And she elicits deep emotional reactions to the more serious turns in her life and in the lives of others.

Lucy's most recent love affair was with Dr. Kevin Collins, the identical twin brother of the late Dr. Ryan Chamberlain. Kevin, a psychoanalyst, was obviously falling for the lovely Lucy. But each time he tried to take her to bed, something made it impossible for him to follow through. He began to have nightmares about killing his late wife, Grace. These unresolved feelings of guilt were responsible for his inability to make love to Lucy. But under hypnosis, Kevin recalled that Grace was driving drunk the night she died, absolving him of blame in her death. Kevin and Lucy celebrated his breakthrough by making love.

Special Stories

Soap operas are fun. No one really believes that yesterday's infant can go from tot to teenager in just a few years, but if the object of entertainment is to have us suspend belief for a while, soaps do that especially well.

But the soaps are also dramas, and sometimes they tell stories that remind us that life presents challenges that may not have easy solutions. In recent years, *General Hospital* has presented at least four major stories in which individuals have to face such challenges; and, despite the support of others, they ultimately fight their battles alone.

Alcoholism

Alan Quartermaine, Jr. is a recovering alcoholic who has spent time in a rehabilitation facility. Sean Kanan, who plays A.J., says, "A.J. is tortured. A vulnerable guy who covers his pain with bravado. But his temper and his alcoholism are where he frequently stumbles."

A.J. feels the pressure of being who he is. His parents are super-achievers; Dad: Dr. Alan Quartermaine, holds a major position in *General Hospital,* both by dint of his medical skills and his family's considerable (financial) influence in the institution. His mother, Dr. Monica Quartermaine, is a well-respected heart surgeon. His grandfather, Edward, loves him, but respects his cousin Ned for his business acumen (make that, wheeling-dealing). The only people for whom he feels he doesn't have to be anyone but himself are his brother, Jason, and his grandmother, Lila. For A.J., the next drink is always just one emotional blow away.

The death of a child

Maxie Jones, the eldest daughter of Felicia and Frisco Jones, fell ill. She developed a serious heart defect which could prove fatal. The only thing that could save her was a heart transplant.

Felicia and Frisco both kept vigil over their daughter. In another area of the hospital, Tony found Damian kissing Bobbie. The jealous husband knocked Damian down. Bobbie railed at Tony, and as they argued, Laura's adopted sister, Amy Vining (Shel Kepler), told them their daughter, B.J., had just been brought into emergency: a drunk driver had hit her school bus. The child was found to be brain dead. Tony, the grieving father, made a decision: his child's heart would save the life of his brother's child. Monica performed the surgery, which she said was the most difficult thing she had ever done.

Felicia was grateful that her child would live, then fell to her knees in shock and horror when she learned that the donor was Maxie's beloved cousin, B.J.

225

Cancer

Monica Quartermaine learned she had breast cancer. The news was devastating. As a woman, she shrank from the idea of having a mastectomy. But as a doctor, she knew that for her, there was no choice.

The story of Monica's battle with cancer involved every aspect of a struggle that millions of women go through every year. She came through the surgery, but was reluctant to take the next step. She had to be coaxed to undergo post-surgical therapy. Part of it was physical: with the removal of so much tissue, the body has to learn to adapt to the loss. Part of it was psychological: she had to come to terms with her image of herself as a person, as a woman, and as a survivor.

Monica underwent chemotherapy. The scenes showing her reactions to this drastic, but often necessary, life-sustaining treatment were graphic. There were times when she almost gave up. Alan, who tried to be supportive, was sometimes thrown by her mood swings. Monica did stay with the chemotherapy, but she knew that wasn't enough. Besides working to heal her body, she also had to deal with healing her mind. She went to a retreat for people with cancer, and learned a lot about her disease and herself; she also learned about the reactions people have to death, which seems imminent to some and unthinkable to others.

(In the late 1960s, *GH* had a breast cancer story line that involved the character of Meg Baldwin, played by Patricia Breslin and Elizabeth Macrae. There was also a story on alcoholism involving the character of Iris Fairchild, played by Peggy McCay, who now plays Caroline Brady on *Days of Our Lives*.)

Monica returned with a friend named Paige whose illness was terminal. Monica persuaded the Quartermaines to take in Paige's daughter, Emily. The youngster came to Port Charles, but Monica realized Emily was not able to deal with her mother's death as well as she had hoped. She also seemed to reject Monica. Only Alan seemed able to reach her. Perhaps it was because Monica had had cancer and the girl was unwilling to let herself care for someone who might be taken from her. In any event, Monica's cancer showed how the disease affects not just the patient, but everyone in that patient's life.

AIDS

The fourth major story involved the character of Stone Cates (Michael Sutton) who learned that he was HIV-positive. As Sutton described his character, "He had been sexually active for much of his life but since he didn't do drugs, and was a heterosexual, it never occurred to him that he'd be infected with HIV."

By this time, Stone and Robin Scorpio had fallen in love. They became intimate. But she insisted, and he agreed, that he would wear a condom each time they made love. Just once, they let passion overrule their senses and had sex without protection.

Stone had been feeling ill for months. Robin persuaded him to have a physical. When Alan told him the news, Stone retreated into himself and hoped he could keep this terrible thing secret. When he finally broke the news to Robin, she was overwhelmed, but vowed to stay with him. Robin was advised to have an HIV test, and to everyone's relief, it came out negative. However, she had to be tested again to be certain the virus had not been transmitted to her.

Most of the soaps have dealt with AIDS. But none has dealt with it as *General Hospital* chose to tell the story. Instead of telescoping time, the audience shares Stone's experience day by day. Head writer Claire Labine and executive producer Wendy Riche report they are being advised by doctors who work closely with AIDS patients. Stone reflects the emotional and physical reactions that happen to real people with AIDS.

In 1993, the author interviewed John Beradino (Dr. Steve Hardy) for a thirtieth anniversary story on *General Hospital*. He spoke about the story lines that were played out over three decades. "We've done a lot of good things," he said. " But what I'd really like to see us do at some point is a really good story about AIDS." Reminded that most soaps had done such stories, Beradino said, "That's true. But since our show revolves around a hospital, I feel we could do something more...." "Beradino, who thirty years earlier told his cast mates that the show would succeed in spite of its early dim ratings, proved, once again, to be right in his prognosis.

The Founding Family

Unlike most soaps that debut with core families, *General Hospital* went on air with unrelated characters except for Jessie and Phil Brewer, who were married. They were two-thirds of the three most important characters — the third being Steve Hardy — who would go on to have significant story lines in upcoming years. Other characters who would soon become part of their lives were discussed in the preceding Port Charles Chronicles.

Dr. Steve Hardy, played by John Beradino, is the adoptive father of Tom Hardy, Jr., son of Steve's wife, Audrey, and the late Tom Baldwin; the father of Jeff Webber; grandfather of Steven Lars Webber and of Tommy Hardy, son of Tom and Simone Hardy.

Dr. Hardy established a tradition of reading the Christmas story to his young patients every Christmas. The event has become one of daytime's most anticipated holiday treats.

Nurse Jessie Brewer, played by the late Emily McLaughlin. Jessie, a member of the original cast, won praise from real nurses for her performance as the dedicated Nurse Brewer. She once told the author, "One of the greatest days of my life was to be invited to speak at a graduation ceremony for young nurses, and being given one of their caps."

227

Breaking A Taboo

One of the nurses, Lucille March, Audrey's sister, played by radio soap star Lucille Wall, was to be married for the first time; she admitted to being a virgin, and lamented that on this wonderful day she wouldn't be able to wear white — because she was middle-aged — while so many women who no longer had the "right" to do so, did so. Jessie Brewer encouraged Lucille to get the gown and veil of her girlhood dreams and walk down that aisle — and never mind who gapes and gasps.

Lucille did — and the ratings soared that day.

Jessie was married several times, but none of her marriages brought her happiness. In the early 1980s, Jessie's friendship with hospital administrator, Dan Rooney (played by Frank Maxwell) went to another level. She found herself drawn to him, but refused to have an affair with him and, eventually, he found someone else.

Emily McLaughlin wasn't happy about the way her character was being written at this time: "I feel some of the writers may think the viewers wouldn't like to see people of Jessie's and Dan's age get involved in a love affair. I don't agree: I think the viewers would be happy for both of them. I also feel they aren't giving Jessie enough credit for being a survivor. I believe Jessie's unfortunate experiences with relationships would not keep her from finding a new love in her life. Jessie is a woman who believes in love...."

Emily, who was divorced from the late Robert Lansing (one son), married actor Jeffrey Hunter, who starred as Jesus in *King of Kings* and also starred in the first episode of *Star Trek*. Hunter died early in their marriage. Emily told the author, "I was crushed by his death, but I'm comforted that while we had a short time together, the time we had was wonderful...."

Dr. Phillip Brewer, played by Roy Thinnes, was one of soapdom's classic cads. The husband of Jessie Brewer, who worked to put him through medical school, he was involved with many women before he was finally killed by a woman named Augusta McLeod, who said he threatened to kill her unborn baby.

Fans of the syndicated series *Mystery Science Theatre 3000* — who usually watch films such as *Plan 9 from Outer Space, Attack of the Killer Tomatoes, Attack of the 50 Foot Woman, Hercules and the Maidens from Mars* (not the flick's real name, but you get the picture) — were surprised when the series aired scenes from *GH*'s early days, showing Phil Brewer seducing other women while Jessie tried to put up a brave front. Ironically, Allison Hayes, who played the *50 Foot Woman*, was in the original *GH* cast, and Roy Thinnes would become the star of a sci-fi cult classic, *The Invaders*.

Closeups: Current Cast and Characters

Actor: Rachel Ames

Birthplace: Portland, Oregon
Birthdate: November 2

Rachel is the daughter of two actors, Dorothy Adams, and the late Byron Foulger. She made her professional debut with her parents in the play, *One Foot In Heaven,* and went on to accumulate impressive theater credits. In 1992, she joined with *General Hospital* cast mates Peter Hansen (Lee Baldwin) and Susan Brown (Dr. Gail Baldwin) in co-producing and co-starring in a production of *Pieces of Time.*

Ames was under contract to Paramount Pictures and a member of their "Golden Circle" of talented young performers. She made her film debut in *When Worlds Collide,* and also co-starred in *Daddy's Gone A-Hunting.*

Prior to joining *GH* on February 23, 1964, Rachel guest starred on each major series at least once per season.

Rachel and actor Barry Cahill (formerly on *The Young and the Restless* and *For Better or Worse)* were married in 1968. They have a daughter and a granddaughter.

Character: Audrey March Baldwin Hardy
See Port Charles Chronicles.

Actor: Senait Ashenafi

Birthplace: Addis Ababa, Ethiopia
Birthdate: March 10

Senait's family moved from Ethiopia to the United States where she was able to pursue her interest in music and theater at Florida State University. She began working with the jazz band, Silk.

In Los Angeles, Senait continued to develop her career as a singer. A talented dancer and a gifted model, she found work in television commercials and music videos, including Michael Jackson's *Remember the Time.* She appeared over twenty times as a model on *The Price Is Right.* Her previous soap was *Generations.*

Senait, whose name means "The Peaceful One," continues to study dance and music.

Character: Keesha Ward

Keesha came to Port Charles just when her grandmother, Mary Mae, and her cousin, Justus, were going through several family crises. She met Jason Quartermaine, and the look he gave her was the look every young woman hopes to see in the eyes of that (maybe) very special man.

While Keesha's cousin, Justus, learned he was Jason's cousin as well (they both have Edward Quartermaine as their grandfather), Keesha's potential for joining PC's most prominent family probably lies in ultimately marrying Jason.

Actor: Matthew Ashford

Birthplace: Davenport, Iowa

Matt, who spent his younger years both in Davenport, Iowa and Fairfax, Virginia, attended North Carolina School of Arts in Winston-Salem, N.C. He went on to perform with Ragamuffin Magic & Mime Company in Myrtle Beach, S.C.

The sound of applause reinforced Ashford's goal of becoming an actor. Not that he didn't consider mime acting. As he once told the author, "I think working in mime may be the most difficult acting I'll ever do."

Ashford came to New York and was soon cast as Cagney McCleary on *Search for Tomorrow.* He later played Drew Ralson on *One Life to Live* before joining *Days of Our Lives* as Jack Devereaux.

Ashford assumed the role of Dr. Tom Hardy on *General Hospital* in early 1995.

He and Christina Saffran were married in 1987.

Character: Dr. Tom Hardy

Tom Hardy began life as Tom Baldwin, Jr. He was the son of lawyer Dr. Tom Baldwin and Audrey March Baldwin. She later married her first love, Dr. Steve Hardy. After Tom's death, Steve adopted his stepson.

Scotty Baldwin, Laura Spencer's former husband, is Tom's cousin. He was adopted by Tom's uncle, Lee Baldwin (Peter Hansen) after the death of his mother, Meg.

Tom's adoptive brother is Dr. Jeff Webber (Richard Dean Anderson), Steve Hardy's son.

Tom and his wife, Simone, also a doctor, have a son. Their marriage has been rocky for years. Most recently, Tom returned from a stint with a Somalian relief agency to find Simone being wooed by Justus Ward.

Will Tom and Simone finally break up? Or will these two doctors who have overcome so many problems in their past, including racial prejudice (Simone's African-American parents didn't approve of her marrying a Caucasian) manage to keep their marriage going?

Stay tuned.

Actor: Maurice Benard

Birthplace: San Francisco, California
Birthdate: March 1

Maurice was first introduced to daytime audiences as Nico Kelly in *All My Children*. He was a fan favorite from his first appearance.

After leaving *AMC,* he moved to Los Angeles where he was cast in several guest-starring roles on various nighttime shows. He won the coveted role as Desi Arnaz in the film, *Lucy & Desi: Before the Laughter* opposite former *Edge of Night* star Frances Fisher as Lucille Ball.

He joined *General Hospital* as Sonny Corinthos in August 1993.

Benard's parents were from Nicaragua and San Salvador. He can also trace his roots to France. Maurice and his wife, Paula, share their home with their child, their four dogs, and their cat. Maurice relaxes by working out with the martial arts.

Character: Sonny Corinthos

Sonny was raised in a milieu of crime and criminals. He fell in love with Brenda, and promised her he would cut his ties to the mob. But his promises were more easily spoken than kept.

Sonny assumed control of Frank Smith's "business" after the mob boss died. This did not please Frank's son, Damian, who insisted his father meant for him to inherit the mantle. But it did find favor with Lily's (Lilly Melgar) father, Rivera, who wanted him to inherit his Puerto Rican mob operations.

Meanwhile, Sonny must deal with his feelings for Brenda and for Lily, and the fact that his friend, Stone, is HIV positive. He also must deal with the fact that his criminal ties have hurt his friends, Luke and Laura. Whatever choices Sonny makes about his future will affect the future of many other people.

231

Actor: John Beradino

Birthplace: Los Angeles, California
Birthdate: May 1

John Beradino was a member of the "Our Gang" comedy movies. When he was nine, he was given some baseball equipment by his parents. Over the next six years, he became proficient enough at the game to play semi-pro ball on weekends. During the week, Beradino punted and grunted with his high school football team, which eventually led to a football scholarship at the University of Southern California.

In 1939, Beradino was picked for the St. Louis Browns baseball team. When World War II broke out, he traded in his Browns cap for Navy blue and served Uncle Sam for four years. He returned to St. Louis and then was traded to the Cleveland Indians, and wound up with a 1948 World Series ring.

He left baseball in 1953 and returned to acting. After a decade of feature roles on prime-time series, he joined the original cast of *General Hospital* in 1963. Thirty years later, on April 1, 1993, John Beradino was honored with a star on the Hollywood Walk of Fame. The kid who once dreamed of being in the Baseball Hall of Fame in Cooperstown, New York, has been hitting grand slams both as a performer and a great human being.

John and his wife, Marjorie Binder, have two children, Katherine Ann and John Anthony.

Character: Dr. Steve Hardy

See Port Charles Chronicles and Founding Families.

Actor: Steve Burton

Birthplace: Indianapolis, Indiana
Birthdate: June 28

Although raised and largely schooled in the midwest, Steve moved to California with his father in time to be graduated from Beverly Hills High School. He describes his experience in the 90210 postal zone as "a world apart from the environment I was accustomed to." Beverly Hills High gave him the opportunity to study drama and join their acclaimed "Theatre 40."

Steve had a successful career in commercials and another successful run (three years) as Chris Fuller in the syndicated comedy series, *Out of this World.* His first daytime role was as Harris Michael on *Days of Our Lives.*

Steve Burton is an all-around athlete. His favorite activity is surfing.

Character: Jason Quartermaine

The late Elsa Lanchester, the English actor who was married to Charles Laughton, was once asked if it bothered her that her parents never married and that she was a "love child." Ms. Lancaster replied, "Indeed, I'm proud of the fact that I'm the child of people who loved each other."

Jason Quartermaine is the "love child" of Alan Quartermaine and his former mistress, the late Susan Moore (played by Gail Rae Carlson). He was accepted as an infant by Alan's wife, Monica, who raised him with the same love she showed for her own son, Alan, Jr. Steve Burton, who plays Jason, says, "He never wanted an easy ride, and he never wanted something he didn't work for."

Jason has a family tie to Steve Hardy: his mother, Susan Moore, was a cousin of Heather Grant Webber (Robin Mattson), wife of Steve Hardy's son, Jeff Webber (Richard Dean Anderson). Their son, Steven Lars, is Steve's grandson and Jason's second cousin.

And speaking of cousins, Jason and Keesha Ward, the cousin of his cousin Justus Ward, may soon provide a link between the Quartermaines and another side of the Ward family.

Actor: Rosalind Cash

Birthplace: Atlantic City, New Jersey
Birthdate: December 31

Rosalind knew from childhood that she wanted to be a performer. After attending the City College of New York, she worked on road shows. Her first big break was in the Broadway play, *A Raisin in the Sun*. After that, the offers never stopped coming.

Among her many credits are feature roles in films such as *Buckaroo Banzai, Amazing Grace, The Omega Man*, and *Uptown Saturday Night*.

Cash's television credits include roles on *China Beach, thirtysomething, Cagney & Lacey, Hill Street Blues* and *The Mary Tyler Moore Show*.

Character: Mary Mae Ward

Mary Mae Ward was a woman of many secrets when we first met her in Port Charles on January 7 1994. Rosalind Cash, who plays the African-American matriarch, says, "Mary Mae is a survivor. Although most of her wars have been internal, she has weathered them all...."

Mary Mae endured the agony of believing that her son, Bradley Ward, had committed suicide, and hid his body to avoid anyone learning about it. Later, when it was discovered that he had been murdered, Mary Mae was faced with another crisis of the heart: the man she once loved, Edward Quartermaine, was accused of killing him. It was time for Mary Mae to break her silence. She revealed that Bradley was not the son of her husband, but rather Edward's child through that brief wartime romance. Edward was cleared of the charge (his friend, Jack Boland, was Bradley's killer).

Mary Mae now sings in Luke's nightclub and it wouldn't surprise anyone if she didn't soon find romance again. After all, as Rosalind Cash says, "[S]he continues to have a great capacity to love...."

233

Wallace Kurth and Leslie Charleson.

Actor: Leslie Charleson

Birthplace: Kansas City, Missouri
Birthdate: February 22

Leslie Charleson was voted Outstanding Theatre Arts Student by her graduating classmates in Bennett College in Millbrook, New York. She soon proved they knew what they were doing when she quickly landed a role in the daytime drama, *A Flame in the Wind* (which was later changed to *A Time for Us*).

Leslie's next daytime series was as Iris Donelly Garrison in *Love Is A Many Splendored Thing* which earned her the first of several Emmy Award nominations. Charleson recalls one story line in which she was blind, pregnant, and dying. "And that was all at once," she said.

Charleson continued her drama studies with Uta Hagen at the Herbert Berghof Studio in New York. When she moved to Hollywood, she attended Joan Darling's classes. She worked on a number of prime-time series, including *Adam 12, Kung Fu, The Streets of San Francisco, Wild Wild West,* and *Baa Baa Black Sheep.* She recently did a television movie with Deidre Hall (Marlena, *Days of Our Lives*) called *Woman on the Ledge.*

Leslie co-starred with George C. Scott in the acclaimed feature film, *Day of the Dolphin,* under Mike Nichols' direction.

Leslie Charleson has been an active fund raiser and celebrity chairperson for the Cystic Fibrosis Foundation since 1982. She has an Andalusian horse, Andarra, which she rides in horse shows.

Character: Dr. Monica Bard Webber Quartermaine

Monica Bard was an intern at *General Hospital* when she fell in love with Rick Webber (Chris Robinson). But he left her, and she married his brother, Jeff (Richard Dean Anderson), who had an affair with Heather Grant (Robin Mattson) and became the father of a little boy named Steven Lars.

After her divorce from Jeff, Monica hoped to be reunited with Rick, whom she never stopped loving. But he married Dr. Lesley Williams after her husband died. Monica schemed to break them up, but when she learned she had caused Lesley to have a miscarriage, she vowed to leave them alone.

Monica married the wealthy but insecure Dr. Alan Quartermaine. Rick, meanwhile, had been drawn back to Monica when Lesley's frigidity (brought on by her problems with her daughter, Laura — see Chronicles) caused her to reject him. They had a brief affair and Monica became pregnant. She believed Rick was the baby's father. She and Lesley were trapped alone in a cabin during a blizzard when she went into labor. Lesley delivered the baby. A delirious Monica cried out that it was Rick's.

Monica then tried to divorce Alan. Unwilling to let anyone know that he couldn't keep his wife, Alan refused to let her go. He threatened to take the child from her if she tried to leave him. Sophisticated blood tests proved the child was Alan's, not Rick's. Hoping to marry Rick someday, Monica kept the test results from him, but he eventually learned the truth.

Monica raised Jason, Alan's son with Susan Moore, with her own son, Alan, Jr. Monica later met Dawn, the daughter she had had and given up for adoption when she was a medical student. Dawn came to Port Charles and, for a while, competed with her mother for the same lover, Ned Ashton, son of Monica's sister-in-law, Tracy Quartermaine. More recently, Monica has been fighting a (so far) winning battle with breast cancer.

Actor: Stuart Damon

Birthplace: Brooklyn, New York
Birthdate: February 5

Stuart Damon always wanted to be a performer. At age eleven, he played the Cowardly Lion in a production of *The Wizard of Oz*. He later starred in musical comedies at a summer camp in Connecticut. There was no doubt the young Damon had talent. But his Russian immigrant parents thought he should enter a nice, secure profession, like the law.

Damon obtained a B.A. in psychology from Brandeis University, and seriously considered going to law school. But he was drawn back to the theater world with roles in summer stock productions. After some fifty musicals in stock and on the road, he landed his first Broadway role in the chorus line of *Irma La Douce*. One of his chorus mates was another guy from Brooklyn named Elliot Gould.

Stuart went on to become a Broadway star. He was asked to come to Hollywood to co-star with Lesley Ann Warren in the acclaimed television production of *Cinderella*. That role won him worldwide attention. He was then offered the lead in a new English television series, *The Champions*. Stuart and his English-born wife, actor, Deirdre Ottewill-Damon, and their daughter, Jennifer, moved to England where, for the next twelve years, he worked both in British television and London's West End (the equivalent of New York's Broadway).

Stuart and his family returned to the States in 1977 when he was signed by *General Hospital* to play the role of Dr. Alan Quartermaine.

Damon continues to do television and feature films. In 1982, he and Deirdre worked together for the first time in over ten years when they co-starred in a San Diego production of *Camelot*. He was King Arthur; she was Guinevere. He described the experience as romantic.

Stuart Damon's son, Christopher, has been diabetic since childhood. Stuart has been active with the Juvenile Diabetes Foundation for years, helping to raise funds for the research that he believes will one day lead to a cure.

Character: Dr. Alan Quartermaine

Although Alan Quartermaine has had many liaisons during his marriage to Monica Quartermaine, he likes to think of himself as a good husband whose occasional lapses from marital fidelity are her fault. He had a son, Jason, during his affair with Susan Moore. He's had affairs with Lucy Coe (whom he briefly married) and Charity Gatlin, who left him for his half-brother, Jimmy Lee Holt.

When Alan thought Monica's infant son was actually the child of Rick Webber, he fantasized about ways to punish his errant wife. If he had had a mustache, he would have twirled it in true villain-fashion. But while Alan seemed bent on revenge, viewers could see that he loved this child regardless of who its father was. Of course, when blood tests proved he was the daddy, it was one of the great days of his life.

Alan has always felt he was a pale shadow of his father, Edward Quartermaine. His sister, Tracy, was much more the child of their father. And, in many ways, so was Jimmy Lee, who was not above putting tenants into unsafe properties for a profit. Whenever Alan tries to be ruthless, he doesn't really succeed at it. In spite of himself, he's a pretty nice guy. (Although he did accidentally kill Ray in self-defense, which was followed by a lengthy cover-up.)

In mid-1995, the strains that were put on his marriage by Monica's breast cancer seemed to be creating a new distance in their relationship. All of Alan's previous liaisons had begun when Alan turned to a sympathetic woman for comfort whenever things went awry with Monica. This time, he and Bobbie (Jackie Zeman), who was having marital problems with Dr. Anthony Jones (Brad Maule), comforted each other.

Will this lead to a new romantic relationship? Stay tuned.

Actor: Mary Beth Evans

Birthplace: Pasadena, California
Birthdate: March 7

Mary Beth's fourth-grade classmates were sure she was going to be an actor because she loved doing school plays. They were right. When she was fourteen, she took a part-time job in a fast-food restaurant to earn money for acting classes. After she was graduated from Huntington Beach High School, she enrolled in the South Coast Repertory Conservatory, and went on to do a number of plays.

Before joining *General Hospital*, she guest-starred in a number of prime-time series including *Murder, She Wrote, Crime & Punishment, Father Murphy,* and *Toy Soldiers.* She also appeared in the syndicated soap, *Rituals,* and played Kayla Brady on *Days of Our Lives.*

Mary Beth and her husband, Dr. Michael Schwartz, have three children: Danny, Katie, and Matthew.

Character: Katherine Bell

Katherine Bell tries hard to be tough, but usually winds up being tough out of luck.

She came to Port Charles claiming to be a cousin of the late Dominique Baldwin, Scotty Baldwin's wife; she almost immediately started insinuating herself into his life, much to the chagrin of Lucy Coe, who had her own plans for Mr. Baldwin.

Katherine later manipulated Ned Ashton into marrying her by threatening to reveal information that could link the Quartermaines to a murder. She happily called herself Mrs. Ashton, until she learned he had previously married Lois Cerullo. This did not elate Kate at all. She insisted Lois divorce Ned. Lois said no. Katherine threatened dire doings, and then collapsed. It turned out that she was poisoned. When she came out of her coma, she insisted a Quartermaine did it. But evidence pointed more and more to Katherine as the culprit.

Meanwhile, Katherine maintained a business relationship with Damian Smith (Leigh J. McCloskey), son of the notorious mob boss, Frank Smith. Together, they tried to undermine the foundation A.J. headed: and performed other nasty deeds in tandem.

Luke discovered that Katherine and Damian may have worked together to help launder Frank Smith's mob money through the perfume company Deception.

In mid-1995, Katherine found herself attracted to Mac Scorpio (John J. York). Will Katherine find love with Mac, or will she learn how painful a Scorpio sting can be?

237

Actor: Genie Francis

Birthplace: Englewood, New Jersey
Birthdate: May 26

Few young actors have a chance to create as many roles as Genie Francis. Among them are Ceara Connor, an incest survivor on *All My Children,* Tyger Hayes in both the movie and the series, *Bare Essence,* Brett Main in *North and South, Books I and II,* and Diane Colville in *Days of Our Lives.*

But she is best known for a role she inherited and then made very much her own. The first Laura was Stacey Baldwin, who played the role from 1975 to 1976. Genie assumed the role in 1976 and played it until 1981. She returned briefly in 1983, then again in 1984. Nine years later, Genie, along with her long-time co-star, Anthony Geary, returned in October 1993.

Genie's credits include guest starring roles as Angela Lansbury's niece in *Murder, She Wrote,* and in a television movie with the late Raymond Burr, *Perry Mason and the Case of the Killer Kiss.* She made her New York stage debut in *Baby Dance.*

Genie met her husband, actor/director Jonathan Frakes (*Star Trek: The Next Generation*) when they co-starred in *North and South.* They plan to work together in films and have already done some theater in tandem. Their son is named for Genie's late father, character actor Ivor Francis. The Frakes-Francis family also includes two stray cats, Bix and Alfred, and their goldfish, Thelonius.

Character: Laura Williams Vining Baldwin Spencer Cassadine Spencer
See Port Charles Chronicles.

Actor: Anthony Geary

Birthplace: Coalville, Utah
Birthdate: May 29

Anthony Geary was a Presidential Award Scholar in theater at the University of Utah. Jack Albertson was in the audience during a school production and cast him in a production of *The Subject Was Roses* which starred Albertson and Martha Scott. (Martin Sheen became a star when he appeared in the original Broadway production of the play.) The production toured Hawaii, and then came to Los Angeles where Tony decided to stay and pursue a career in musical theater. One of his early career highlights was appearing with Sid Caesar and Imogene Coca in a Las Vegas production of *Your Show of Shows.*

Some years after working with Sid Caesar, Tony played Caesar — as in Octavious Caesar — in a PBS/BBC production of Shakespeare's Antony and Cleopatra, co-starring Lynn Redgrave and Timothy Dalton.

Tony has chalked up roles in over fifty stage productions, ranging from Ibsen to Shakespeare, Shaw, Tennessee Williams, and others.

He has a long list of guest-starring roles on prime-time, including *The Streets of San Francisco, All in the Family, The Six Million Dollar Man,* and *Murder, She Wrote.* His feature film credits include *The Disorderlies, Johnny Got His Gun, You Can't Hurry Love,* and *Night of the Warrior.* On television, his movies including *Perry Mason* and *the Case of the Murdered Madam, Do You Know the Muffin Man,* and *Sins of the Past.*

Before *General Hospital,* Tony had roles in the daytime series, *Bright Promise.* (Gloria Monty was the director and when she moved to *GH* later on, she brought three of her brightest stars from *Bright Promise* with her: David Lewis, the original Edward Quartermaine; Susan Brown, who played Dr. Gail Adamson Baldwin; and Anthony Geary.)

He also appeared in *The Young and the Restless* as George Curtis, the man who raped Chris Brook.

Tony Geary won a Cindy Award for the drama, *Sound of Sunshine, Sound of Rain,* a children's play for Public Radio. He also teaches improvisation and story-theater techniques. And when he has time, he likes to scuba dive.

Character: Luke Spencer
See Port Charles Chronicles.

Actor: Lynn Herring
Birthplace: Enid, Oklahoma
Birthdate: September 22

When Lynn Herring joined *General Hospital* in 1986, it was supposed to be for a short run; just long enough for the character, Lucy Coe, to bridge a story line. But ten years later (and with a brief time-out for a stint on *Days of Our Lives,*) both Lynn and Lucy remain popular with the fans.

As a child in an air force family, Lynn moved around the country frequently. She attended fifteen primary schools and four high schools. She was graduated from Woodson High in Fairfax, Virginia, and from Louisiana State University with a degree in psychology. (She counts Jennings, Louisiana as her home base since most of her relatives live there now.) She was accepted for graduate work by the University of Southern California, UCLA, and Loyola-Marymount. But she chose to go to New York to pursue an acting career and was accepted to study at the Actors Company.

239

When she returned to Los Angeles, she enrolled at Loyola-Marymount and earned credits towards what she called "half a Master's degree." She also began accumulating credits with roles on episodic television.

In 1986, she turned up for a reading for the role of Lucy Coe in *General Hospital*. The casting director thought she was too attractive for the Lucy they had in mind. But executive producer Gloria Monty liked the way Lynn injected humor into her reading and she got the part.

Lynn is married to Wayne Northrop, formerly Roman Brady on *Days of Our Lives*. When she was on *Days*, she told the author that she looked forward to sharing a scene with her husband, "But it never happened. Sometimes we weren't even in the studio on the same day."

Lynn and Wayne have two sons, Hank and Grady.

Character: Lucy Coe

If Lucy Coe had to be summed up in a description of just two words, it might be something like: she tries.

Lucy skimmed some money that didn't belong to her. A man named Ted Holmes learned about it, and was later murdered. Lucy was suspected of killing him. Jake Meyer (Sam Beherens) believed her claim of innocence, and agreed to be her lawyer. The next thing Bobbie Spencer Meyer knew, Lucy was moving in on her marriage. Or, at least, she tried to.

Lucy skipped town and Jake followed in hopes of bringing her back before she made herself look guilty. The two were trapped in a storm. As the elements railed, their passions rose and they made love.

Lucy was cleared of the murder when the real culprit was unmasked. Meanwhile, Lucy learned she was pregnant. The news was a shock to Jake, but Bobbie, who couldn't have children, saw it as a blessing in disguise. She and Jake would adopt Lucy's child. Unfortunately, Lucy miscarried.

After the death of Tanya Jones, Tony Jones asked Lucy to care for his young daughter, B.J. Lucy agreed. She moved into his place and they became lovers. But although he told her he could never love her, he agreed to marry her.

Later, Lucy's Aunt Charlene became Tony's housekeeper. She brought along her son, Lucy's cousin, Colton Shore, who would later become the lover of several of Port Charles' lovely ladies.

Lucy's most recent love affair has been with Dr. Kevin Chamberlain. She's also been busy as an executive with the Deception perfume company. She discovered that her once and apparently permanent nemesis, Katherine, had been "watering" the perfume with cheap ingredients.

Damian Smith, son of the notorious crime boss, Frank Smith, and Katherine's sometime bedfellow and frequent partner in crime, had Lucy believing in the powers of a television psychic for nefarious reasons of his own. But his plans may take a surprise twist because, when it comes to Lucy Coe, the best made plans often go haywire.

Actor: John Ingle

When David Lewis decided to retire from the role of Edward Quartermaine after some two decades of playing Port Charles's testy tycoon, his good friend, John Ingle, stepped into the role. "I am," says the famous actor and acting teacher, "the luckiest actor in town. I'm having a wonderful time playing this wonderful character and I hope to play him for as long as it's supposed to be."

Ingle has been a part of the wonderful world of actors and acting for much of his life. But it's only within the last fifteen years or so that he's been an actual "working actor" — that means someone who can make a living at it. For some thirty years prior — he established a reputation as one of Hollywood's finest acting teachers. Some of his students include Swoozie Kurtz, Julie Kavner, Mike Farrell, Barbara Hershey, Meredith Baxter, Stefanie Powers, Nicholas Cage, and Richard Dreyfuss.

Ingle established the Performing Arts Departments in both Beverly Hills and Hollyood High Schools. "I loved teaching," Ingle said. "I come from a family of teachers and we all grew up appreciating the importance of education...."

John decided to do what he so brilliantly taught for so many years, when a friend suggested he go out for commercials. He got several. "This made me feel that I might, somehow, have a future in this business," he said with a chuckle.

He was cast in films such as *Death Becomes Her* with Meryl Streep and Goldie Hawn, *Heathers,* and recently appeared in *Batman Forever.* He did the prime-time soap circuit from *Dallas* to *Beverly Hills 90210* (ironically, the fictional postal zone where he actually taught school for so long). "I was cast mostly as judges or priests. I used to say, my characters judge them, and lecture to them, but rarely talk to them."

John Ingle, Nancy Lee Grahn (formerly Julia, Santa Barbara), and Matt Ashford.

241

A dog lover in real life, he was delighted to share scenes with Foster, the dog that belongs to Lucky Spencer, Luke's son, and Annabelle, the Quartermaine's canine, and Annabelle's pup. "I know all about the hazards of actors working with animals and children," he told the author (they steal scenes!), "but I feel privileged to work with everyone on this show."

John Ingle and his wife of forty-two years plus, have five daughters and nine grandchildren, all of whom are proud that John is a soap star.

Character: Edward Quartermaine

Husband of Lila Quartermaine; father of Alan and Tracy Quartermaine, Jimmy Lee Holt, and the late Bradley Ward. Grandfather of Alan, Jr., (A.J.), Jason Q., Ned Ashton, Justus Ward, and Dillon Albert Quartermaine Hornsby, Tracy's son with Paul.

One of the most colorful characters in soap opera, Edward Quartermaine has been, and probably always will be, a man of many colors. Although he can be a bulldog in business, he can also be a pussycat with his family.

No one knows him better than his loving wife, Lila, who has stood with him during his many triumphs and fiascos.

When the beautiful Mary Mae Ward revealed he was her handsome Naval officer lover during World War II, he also learned, for the first time, that he was the father of her late son, Bradley Ward, and the grandfather of Bradley's son, Justus.

Edward has been accused of many things, including murder, but there's one thing he has never been charged with, and that's not loving his family enough. Even though he has railed at his daughter Tracy for her manipulations that so often cause grief to others, she is still his little girl. If only she would learn to direct all that machinating talent against business rivals instead of family members.

See Port Charles Chronicles for more on Edward Quartermaine.

Actor: Jonathan Jackson
Birthplace: Orlando, Florida
Birthdate: May 11

Jonathan's older brother, Richard, is also an actor. Jonathan recently made his first feature in the comedy, *Camp Nowhere*. He, his brother, sister, and mother, have homes in Los Angeles and Washington State, where his dad lives. Jonathan won an Emmy in 1995 for best younger actor, appropriately presented by his on-screen parents, Genie Francis and Tony Geary.

Character: Lucky Spencer

Lucky is the son of Luke and Laura Spencer and brother of Lesley Lu. His dog, Foster, completes the family circle.

Actor: Sean Kanan

Birthplace: Cleveland, Ohio
Birthdate: November 2

Sean was raised in Newcastle, Pennsylvania. His parents encouraged him to follow his various interests. He enjoyed writing; he liked acting in school productions; he started studying karate and kick boxing when he was just thirteen.

He majored in political science at UCLA. Still interested in acting, he went to an open call for director John Avildsen's new feature film, *Karate Kid.* The martial arts skills he developed as a youngster stood him in good stead. He got the co-starring role opposite Ralph Macchio.

Other credits include the feature, *Rich Girl,* and the television film, *Perry Mason's The Case of the Killer Kiss,* which co-starred his *General Hospital* cast mates, Stuart Damon and Genie Francis.

Sean has written two screenplays; one of them, *Beyond the Edge* will star Sean Kanan.

Character: A.J. (Alan, Jr.) Quartermaine

A.J. spent time in a rehabilitation facility and returned to Port Charles as a recovering alcoholic. His parents, Monica and Alan, are aware of how desperate he is to find his own way within a family that sometimes seems to overwhelm him.

A.J. was put in charge of an important foundation, but he's been undermined by adversaries, including Katherine and Damian. Will A.J. be able to stand up to the pressures of trying to be his own person, and will he be able to stay sober? As Sean Kanan told the author: "A.J. has some great qualities he's still unaware of...." Let's hope he finds them in time.

Actor: Wallace Kurth

Birthplace: Billings, Montana
Birthdate: July 31

Wallace Kurth grew up loving music and playing music (mostly piano and guitar) and was absolutely certain that he'd make music his life and his living. Very early in his performing career, he translated his musical talents to musical theater, and added song writing to his complement of achievements. He has appeared in regional productions, the Kennedy Center, and

the Mecca of America's Musical Theater — Broadway. He played the Pirate King in *The Pirates of Penzance* and has some very nice reviews from the tough New York Critics to show for his efforts. And, of course, he does his own singing and accompaniment on *General Hospital* whenever the script calls for his character, Ned Ashton (or his character's previous alter ego, still his stage persona, Eddie Maine), to do the vocals and the riffs.

Kurth's drama credits include a television movie of the week, *Miracle in Caulfield, USA,* and the cable chiller, *The Final Embrace.* Kurth and his musical partner, Christian Taylor, perform throughout Southern California.

Wally Kurth doesn't mind the frantic pace of doing a soap, especially one that gives Ned Ashton so many different shadings from script to script. "Working on *General Hospital* is the best of both worlds. It affords me the opportunity to practice my acting skills with an entirely new script each day, and also provides the time to enjoy music and writing." *GH* also is responsible for his off-screen happiness with co-star Rena Sofer.

Kurth's former soap role was as Justin Kiriakis, Victor's nephew, on *Days of Our Lives.*

Character: Ned Ashton

He was born with the proverbial silver spoon in his mouth, but soon made plans to substitute it for gold, even if it meant pulling one out of someone else's mouth. The son of Tracy Quartermaine (Jane Elliot) and one of her several former husbands, Lord Ashton, Ned is the apple of his grandfather, Edward Quartermaine's eye. Like granddad, Ned sees business as an arena where the aim of the game is always to beat the other guy by fair means or foul.

For most of his life, Ned was his mother's only child. She doted on him, and encouraged him to be the man his grandfather is. (Or, more to the point, to be more like her.) But now, Ned has a half-sibling named Dillon Albert Quartermaine Hornsby, born to Tracy and another one of her former husbands, Paul Hornsby. Again, ironically, Tracy helped break up Ned's marriage to Jenny Eckert before causing her own marriage to collapse. Ned then lost Jenny to Paul. Meanwhile, Tracy took her baby and left town.

Ned and his aunt Monica, Alan's wife, were lovers. They met when she was at a spa and he was the Spa Stud. They made love and decided they wanted more than a one-day roll in the hayloft. They continued their affair when they got back to Port Charles. They later learned they were related by marriage, and although the affair cooled, it took a long time for Ned to get Tracy to cool her heated ire.

Currently, Ned is wed to Lois Cerullo, the bright-eyed Brooklyn-born beauty he first wooed as Eddie Maine. How long will they stay married? Maybe long enough for Dillon Albert Quartermaine Hornsby to become a rival for her affections. He may have been an infant just a couple of years ago, but in the way soaps have of telescoping time, it probably won't be too long before Ned is in competition with his sibling.

For more about Ned Ashton, see Port Charles Chronicles.

Actor: Anna Lee

Birthplace: Ightham, Kent, England
Birthdate: January 2, 1913

Born Joan Boniface Winnifrith, the daughter of the Rector of St. Peter's Church in Ightham, Joan was not expected to choose a life in the theater. But she loved plays and loved to put on performances for her friends. At seventeen, Joan went to London to study at the famous Central School of Speech Training and Dramatic Art at the Royal Albert Hall. She would join an illustrious list of alumni that included Laurence Olivier, John Gielgud, and Ralph Richardson. By then known as Anna Lee, she was soon touring with the London Repertory Theatre in productions such as *The Constant Nymph* and *Jane Eyre.*

Anna Lee with son Jeffrey and a friend.

In 1935, Anna Lee made her first film. By 1939, she had appeared in over a dozen flicks, including *King Solomon's Mines,* which co-starred Paul Robeson; *Young Man's Fancy;* and *Non-Stop, New York.*

She was asked to come to Hollywood, where she was immediately put into a film with Ronald Coleman in the delightful *My Life With Caroline.* She also played Bronwen in the Academy Award-winning movie, *How Green Was My Valley,* starring a very young Roddy McDowall.

During World War II, Ms. Lee continued to make movies, including the classic *Flesh and Fantasy* with Charles Boyer. She also took time out to travel with the USO, and entertained allied troops in Africa and Sicily. General Patton made her an honorary private in the Sixth Army. Incidentally, it's interesting to note that the fictional hero of *King Solomon's Mines* was named Allan (with two "lls") Quartermaine.

Anna Lee continued to work in films after the war, such as *The Ghost and Mrs. Muir* with Rex Harrison and Gene Tierney, and *The Sound of Music.* She increasingly appeared in prime-time series, including ABC's live

245

weekly show, *A Date with Judy*. She is probably the only soap star to have shared a program with Walter Cronkite in the CBS panel show called *It's News to Me*. Anna Lee's film and television career continued throughout the 1960s and '70s. In 1976, she created the role of Lila Quartermaine on *General Hospital*.

Anna Lee, who is an MBE (Member of the Most Excellent Order of the British Empire, which was awarded to her by Queen Elizabeth in a 1982 ceremony at Buckingham Palace) was married to the late novelist Robert Nathan. They had five children, one of whom, Jeffrey Byron, played Jeff Martin on *All My Children*. (Nathan died in 1985; her eldest died a year later.) Anna is the proud grandmother of five grandchildren. She is active in charitable causes and is completing her autobiography.

Character: Lila Quartermaine

Lila Quartermaine, matriarch of the Quartermaine family, could be called husband Edward's conscience. But it would probably be closer to the mark to call her his confidante and his counselor.

Over the years, Lila has been able to keep the querulous, quarrelling, and sometimes quixotic Quartermaines from tearing each other to pieces. Lila is the mother of Alan and Tracy Quartermaine; the grandmother of Alan's sons, Jason and A.J., and of Tracy's son, Ned Ashton, and Tracy's infant, Dillon Hornsby. She is the mother-in-law of Monica Quartermaine, with whom she shares a loving and mutually respectful relationship. She was also, briefly, the mother-in-law of Lucy Coe, Alan's wife during a break in his marriage to Monica.

With Tracy, the title mother-in-law has been used by several men who had the dubious distinction of exchanging I do's with her.

Lila has been understanding of Edward's occasional flings, which go back to his younger days, two of which produced sons, Jimmy Lee Colt and the late Bradley Ward. Bradley was born of the wartime affair Edward had with Mary Mae Ward. (Justus Ward is Bradley's son.)

During Edward's disappearance and presumed death about ten years ago, Lila "heard" Edward's voice when they discussed matters relating to family and finance.

Actor: Jon Lindstrom

Birthplace: Medford, Oregon
Birthdate: October 18

"They wanted me only as a recurring character," Jon Lindstrom said of his role as Dr. Ryan Chamberlain, the sociopathic murderer. "But then they decided they wanted me to stay on...." And the next thing Lindstrom knew, he was not only playing Ryan, but also Ryan's identical twin, Dr. Kevin Collins.

Jon grew up in the Pacific Northwest. His father, an advertising executive who also directed commercials, introduced him into the performing life. Jon, who is also a drummer, studied both music and drama at the University of Oregon.

When he moved to Los Angeles, he studied drama with several well-known teachers including Lee Strasberg and Stella Adler. He earned his tuition fees as a bartender, developing skills which he would later use in his first professional acting role on the ABC series *Call to Glory.*

Lindstrom's credits include the Jim and Tammy Bakker story, *Fall from Grace,* and the television film, *The Alamo: Thirteen Days to Glory,* starring a famous soap alumnus, Alec Baldwin (formerly of *The Doctors*). His feature films include *Listen to Me* with Roy Scheider, and *Point of Seduction,* with Morgan Fairchild (who stars in the revamped *Loving* now called *LOV♥NYC*). His previous soap was *Santa Barbara.*

Jon and *Days of Our Lives* star Eileen Davidson (Kristen Blake DiMera) have been an "item" for several years.

Character: Kevin Collins

Kevin's late twin brother, Dr. Ryan Chamberlain, was "killed" several times before he was finally dispatched. Although Kevin liked to think of himself as the good twin, he sensed dark places in his mind and was worried that if he probed too deeply, he might discover that he and Ryan had more in common than the same DNA. How will that affect his future with Lucy? Stay tuned.

Jon on playing a dual role:

"Ryan was a challenge because his mind was so dark. Kevin was also a challenge, because he has secrets buried in his mind that he's afraid of."

Actor: Vanessa Marcil

Birthplace: San Diego, California
Birthdate: October 15

Vanessa Marcil was born in sunny San Diego and moved almost immediately with her family to Anchorage, Alaska, where her father is credited with building the first earthquake-proof structure in the state. Later on, the Marcils moved to Palm Desert, California where Vanessa began acting in local theater at the age of eight.

Vanessa's earlier goal was to study law. But she loved performing in front of people (isn't that what a lot of lawyers do?) and opted for an act-

247

ing career instead. She studied by doing, taking roles in stage productions of *The Miracle Worker, Sweet Bird of Youth, Pygmalion,* and others.

Her role as Brenda Barrett on *General Hospital* marks Marcil's first professional assignment. Prior to *GH* Vanessa was best known for her role in a video by the Artist Formerly Known as Prince.

She's active in charitable causes, and she loves to ride motorcycles.

Character: Brenda Barrett

Brenda came to Port Charles as the rich spoiled daughter of the late Harlan Barrett. She spent freely, but soon realized her sister Julia was in control of her trust fund, so she had to put the brakes on.

Brenda's relationship with Sonny Corinthos (Maurice Benard) took a turn when she agreed to wear a wire to learn where he gets his money. Although Sonny accused her of betrayal and walked out when he learned about it, she had already decided not to turn over anything that might be incriminating.

Brenda's friendship with Miguel proved comforting when she and Sonny had their big blowup. Will Miguel become more than a provider of a shoulder to lean on, or will Sonny and Brenda reconcile? Stay tuned.

Vanessa on Brenda:

"She always thought all she needed was money and her looks. But she began to learn that she also needed a family. She found that with people like Lois, Sonny, Robin, Miguel, Lily.... She can still be headstrong, but at least she knows there are people who care about her."

Actor: Ricky Martin

Birthplace: San Juan, Puerto Rico
Birthdate: December 24

Ricky was a member of the famed *Menudo* singing group. After leaving them, he went on to a successful musical career. He was named Best New Latin Artist at the 1993 Billboard Video Awards for his hit album, *Me Ameras.* Ricky has appeared in concerts in over twenty countries, including Spain, Portugal, most countries in South America, Mexico, and, of course, the United States.

He is also a popular actor in the Latin countries. He won The Heraldo, the Mexican equivalent of an Oscar, for his work in the film, *To Reach a Star.* He also appeared in the television version of the movie. Martin made his American acting debut in a recurring role in *Getting By.*

Character: Miguel Morez

Miguel came to Port Charles in 1994. As with many soap characters, he had secrets in his past. One of them, his ability to sing, was soon unveiled. But the deeper secret involved his love for a beautiful young woman named Lily whom he left behind in Puerto Rico because her father, who made his living in the shadier side of the business world, wanted him out of her life.

Lily later came to Port Charles and shocked him with the news that she had given birth to their son, whom she had given up for adoption. Miguel and Lily resumed their romance, but there were continuing problems that interfered with their plans to marry. Will they marry or go their separate ways? As Ricky Martin told the author, "What I love about doing a soap opera character, is you can never be sure what will happen to him next...."

Ricky on Miguel:

"It gives me a chance to do everything I love to do: act, sing, play music, and visit Puerto Rico."

Actor: Brad Maule

Birthplace: Camp Springs, Texas
Birthdate: October 11

Brad Maule was graduated from Stephen F. Austin College cum laude with a B.F.A. in theater and English. (Maule, who grew up on a farm in rural west Texas, attended one of the few remaining country schools with an enrollment of 150 students in twelve grades.)

Maule's theater credits include Billy Barnes's musical revue, *Movie Star*. He then played Hamlet in *Somethin's Rockin' in Denmark*. He won the Drama-Logue Award for his performance in Stephen Sondheim's *Marry Me A Little*.

Maule's television credits include guest starring roles in *The White Shadow, Three's Company, Too Close for Comfort,* and *Charlie's Angels*. He also appeared on the ABC miniseries, *Malibu*. Brad Maule wrote and performed songs before he became an actor. He worked as backup singer for Bobby Gentry and Jim Nabors, among others, and has released a couple of albums.

Brad and his wife, Laverne, have three children: daughter Lily Alexandra Nix, and sons Michael Benjamin and Hunter Nix.

Character: Dr. Anthony Jones

Dr. Anthony Jones came to Port Charles in 1984. His flamboyant brother, Frisco, arrived a year earlier. Tony Jones joined the staff of *General Hospital* and soon established himself as a skilled neurosurgeon. As a doctor, his accomplishments were phenomenal. As a human being, however,

249

Anthony Jones would see one precious thing after another in his life slip away.

He married the beautiful Tanya Roskov (who should probably be more properly called Roskova), played by Hilary Edson. He became the father of a baby girl named Barbara Jean, B.J. for short.

Soon after the child's birth, Tanya died. Lucy Coe married Tony, albeit briefly. Tony and Bobbie Spencer turned to each other for comfort when their respective marriages ended. He agreed to help Bobbie pay for a child who was being offered by a baby broker, and they were married. He was ecstatic about having a little brother for B.J. But then Bobbie learned the child had been stolen from its mother, Cheryl, Tiffany Hill's late sister, and the couple were forced to give him up.

Several years later, Tony's beloved B.J. was left brain-dead after an accident that had been caused by a drunken driver; he made the decision to donate her heart to her cousin, Maxie (Frisco's daughter) who would have died without a transplant.

Tony and Bobbie's marriage became strained. She had been involved with Damian Smith. He found himself drawn to his sister-in-law, Felicia, although he would not make the first move.

A former writer for *General Hospital* once told the author that he would have loved to have written a "happily ever after story" for Dr. Anthony Jones. And maybe one day soon, someone will.

Actor: Leigh J. McCloskey

Birthplace: Los Angeles, California
Birthdate: June 21

Leigh J. McCloskey studied acting at the famous Juilliard School in New York. He made his professional debut in the 1975 classic miniseries, *Rich Man, Poor Man* which helped launch the careers of Nick Nolte and Peter Strauss, and turned a long-time character actor, Ed Asner, into a television star.

He went on to appear in other television movies, including *Dawn: Portrait of a Teenage Runaway*, and its sequel, *Alexander: The Other Side of Dawn*. McCloskey landed the role of Mitch Cooper on *Dallas*. His feature films include the cult favorite, *Inferno*, as well as *Lucky Stiff* and *Just One of the Guys*.

Leigh seems to be a two-time winner on daytime television: he played Zack Kelton on *Santa Barbara* and was so popular in that role that, after it ran its course, the producers planned to use him again as soon as possible; and they did, with the character of Ethan Asher.

Leigh's original role on *General Hospital* was the recurring character of Dr. Michael Barnaski. Again, he scored high marks with the audience, and when it was time to cast Damian Smith, Leigh got the call.

A well-known artist, he's had several showings of his work, which includes acclaimed pen-and-ink drawings.

McCloskey and his wife, Carla, a film director, have two daughters, Caytlyn and Brighton.

Character: Damian Smith

Like pop, like pup? Damian Smith would like to believe he's every bit the man his father was, even if his father was an underworld crime boss. So far, Damian has yet to have his handsome face and profile turned into police mug shots, but he often comes close to crossing the line between what is merely nasty and deceitful to being purely criminal.

Damian has teamed with Katherine Bell in their mutual pursuit of wealth and power by any means necessary. Since Lucy Coe stands in the way of one of their enterprises — which involves laundering mob money — Damian arranged for Lucy to come under the influence of a TV psychic whom he paid to offer Lucy "advice."

Damian seemed upset when control of Frank Smith's mob went to a streetwise hood named Sonny Corinthos (Maurice Benard). Though they have an "agreement" for Sonny to play front man while Damian operates behind the scenes, Sonny has been trying to call the shots and Damian will do what he has to do to make sure Sonny doesn't permanently usurp the role he should have been given to play.

In other words, let the Son rise, while Sonny fades into the shade.

Actor: Kimberly McCullough

Birthplace: Bellflower, California
Birthdate: March 5

Kimberly was a youngster when she came aboard *General Hospital* as the daughter of Anna Devane and Robert Scorpio in 1985. In the decade since, she has grown from a young girl to a young woman, and her character, Robin Scorpio, has taken on remarkable depth.

Ms. McCullough has been a straight-A student throughout her educational career. She has a letter from President Bush commending her as a recipient of the 1989 Presidential Academic Fitness Award. "I expect to go on to college," she told the author. "I love acting, but I also love school, and I feel I'll be able to do both...."

Kimberly started her acting career at age seven — months, that is. She co-starred in a diaper commercial with English actor, Juliet Mills. She

251

has danced in *Fame, Solid Gold,* and in the feature film, *Electric Boogaloo: Breakin'2.*

Kimberly has appeared in *Les Miserables* as Little Cosette. She played Warren Beatty's daughter in the feature film, *Bugsy,* and Kevin Kline's daughter in the feature, *Consenting Adults.* She's a 1989 Emmy winner, and frequent Emmy nominee. She has also won two Soap Opera Awards. Kimberly enjoys collecting coins, bells, and European dolls.

Character: Robin Scorpio

"Robin has grown up physically, but it took a little longer for her to grow up emotionally." That's how Kimberly McCullough described her character after Robin and Stone Cates (Michael Sutton) became lovers.

Robin, the child of Anna Devane and Robert Scorpio, was left in the care of her uncle, Mac Scorpio (John J. York). He was protective of his niece, but as Kimberly put it, "As much as she loves her uncle, she sometimes felt she had to rebel."

One rebellious act was to go to a concert with Stone. When Mac reacted angrily, Felicia Jones helped him cool down. She also tried to provide motherly advice for Robin, telling her to wait before having sex (although that bit of wisdom was a little late), also advising her about the importance of protection should she decide she could handle a sexual relationship.

Robin and Stone used protection every time except once. Later, when he learned he was HIV-positive, Robin was tested and proved to be HIV-negative. Robin has persuaded Stone not to push her away. She has vowed to stay with him, and will record their day-by-day experiences in a journal.

Robin's future with Stone is marked by the prognosis of his disease. If a cure for AIDS is found in time, they can make plans that are far more long-ranging than any they can make now. If there is no cure, as Robin has told Stone, "we'll live each day as it comes...."

Actor: Joseph C. Phillips

Birthplace: Denver, Colorado
Birthdate: January 17

Phillips started his career on the Broadway stage. He starred in *Six Degrees of Separation* and appeared opposite Danny Glover and Esther Rolle in *A Raisin in the Sun.* He also co-starred with Christopher Walken in Shakespeare's *Coriolanus.*

His features include *Strictly Business* with Halle Berry, and *Playing for Keeps.* On prime-time, he guested on *The Bill Cosby Show, A Different World,*

A Man Called Hawk, and *Virtual Reality,* among others. His previous daytime role was as Cruiser McCullough on *Search for Tomorrow.*

Joseph C. Phillips — whose character, Justus Ward, hopes for a political career — began studying law at Rutgers University, and intends to complete his work toward a law degree.

Joseph and his wife, Nicole, were married in Chicago.

Character: Justus Ward

Justus Ward arrived in Port Charles when his long-missing father, Bradley, turned up dead and buried in the backyard of his childhood home, now occupied by Luke and Laura Spencer.

For twenty years, Justus wondered where papa was. But as soon as that mystery was solved, the mystery of who killed papa began: suspicion fell on Edward Quartermaine, but it turned out one of Quartermaine's cronies, Jack Boland, committed the murder.

But it seems there was more to the Edward-Bradley connection than a possible murder charge. Justus's grandmother, Mary Mae, revealed that Edward was Bradley's father, which made Edward Justus's grandfather.

Justus plans a career in politics, starting with Port Charles's city council. He's a man of principle — something that, one would hope, wouldn't keep him from becoming the first African American to take up residence at 1600 Pennsylvania Avenue.

Actor: Rena Sofer

Birthplace: Arcadia, California
Birthdate: December 2

After her parents' divorce, Rena moved to Pittsburgh, Pennsylvania, and then to North Bergen, New Jersey, where she finished high school. Her mother teaches psychology in Boston. Her father is an Orthodox Jewish rabbi in New Jersey. Like her character, Lois Cerullo, Rena is devoted to her family, all of whom have supported her acting career.

A New York talent agent directed her to a modeling career when she was fifteen, and advised her to take acting classes. She moved into roles on stage and features, including flicks such as *The Only One* and Sidney Lumet's *A Stranger Among Us.*

Rena's previous daytime roles were on *Another World* and *Loving.*

Rena won a best supporting actress Emmy in 1995. In addition to praising the cast and crew of GH, she extended a special thank-you to her on- and off-screen co-star, Wally Kurth.

Character: Lois Cerullo Ashton

Lois comes from a warm, loving Italian-American family with roots in the Brooklyn, New York, neighborhood of Bensonhurst. She came to Port Charles as the manager of a rock band and met a rock singer (and pharmaceutical salesman) named Eddie Maine — and promptly fell head-over-high-boots for him. They were eventually married, but she was stunned to learn he wasn't Eddie; he was Ned Ashton, of the wealthy Quartermaine family. She was stunned to learned he had also married Katherine Bell, whose chimes Lois had long wanted to ring. (She never trusted cute Kate.) But things worked out for the couple. Ned was able to prove that Katherine blackmailed him into marriage, and that the marriage wasn't valid because he had first married Lois. And, he had wisely used his own name on the marriage certificate.

Lois and Ned later had a great big happy Italian-American wedding, Brooklyn-style, with the Quartermaines and all their friends in attendance. While it probably wasn't the highlight of the Brooklyn social season (there's always the Bocci ball tournament in Fort Hamilton Park, for example) it was big enough.

Lois has run into problems with her recording company, thanks mostly to her colleagues, Brenda, Sonny, Miguel, and Lily, whose personal lives are still in a state of flux.

But being married to Ned Ashton also carries some risks. He hasn't exactly been the most stable person in the past and who knows what can set him off again in the not-so-distant future. But Lois is a survivor. And whatever happens, she won't be left out in the cold.

Actor: Michael Sutton

Birthplace: Los Angeles, California
Birthdate: June 18

The role of Mike "Stone" Cates marks Sutton's professional debut as an actor. But it's not his first exposure to the wonderful world of show business. Michael's father, Joe Sutton, owns one of Hollywood's best-known public relations firms, and the younger Sutton grew up in the company of some of the town's most famous players.

He was a Beverly Hills High School classmate of Steve Burton, who plays Jason Quartermaine on *General Hospital*. Michael Sutton was graduated from California State University at Northridge with a degree in film. He has directed and plans to produce films one day.

"Although acting is my profession of choice," he says, "I strongly believe that my knowledge of all the various facets of production contribute to my performance before the camera."

254

Character: Mike "Stone" Cates

Stone Cates came to Port Charles as one of Jagger Cates's younger brothers. He was street-savvy, and often let his fists do much of his talking. Stone had been a teenage runaway and lived, as our English cousins describe it, "rough" for several years.

In Port Charles, he fell for the lovely Robin Scorpio. Despite her uncle Mac's dislike of him (he felt Stone was not a suitable suitor for his young niece), Robin returned his feelings and they eventually became lovers. Robin and Stone used protection each time they loved — except once, when passion overwhelmed them.

Stone had been feeling ill for several months. Robin persuaded him to see a doctor. He underwent an AIDS test and, to his horror, learned he was HIV-positive. (Robin was later tested and found to be negative, but must be tested again.)

Stone Cates had had many sexual encounters over the years he was living pretty much on the streets including, as he recalled, an affair with a young woman who had been an IV drug user.

Kristina and Jack Wagner, in early Felicia-Frisco days.

At first, Stone wanted to run away. He didn't want anyone he cared for to know the truth. He hid out but Robin found him and persuaded him to come into her life and the lives of his family and friends. His friend, Sonny, asked him to live in his apartment. Jason Quartermaine opened the Quartermaine gym to him (although brother A.J. was a mite nonplussed to find Stone's sweat on some of the equipment, and had to be taught how the disease is transmitted AND HOW IT'S NOT).

For Stone, life is a day-by-day experience in which an early death seems to be his destiny. But he'll learn that while he'll have bad days physically and emotionally, he mustn't give up hope.

255

The author asked head writer Claire Labine if she thought it was credible for Stone to believe in a cure. Labine replied: "Yes, I do. I think hope is something we all need to hold onto at different times in our lives. Stone is facing something especially cruel, but it doesn't mean he should stop hoping...."

Actor: Kristina Wagner

Birthplace: Indianapolis, Indiana
Birthdate: October 30

Kristina is married to actor/singer Jack Wagner, who played her on-screen husband, Frisco Jones. She started her career dancing and acting in high school productions and, later, at Indiana Central University, where she majored in drama. She transferred to Indiana University-Purdue University at Indianapolis where she earned her degree in theater.

Kristina worked in commercials for local companies while performing with the University Theater Group. Her brother suggested she send a picture and resumé to a modeling agency. That led to auditions for roles on *All My Children*, *Ryan's Hope* and, eventually, *General Hospital*. She joined *GH* in 1984. (She was then known as Kristina Malandro.)

Kristina's visit to Africa a few years ago led to her becoming a member of the Africa Wildlife Foundation, a group dedicated to preserving the continent's magnificent and endangered wildlife. Like their on-screen counterparts, the Wagners have two children, Peter and Harrison.

Character: Felicia Cummings Jones
See Port Charles Chronicles.

Actor: John J. York

Birthplace: Chicago, Illinois
Birthdate: December 10

John J. York studied marketing at the University of Whitewater in Wisconsin when he realized that what he really wanted to market were his talents as an actor. He returned to Chicago and began to study with the renowned Edward Kaye-Martin. He soon made his acting debut in theater in such plays as *Picnic, Loss of Roses, Career,* and *Golden Boy.*

In 1983, he moved to Hollywood and began getting prime-time guest roles on various series including *21 Jump Street, Murder, She Wrote, Family Ties, Sydney, Newhart,* and others. He played Eric Cord on *Werewolf,* a sci-fi horror-action series, for two seasons.

His feature films include *Steel and Lace, House of the Rising Sun,* and *The Bear,* about the University of Alabama Coach Bear Bryant, starring Gary Busey. It was while he was making the feature, *Chattanooga Choo Choo,* that he met his wife, Vicki, a casting director. They share their home with daughter, Schuyler and two cats, Alex and Smokey.

Character: Malcolm "Mac" Scorpio
It's not easy being the kid brother of anyone. It's really rough being the kid brother of the famous crime fighter, Robert Scorpio, especially

when you only found out about him when you were already an adult. But somehow, Mac has managed to make himself his own man in Port Charles.

His most important responsibility is raising the orphaned daughter of Robert and Anna Devane. Learning that young Robin's lover, Mike "Stone" Cates, has AIDS, has not been easy for Mac to deal with. But for her sake, he'll have to overcome his fears and provide her with a comforting source to which she can turn when life gets rough. Meanwhile, Mac wonders if Felicia Jones will turn to him if she decides she's had it with a marriage in which her husband, Frisco, makes guest appearances. They had been lovers (he believed he was the father of her baby daughter, Georgie, but Frisco was the child's daddy) and, perhaps, they'll be lovers again.

As for Katherine Bell? Well, Mac could have some thoughts about her, as well.

Actor: Jacklyn Zeman

Birthplace: Englewood, New Jersey

Jacklyn Zeman began her career training as a classical ballet dancer. She was accepted into the New Jersey Dance Company while continuing her dance and academic studies. She was graduated from high school at fifteen and went to New York University on a scholarship. She majored in dance and occasionally worked as a model while continuing her college studies.

When she decided to switch from dance to drama, she enrolled in a school that taught television acting techniques. Three months later, she was playing Lana McClain on *One Life to Live*.

Zeman went on to work in theater in various off-Broadway productions. In 1977, she moved to Los Angeles to create the role of Barbara Jean (Bobbie) Spencer in *General Hospital*.

Jacklyn Zeman's credits include an ABC movie, *Jury Duty: The Comedy*, with Alan Thicke and Bronson Pinchot, and the feature films, *The Groove Tube* and *The Day the Music Died*. She also did two ABC movies, *Young Doctors in Love* and *National Lampoon's Class Reunion*.

Zeman is the author of *Beauty on the Go*, published by Simon & Schuster. She is active in charitable causes, including helping to raise public awareness, through the Easter Seals campaigns, of the problems of the disabled. Unlike her oft star-crossed character, Jacklyn Zeman is happily married. She and her husband, Glenn Gordon, have two daughters, Lacey Rose and Cassidy Zee.

Character: Barbara Jean (Bobbie) Spencer Meyer Brock Jones
See Port Charles Chronicles.

257

Guiding Light

I f Irna Phillips can be called The Mother of Soap Operas, then radio has to be called The Midwife. It was radio that delivered the soaps to audiences from the 1930s until 1960.

Many radio soaps tried to make the transition to television. Every one of them — except *The Guiding Light,* which Irna had created in 1937 — failed. Those who have a spiritual turn of mind might like to think the reason *The Guiding Light* (the series used an introductory article then) succeeded where others didn't is that it was, and still is, watched over by the original "Guiding Light," the Reverend Dr. John Rutledge. (Phillips had based Rev. Rutledge on a real-life Protestant minister, Dr. Preston Bradley, whose speeches on peace and tolerance inspired the young Jewish writer.)

The Guiding Light made a lateral move in 1952. It stayed on radio, using the same story lines for years, until 1956. In terms of television longevity, *Guiding Light* is five years younger than *Meet the Press,* which first aired in 1947. In theater, the TV soap is the same age as Agatha Christie's *The Mousetrap,* which debuted in London in 1952 and continues to attract audiences. (In some ways Christie and Phillips were very much alike: Both loved telling stories; both loved being lionized by literary types; and both were perfectionists. Phillips was uncomfortable with actors ad-libbing in any of her soaps, even when they were done live on television and sometimes had to fill in their own words when they momentarily forgot hers. Christie felt the same about her work when it was transferred to the screen: She had to be consulted on all aspects of the adaptation. And, of course, both were prolific writers.)

Beyond Family Values

Guiding Light has told the story of the Bauer family. Even though other families have come and gone, a Bauer has always been present. The first Bauer, Meta, appeared in the original radio cast. The other Bauers were introduced on radio soon after. Among those who went on to dominate the television version of the series were Papa and Mama Bauer, and their children Bill, Trudy, and Meta.

Original Cast — Radio

Mercedes McCambridge . . . .Mary Rutledge	*Ruth Bailey* . . . . .Rose Kransky
John Hodiak . . . . .Ned Holden	*Sarajane Wells* . . . . Also played Mary Rutledge
Raymond Edward Johnson . . . . .Mr. Nobody from Nowhere	*Ed Prentiss* .Also played Ned Holden
Arthur Peterson . . . . .The Reverend Dr. Rutledge	*Gladys Heen* . . . . .Torchy
	Jone Allison . . . . .Meta Bauer*

*The character remained with the series when it moved to television.

First Air Date: January 25, 1937

Original Cast — Television

Jone Allison . . . . .Meta Banning	*James Lipton* . . . . .Dr. Richard Grant
Charita Bauer . . .Bertha (Bert) Miller Bauer	*Herb Nelson* . . . . .Joe Roberts
Susan Douglas . . . . . . .Kathy Grant	*Lyle Sudro* . . . . .Bill Bauer
Theo Goetz . . . . .Papa Bauer	*Alice Yourman* . . . . .Laura Grant

First Air Date: June 30, 1952 / CBS

259

Long before a movie house near Times Square was converted to the hippest nightclub in New York, there was a Studio 54 with its own claim to fame: It's where *The Guiding Light* broadcast the show in the early 1950s.

Bill married Bertha (Bert) Miller. They had two sons, Michael and Edward. The original Bert Bauer was played by Ann Shepherd until 1950. She was replaced by Charita Bauer (the last name is coincidental) who played the part until her death in 1985.

Before the series settled in Springfield, Irna Phillips moved the show from its original studios in Chicago to Hollywood, changing the soap's locale from Five Corners, a Chicago suburb, to Selby Flats, a Los Angeles suburb. But Irna was used to the pace of a big city, which Los Angeles was not back in the 1940s. She packed up and headed East to New York in 1949, and relocated her soap to Springfield. Previously, the core of her story lay with the various ministers who replaced the original Reverend Rutledge. In Springfield, the central focus would be on the people of Cedars Hospital.

By the time the soap had moved to New York, Phillips had also moved the Bauers in as the main family. Incidentally, the name Bauer is German for farmer. The original name for the family was Baum, which is German for tree. Why did Irna change it? There have been all sorts of stories: one is that she preferred the sound of Bauer over Baum, which she thought some would pronounce "Bum." Another is that she had a friend named Bauer. There's a story that her secretary misheard the name on her dictaphone (an early recording device) and typed it as Bauer, and Irna liked it, and kept it. Still another story seems to make the most sense: Because she wanted to.

Most of the characters who went on CBS Television on June 30, 1952, had been introduced to the viewers through the radio version of *The Guiding Light,* which continued to run parallel stories on both media for four years. During those concurrent runs, an actor's typical day consisted of rehearsing for the television show in the morning; going in front of the cameras from 12:45 to 1 PM; then rushing from the CBS television facility in Liederkranz Hall (*The Secret Storm* and *Captain Kangaroo* were also produced there) down to the radio studio on East 52nd Street, where the cast worked until four in the afternoon. Then it was back home to study the new script.

About a year before she died, Charita Bauer told the author, "We used to do the radio show live, of course. But when we moved into television, we started to record the radio shows the day before they aired ... they were our rehearsals for the TV shows, which, in those days, we did live.... It was exhausting, sometimes, but very exciting."

Other soaps that started on radio — and *Guiding Light* was no different — had a problem adapting to television. *Search for Tomorrow* and *Love of Life,* for example, which began on TV, were produced by people who

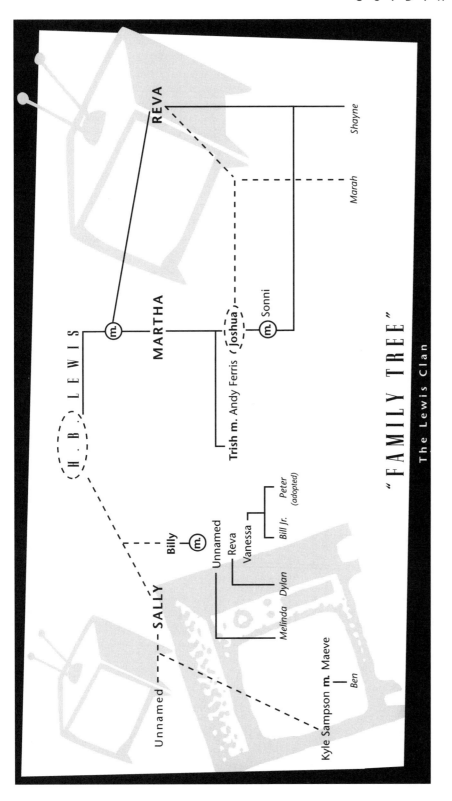

"FAMILY TREE"

The Lewis Clan

H B. Lewis struck oil and headed for Springfield, where his various offspring—Billy, Trish, and Joshua—soon became business leaders and, of course, lovers like nobody's business. All the Lewis men, plus Kyle, Billy's half-brother, have been involved with Reva Shayne Lewis, though her heart (and her two children) belongs once and forever to Josh.

261

A Personal Note about Irna

A young woman from the University of Chicago contacted Irna Phillips, wanting to work for her during her summer break. Phillips told her to watch *The Guiding Light* for a month, and then come back with one suggestion on how to improve it. The young writer felt she was put in a corner. How do you tell the creator that her work could be improved? But she tried. She handed in a suggestion and Phillips gave her the job. That young writer was the author's aunt, who went on to a teaching career. Her submission? Put teachers into your stories.

had worked in other television shows or in films. They were used to scripts that said less and allowed them to show more. Irna was advised to make changes. At first, she didn't think it was necessary. But after watching some of the episodes, she agreed that her characters didn't need quite as much dialogue to get the story across.

A thrifty woman, Irna must have loved the idea of writing less but earning more as the soap became increasingly popular.

Irna's reluctance to change delayed the soap's move into colorcasting. Irna was against the whole idea; she thought black and white was the most dramatic background for her stories. This belief may be traced to the fact that the show started on radio and Irna believed her listeners were influenced by the movies. Only the musicals were in color; the dramas were not. She felt keeping the shows uncolored would help keep the dramatic effect viable. But CBS, which was airing *Search for Tomorrow* and *Love of Life* in color, set a date for the first color show, and Irna gave in.

Or did she?

On that fateful date, Irna arranged to have the action take place in Cedars Hospital: all those white walls, white uniforms, black stethoscope tubings — and all shot by expensive new color cameras.

Guiding Light ended its radio run in 1956 as the top-rated show in that medium. On television, *GL* would be at the top of the ratings ladder, and sometimes it would fall to the lower rungs. Rumors predicted that the "Light" was about to be turned off. But there was always a story line that reignited the spark and kept it going. And if it isn't the fictional Dr. Rutledge who's been relighting the lamps this time, it may be Charita Bauer, who loved the soap and told a magazine editor shortly before she died, "I've been so lucky to have two wonderful families: my own, and everyone on the show."

Springfield Chronicles

Papa and Mama Bauer were immigrants. They loved America and loved telling their three children, Meta, Trudy, and Bill, how fortunate they were

Charita Bauer.

to have been born and raised in this country. Trudy married early in the story and never made it to the television version.

Meta was continually involved in problems, often of her own making. She was married and had a stepdaughter, Kathy, with whom she had a strained relationship. Perhaps there was a touch of jealousy involved. Kathy was the apple of her doting father's eye, and Meta warned Joe Roberts about being overprotective.

Kathy was widowed while pregnant. She married Dr. Dick Grant (played by James Lipton), who was wealthy and handsome, and for a doctor, quite naive: He believed that he was the father of Kathy's daughter. After Joe died of cancer, Meta and Kathy competed for the same man, Mark Holden, a friend of Meta's brother, Bill. Kathy won.

When Susan Douglas, who played Kathy, became pregnant, Irna realized she would not be available for crucial scenes she had planned for Kathy and Mark. So Kathy had to die; and what a way to go! She was in a wheelchair when youngsters on bicycles bumped into her and pushed her into oncoming traffic.

The country rose up against the death of Kathy Roberts Grant Holden. Irna sent a letter to everyone who wrote in to complain, pointing

263

Stars who appeared on Guiding Light include:

Kevin Bacon • Barnard Hughes • Meg Mundy • Carrie Nye • John Wesley Shipp • JoBeth Williams • Chris Sarandon • Michael Wilding, Jr. • Phillip Bosco • James Earl Jones • Billy Dee Williams • Sandy Dennis • Cicely Tyson • Don Scardino • Zena Bethune • Christopher Walken, who would sometimes fill in for his brother, Glenn Walken.

out that we must expect people to die: in life, there is happiness and there is sorrow.

She ended her letters with, — "We hope you will continue to watch *The Guiding Light* so that you may see reflected the wonderful moments there are in living as well as the tragic."

The Queen Departs — Hail to the Queen

Irna Phillips left *Guiding Light* shortly after Kathy's death to concentrate on her new series for Procter & Gamble, *As the World Turns.* Coming in to take over the show and ultimately make it very much her own was Agnes Nixon. With Nixon's arrival, the series would soon show her trademark "social relevance" story lines. She would also create something more substantial in Bert, so that she would become a woman other women could look at and, as Agnes said, think, "there, but for the grace of God, go I."

Bert began as a compulsive butter; that is, she would butt into everyone's business. Even her patient father-in-law, Papa Bauer, would throw up his hands and say something like, "Ach, liebling, give it a rest."

But Bert's life was not an easy one, thanks largely to Bill's behavior. They fought often; taunted each other with promises to get a divorce; and seemed determined to inflict as much pain as possible on one another — each believing the other one deserved it more.

Rotters, Drinkers, and Womanizers

The fact is, Bill Bauer was no good. In England he would have been called a rotter. To his wife, he was just plain rotten. To his father, he was a disappointment. But Papa always hoped he would straighten out.

Whenever the mood moved him, Bill Bauer would leave home for long periods. On at least two occasions, he was assumed to have left this earthly plane, but was resurrected in time for a story line turn.

Bill was not only an alcoholic, he was also a womanizer. One of his mistresses bore him a daughter, Hillary, who grew up to become a nurse at Cedars (played by Marsha Clark).

Michael Bauer grew up to be a lawyer, which made Papa and Bert very proud. But Mike (played in adulthood by Don Stewart) was a womanizer just like dad.

Edward Bauer grew up to be a doctor; again, grandpa and mother were very proud. But Ed inherited his father's gene for alcoholism, and over the years, it's created problems for him and his loved ones.

Guest Stars Who Have Shined Brightly on Guiding Light

• Keir Dullea • Maureen O'Sullivan (Mia Farrow's mother) • Taina Elg • Teresa Wright • Adolph Caesar • Joan Bennett (playing herself) • Elizabeth Allen • Jan Sterling • Ed Begley, Sr.

More Amorous Adventures

Michael's first love was a young woman named Robin Holden, his aunt Meta's step-granddaughter. (Robin's mother was the late Kathy Holden.) Robin's stepfather, Mark, married his housekeeper, who had a son, Karl. Michael and Karl were friends. One night they argued over Robin. Karl fell to his death. Michael went on trial but was acquitted. He married Robin, but Bert forced them into an annulment. (She hadn't yet learned how to channel her proclivity for butting in into more positive areas.)

Mike became a law clerk and soon found himself less concerned with legal briefs than brief encounters with his employer's secretary, Julie Conrad. Those brief moments became trysts, and Julie became pregnant. Bert insisted Mike marry her. Julie had a nervous breakdown after giving birth to their daughter, Hope. She later took her life in a mental hospital.

Bert took Hope into her home and her heart. Mike was upset that Bert was both smothering and spoiling the child. He accepted a position in Bay City (the fictional site of Irna Phillips's soap, *Another World*). There he met Pat Randolph, the wife of another lawyer. But for probably the first time in his amorous adventures, he was turned down. Pat fantasized about him, but she didn't want to betray her husband.

Mike returned to Springfield, and once again, fell in love with a married woman. But this time the other spouse wasn't a Brother at the Bar of Justice: it was Edward Bauer, a brother at the bar, or wherever else he could get a drink.

While Mike was in Bay City, Ed, who was now a doctor, was encouraged by his mentor, Dr. Steve Jackson, to marry his daughter, Leslie. He felt Ed was the right man for her. They married, and things went well until Leslie pressured him about having a child. Like his father, Ed reacted to pressure by drinking. And, while Bill's abuse was largely verbal, Ed actually beat Leslie in his drunken rages.

By the time Mike had come back to town, Leslie was very much a vulnerable woman looking for a loving, caring man.

Ed was fired by Cedars and ran off. He had an affair with a woman named Janet Mason. The news gave Leslie the courage to tell Mike she loved him. But Ed returned and persuaded her to take him back. She did. She became pregnant. A disappointed Mike turned to a comforting Charlotte Waring and they were married. But the marriage ended early.

Leslie gave birth to a son she named Frederick after his great-grandfather. This was the first time most viewers learned that this was Papa Bauer's given name. In time, the little boy would be called Freddy, then Rick. He would grow up to become a popular character. (When the character and the actor who played him, Michael O'Leary, left the show in the mid-1980s, fans hoped for a return. They got their wish a decade later.)

Somewhere between the adventures and misadventures of the Brothers Bauer, Bill and Bert had one of their frequent "troublesome" periods, which ended in a curious way. Bill used the excuse of Bert's devotion to granddaughter Hope to claim he was being ignored, so he might as well start drinking again. His secretary, Maggie Scott, comforted him.

Maggie's estranged husband, Ben Scott, returned to rebuild a relationship with her and their daughter, Peggy. When Peggy learned of Maggie's affair with Bill, she turned to a young man named Johnny. Ben was so upset that he died of a heart attack. Maggie died soon after. Bert and Bill had reconciled, and took young Peggy into their home. Peggy would later become part of the Thorpe story, which would introduce one of the longest running antiheroes in soapdom, Roger Thorpe.

An Adopted Bauer Takes Center Stage

Also coming into prominence at this time was the Norris family, which would eventually link up with Roger Thorpe and back to the Bauers.

Peggy and the young man she cared for, Johnny Fletcher, hoped to marry but fate, in the person of a beautiful woman named Tracy Delmar, interfered. But to tell that story, we have to backtrack a few paragraphs.

Johnny's father, Dr. Paul Fletcher (last played by Bernard Grant), was reunited with an old friend, Dr. Sara McIntyre (last played by Millette Alexander) when she joined Cedars Hospital. Hard-luck Robin, now married to Paul, grew increasingly jealous.

By this time, Agnes Nixon left as head writer. A series of writing teams were brought on. Two actors who had been on the soap, John Boruff and James Lipton, joined the scribe tribes for a spell. (And speaking of spells — it was at this point that the locale of *Guiding Light* made a magical blink-of-an-eye change from Los Angeles to Springfield, U.S.A.)

Irna Phillips returned to take the reins of her creation and immediately decided that Robin was in the way, and had to go. A decade earlier,

Irna had sent Kathy, Robin's mother, into soap oblivion via an auto accident. This time poor Robin had her wings clipped via a speeding truck. There was the usual outraged reaction from the fans, but it subsided in time. Irna went back to *As the World Turns* and *Guiding Light* moved on.

In March, 1967, the show began broadcasting in color. In September, 1969, it expanded from fifteen minutes to a half hour. It also stopped telecasting live shows. Instead, each episode would be videotaped for airing the next day. (Today, taping typically takes place a week before air time, unless special location shots are being stockpiled for future airing.)

> *Guiding Light* had a number of favored methods of removing characters. These included car accidents, if the removal was to be permanent; commitment to a sanitarium if there was a chance the character might return; and a fall from a great height — which left both possibilities open.

A Heart-Stopping Beginning

The first half-hour episode opened with a dramatic story being played out in Cedars Hospital. Bill Bauer was undergoing the first heart transplant on daytime television. (Ed Bryce, who played Bill, was supposed to lie deathly still as the make-believe doctors, buttressed by a group of professional nurses and medical advisers, stood around him. When the scene was over, Ed didn't get up. There was momentary concern, but eventually he opened his eyes. He had simply fallen fast asleep.)

Now, back to our continuing story.... After Robin's death, Paul Fletcher made romantic overtures to Sara McIntyre, but she was not receptive. (Poor Robin: she had no reason to feel jealous.)

Meanwhile, just as Paul's son, Johnny, was hoping to work things out romantically with Peggy (and vice versa), Sara's niece, Tracy Delmar, turned up, and Johnny was turned on and married her. Peggy (Fran Myers) married on the rebound to Marty Dillman (last played by Christopher Wines), a rich guy whose money came from shady sources. And those sources provided him with information about Tracy Delmar: To wit: that she was really Charlotte Waring (last played by Victoria Wyndham) who posed as Tracy to get Sara's money.

Sadly, for Marty, he was killed, and poor Peggy was charged with his murder. But Mike Bauer came to the rescue, and with Charlotte revealing her true identity, Peggy was acquitted. Someone named Flip Malone did poor Marty in.

Johnny divorced Charlotte and married Peggy Scott Dillman, who had a son, Billy. Peggy's happiness was short-lived. Johnny cracked under the pressure of trying to be the kind of doctor his father, Paul, was, and had a nervous breakdown. He was sent to a sanitarium.

267

More Bauer Struggles

After divorcing Ed Bauer, Leslie Bauer (played by Barbara Rodell, Kathy Hays, and Lynne Adams), now the mother of little Frederick (Rick) Bauer, was courted by the wealthy Stanley Norris (Michael Higgins). Her father, Dr. Jackson, was against the marriage, but Leslie defied him. Leslie's step-daughter, Holly Norris, was an insecure young woman desperate to reconcile with her father after he had alienated himself from his family.

Holly (originally played by Lynn Deerfield and most recently by Maureen Garrett) would go on to become an increasingly important character, involved with some of the most fascinating of *GL*'s gentlemen, including Roger Thorpe (Michael Zaslow), the father of her daughter, Cristina (Blake).

Stanley's son, Ken, married Janet Mason, the woman with whom Ed Bauer had had an affair. It was at this time (1971) that Holly met Roger Thorpe, who worked for her father. They had an affair, and she expected they would marry. But Roger's libido was jarred by Mason, and he wanted no one else.

Holly's mother, Barbara, meanwhile (originally played by Augusta Dabney, then by Barbara Berjer) had fallen for, and married, Roger's father, Adam (Robert Milli).

Murder in the First Degree

Leslie's marriage to Stanley Norris ended when he was murdered. She was tried for the crime, but acquitted. Holly, who was still dealing with her father's death, was horrified when she saw Roger come out of her sister-in-law, Janet's, apartment wiping lipstick off his face. She was so dazed, she ran into the street in front of a speeding car and....

She was hit; she was hurt; but unlike previous characters caught in auto accidents, she didn't die. Holly told Ken what she'd seen, and his jealousy flared. Janet tried to explain that Roger had forced his way into her place, but she'd fought him. Ken left her.

Holly entered Cedars when she was overwrought by the events of her life, including Roger's betrayal. She met Ed Bauer, who was nursing a few emotional problems himself: His ex-wife, Leslie, was about to marry his brother, Mike, and to make matters worse, Ed was living at home with his mother, Bert.

One night, Ed got drunk and married Holly. The next morning, she claimed they had consummated the marriage, and that an annulment was out of the question. (But if we recall our Shakespeare, wine does rob the "performance" and Ed was nowhere near performing that night.) In any event, Bert welcomed her new daughter-in-law.

Mike and Leslie were married and were sure they would live happily ever after. But Leslie's presumed dead mother resurfaced and tried to insinuate herself into her daughter's life again. She also tried to rekindle her relationship with husband, Steve Jackson, but he rejected her. At first he was furious, but an old lover turned up, and she left with him. Her farewell message to Leslie was a shocker: Steve, the father she loved, was not her father after all.

Meanwhile, Ed and Holly had mounting problems. It got so bad, he demanded separate bedrooms. But Holly soon found another bed mate, her old beau Roger Thorpe. She became pregnant, but realized she and Ed hadn't had sexual relations in a long time. So she quickly revived their sex lives and eventually felt safe in telling him "they" were going to have a baby.

Many actors began successful soap careers on *Guiding Light. AMC*'s Ruth Warrick played her former radio soap character, Janet Johnson, R.N.; Helen Wagner is the original Nancy Hughes of *ATWT;* Gillian Spencer became Daisy Cortlandt on *AMC;* Virginia Dwyer and Victoria Wyndham, both of whom found stardom on *AW;* Anthony Call, who played Herb Callison on *OLTL;* and Chris Marcantel, who appeared on several daytime shows, including *Loving.*

Ken saw Ed and Janet in an innocent hug, and shot him in the chest. Ed survived, but he was left with a partially paralyzed hand. He went into a deep depression when he thought his surgical career was over. However, he was buoyed by the birth of daughter Cristina. Although Holly was happy that Ed seemed to accept the baby as his own, she still yearned for Roger. But Roger now yearned for Peggy Scott Fletcher.

Cristina fell ill and needed a blood transfusion. Ed's blood was the wrong type. Rather than let her child die, Holly confessed Roger was the father. Ed left her and the baby, and he made sure that Peggy — who was in the process of divorcing Johnny — knew about Roger. She was shaken by the revelation, but married him anyway. Their only witnesses were Adam and Bert.

Others May Come and Go, but the Bauers are Here to Stay

Meanwhile, Ed turned to a Cedars nurse, Rita Stapleton (Lenore Kasdorf) for comfort and friendship, and she came through. Another nurse named Hillary Kincaid (Linda McCullough and Marsha Clark) needed an emergency appendectomy. Her father went to see her. No one recognized him until he later introduced himself to Mike Bauer with words to the effect of, "I'm your daddy and I didn't die in that plane crash ten years ago."

The late Doug Marland once told the author, "our show is a resource for New York's theaters. Whenever a producer needs an actor, they can find one in our cast ... (and) I try to write a story that will allow them time to appear...."

Bill admitted he ran away when he could no longer handle his drinking or his family responsibilities. He went to Canada and became Bill Moray, and married a woman named Simone. Hillary was their daughter.

Mike accepted his half-sister. Bert, as usual, accepted the situation. But Ed turned to drink. Bill helped him learn how to deal with his alcoholism. Ed finally welcomed Hillary into the family. Bill left for Chicago.

The Norrises, except for Holly, were beginning to be phased out of Springfield by the mid-1970s. Ready to come in and stake out a major part in the ongoing story of *The Guiding Light* were the Spauldings and the Marlers, followed by the Reardons and the Lewises. And still at the center, like some giant Maypole, are the Bauers. There may be fewer of them than there once were, but, as a former writer for the soap told the author, "as long as there's a Bauer, there's a story we can write...."

The Young and Zestful

In 1980, Douglas Marland — who brought young characters into *General Hospital* during his tenure as head writer (although he told the author that he would never have had Laura raped by Luke later to accept him as her lover) — had assumed head writing duties for *Guiding Light*. He introduced the first teenage story line in the soap's history.

"I recalled my own teenage years," Marland told the author, "and remembered that there were times when I was confused and unhappy ... and I realized this was true for most people.... I thought I would bring in young characters who face many of the same problems we all do while we're living through those difficult years...."

Marland also spoke with his then fifteen-year-old niece and asked her what would be the most fantastic romantic thing that could happen to her. She said it would be having a college man fall for her — not a high school boy! Marland kept that in mind as he began writing stories for his newly introduced youth brigade. They included Tim (T.J.) Werner, Sara McIntyre's adopted son (played by Kevin Bacon, and then by Chris Marcantel when Kevin left to do a play); Morgan Richards (Kristen Vigard and Jennifer Cook), whose mother was Jennifer Richards (Geraldine Court), a lady with a very important secret; Kelly Nelson, Ed Bauer's godson, (John Wesley Shipp); Nola Reardon, (played by Lisa Brown); Hillary Bauer (Marsha Clark); and Floyd Parker (Tom Nielsen).

Nola's really big adventure with the mysterious Quinton McCord (Michael Tylo) was still a year away when she fell for and tried to snare the handsome and noble Kelly. The problem was, Kelly was in love with Morgan, who was dating Tim.

Nola arranged for her accommodating boyfriend, Floyd, to help her become pregnant so she could claim Kelly as the father. (She had gotten Kelly drunk and into bed, and the next day lied about their having made love.) But Nola's no-nonsense mother, Bea Reardon (Lee Lawson) revealed the truth.

Coming so close to losing Kelly, Morgan realized she loved him. Tim and Kelly had been the best of friends, but were now seeing their friendship torn by their love for the same young woman. But Tim eventually accepted the situation. Kelly and Morgan were married, but were divorced soon after, and each made their separate way out of Springfield. Although Morgan left town without a husband, at least she learned she had a sister. This will soon be explained.

Kristin Vigard and John Wesley Shipp.

The Spauldings

Until 1977, the name Spaulding would elicit certain reactions from certain people. If you came from Brooklyn, and played stick ball, you usually used a "spaldeen" ball, which was actually a Spaulding ball. If you were a Marx Brothers fan, you remember Groucho playing Captain Spaulding in one of his movies. But from 1977 on, Spaulding would come to mean Alan, Elizabeth, Phillip, Brandon, Alexandra, Alan-Michael, and so on. Because in 1977, the first members of the powerful clan arrived in Springfield.

Alan Spaulding (first played by the late Christopher Bernau, then by Daniel Pilon, and currently by musical theater star Ron Raines) has been involved in murder, mayhem, and all sorts of mischief over the years. He has also been an unfaithful husband. (Surprise!)

Mike Bauer was hired as counsel to the Spaulding company. He became friendly with Alan's wife, Elizabeth and encouraged her to resume her photography career. (Some years earlier, Mike at first resisted Leslie's

271

Phillip Spaulding's Family "Square"

Talk about "squaring" the family roots! (1) Phillip's biological parents, Jackie and Justin Marler, were married to each other. (2) Phillip's adoptive parents, Alan and Elizabeth Spaulding, were married to each other. (3) Phillip's real mother, Jackie, married his adoptive father, Alan. (4) Phillip's real father, Justin, married his adoptive mother, Elizabeth.

plan to return to college, but later supported her.) Alan, however, thought Elizabeth might neglect their son, Phillip (Grant Aleksander and John Bolger) who had a heart condition. But Elizabeth suspected Alan's motives were more selfish: He didn't want her to neglect him, although he was already involved in an affair with his secretary, Diane Ballard.

Elizabeth sued for divorce and custody of Phillip. Mike took her case. He also hoped to win her heart. When Alan learned of Mike's proposal, he taunted her with the fact that she couldn't have children. Elizabeth broke her engagement to Mike.

After the Spaulding divorce, Jackie Marler, who had been dating Mike, turned to Alan and showed an extraordinary interest in young Phillip. (Naturally, she was his mother.)

Jackie had divorced Justin Marler on the grounds of adultery. She went to Europe where she gave birth to their son, and gave the boy to an obstetrician — who was also Elizabeth's doctor — for adoption. Elizabeth had given birth to a stillborn child. Alan arranged for the doctor to substitute the infant given up by its natural mother. Jackie learned who had her child, and later married Alan so she could raise him.

Mike made up with Elizabeth and filed to have her regain custody of Phillip. About this time, Phillip collapsed and was rushed into surgery where Dr. Justin Marler performed the life-saving procedure on the boy, unaware that it was his son.

Elizabeth drew closer to Justin and married him.

Although Alan had no great love for Mike Bauer, he fell in love with Mike's beautiful daughter, Hope. The marriage eventually proved a disaster. But there was one bright light: the birth of their son, Alan-Michael Spaulding, named for his father and grandfather.

It would seem that in adding up Alan Spaulding's progeny, the sum would come to one son and one adopted son. But remember Jennifer Richards? A young woman named Amanda Wexler arrived in town with her mother, Lucille. Amanda had been left a part of the Spaulding Enterprises by Alan's late brother, Brandon. No one knew why. That is, no one except Lucille.

Lucille hired Jennifer Richards as her housekeeper. A close friendship developed between Jennifer and Amanda. Lucille was furious and eventually learned that Jennifer was actually Jane Marie Stafford, Amanda's real mother. Lucille tried to kill Jennifer, but instead fell on her knife and died.

Jennifer went on trial, but was acquitted when she revealed Amanda was the child she had had with Alan when they were lovers. Brandon knew the truth, which was why he arranged for Amanda to be an heir to her family's holdings.

That's "Oil" Folks

Jennifer's other daughter, Morgan, divorced Kelly because of his jealousy over her friendship with Josh Lewis (Robert Newman), a member of the newly arrived oil-rich Lewis clan.

Ed Bauer, meanwhile, fell in love with and married Maureen Reardon. Maureen's sister, Nola, met a mysterious stranger named Quinton McCord, played by Michael Tylo, who lived in a gloomy mansion presided over by a gloomy housekeeper, played by Beulah Garrick. Nola had wonderful fantasies about herself and Quinton. She saw Quinton and herself as the lovers in *Wuthering Heights;* she saw herself as a beautiful woman about to be burned at the stake for witchcraft, but rescued in time by her dashing knight; and she saw Quinton as Dracula and herself as a willing victim.

Nola's Wizard of Oz *fantasy. From left: Michael Tylo, Lisa Brown, William Roerick, and Gregory Beecroft.*

Quinton, an archaeologist, was reluctant to talk about his past. But after the death of a long-time nemesis, he revealed that he was the illegitimate son of Henry Chamberlain, a business associate of Alan Spaulding. This made Quinton half-brother to Vanessa Chamberlain. Quinton became Quinton McCord Chamberlain, and Nola became Nola Reardon Chamberlain.

Vanessa had an affair with Nola's brother, Tony, but they broke up when he found out that she was spoiled and immature. Meanwhile, Trish Lewis, Josh Lewis's sister, became friendly with Alan, which sparked more problems for Alan and Hope. Hope divorced Alan, but Trish's real interest was in Justin's lawyer brother, Ross Marler (Jerry ver Dorn).

Just to remind those who may have forgotten, Ross had been married to Carrie (played by Jane Elliott), who had a nervous breakdown and

A Literal "Skeleton" in the Spaulding Closet

Tony Reardon and Annabelle Sim were married and moved into their "dream house," which soon proved to be a nest of nightmares. Annabelle realized she had psychic abilities and was able to direct Tony to the tunnel under the house where she had seen the skeleton of a black man in her visions.

Tony, Annabelle, Jim Reardon, Dr. Claire Ramsey, and a newspaper reporter named Fletcher Reade went to Barbados where they learned that the dead man, Conrad, had had a sister named Sharina, who had had a love child with Alan's brother, Brandon. Brandon's wife tried to kill the lovers, but Conrad was killed instead. Brandon faked his death and went to Barbados with Sharina.

was sent to an asylum. And Justin's former wife had also been Alan's wife at one point. So Trish would have become involved in a lot of Spaulding/Marler history.

The Lewises continued to arrive: Billy (Jordan Clarke) came with his teenage daughter, Mindy (Krista Tesrau). Billy fell in love with Vanessa but Billy's ex-wife, Reva (Kim Zimmer) wasn't about to let him marry her.

Mindy, meanwhile, fell in love with Phillip Spaulding. But Phillip was interested in Rick Bauer's girlfriend, Beth Raines, whose mother, Lillian, was a nurse at Cedars.

Beth's stepfather, Bradley, had sexually abused her — a fact that would come out later. Seeing Phillip's interest in the girl, Bradley told him the truth about his parentage: he was not a Spaulding. Justin and Alan were forced to confirm Bradley's charge. Phillip was upset. Jackie had died in a plane crash the year before. Justin took their baby, Samantha, to Arizona. Phillip felt alone and turned to Beth for comfort. Bradley's jealousy erupted and he raped his stepdaughter. She was overwhelmed with shame and refused to see Phillip.

Blackmail, Black Gold, and a Baby Girl

In 1985 Alan Spaulding's sister, Alexandra Spaulding von Halkein (originally played by Beverlee McKinsey and currently by Marj Dusay) returned from Europe where she'd been living as the wife of a German baron.

Beth Raines began dating Lujack, a young street-wise nightclub owner played by Vincent Irizarry. (Lujack's full name was Brandon Luvonaczek). Alexandra learned he was her son. A jealous Phillip tried to sabotage Lujack's place, but wound up blinding Beth.

India von Halkein, Alexandra's stepdaughter, knew about Phillip's part in the explosion that hurt Beth, and blackmailed him into marrying her. It was not a happy marriage, and eventually, India left him and Springfield and returned to Europe.

Reva Shayne Lewis may have been the ex-wife of Billy Lewis, but the failure of that marriage didn't deter her from pursuing two more Lewis men: She had an affair with Billy's younger brother, Josh. She then fell in love with their father, H.B. Lewis, and married him. No one knew, at the time, that Reva had had a child with Billy named Dylan. He would come to town much later.

Although Reva and H. B. agreed they'd have a platonic marriage, they did sleep together once, and she became pregnant. Sadly, she later miscarried. Meanwhile Billy's wife, Vanessa, gave birth to their son Bill, who had a heart defect. Vanessa turned to drugs to lessen her anxiety over her son's problem, but she eventually straightened out.

The Bauers learned that Bert had developed a blood clot and would have to have a leg amputated. (In reality, Charita Bauer underwent the amputation because her cancer had spread to her leg.) A year later, in 1985, Bert (and Charita) died.

Lewis Oil was a thriving business. Only someone with the strength of Samson could shake it from its solid moorings. Along came Kyle Sampson (Larkin Malloy) who had a grudge against the Lewis men. He tried to become friendly with Reva. But he and Reva's lovely sister, Roxie Shayne, (Kristi Ferrell) had some history together, and she was afraid he might tell her boyfriend, Rick, that Kyle was once one of her johns when she was a hooker. She ran off to Alaska, lost her memory, met a man named Kurt Corday, and, when she regained her memory, brought him back to Springfield. Kurt later married Mindy Lewis.

Kyle and the Lewises learned that he was a member of the family. It seems Kyle's mother, Miss Sally, was also Billy's mother.

Meanwhile, Ed and Claire Ramsey learned that their respective spouses, Maureen and Fletcher, had been killed in an explosion. They turned to each other, and comfort led to passion, and passion led to pregnancy and a baby daughter. But when Maureen and Fletcher returned, all was forgiven.

Plenty of Bad News to Go Around

Reva, by now, had broken up with H.B. They remained close friends, but agreed they shouldn't be married. Kyle proposed to her, but his mother, Miss Sally, was against the marriage and got one of Kyle's old flames, Maeve Stoddard (Leslie Denniston) to seduce him. She became pregnant. Reva knew about the baby, but hoped to keep it from him until after their marriage. But at the altar, she told him everything. They parted and he married Maeve. Maeve later told Kyle their child was stillborn, so he would

275

When you think of it: Reva Shayne bedded all the Lewis men, from H.B. to Billy to Josh to Kyle. One wonders if they'll ever consider singing the old Andrews Sisters hit, "Bei Mir Bist Du Shayne" to her someday.

feel free to marry Reva. The baby, actually, was well and left Springfield with Maeve soon after.

Mindy's husband, Kurt, died in an accident. Lujack died trying to rescue Beth from an underworld group. Chelsea Reardon's fiancé died from car accident injuries while he was under Rick's care, and she planned to sue him for malpractice. Instead, she decided to put her energy into a romance with Phillip.

Vanessa shocked Ross with the news that they were parents of a little girl, Dinah, to whom she had given birth when they were teenagers. Billy and Vanessa divorced, and he moved to Venezuela. (He would return; they would remarry; they would divorce again.)

Reva's father, Hawk Shayne, and her brother, Rusty Shayne, came to town. Hawk proposed to Beth's mother, Lillian.

Reva and Josh had an affair and became parents of a little girl they named Marah. Josh was delighted to be a father, but Reva worried that the child might be Kyle's. Although the blood tests proved Josh was Marah's dad, Alan had the tests tampered with so that it looked as if Kyle was the father of the baby.

Johnny Bauer (James Goodwin), a cousin, came to Springfield. He developed throat cancer. Drs. Rick Bauer and Meredith Reade (Nicolette Goulet) wanted to provide conventional treatment. But Johnny chose to deal with his illness in his own way. He went up in a plane, and circled Springfield's Light House, and came down, cured.

Meanwhile, Josh learned his dead wife, Sonni, hadn't died in Venezuela as he thought. He left Reva and remarried Sonni, who was actually his wife's identical twin, Solida, who'd been put up to the scam by Dr. Will Jeffries, who wanted to kill Josh. Alan was also part of the scheme, since he was still lusting after Reva.

The truth about Marah's parentage came out, much to Alan's dismay. Later, Sonni told Reva her tragic story: She had slept with Will when she was a teenager. Her father assumed Solida was the guilty twin and whipped her severely. That night, Solida killed herself. Her body was buried secretly, and Sonni took her sister's identity in addition to her own. She was both Sonni and Solida.

276

The Return of the Natives

Blake Lindsey came to town and was later found to be Cristina Blake Thorpe, daughter of Holly Norris Thorpe Marler Bauer, and Roger Thorpe.

Alan-Michael, the son Alan had with his former wife, Hope Bauer, returned to Springfield as well.

Blake and Phillip became involved and decided to marry. Only one thing marred Blake's happiness: her father, Roger, had died in a fall from a cliff years earlier. Meanwhile, a mystery man turned up in Springfield and attended the wedding. Alan recognized him as Roger and leveled a gun at him. They struggled, and the gun went off. Phillip was accidentally wounded. Alan shot again and this time the bullet found its mark in Roger's body.

Ed operated to save Roger's life, while Holly opted for Ed's scalpel to make a wrong cut. Roger Thorpe had been a wanted man when he supposedly died. But as it turned out, Roger had been working as a CIA agent and while no one could call him a good guy, at least he did his nasty deeds in the name of patriotism. Alan was arrested and sentenced to jail. Before leaving, he told Phillip that his former love, Beth, was still alive.

Alan-Michael, meanwhile, married Harley Davidson Cooper as part of a business ploy. Phillip Spaulding had taken over Spaulding Enterprises, which upset A-M. He knew if he were married, he would be entitled to part of his trust fund, and would turn it over to his father. However, to A-M's surprise, he fell in love with Harley.

A Reva-Josh glam shot: Kim Zimmer and Robert Newman in the 1980s.

Later, A-M learned that Harley had had a child with Dylan, Reva's son with Billy Lewis. Although Dylan considered their relationship over, he slept with Harley again. Alan-Michael and Harley were divorced and she left town with her child, who is, of course, Reva and Billy's granddaughter.

Reva's brother, Rusty Shayne, helped rescue Mindy when the mad Will Jeffries held her prisoner. Will fell to his death. Mindy went into a drug-induced coma, and had an out-of-body experience.

Blake thought Phillip was having an out-of-mind experience because of his obsession with finding Beth, and had him committed. This proved to be a blessing for Phillip. He saw Beth on the hospital grounds and, eventually, they were reunited. She had aphasia — an inability to speak — caused by her many traumas. But Beth began to remember him, and remembered, most of all, that she still loved him.

277

When Roger Thorpe was shot in that green-house, nearly everyone in Springfield had a motive. But when Billy Lewis was convicted of the attempted murder, it marked a rare occasion: soaps don't usually send major characters to jail.

Alexandra became involved with Roger.

Blake became involved with Ross, who had also been involved with her mother, Holly.

Reva and Josh finally married in a sunny picnic wedding; Marah served as flower girl for her parents. Reva gave birth to their second child, and while tormented by post-partum depression, drove off a bridge. For some five years, she was assumed to have died in the raging river waters.

Recent Turnings of the Wheel

In 1991, a young man named Nick McHenry turned up in Springfield. To Alexandra's shock, she learned he was Lujack's identical twin, who had been taken from her at birth. She never knew he existed, until she saw him and was drawn to him. Nick is played by Vincent Irizarry, who previously played Lujack.

In 1991, Bridget Reardon came to Springfield. She and a young man named Hart (who was later revealed to be Roger's illegitimate son) had a child. Bridget spent her pregnancy locked in the attic of Nadine Cooper (played by Jean Carol). Nadine wanted her then-husband, Billy, to believe this was their baby. Billy discovered the ruse, divorced Nadine, and remarried Vanessa; they adopted baby Peter.

After Billy went to jail for shooting Roger, Bridget challenged Vanessa's custody of the child. So did Roger. This was, after all, his first grandchild. Bridget and Vanessa were given joint custody, but Vanessa had liberal visiting rights. Roger could visit, but only with supervision.

A Young Man in Disguise

Vanessa met a younger man, Matt Reardon, Bridget's brother. They defied their families' outraged reactions and decided to marry.

Alan had been released early from jail after helping to save lives in a riot. But for months, he kept his presence in Springfield a secret. He disguised himself as an Asian business man, and playing on Roger's greed, got him to do his bidding in a business deal.

*Melina Kanakaredes
(who created the role of
Eleni Cooper), Melissa
Hayden, Jean Carol, and
Frank Dicopoulos.*

Alan also hid between the walls of his Spaulding mansion so he could overhear sister, Alexandra, whenever he thought she might have something to say that he could later put to good use.

Alexandra, who had had an affair with Fletcher Reade, was upset about Roger (her former lover) wooing his former wife, Holly. She arranged to make it look as if Roger had spent a night with her.

Holly turned to Fletcher for emotional support. Fletcher was happy to supply a strong shoulder to lean on; eventually, he proposed. Roger and Alexandra had each other, but, to their dismay, they lost the people they really loved. Alan finally revealed himself to his family and was warmly welcomed by Alexandra.

Tangie Hill (Marcy Walker) came to town and she and Josh Lewis became involved. When that relationship ended, she found herself the object of desire of the Spaulding men, *père et fils*. Alan was upset that Alan-Michael had designs on Tangie when it should have been clear to his sprig that she loved daddy. (Actually, she liked Alan, and could have easily fallen in love with A-M.)

Nadine's former husband, Buzz Cooper (Justin Deas) returned to Springfield and reconciled his differences with his estranged son, Frank

279

THE ULTIMATE SOAP OPERA GUIDE

Blake and Ross's wedding portrait (l-r): Marcy Walker, Michael Zaslow, Maureen Garrett, Elizabeth Keifer, Jerry ver Dorn, Peter Simon.

(Frank Dicopulous). After an affair with Jenna Bradshaw (played by Fiona Huchinson), Buzz — who had rejected Nadine's overtures for remarriage — now considered the idea more favorably. But Nadine seemed to be less interested now that she'd found Detective Cutter (Scott Hoxby) showing interest in her.

Eleni, Frank's Greek-born wife, had to return to Greece to settle a family "scandal." It seemed she had been promised in marriage to someone else while she was a child. That promise was now being called in, and Eleni's family would be shamed if it were not kept. But Frank was not going to lose his wife. He almost lost her to Alan-Michael a few times; he was not going to let Hellenic tradition undo their happiness. The ancient Greeks used to warn of hubris; was Frank daring the gods by going against tradition? Eleni's family and the family of her "betrothed" settled the problem and Eleni came home, to stay.

Lucy Cooper (Sonia Satra), Buzz's daughter, had begun working at Spaulding Enterprises, where Alan-Michael was now president. A-M was falling for her. An employee named Brent had made a pass at her, but she was persuaded that it was not meant to be serious. He later took her out and, to her shock and horror, he raped her. Lucy tried to hide the rape, but Bridget suspected something was wrong. Eventually, Lucy told her story.

It turned out that among other nefarious things Alan had done to try to wrest back control of the company from his son, he had made a deal with Brent. Brent later proved to be HIV-positive and Lucy and Alan-Michael faced the possibility that she, too, may have been infected.

The Trouble with Daddy's Girl

Blake, meanwhile, had married Ross Marler in 1994. To her surprise, his daughter, Dinah, whom Vanessa had borne when they were teenage lovers, came back to live with daddy. Dinah created problems from day one. Blake tried to tell Ross about them, but Ross wouldn't hear a nasty word about his little girl.

It turned out that Dinah was in deep debt to some unsavory types. She joined with her hitman in a phony kidnapping-for-ransom scheme. She was rescued, and later, at Matt's (her future stepfather) urging, she confessed all.

Roger tried to separate Fletcher and Holly. He even faked amnesia following a car crash, hoping Holly would take care of him, and realize she still loved him. But his plot was a flop. Holly finally got Blake's blessing to marry Fletcher, although she knew Blake desperately wanted to see her parents reconciled and remarried. Holly's mother, Barbara (Barbara Berjer) came to the wedding. So did Roger. But he behaved. Dinah and Roger became lovers.

Alan was charged with a series of legal problems and was put in jail while awaiting trial. He was hurt trying to escape. He and Alexandra became closer as they recalled their troubled childhood. At the trial, Tangie testified against him, as did Alan-Michael. Alan faced the terrible truth: He had lost his battle for power, but had not conceded the fight.

A Ghostly Apparition

Reva, in the interim, had returned to Springfield. At first, she appeared as a ghostly figure, taunting Josh, who had begun a relationship with a nurse, Annie Dutton (Cynthia Watros). But after a few months, Reva's "spirit" gave Josh and Annie her blessing, and left.

Meanwhile, in a small community, a woman (Reva) opened her eyes in a clinic, and was told that everything would be all right. Alan Spaulding found himself in that community, and suddenly, Reva and Alan would discover that the past was now coming at them. And what of the future? Stay tuned.

The GL *cast celebrates a milestone for the show.*

Rick Bauer (played by Michael O'Leary) returned to Springfield. He was immediately thrown into a controversial situation involving his father's fiancée, Dr. Eve Guthrie (Hilary Edson). She collapsed before she and Dr. Ed Bauer could marry. Diagnosed as terminal, Eve insisted on an alternative procedure which, although risky and unproved, might save her life. Ed reluctantly agreed to it. And despite his misgivings, Rick chose to support his father. Eve died, and the Doctors Bauer knew they would have to face very serious charges from the hospital board.

Rick had another choice to make. He and Annie Dutton (Cynthia Watros) had known each other before she came to work at Cedars. He warned her that if she didn't tell Josh about her past, he would. He agreed not to say anything after she assured him she would be completely candid with Josh. But Rick had reason to believe she would not tell everything — and he had reason to worry that Annie's past could create problems for other people as well.

Nick stopped Alexandra from attempting to blackmail a judge involved with Alan's case. After Tangie rejected him, a furious Alan ordered his lawyer, Sid, to destroy her and his son, Alan-Michael, on the stand. But it was Alan, not his accusers, who faced the terrible consequences of the truth.

Some *Guiding Light* Guide Posts

Under Agnes Nixon's stewardship as head writer, *Guiding Light* introduced black characters who had important story lines and weren't simply *reactors* to situations. Her Nurse Martha Frazier was played by both Ruby Dee and Cicely Tyson. Dr. Jim Frazier, Martha's husband, was played by both James Earl Jones and Billy Dee Williams.

Agnes stressed the importance of regular pap tests in *GL* story lines. It was a subject that was rarely discussed in public, and, except for an article or two in women's magazines, was never discussed in any other medium at any great length.

In the story, Bert Bauer tells Dr. Paul Fletcher she hadn't had a full physical examination since giving birth to her son, Edward. Like many — if not most — women, Bert felt it was unnecessary, but she agreed to have an exam. Fletcher told her he was going to take a pap smear. She asked about it and he explained, in detail, its purpose. Later, Bert was told the smear showed irregular cells. She had cancer and would require surgery. Because the cancer was diagnosed relatively early, Bert would survive.

Agnes Nixon recalled that women from all over the country later wrote to say their lives had been saved because they followed Bert's example, and had a pap test done. Nixon's own gynecologist told her the show resulted in appointments with six patients he hadn't seen in years.

The network was shocked at the positive response to the story; ditto Procter & Gamble. They were a conservative lot who feared the worst when they reluctantly agreed to it. Nixon wrote the story six months before it aired because it had to get past the censors.

Agnes Nixon also introduced the first wife-beating story line on daytime with Ed Bauer assaulting his wife, Leslie, in one of his drunken rages.

The Founding Families

Meta Bauer Roberts Banning, played by Jone Alison on both the radio and television versions of the soap. She was one of three children of Papa Bauer and his late wife. Her sister was Trudy Bauer; her brother, Bill Bauer. Her child, Chuckie, was adopted by Ray and Charlotte during the soap's radio days. Later, Ted White, the boy's natural father, learned Meta had recovered custody of the child and came back into her life. She agreed to marry him to give the boy a father. Chuckie enjoyed painting; Ted wanted him to experience more "manly" pursuits. The child sustained a skull fracture during boxing practice and died. Meta was shattered with grief and stalked Ted. When she found him she killed him, but blotted the whole thing out of her mind. Later, she stood trial but was acquitted.

Meta married Joe Roberts, and became stepmother to his children, including his daughter Kathy. Meta, Joe, and Kathy moved to the television version of the soap.

After Joe's death, Meta and Kathy competed for the love of the same man, Mark Holden. Although Kathy won him, Meta was free to find Mr. Right — who turned out to be Dr. Bruce Banning.

Bertha (Bert) Bauer,

played by Charita Bauer until her death in 1985. Bertha Miller married Bill Bauer during the soap's earlier radio phase. They had two children, Mike and Ed.

Bert's grandchildren include Hope Bauer, Mike's daughter; Rick Bauer, Ed's son; Michelle Bauer, Ed's daughter. Her great grandson is Alan-Michael Spaulding, son of Hope and Alan Spaulding.

Bert started on the series as a nagging, immature young wife who butted into everyone's business. As she dealt with her husband's drinking and womanizing, she matured and became the heart of the Bauer family.

Kathy Roberts Lang Grant Holden,

played by Susan Douglas. Kathy was the daughter of Joe Roberts, Meta Bauer's husband. She married Dr. Richard Grant without telling him she'd been secretly married before to Bob Lang. She gave birth to a daughter, Robin, and was so preoccupied with raising the child, that she didn't realize she had a rival for Richard's affections in his nurse, Janet Johnson (Ruth Warrick).

When Susan Douglas became pregnant — and would be unavailable for six months — the show's producers decided to have her character die. Irna Phillips arranged for a wheelchair-bound Kathy to be hit by young bicyclists and pushed out into open traffic.

Papa Bauer,

played by European actor Theo Goetz until his death in 1972. Papa and his late wife came to America to find the American dream. They had three children: daughters Trudy and Meta, and a son, Bill. Trudy married early and left the show while it was still just on radio.

Papa Bauer's namesake is his great-grandson, Rick (Frederick) Bauer, son of grandson Ed Bauer and his wife, Leslie. His other great-grandchildren are Michelle, Ed's daughter, and Hope Bauer Spaulding, Mike's daughter. His great-great grandson is Alan-Michael Spaulding, son of Alan and Hope.

Dr. Richard Grant

(James Lipton, who would later become one of *Guiding Light*'s head writers). Dr. Grant was married to Meta Bauer's stepdaughter, Kathy Roberts, who gave birth to a daughter, Robin. He and

Kathy had their marriage annulled when she confessed that her late husband was Robin's real father. Although they were no longer married, Dick still loved Kathy and was upset when another doctor came into her life. He was unable to proceed with surgery one day, and left the hospital and moved to New York.

He met and married an artist, Marie Wallace, despite the disapproval of his mother, Laura.

Joe Roberts

(Herb Nelson) was a widower with two children when he married Meta Bauer. She tried to be a mother to his son, Joey, and daughter Kathy. But Kathy resented her. She wanted Joe to marry someone else.

Joe and Meta loved each other, and the marriage worked. He died of cancer, leaving Meta devastated. She later fell in love with Mark Holden because she saw in him many of the qualities she loved in Joe. Ironically, it was Kathy who would marry Mark.

Bill Bauer,

originally played by Lyle Sudro, then by Ed Bryce. Bill was the son of Papa Bauer and the brother of Trudy and Meta. He was married to Bertha (Bert) Miller Bauer. They had two sons, Michael and Edward (originally named William Edward, Jr., after him). He was also the father of Hillary Kincaid Bauer, whose mother was his one-time mistress, Simone Kincaid.

Bill was an alcoholic who frequently left when life at home got rough. He had the first heart transplant on daytime. He was also reported dead at least twice, but returned to Springfield to disprove the reports. At last count, his reported death "took."

Laura Grant

(Alice Yourman), Richard Grant's mother, was fiercely protective of her son. She never liked any of the women he loved, and gave wife, Kathy, a difficult time; ditto wife, Marie.

Closeups: Cast and Characters

Actor: Jean Carol

Birthplace: Hillside, New York

Birthdate: April 13

Jean started acting at age three as part of a junior repertory company that performed in Carnegie Hall. She is a Phi Beta Kappa graduate of Florida State University and holds a B.A. and M.S. in theater arts and broadcasting. She hosted *PM Magazine* for six years. Her prime-time credits include *Simon & Simon* and the miniseries *Space*. She was also on *The Young and the Restless*. Jean and her husband Gerry Rand, live in New York.

Character: Nadine Cooper Lewis Cooper

Nadine is the former wife of Buzz Cooper (Justin Deas) and Billy Lewis. She is an ambitious woman who tried to climb Springfield's social ladder via her marriage to Billy: But her social ascent crashed when he discovered that their son, Peter, was actually the child Bridget Reardon was carrying in secret (and gave birth to in secret), while Nadine put more stuffing under her skirt every month.

Nadine has become close to her stepson, Frank, and his wife, Eleni. From time to time she considers trying to get her former husband back, but one or the other is often diverted.

Actor: Justin Deas

Birthdate: March 30

Emmy winner Justin Deas studied theater at the Julliard School in New York City, and took a degree in theater arts at the College of William and Mary. He taught theater at Florida State University before joining the Asolo Repertory Company. He went on to roles in several Shakespearean plays, including *Romeo and Juliet* at the Guthrie in Minneapolis. He has also been on Broadway and starred as Konicke in the first national production of *Grease*. His prime-time work has included *Foley Square* which starred his wife and former *As the World Turns* cast mate, Margaret Colin. He also appeared on *Santa Barbara*. Justin and Margaret live in New York with their two young sons.

Character: Frank (Buzz) Cooper, Sr.

Buzz is the father of Frank Cooper, Harley Davidson Cooper, and Lucy Cooper. He is also the ex-husband of Nadine Cooper. He left his family years earlier and became involved with another woman. In 1993, he returned to his family, who greeted him with mixed feelings. A few months later, a young woman named Lucy Cooper turned up and announced she was his daughter by that previous liaison. Buzz, who may still love Nadine, was involved with Jenna Bradshaw (played by Fiona Hutchison), who left town pregnant. Was it his child she carried? Probably.

Actor: Frank Dicopoulos

Birthplace: Akron, Ohio
Birthdate: January 3

Frank is a graduate of Kenyon College in Gambier, Ohio. His previous credits include *Falcon Crest, The Tracey Ullman Show, Silver Spoons* and *Dynasty*. He was also on *The Young and the Restless, General Hospital*, and *Capitol*. He joined *Guiding Light* in 1987. He and his wife, Teja, have a son, Jaden, born July 1993.

Character: Frank Cooper, Jr.

Frank and his wife, Eleni, ran a diner. He also became involved in a detective agency. But more recently, he's considered joining Springfield's police force, which does not please Eleni.

Frank has come through several personal problems. He almost lost Eleni permanently to her first husband, Alan-Michael Spaulding, who used under-handed methods to get her away from Frank. His daughter with Eleni had a hearing defect. He's had problems with his father, Buzz, and his former stepmother, Nadine — not to mention Eleni's family in Greece, who wanted her to leave him to marry the man to whom she was betrothed as a child. He also lived through the campaign of a jealous woman out to destroy his marriage so that she could have him for herself.

Frank could be called the Job of Springfield. Much happens to him, but he rarely complains: He simply works it through.

Actor: Marj Dusay

Birthplace: Russell, Kansas
Birthdate: February 20

Marj Dusay began her acting career with a Los Angeles improvisational group called "The Session," which included Rob Reiner and Richard Dreyfuss. She went on to do comedy on *The Steve Allen Show.* Her 200-plus prime-time credits include *Dallas, In the Heat of the Night, Murder, She*

Wrote, Fresh Prince of Bel Air, Perfect Strangers, Star Trek, and *WKRP in Cincinnati.* Her features include *MacArthur, Made in Heaven* and *Sweet November.*

Dusay joined *Guiding Light* in September, 1993.

Character: Alexandra Spaulding von Halkein

Alexandra could well be called the "poor little rich girl." Despite her wealth and social standing, Alex has had a great many personal problems. She gave birth to twin sons who were taken from her. (She thought she only had one son.) She eventually found her son, Lujack (Vincent Irizarry), who had a nightclub in Springfield, only to lose him when he was killed. The arrival of Nick McHenry (also played by Irizarry) in Springfield disturbed her. The young man was a double for the dead Lujack. She discovered he was Lujack's twin; the child she never knew she had.

Alexandra is the former wife of a German baron, and the stepmother of the beautiful India von Halkein (Mary Kay Adams).

Alexandra has a love-dislike relationship with her brother, Alan. They compete for control of the family business, and often have violent disagreements about each other's personal life. But there is a deep well of love between them.

Alexandra had a long affair with Fletcher Reade (Jay Hammer) but lost him to Holly Lindsey Thorpe, the ex-wife of another lover, Roger Thorpe. Alexandra set up a ploy to thwart the Thorpe remarriage. Unwittingly, she set up a situation where Holly found Fletcher, Fletcher responded, and the two married.

Has Alexandra learned her lesson not to manipulate and machinate? Of course not. She'll simply try to be better at it next time.

Actor: Maureen Garrett

Birthplace: Rocky Point, North Carolina
Birthdate: August 18

Maureen originally played Holly from 1976 to 1981. The character then left the story. When Holly was brought back in 1989, the producers said they couldn't imagine anyone but Maureen in the role.

Garrett grew up in various parts of the United States and Europe. She studied at the Universitat Munchen in Germany and in the United States, she attended Villanova and Temple Universities. She has an extensive background in theater.

Character: Holly Norris Bauer Marler Thorpe Lindsey Reade

Holly, the daughter of Stanley and Barbara Norris, has been involved with many of the more fascinating men folk of Springfield. Most recently, she ended an unsuccessful attempt at reconciling with Roger Thorpe, father of her daughter, Blake, by marrying journalist Fletcher Reade.

See Springfield Chronicles for more on Ms. Lindsey-hyphen-Reade.

Actor: Jay Hammer

Birthplace: San Francisco, California
Birthdate: November 16

Jay Hammer, a graduate of the University of the Pacific, studied with Sanford Meisner at the famed Neighborhood Playhouse School in New York. He worked mostly in theater, but also accumulated a long list of prime-time credits including *The Blue Knight, The Jeffersons, Mannix, Kojak,* and *Adam 12.*

He started with *Guiding Light* as a writer, using the name Charles Jay Hammer. ("I felt my family would be happy to see my full name on the credits roll," he said.) In March 1984, he was persuaded to play the short-term role — one day of taping is as short as they get — of Fletcher Reade, a dashing newspaperman. "They were as surprised as I was to find the audience liked Fletcher and so he stayed," said Jay.

Hammer, the father of one daughter and three sons, lives in Manhattan.

Character: Fletcher Reade

Fletcher was not supposed to become a major part of tho *Guiding Light.* But the audience reacted to his first (and supposedly only) appearance, and the writers, including the man who played him, Charles Jay Hammer, quickly scrambled to give him a story line.

Fletcher had a long, torrid affair with Alexandra Spaulding. When Holly was upset with her former — and potentially future — husband, Roger, for allegedly sleeping with his former lover, Alexandra, Fletcher provided a comforting presence. (Ironically, Alexandra had set Roger up because she didn't want him to return to Holly.) Soon comfort turned to love and Fletcher and Holly were wed, much to the chagrin of Alex who thought she could get him back into her bed again.

Actor: Melissa Hayden

Birthplace: Santa Monica, California
Birthdate: November 13

Melissa is pleased that she has the same name as the famed ballet dancer. "I love dancing," she said, "but I love acting more."

289

Ms. Hayden started her career in feature films, including *Punchline,* *Pennies from Heaven,* and *Annie.* Her first soap was *General Hospital.* She joined *Guiding Light* in 1991 as Bridget Reardon, a role that has so far brought her an Emmy.

Character: Bridget Reardon

Bridget was a confused teenager in love with the gentle, handsome Hart, the illegitimate son of Roger Thorpe. (Unfortunately, Hart wanted Julie, whose brother Mallet wooed Harley Cooper.) She became pregnant, and was so upset and ashamed by her situation that she allowed Nadine, who was then married to Billy Lewis, to hide her, and she agreed to give Nadine the baby when it was born. In the meantime, Nadine would pretend to be pregnant.

Bridget later recovered her child when Billy learned about the deception. However, Billy, now remarried to Vanessa Chamberlain, wanted to adopt the baby, claiming they could give it a better life than Bridget could offer. When Billy went to jail, Bridget went to court; she and Vanessa were granted joint custody of baby Peter. Roger, having learned Hart was the father, immediately tried to win custody of his grandchild; he was granted visitation rights.

Hart (who was played by Leonard Staab until the actor had a tragic hang-gliding accident) had left town suddenly. (The character was slated to return in 1995.) Dylan Shayne Lewis, the son of Reva and (ironically) Billy Lewis, became her friend and confidante; they might have married, but he became blind and left Springfield.

Bridget's father is Sean Reardon; her brother is Matt Reardon who (again ironically) planned to marry Vanessa Chamberlain Lewis, another "ex" of Billy's.

Actor: Rick Hearst

Birthplace: Howard Beach, New York
Birthdate: January 4

Rick grew up in New York, New Jersey, and Texas. He studied at the University of Texas at Austin, and at the Circle in the Square Professional Workshop in New York City. His feature film credits include *Crossing the Line* and *Brain Damage.* His previous soap role was on *Days of Our Lives.*

Rick won his Daytime Emmy for Outstanding Younger Actor in 1991, the day after his wife, Donna, gave birth to the first of their two children. He was nominated for Best Supporting Actor in 1995, only to lose to cast mate Jerry ver Dorn.

Character: Alan-Michael Spaulding

Alan-Michael is the son of Alan Spaulding and his former wife, Hope Bauer, daughter of Mike Bauer. His great grandmother is the late Bert

Bauer. Alan-Michael is the half-brother of Amanda Spaulding, Alan's daughter with Jennifer Richards. He is also the adoptive brother of Phillip Spaulding.

Alan-Michael has been married to Blake, Roger Thorpe's daughter; Eleni, currently the wife of Frank Cooper; and (as this is written) should be exchanging I dos with Buzz Cooper's daughter, Lucy.

Alan-Michael has often been a pawn on his father's chessboard. Alan put him in charge of Spaulding Enterprises when it suited him, then tried to have him removed by devious means. A-M has matured and has stood up to his father, whom he loves, in spite of his less-than-noble tendencies.

Actor: Vincent Irizarry

Birthplace: Queens, New York, N.Y
Birthdate: November 12

Vincent Irizarry was graduated from the Berklee College of Music in Boston and is a classically trained pianist. He studied jazz dance at the Morelli Ballet and won a scholarship to the Lee Strasberg Theatre Institute.

Rick Hearst and Jerry ver Dorn.

He's worked on off-Broadway and off-off-Broadway in productions that include *The Death of von Richthoven* and *Lennon*. After leaving *Guiding Light* in 1985, Vincent starred in several miniseries, including *Echoes in the Darkness,* and *Lucky Chances.* He was in the feature film, *Heartbreak Ridge* with Clint Eastwood. He also appeared in the soap, *Santa Barbara.* He was formerly married to Signy Coleman (Hope, on *The Young and the Restless*) with whom he had a daughter, Sienne. Vince commutes frequently from New York to spend time with his child.

Character: Nick McHenry Spaulding

Nick is the surviving half of a set of twins born to Alexandra Spaulding. Nick came to Springfield unaware of his kinship to the town's most important family. Alexandra saw his striking resemblance to Lujack and later was able to find proof that Mr. McHenry was Lujack's twin.

Nick was married to Mindy Lewis, but the marriage was in trouble almost from the start since Alexandra didn't like Mindy and Mindy didn't like mama. He left the presidency of Spaulding Enterprises to return to his first love, writing, at the *Springfield Journal*.

Actor: Elizabeth Keifer

Birthplace: Santa Monica, California
Birthdate: November 14

Elizabeth studied at the Academy of Stage and Cinema Arts in Los Angeles. She also studied voice at U.C.L.A. Her previous soaps include *The Young and the Restless, One Life to Live* and *General Hospital*. She's also done a slew of prime-time guest roles. She holds a brown belt in karate.

Character: Blake Thorpe Spaulding Marler

Blake (Cristina) was born the daughter of Holly and Roger Thorpe. She was unaware of the identity of her real father for several years and resented Holly for keeping the secret for so long.

Blake has been married to Alan-Michael Spaulding and later became involved with Ross Marler, her mother's former husband whom Holly considered remarrying. However, Blake made it to the altar with Ross first.

Blake had hoped her parents would remarry, and was upset when Holly passed over Roger to marry Fletcher Reade. But she gave her mom her blessing.

The return of Dinah, the daughter of Ross and Vanessa Lewis, has created problems in her marriage. It remains to be seen if Ross is more interested in meeting the needs of his wife, or assuaging the guilt of a parent who was not there for a child when she needed him most.

Actor: Maeve Kinkead

Birthplace: New York City
Birthdate: May 31

Maeve won an Emmy for Outstanding Supporting Actress in 1992. Both of her parents worked for the *New Yorker* magazine. Maeve majored in English at Radcliffe, and planned to teach. While doing graduate work at Harvard, she became involved with the University's famed Loeb Drama Center. She went on to study at the London Academy of Music and Dramatic Art.

292

Besides theater, Kinkead's previous credits include three productions for WGBH, the Public Broadcasting station in Boston, and three years on *Another World*. She joined *Guiding Light* in 1980. Maeve Kinkead and her husband, Harry Streep (yes, he's Meryl's brother) and their two children, live in a suburb of New York.

Character: Vanessa Chamberlain Lewis (and maybe Reardon)

Vanessa was introduced as the spoiled, willful child of Henry Chamberlain (William Roerick). She became involved with Tony Reardon. But he found her shallow and immature, and he left her.

She later fell in love with Billy Lewis, but his ex-wife, Reva, tried to keep them apart. Eventually, Billy and Vanessa were married. They broke up over his drinking.

Vanessa had had an affair with Ross Marler when they were teenagers. She had a daughter whom she gave up for adoption. Ross was unaware of the baby until Vanessa told him about little Dinah many years later. Recently, Dinah has come back into her parents' lives, and she's stirred things up for them.

Ironically, Vanessa, who never got to be a Reardon with Tony, will probably do so now with a much younger Reardon, Matt. She also shares custody of Matt's nephew, Peter, born to Bridget Reardon. Also, Dinah started sleeping with Roger Thorpe, little Peter's grandfather. Well, nothing like keeping it all in the family.

Maeve Kinkead and William Roerick.

Actor: Kurt McKinney

Birthplace: Louisville, Kentucky
Birthdate: February 15

Kurt became a fan favorite when he played Ned Ashton in *General Hospital*. He also had a recurring role on *Day of Our Lives*.

He has guested on several prime-time shows, and has also appeared in the television film, *Sworn to Vengeance*. On stage, he appeared in *No One Went for Cookies* at the Genesian Theatre Group in Los Angeles.

Kurt and his wife live in New York with a pet dog they found as a stray in L.A.

Character: Matt Reardon

Matt is Bridget's brother and Sean's son. He came to Springfield in 1994 and met Vanessa Lewis, an older woman whom he found absolutely

293

entrancing. They fell in love, but agreed to keep their romance secret until Vanessa could somehow break the news to her family. Eventually, their secret came out, and while most of Vanessa's kinfolk were against her involvement with the much younger man, she defied them and their relationship grew stronger.

Matt even proved helpful when Dinah staged her own kidnapping to help raise money for her dangerous creditors.

Actor: Wendy Moniz

Birthplace: Kansas City, Missouri
Birthdate: January 19

A long-time *Guiding Light* fan ("I started watching when I was six"), Wendy was overwhelmed at the idea of joining the cast of her favorite soap in 1994 when she recreated the role of Dinah Chamberlain Marler, the often difficult child of Vanessa Lewis and Ross Marler.

She holds a B.A. in English and Acting from Siena College in Albany, New York. Her theater credits include *Agnes of God, Grease, Crimes of the Heart,* and *Baby with the Bathwater.*

Wendy and her husband, David, live in New Jersey.

Character: Dinah Chamberlain Marler

Dinah is the child of a teenage affair between Vanessa Chamberlain Lewis and Ross Marler. She was adopted, but later learned who her real parents were.

Dinah came back to Springfield soon after her mother became engaged to Matt Reardon. She caused problems in her father's marriage to Blake Thorpe, and arranged her own kidnapping for ransom to raise money to pay off her mob-connected creditors.

Dinah and Roger Thorpe became lovers, more for expediency than for passion. (Roger feels he can get to Lewis Oil through Dinah's relationship with Vanessa, and she feels she can use Roger in any way she has to.)

Actor: Robert Newman

Birthplace: Los Angeles, California
Birthdate: June 27

Robert Newman came to New York after an extensive career in theater in Los Angeles. He has a bachelor's degree in theater from California State University in Northridge. He created the role of Joshua Lewis on *Guiding Light* in October, 1981. He left the series in 1983, and then returned in

1986. Between his *GL* residences, he worked in *General Hospital* and *Santa Barbara,* and starred in the pilot for *Destination America.*

Bob has been involved with children's organizations both in the United States and abroad. He and his wife, actor Britt Helfer, live in Westchester County in New York with their two children.

Character: Joshua Lewis

Josh is the son of oil tycoon H.B. Lewis. His half-brother is Billy Lewis, Jr; his sister is Trish Lewis.

Although Josh has been involved with many women in Springfield, the woman with whom he has been most deeply in love is Reva Shayne Lewis (played by Kim Zimmer).

Josh and Reva had two children before she disappeared and was presumed dead. He left Springfield to search for her but was unsuccessful. He returned in 1993. There was a new woman in his life, Tangie Hill (Marcy Walker). But that didn't work out. He later met a nurse, Annie Dutton, and became closer to her. Eventually, they fell in love.

But Reva — or at least, Reva's ghost — returned to try to get him to leave Annie. However, when Annie helped save the life of Josh and Reva's daughter, Marah, Reva relented and wished Josh well.

As 1995 moved into autumn, Reva had awakened in a clinic; Alan Spaulding, who once tried to break up Reva and Josh (even planting false evidence that Kyle was Marah's father) had met Reva in a small community, and Rick Bauer, who knew Annie's secrets from the past, was considering telling Joshua everything.

Actor: Michael O'Leary
Birthplace: St. Paul, Minnesota
Birthdate: March 27

In 1995, Micheal O'Leary made his second return trip to *Guiding Light.* He first played Rick Bauer from 1983 to 1986. He came back to the role in 1987, and then left in 1991. He told the author, "Coming back here is really like coming back to a family. Just about everyone I'd known before is still here…. I always had a great time on the show, and I know it'll be the same this time…."

O'Leary was raised in Diamond Bar, California. He majored in television production at California State University. His credits include the recurring role of Dr. Stewart Farmingham on *Doogie Howser, M.D.* He co-starred with Bess Armstrong in a Los Angeles theater production of *Tea and Sympathy.* He also wrote and co-starred in *Scars,* and has a new play, *Rain* in the process of being produced.

O'Leary spent some of his off-*GL* time visiting Ireland, his ancestral homeland. He and his wife, Joni, also spent time in Scotland, where she can trace part of her ancestry.

Character: Rick Bauer

See Springfield Chronicles.

Actor: Ron Raines

Birthplace: Texas City, Texas
Birthdate: December 2

Ron Raines took up the reins (really, no pun intended) of Alan Spaulding in 1994, and has played him to his charmingly villainous hilt since the character reemerged in Springfield after several years away. (Actually, he was in jail.)

Ron has played the lead role in virtually every major American musical and operetta. He also appeared in Grand Opera, and now he's starring in *Soap Opera*. His musical theater credits include *Show Boat, Teddy and Alice, Colette,* and *The Unsinkable Molly Brown* (which he did with Debbie Reynolds). He was nominated as Best Actor by the *Detroit Free Press* for his role in *Follies*.

Ron is a frequent guest artist with various philharmonic orchestras. He and his wife, stage director Dona Vaughn, live in Manhattan with their young daughter.

Character: Alan Spaulding

Created by the late Christopher Bernau, and later played by Daniel Pilon after Bernau's death, and now by Ron Raines, Alan Spaulding has been part of Springfield's history since 1977. He arrived with his wife, Elizabeth, and soon became involved with other women, including Hope Bauer, whom he married, and with whom he had his son, Alan-Michael.

Alan is the father of Amanda Wexler Spaulding (Kathleen Cullen) who was born to his former lover, Jennifer Richards (née Jane Marie Stafford). Alan was also involved with one of Ed Bauer's wives, Rita Stapleton. Their affair led to her divorce from Ed.

In mid-1995, Alan's pecadilloes caught up with him again, and he found himself in a peck of legal trouble. He left Springfield and headed into a small community where, unbeknownst to him at first, the woman he once loved, Reva Shayne Lewis Lewis Lewis, was living.

For more of Alan Spaulding — see Springfield Chronicles.

Jennifer Roszell

Birthdate: March 7

Jennifer is of Greek descent (as is her husband, Constantine) and she plays Greek immigrant Eleni Cooper on the soap. Besides her acting career, Jennifer is also an accomplished singer (soprano) and was the voice of Constance in the animated feature, *The Mark of the Musketeers.*

Character: Eleni Cooper
    See Springfield Chronicles.

Actor: Sonia Satra

Birthplace: Glen Ridge, New Jersey
Birthdate: December 17

Sonia had a role in the TV movie, *Bonanza: The Next Generation,* and has also appeared in several syndicated series. Her feature films include *Brand New Life* and *Sam and Ed.* She made her daytime television debut as Lucy Cooper in September 1993.

Character: Lucy Cooper
    Lucy is the daughter of Buzz Cooper and the half-sister of Frank, Jr., and Harley.

    She and Alan-Michael Spaulding became friends. She went to work for him when he took over Spaulding Enterprises. One of the employees, a man named Brent, asked her out on a date and raped her.

    Lucy was ashamed to tell anyone about it; Brent warned her that if she did tell someone, he would say she wanted to have sex, and then panicked afterward. But eventually she revealed what had happened to her. As part of her therapy, Lucy attended rape counseling sessions where she learned she had no part in the rape and that full blame must be put on her rapist.

    Barring any of the complications that often befall Alan-Michael's plans for a happy love life, Lucy may marry him. But perhaps not.

Actor: Peter Simon

Birthplace: New York City
Birthdate: September 27

Peter is a graduate of Exeter Academy and Williams College. He has appeared frequently in off-Broadway plays and with the New York Shakespeare Festival. He has two previous soaps to his credit: He played Scott Phillips in *Search for Tomorrow* (his wife, Courtney Sherman, now a writer, played his wife on the soap) and he played Ian McFarland on *As the World Turns.*

Peter left *Guiding Light* in 1984 and returned in 1986.

Character: William Edward Bauer, Jr.

Surprised? Although we think of the character mostly as Ed Bauer, his father, Bill, insisted the boy also carry his first name; hence the William. But the character soon became just Ed.

Ed is one of two sons of Bill and Bertha (Bert) Bauer. He's the brother of Mike Bauer, and the half-brother of the late Hillary Bauer. He's the uncle of Mike's daughter, Hope. Ed is the father of Frederick Bauer, later known as Freddy, and finally as Rick. Like his dad, Rick, too, is a doctor. Rick's mother is the late Leslie Jackson Bauer Bauer (she was also married to Mike). Ed's other wives include Holly Norris Thorpe and Rita Stapleton.

Ed is a recovering alcoholic. In the past, he's been guilty of spousal abuse during his drunken rages.

Most recently, Ed was engaged to marry Dr. Eve Guthrie, but she collapsed before the wedding and died soon after. Ed and Rick both faced serious charges from the hospital board for taking part in an unorthodox procedure that Eve urged them to perform.

For more on Ed Bauer, see Springfield Chronicles.

Actor: Jerry ver Dorn

Birthplace: Sioux Falls, South Dakota
Birthdate: November 23

Jerry ver Dorn attended Moorehead State University in Minnesota and then spent a year at London's Studio 68, an acting academy founded by several British actors, including Sean Connery.

His big break as an actor was in a Rutgers University production of Eric Bentley's stirring play about the 1950s political witch hunts, *Are You Now, or Have You Ever Been?* The production moved from the campus to off-Broadway's Promenade Theater and then to Broadway. Jerry did the evening performances, while winning applause at the matinees of Shaw's *Man and Superman* at the Circle in the Square, where he was seen by *Guiding Light* casting people. He joined the show in 1979 as Ross Marler, the lawyer-brother of Justin Marler.

Some years later, ver Dorn recreated the role for the television film, *The Cradle Will Fall.*

Jerry and his wife Beth have two sons.

Character: Ross Marler

Ross is the father of Dinah Chamberlain Marler. Her mother was his teenage lover, Vanessa Chamberlain Lewis. He is also the uncle of Phillip Spaulding, the adoptive son of Alan Spaulding, whose real father was Ross's brother, Dr. Justin Marler.

Ross is married to Blake Thorpe Spaulding, daughter of ex-wife, Holly Reade, and Roger Thorpe.

Dinah has recently come back into his life, and has caused him and Blake quite a lot of trouble since his return. Perhaps most irksome for both of them is the fact that Dinah has been having an affair with Roger Thorpe.

Actor: Cynthia Watros

Birthplace: Lake Orion, Michigan
Birthdate: Sept 2

Cynthia, who is of Native American ancestry on her father's side, says her last name, Watros, means Water Lily in the language of her ancestors.

She started acting when a professor at Macomb Community College in Macomb County, Michigan suggested that she had a flair for it. She went on to receive a Bachelor of Arts degree from Boston University's School for the Arts. She appeared in several of the school's productions before heading to New York, where she found herself on stage at the Lucille Lortel Theater in New York's Greenwich Village, in the hit comedy, *Four Dogs and A Bone,* co-starring with Grant Shaud of *Murphy Brown* and Kim Zimmer, who had played Reva Shayne Lewis in *Guiding Light.*

About a year later, Cynthia was told she had the newly created role of Annie Dutton on *GL.* And, to her surprise and delight, she learned Kim, her cast mate from *Four Dogs* would be returning to the show — first as a spirit and then, as it turned out, on a long-term contract status.

Character: Annie Dutton

Annie is a nurse with a secret in her past; Dr. Rick Bauer knew her secret and wanted her to reveal it to Josh Lewis. But Annie hesitated. Would Josh understand what she would tell him?

Annie and Josh grew closer. When he was visited by Reva's spirit, Annie felt she was being pushed out of his life. After Josh finally told her about Reva, Annie "saw" her too, and insisted she would fight Reva for Josh's right to put the past behind him to live a new life with her.

Dutton won over the rather jealous spirit by saving the life of Reva and Josh's daughter when Reva told her the child had been hurt and was lying unconscious.

Whither the fortunes of Annie and Josh? Stay tuned.

299

Actor: Michael Zaslow

Birthplace: Inglewood, California
Birthdate: November 1

Michael Zaslow is married to Susan Hufford, whom he met when they were on Broadway in *Fiddler on the Roof*. The Zaslows have two daughters, Marika and Helena, whom they adopted from Korea. Zaslow is a Phi Beta Kappa graduate of UCLA (political science major). He enjoys family musicales: His daughters play their violins and he plays the piano and sings along with Susan.

On *Guiding Light*, Zaslow created a classic soap villain: Roger Thorpe is slick, smart, sexy, and almost always ruthless. In *One Life to Live*, the soap he did between his two stints on *Guiding Light*, he played pianist David Rinaldi. "As much as I love doing well-written villains like Roger," Zaslow said, "I enjoyed the chance to be a nice guy for a little while, and also play the piano on camera."

His other daytime credits are Dick Hart on *Search for Tomorrow*, and Dr. Peter Chernak on *Love Is a Many Splendored Thing*.

Zaslow's other theater credits include *Carousel*, and *Cat On A Hot Tin Roof*. He has appeared as a guest star on *Star Trek*, and other episodic television programs. He played Jonathan Hadaray on the nighttime soap, *King's Crossing*.

Michael Zaslow is active in environmental causes.

Character: Roger Thorpe

Roger Thorpe may be daddy to his daughter Blake, and has finally been accepted as a father by his son, Hart, but in his time, he's been a real rotter and a rapist.

He raped Blake's mother, Holly, at least twice. He raped Rita Stapleton, and later kidnapped her when she was pregnant with her husband Ed Bauer's child. He tied her to the bed and when she went into labor, he fled after hearing police sirens. In his haste to get out, he threw over a lantern and the cabin was set ablaze. Mike and Ed saved Rita, but she lost her child.

Later, Roger traced his former wife Holly and their daughter Cristina (Blake) to their remote hiding place, where Ed thought they'd be safe. But Roger had bugged their phones and knew where to find them. He tried to abduct Cristina, but Holly distracted him, and he wound up dragging her into the jungle instead.

Mike and Ed arrived and as Mike led Holly away Roger shot at Ed and then fell backward over a cliff. Although shot by Roger's bullet, and furious at what he had done to his family, Ed tried to save Roger's life; but Thorpe fell, and with a bloodcurdling scream, presumably died on the rocks below. Roger, of course didn't die then — or any other time he was presumed to have expired.

For more about Roger Thorpe, see Springfield Chronicles.

Michael on Roger:

"No one trusts Roger very much. And he doesn't seem to understand why."

Actor: Kim Zimmer

Kim Zimmer, who created the role of Reva Shayne for *Guiding Light* in 1983, has been acting in television and theater for several years. Her most recent stage credit is *Four Dogs and a Bone,* which she did with *Murphy Brown* star Grant Shaud; ironically, the cast also featured Cynthia Watros, who later joined *Guiding Light* as Annie Dutton, Reva's rival for Josh Lewis.

Her prime-time credits include roles on *Designing Women, Seinfeld, University Hospital, Models, Inc.,* and *Babylon 5.*

Kim's daytime credits include *The Doctors, One Life to Live* and *Santa Barbara.*

Kim returned to *Guiding Light* in May 1995, after an absence of five years. It was to be a limited run. But in June she agreed to a long-term contract with the soap.

Kim and her actor husband, A.C. Weary, and their children, have relocated to New York from their home in California.

Character: Reva Shayne Lewis Lewis Lewis
See Springfield Chronicles.

Supporting Cast

Actor: Lisa Brown

Lisa Brown, who created the role of Nola Reardon Chamberlain on *Guiding Light,* returned to the series in August 1995.

Previous to her move back to Springfield, she had a short-term role on *Loving.* Lisa also appeared as Iva Snyder, mother of Lily Walsh, on *As the World Turns.*

She was the toast of Broadway in David Merrick's production of *42nd Street,* but after the birth of her child (she was married to former *GL* co-star Tom Nielsen (Floyd), she concentrated mostly on her soap career.

She was cast in *Guiding Light* by the late Douglas Marland, who had seen her in theater productions previously. There was resistance to bringing someone into the soap who had relatively little television experience, but Marland was adamant: He felt she was a great talent they could not afford to pass up. As usual, he was right.

Marland again cast her in *As the World Turns* when he created the Snyder family on that series.

Character: Nola Reardon Chamberlain
See Springfield Chronicles.

Actor: Bryan Buffinton

Birthplace: Ridgewood, New Jersey
Birthdate: April 1

Bryan's character was first listed on the credits roll of *Guiding Light* as Little Billy Lewis. He eventually became just Bill. The son of Billy Lewis and Vanessa Chamberlain, his grandfather is H.B. Lewis. He is friendly with Michelle Bauer, daughter of Dr. Ed Bauer.

The role on *GL* is the young actor's first for television. He has had several Daytime Emmy nominations as Outstanding Younger Actor in a Drama Series. He was in the feature film *Mr. Destiny* with Jim Belushi and Michael Caine.

Actor: Scott Hoxby

Birthplace: Cincinnati, Ohio
Birthdate: June 10

Scott plays Detective Patrick Cutter, whose interest in Tangie was thwarted by two Spauldings, Alan-Michael and his father, Alan. In real life, the only woman who interests Scott is his wife, Judy.

Actor: Amelia Marshall

Birthplace: Albany, Georgia
Birthdate: April 2

Amelia plays Gilly Grant, a successful reporter at WSPR, the local TV station. She doesn't know that Alan Spaulding cost her a coveted job in Los Angeles, in order to keep Sid Dickerson in Springfield (working for Alan).

Actor: Kelly Neal

Birthplace: Philadelphia, Pennsylvania
Birthdate: February 3

Kelly plays Sid Dickerson, a bright young lawyer who works for Alan Spaulding. He's devoted to reclaiming his old neighborhood, "Fifth Street," and finding happiness with Gilly Grant.

Actor: William Roerick

Birthplace: Hoboken, New Jersey
Birthdate: December 17

The distinguished film and theater actor plays Henry Chamberlain, father of Vanessa Chamberlain Lewis and Quinton McCord Chamberlain.

Actor: Tina Sloan

Birthplace: Bronxeville, New York
Birthdate: February 1

Tina plays nurse Lillian Raines, mother of Beth Raines. Lillian developed breast cancer, and her story revealed both the fear that grips a woman when she first learns about the diagnosis, and the courage that makes her decide to fight for her life.

Tina Sloan was educated at the Ursuline School of New Rochelle in Westchester County in New York, and at Manhattanville College.

Loving

A gnes Nixon and Douglas Marland combined their talents to create a soap opera that was a small but beautiful gem. It went on the air as a two-hour movie the evening of June 26, 1983, starring Lloyd Bridges and the late Geraldine Page. It went on daytime the following Monday.

In an interview, Bridges told the author that he regretted being killed off in the movie. "I would love to have survived so that I could make an occasional appearance on the daytime version.... [It] all sounds very exciting and very much the kind of thing actors love to do...."

The show was given an official welcome into the wonderful world of soaps at a party in New York's Gracie Mansion, the home of the Big Apple's mayors. Mayor Edward Koch openly hinted to Agnes that he wouldn't mind making an appearance on the show every now and then. When he was reminded that the show is set in Corinth, a fictional town in Pennsylvania, he quipped, "so have an excuse for me to go there, and for some of your characters to come here."

Ironically, thirteen years later, *Loving* (which, of course, is actually produced in the ABC studios on Manhattan's West Side) moved its fictional site to the real thing: New York City. The core location is in Soho, a wonderful neighborhood filled with art galleries, great loft space for apartments and studios, fine shops, Class-A restaurants and, most of all, some of the most interesting people who live and work in the Big Apple. The show's title has been changed to *LOV❤NYC*, with a "Big Apple" in its logo.

Change may be good for the artistic soul, but it comes with a price: Many of the characters fans have come to know and love over the years will not make the move. Indeed, many of them will not survive the serial killer who will be stalking Corinth over several months, starting July 14, 1995, when the first victim, Stacey Donovan Forbes, was found dead. Ironically, Stacey was played by the only remaining member of the original cast, Lauren-Marie Taylor. (Chris Marcantel, who played Curtis Alden, was also a member of the original cast, but he left the show several times while Lauren-Marie stayed with it.)

Clues to the killer's identity were given in the episodes. By the time the move is made in November, the murderer will be unmasked, and the show will go on.

Morgan Fairchild — The First Lady of Soho

LOV❤NYC debuts with a new first lady in residence: Morgan Fairchild. Her credits include *Search for Tomorrow* (she played the paranoid killer Jennifer Pace Phillips) and *Flamingo Road*, on which she played Constance Weldon Carlyle. She's had recurring roles on *Dallas*, *Roseanne*, and *Mork and Mindy*. She earned an Emmy nomination for her guest starring role on *Murphy Brown*. Her television movies include *North and South*, *Street of Dreams*, and *Writer's Block*.

Fairchild's feature films include *The Seduction*, *The Red-Headed Stranger*, *Deadly Illusions*, *Campus Man*, and her most recent, *Gospel* with

Original Cast

Wesley Addy . . . . .Cabot Alden	*Tom Ligon* . . . . .Billy Bristow
Jennifer Ashe . . . . .Lily Slater	*Marilyn McIntyre* . . .Noreen Vochek Donovan
Pamela Blair . . . . .Rita Mae Bristow	
Brian Cranston . . .Douglas Donovan	*Chris Marcantel* . . . . . .Curtis Alden
John Cunningham . . . . .Garth Slater	*Augusta Dabney* . . . . .Isabelle Alden
Peter Davies . . . . .Father Jim Vochek	*John Shearin* . . . . .Roger Forbes
Shannon Eubanks .Ann Alden Forbes	*Perry Stephens* . . . . .Jack Forbes
Patricia Kalember . . . .Merrill Vochek	*Lauren-Marie Taylor* Stacey Donovan
Teri Keane . . . . .Rose Donovan	*Susan Walters* . . . . . . .Lorna Forbes
James Kiberd . . . . . . .Mike Donovan	*Ann Williams* . . . . .June Slater

First Air Date: June 27, 1983 / ABC

305

Martin Sheen. Morgan's pact with ABC includes a two-year contract for the soap, and also commitments for other projects. She will continue making films during her stay with the soap.

Looking Back As We Look Ahead: Milestones in Corinth

Loving was set in a college town in Pennsylvania where four families would have their lives intertwined. And what sometimes seemed so obvious on the surface frequently hid some terrible truths.

Roger and Ann Alden Forbes had two children, Jack, whom they adopted, and Lorna, a college student. Jack was in love with the gentle Lily Slater, who would later have a nervous breakdown and the ugly story of her having been a victim of her incestuous father would come out.

Loving took a stand on an issue that had been largely ignored by the soaps: It dealt with the tortured soul of a Vietnam War veteran, Mike Donovan, played by James Kiberd, as he tried to find his way back to a normal life. In a story line that helped remind people of what these war veterans had gone through, Mike would get drunk and lash out about his buried demons, and speak bitterly about the war. In the mid-1980s, *Loving* went to the Vietnam War Memorial in Washington, D.C., where Kiberd gave a moving performance as a man coming to confront his painful memories.

The character of Noreen Vochek was a nurse involved in AIDS research. Her brother, Jim, was a priest, who would later find himself in love with Shana Sloane, Cabot Alden's illegitimate daughter, played by Susan Keith. (Susan met her husband, James Kiberd on the show. "I almost didn't get the role," she told the author. "He didn't like me and thought they should bring someone else on. But they persuaded him that I could do the work." And the rest has been a wonderfully successful marriage.)

Merrill Vochek, sister of Father Jim and Noreen, was a television reporter who got the scoops, but never seemed to get the man she wanted. Jack, who disappeared from the soap in the late 1980s, had a lot of problems to deal with in the course of his life in Corinth. He was arrested for killing Lily's incestuous father, but at his trial, Lily's mother, June, suddenly recalled pulling the trigger. She had tried to blot out not just her act, but also the reality of her husband's abuse of their daughter with drugs and alcohol.

Jack's real father, the notorious Dane Hammond, played by Anthony Herrera, turned up with the intention of destroying Alden Enterprises because Cabot fired him for embezzlement. Dane planned to use Shana in his scheme, but Shana began to love her father, and refused to hurt him.

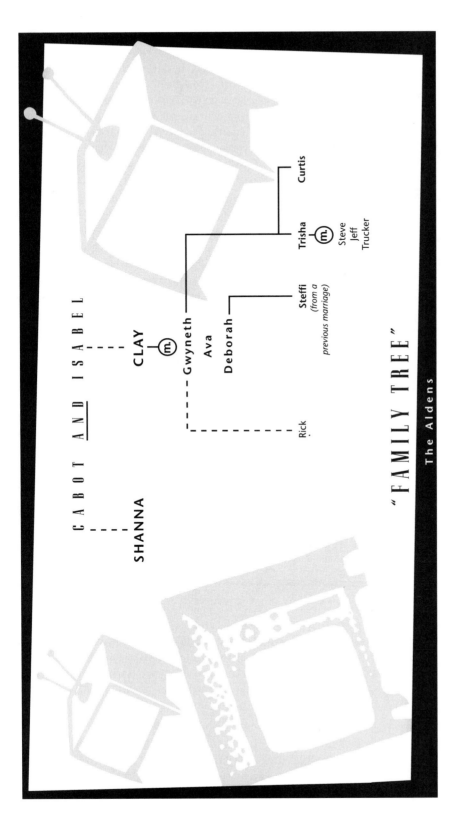

"FAMILY TREE"
The Aldens

CABOT AND ISABEL — — — CLAY — (m) — Gwyneth
Ava
Deborah

SHANNA — — —

Curtis

Trisha — (m) — Steve
Jeff
Trucker

Steffi
*(from a
previous marriage)*

Rick

L oving has had its
share of good and
bad experiences—
and an Alden has been
involved in each of
them. Sometimes in a
"loving" way; often as
not, not!

Jean LeClerc and Kate Collins, who created the role of Natalie on AMC.

To pressure Shana into doing his bidding, Dane had a private detective show her photos of herself and Father Jim in compromising positions. (Shana and Jim were involved when he was studying for the priesthood in Rome.) When Shana was kidnapped by the devious P.I., she was saved by Mike. Cabot then went public with the announcement that she was his daughter. Shana later married Jim when he was released from his vows; but not before he faced the devil himself in church, and won the battle for his soul.

The character of Paul Slavinsky (Joseph Breen) was paralyzed following an explosion. The soap dealt with the plight of a paraplegic who not only has to come to terms with his disability, but also his sexuality. Does he have the right to ask a woman to share his life and be his lover? Can he be a lover?

Clay Alden, played by Randolph Mantooth, came to Corinth after being missing for years. He reconciled with his wife, Gwynn and his family. But the real Clay Alden (Dennis Parlato) turned up later on. It seems the fake Clay, whose real name was Alex Masters, had taken Clay's identity. Cabot Alden was a mite confused about which son was who. In any event, some years later, Clay learned that while he was his mother's son, her lover had fathered him; but Cabot accepted him as his own.

Ava Rescott (Lisa Peluso), the brunette beauty from the other side of the tracks, managed to bed and wed some of the town's hoi polloi, including Jack Forbes and Clay Alden. She later married Alex Masters.

Jeremy Hunter (Jean LeClerc), who started soap life as Erica Kane's protector and lover on *All My Children,* moved to Corinth to become an art professor at the University. He became involved with Ava and Gwyn, Clay's former wife. He also discovered he had a twin brother who had been kidnapped as a baby and was out to get Jeremy for having the good life while he had to grow up with a nasty kidnapper.

Trisha Alden, Clay's daughter, and the apple of his eye, seemed to fall in love with men daddy just didn't approve of. One of them was Trucker McKenzie, who drove a truck for Clay years earlier, and who took the rap for Clay for vehicular manslaughter. Trisha proposed to Trucker. Gwynn was determined to keep her daughter from marrying him and arranged to make it look as if Trucker beat her up and slept with her. He was a dumped Trucker after that.

Trisha married the strange Jeff Hartman. Trucker found her and explained what her mother had done to break them up. Jeff tried to knife Trucker; they fought. Jeff fell and claimed he was paralyzed. Trucker and Trisha were eventually married, but she disappeared and was presumed to have died. Trucker, however, never believed she was gone and years later, he found Jeff in Rome who admitted Trisha was with him. But Jeff vanished before Trucker could get anything more out of him.

A major story line involved Kate Rescott, Ava's mother, played by Nada Rowand. Her gynecologist told her she had cancer and would have to undergo a hysterectomy. He reminded her (and the audience) that if she had had a regular examination, this might have been avoided. To Ava's shock, she learned her mother's cancer had spread beyond the focal site first mentioned by the doctor. Kate might die. In a well played story line, Kate goes through post-surgical treatments and learns to deal with having her hair fall out. But she also finds love in the person of a widower named Louie (Bernard Barrow). They marry and live happily together until Louie died. (The death of Bernard Barrow was also the death of Louie.) Kate later met Neal (Larry Haines) a man from her past. Perhaps he might also be the next man in her future?

After the death of Jim Vochek and their child, Shana buried herself in work for Alden Enterprises. But she later met and fell in love with Leo Burnell (James Carroll) who owned a department store. They were married and she became pregnant. The child was born with a genetic defect. Shana was aware of the risk before the baby's birth, but resisted the suggestion of an abortion. Leo was distraught and angry. Shana should have aborted the baby. But he realized he was acting out of fear of the unknown. Like her, he wanted this child. He, Shana, and their baby left for Rome where she had a great job offer waiting.

In the years before *Loving* was set for its changeover, two *All My Children* alumni arrived to keep Jean LeClerc company in Corinth: Debbi Morgan recreated her role as Dr. Angie Hubbard, and a few years later, Darnell Williams, who played Angie's late husband, Jesse, turned up as Jesse's look-alike, Jacob Johnson. He fell in love with Angie, but despite her feelings for him (are they for Jacob or for Jesse?) she married Charles.

Curtis Alden, who seemed to be playing with more jokers in his deck than he should have, was committed to a sanitarium, but later got out and just as the killings began, started doing strange things, including lavishing gifts on the lovely model, Steffi, and buying his father, Clay, his favorite brandy.

Could Curtis have been the killer?

Or was it Tess (Catherine Hickland) who was so upset with Stacey for barging into an important party? Or for taking Buck back when Tess began to hope he'd be hers?

309

Or Deborah, Clay's wife, who was upset with all the Alden men because her beautiful model daughter, Steffi was pregnant — probably by Cooper (Michael Weatherly)?

Or could it be Buck Huston, Trucker's brother (Philip Brown) who may have killed Stacey because she may have changed her mind about marrying him, and killed others to confuse the investigation?

Or did Dane Hammond return to wreak vengeance on his old adversaries? Or did his son, Jack, return to find Stacey hadn't kept the vigil while he was gone?

(How close were you to finding your way through the maze-o-clues?)

Goodbye, Corinth

Although we'll no longer be in a Corinthian "lather," here's to *LOV♥NYC* making it for at least another thirteen years as *the little soap that could.*

A Last Look at the Last Cast of *Loving*

Nancy Addison–Altman, who was born in Brooklyn, New York on March 21, created the role of Jillian Coleridge on *Ryan's Hope.* In 1989, she played Marissa Rampal on *All My Children* opposite her *Loving* co-star, Jean LeClerc. On *Guiding Light,* she played Kit Vested from 1970 to 1974. She starred opposite Claudette Colbert in Broadway's *A Talent For Murder.*

Deborah Brewer Alden is less loving toward her daughter, Steffi, than she is ambitious for the young model. She was jealous of Clay Alden's attentions to Steffi and managed to insinuate herself into his home where she got hold of material that "persuaded" him to marry her. Deborah recovered from a heart attack, and was touched that Clay didn't let her die when she was first stricken. Later, she vowed to make all the Alden men "pay" when she learned Steffi was pregnant. Soon after, Clay was found dead.

Wesley Addy, a film, theater, and television star, created the role of Cabot Alden in 1983 and played it until 1991. He returned to the series in 1994. Wesley has worked on screen and the stage with Helen Hayes, Laurence Olivier, Vivien Leigh, Bette Davis, and other great stars, including Celeste Holm, who happens to be his wife. (Holm briefly played Cabot's wife, Isabelle, on the soap.) His previous soaps were *Days of Our Lives* and *Edge of Night.*

Cabot Alden is the patriarch of the Alden family. His wealth and his position of power within Corinth have not prevented many family tragedies, including the disappearance of his grand-child, Trisha, and the death of a grand-child born to daughter Shana and her late husband. Cabot was presumed dead for several years but returned to Corinth much to the chagrin of his son, Clay, and his wife, Isabelle, both of whom knew he was alive, and knew he could wreak destruction on all of them.

Alimi Ballard made his network televi-sion debut in the role of Dr. Angie Hub-bard's teenage son, Frankie. His previous TV experience was with PBS' well-received magazine series for teenagers, *In the Mix,* on which he still appears. The New York-born Ballard (birthdate, Octo-ber 17) studied at the Harry Truman High School in the Bronx with an eye to becoming a lawyer. But he wandered into a neighborhood arts center and found himself agreeing to take a role in an orig-inal play. With that move, the law was put on the back burner. Alimi hopes one day to complete his law studies while continuing his performing career.

Frankie Hubbard has had problems adjusting to his widowed mother's rela-tionship with another man, but he learned to accept him.

Philip Brown.

Philip Brown has done more than 250 commercials. The Coalinga, Cal-ifornia native (March 26) made his television debut as Billy Martin on *The Doris Day Show* when he was ten. He loved working with Doris, and shares her love of animals. (Doris has saved thousands of stray dogs over the years.) Philip owns two Staffordshire terriers, Cassie and Zelda, whom he admits he spoils. He previously appeared on *General Hospital* and *Search for Tomorrow.* He's also done episodic television and made movies in Namibia and Mozambique. He also played the good guy-turned-bad-guy Brian Johnson in *Knots Landing.*

Buck Huston is the brother of former *Loving* character, Trucker McKenzie. Buck was deeply in love with Stacey Forbes, the first of the Corinth serial killer's victims. He found her body after bringing her children to summer camp. He was a suspect.

311

Augusta Dabney played Isabelle from 1983 to 1987; then returned in 1988 and played the role until 1991. She returned again in 1994. Dabney has been on Broadway in several major productions such as *Children of a Lesser God,* and has been featured in films including *The Heartbreak Kid, Plaza Suite,* and *Violets Are Blue.* Her previous soaps were *Another World, As the World Turns,* and *Love is A Many Splendored Thing.*

Isabelle Alden is the matriarch of the Alden family. For years she kept secret from Clay Alden the fact that he was her son through a love affair. But Cabot Alden accepted him as his child.

Geoffrey Ewing was born in Minneapolis, Minnesota on August 10. He played college baseball at the University of Minnesota with Dave Winfield. At one time he considered making the sport his career, but decided he'd rather be an actor. Ewing has an OBIE (an Off-Broadway award) for *Ali,* the show about Muhammed Ali that he starred in and co-wrote. Geoffrey's wife, actor Nan-Lynn Nelson, played Harrison's dead fiancée in flashbacks on *Loving.*

Charles Harrison is a police detective who came to Corinth during an investigation and found himself falling in love with the widowed Dr. Angie Hubbard (Debbi Morgan). He had a problem with her son, Frankie, who was in danger of becoming a drug addict. Eventually, that worked itself out. Then a ringer for Angie's dead husband, Jesse Hubbard, arrived, and Charles wondered if she would choose to marry the newcomer, Jake Johnson, or him. She chose him. But Jake never left town.

Meta Golding was born in India while her father was stationed there as part of his work for the United Nations. She is a graduate of Cornell University in New York with a double major in theater and political science. Meta originally tested for a role on *One Life to Live.* She didn't get the role, but got a recommendation for another role that was being cast on *Loving.* She learned four days later that she got it, and had to fly to New York from Los Angeles in two days.

Bree works for Tess at the ad agency and may be a new love interest for Frankie Hubbard.
"I could hardly believe it, but I packed my bags and went to New York and realized I hadn't been dreaming the whole thing."

312

Larry Haines, a New York native, became one of soapdom's longest-running actors when he co-starred with Mary Stuart on *Search for Tomorrow.* He started his career in radio ("which is still my favorite medium," he says) and has done prime time, theater, and film work.

Neal came to Corinth shortly before the killings began. He is from Kate's past. But did he really come to see her after all these years?

Amelia Heinle was born in Casa Grande, Arizona on March 17, and moved to Cherry Hill, New Jersey with her parents when she was in high school. After graduating, she started her successful modeling career. Her role as Steffi Brewster is her acting debut. However, daytime audiences saw her photo on *One Life to Live* as Rose, one of Asa Buchanan's many lady friends.

Stephanie (Steffi) Brewster is the daughter of Deborah Brewster. She is a successful model and has worked for Tess Wilder's agency. She has also been in love with Cooper Alden, and was about to marry him and go off to Paris with him but her mother had a heart attack and she chose to stay with her.

Steffi has been bulimic and has been the target of a stalker. (Tess, anxious for publicity, was the stalker.) She is also pregnant with a child by Cooper.

Catherine Hickland, who was born in Fort Lauderdale, Florida, on February 11, starred in *Capitol,* where she played the dual roles of Jenny Diamond and Julie Clegg. She also played Dr. Courtney Marshall on *Texas.* She guest starred in a great many prime-time shows, including *Knight Rider,* which starred her former husband, David Hasselhoff, as the dashing Michael Knight. She is now married to the real Michael Knight, who plays Tad Martin on *All My Children.* The couple's one dog and four cats share their apartment with them.

Tess Wilder came to Corinth and immediately set her cap for the recently widowed Trucker McKenzie, but Trucker found someone else. She opened a model's agency and ran into trouble with Clay Alden, who tried to blackmail her into giving up control, using the information he had that she was the Stalker; the person who was making Steffi's life a nightmare. Tess vowed to pay back Stacey for upsetting a party; the next day, Stacey was dead.

T. W. King was born Theodore William King in Hollywood, California, and moved around a great deal while growing up. At one point, the family lived on a ranch, which T.W. recalls fondly. "We had two horses, chickens, pet fish, hamsters, dogs and a donkey.... It was great. Oh, yes, we also had rabbits. We started with two and in three years we had forty-two." T.W. started his career in theater, doing off-off Broadway, way off Broadway, and off-Broadway. He has studied film editing and directing. He believes every actor should know all facets of the business.

Danny started as a sleazy drug dealer who was instrumental in the death of Casey Bowman, and then became obsessed with Casey's widow, Ally

313

(Laura Sisk). Will the character be redeemed? T.W. thinks it's possible. Of course, the question to ask is, will Danny survive the serial killer? Then we can wonder about redemption.

Jean LeClerc is a native of Montreal, Quebec. His birthdate is July 7. His parents were born in France and moved to Canada. Jean originally planned a career in medicine, but was increasingly fascinated by acting. He has extensive theater credits, including playing Dracula on Broadway; in 1995 he signed to play the Transylvanian vampire in a film for cable. Before joining *Loving,* he was Jeremy Hunter on *All My Children* and became one of Erica's (Susan Lucci) lovers. Like his on-screen character, Jean is an artist and an art collector. LeClerc is active in the Children With AIDS Foundation. He is also a correspondent for national Canadian television.

Jeremy Hunter is the son of the late Alex Hunter, and the stepson of the late Natalie Hunter. His half-brother is Timothy Hunter Dillon. Jeremy moved from Pine Valley to Corinth to accept a position as professor of art. He was involved with several women, including Gwyneth Alden and Tess Wilder. He survived an attack by his long lost twin brother.

Randolph Mantooth was born in Sacramento, California on September 19. He has had a long career in theater and prime time. He created the role of Alex Masters on *Loving.* He formerly starred in the prime-time series, *Emergency,* and in the short-lived *Under Cover.* Mantooth continues to do theater when time allows. He starred in the world premiere of *Evil Little Thoughts* at the Denver Center for the Performing Arts. Proud of his Native American heritage, Mantooth attends pow-wows when his schedule allows.

Alex Masters, a police detective, first came to Corinth as the long missing Clay Alden. The real Clay later turned up. Alex has been involved in cloak and dagger stuff for years. He has a child with his current wife, Ava Rescott Alden Masters (whom he married and divorced once before). He was finding clues to the serial killer, but ran into a lot of dead ends — with the emphasis on dead.

Christopher Marcantel is a soap opera veteran. He created the role of Curtis Alden on *Loving.*

Curtis Alden has been operating with several cards short of a full deck. He was released from a sanitarium shortly before the killings began. Is he the killer? Well, he did give daddy Clay a bottle of his favorite brandy before Clay died. Was it for a farewell toast?

Debbi Morgan was born in Dunn, North Carolina on September 20. She created the role of Dr. Angie Hubbard on *All My Children,* leaving to join *Generations.* When that series ended, she returned to New York and was asked to reprise the role of Angie on *Loving.* She agreed. Debbi also played Alex Hayley's Aunt Elizabeth Harvey in *Roots: The Next Generation* and went on to do TV films such as *The Jesse Owens Story* and *The Lenney Jeter Story.* She was formerly married to actor Charles Dutton *(The Piano Lesson).*

Angie Hubbard, mother of teenager Frankie Hubbard, has had some rough times in recent years. She continued to grieve for her late husband, Jesse, but thought she found love with a new man, Charles Harrison whom she married. But Jesse's double, Jacob Johnson, appeared, and Angie wonders if she can stay faithful to Charles and not be drawn into an affair with Jake. Then again, the Corinth killer might make all that angst moot.

Christine Tudor Newman was born and raised in Baltimore, Maryland. She earned a scholarship to the Peabody Conservatory of Music in Baltimore and developed her strong stage voice, which she has used in such productions as *Cat on a Hot Tin Roof, Plaza Suite,* and *Pajama Tops.* She is a partner in "Youth at Risk," which works with teens in trouble.

Gwyneth Alden is the ex-wife of Clay Alden and the mother of the missing Trisha and the unbalanced Curtis. She was also involved with Dane Hammond, the real father of Jack Forbes, husband of Victim No. 1, Stacey Forbes. Jack has also been missing. Did he return to do in his family? And will Gwyneth's recent affair with Jeremy last beyond the killer? Or will it matter?

> *P.S. Gwyneth had another son who died some years ago after causing a lot of mischief among the Corinthians.*

George Palermo is a native of Hoboken, New Jersey, whose other famous son is Frank Sinatra.

Tony was the bodyguard hired to guard Steffi during the stalking period. He's since been made a partner with Alex Masters. He arrived shortly before the killing started. Does that indicate anything significant? We'll see.

Dennis Parlato was born in Los Angeles, California on March 30. His father was a well-known trumpet player. Dennis was a high school English teacher, but left teaching to pursue a career in dance. He performed with several ballet companies before deciding to try his luck as an actor. He made his acting debut as King Louis VII in an off-Broadway production of *Becket.* He also appeared as Zack in *A Chorus Line* and in several other productions. Parlato has appeared in episodic television and in films. Dennis

Lisa Peluso.

admits he's typecast for roles as wealthy and powerful men. His previous soap role was as Michael Grande on *One Life to Live.*

Dennis decided to leave *Loving* before he knew he would be the second victim. The problem was that the soap needed to have him around so that they could kill off his character according to their time table. Dennis agreed to stay on for three more months.

Clay Alden is the scion of the Alden family. (Actually, he's Isabelle's son through an affair, but Cabot raised him as his own.) Clay and Gwyneth are the parents of the missing Trisha and the mentally challenged Curtis. The couple have long been divorced, but never quite cut the passionate links. His most recent wife was Deborah Brewster, who blackmailed him into marriage, and detested him for being involved in her daughter Steffi's life. (Clay warned Deborah to be a better mother to her bulimic child.) Clay died soon after Deborah vowed vengeance on the Alden men when she learned Steffi was pregnant.

Lisa Peluso, born July 29 in Philadelphia, previously worked on *Search for Tomorrow* as Wendy Wilkins. She created the role of Ava Rescott on *Loving.* Lisa started modeling at four months as the Philadelphia Phillies' caption baby. (Her photo was used in the papers with cute captions about the team.)

Ava Rescott Alden Masters has been a scrapper for much of her life. She was born into a blue collar family and married into wealth. Her great love remains Alex Masters, to whom she was married for the second time. She sometimes gets dark premonitions, but even when things get really hairy (the name, Peluso, means hair in Italian), she works them out.

Lisa on Ava:

"[She's] one of the best characters a woman could want to play. Ava gets involved in everything."

Nada Rowand entertained the troops in Vietnam in 1970 and 1972 with a USO tour. "I was the only woman in a helicopter with five men that dropped down to a fire base near the front line...." It was, she said, "like being in the movies."

A native of Melvin, Illinois, Nada majored in music and drama at the University of Illinois before coming to New York for a career in theater. She's also made several films. She's active in Broadway Cares/Equity Fights AIDS.

Kate Rescott Slavinsky is Ava's widowed mother. She has lost one son and has had problems with all of her children, including Ava. She also developed cancer and was close to death. She underwent chemotherapy and survived and remarried. Her second husband, Louie, died. (He was played by the late Bernard Barrow.) Most recently, an old friend from the past, Neal (Larry Haines) came into her life. Is he the serial killer?

Laura Sisk was born in Washington, D.C. on September 11. She was voted one of soaps' ten most beautiful women by *Soap Opera Digest* in 1995. She started her career with a music video that was shown on a local Maryland station; soon after she got some commercials and then the role of Ally.

Allison Rescott Bowman is the widow of the slain Casey Bowman. She blames the drug dealer, Danny, for his death. She's aware that Danny lusts after her, and she intends to use that obsession to try to destroy him.

Darnell Williams was born in London, England on March 3. He became a soap favorite in his role as the late Jesse Hubbard on *All My Children*. He went on to do theater and feature films. He returned to soaps in the early 1990s in *As the World Turns* and then went to *Loving*.

Jacob Johnson brought mystery to Corinth when he turned up as the ringer for Angie Hubbard's late husband, Jesse. Jacob fell in love with Angie and would have tried to stop her from marrying Charles Harrison, but he decided to leave town instead. On his way out, "Jesse" appeared and told him to go back. Will Jake break up Angie and Charles? Or will he find love with another woman? And will he survive the serial killer?

And who, out of the foregoing, will be here for us to write about in the book's next edition?

One Life to Live

A gnes Nixon began her daytime career almost twenty years before *One Life to Live* debuted. In 1951, she and Roy Winsor co-created *Search for Tomorrow*. In 1956, she and Irna Phillips co-created *As the World Turns*. In 1958, Agnes Nixon took over as head writer for Irna's long-running soap, *The Guiding Light*. In 1965, Agnes Nixon took over head writing duties on *Another World*, which she saved from imminent cancellation.

The American Broadcasting Company had launched nine soaps since 1960, but by 1967, only three were still airing: *General Hospital, Love Is a Many Splendored Thing*, and the delightfully campy *Dark Shadows*. ABC asked Nixon to create a daytime show for them, and she obliged with a series she called *Between Heaven and Hell*. The network loved it, but balked at the title, thinking it would offend the audience. She changed the name, and on July 15, 1968, *One Life to Live* joined ABC's daytime schedule. *One Life to Live* premiered as a half-hour serial. In 1976, it expanded to forty-five minutes, and in 1978, it went to a full hour.

OLTL was the first soap to feature an ethnically, socially, and racially diverse cast of characters. There were Episcopalians, Polish and Irish Catholics, Jews, African Americans, factory workers, waitresses, truckers, publishing tycoons, beat reporters, doctors, nurses — the whole gamut of American society in the town of Llanview, Pennsylvania.

OLTL introduced the first black "front burner" characters on soaps. The series also boasted the first black actor, Al Freeman, Jr., to win a Daytime Emmy. The soap also had interreligious relationships — Eileen Riley Siegel was Irish Catholic; her husband, Dave, was Jewish. In Nixon's Llanview, social strata are rungs on a ladder that anyone can climb: All it takes is intelligence, courage, and gumption. Over the years, new executive producers have come in and each has brought her or his special vision to the series. But the soap remains essentially true to its origins.

Sammy Davis, Jr.'s favorite soap hangout when he was in New York City was at *Love of Life,* where he could sing in the soap's nightclub whenever he liked. When *Love of Life* ended, *One Life to Live* created a character, Chip Warren, for Sammy Davis, Jr. to play whenever he was in New York City.

One Life to Live's stories over the years have involved prostitution, spouse abuse, homophobia, split personalities, drug addiction, gang violence, childhood sexual abuse, rebellious young people, illegitimacy, post-partum depression, embryo transplantation, a woman who never knew she had been pregnant as a teenager and had given birth to a daughter, the same woman discovering that she had a half-sister and two half-brothers (and maybe more; daddy was quite prolific in his time), and occasional flights-of-fancy that included visits to departed kith and kin in heaven, and a romp with the old ancestors back in the old West.

Some of the most dynamic characters in soap history have called Llanview home, and some of the best actors anywhere have played them, to wit: Karen Wolek, a hooker with the proverbial heart of gold (Judith Light); Victoria Lord (Erika Slezak); Dorian Lord (Robin Strasser); Victor Lord (Shepherd Strudwick); Asa Buchanan (Phil Carey); Bo and Clint Buchanan (Robert S. Woods and Clint Ritchie); Marco Dane and his twin brother, Dr. Mario Corelli (Gerald Anthony); Dr. Mark Toland (Tommy Lee Jones); Ed Hall (Al Freeman, Jr.); Joshua Hall (Laurence Fishburne); Jenny Vernon (Brynn Thayer); Renee Divine (Patricia Elliott); and Max Holden (James DePaiva).

Original Cast

Doris Belack	. . . . .Anna Wolek	Joe Gallison	. . . . . . .Tom Edwards
Lynn Benish	. . . . . . .Meredith Lord	Ellen Holly	. . . . .Carla Gray
Peter Deanda	. . . . .Dr. Price Trainor	Allan Miller	. . . . .Dave Siegel
Niki Flaks	. . . . .Karen Martin	Lee Patterson	. . . . .Joe Riley

First air date: July 15, 1968 / ABC

The Lord's Dominion

In the beginning, the Lord of Llanview dominated the town and the lives of many of the people who lived there. He was a man who believed in owning what he wanted: Victor Lord owned the newspaper, and, it was said, he "owned" many people who were beholden to him — not always by choice. But what he wanted most was to own his two daughters, Victoria and Meredith. However, in spite of their awed respect and undoubted love for him, the girls proved to have minds of their own — especially, where their hearts were concerned.

Meredith (Merri) fell in love with Larry Wolek. Although he was a doctor, Victor Lord considered the son of a Polish-American blue-collar family to be eminently unqualified to marry his daughter.

Meanwhile, Victor's older daughter, the "sensible" Victoria whom he was grooming to take over the business, fell in love with one of *The Banner*'s reporters, Joe Riley (Lee Patterson). But Victor refused to accept anyone from the wrong side of tracks wooing and (Lord forbid) winning Victoria's heart.

Although Victoria played the dutiful child for all she was worth, the pressures of living under Victor's autocratic rule caused her to split into an alternate personality, the fun-loving Niki Smith. Wherever Victoria feared to go, Niki, in her red wig and provocative get-up, would rush in eagerly.

Niki developed a crush on Larry's brother, Vinnie (Anthony Ponzini), an auto mechanic (later a policeman). She made a play for him. At first Vinnie was stunned, then delighted, then shocked when he realized who Niki Smith really was. He gallantly declined her overtures and told Viki about her "other" self. At first, Victoria rejected the possibility that she could be "two people." But she finally agreed to see a doctor.

Victor, in the meantime, found young Tom Edwards (Joe Gallison) to be a more suitable suitor for Merri. (Unbeknownst to anyone, including Tom, he had amnesia.) Merri turned down his proposal and returned to Larry.

Both Lord sisters married the men they loved. Viki was proud of Joe when he was promoted to editor-in-chief. He got a tip on a story involving a criminal syndicate and left to check it out in California. To Viki's horror, he disappeared and was reported dead.

Meredith desperately wanted children, but Larry was reluctant to have her risk her life. She had had a heart problem since childhood and pregnancy could be dangerous. But Merri became pregnant, and although she had to spend most of the nine months in bed, she told Larry she would endure anything to be the mother of their child. Merri gave birth to twins, but only one of her boys, Danny, survived.

Dr. Jim Craig (originally played by Robert Milli, who later played Adam Thorpe on *Guiding Light*, and then by Nat Polen until his death in

Victor Lord had five children (and perhaps more yet to be revealed). Though Meredith and Tony have died, his influence continues to be exerted through Viki, Tina, and Todd. In some way, there will always be a Lord to dominate Llanview society.

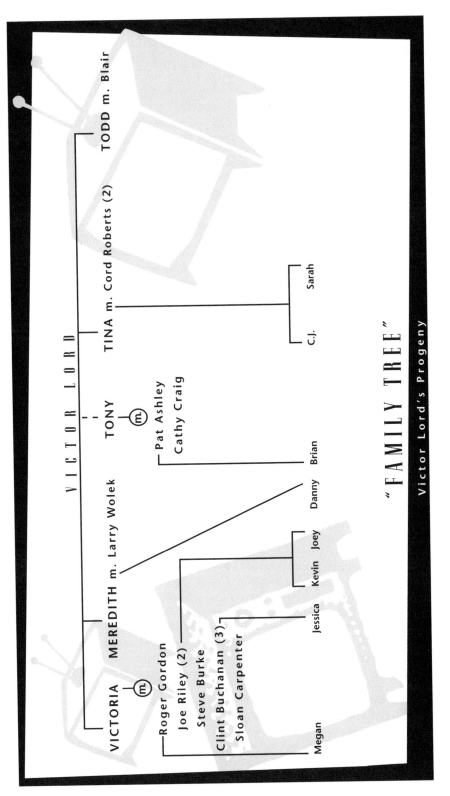

VICTOR LORD

TODD m. Blair

TINA m. Cord Roberts (2)
- C.J.
- Sarah

TONY —(m.)
- Pat Ashley
- Cathy Craig

MEREDITH m. Larry Wolek
- Brian
- Danny

VICTORIA —(m.)
- Roger Gordon
- Joe Riley (2)
- Steve Burke
- Clint Buchanan (3)
- Sloan Carpenter

- Kevin
- Joey
- Jessica
- Megan

"FAMILY TREE"

Victor Lord's Progeny

1981) was the hospital chief of staff. He married Larry's sister, Anna (Phyllis Behar). Jim had a daughter, Cathy (last played by Jennifer Harmon), who rebelled against his strictness and took to drugs. Anna tried to be a mother to her, but Cathy's drug addiction had become acute. Jim refused to believe his little girl was an addict. But he finally allowed her to enter Odyssey House (a real facility) for treatment.

Viki, meanwhile, was lost in a limbo of not knowing whether Joe was really dead or might still be alive. Victor brought in Steve Burke (Bernard Grant) to *The Banner,* and encouraged him to pursue Viki. That was a welcome assignment from the boss, since Steve had already fallen in love with her. Viki was especially vulnerable and obviously needed the quiet comforting love that Steve offered. And so, they were wed.

Meanwhile, a stranger who had lost his memory stumbled into the diner where Wanda Webb (Marilyn Chris), a friend of Vinnie Wolek, worked as a waitress. When the man collapsed, Wanda helped take care of him. He later remembered he was Joe Riley. But when he learned of Viki's new marriage, he decided not to interfere in her life. Meanwhile, Joe, Wanda, and Vinnie became close buddies.

Cathy's friend, Julie Siegel (originally played by Lee Warrick), daughter of Eileen and David Siegel (Alice Hirson and Allan Miller), shocked her parents when she moved out of the family home and moved in with her boyfriend, Jack. But when he told her he had no intention of marrying her, she realized her folks were right about him, and nearly had a nervous breakdown. (It might be argued that the breakdown was caused by Jack's callousness. But for a young person, the idea that one's parents can be right about something can be literally mind-boggling.)

Julie met and married Dr. Mark Toland (Tommy Lee Jones). However, although she said, "I do," she didn't. At least, not often. Her emotional scars with the unfaithful Jack had left her frigid. Toland tried to be understanding, and one imagines he probably ordered a lot of corned beef from the hospital commissary. (It's cured with saltpeter.)

Life continued to hold surprises — some of them tragic — for the Lord sisters. Joe had an affair with Cathy Craig, and she became pregnant. By this time, he had persuaded Viki to divorce Steve and marry him. But with Cathy's news, he was prepared to marry her instead, and give their child a home. Cathy turned him down: She would rather raise her child alone than marry a man who not only didn't love her, but who loved someone else.

Viki and Joe were quietly married, and hoped they could settle down in domestic bliss. (Remarrying the same man would later become a pattern in Viki's life with Clint Buchanan.)

Meredith, meanwhile, had come home from the hospital with her newborn son. Her brother-in-law, Vinnie, was with her. Burglars broke in, and when Vinnie tried to catch one of the culprits, Meredith fell and hit her head. She developed an aneurism and died. Vinnie blamed himself, while a grief-stricken Larry threw himself into his work.

Black, White, and Gray

Amid a soap-like series of loves gone right and wrong, a taboo-shattering story line was being played out. Jim Craig hired a beautiful young woman (Ellen Holly), who said her name was Carla Bernari. Although she was black, she was trying to pass as white, and hid the fact that Sadie Gray was her mother.

Carla was first attracted to the handsome Dr. Price Trainor, an African American. The audience was upset about a white woman being involved with a black man. Price's mother felt she was all wrong for him. Later, when she acknowledged being Sadie's daughter, audiences were shocked when Carla showed interest in her white boss, Jim Craig.

Carla finally met the man of her dreams, police Captain Ed Hall (Al Freeman, Jr.), who called her stuffy and stuck-up, and then kissed her and proposed. She said yes.

Along Came the Spider

Dr. Dorian Cramer and her sister, Melinda, came to Llanview. (Dorian was first played by Nancy Pinkerton, then by Claire Malis. Robin Strasser has played Dorian since 1979; Elaine Princi played the role for two years while Robin was in California. Melinda was played by Patricia Pearcy, Jane Badler, and Sharon Gabet, formerly Raven on *Edge of Night*.)

Dorian was a brilliant doctor and a beautiful, scheming woman whose bedside manner included sharing pillow talk with other women's husbands. Mark Toland, with his marital problems, was perfect prey for Dorian, who soon entered into an affair with him. Melinda, whose view of the world was skewed by her mental problems, was jealous of Dorian and Mark and tried to kill them. When Mark stopped her, she went into a catatonic state.

Mark and Dorian inadvertently killed a patient with an overdose of medicine. Dorian wanted to report the incident, but Mark turned on her. She had an accident and slipped into a coma. She revealed everything when she regained consciousness, but by that time the hospital board had fired them both. Instead of accepting the situation and working to reestablish her reputation, Dorian planned to give those who destroyed her career a taste of their own medicine.

323

Mark chose to leave town. Julie, whose beloved father, David, had died, went home to mother. She was shocked that mom was seeing Ben Howard. She railed at Eileen for betraying her father's memory. Deep down, however, she was upset that Eileen might find the happiness that eluded her.

Cathy gave birth to Megan, the baby fathered by Joe Riley. The child underwent surgery for a congenital heart defect. Cathy was never told Megan would probably not live past adolescence.

While Viki was watching Megan one night, the baby had an attack. Viki rushed her to the hospital, but crashed her car. Megan died and Viki was left in a coma, but ultimately recovered. Cathy, however, never recovered from her baby's death, and plotted revenge against Viki.

Dorian charmed Victor Lord, and when she saved his life during a heart attack, he realized this was the woman for him. They were married, and Dorian Cramer became Dorian Lord, the Lady of Llanfair. Victoria, however, remained a problem for Dorian. She was against the marriage, and would not accept Dorian as her stepmother. Dorian knew that while Victor doted on his new bride, he also adored his daughters — especially Viki; Dorian could not afford to let Victor feel that he had to choose between her and his children, especially Viki.

A handsome young stranger named Tony Randolph (played by George Reinholt, who had just been fired from his role as Steve Frame on *Another World*) came to town. Dorian snooped around and learned he was Victor's illegitimate son. Rather than encourage Victor and Tony to bond as father and son, Dorian told lies that kept each man feeling hurt and bewildered by the other.

Meanwhile, Cathy Craig decided to visit her friend Pat Ashley (played by Jacqueline Courtney, who had just been fired from her role as Alice Frame on *AW*) in New York. Cathy told Pat that Megan was alive, but Steve Burke told her the child had died. He offered her a job at *The Banner,* she accepted, and moved to Llanview with her young son. Surprise! Pat and Tony had once been lovers, and Tony was the father of her son, Brian.

Viki became pregnant and was faced with a difficult decision. She realized that her child could be born with the same congenital heart defect that Megan had inherited from Joe. She considered aborting the baby, but waited until it was too late for the procedure.

Cathy was increasingly resentful of Viki's presence. When she learned that Megan was doomed to an early death, even if she had not been killed in the crash, she was upset that people had lied to her. Tony proposed to her and she accepted, mostly because she hoped she would again have a child of her own.

Anna's cousin, Jenny Wolek (Brynn Thayer), a novice nun, came for Vinnie's wedding to Wanda. She and Tim Siegel (Tom Berenger) were attracted to each other. She fought her feelings, but eventually agreed to marry him. But first, there were the poor people in South America whom she had promised to help.

When she returned from her mission, she and Tim planned their wedding. Vinnie, however, was against it. He felt Tim had stolen her from the church. The two men argued. Vinnie accidentally knocked Tim down a flight of stairs and he was critically hurt. That night, Jenny married him in his hospital room just moments before he died.

Victor learned about Dorian's scheming, and when she confessed that the rumors about her were all too true, he had a stroke. Dorian arranged for him to leave the hospital early, claiming she would care for him. He died at home, and Dorian Cramer Lord was now a wealthy widow with a great deal of power that derived from the Lord holdings.

Viki was sure Dorian had killed her father, and vowed one day to bring her to justice.

Obsesssed with having a child, Cathy kidnapped Viki's newborn son, Kevin, but the baby was ultimately found safe and well.

The new chief of psychiatry at Llanview Hospital, Dr. Will Vernon (originally played by Farley Granger, then by Anthony George), arrived with his wife, Naomi (Teri Keane), daughter, Samantha (first played by Susan Keith, then Julie Montgomery, and then Dorian LoPinto), and son, Brad — the original soap cad — first played by Jameson Parker, then by Steve Fletcher (who once upon losing a bet changed his name to Steve Blizzard).

Naomi killed herself in the mistaken belief that Will Vernon was involved with Jenny. Actually, Jenny Wolek Siegel was falling in love with Brad. They planned to marry until he was implicated in the murder of his pregnant former girlfriend (played by Jackie Zeman, now on *GH*). Although he was not convicted of the murder, he was found guilty of lying to the grand jury and sent to jail for three months. Jenny tried to have the marriage annulled, but he assured her he reformed in prison. But he was still the same scoundrel; perhaps even more so.

Paul Kendall, who Pat believed had died, turned up to reveal that he had been a top secret agent and was now coming back to rebuild his life with her. Although Pat was happy he was alive, she thought his timing was a bit awkward, since she was getting ready to marry Tony. But she had to accept things as they were. However, when young Brian learned Tony, not Paul, was his real father, he rushed out into the street in tears, was hit by a car, and died.

Larry married his beautiful cousin, Karen (Judith Light), Jenny's sister. They seemed happy, but Karen had a problem living on the budget Larry drew up for them. She wanted the luxuries she felt a doctor's wife deserved. When a wealthy businessman named Talbot Huddleston offered to buy her an expensive dress, she was overwhelmed. How could she ever repay him? Symbolically twirling his invisible mustachio, and silently gloating — "heh, heh, heh" — Talbot suggested she provide him with certain "favors."

Karen agreed to provide these "favors" regularly in return for gifts. But Marco Dane (Gerald Anthony) blackmailed her into taking him on as her pimp, to work for money instead of things. Karen eventually confided in Dr. Will Vernon and Viki, who helped her escape from Marco's dominance. Marco vowed revenge. A young girl named Tina Clayton moved in with Viki and Joe after her mother died. Marco put a photograph of Tina's face on a picture of a nude woman and tried to blackmail Viki with it. He was later found murdered.

Viki was charged with the murder, but was acquitted when Katrina Karr (Nancy Snyder) testified that she had seen Talbot murder Marco. Karen also testified for Viki, revealing her double life as housewife and hooker.

Dorian used the possibility of scandal to try to force Larry out as chief of staff, in order to install her own choice, Dr. Ivan Kipling (Jack Betts), in his place. Larry, meanwhile, was drawn to Ivan's wife, Faith (Mary Lyn Rapaleye), who looked like his beloved Meredith.

Karen learned that Marco was not dead, after all, but had returned as his own twin brother, Dr. Mario Corelli, who had been killed by Talbot in the mistaken belief that he was killing Marco. (If that sounds confusing, it confused Marco too, as you'll read later on.)

Melinda was released from the sanitarium and returned to Llanview. By this time, Dorian had become involved with Dr. Peter Jansen (played by Denny Albee, Robert Burton, and Jeffrey David Pomerantz). Melinda became her rival and eventually won Peter's heart. Dorian tried to recommit her sister, but finally accepted the marriage. Melinda, however, continued to live in a world of her own.

Jenny had a difficult pregnancy. While she was in the hospital, Brad was out looking for other women. He raped Karen, and when Jenny found out, she said they were through.

Katrina was also giving birth at the same time. When Karen realized Jenny's baby had died, she wanted to save her anguished sister more pain, and with Marco's help (he was pretending to be his dead brother, Mario), arranged to swap the stillborn child for Katrina's daughter. Katrina was told her baby was dead; Jenny was told she had a little girl, whom she named Mary. Later, Jenny would learn the truth about little Mary, and although her heart was breaking, she returned the child to Katrina.

Ironically, both Jenny's baby and Mary had the same father: Brad Vernon; and had Jenny's baby lived, they would have been half-sisters.

Marco eventually cracked under the strain of pretending to be Mario when he was really Marco, and became both Mario and Marco for a while. He underwent treatment. Edwina Lewis, a newspaperwoman, stood by him when he went to jail for a month for impersonating a doctor; she

*Clint Ritchie on location
in Old Tucson, Arizona.*

then married him and they left town. Marco later returned when the marriage ended. (He and Gerald Anthony also later turned up on *General Hospital* in the course of a story line requiring Marco's special contacts with the less savory members of society.)

Larry forgave Karen for becoming a prostitute, but there were other problems in the marriage that eventually undid them. Ed and Carla Hall also found themselves drifting apart and were divorced. Carla left town.

Victoria Lord Riley Burke Riley's hope for a long happy life with Joe ended when he died of an inoperable brain tumor while Viki was pregnant with their second child. With Larry as her Lamaze coach, Viki gave birth to Joey, who would later grow up to become involved with Dorian. But that's several pages and years to come.

The Buchanan Buckaroos Come to Town

327

Prime time had *Dallas* and NBC was gearing up for a 1980 debut of *Texas,* which would be spun out of *Another World,* when *One Life to Live* blazed the daytime trail with the introduction of the Buchanan clan, the oil-rich Texas cousins of the Woleks. They came to Llanview in 1979, and nothing would ever again be the same. Patriarch Asa (Phil Carey) had two sons, Bo (Robert S. Woods) and Clint (Clint Ritchie). They were the Testosterone Trio from Texas, and you messed with them at the risk of being either romanced or run-off, pardner.

Pat's twin sister, Maggie, imprisoned her in her basement and took her place in hopes of winning Clint's love. But in a struggle with a gun-toting Maggie, Pat managed to turn the pistol away from her and toward Maggie, who was struck by a bullet when the gun went off.

Later, Pat went to Paris and met a woman named Nicole, who she learned had once been married to Asa and had given birth to Bo (now Pat's lover) after sleeping with Asa's long-time employee, Chuck Wilson (Jeremy Slate). Asa was upset about Nicole, who knew too much about the Buchanans, and ordered that she be brought to Llanview, where he put her into a wing of his mansion and held her against her will. The woman was eventually identified as Olympia Buchanan (played by ballet star Taina Elg). She died in a fall while guests downstairs reveled in a grand masquerade party.

Oh, yes — Bo was not Chuck Wilson's son after all. But while his Buchanan paternity seemed safe enough now, it would be questioned again, later on.

Asa was also upset about Bo and Pat's plan to marry, and ordered his nubile cheerleader mistress, Mimi King (Kristen Meadows), to seduce Bo. Asa, in the meantime, wasn't worried about his emotional needs while Mimi was following his orders. He had been lusting after Samantha Vernon, although she was young enough to be his daughter. (But then, so was Mimi.)

He wooed her with gifts and plied her with promises of a happy life together. But to his chagrin, she remained wary and unwilling to return his ardor. (No word, though, whether she ever returned his gifts.)

Samantha did eventually marry Asa, but their marriage was short-lived. His then-wife, Nicole, tried to make it even shorter when she attempted to kill Asa's young bride.

Meanwhile, Karen left Llanview with Steve Burke. Larry and Jenny became closer, but her old feelings for Brad returned. However, when Brad pulled one of his nasty moves against Katrina, Jenny broke off their relationship.

Tina Clayton's father, Ted, turned up, and when Vinnie discovered he was part of a counterfeit ring, Ted killed him, but he managed to make it look as if he'd had a heart attack.

Echo di Savoy (Kim Zimmer) and Giles Morgan (Robert Gentry), who were actually brother and sister out to ruin Clint, arrived in town. She seduced him for a night of passion, and let Viki (who was beginning to return Clint's feelings for her) know about it. They had a bitter fight and

Echo supposedly killed herself by jumping off a bridge. Dorian, ever eager to undo any rival — and she saw the Buchanans as major contenders for power in Llanview — testified that she saw Clint push Echo. But Echo turned up at the trial and admitted she jumped. She then revealed that she and Giles were out to avenge their mother, Giselle, whom they thought Clint had killed. They subsequently learned their father was the murderer.

The Checkered Ralstons

Bo was falling for the lovely Delilah Ralston (Shelly Burch, whose family back in Arizona were close friends and supporters of Senator Barry Goldwater), but had to hide his feelings because he'd been told he was actually a member of the Ralston family — who were neighbors of the Buchanans back home in Texas. Asa, however, knew Bo was actually his own beloved little baby Buckaroo Buchanan, but wouldn't tell him because the Samson of the Oil Patch wanted the beguiling Delilah for himself.

When Bo discovered he wasn't who he thought he was, but was who he always believed he was (in other words, when he realized he was really a Buchanan), he proposed to Delilah and she said yes.

Rebecca (Becky) Lee Abbott (Mary Gordon Murray), a beautiful folk singer, had had an affair with Bo and was pregnant with their child. She planned to marry Drew Ralston (Matthew Ashford, later Jack on *Days of Our Lives* and Tom Hardy on *General Hospital*), but he was killed on their wedding day. Asa was delighted to have a new grandson, and persuaded Becky to marry him so that they could raise the boy together.

Bo was delighted to learn he was a new father, and left Delilah when he found out she knew about the baby all along.

Dorian had married the soft-spoken district attorney Herb Callison (Anthony Call). She was impressed by him when he prosecuted Victoria Lord for murder. Although Viki was acquitted, Dorian felt he had done a wonderful job and, but for the grace of an infallible bit of truthful testimony, Viki would have gone to the chair. (Years later, Viki would feel a sense of satisfaction in seeing her former stepmother in the dock and later in the can.)

Dorian and Herb were happy together, although she wished he were more politically ambitious. When she learned the daughter she thought had died years earlier was still alive, she was overjoyed. Cassie came to stay with her and Herb.

Dorian felt secure for the first time in years. She had a husband who loved her and a daughter who was learning to love her. And she had a lot of money, power, influence, and so on.

329

Then came David Rinaldi, a.k.a. David Reynolds (Michael Zaslow on his "good guy break" from playing *Guiding Light*'s Roger Thorpe), Cassie's father. He was a world-famous pianist, but he may also have had a secret life she had never known about; for example, he might have been a terrorist.

Herb and Dorian separated. Cassie chose to live with her stepfather. Dorian still had feelings for David, but he was becoming interested in Jenny.

Samantha had married police officer Rafe Garrison (Ken Meeker), and was expecting their baby. She was brutally assaulted and was brain dead. Her friend, Delilah (ironically the woman Asa married when he couldn't marry Samantha), agreed to have Samantha's embryo implanted in her womb. After the procedure, her heartbroken father, Dr. Will Vernon, tearfully pulled the plug.

Cassie fell for the dashing Rob Coronal (Ted Marcoux), whose grandfather had been a mob boss. Alex Crown (Roy Thinnes, in his first appearance on the soap; he would later play Cassie's father-in-law) was revealed as Alessandro Coronal, Rob's father.

Bo left Llanview when his marriage to Delilah ended, and went to work at one of Viki Buchanan's properties run by Harry O'Neill and his daughters, Joy, Connie, and Didi. Realizing the O'Neills didn't like the Buchanans, he called himself Bill Brady. He helped expose an embezzling scheme and later married Didi.

Meanwhile, Tina Clayton learned her real father was Victor Lord, who had secretly married her mother, Irene Manning, before he married Dorian. Already rocked by the fact that her beloved daddy had fathered an illegitimate son, Tony, Victoria was shocked by the fact that he had also fathered another daughter whom he never spoke of. She turned into Niki.

Tina's boyfriend, a dastard named Mitch, found a letter from Victor naming Tina as his sole heir if Niki ever returned. While trying to prove Niki was back, Mitch killed Harry O'Neill in the process. Tina was put on trial for the murder, but was acquitted when both Niki and Viki testified for her.

Jenny and David were reunited and left town.

Dorian agreed to work for Asa once she realized she would have to move out of Llanfair, since Victor's marriage to Tina's mother was still in effect when she married Victor.

Meanwhile, the much-married Asa Buchanan was said to have another secret wife named Pamela living on an island. When Asa admitted it was true, Bo and Clint commiserated with each other about daddy's checkered nuptials history.

Clint and Viki were happily married — and then came Joe. No, not Joe. Tom, Joe's look alike.

It turned out that Tom Dennison was actually Joe Riley's twin brother — Viki's brother-in-law, and uncle of her two sons.

Clint knew how much Viki had loved Joe, and suspected she was having an affair with Tom as a way of recapturing her love for her dead husband. He took the boys to Arizona, but then returned when he learned the reason for Viki's strange behavior was not guilt over an affair, or even being Niki Smith. Viki had a brain aneurysm.

She underwent surgery with both Clint and Tom keeping vigil. She slipped into a coma and found herself in heaven with all of her loved ones: her parents, her sister, and others. She had two choices to make: she could stay in heaven or return to earth. She chose to return — and she could choose either Clint or Tom; she chose Clint.

Clint's former lover, Maria, turned up in town with their son, Cord (John Loprieno). Tina and Cord were married, but when he suspected she only wanted his money, he turned to another woman, Kate. Tina left Cord a message on his answering machine that she was pregnant, but he never got it.

To make sure Tina stayed away from her son, Maria arranged with Max Holden (James De Paiva) to lure Tina to Argentina. He took her to his ranch, which they discovered was being used by drug dealers, including Kate's brother, Jamie. They fled, and when Tina was washed over a waterfall, she was assumed to have died.

Cord was upset about Tina's death, but then proposed to Kate. Max learned Tina was alive. Gabrielle (Fiona Hutchison) gave birth to a child fathered by Max, and rather than admit to being an unwed mother, she gave the baby to Tina.

Just as Kate was about to tie the knot with Cord, Tina turned up with "her" child in her arms. Kate left town. When Cord learned Tina's "baby" was Gabrielle's and Max's, he was desperate to find the son Tina had given birth to and was forced to leave behind. Eventually the baby was found and named Clint — C.J.

Cord was upset with Tina for lying to him, and wanted to divorce her; Max then proposed to her. Gabrielle wanted Max for herself, but married his brother Steve instead. Tina said no to Max when she realized she couldn't live without Cord. They reconciled; Gabrielle divorced Steve and pursued Max.

Meanwhile, Clint went blind and the Buchanans returned to Arizona where they had a ranch. When Clint was thrown from a horse, he found himself back in 1888, one hundred years in the past, where he would have to stay until he worked out some problems with Viki's ancestors. Viki followed him into 1888, and stopped him from marrying her great grandma.

331

Cord had once again broken up with Tina and began dating a lovely young woman named Sarah Gordon.

Grandpa Asa was courting Renee Divine (Patricia Elliott). Suddenly, he seemed to be losing his mind and his memory. Renee was arrested for poisoning him. But the real culprits were Patrick London, the Faux Bo, and Elizabeth Saunders, who were out to do in the Buchanans.

The real Bo was being kept prisoner along with his once and current wives, Delilah and Didi. Meanwhile, Patrick seduced Tina, but Cord turned up in time to stop her from marrying Bo. Didi was killed in the attempt to free the hostages. Becky Lee, Bo's former wife, came to the funeral with their son, Drew.

So many of the men were discovering they had children they didn't know they had, it was time for equal play for the womenfolk of Llanview. Victoria Lord Riley Burke Riley Buchanan discovered that her former lover Roger Gordon, father of Sarah (Jensen Buchanan) and Megan Gordon (Jessica Tuck), was in an underground enclave called Eterna. He told her Megan was their child, and Victor had brainwashed her into forgetting she had given birth to the little girl.

It took time for Megan to accept Viki as her mother. But eventually, she came around and Viki was overjoyed to have her oldest child back again. Clint, however, was increasingly jealous of Viki's relationship with Roger. And he soon found he had good reason to be worried.

Roger had been poisoned by Gabrielle, but Megan found the antidote in Eterna in time to save him. It also transpired that Viki and Roger had been secretly married. This made Viki's subsequent marriages to Joe Riley, Steve Burke, and Clint Buchanan invalid.

Bo was falling for Megan's sister, Sarah, while Max was falling for Megan. Danny Wolek, who had become a doctor like his dad, Larry, fell for Brenda, who was pregnant with the late Steve Holden's twins, although he knew she cared more for his father.

Asa's nephew, Austin, came to Llanview determined to destroy Bo for testifying against him and causing him to be sent to jail. He raped Sarah when she tried to get him to confess that he planted evidence implicating Bo in vehicular homicide. She found his gun and shot him, and everyone assumed he was dead. Poor Sarah was bedeviled by "seeing" Austin, but no one would believe her. Eventually, Austin's scheme was undone. Clint killed Austin after he shot Viki. Megan went into shock when she thought her mother was dead. When she revived, like her mother, she emerged with a new personality, Ruby Bright.

Megan, who had married Jake (Joe Lando), later died of lupus. Viki was heartbroken to lose the child she had only just come to know. Sarah Gordon also died, leaving Bo, once again, devastated. Viki and Clint reconciled and tried to start a new life with their three children, Kevin, Joey, and daughter, Jessica.

Cassie married a minister, Andrew Carpenter, whose brother William, a homosexual, was dying of AIDS. Llanview was torn by the homophobic bigotry that suddenly descended on their town. People started to examine their prejudices, and in time most of them came to realize that AIDS was not a divine visitation meant to punish homosexuals; it was a disease that could affect anyone. The AIDS Quilt became part of the story line.

Viki helped counsel a woman whose husband abused her. She brought the woman into a circle of other women, so that she would feel safe within this comforting group of "sisters." The women persuaded the beaten wife to stand up to her husband, to insist that he go for treatment. He was the one who was doing wrong; she was not to blame for being a victim.

Dorian discovered a lump in her breast and went to a doctor. The story line took Dorian through the different options she had for treatment. Most of all, it showed the importance of self-examination and mammograms.

Roy Thinnes at a celebrity fund raiser.

Viki became close to Andrew's father, Sloan (played by Roy Thinnes). In spite of herself, she began daydreaming about him and felt as if she were falling in love. She resisted. After all, she had this wonderful man, Clint, and all the history they had shared. But finally, she had to admit to herself, and to Clint, that she loved Sloan. He had long since admitted his love for her.

Clint reluctantly agreed to give Viki a divorce. It was something they had discussed several times before; perhaps they would remarry, as they had several times before.

Suddenly, Sloan seemed to be drawing away from her. She learned he was dying of cancer, and he didn't want to involve her in his death. But she insisted, and they were together before he died.

The story line also treated a gang rape that involved Kevin Buchanan and three of his fraternity brothers, accused of attacking a student, Marty Saybrooke (Susan Haskell), at a frat party. One of the rapists was Todd Manning (Roger Howarth), who was sent to jail for the crime. But he escaped and had a chance to do something heroic. This led to his sentence being reduced.

Blair Daimler (Kassie Wesley), Dorian's niece, came to Llanview, and would later become involved with Asa. And with Max. And with Todd.

For Dorian, Sloan's death was a mixed blessing. She didn't mourn him, certainly. After all, he had written the book about Victor Lord that seemed to confirm that she had smothered her husband with a pillow. If only he had died before he got to that chapter.

Dorian was put on trial and to Viki's delight, was found guilty. Cassie was heartbroken. Dorian, who usually could find a way out of any problem, felt she was doomed to spend the rest of her life in jail. And doomed to wear that awful prison garb.

But help arrived in a strange way. A young man named David Vickers (Tuc Watkins) came to see Dorian with a diary written, he said, by the late Irene Manning Clayton — Tina's and his mother. He was the long-lost other son that Victor was rumored to have sired. And the diary would prove that Dorian did not kill Victor.

Viki was dubious about accepting David as her brother, especially since he had evidence that could clear Dorian. But there was nothing she could do about it. Dorian was released, but was cautioned that she had not been cleared, and that if evidence turned up to prove she had done the deed, she'd be back in prison grays in a trice.

Dorian's anger at Viki, whom she blamed for getting her indicted on the basis of Sloan's book, burned inside her. The only revenge that would really get to this woman, Dorian felt, was through one of her children.

Dorian seduced young Joey Buchanan, who was entranced by this beautiful, sophisticated woman. She arranged to have Viki "catch" them in bed together in a New York hotel. Viki was devastated. Clint would have gladly killed Dorian if he could have. Dorian gloated. And then, strangely, felt guilty for using Joey as she had. She realized, to her shock, that she was falling in love with the young man and knew that he felt the same about her. This could get very complicated, Dorian reckoned. But she would deal with it when she had to.

David was drawn to Tina, and she was drawn to him. But she was also drawn to her once and always husband, Cord. David had to tell her that he wasn't really her brother. That was a relief to hear, because she rather liked the non-brotherly kiss he suddenly planted on her lips. She promised to keep the secret, but Dorian, who already knew the truth, learned that David had confided in Tina.

More evidence was produced to prove that Todd Manning, the man who raped Marty, was actually Victor Lord's son. As soon as Todd had the news confirmed, he went overboard with flexing his newfound wealth and position.

Dorian realized that David could be a problem if the Victor Lord case were reactivated. She "persuaded" him that for both their sakes, they'd be better off married, since neither could then be forced to testify against the other if they were both charged with a crime. It would be a loveless marriage, she cautioned. He agreed, and later tried to explain the situation to Tina, who, to his dismay, didn't seem to care anymore.

Dorian forced herself to make Joey believe she was no longer interested in him. Dorian's niece, Kelly (Gina Tognani), was becoming interested in Joey, and seemed flattered by the interest David showed in her. (Incidentally, both of Dorian's sisters, Kelly's mom Melinda and Blair's mom Addie, have a history of mental problems.)

Meanwhile, Dorian had learned a terrible truth about Viki's past and had to confront her with it: her father had molested her as a child. That was why she developed the Niki Smith personality.

Viki flipped. Other personalties began to emerge including Jean, Tori, Tommy, and Princess. They had been inside Viki all these years. Jean, Tori, and Tommy, especially, wanted to protect both Viki and "little" Princess, who was particularly fragile and vulnerable, from the truth about their father.

Jean imprisoned Dorian in the secret room Victor had built beneath Llanfair, and ultimately persuaded her to help her with her plan for destroying the Lord legacy.

Dorian went along as best she could, hoping to persuade Viki's alters to relinquish control, to let Viki emerge as herself. But Jean, et al, had too much to do before that could happen.

Tori planted story "tips" with Todd, who ran them in his newspaper without checking them out. She also arranged to have *Banner* equipment sabotaged. She set fire to Llanfair, hoping to destroy forever any remnant of an unhappy childhood that she had suppressed, and had never come to terms with.

When she realized Jessica was trapped in the blaze, Viki reemerged and rushed to save her. Later, in a hospital room, Viki realized she would need help to deal with her past. Susannah, the psychologist sister of Bo's wife, Nora (Hillary B. Smith), volunteered to help Viki deal with her problems. Viki's fight to regain her integrated self was written to be a long struggle that the audience will share as they watch a woman come to terms with the buried terrors in her mind.

Other story lines that developed in the mid-1990s involved street gangs and the fight of a mother, Carlotta (Patricia Mauceri), to keep her son, Cristian, from becoming a criminal like his brother, Antonio. And what about the friendship between Jessica Buchanan and young Cristian? Is there a chance for them?

Blair became addicted to gambling, as did Max. She needed money to pay off her debts and to fund her business enterprise. When she realized Todd was the Lord heir, she seduced him and later persuaded him to marry her when she said she was pregnant. (To her surprise, she was.) She was later mugged by the gang and lost the child. Max, who had grudges against her, blurted out to Todd that she had lied to him about the pregnancy.

Todd was furious with her, and during an argument, tried to rape her. Is there a future for Blair and Todd? Indeed, is there a future for Todd, if he still has to work out his anger against women by attempting to rape them?

It may be technically called *One Life to Live* — but Agnes Nixon was probably right to originally name it *Between Heaven and Hell* — because that's where a lot of the action seems to be going on.

The Founding Families

There were three major families in the early days of *One Life to Live* — the Lords, the Woleks, and the Rileys. Over the years, the Lords and Woleks have stayed pretty much in place while the Rileys are represented by Kevin and Joey, the two sons of Viki and the late Joe Riley.

The Lords

Victor Lord, originally played by Ernest Graves, then Shepperd Strudwick, Tom O'Rourke, and Les Tremayne, was the patriarch of the Lord family. A wealthy newspaper tycoon, he lived in Lordly splendor in a mansion called Llanfair, which overlooked the town of Llanview, much of which he owned.

He was the father of two daughters, Victoria and Meredith, by his first late wife. It was later learned the Lord of Llanfair lived up to his concept of *le droit de Seigneur*. (This was the medieval *Right of the Lord* to sleep with every new bride in his domain.) Victor Lord fathered at least three other children: they include the late Tony Randolph Lord, Tina Clayton Lord, and Todd Manning. There may be more Lords a-leaping out of the writers' computers at some future sweeps period.

Victor's last wife was Dr. Dorian Cramer Lord, who was suspected of killing him to inherit his estate. In 1995, Dorian confronted Victoria with proof that she had suppressed memories of Victor sexually abusing her in childhood. (See Victoria Lord.)

Meredith (Merri) Lord, played originally by Trish van Devere, then by Lynn Benesch, who played her from 1969 to 1973, and then reappeared in

1987 to greet Victoria, who was meeting family and friends in Heaven after brain surgery.

Meredith was the often-overlooked daughter of Victor Lord, who doted on Victoria, whom he groomed as the son (he said) he never had. Meredith was the first to cross class lines by daring to fall in love with a member of the blue-collar Wolek family. Although Larry Wolek was a doctor, Victor did not approve of his daughter mixing Lord and Wolek DNA. Meredith, who had a heart condition since childhood, defied Larry, whom she ultimately married, and became pregnant although she knew pregnancy could cost her her life. She bore twins, one of whom died at birth. The other, Danny, grew up to be a doctor like dad.

Dr. Joyce Brothers made several appearances on *OLTL* playing herself. She counseled Meredith, who suffered from depression after the birth of Danny and the loss of his twin. Meredith later died of a brain injury when she was injured during a burglary at Llanfair.

Victoria Lord Gordon Riley Burke Riley Buchanan Carpenter.

Played originally by Gillian Spencer, who later became Daisy Cortlandt on *All My Children*; then by Joanne Dorian; then by Erika Slezak, who has played the role non-stop since 1971.

Although born to be the Lady of Lord Manor, Victoria early showed signs of the true democrat (that's with a small d). She believed that the privileged circumstances of her birth were not as important as the choices she would make in life.

Victoria's lifetime devotion to the memory of her father was severely tested when she was forced to recall that he had sexually abused her as a child. Victoria had had a split personality for years. Niki Smith was the alter ego who always emerged. When the shock of the sexual abuse struck home, Viki's other alters, Jean, Tori, Tommy, and little Princess, also emerged.

Victoria has been deeply in love three times. The first was with the late Joe Riley, her second and fourth husband, and father of her two sons, Kevin and Joey. The second was with Clint Buchanan, father of her daughter, Jessica, whom she has married and divorced several times and may well ultimately remarry. (Clint and Viki are the Victor and Nikki Newman of *The Young and the Restless*: they merge; they split; they wander into other relationships; but they inevitably come back to each other.)

The third great love of Victoria's life was the late Sloan Carpenter, whose book about Victor Lord seemed to expose Dorian Lord as Victor's killer — which Victoria had always believed. Viki rushed to have Dorian indicted and, uncharacteristically for this usually super-fair lady, gloated when Dorian was convicted. (She later apologized for the rush to judgment when proof was offered that seemed to clear Dorian.)

Sloan's book eventually led to circumstances that opened up the dark places in Viki's mind and threw a painfully glaring light on her secret fears and memories. Since Victor Lord had brainwashed her into forgetting her marriage to Roger Gordon and the child, Victoria assumed that Joe was her first husband and that she had no other children before bearing her sons, Joey and Kevin Riley.

The Latter Day Lords

Three of Victor Lord's children emerged into the story long after the show went on the air.

Tony Randolph Lord, originally played by George Reinholt, then by Chip Lucia, and finally by Philip McHale, who made two appearances on the show. McHale played Tony from 1977 to 1979, then reappeared in 1987 as one of Victoria's kin and kith whom she visited on her tour of heaven after brain surgery.

Most soap savants would agree that Tony Lord's emergence was a clever way to introduce George Reinholt, newly fired as Steve Frame from *Another World,* into the series. Jacqueline Courtney, George's fired co-star on *AW* (she played Alice Frame), was brought on as Pat Ashley Kendall, Tony's former mistress and mother of his son. They later married.

Tony was also married to Cathy Craig, who had been Joe Riley's lover and mother of their daughter, Megan. The child died in a car crash, and Cathy was obsessed with having another child with Tony, but it never happened. (It was through Cathy that Tony and Pat were reunited: Cathy visited her old pal, Pat in New York, and brought her back to Llanview to take a job with Victor's paper, *The Banner.*)

George Reinholt left the soap in 1977; Tony was killed off in 1983. That same year, Courtney left the series, taking her character, Pat Ashley Lord, to Europe.

Tina Clayton Lord Roberts, originally played by Andrea Evans, then Karen Witter, and currently by Krista Tesreau (formerly Mindy Lewis on *Guiding Light*), is the second of the three emergent latter-day Lords. She was a trouble-making young woman whose (presumptive) father, Ted Clayton, was a nasty piece of work; a blackmailer, kidnapper, and all-around rotter. He was killed by Clint Buchanan after he tried to kill Viki.

Tina learned of her true paternity through evidence found in Victor Lord's secret room beneath Llanfair. It was later learned that Tina was not illegitimate, as she believed. Apparently, Victor and her mother, Irene Clayton, had been secretly married.

Tina has had many loves in her young life, but like her sister, Victoria, who seems destined to be forever linked to Clint, there is one man in

Andrea Evans as Tina
Lord Roberts and John
Loprieno as Cord
Roberts.

Tina's life who is her great love: Clint's illegitimate son, Cord Roberts, the father of her son, C.J., and daughter, Sarah.

Most recently, Tina has had a fling with her "brother," David Vickers, who then married Dorian. But that's not the end of their story, yet.

Todd Manning, played by Roger Howarth, started on the soap as a rapist; one of several young men who gang-raped a young woman, Marty Saybrooke (Susan Haskell), and was sent to prison for the crime. Howarth, who created the role, was told it would be for a short run. But the audience liked him, and since nothing redeems as well as an appreciative viewership (remember Luke Spencer of *General Hospital*?), the writers decided to rewrite the soap's projected story to keep Howarth around.

Todd was given an early release for a display of heroics he performed while on the run following his escape from custody. It was later learned that Todd grew up with an abusive father who never showed him any love.

Todd learned he was the true Lord heir after the *poseur*, David Vickers, admitted he was not Irene Clayton's son. A Lord family legal adviser found evidence that Todd was Victor's offspring.

339

The Woleks

A Catholic Polish-American family, the Woleks represented the hard-working families who came from eastern Europe to work in the coal mines and steel mills of Pennsylvannia to make the American dream happen for their children. Agnes Nixon knew people like the Woleks in her native Chicago; she came to know more of them when she moved to Pennsylvania. They became part of the strong foundation of her new series.

Anna Wolek, who was first played by Doris Belack, then Kathleen Maguire, and finally by Phyllis Behar, was the first member of the family to appear on screen. She was married to Dr. Jim Craig (Nat Polen), who died in 1981, and was a loving stepmother to his troubled daughter, Cathy. She was the sister of Larry and the late Vinnie Wolek; the aunt of Danny, Larry's son with Meredith; the sister-in-law of Wanda Webb Wolek; and the step aunt of the late Megan Craig, Cathy's child with Joe Riley.

Vincent Wolek, played originally by Jordan Charney, then Michael Ingram, and by Anthony Ponzini, until 1975. Ponzini reappeared in Viki's heaven sequence in 1987. He was Larry and Anna's brother; uncle of Danny Wolek; step uncle of Cathy Craig; and the husband of Wanda Webb Wolek. At one time, Viki's alter-ego, Niki Smith, made a play for him, but when he realized who Niki was, he gallantly said no and then informed Viki about Niki's appearance.

Vincent felt guilty over the death of his sister-in-law Meredith Lord Wolek because he went after robbers who had broken into Llanfair. In the ensuing struggle between Vinnie and the crooks, Meredith sustained a brain injury and died shortly after.

Vinnie was more directly involved in the death of his cousin Jenny's husband, Tim Siegel, whom he blamed for taking her away from her vocation in the church. Vinnie wanted the novice nun to return to the convent, but Jenny and Tim insisted on marrying. During their argument, Vinnie pushed Tim, who fell down a flight of stairs and was critically injured. He and Jenny were married on his deathbed.

Vinnie discovered Ted Clayton (see Tina Clayton Lord Roberts) was part of a counterfeit ring. Clayton killed him, but made it look like a heart attack.

Larry Wolek, originally played by Paul Tulley, then by James Storm, and since 1969, by James's brother, Michael. When James Storm wanted to leave the series in 1969, his character was trapped in a fire in the hospital. The badly burned Larry Wolek was rescued by Nurse Karen Martin. When the bandages came off, the man who looked into the camera looked like Larry Wolek, but not quite like the Wolek of yore. That's because James (who recently had a role on *The Bold and the Beautiful*) had been replaced by his brother, Michael, who has played the role since.

Larry's great love was his wife, Meredith Lord Wolek, who died of a brain injury suffered during a robbery. (See Vincent Wolek.) He was also married to the troubled Karen Wolek (Judith Light), who performed sexual favors for a wealthy man in return for gifts, and was later blackmailed into prostitution. Larry loved Karen, and forgave her, but their marriage ended when she left town.

At one point, Larry's son, Danny, fell for Brenda, the woman Larry hoped to marry, but she fell in love with someone else. Larry experienced something like that years earlier when he fell for his and Karen's cousin, Jenny; but she fell back in love with her former husband, Brad, and eventually married and left Llanview with Cassie Callison's father and Dorian's former lover, David Reynolds (a.k.a. Rinaldi).

Michael Zaslow and Brynn Thayer as David and Jenny Rinaldi.

The Rileys

An Irish-Catholic family, the Rileys were represented by two family members in the early years, Joe Riley and his sister, Eileen Riley Siegel. A "cousin," Tom Dennison, who came along a decade later, turned out to be Joe's long-missing identical twin.

Joe Riley, played by Lee Patterson, was a reporter who had an instinct for news, an appreciation for liquor, and a great love for Victoria Lord. He and Victoria were married; he then "disappeared" on the trail of a story and developed amnesia. When he regained his memory, Vinnie Wolek told him Viki had allowed herself to be talked into marrying her father's employee, Steve Burke. Joe decided not to interfere in her life.

He drifted into an affair with Cathy Craig, stepdaughter of Vinnie's sister, Anna Wolek Craig. She gave birth to their daughter, Megan, who inherited a condition from the Rileys that would have caused her to die in adolescence. The child, however, died in a car crash.

341

Victoria later divorced Steve when she learned Joe was alive; she and Joe remarried, and they had two sons, Kevin and Joey. Viki considered an abortion when she learned about Megan's congenital condition, but decided to take a chance. Joey was born completely healthy; so was Kevin.

Joe died of a brain tumor. Joe's long-lost twin brother, Tom Dennison (also played by Patterson), turned up in Llanview in the early 1980s causing a flutter in Viki's heart, and a near-stoppage of husband Clint Buchanan's. But as attracted as Viki was to her late husband's dead-ringer brother, she stayed faithful to Clint.

Eileen Riley Siegel
was Joe Riley's sister and the wife of a Jewish attorney, David Siegel; mother of Julia and Tim Siegel; mother-in-law of Jenny Wolek Siegel and Dr. Mark Toland; sister-in-law of Victoria Lord Riley; aunt of Kevin and Joey Riley and the late Megan Craig. Eileen left Llanview a decade before her long-lost brother, Joe's twin, Tom Dennison, turned up.

Current Cast and Characters

Actor: Laura Bonarrigo

Birthplace: Brookline, Massachusetts
Birthdate: October 29

Laura says she always knew she wanted to act. She appeared in school and community theater productions. When her family moved to Thomaston, Maine, she competed three times in the Miss Maine National Teenager Pageant, and each time won for congeniality.

She later attended the Mason Gross School of the Arts at Rutgers University in New Jersey. After graduation, she traveled to Europe and lived for several months in Greece.

Laura previously played Lindsay on *Another World*.

Character: Cassie Callison (Reynolds) Carpenter

Cassie is Dorian Cramer Lord Callison's daughter, who she thought had died years earlier. (The first Cassie was teenager Cusi Cram, great granddaughter of legendary publisher, Lord Beaverbrook; the role has also been played by Ava Haddad and Holly Gagnier). Cassie became close to her mother's husband, Herb Callison (Anthony Call) and remained close to him after their divorce.

She discovered that her biological father was Dorian's former lover, pianist David Reynolds, a.k.a. David Rinaldi (Michael Zaslow). Her new stepfather is David Vickers (Tuc Watkins).

Cassie is married to a minister, Andrew Carpenter (Worthan Krimmer). Their child died when she went into labor prematurely. The tragedy occurred when she reacted to news about Dorian's attempt to ruin the reputation of her father-in-law, Sloan Carpenter (Roy Thinnes), in an effort to get him to stop writing a book about the Lord family. Dorian was afraid it might make her look as if she had murdered her former husband, Victor Lord. Cassie and Andrew had marital problems when he became involved with Marty Saybrooke. Cassie went into a deep depression over the loss of her child. She and Andrew have since reconciled and adopted a son, River.

Daughter and mother were reconciled when Dorian appeared to have breast cancer. They became closer again when it looked as if Dorian would be sentenced to a long term in prison for Victor's murder.

After a career as a private investigator (and a relationship with John Walker), Cassie is following in her mother, Dorian's, footsteps: Dorian owns *The Naitonal Intruder* with Max Holden, and Cassie joined *The Banner*.

While never manipulative or scheming, as mama has been, Cassie is her mother's daughter in terms of becoming her own woman. Look for her to become increasingly independent.

Actor: Philip Carey

Birthplace: Hackensack, New Jersey
Birthdate: July 15

Philip Carey was a well-known film actor when he decided to accept a bid to do a soap opera in New York. As he told the author soon after he joined *One Life to Live,* "I don't know how long this will last, but it's been a lot of fun so far."

That was in 1980. (He actually started in 1979.) He also confided that the work is a lot tougher than doing a movie. But nothing daunts an ex-marine for long, and pretty soon Philip Carey was on his way to becoming a favorite with daytime audiences.

Carey saw action with the marines in World War II and the Korean War. His first feature film was *Operation Pacific,* starring John Wayne, who became a close friend. (Carey is said to be a distant cousin of the late film star, Macdonald Carey, who created the role of Dr. Tom Horton on *Days of Our Lives* and who was also a marine.)

Other actors with whom Carey shared celluloid were Henry Fonda (*Mister Roberts),* Gary Cooper (*Springfield Rifles*), Peter Fonda (*Fighting Mad*), Tyrone Power (*The Long Gray Line*), and Fred MacMurray and Kim Novak (*Pushover*).

He starred in several television series, including *Philip Marlowe, The Bengal Lancers, Laredo,* and *The Untamed World.* He's also done a slew of

343

guest spots on episodic television and has appeared on stage in plays such as *All My Sons* and *Cyrano de Bergerac*.

Philip Carey has three children. He's done many westerns and continues to ride, often along New York's Central Park bridle path. He likes to say, "I'm an actor who rides, not a rider who acts."

Character: Asa Buchanan

In 1995, Asa Buchanan, a cousin of the Wolek family, married his eighth wife, Alex Olanov Hesser, played by Tonja Walker. Some of his wives have been former mates or lovers of his son, Bo (Robert S. Woods). But then, Bo has wedded or bedded women who were formerly married to or simply tarried with Asa. One of Asa's former wives, Becky Lee Abbott (Mary Gordon Murray) is also the mother of his grandchild, whom she conceived during an affair with Bo.

Asa's two sons have provided him with numerous daughters-in-law. Bo's most recent wife is Nora Gannon (Hillary B. Smith). He has the aforementioned grandchild from Becky and Bo; a granddaughter, Jessica, from Clint and Viki; a grandson, Cord, from Clint and his former mistress, Maria; a great grandson, C.J., and great granddaughter, Sarah, courtesy of Cord and Tina Lord; and two step grandsons, Kevin and Joey Buchanan.

He has survived plots against his life from wives and other adversaries, and will probably survive being the husband of the new mayor of Llanview — if he can buy Alex enough votes.

Actor: James De Paiva

Birthplace: Hayward, California
Birthdate: October 8

The son of a musician, De Paiva started his own band when he was fifteen. But the theater interested him more than any riffs he could lay down and he eventually found himself turning in his guitar for the stage.

After studying theater arts, which included fencing and ballet and jazz dance, he worked with a repertory company in Solvang, California. This led to getting an agent, and the agent got him a role on *General Hospital* as a waiter who tried to romance Holly Scorpio (Emma Samms).

Although his character struck out with Holly, he struck an interest in a casting director looking for an actor to play *One Life to Live*'s new character, Max Holden.

James is currently separated from his wife, actor Misty Rowe; they have a daughter, Dreama Marie, born in 1992.

Character: Max Holden

Max has been in a lot of trouble since he first appeared in Llanview in 1987. He's been involved with some of the most beautiful women, including Kate Saunders, Megan Gordon (Viki's daughter with her first husband, Roger Gordon), Tina Lord, Gabrielle Medina, and Blair Daimler. He is the father of Gabrielle's son, Al, and has twins with his late wife, Luna. When Gabrielle was charged with complicity in kidnapping a child and sent to prison, Max broke in and saved her when she nearly died in the prison laundry. Max produced a series called *Fraternity Row* and hired Gabrielle to work with him.

Max subsequently became involved with the lovely Luna Moody, who seemed to be in touch with new age philosophy. They were married, but his dalliance with Dorian's niece, Blair Daimler — and their mutual addiction to gambling — almost destroyed the marriage. Later, Max became obsessed with outmaneuvering Blair, who had become his most intense business rival.

When James De Paiva left the show at one point, he was replaced in the role by Nicholas Walker, formerly of *Capitol* and other soaps. As with James and Michael Storm's replacement gimmick, Max was burned, and when his bandages came off after plastic surgery, he was no longer James; he was Nicholas.

Later, when De Paiva came back, there was no explanation as to why Max no longer looked like Walker. Maybe a variation on the old adage will explain ... *twice burned is enough.*

Actor: Nathan Fillion

Birthplace: Edmonton, Alberta
Birthdate: March 27

Nathan's parents are educators and although they expected him to follow an academic life, "they supported my decision to become an actor, nonetheless," he told the author.

Nathan got the role of Joey Riley Buchanan while he was finishing his last semester at the University of Alberta, and headed for New York as soon as he could get his bags packed.

"Yes, I was excited," he said. "I didn't know what I was getting into in terms of the role and the soap, but I did know that this was a wonderful opportunity and I was determined to do my best with it...."

Fillion, who is related to a famous Canadian jockey of the same name, had a feature role in ABC's film *Ordeal in the Attic,* which starred Richard Chamberlain and Melanie Mayron. He has also appeared in several Canadian productions.

345

Character: Joey Riley Buchanan

The son of the late Joe Riley and Victoria Lord, Joey has been close to his stepfather, Clint Buchanan, although Victoria divorced him and married the late Sloan Carpenter in 1994.

When Dorian decided to strike back at Victoria for having her charged with the murder of her former husband, Victor Lord (Victoria's father and Joey's grandfather), she seduced Joey and then let Viki know about their affair.

Joey fell in love with Dorian and Dorian began to return his feelings when she abruptly ended their liaison. He didn't know that one of his mother's alters, Jean, forced Dorian to marry David Vickers. (The loveless marriage was an expedient way of keeping both David and Dorian out of prison.)

Joey has since found a new friendship with Kelly, Dorian's niece, although Kelly is also interested in David. Joey also faced problems involving his sister, Jessica, and her involvement with Cristian, who is the target of some gang kids who hang out at the local community center.

Actor: Roger Howarth

Birthplace: Westchester, New York
Birthdate: September 13

Howarth has performed at several prestigious regional theaters, such as Williamstown in Massachusetts (where castmate Robin Strasser often appears) and the Cleveland Playhouse. He has played a lot of Shakespearean roles, and three fraternity brothers. The latter reflect his roles on all three soaps on which he's worked: *Loving, Guiding Light,* and *One Life to Live.* In real life, Howarth never joined a fraternity.

His one-day role on *OLTL* turned into a long-term contract and eventually led to his character being revealed as another of Victor Lord's long-lost sons.

Howarth and his wife, Cari, have a son, Julian, born in 1992.

Character: Todd Manning

See The Latter-Day Lords under Founding Families.

Actor: Wortham Krimmer

Birthplace: Chicago, Illinois
Birthdate: November 24

Wortham Krimmer was graduated with a B.A. from Colorado College in Colorado Springs, where he met his future wife, Mary Ellen, who is a photographer and a Denver native. After graduation, he headed off to law school at the University of California at San Francisco. But two years into studying tort law and all those other *res adjudicata* subjects, he decided he'd rather follow a long-time love, acting. He received a scholarship to the American Conservatory Theatre, where he earned his master's in fine arts. He also studied with Stella Adler.

After graduation, Krimmer toured in regional theater productions and also landed guest roles on prime-time series such as *St. Elsewhere, Hill Street Blues, The Twilight Zone, The Paper Chase* (which is based on the lives of law students), *Max Headroom,* and *Knots Landing.*

He also played the evil Cal Winters on *Days of Our Lives.*

Wortham, born Bob Krimmer, has adoped Mary Ellen's birth name as his own. They have two children, son Max and daughter Tess.

Character: Reverend Andrew Carpenter

The good reverend is married to Cassie Callison, daughter of Dorian Lord Callison. When his brother died of AIDS, Andrew was successful in helping to overcome the overt homophobia of many of his flock.

He and Cassie endured several trying periods in their marriage. The death of his brother; the death of his father, Sloan, who was married to Victoria Buchanan before he died; and the death of their prematurely born son. He also caused Cassie no end of grief over his close relationship with Marty Saybrooke (Susan Haskell).

Has the good reverend learned not to be tempted to break the commandment against adultery, or will he succumb to his still unresolved feelings for Marty? And will Cassie even care by that time?

Then again, while Reverend Andrew may ignore the Bible's warnings, would he dare incur the wrath of his mother-in-law, Dorian, who is a fierce Mama Lioness when it comes to protecting her cub?

Well, they say that because God couldn't be everywhere, so He created mothers.

Actor: John Loprieno

Birthplace: Chicago, Illinois
Birthdate: October 7

347

John Loprieno made his theatrical bow in high school productions in Elk Grove, Illinois, at the insistence of his sister. Although he was busy with football and baseball, he indulged his sibling, and suddenly it seemed he preferred meeting his marks on stage to sliding into home base.

Loprieno earned a B.A. in theater at Lewis University in Romeoville, Illinois. He went on to do summer stock and obtain his master's degree. He also taught acting in Chicago.

John was cast as Danny Walton in *Search for Tomorrow* in 1985. In 1986, he joined *One Life to Live* as Clint Buchanan's son, who was born to former mistress Maria Roberts, played by Barbara Luna.

John and Lisa Loprieno have set up a nonprofit theater company, Theatrical Education Workshop, where he teaches novice and more advanced students such subjects as acting techniques and cold reading and monologue preparation.

Although he has a busy schedule with the soap and his script writing commitments for movies and television, John Loprieno makes sure there's plenty of time to spend with his daughters, Daniele and Anna Elise.

Character: Cord Roberts

Once upon a time, Clint Buchanan fell in love with a beautiful woman named Maria. Several years later, when Clint was an established businessman in Llanview, Pennsylvania, Maria Roberts came to town and told him that he was the father of her son, Cord, who had been raised by her and the man she later married. Maria's feelings for her former lover may have been passionate, but they weren't kind. She schemed schemes. Cord and Tina realized they loved each other. What's more, Cord decided he liked — and even loved — his dad; and he loved his grandfather, Asa, who doted on this newly discovered grandson; and, durn it all, he really liked his Llanview kinfolk, including Tina's sister and Clint's wife, Viki.

Cord and Tina became lovers, spouses, and ex-spouses; kind of like her sister, Viki, and his daddy, Clint.

Actor: Clint Ritchie

Birthplace: Grafton, North Dakota
Birthdate: August 9

Clint Ritchie may play a Texas-cowboy-turned-businessman on *One Life to Live*, but he prefers to describe himself as "just one of your usual North Dakota plowboys."

Although he always wanted to be an actor, he was too shy to do plays in school. But at sixteen, he headed for Hollywood and began taking acting lessons. The long-time horseman made his acting debut as a cavalry lieutenant in the pilot of *The Wild Wild West*. He also appeared in segments of the miniseries *Centennial* and in an episode of *Dallas*. His work as McMurphy in a stage production of *One Flew Over the Cuckoo's Nest* earned him a contract with 20th Century Fox Studios, leading to roles in such features as *Patton, A Force of One, The St. Valentine's Day Massacre,* and *Bandolero.*

Ritchie owns a ranch in Northern California where he enjoys training his horses. In 1979, he came to New York as Clint Buchanan, one of the Buchanan trio, and has been a fan favorite ever since his first appearance on the soap.

Character: Clint Buchanan

Son of Asa Buchanan, brother of Bo Buchanan, cousin of the Wolek family, and frequently former husband of Victoria Lord, Clint is the father of Jessica Buchanan with Victoria, and of Cord Roberts with his former lover, Maria Roberts. He is also the loving stepfather of Victoria's sons, Kevin and Joey, and grandfather of Cord and Tina's children.

Although their last marital problem started with Viki's undeniable love for Sloan Carpenter, Clint has been largely to blame for making most of the couple's problems worse. His love for Viki has often made him overly jealous, and he has often gone to his ranch in Arizona to cool off while leaving things to heat up back in Llanview.

On one such visit to the ranch, he fell from his horse, hit his head, and wound up in 1888, where he would have to stay until he fixed some problems his forebears had had with the Lords. Viki joined him just in time to keep him from marrying her great grandmother.

Clint was tempted to stray off the marital path with a journalist he hired for *The Banner,* Julia Medina, played by Linda Thorson of *Avengers* fame. Julia was Gabrielle's mother. Basically, Clint is a devoted family man who will always love Viki, and will probably always be willing to go through another marriage ceremony with her.

Actor: Erika Slezak

Birthplace: Hollywood, California
Birthdate: August 5

Erika Slezak has won five Daytime Emmys for her work as Victoria Lord Buchanan.

The daughter of the late great actor Walter Slezak, who played Lazslo Braedeker on *OLTL* in 1974, and the granddaughter of European and Metropolitan Opera star Leo Slezak, Erika is the only member of her family currently in show business. Her sister, Ingrid, is a lawyer; her brother, Leo, is a pilot.

Erika told the author, "I believe I always wanted to act, and my parents respected that. My father did not discourage me, but he made it clear that I would need to be trained well, and to accept the fact that since I was

349

the daughter of a famous actor, I would have to prove myself more than others would, and, as usual, he was right."

Ms. Slezak was, at seventeen, the youngest student to be admitted to the Royal Academy of Dramatic Arts in London.

Before joining *One Life to Live* as Victoria Lord in 1971, Erika established herself as a fine stage performer, appearing in everything from Chekhov to Coward, and from Shakespeare to Shaw.

Erika and her husband, actor Brian Davies, have two children: son Michael Lawrence, born in 1980, and daughter Amanda Elizabeth, born in 1981.

Character: Victoria Lord Gordon Riley Burke Riley Buchanan Buchanan Buchanan Carpenter
See Founding Families.

Hillary B. Smith with the Outstanding Lead Actress Emmy she earned in 1994.

Actor: Hillary B. Smith
Birthplace: Boston, Massachusetts
Birthdate: May 25

Hillary, who commuted from New York to Los Angeles in 1994 to co-star with Gene Wilder in the series *Something Wilder,* told the author that doing both the daytime and nighttime shows, "was difficult, but since I love to act, I enjoyed it. The only downside was not having enough time with my family."

Smith and her husband, Phillip "Nip" Smith, have two children, Courtney and Phips.

Hillary worked with a geneticist at the New England Medical Center and planned a career in genetics. But she was also intrigued by acting. She enrolled at Sarah Lawrence College because it had a masters program in both genetics and theater.

Hillary has appeared on stage and in films, including *Hair* and *Purple Hearts.*

Her previous soap roles were as Kit McCormick on *The Doctors* and Margo Hughes on *As the World Turns.* Her son, Phips, played Margo's son, Adam, as an infant.

Character: Nora Gannon Buchanan

Nora, a lawyer, was formerly married to Hank Gannon, a district attorney. Their interracial and interreligious (Nora is Jewish; Hank is Christian) marriage produced a daughter, Rachel, who is a law student with an addiction to prescription drugs.

Nora's marriage to Bo Buchanan almost didn't happen. She was injured and blinded. She also was afraid Bo would find out that she had had an affair with Hank's brother, R.J., during her first marriage. But love won out, and Nora became Bo's most recent wife.

Actor: Robin Strasser

Birthplace: New York, New York
Birthdate: May 7

Robin was born in the Bronx and raised in Manhattan. She attended the High School of Performing Arts (the school memorialized in the movie and series *Fame*). She entered Yale School of Drama on a scholarship.

Strasser, who has a long credits list in theater, is a founding member of the American Conservatory Theatre and has appeared in productions at the Williamstown Theatre Festival, the Mark Taper Forum in Los Angeles, and on Broadway in *The Shadow Box, Chapter Two,* and other productions. She has also created two memorable roles in daytime: she was the first Rachel Davis Frame on *Another World* and Dr. Christina Karras on *All My Children.*

On prime time, she starred in the powerful film *Baby M,* played recurring roles on *Knots Landing* and *Coach,* and had guest roles on *Murphy Brown; Murder, She Wrote; Civil Wars; China Beach;* and others.

She is a tireless worker on behalf of S.O.S. (Soap Opera Supports) — an organization that she helped found — which is involved in promoting AIDS awareness and raises funds for AIDS research. She is the mother of two sons, Nicholas and Benjamin.

Character: Dorian Cramer Lord Callison Vickers
See Llanview Chronicles.

Actor: Krista Tesreau

Birthplace: St. Louis, Missouri
Birthdate: January 10

Krista first assumed the role of Tina Lord Roberts in 1994. She was welcomed back to soaps by fans who were introduced to her as Mindy Lewis on *Guiding Light.*

Tesreau first performed in public at the age of two, when she just got up and made an impromptu appearance before a group of family members. At three, she started to play the piano. At four, she began piano lessons. At fourteen she was among the top ten finalists of the Liberace Talent Search, and a year later she won the Missouri Piano Concerto Competition. Her first professional role was as the daughter of Jerry Stiller and Anne Meara in an industrial film for a telephone company.

While she was on *Guiding Light,* Krista made her stage debut in the off-Broadway musical *Buskers.* After leaving *GL,* she appeared in such prime-time series as *My Two Dads, Elvis, Silk Stalkings,* and *Who's the Boss?* She also guest-starred in the TV film *Perry Mason: The Case of the Killer Kiss.*

Krista played Andi Klein in *Santa Barbara* before returning to New York. She is active with the Big Sisters of America organization and is an avid motorcycle rider.

Character: Tina (Clayton) Lord Roberts

See The Latter-Day Lords under Founding Families.

Actor: Tonja Walker

Birthplace: Huntington, New York
Birthdate: September 19

Tonja's soap opera credits include Olivia Jerome on *General Hospital,* Lizabeth Bachman on *Capitol,* as well as, of course, the sometimes mercurial, sometimes funny, and always interesting Alex Olanov Hesser Buchanan.

A former Miss Teen All-America and a Miss U.S.A. finalist, Tonja attended Towson State University and UCLA. She also studied music at the Peabody Conservatory of Music in Boston.

Besides being a singer and songwriter, she's an avid football fan and sang at the Aloha Bowl in Hawaii. She's active in an organization called Broadway Cares/Equity Fights AIDS and helps raise funds for the Starlight Foundation.

She and Sammy the Dog share the home of Shauna the cat.

Character: Alex Olanov Hesser Buchanan

The eighth wife of Asa Buchanan, Alex's background includes working both sides of the law. A former federal agent, she became involved in "the mob," and then became a torch-song singer, before finally seducing Asa Buchanan into marriage. At last report, Asa was prepared to help her become the Mayor of Llanview. If that should happen the old saying, you can't fight city hall, will probably be changed to *Don't even try it!*

Actor: Robert S. Woods

Birthplace: Maywood, California
Birthdate: March 13

Robert S. Woods created the role of Bo Buchanan when he joined *One Life to Live* in 1979.

A former Green Beret, Woods has been an outspoken advocate on behalf of his fellow Vietnam veterans, who were ignored for years and made to feel guilty for participating in a war that most Americans have come to believe should not have happened.

Acting was always Bob's goal, and after he left the service he studied at the Film Actors Workshop in Los Angeles, the James Best Theater Center, and the Directors Lab.

Some of his prime-time roles included the part of Dr. David Spencer in *The Waltons*, and Lt. Bob King in *Project UFO*. He also appeared on *Family, City of Angels*, and *Newhart*. He was in the films *The China Syndrome* and *Big Wednesday*. His theater credits include co-starring with Dorothy Lamour in *Barefoot in the Park* and a series of Disney Drama Workshop productions.

Bob plays a Texan, and although he was born in California, he comes from a long line of Texans, many of whom moved along the famous Chisholm Trail on their trek west. He and his actor wife, Loyita Chapel, have a son, Tanner.

Character: Bo Buchanan
See Llanview Chronicles.

Supporting Actors and Characters

Actor: Patricia Elliott

Birthplace: Gunnison, Colorado
Birthdate: July 21

A distinguished theater actor (she made her Broadway debut in 1972 in Stephen Sondheim's *A Little Night Music*), Elliott has won New York's triple crown: A Theatre World Award; a Drama Desk Award; and a Tony. She works with a group called Plays for Living, which produces inspirational works for schools, shelters, prisons, churches, and corporations. The productions deal with AIDS, homelessness, and other social issues.

Patricia's character, Renee Divine Buchanan, is a former madam and a former wife of Asa Buchanan.

353

Actor: Susan Haskell

Birthplace: Toronto, Ontario
Birthdate: June 10

A *cum laude* graduate of Tufts University with a degree in biopsychology, Susan started acting in college and then continued to study at the American Academy of Dramatic Arts. A former model, she has a slew of television commercials to her credit. And, yes, she plans to go to medical school one day.

Character: Marty Saybrooke
See The Latter Day Lords.

Actor: Patricia Mauceri

Birthplace: New York

Patricia has a long list of television, Broadway, and off-Broadway credits, including being standby for Glenn Close in *Death and the Maiden*. She played Dona Querida in the film *Don Juan de Marco,* starring Johnny Depp and Marlon Brando. She now plays Carlotta, Dorian's maid.

"For a long time, Dorian would call out to Carlotta and she was never seen. Now, Carlotta, who is the mother of Cristian and Antonio, is not only seen; she plays a pivotal part in the lives of many people, including the Buchanans."

Actor: Nathan Purdee

Nathan plays Hank Gannon, Llanview's district attorney. He's Nora Gannon's former husband and the father of their daughter, Rachel. His brother is R.J. Glover, a gentleman with some shady secrets in his past.

Nathan starred in the film *The Return of Superfly,* in which his *OLTL* brother, Tim Stickney, played his taxi driver. Purdee formerly appeared in *The Young and the Restless.*

Actor: Timothy D. Stickney

Birthplace: Wichita Falls, Texas
Birthdate: January 31

Timothy's background is largely rooted in Shakespeare. "I fell in love with his plays when I was very young," he said, "and I find them increasingly relevant even today." He is also an accomplished musician and singer.

Timothy plays R. J. Glover, Hank Gannon's brother, who has had a career on the wrong side of the law for years, but now seems ready for redemption.

Actor: Tuc Watkins

Birthplace: Kansas City, Missouri
Birthdate: September 2

The role of David Vickers on *OLTL* is Tuc's first daytime television. Much of his past work has been on episodic TV, including *Sisters*, *Melrose Place*, *Laurie Hill*, *Sibs*, and *Get A Life*. He is an award-winning theater actor who made his New York stage debut in 1995 in *Fortune's Fools* at the famous Cherry Lane Theater.

Character: David Vickers

David Vickers came to Llanview to help get Dorian out of jail; to do so, he posed as Victor Lord's long-lost son and revealed a portion of a diary that appeared to prove that Victor had been killed by Irene Clayton, and not Dorian. For more about Tuc, see Llanview Chronicles.

Susan Haskell with the Best Supporting Actress Emmy she won in 1994.

Actor: Kassie Wesley

Birthplace: Morganfield, Kentucky
Birthdate: March 21

Kassie Wesley grew up in Kentucky with two older brothers and a younger sister. She worked at Nashville, Tennessee's Opryland as a singer; at 18 she debuted as a soloist at the legendary Grand Ole Opry, performing two songs. She attended Indiana University and, later, the University of California at Los Angeles, studying theater. At UCLA, she became a member of a four-part harmony band called Newport. Kassie ultimately left school to travel with the USO on a tour of Japan, Korea and Okinawa. Later, Kassie sang backup for soul singer Bobby Womack during two United States and one Great Britain tour.

Kassie's first professional acting role was as Bobbie Jo in the feature film *Evil Dead II*. She's done several guest shots on prime-time shows; her previous daytime experience was on *Guiding Light*, where she played nice-girl Chelsea Reardon from 1986 to 1991.

Kassie and her husband, production designer Richard Hankins, live in New York. Kassie serves as co-host of the syndicated television golf show, "The Pro Shop," and is actively pursuing her singing career.

Character: Blair Daimler Manning

See The Checkered Ralstons.

355

The Young and the Restless

T*he Young and the Restless* was a series whose time had come. By 1973, when the show debuted, it was apparent that many of the social changes wrought by the 1960s were permanently etched into the American ethos. When William J. Bell and Lee Phillip Bell were crafting their new soap, they recognized that the young were, indeed, still restless. The social revolution was still going on, and, for many, the daytime dramas their parents watched no longer reflected the society they were building.

While the Bells recognized the increasing influence of the younger generation on American values and mores, they did not create a daytime version of *Logan's Run* (the film in which a society considers anyone over thirty too old to be allowed to live). Members of *Y&R's* older generation have continually been involved in powerful, vibrant storylines that deal with everything from boardroom intrigues to bedroom escapades. Indeed, if the Bells ever decide to spin off a soap peopled just by these folks, they probably could call it *The Strong and Zestful*.

Y&R looked very different from all the other soaps that were on the air in 1973. John Conboy, the series' first executive producer, understood that television audiences were used to seeing both feature films and prime-time TV productions that emphasized enhanced production values. Because the soap was taped, not filmed, it could never duplicate the special depth and gloss that film provides. However, Conboy showed that with the right lighting, and with camera angles borrowed from the movies, the soap could achieve a remarkably film-like effect.

Y&R's people looked different, too. Both the Bells and Conboy recognized that part of the social revolution involved the way people dressed. Through flouting fashion rules, the late 1960s and 1970s evolved into a period of sartorial independence. People expressed how they felt by the way they dressed — or undressed! While the soap's clothing allowance was the highest ever budgeted for a daytime show, the series also set a record for the number of times its characters acted *au naturel*. This penchant for doffing one's duds was a new phenomenon in daytime.

When Jill Foster and Jack Abbott were played by Deborah Adair and Terry Lester in the early 1980s, they had the first love scene on a soap that could literally be called steamy. Standing in a shower stall, the latter-day Jack and Jill happily lathered one another. But not without one restriction: Lester had to keep his hands in the camera's view lest the viewers imagine where they might be if they were out of sight.

Bell recalls, "The title I had had in mind for *The Young and the Restless* for some four or five years before it was produced was 'The Innocent Years.' Then I became aware of the obvious: that between the time when I first thought of the title, and the time the show was ready to air, the word — 'innocent' — was no longer an operative word. We, as a country, had lost our innocence. We were facing new challenges and undergoing rapid social changes.

"We wanted our soap to reflect what was happening in the country, and we felt the new name better reflected what the soap was all about."

Another pair who got into a real lather while showering together were Lauralee Brooks (Jaime Lyn Bauer) and Jed Andrews (Tom Selleck of pre-*Magnum* fame). Talk about soap opera! These two sudsed each other as if they were training to work as back scrubbers in a Japanese bath house. Years later, asked what he was thinking of while doing the scene, Selleck grinned, and replied, "I wondered what would happen if we ran out of soap...."

Nikki Reed (played by Melody Thomas Scott) — one of the most important characters in daytime — was the first disco strip dancer in the soaps. Although she had never "stripped" before, Thomas Scott, a trained dancer, quickly learned the technique. "You just pull the right strips on your costume," she said. But one day, while doing one of Nikki's routines on camera, she accidentally pulled the wrong strip. The scene didn't air, of course, but we'd like to think that some day, when Nikki Reed Foster Bancroft Newman Abbott is a lady of a certain age, she will gather her grandchildren to show that tape — and will then prove that she's still got the moves!

The Young and the Restless has broken ground in many areas. "We were the first to do a story on breast cancer," Bill Bell said, referring to one

357

of the soap's original characters, Jennifer Brooks, played by Dorothy Green. "We showed how the woman learns to recover her self-esteem after the operation," Bell said. "We also showed how her family reacts to her, and how she relates to them after this experience. It was a powerful story. We received letters from people who said it helped them understand what happens to a woman from the time she learns she has cancer, on through the recovery."

In 1992, *The Young and the Restless* introduced a story line involving sexual harassment. The character of Christine (Cricket) Blair Romalotti (played by Lauralee Bell) was harassed by her employer, Michael Baldwin (Christian LeBlanc). Warned that no one at the law firm would take her complaints seriously, Christine insisted on bringing charges. She was accused of everything from being mentally disturbed to being hopelessly in love and fantasizing about her alleged tormentor; she was also charged with being vicious and vindictive when — as Michael claimed — he rejected her advances. Finally able to prove her story, Christine scored one for the good guys.

Most recently, *The Young and the Restless* presented a powerfully written story about stroke, featuring the character of John Abbott (Jerry Douglas) whose life changes dramatically when he's suddenly stricken with a cerebral hemorrhage.

The history of soap spinoffs has been a dismal one with one exception: In 1987 *The Young and the Restless* spawned *The Bold and the Beautiful*. Some of the characters have moved between the two series, but essentially they've maintained their separate identities. As this book goes to press, there's talk about a third series coming out of the Bells' shop.

Original Cast

Robert Clary . . . . . .Pierre Boulland	*Pamela Peters* . . . . . .Peggy Brooks
Robert Colbert . . . . . .Stuart Brooks	*Tom Hallick* . . . . .Brad Eliot
Dorothy Green . . . . .Jennifer Brooks	*James Houghton* . . . . . .Greg Foster
Trish Stewart . . . . . . .Chris Brooks	*Julianna McCarthy* . . . . . .Liz Foster
Jaime Lyn Bauer . . .Lauralee Brooks	*William Gray Espy* . . .Snapper Foster
Janice Lynd . . . . .Leslie Brooks	*Lee Crawford* . . . . . . .Sally McGuire

First Air Date: March 26, 1973/CBS

Created by William J. (Bill) Bell and Lee Philip Bell for Columbia Pictures Television

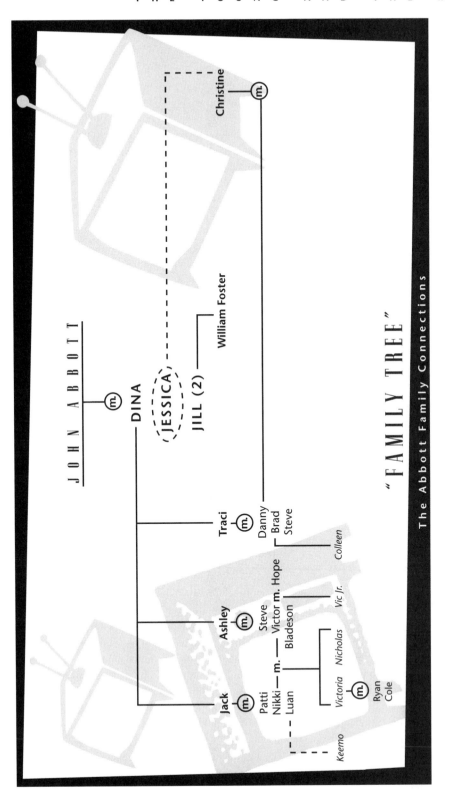

"FAMILY TREE"

The Abbott Family Connections

John Abbot is Genoa City's patriarch. He and his eldest son, Jack, have bedded and/or wedded some of the town's most desirable women. (At one point, Jack was stepmother Jill's lover.) His daughters, Ashley and Traci, have loved and lost, but have never given up on the chance to love again.

359

Home Sweet Genoa

Bell had already introduced the middle-class Williams family in 1980 (the Paul Williams character had come on in 1979). Jill Foster, Kay Chancellor, Victor Newman, and Nikki Reed stayed on in Genoa City after the major cast and character change, and continue to influence most of the heavy "front-burner" stories to this day.

The series is set in Genoa City — which is said to be based on a small town in Wisconsin, population 1,005, close to where Bill Bell grew up, and not too far from Lake Geneva where the Bell family spent most of their summer vacations when they lived in Chicago.

The soap's Genoa City is primarily an upscale town. However, families of more modest means are well represented and the story line often involves their efforts to rise above their economic and social situations. The series started in 1973 with two core families: The blue-blood Brooks, and the blue-collar Fosters. But while the Fosters may have come from humble means, their children were soon upwardly mobile: One of the Foster sons, Greg, became a lawyer, while another, William, Jr. (nicknamed Snapper), became a doctor.

William J. Bell was a medical student in Chicago when he took a summer job working for Irna Phillips. The experience was to be, literally, life-changing: He decided to become a writer rather than a doctor (although his early interest in medicine continues to be expressed in his story lines over the years).

The Foster daughter, Jill, took a different upwards path: She became a beautician to help put her brothers through school. She also used her considerable beauty and intelligence to marry her way up into Genoa City's high society. (The character of Jill Foster is the only member of the family to survive Bell's reconstruction of Genoa City's population in 1981.)

Phillip and Katherine (Kay) Chancellor, and Kay's son by her first marriage, Brock Reynolds, came to Genoa City early in the soap's first year. Jill Foster would soon interact with the high-on-the-hill Chancellors, setting in motion the longest story line in soap opera history involving the often stormy and sometimes surprisingly warm relationship between Kay and Jill.

Other major characters who moved to Genoa City in the 1970s included Dr. Casey Reed, who arrived in 1978; followed in 1979 by her disco dancer sister, Nikki; and in 1980, by their father, Nick, who was to be one of the first incestuous fathers shown on daytime television. In 1980, the mysterious businessman, Victor Newman, arrived. He would interact with Lauralee Brooks, and later, with just about every beautiful young woman in Genoa City, including Nikki.

In 1981, a year before *The Young and the Restless* won its second Emmy for Best Daytime Drama (it won its first Emmy in 1976), the soap faced a major challenge: Several of its original cast members were leaving.

Rather than recast the roles, Bell decided to disassemble the original family groupings and begin repopulating Genoa City with two new core clans.

The upper-income entrepreneurial Abbotts came on to replace the fading Fosters and Brooks clans. In 1981, Bell also brought in the socially elite Bancrofts: Earl (with whom Kay had once had an affair), Alison, and Kevin. The Bancrofts never quite caught on, and by 1983, they left town and no one has gotten so much as a postcard from Gstaad or Côte d'Azur since their departure.

One reason the Bancrofts didn't generate viewer excitement was that no one could really be sure what they did beyond being rich. The audience tended to like characters who were actually involved in something. Victor Newman was a businessman, and John Abbott owned a cosmetics firm: These were wealthy and productive people.

The People of Genoa City

Over the past twenty plus years, Genoa City has been a place where some of the most vibrant characters in daytime television reside. On the following pages, you'll find a history of the two founding families — the Brooks and the Fosters — as well as profiles of the most prominent current characters and the actors who portray them.

Jaime Lyn Bauer and Eric Braeden.

The Founding Families

The Brooks

361

Chris Brooks (originally played by Trish Stewart, then by Lynn Topping). Daughter of Stuart and Jennifer Brooks; sister of Lauralee, Leslie, and Peggy. Wife of Snapper Foster. Chris — a journalist — and Snapper were the first characters to discuss sex on a daytime soap. She was raped by George Curtis, who followed her home and broke into her apartment. Curtis was freed for lack of corroborating evidence. Chris felt as if she'd been assaulted twice: Once by the rapist, and once by the judicial system. She had a miscarriage when she learned Snapper had fathered a child with another woman before their marriage. The couple reconciled, but Chris later learned that Snapper had also become involved with his medical colleague, Dr. Casey Reed. Chris left town in 1982 to return only for the wedding of Casey's sister, Nikki, to Victor Newman in 1984.

Jennifer Brooks (Dorothy Green). Wife of Stuart Brooks; mother of four daughters, Chris, Lauralee, Leslie, and Peggy. Jennifer was the first soap character to have a mastectomy. Having once had an affair with Bruce Henderson, she was eventually forced to reveal that he, not Stuart, was Lauralee's father when Lauralee fell in love with Bruce's son, Mark, who proved to be her half-brother.

Leslie Brooks (originally played by Janice Lynde; then by Victoria Mallory). Daughter of Stuart and Jennifer Brooks; sister of Chris, Lauralee, and Peggy; ex-wife of Brad Eliot and of Lucas Prentiss; mother of a daughter, Brooks. She was a gifted pianist. Many of her emotional problems were caused by her sister, Lauralee, who broke up her romance with Brad by telling him he was thwarting Leslie's musical career, then duping him into believing Leslie jilted him. Leslie had a nervous breakdown, resulting in amnesia. When she recovered, she married Brad — though not for happily ever after. Brad began to go blind, and, unaware the condition was treatable, he decided to force Leslie out of his life rather than become a burden to her.

The oft-rejected Leslie found comfort in the bosom of her family. Actually, it wasn't exactly the bosom, and the comfort-giver was family only in the legal sense: He was her brother-in-law, Lance. She became pregnant with their daughter Brooks. She then married Lance's brother, Lucas. When that union ended, she had another breakdown. Finally, she decided to revive her musical career and left with young Brooks to tour Europe. She's still touring.

Peggy Brooks (originally Pamela Peters, then Patricia Everly). Daughter of Stuart and Jennifer Brooks; sister of Chris, Lauralee, and Leslie Brooks. Peggy started out on the series as a typical college coed. She was raped and later identified her rapist by hearing his voice. She later had an affair with Jack Abbott, then left town in 1982, returning in 1984 for the wedding of Victor Newman and Nikki Reed.

Stuart Brooks (Robert Colbert). Father of four daughters, Lauralee (Lori), Chris, Peggy, and Leslie. He was married three times. His first wife

The Y&R cast celebrates
a milestone episode.

was Jennifer, the mother of the four Brooks sisters. She shocked him many years after their marriage by revealing that a former lover was Lauralee's real father. He later fell in love with Liz Foster, but their plans to marry were thwarted by her daughter, Jill, who had seduced him and told him she was pregnant. He did the noble thing and married her. After learning that Jill's claim of an imminent visit from the stork was a lie, he divorced her and finally married the woman he loved, his one-time mother-in-law, Liz Foster. They moved out of town. Liz returned a few years ago for the birth of her grandson, William, born during Jill's second marriage to John Abbott.

The Fosters

Greg Foster (originally played by James Houghton, then by Brian Kerwin, and Wings Hauser). Son of Liz and William Foster, Sr.; brother of William, Jr. (Snapper) and Jill; husband of Nikki Reed. He was attracted to Chris Brooks, who loved his brother, Snapper. A lawyer, Greg later fell in love with and married Nikki, a beautiful honky-tonk dancer. The marriage was a troubled one, and Greg turned to April Stevens, a bright young woman who had been a victim of a drug cult. He, April, and her child left Genoa City to start a new life together. (April and her daughter returned to Genoa City in 1993 for a year's stay. Her marriage to Greg was over and

363

her second husband was abusive; she wound up shooting him, but was found not guilty when the jury learned that he had threatened her life).

Liz Foster (played by Julianne McCarthy). Mother of Jill, Greg, and William, Jr. (Snapper); married to William Foster, Sr., then to Stuart Brooks. Liz became a servant after her husband, Bill, left her when the children were small. With the help of her ambitious daughter, Jill, she put Greg through law school and Bill, Jr. through medical school.

Liz was part of the first euthanasia story line on soaps, which involved her terminally ill husband, Bill, Sr., who returned to his family when he realized he was dying. Liz later married Stuart Brooks after his divorce from Jill. (See Stuart Brooks and Jill Foster.) Although the couple left Genoa City in 1982 to start a new life together, Liz returned in 1994 for the birth of her grandson, William Abbott.

William Foster, Jr., a.k.a. Snapper, (originally played by William Grey Espy, then by David Hasselhoff). Son of Liz and William, Sr.; brother of Greg and Jill Foster; husband of Chris Brooks; father of Chuckie. Snapper was a doctor who devoted most of his practice to caring for inner-city patients. He was in love with Chris Brooks; before marrying Chris, however, he had an affair with Sally McGuire, who became pregnant with his son, Chuckie. Snapper married Chris soon after breaking up with Sally. After Chris left him, he became involved with Dr. Casey Reed.

David Hasselhoff described Snapper as "a typical American success story. He came from humble beginnings and made something of himself and even though he had a lot of problems, he remained basically a good guy...." Snapper left Genoa City in 1982.

William Foster, Sr. (played by Charles Gray). Husband of Liz Foster; father of Greg, William, Jr. (Snapper), and Jill. A ne'er-do-well who walked out on his family, leaving his wife, Liz, to raise three children, William returned when he became terminally ill. He and Liz tried to help Kay Chancellor deal with her alcoholism. He was the first soap character whose life support was turned off when his wife realized he was terminally ill and in great pain.

Firsts

The Young and the Restless has assembled an impressive list of daytime television "Firsts." Here's a sample of them:

The first hint of what might have developed into a lesbian relationship took place between Katherine Chancellor and a character named Joann Curtis. The story line was cut when the audience protested.

Jennifer Brooks was the first soap opera character to have a mastectomy. The story line, which aired in the early 1970s, also featured the first discussion of breast cancer on daytime.

The first case of bulimia dramatized on a soap (1983), featured the character of Traci Abbott, who almost killed herself trying to be fashionably thin.

The first story to deal with euthanasia (1976): Liz Foster pulled the plug on her suffering, terminally ill husband, Bill.

The first vasectomy: Victor Newman's.

The first failed vasectomy: Victor Newman's.

The first disabled character — Carol Robbins Evans — played by Christopher Templeton, who has an impaired leg from childhood polio.

The first presidential offspring on a soap was Steven Ford (1981–1987) — the son of Gerald and Betty Ford — who played Andy Richards. (Michael Reagan would later have a guest appearance on *Capitol*.)

The first "white face" story line on a soap: Phil Morris played private detective, Tyrone Jackson, who wore makeup to look Caucasian while he was on a case.

In 1981, the first soap gigolo was introduced: Jerry Cashman, a stripper nicknamed Cash. He romanced wealthy — usually older — women including Kay Chancellor. When she realized he was making a passion ploy to get her money, she dropped him. (The late John Gibson, a Chippendale dancer-turned actor, played Cash.)

The first story line on cults and drugs appeared on the *Y&R* in the early 1980s. It featured the characters of Paul Williams and April Stevens who were mesmerized by an evil cult leader.

The Young and the Restless was the first soap opera to become part of a feature film: In the 1976 movie *Taxi Driver*, Robert DeNiro watched scenes between Brock Reynolds and Jill Foster.

Alcoholism as it really is: Kay Chancellor's struggle with alcoholism continually shows that while the recovering alcoholic may be in control at any given moment, she is always vulnerable to lapses.

365

The first "torture-by-erotic films" story line (1980–1981) was set in the Newman mansion. After learning that Michael Scott had been sleeping with his wife, Julia, Victor Newman caged Michael in a special cell beneath his mansion and tormented him by showing movies in which he and Julia make love.

The Second Coming

In 1981, William and Lee Phillip Bell had established a second set of core families with the Abbott and Williams clans. Also included in the repopulation of Genoa City were the mysterious Victor Newman and the beautiful Nikki Reed. On the following pages, you'll find profiles of the actors who play the soap's most important current characters, as well as a description of their dramatic alter-egos.

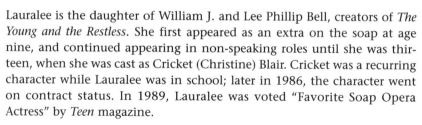

Closeups: Current Cast and Characters

Actor: Lauralee Bell

Birthplace: Chicago, Illinois
Birthdate: December 22

Lauralee is the daughter of William J. and Lee Phillip Bell, creators of *The Young and the Restless*. She first appeared as an extra on the soap at age nine, and continued appearing in non-speaking roles until she was thirteen, when she was cast as Cricket (Christine) Blair. Cricket was a recurring character while Lauralee was in school; later in 1986, the character went on contract status. In 1989, Lauralee was voted "Favorite Soap Opera Actress" by *Teen* magazine.

Lauralee enjoys doing rug art and stitchery between scenes on the set of *Y&R*.

Character: Christine (Cricket) Blair

Much has happened to Cricket Blair in the last decade. She was a victim of date rape and courageously decided to charge her attacker with the crime, although she was warned of what could happen to her on the stand. Her experiences in the courtroom led her to become a lawyer. Her clients include abused spouses, exploited seniors, the homeless, and other people who would otherwise be denied their legal rights.

Christine fell in love with Dr. Scott Grainger (Peter Barton), son of Dr. Jim Grainger (John O'Hurley). But before the couple could consummate their relationship, Christine's long-missing mother, Jessica (played by Roberta Street) returned to Genoa City. Dying of AIDS, which she contracted from her lover, she was determined to find her child and make peace with her. When she learned about Scott, she told Christine that her real father was Dr. Jim — making Dr. Scott her half-brother.

Jessica married John Abbott, making Christine John's stepdaughter. When she was close to death, John agreed to divorce her so that she and Jim could marry and give Christine the family she never had.

Christine married Danny Romalotti (Michael Damian), who supported her when she brought charges of sexual harassment against a lawyer named Michael Baldwin. The Romalottis were happily wed until Danny went off to star in a Broadway show and became involved with another woman. After their divorce, Christine turned to a long-time friend, Paul Williams (Doug Davidson). But their plans for marriage ended when he was hit by a car driven by Danny's wife, Phyllis (she was aiming for Christine). When Paul learned he'd been left impotent by the accident, he refused to marry Christine. Meanwhile, Keemo Abbott (Philip Moon), Jack Abbott's son, dreams of making the lovely Ms. Blair his wife.

Lauralee Bell and Michael Damian.

Actor: Peter Bergman

Birthplace: Guantanamo, Cuba
Birthdate: June 11

Peter Bergman, who was born into a naval family, assumed he would make the military his career. But after discovering he had a flair for acting in college, he decided to study drama. Peter worked in construction to earn tuition for the prestigious American Academy of Dramatic Arts in New York. After graduating, he landed roles in off-Broadway plays, and his television career began with a series of well-received commercials. In 1979 he made his soap opera debut as Dr. Cliff Warner on *All My Children*.

After leaving the New York-based series in 1989, Bergman headed to Hollywood to replace Terry Lester as Jack Abbott in *The Young and the Restless*. Bergman earned an Emmy in 1991 and again in 1992, and has also been honored with awards from *Soap Opera Digest*.

In his off-screen life, Peter Bergman enjoys playing the piano (he loves both classical and contemporary music) and likes to work around the house. He and his wife, Mariellen, have two children, Connor and Clare Elizabeth.

367

Character: Jack Abbott

Jack Abbott was originally played by Terry Lester, who gave the character a shiny hard edge that made him an attractive villain who never lacked for female company, no matter how badly he treated the women in his life. Later, when Peter Bergman took over the role, Jack became a more sympathetic figure.

Jack is the son of John Abbott and Abbott's first wife, Dina Abbot Mergerson — which makes him the brother of Ashley and Traci Abbott. Jack also has quite a résumé as a brother-in-law: He was brother-in-law to Victor Newman when Ashley was married to him; he was brother-in-law to Brad Carlton and to Danny Romalotti when Traci was married to them; and he was brother-in-law to Paul Williams when he was married to Paul's sister, Patty.

Christine (Cricket) Blair Romalotti was his stepsister when his father, John, was married to Christine's late mother, Jessica. He was the stepfather of Victor's children when he was married to Nikki, one of his former lovers. (He made a play for her soon after she married Victor in 1984; just about the same time, his sister, Ashley, let Victor know she was available.) Jack is the former lover of Jill Foster and has twice been her stepson. Her son, William Foster Abbott, is Jack's half-brother.

Jack was the typical playboy of the 1980s. He had money, and he knew how to use it to get whatever he wanted. At one point, he tricked photographer Lindsey Wells into a phony marriage to get blackmail photos she had taken of him and Jill in a compromising position. When she gave him the negatives on their "wedding night," he confessed to the hoax. Furious, Lindsey sold a set of prints to Kay Chancellor, who blacked out Jack's face, but left Jill's face and body untouched before giving them to John. That ended Jill's first marriage to the patriarch of the Abbott clan. In 1993, Jack discovered that the great love of his life, Luan, a woman he had to leave behind in Vietnam when his outfit was airlifted out of Saigon, was still alive; what's more, her son, Keemo, was his child.

In 1995, Jack and Luan were married. How long the marriage will last may well depend on how sick Luan really is. (She decided not to tell him about her illness when he asked her to marry him.) Jack's most recent ex-wife is Nikki Reed Foster Bancroft Newman Abbott, who has become one of his closest friends.

Actor: Eric Braeden

Birthplace: Kiel, Germany

Eric Braeden came to the United States in 1959. He attended Montana State University where he and a fellow student made a documentary on their boat trip along the Salmon River in Idaho. While trying to find a distributor for the film in Los Angeles, Braeden decided to stay on and enrolled in Santa Monica College where he met his future wife, Dale. When he learned that German actors were needed for various film and TV projects, he hired an agent; before long, he found himself working in a series of films, among them *Operation Eichmann, Morituri* with Marlon Brando, and *Escape from the Planet of the Apes* with Roddy McDowall.

In 1967, still using his real name, Hans Gudegast, he was cast as Captain Dietrich in *The Rat Patrol.* He then went into the now classic sci-fi flick, *Colussus: The Forbin Project.* He bowed to studio pressure and shortened his name to Eric Braeden. (Eric is a family name; Braeden is the name of a village in Germany where he was raised.)

In 1980, he joined the cast of *The Young and the Restless* in the role of the mysterious businessman, Victor Newman. Braeden's career, both before and after he joined *Y&R,* has included over 125 guest-starring roles in miniseries and episodic television.

Braeden, who started kicking a soccer ball around in childhood, has played with several teams since coming to the United States, including the Maccabees, with whom he won the 1972–1973 National Soccer Championship. He also enjoys boxing, running, skiing and tennis.

In 1991, Eric Braeden, the son of a German military officer, was awarded the Federal Medal of Honor; presented by the president of Germany, the medal recognizes Braeden's work promoting a positive, realistic image of Germans in America while, at the same time, helping to advance German and Jewish dialogue. He co-founded the German-American Cultural Society to continue to foster these dialogues. Others in the society include Dr. Henry Kissinger, *Washington Post* publisher Katherine Graham, General Alexander Haig, tennis star Steffi Graf, and former head of the Federal Reserve, economist Paul Volker.

Braeden and his wife, Dale, have a son Christian, who, like his dad, enjoys boxing and playing soccer.

Character: Victor Newman

The dashing Victor Newman came to Genoa City in 1980, and has been involved with a number of lovely ladies, including Lauralee Brooks. Theirs was the hottest affair on soaps; even after Lauralee left Genoa City in 1982, fans believed that one day she would walk back into his life and they would resume their torrid relationship — and maybe even get married.

And marry Victor did — many times, although not to the beauteous Ms. Brooks. His first marriage to Julia (Meg Bennett) ended when he learned of her affair with Michael Scott (Nick Benedict). But before the couple could leave town, Victor arranged to put Michael into a special room in the basement of his house, forcing him to watch films of him making love to his wife.

Some years later, Julia returned just in time to save Victor from being poisoned by his newest lover, Eve Howard. Victor and Julia became good friends. (By that time, Meg Bennett had established herself as one of Bill Bell's team of writers.)

After Lauralee left town, Victor found himself drawn to Nikki Reed Foster (Melody Thomas Scott), the stripper sister of Dr. Casey Reed (Roberta Leighton) and ex-wife of lawyer Greg Foster. They became lovers. When Nikki became pregnant, Victor lied about the paternity test results and persuaded her to marry her rich and much younger lover, Kevin Bancroft. After Nikki divorced Kevin, Victor proposed. Their 1984 marriage drew one of the largest audiences in soap history. With his new bride and his daughter, Victoria, Victor set out to live a happy domestic life. However, the lovely Ashley Abbott was attracted to Victor, while her brother, Jack, found himself drawn to Nikki. The Newmans divorced, and Nikki left town for a while without telling Victor she was carrying their second child.

Meanwhile, Victor learned that Ashley had aborted their child. His furious reaction led her to have a nervous breakdown. Ashley later married her psychiatrist, Dr. Steven Lassiter, who died soon after their nuptials. Eventually, Victor and Ashley were married and divorced. He married Leanna Love (Barbara Crampton), who, like Ashley, had also been Dr. Steve's patient. They divorced. By that time, Nikki decided to marry Jack Abbott. Victor found comfort for a short while in the arms of Jack's former lover and erstwhile stepmother, Jill Foster.

In 1994, Eve Howard became ill on her way to Genoa City. Unable to speak, she tried to make Victor believe that her son, Cole Howard (J. Eddie Peck), the young writer whom his daughter, Victoria (Heather Tom), had fallen in love with, was also Victor's son. Cole and Victoria eloped before Victor could stop the wedding. Although they consummated their marriage, they didn't commit incest: It seems one of the mourners at Eve's funeral was Cole's real father. (Victor managed to get a blood sample from the man, and had a paternity DNA test run in record time.)

Victor's most recent wife is the beautiful blind Hope Adams Newman (Signy Coleman), who gave birth to his third child, Victor, Jr. However, Hope has decided that, for a while, at least, she'd rather raise the baby at her farm in Kansas than share Victor's luxurious lifestyle in Genoa City.

Does this mean that Victor and Nikki will now have a chance to reconcile? Maybe. Maybe not. But Victor's longtime friend, Douglas Austin, says they are destined to be together. And Douglas is never wrong — at least not that you'd notice.

J. Eddie Peck

Actor: Sharon Case

Birthplace: Detroit, Michigan
Birthdate: February 9

Sharon was still starring in the limited-run syndicated series *Valley of the Dolls* when she was asked to join *The Young and the Restless* in the role of Sharon Collins. Until *Valley* ran its course, she managed to do both shows.

Sharon previously played Debbie on *As the World Turns* and Dawn on *General Hospital.* She's also done guest roles on several prime-time shows including *Cheers, Beverly Hills, 90210,* and *Silk Stalkings.*

Character: Sharon Collins

Sharon Collins has had some nasty turns in her young life. She became pregnant by a high school jock who refused to pay child support. She was later the victim of date rape: Matt Clark (Eddie Cibrian) forced himself on her, although she told no one about it. Nicholas Newman (Joshua Morrow), the son of Victor Newman and Nikki Newman Abbott, had fallen in love with her, and assumed she was a virgin because she was reluctant to "go all the way" with him. While Nick was taking cold showers, Sharon's mother, Doris, was advising her to tell him about the baby; but Sharon refused, fearing that Nick would leave her if he knew she had had a child.

Seething with jealousy over Sharon's relationship with Nick — and the fact that Sharon and Nick had won the title of Most Popular Couple in Genoa City High School — Matt vowed to break them up as painfully as possible. In May, 1995, just as the soap was moving into its summer story line mode (where the emphasis on the younger characters is heightened) Matt learned about the baby and began his campaign of psychological terror against Sharon.

Actor: Tricia Cast

Birthplace: Long Island, New York
Birthdate: November 16

Tricia's first role was in the television series *The Bad News Bears.* She later co-starred with Jason Bateman in the NBC series *It's Your Move.* Her first soap stint was as Kristy Duvall in the now canceled *Santa Barbara.*

Tricia is married to composer Jack Allocco, whose credits include the music for both *The Young and the Restless* and *The Bold and the Beautiful.* She is concerned with protecting the environment and considers herself a devout recycler.

Tricia won both a Daytime Emmy and a *Soap Opera Digest* award in 1992.

371

Character: Nina Webster Chancellor Kimble McNeil

Daughter of Florence Webster; ex-daughter-in-law of Jill Foster; widow of Phillip Chancellor, Jr. and David Kimble; mother of Phillip

Chancellor, III; and wife of Ryan McNeil, Nina came from way across the tracks. Determined to move up in the world, she started with a glamorous career and then married a wealthy man.

She and Christine (Cricket) Blair became friends when they were models for John Abbott's company, Jabot. When Cricket and the wealthy young Phillip Chancellor (played by Thom Bierdz) fell in love, Nina decided to steal him away for herself. She got him drunk and seduced him. (On the soaps, there's no such thing as wine stealing the performance, as Shakespeare tells us.) When she became pregnant, both Jill Foster, Phillip's mother, and Kay Chancellor (Jeanne Cooper), who had taken the son of her late husband into her home and her heart, rejected her claim that Phillip fathered the child. But much to the chagrin of Phillip, Jill, and Kay, blood tests proved the baby was his. He married Nina, but died soon after in a car accident, leaving her a wealthy, but very vulnerable young widow. Kay and Jill tried to set her up with a lover, so that she could be charged as an unfit mother, allowing them to take custody of the baby. But their plan failed.

Nina married a sweet-talking villain named David Kimble (Michael Corbett) who tried to kill her and her son in order to inherit her fortune. But Cricket and Danny (Michael Damian) thwarted his scheme.

Nina went on to marry Ryan McNeil (J. Eddie Peck), former husband of Victoria Newman (Heather Tom). Encouraged by Christine, Nina enrolled in college. After miscarrying their child, Nina told Ryan about her first baby, which had been sold to a couple by the ruthless baby broker, Rose DeVille (played by Darlene Conley, who is now Sally Spectra on *B&B*).

If the devil is in the details, as they say, we can assume that in soap operadom, future story lines often lurk in seemingly insignificant lines. This allusion to Rose DeVille could foreshadow a story line in which Nina finds her lost first-born. Perhaps it will happen when young Phillip suddenly finds himself past puberty. (Soaps have a way of telescoping time, turning toddlers into teens almost overnight.) Perhaps he'll meet a lovely young woman just a little older than he is — and she'll turn out to be his long-lost half sister.

Stay tuned.

Actor: Signy Coleman

Birthplace: Bolinas, California
Birthdate: July 4

Signy came to *The Young and the Restless* with a remarkably long list of credits for someone who started her career in 1987. Some of her past shows include the daytime series *Santa Barbara,* and prime-time shows such as *The Human Target, Fast Forward, The Steens Banks Series, Jake and the*

Fatman, Silk Stalkings, Doors, Dark Justice, The Flash (which starred soap veteran, John Wesley Shipp) and the TV movie *Stingray*. Her feature films include *Relentless III* and *Indecent Exposure* starring Robert Redford and *General Hospital* veteran Demi Moore.

Signy has a daughter, Sienne, by her former husband, Vincent Irrizary (who plays Nick on *Guiding Light*). Coleman is devoted to healthy living. She runs daily and works out frequently.

Character: Hope Adams Newman

Victor Newman met Hope Adams, a courageous young blind woman, when he took a job on her farm in Kansas after his Rolls Royce was stolen. The car had been crashed and authorities assumed that the burned body was Newman's. Victor let people believe he was dead while he stayed on with Hope. Eventually, they fell in love and she persuaded him to tell his family he was alive.

Hope and Victor were married and she moved to Genoa City with him while her longtime friend, Cliff Wilson (David Cowgil) agreed to take care of her farm. At Victor's insistence, Hope consulted leading ophthalmologists, all of whom agreed her blindness was probably irreversible. When she became pregnant, Victor suggested she abort the baby in case her blindness was hereditary. She refused.

Hope, who always sensed Victor had never really broken from Nikki, felt less connected to him as her pregnancy continued. She gave birth to her baby son, Victor, Jr., at the farm and told Victor that although she loved him, she wouldn't return to Genoa City with him. When Victor returned to Genoa City with a heavy heart, viewers wondered if he had, indeed, lost Hope for good. Would she ultimately turn to Cliff? Or would Hope decide to return to Victor just when he and Nikki prepare to make a decision about their future? It could happen.

Actor: Jeanne Cooper
Birthplace: Taft, California

Jeanne Cooper has been nominated four times for a daytime Emmy. She also earned two Emmy nominations for her work in the 1960s prime time series *Ben Casey*. Cooper also made another Emmy bid for her more recent guest starring work on *L.A. Law,* in which she played the mother of lawyer Arnie Becker — played by Corbin Bernsen, her real-life son.

Cooper also played Corbin's mother in the film *Frozen Assets,* which co-starred Shelley Long and featured Jeanne's other son, Collin. Jeanne's most recent teaming with Corbin was in the TV film *Appointment For a Killing.* "Corbin told me he would like me to appear at least once in every show he does," Jeanne told the author. "He says I'm his good luck charm."

373

Jeanne Cooper and Jess Walton in a special Y&R masquerade episode.

Jeanne Cooper's long and distinguished career began in films when she was put under contract to Universal. Her first feature was opposite Maureen O'Hara in *Redhead from Wyoming.* From there, she went into *The Man from the Alamo,* which starred Glenn Ford.

The French might call Katherine Chancellor a "woman of a certain age." Cooper rejects that label: "I don't believe in putting people into categories. At what age are you a 'certain age?' I prefer to think of Katherine as a woman who has lived a life full of experience, both joyful and painful, and still feels she has a lot of life and a lot of living to do."

When she's not working on the soap or in a film, Jeanne devotes a good deal of her time to her work with human rights organizations. She's an activist with a pro-choice group, and is a supporter of Greenpeace and the National Wildlife Association. Recently, she established the Katherine Chancellor Society, which works to revitalize the American community through a volunteer support network.

Jeanne Cooper is the proud grandmother of Oliver, Westin, and Harrison Bernsen. "My sons, Corbin and Collin, have given me wonderful grandsons whom I dearly, dearly love," Cooper explains. "But when I shop for the boys, I see these lovely things for little girls, and I would so love to have a granddaughter for whom I can buy these beautiful clothes. Perhaps one of my sons or my daughter, Caren, will make that happen for me."

Character: Katherine Reynolds Chancellor Thurston Sterling

Katherine and Phillip Chancellor arrived in Genoa City in 1973 and immediately set themselves up as the wealthy equals of the Brooks family. The mother of Brock Reynolds, Kay had a drinking problem, which affected her marriage to Phillip. After firing her secretary during a drunken binge, she arranged for Jill Foster, a young woman who worked in a beauty salon, to take up her former secretary's duties. Phillip Chancellor encouraged Jill to keep an eye on his often inebriated wife. Jill's friendship with Phillip deepened and they finally shared a night of passion. Meanwhile, Kay persuaded her son, Brock, to marry Jill so that she would stay away from Phillip. He obliged, but the marriage was never consummated, and eventually ended. Jill, meanwhile, learned she was pregnant with Phillip's child. Phillip divorced Kay. Raging with jealousy, Kay caused the car crash that ultimately took the life of Phillip Chancellor, who married Jill on his deathbed. Jill inherited his fortune, including his mansion. Kay was dispossessed, but eventually managed to prove in court that she had been duped into signing the divorce papers while she was drunk; the divorce therefore was invalid, and so was Phillip's marriage to Jill. Katherine moved back into her mansion, and then tried unsuccessfully to "buy" Jill's child — Phillip's baby — from her for $1 million.

Kay thwarted Jill's effort to sue for part of the Chancellor estate on behalf of her son by claiming the child was actually Brock's baby. (Years later, the boy's birthright was acknowledged; while his mother had once refused to give him up to Katherine, he now voluntarily chose to live with her.)

Katherine married twice after Phillip's death. Her marriage to Derek Thurston, a much younger man, was marked by quarrels over his affairs with other women. At one point, she jumped off a cruise ship to try to kill herself. Later, she returned to Genoa City, claiming that she'd been rescued by a Cuban refugee.

Katherine had an affair with the charming gigolo, Jerry Cashman (Cash). When she realized his passion for her was fueled by his desire for her money, she ordered him out of her life. Meanwhile, she continued to battle her addiction to alcohol, and was finally able to get the help she'd been avoiding for years.

Katherine married the handsome, dashing, Rex Sterling. She learned, later, that he was actually the father of Gina Roman (Patty Weaver) and Danny Romalotti (Michael Damian). She also learned that he'd been in jail. But he was obviously on the straight and narrow, and, besides, she loved him.

Kidnapped along with her faithful maid, Esther (Kate Linder), Katherine was kept prisoner by one of Rex's cronies (from his bad guy days). Having found a waitress who looked remarkably like Kay, this man had her undergo a make over that turned her into a virtual doppelganger of the wealthy Katherine Chancellor Sterling. The woman was so convincing that Rex was completely taken in. He was a bit puzzled, at first, at how uninhibited she'd become in bed, but counted that as a welcome sign of their growing compatibility.

After Kay and Esther were rescued, Katherine realized the experience had put a strain on their marriage. The Sterlings split, but eventually reconciled.

In 1995, Rex was killed by Esther's husband Norman, when Rex caught Norman cleaning out Katherine's safe. Kay was shattered by his death and almost took her first drink in years, but recalled how proud Rex was of her success in dealing with her alcoholism.

375

Actor: Michael Damian

Birthplace: San Diego, California
Birthdate: April 26

Both Michael Damian and his *Y&R* alter-ego, Danny Romalotti, started their careers as singing waiters and became top pop and rock idols. Both also went on to star on Broadway: Michael in Andrew Lloyd Weber's *Joseph and the Amazing Technicolor Dreamcoat,* and Danny in the show's fictional equivalent.

So far, however, Danny hasn't quite kept up with all of Michael's accomplishments, which include starting his own production company, Michael Damian Entertainment. In the summer of 1995, Michael began production of the company's first full-length feature called *Finders Keepers,* written and directed by Damian. Actor/screenwriter Quinn E. Redeker, who played his father, Rex Sterling, on *Y&R,* was also involved in the production.

Earlier in 1995, Damian worked on a film for CBS called *Murder on the Iditarod Trail,* co-starring Corbin Bernsen. The movie marks the soap star's first role as a villain.

Michael, whose real name is Michael Damian Weir, is one of nine children, all of whom are musically talented. He studied classical piano with his concert pianist mother, and then went on to master several other instruments. "The one you picked up was the one your siblings weren't using," he recalls.

Michael's off-screen activities include working with anti-drug groups and playing golf.

Character: Danny Romalotti

Danny is the brother of Gina Romlotti (Patty Weaver) and the son of the late Rex Sterling and stepson of Katherine Chancellor Sterling. He is married to Phyllis Romalotti (Michelle Stafford), who pursued him while he was appearing on Broadway. They slept together once and she became pregnant. Although Danny was still married to Christine Blair (Lauralee Bell), she agreed to give him a divorce so that he could marry the mother of his child.

It was, for Danny, a loveless marriage. But Phyllis followed Danny to Genoa City after the production closed in New York and persuaded him to share her home for the sake of their child.

Meanwhile, afraid that Danny might reconcile with Chris (which came to pass), Phyllis even went so far as to try to kill Chris rather than risk losing Danny to his former wife.

And speaking of former wives, Danny Romalotti has several exes: The sad little rich girl, Traci Abbott (Beth Maitland) developed a crush on

Beth Maitland, Michael Damian, and Tracey Bregman in a classic soap triangle.

Genoa City's rock idol in the early '80s, but Danny was dating Lauren Fenmore (Tracey Bregman Recht) at that time. Unable to break them up, Traci tried to commit suicide. When she became pregnant by one of her professors, Danny (always eager to do the right thing) offered to marry her and stay with her until the baby was born.

At this point, Patty Williams, newly divorced from Traci's brother, Jack Abbott, had hoped to make Danny her next husband. She confronted Traci about Danny. The two women argued, and, after Traci miscarried, she and Danny divorced.

Danny became closer to his father, the ex-con Rex Sterling (Quinn Redeker), and to his stepmother, Kay. After Rex was killed trying to stop a robbery in the Chancellor mansion, Danny was devastated.

Whether Danny and Christine will ever remarry depends on several factors: The most obvious impediment is Danny's relationship to Phyllis; another sticking point involves whatever unresolved feelings Chris might still have for him; and finally, there are at least two other men who love Chris — Keemo Volien Abbott (Phillip Moon), Jack Abbott's long-lost half-Vietnamese son, and Paul Williams (Doug Davidson), to whom she was engaged when Phyllis tried to run her down, injuring Paul instead.

377

RELATIVE-ITY

It would be ironic if Paul married Chris since it was Paul's sister, Patty, whom Danny jilted when he married Traci Abbott out of sympathy for her condition. It would also be ironic if Keemo married her, because Traci is Keemo's aunt.

Actor: Doug Davidson

Birthplace: Glendale, California
Birthdate: October 24

Doug Davidson had two interests when he started college: Acting and marine biology. Would he devote his life to the theater, or would he explore the depths as a successful marine biologist? Apparently, Davidson decided he'd rather be an actor (even if he never worked for more than scale) and worked at a number of odd jobs, including driving taxis and waiting on tables, to earn a living while studying his craft. Davidson's break came with a series of major TV commercials, which led to parts in films and television shows.

Doug first appeared on *The Young and the Restless* through a chance meeting with the producers while he was visiting a friend on the set. He did several guest shots before being cast as Paul Williams.

Proud of his Scottish heritage, Doug owns a Clan Davidson tartan and plays the bagpipes. He and his wife have two children, Calyssa Rae and Caden Douglas.

Character: Paul Williams

Paul Williams, who heads up a private detective agency, is the son of Mary Williams and Genoa City police official, Carl Williams. He is also the brother of Patty and Steve Williams.

In 1980, Paul and a beautiful young woman named April Stevens became involved with a cult. After the two finally broke free, they had a daughter, but Paul seemed unable to take responsibility as a father. April turned to Greg Foster, a young lawyer who had been married to Nikki Reed, and the couple left Genoa City with her child in 1982. In 1993, having remarried, April returned to Genoa City for a brief time. Her husband, Robert, a dentist, beat her, and she finally killed him when he implied he might abuse her daughter. She was found not guilty and left Genoa City after realizing she had no future with Paul.

When Christine Blair Romalotti's marriage to Danny Romalotti ended, she and her longtime friend, Paul Williams, became closer. They finally decided they loved each other and wanted to marry. Danny's jealous wife, Phyllis, tried to run Christine down, hoping to get her out of the picture forever. Instead, Paul suffered nerve damage that resulted in his becoming impotent. Although Chris insisted his physical condition made no difference to her, he refused to marry her.

His former wife, Lauren Fenmore, was curious about the broken engagement, and when she realized he wasn't responding to her very sexy dance movements, she deduced that Paul's once dependable reaction to sexual stimuli was no longer functioning.

Of course, no one should doubt that one day Paul Williams will regain his virility. That will make Christine very happy since his mother, Mary, blames Chris for what happened to her son.

Actor: Don Diamont

Birthplace: New York, New York

Birthdate: December 31

Discovered by a modeling agency while he was in college in Los Angeles, Don was sent to Europe to work the fashion shows on the Continent for a year. When he returned to L.A., he added acting to his modeling work. He auditioned for classes with Nina Foch and was accepted — later to learn he was the first newcomer Ms. Foch had agreed to take as a student.

He went on to acquire an agent who lined up acting jobs for him. Don landed the role of Carlo Poenza on *Days of Our Lives,* and when that job ended nine months later, he was cast in the role of Brad Carlton on *The Young and the Restless.*

When he's not on the set, Don enjoys being with his wife and family. However, he makes time to help support various groups such as the American Cancer Society and the Juvenile Diabetes Foundation.

Character: Brad Carlton

Brad, who is a major executive with Jabot, has had quite an eventful life since arriving in Genoa City in 1985. He has been kidnapped by a love-obsessed woman, and he was married to — and divorced from — the wealthy and powerful John Abbott's daughter, Traci Abbott. And although their relationship has at times been bitter, he's aware, as is she, that they still love each other.

In the spring of 1995, Traci seemed ready to leave her husband, Steve, to return to Brad with their daughter, Colleen. But as much as he was tempted to reclaim his family, Brad realized that the noble choice would be to persuade Traci to try to make her marriage work.

Although he's bedded most of the lovely women of Genoa City, including Jill Foster and Lauren Fenmore, who has never quite gotten over him, he doesn't let his libido dominate his thinking: He's said no a few times.

In 1995, Victoria Newman Howard (again a boss's daughter) hinted that she wouldn't mind if their working relationship developed into something more intimate. Brad, however, encouraged her to go home to her husband, Cole. Brad then turned to Nikki Abbott, Victoria's mother.

Actor: Jerry Douglas

Birthplace: Chelsea, Massachusetts
Birthdate: November 12

Jerry Douglas might have become a football player instead of a performer. He attended Brandeis University on a football scholarship, but decided that instead of making a living passing and punting, he'd rather sing and/or act for his supper.

Before Douglas joined *The Young and the Restless* in the role of the wealthy John Abbott in 1982, he had already compiled a lengthy list of credits that included guest shots on over fifty television shows, and a slew of feature and television films.

Like Abbott — who raised Jack, Ashley, and Traci on his own after his wife, Dina, left him — Douglas raised his kid alone. Today, Douglas is very happily married.

When he's not on camera as John Abbott, or appearing in musical productions, or making records, Jerry Douglas enjoys going to movies, plays, and sporting events. He is also active with Variety Clubs, which helps support the homeless.

Asked once to describe John Abbott, Douglas said, "He is strong-willed and powerful. However, the most important thing in John's life is not his wealth or his power; it's his family."

Character: John Abbott

Film and television actor Brett Halsey was the first to portray John Abbott from 1981 to 1982. Jerry Douglas assumed the role in 1982, and has played it ever since.

John Abbott is well named — since Abbott comes from the Hebrew word "abba," meaning father, which was eventually adapted to indicate the head or "father" of any Catholic monastic order.

If anyone can be said to be the patriarch of Genoa City, it would be John Abbott; he's been father, stepfather, father-in-law, etc., to a large contingent of Genoans over the past fifteen years.

He's the father of Ashley, Jack, and Traci; he was father-in-law of Victor Newman (when Newman was married to Ashley) and Newman's former wife, Nikki, when she was married to Jack; he's the former father-in-law of Patty Williams, Jack's first wife, and of Brad Carlton and Danny Romalotti, when they were married to Traci. He is also the current father-in-law of Steve Connelly, Traci's husband; of Luan Volien Abbott, the Vietnamese woman Jack loved in Vietnam and thought he'd lost forever after the war; and of Alex Bladeson, Ashley's husband. John's most recent wife, Jill Foster, was also his second wife. He was previously the stepfather of her late son, Phillip Chancellor, Jr., and is the step grandfather of Phillip's son, Phillip III.

John is also the grandfather of Traci and Brad's daughter, Colleen, and Keemo Volien, Jack's child with Luan. John and Jill also have a son of their own, William Foster Abbott, named for her late father, William Foster. Another former stepchild is Christine Blair, Danny's former wife.

Abbott's first wife, Dina Abbott Mergeron, is the mother of the three Abbotts, although John is the biological father of only two, Traci and Jack. Although Ashley's real father was Dina's lover, Brent Davis, John has always considered Ashley his own, and couldn't have loved her more if she were his genetic child.

John is an ethical man. He's also a man who holds love dear even if that love has been abused. Over the years, he's forgiven Jill for her trespasses and might even nurture some affection for Dina, even though she treated him and the children so shabbily.

John's second wife was Jill Foster. That marriage ended in divorce when he saw her in Jack's bed. But, again, although she betrayed him, there was still a spark of love left, and it wasn't too difficult for Jill to help ignite it again several years later.

Peter Bergman, Jess Walton, and Jerry Douglas all play Abbotts on Y&R.

John's third wife was the lovely, doomed, Jessica Abbott Grainger. She had been the former mistress of a wealthy man who infected her with the AIDS virus. When she learned she was dying, she came to Genoa City to find, and reconcile with, Christine (Cricket) Blair, the daughter she had left in someone else's care years earlier. Jessica also wanted to tell Cricket who her father was. (This information was especially timely since Cricket was in love with handsome, young Dr. Scott Grainger, the son of Dr. Jim Grainger who, Jessica told Cricket, was her father.)

Cricket and Scott were stunned to learn they were half-siblings. They realized that the attraction they felt for each other came out of a sense of "belonging" to one another that they didn't understand until their relationship was explained.

John Abbott and Jessica fell in love. He proposed. She rejected him. He persisted. She finally accepted. They were married. (It's interesting that Irna Phillips's brightest protégés, Agnes Nixon and William J. Bell, both did story lines about marriages between healthy men and AIDS-infected women. [Nixon's story revolved around Stuart Chandler and Cindy Parker of *All My Children*.] These stories helped break the stereotype of AIDS victims as mostly gay men. Since the stories involved marriage, they also helped reinforce the concept of practicing "safe sex.")

Despite objections from Jack, John brought Jessica into the Abbott mansion. He told anyone who didn't like it that they could leave his wife's home. As Jessica's condition worsened, John Abbott divorced the woman he loved so that she could marry Jim Grainger and give Cricket the family unit she never had.

In 1993, John Abbott remarried Jill. Their first crisis involved Jill's going off her birth control pills, even though she knew John didn't want to start another family. With some good wine and a seductive massage, Jill got John to make love to her without being concerned about her fertility, or lack thereof. The next day he underwent a vasectomy — which came 12 hours too late. Jill had become pregnant. Fearing he would be a laughing stock among his friends and business colleagues, John asked her to abort the child. When offered nothing but congratulations, however, John came to accept the prospect of imminent fatherhood; by the time young William was born, hardly a prouder new papa there was than the patriarch of Genoa City himself, John Abbott.

When John was temporarily impotent, Jill had an affair with the architect he hired to do some fixing up around the house. The Abbott housekeeper, Mamie Johnson, who never liked Jill, knew what was going on and eventually confirmed John's growing suspicions. Furious, John ordered Jill out, but insisted on keeping custody of the baby. The whole mess finally went to court. Mamie testified for a grateful John, who impulsively kissed her on the lips, shocking Jill, who saw the whole thing.

John's feelings for the beautiful African-American woman grew stronger. Her feelings for him intensified. The two made plans to go on a cruise. Meanwhile, Jill tried to talk John out of the divorce. To her shock, John had a stroke and, for a while, had no memory of recent events — not even his relationship with Mamie. But as he recovered, Mamie's image in his memory became stronger.

Ironically, one of his old-time adversaries, Victor Newman, who managed to obtain control of Jabot after John had gotten into a bad business deal, became a friend. As Jerry Douglas said of John, "There isn't a mean bone in his body. If anything, he'll eventually win over any enemy he has simply by being stronger and better and nicer than they are."

Actor: Brenda Epperson

Birthplace: North Hollywood, California
Birthdate: September 9

Brenda grew up in the logging town of Dallas, Oregon. After high school, she came to Hollywood and enrolled in workshop classes. Soon, she was

making personal appearances on *Saturday Night Live* and *Stop the Music* and she also appeared on her first daytime drama, *The Bold and the Beautiful*. In 1988, Brenda Epperson took over the role of Ashley Abbott; she describes her character as "someone people can admire and look up to...."

Brenda has been active with the National Missing Children's Foundation in Oregon. She and her husband had their first child in 1995.

Character: Ashley Abbott

The role of Ashley Abbott was first played by Eileen Davidson from 1982 to 1988. Brenda Epperson, who was told in high school that she looked like Eileen, assumed the role after Davidson left the show. The daughter of John Abbott and Dina Abbott Mergeron, Ashley is the sister of Traci and Jack. She is a chemist in Jabot, the company her father founded and which has for years been controlled by her former husband, Victor Newman.

Wealth and social standing could not insulate Ashley from more woes than are suffered by the heroine of a Russian novel. Like Lauralee Brooks before her, this young woman of privilege also learned that the father she adored was not her dad after all. Her father was Brent Davis, one of Dina's lovers. The news devastated Ashley: She ran off, developed amnesia, was kidnapped by a truck driver who held her for ransom, and was ultimately saved by her father's long-time adversary, Victor Newman. (Newman, incidentally, was also the lover of Lauralee Brooks.)

In 1985, Ashley fell in love with Eric Garrison, an executive with Mergeron Cosmetics. When the mysterious Madame Mergeron arrived in town, she turned out to be Ashley's mother, Dina. Eric, as Ashley would learn, was also Dina's current lover.

Once again, Ashley's romantic dreams were shattered. She turned to Victor for comfort and the two were soon lovers. She became pregnant, and Victor assured her they would marry just as soon as his divorce from Nikki was final.

Nikki, however, became ill, and Victor felt they should put their plans on hold until she recovered. Ashley agreed, but rather than wait for the marriage that might never come, she aborted the child. Victor's anger about the abortion propelled Ashley into a nervous breakdown. After recovering, she married her doctor, Steven Lassiter, who was later killed by the drug-crazed son of a former patient.

Another of Steven's former patients, Leanna Love, came to Genoa City to kill Ashley and marry Steven, but decided it wasn't worth all the trouble. Instead, she married the now divorced Victor. Leanna made several shady deals. Nikki and Ashley teamed up to expose her. When Victor learned the truth about his bride, he divorced her and married Ashley. Nikki, meanwhile, married Ashley's brother, Jack. Ashley thought she and Victor could now settle down into domestic tranquility. However, she hadn't counted on Victoria — Victor and Nikki's teenage daughter — leaving her school in Switzerland to return to life in Genoa City.

Determined to see her parents reunited, Victoria pulled some nasty little deals to unsettle both Ashley and Jack in their respective marriages. Ashley also had to cope with Victor's "can't-live-with-her, can't-live-without-her" obsession with Nikki, and she had to deal with her sister, Traci, who was jealous over her former husband, Brad Carlton. Traci, who claimed she wanted to remarry Brad, believed Ashley was trying to seduce him.

Cupid shafted Ashley again in 1993 when Victor and Nikki admitted they were still in love, and would divorce their respective Abbotts and rewed. As Ashley contemplated her future status as the latest addition to the long line of Newman's exes, Nikki learned she was pregnant with Jack's child, and canceled the divorce. Victor turned back to Ashley who did not, to Victor's amazement, return his retarded emotions.

Nikki miscarried the child, and she and Jack ultimately divorced. After Victor and Ashley were divorced, he found comfort in the arms of Jill Foster, who had once been Jack's lover and would soon be John Abbott's wife again. (Jill also offered comfort to Rex Sterling when he had marital problems with Kay Chancellor Sterling.) Ashley later married the photographer, Alex (Blade) Bladeson. When his evil twin brother turned up, he had Blade held prisoner on a Caribbean island and took his place in Blade's business and bedroom. But Blade managed to escape and sent his brother packing before Ashley could learn that she'd been sharing herself with two men with identical DNA.

Ashley's life took an easier, less stressful path for much of 1995. But for the young woman for whom the term "poor little rich girl" might well apply, an uneventful period is always the proverbial peace before the hurricane.

Actor: Joshua Morrow

Birthplace: Juneau, Alaska
Birthdate: February 8

Joshua Morrow's father was in the Coast Guard. Joshua, his three sisters, and his parents moved several times. He lived in Oregon, Oklahoma, and New Mexico before the Morrows headed for California in 1992. He enrolled in Moorpark College to study acting. He appeared in several student films, but worked mostly on stage and in comedy nightclubs before he got the role of Nicholas (Nick) Newman, the son of Victor Newman and Nikki Newman Abbott (Eric Braeden and Melody Thomas Scott).

Soon after he joined the cast of *The Young and the Restless*, Joshua told the author, "It's strange, but I sometimes feel as if I'm their real son.

They (Eric and Melody) are both so easy to talk to ... Also, when I told Eric that I'm in a semi-pro soccer league, I don't think anything else I could have said would have made him happier. He's been involved with soccer since he was a kid...."

Character: Nicholas Newman

Nicholas is the son of Victor Newman and Nikki Newman Abbott. His older sister is Victoria Newman McNeil Howard. He has a younger half-brother, Victor, Jr., who was born to his father's most recent wife, Hope Adams Newman. His early reaction to his half sibling's birth was anxiety: Will the baby take his father's attention away from him? He also resented the fact that the child was named Victor, Jr., while he was named for his mother's father, Nicholas Reed. He felt the baby had, somehow, usurped what should have been his right to carry his father's name.

Nicholas also became involved romantically with Sharon Collins, a girl from humble origins. Both of them became targets of the envious Matt Clark, who started a campaign to break up the couple by exposing Sharon's less-than-innocent past.

"Nicholas sometimes thinks he's grown up," Joshua told the author. "But he still has a lot of maturing to do." And when it comes to learning the facts of life, you can hardly find a better place than Genoa City.

Actor: Scott Reeves

Birthplace: Santa Monica, California
Birthdate: May 16

Scott joined *The Young and the Restless* in 1991. His previous soap role was as Jake Hogansen on *Days of Our Lives,* the series on which his wife, Melissa Reeves, plays Jennifer.

Scott's credits list includes feature films, such as *Jason Takes Manhattan* and *Big Man on Campus*. He also appeared in several miniseries and made-for-television movies. During their free time, the Reeves enjoy taking their young daughter, Emily Taylor, on day trips. "Fatherhood is wonderful," Scott says. "I recommend it highly." Melissa (Missy), Scott, and Emily, share their home with their several dogs, cats, and birds. They also have a mustang — the four-footed variety that whinnies.

Character: Ryan McNeil

Ryan McNeil joined Jabot, the company Victor Newman controls, full of ideas about getting ahead. When he met Victoria, the boss's beautiful young daughter, it didn't bother him, at first, that her obvious attraction to him could be "helpful." But when he realized Daddy Newman was not happy about his little girl getting involved with the help, as it were, he tried to disassociate himself from Victoria. But she wouldn't go away.

385

Eventually, after many threats, and all sorts of *sturm und drang* episodes, Victor and Nikki accepted Ryan as their daughter's choice. The two married, but didn't live happily ever after. Victoria, who had seemed so uninhibited before, suddenly became frigid. Ryan tried to do all the right things a loving husband should do to reassure his withdrawn young wife, but nothing worked. Eventually, the couple divorced.

To Victoria's dismay, Ryan turned to Nina Chancellor for comfort. Within a short time, Nina's son, Phillip Chancellor III, was calling Ryan daddy. Ryan and Nina married, but problems developed (of course). After miscarrying their child, she told him about a child she had given birth to years earlier, who had been taken by a baby broker and sold. Then there was Nina's decision to finish her college education before (perhaps) getting pregnant again.

And all the while, there's Victoria, now married to Cole Howard, who likes to remind him that she once (once?) loved him.

Actor: Melody Thomas Scott

Birthplace: Los Angeles, California
Birthdate: April 18

Melody Thomas started her training as a performer at age three, studying singing, and ballet, tap, and jazz dancing. Before she was seven, she had already done television commercials and had guest starred on a number of series, including *My Three Sons* and *Ironside*. When she was eight, Melody was chosen to play the role of the young Marnie in Hitchcock's classic thriller, *Marnie*. She also worked in feature films with Clint Eastwood and in *The Shootist,* John Wayne's last movie.

Melody took time out from her career to major in music at the University of Southern California. She returned to films and had a recurring role on *The Waltons*. In 1978 she was offered three prime-time TV pilots and a role on a daytime soap. She chose the soap, and the character of Nikki Reed was born.

Melody is married to Edward Scott, executive producer of *Y&R*. They have three daughters: Alexandra, Jennifer, and Elizabeth.

Character: Nikki Reed

The role of Nikki Reed was originally played by Erica Hope in 1978 and part of 1979. Melody Thomas (as she was known then) assumed the role in 1979, and has played it ever since.

Nikki is one of the most interesting characters in daytime. She's the daughter of Nick Reed (who was played by Quinn Redeker, who later went on to play other roles on the soap, including Rex Sterling, the late husband of Nikki's good friend, Katherine Chancellor.) She's the sister of Dr.

Casey Reed. Both young women were sexually abused by their father. Nikki's first husband was the young lawyer, Greg Foster. She also married Kevin Bancroft, Victor Newman, and Jack Abbott. She has two children with Victor, a daughter, Victoria, and a son, Nicholas.

While sister Casey became a doctor, Nikki became a disco dancer. Her goal was to marry her way up the social ladder. After her divorce from Greg, she became a stripper. It was then that she and Victor Newman met and were mutually attracted; the two became lovers. When Nikki told Victor she was pregnant, he had tests done and then lied to her that Kevin Bancroft, her rich, young admirer, was the baby's father, and urged her to marry him.

After Nikki's marriage to Bancroft ended, Victor proposed and she accepted. Their 1984 marriage attracted one of the largest audiences in soap history. Most of the original cast of Brooks and Fosters returned for the nuptials, including Victor's former lover, Lauralee Brooks.

Melody Thomas Scott and Eric Braeden.

The newlywed Newmans went off to live a happy life with their daughter, Victoria. But soon after they had settled down, Ashley Abbott became attracted to Victor, while brother Jack let Nikki know he wanted to make love to her. As Victor's attraction to Ashley grew stronger, Nikki left town without telling him she was pregnant with their second child.

When Nikki returned to Genoa City, she startled Victor with the news that he was the father of a son. After Nikki married Jack, she injured her back in a riding accident, and became dependent on both pain pills and alcohol. Victor, in the meantime, had married Leanna Love, but much to Leanna's chagrin, he spent a great deal of time with Nikki. (Jack wasn't too keen on this either.) Later, Nikki joined forces with Ashley to expose some of Leanna's nasty dealings, which led to Victor divorcing her and marrying Ashley.

387

When Nikki's painful back problems worsened, she underwent complicated surgery. After she and Victor finally admitted they still loved each other, they planned to remarry. But Nikki learned she was pregnant with Jack's baby and felt it would be wrong to divorce him at this time. News of his imminent fatherhood overwhelmed Jack.

Then, tragedy struck. Nikki developed a fever that threatened the baby's life. She made Jack promise to donate the child's organs if it did not survive. The child died, and a heartbroken Jack kept his word to his wife. When Victor reappeared in her life, she sent him away, feeling that her place was with Jack.

The long-delayed divorce, however, was at last finalized. But by that time, Victor had married Hope Adams, the beautiful blind girl he met when he was in Kansas letting everyone believe he had died in the fiery crash of his Rolls-Royce.

During one of her emotionally vulnerable periods, Nikki had an affair with Jed, the same architect who was fixing up the Abbott household when he was seduced by Jill. Ironically, Victor had sent Jed to do more than renovate the Newman ranch; he felt Jed might help cheer up Nikki. When Nikki learned Jed was doing double duty twixt her and Jill, she told him to pack up his levels and blueprints and get out.

Later, when Nikki sensed a problem in Victor's marriage to Hope, he insisted everything was fine. By the time Hope's baby, Victor, Jr., was born, Nikki had given up on Victor (again) and turned to her old friend, Brad. Meanwhile, Victor realized Hope planned to spend much of their marriage living in Kansas. (Gosh, Toto, we're not in Genoa City anymore.)

Will Nikki and Victor ever reunite? Of course they will. But for how long? Therein lies the rub of their relationship.

Actor: Tracey E. Bregman Recht

Birthplace: Munich, Germany
Birthdate: May 29

German-born Tracey Bregman was raised in London. When her family moved to Southern California, she began studying drama with veteran actor Francis Lederer. She also began studying at the Lee Strasberg Theatre, while continuing her college prepatory education at the Westlake School for Girls.

Tracey's big break came while she was on Easter holiday in 1978: NBC wanted her for a three-day role on *Days of Our Lives*. The role, as Donna Craig, turned into a run of almost three years.

In 1983, Tracey joined *The Young and the Restless* in the role of Lauren Fenmore, the daughter of a well-to-do businessman. Tracey's performance over the years has earned her several awards, including *Soap Opera Digest's* "Best Actress Award," and several Emmy nominations. Like her dramatic alter-ego, Lauren Fenmore, Tracey has a good eye for fashion. (Her designs, however, are more likely to be worn by babies or carried by their mothers. In addition to togs for tots, Tracey also designs handbags.)

Tracey is involved in "The Young Persons Committee," which works with the underprivileged. She is also active with animal rights groups and "The Young Musicians Music Foundation," which funds music education programs. A gifted musician herself, she is both an accomplished singer and songwriter. She wrote the theme for one of her feature films, *The Funny Farm,* and also for the film, *Concrete Jungle.*

Tracey enjoys family life with husband, Ron Recht, and their three children: Son, Austin, and Ron's daughters by a previous marriage, Emily and Lindsay. Also included in the family circle are the Recht dogs, Bagel and Sox.

Character: Lauren Fenmore Grainger

Over the years, Lauren became involved with several of Genoa City's young men — including Paul Williams (her once and, perhaps, always great love, whose plans to marry Christine Blair were undone when he became impotent following a hit-and-run meant for Chris) and Danny Romalotti (Christine's ex-husband, and the spouse of the woman who drove the car that hit Paul). Lauren would also have an on-again, off-again affair with Brad Carlton, Traci Abbott's ex-husband.

Lauren was married to, and later divorced from, the late Dr. Scott Grainger, Christine's half-brother, who married Sheila Carter, his beautiful but mentally disturbed nurse (whom he married because she said he was the father of her unborn child). After Lauren gave birth, Sheila substituted another baby for Lauren's infant, and took little Scotty home.

Lauren eventually learned the truth about the baby switch from Sheila's mother and confronted Sheila, who took her prisoner. Lauren and Sheila's mother narrowly escaped a fire in which Sheila was presumably killed. Sheila, however, survived and moved to Los Angeles where she became a character on *Y&R*'s sister soap, *The Bold and the Beautiful,* and married the wealthy Eric Forrester.

Meanwhile, Lauren hoped to remarry Scott, who had full custody of young Scotty. Scott, however, learned he had terminal cancer. Before dying, he made her promise never to reveal the truth about Sheila.

Lauren, who owned Fenmore's, a big clothing store in Genoa City, became a regular commuter between Genoa City and Los Angeles where she frequently bought some of the Forrester fashions for her emporium. Needless to say, her visits caused Sheila much anguish, and led to several plots to eliminate Fenmore forever. At one point, Sheila believed she had drowned Lauren in the Forrester hot tub, but the plucky Ms. Fenmore managed to suck air from a water pipe, and survived. But then, fans of the bright, resourceful character never doubted she would.

In June, 1995, Sheila gathered her "enemies" around her — including Stephanie, Eric, Ridge and Brooke Forrester, James Warwick, and Lauren Fenmore Grainger — summoning them all to Genoa City. Sheila drank

389

poison. Ironically, the one person she hurt more than any other — Lauren — was the first to beg her not to kill herself; and at the end, Lauren was the one who held Sheila as she lost consciousness.

What next for Lauren Fenmore? An old love affair made new again? Or a new love affair and its bright promise of ... well, whatever.

Actor: Heather Tom

Birthplace: Hinsdale, Illinois
Birthdate: November 4

Emmy Award winner Heather Tom may be the most famous undergraduate at the University of California at Los Angeles (UCLA). Many UCLA students admit to being soap opera fans; but if any of them weren't fans of *The Young and the Restless* before 1995, they were most likely won over to the CBS series once they realized that one of the members of the freshman class that year was Heather Tom — the popular young actor who plays Victoria Newman McNeil Howard on the series.

Heather was raised in Hinsdale, Illinois, a suburb of Chicago, until she was ten. Her family then moved to Seattle where she studied acting and performed with the Seattle Children's Theatre. She studied dance at Pacific Northwest Ballet, and piano at the Academy of Music and Dance.

Three years later, the Tom clan headed south for Los Angeles; soon after they arrived, Heather was getting roles in episodic television shows such as *Who's the Boss?*, *Divorce Court*, and *Trial by Jury*. She also appeared in several television movies, including *Deadly Whispers* and *I'll Take Romance*. In 1991, she joined *Y&R* as the willful teenage daughter of Victor and Nikki Newman (Eric Braeden and Melody Thomas Scott).

Interestingly, Heather's sister, Nicholle Tom, landed a feature role on the nighttime series, *The Nanny,* as the daughter of co-star Charles Shaughnessy, who previously played Shane Donovan on *Days of Our Lives*. Coincidentally, Charles's brother, David, is a producer of *The Young and the Restless*.

Character: Victoria Newman McNeil Howard

Victoria Newman was conceived when her parents — Victor Newman (Eric Braeden) and Nikki Reed Foster Bancroft Newman Abbott (Melody Thomas Scott) — became lovers. Because Victor lied about the paternity test results, Victoria was at first believed to be the child of Nikki's second husband, the handsome and wealthy Kevin Bancroft. Victor later acknowledged he was the child's father, and in 1984 he and Nikki were married.

Victoria is also the sister of Nicholas Newman and the half-sister of Victor, Jr., born in 1995 to Victor and his then wife, Hope Adams Newman (Signy Coleman).

For most of the 1980s, Victoria Newman was in school in Switzerland. When she returned to Genoa City in 1991 for a holiday visit, she had grown into a lovely teenager who decided she was finished with finishing school. Instead, she had an ambitious personal agenda to follow in her home town, starting with the reconciliation of her parents, Victor and Nikki. That entailed breaking up their respective current marriages — which she planned to do by making their respective current mates so miserable that they would file for divorce.

As it turned out, a variety of problems undermined the union of Victor and Ashley (Brenda Epperson), as well as that of Nikki and Ashley's brother, Jack (Peter Bergman). Although both couples were divorced, Victoria's long-hoped-for second chance to be at her parents' marriage didn't work out quite as planned: A series of mishaps interfered.

Meanwhile, Victoria Newman fell in love with Ryan McNeil, an ambitious young executive in her father's company. Despite dad's disapproval, the two were married. But Vicky's previously lively libido suddenly went into a flatline: Try as she might, she couldn't give herself easily to her husband. Maybe it was because she caught him making love to her friend, Nina (Tricia Cast), before they married, or maybe it was everyone telling her how immature she was. Whatever the cause, the level of frustration in the McNeil household reached critical mass.

In the meantime, Victoria met a New York magazine editor who suggested she pose for one of their centerfolds. Eager to prove she could make mature decisions, Victoria left for the Big Apple and signed a contract with the publishers. However, when it came time to pose, she was told to strip to the buff. When she resisted, she was reminded of her contract. Oh well, Victoria thought, as long as Daddy never finds out.

But Daddy did find out, and he began buying up all available issues of the magazine. He and Ryan flew to New York and brought the errant heiress home.

When Victoria's marriage to Ryan ended, he married Nina. Vicky found herself drawn to a young writer named Cole Howard, who worked at the Newman ranch. Nikki, now single and restless, also found herself drawn to the handsome stable hand, and helped him find a publisher for his novel. While Cole was friendly enough with Nikki — he dedicated the book to her — he was falling in love with Victoria; this led to a falling-out between mother and daughter when Nikki accused Vicky of stealing her man.

By this time, Vicky realized her frigidity was thawing. She thought warm thoughts about Cole, and discovered that he felt passionately about her as well. Cole also told Vicky that his mother was Eve Howard, and that he hated his father — whom he never knew — for having left his mother before he was born.

Meanwhile, Eve Howard, who had once tried to poison her former lover, Victor Newman, was in a hospital in Genoa City, stricken by an ill-

391

ness that would prove fatal. When Cole told her he was in love with Victor Newman's daughter, Eve, unable to speak, showed panic in her eyes. Eventually, Eve led Victor to believe Cole was his son. When Victoria eloped with Cole, Victor set off to find the couple "before it's too late." While Victor pursued the elusive couple, however, they were married, and within hours of exchanging vows, Victoria knew she was no longer frigid. Nor was she incestuous: Victor later learned another man had fathered Cole.

Victoria took a job with Jabot, the company her father controlled, and soon showed she had a flair for writing promotional copy. She impressed Daddy, and she impressed Jabot executive Brad (Don Diamont). While Cole devoted himself to writing his second book, and spending time with his attractive young editor, Victoria felt ignored. She let Ryan know she no longer had "that problem." But Ryan, apparently, no longer wanted anything from her beyond friendship. Brad also made it clear that their relationship was to be strictly business. Besides — he was developing something more intimate with her mother, Nikki.

Victoria Newman McNeil Howard can't be faulted for wanting her parents, once and for all, to forsake all others, and remarry. Besides giving the Newman family values a boost, it would ensure that she and mommy won't always compete for the same man.

Maybe.

Actor: Jess Walton

Birthplace: Grand Rapids, Michigan
Birthdate: February 18

Jess Walton grew up in Toronto, Ontario, Canada. She attended high school at Loretto Abbey, and soon after she was graduated she enrolled at the Toronto Workshop Productions' Repertory Theatre, where she studied and worked for three years.

In 1969, Walton came to Los Angeles and began working in episodic television, including *Marcus Welby, M.D, The Bold Ones, Cannon, The Six Million Dollar Man, Ironside,* and *Kojak.* Her TV movies include *Diary of A Madman, Mod Squad II, The Storm,* and *Monserrat.*

Jess Walton's first soap role was as Kelly Harper in *Capitol.* She stayed with the series for three years, and then moved across the CBS lot to *The Young and the Restless* to assume the role of one of daytime's most fascinating females, Jill Foster.

Walton and her husband, renowned grief recovery authority John W. James, have one son. In her free time, Jess is active with recovering alcoholics at the Clare Foundation Los Angeles. She also volunteers at the Adam Walsh Child Resource Center. She enjoys the fine arts, landscaping, redecorating, traveling, bowling, and working out in her home gym.

Character: Jill Foster Reynolds Chancellor Brooks Abbott

Jill Foster was originally played by Brenda Dickson, then by Deborah Adair. Jess Walton assumed the role in 1987.

Jill is the daughter of the late William Foster, Sr. and Liz Foster; sister of William, Jr. (Snapper) and Greg Foster. Her husbands include Brock Reynolds, stepson of her second husband, the late Phillip Chancellor; Stuart Brooks, her third husband, who became her stepfather; and John Abbott, whom she married twice. She is the mother of the late Phillip Chancellor, Jr. and William Foster Abbott, John's son; Jill is also the grandmother of Phillip Chancellor III, and in the course of her two marriages to John Abbott, has been the erstwhile stepmother of Jack (who had been her lover); Ashley (whose former husband, Victor, had also been her bedmate); and Traci (whose former husband, Brad, had boudoir privileges as well). The step grandmother of Brad and Traci's daughter, Colleen, and Jack and Luan's son, Keemo, Jill has also been the stepmother-in-law of Alex Bladeson, Ashley's husband; Steve Connelly, Traci's spouse; and Luan Volien Abbott, Jack's wife. She is the former mother-in-law of Nina Webster Chancellor Kimble McNeil.

Jill is a top executive at Jabot, the company founded and run by her husband, John — and controlled (via a takeover gambit) by her ex-bedmate, Victor Newman.

Jill first appeared soon after the soap debuted. Before her rise to wealth and power, achieved largely through bedding and wedding wealthy and powerful men, she worked in a beauty parlor to help put her brothers through law and medical school.

When Kay Chancellor, one of Jill's customers at the beauty shop, fired her secretary in a drunken rage, Jill, still dreaming of becoming wealthy and socially powerful, persuaded Kay to hire her as secretary. The relationship between the women started as a friendly one. Jill was attentive to Kay whenever Kay became drunk, and Kay was kind to her. Phillip, Kay's husband, appreciated Jill's efforts and found himself drawn to her. They were falling in love, but for Kay's sake, both tried to fight it; eventually, however, they shared one night of passion.

Kay asked her son, Brock, to marry Jill to keep her away from Phillip. He obliged, but never made love to his bride. When Jill learned she was pregnant with Phillip's baby, they divorced. Phillip then divorced Kay. He married Jill on his deathbed, making her a very wealthy widow. She lost her legacy, however, after Kay proved in court that she was drunk when she signed the divorce papers, making Phillip's subsequent marriage null and void.

Brock got Jill a job at a beauty shop owned by Derek Thurston. She and Thurston fell in love and planned to marry. But while Jill promised Derek domesticity and children, one of his clients, Katherine Chancellor, set him up in an exclusive salon. She got him drunk and married him in a quickie ceremony.

Although Jill never got to be the wife of a successful salon owner, she still had plans to raise her son, Phillip, in a manner worthy of his Chancellor heritage — far better than she could offer him on a beautician's income. Setting her cap for the wealthy widower, Stuart Brooks, she seduced him. However, Stuart had already fallen in love with Jill's mother, Liz. When Jill claimed to be pregnant with Stuart's child, he reluctantly parted with Liz, and married Jill. After learning she had never been pregnant, he divorced her and married Liz Foster.

Jill got a job at Jabot and found herself attracted to both her boss, John Abbott, and his son, Jack. Since Jack's attentions were diverted by the return of Stuart's daughter, Peggy Brooks — Jill's former stepdaughter — she concentrated her amorous ambitions on John. They were married, but soon started arguing over John's first wife, Dina. Meanwhile, Jill drifted into a torrid relationship with Jack. After Kay Chancellor made sure that John Abbott learned about his young wife's adulterous behavior, he divorced her.

By this time, however, Jill had established herself as an astute businesswoman, and no longer needed a husband to permit her to lead a life of privilege. Although there were several men in her life following her divorce from John — including a brief affair with Katherine's late husband, Rex Sterling, when the couple was briefly between marriages — it was John she still loved. And, to the chagrin of his three children and devoted housekeeper, Mamie Johnson, John acknowledged he still loved her as well.

John and Jill were remarried in 1993. She avoided signing a prenuptial agreement with him, although Jack Abbott was led to believe that his second-time-around stepmother would be unable to control any of the Abbott fortune should John die before her. She also planned to have a baby with John, despite his reluctance to start a new family at his age. Aware that Jill had stopped taking her birth control pills, John decided to have a vasectomy without telling her. But the night before the day of the procedure, Jill seduced him and they made love. When John found out that Jill was pregnant, he became angry and demanded that she terminate the pregnancy. She refused. Fearing the ridicule from his colleagues, he was instead hailed with congratulations, and John warmed to the idea of fatherhood. Jill named their son for her late father, William Foster.

Jill was prepared to live a life of joyful domesticity as the wife of John Abbott. But when he was temporarily impotent, and seemed unwilling to have the problem treated, Jill seduced an architect, Jed, in the study of the Abbott mansion, and the two indulged in desk-top passion. After Mamie managed to make John aware of Jill's adultery, he filed for divorce. Jill tried to persuade John to reconcile and it seemed that despite his anger at her betrayal, and his growing relationship with Mamie, he was going to agree — at least for the sake of their little boy. But John suffered a stroke before he could tell Jill what he decided.

Will Jill recapture John's love? Will she lose him to Mamie Johnson? Whatever happens, fans of *The Young and the Restless* know Jill is a strong woman and a survivor. After all, Jill Foster Reynolds Chancellor Brooks Abbott is the only founding family member still living and loving in Genoa City.

Jess on Jill

"I see Jill as very much like a latter-day Scarlett O'Hara.... She is very manipulative, and feels she is strongly justified in her actions. "She's a wonderful character to play...."

Supporting Characters

Sharon Farrell: Florence Webster is the mother of Nina Webster Chancellor Kimble McNeil, and the grandmother of young Phillip Chancellor III. She has had a difficult life (the story line alludes to her having been a prostitute). She raised Nina alone after Nina's father deserted her when he found out she was pregnant. She sometimes seems to be a dependent woman but, in reality, she is a strong person: She will survive because, for her, there is no other choice.

Veronica Redd Forrest: Mamie Johnson is the longtime housekeeper for the Abbott family. Without a mother of their own, the younger Abbotts see in her someone who cares for them, and someone in whom they can confide. (Dina, Ashley, Jack, and Traci's real mother left them years ago and has only seen them on sporadic visits; their father has never been married long enough for them to develop a relationship with his other wives.)

Mamie, who is the aunt of Dr. Olivia Barber and Drucilla Winters, has been in love with John Abbott, her employer, for years. When his second marriage to Jill was breaking up, she stood by him. When he had his stroke, she vowed not to let Jill take over his mind. Veronica Redd Forrest told the author, "Regardless of how the relationship between John and Mamie is defined, or where it will go, it will always be something special between them. "

Karen Hensel: Doris Collins is the loving, protective mother of Sharon Collins. She believes in honesty and has counseled her daughter not to keep secrets from Nicholas Newman about her past.

When she needed a potentially life-saving operation, the Collinses were unable to raise the money to pay for it. Victor Newman, however, advanced the amount needed, giving Doris a new lease on life and tying her closer to the Newman family.

395

Kate Linder: Esther Valentine is a pivotal dramatic character. She is a catalyst who doesn't change things, but whose mere presence instigates change. In the late 1980s, the young woman who never acted on impulse, did so one night when she picked up a man and slept with him. She later learned she was pregnant. Kay wondered aloud how it could have happened to Esther, who surprised Kay by saying that she was quite capable, thank you, of attracting a man.

Kay delivered Esther's baby in the Chancellor mansion when a power failure hit Genoa City.

A few years later, Esther was married (or thought she was: Kay hired someone to impersonate a minister). Esther's husband proved to be a scoundrel — just as Kay had suspected — and shot Rex when Rex discovered him rifling through the family safe. Kay refused to allow Esther to blame herself. Instead, the tragedy strengthened the friendship between them.

Kate Linder joined *The Young and the Restless* as Katherine Chancellor's maid in 1982. She was a flight attendant at the time, and remained on call for the airline for years. "When I would ask the passengers if they would like a pillow or a drink, those who recognized me from the soap said what they really wanted was to see Kay find a good man who wouldn't take advantage of her, and for Esther to find a good man who will love her ..."

Beth Maitland: Traci Abbott Romalotti Carlton Connelly is John Abbott's youngest daughter. She is the mother of Colleen Carlton, and the wife of Steve Connelly, the man who published her best-selling novel several years ago. Her previous husbands include Brad Carlton and Danny Romalotti.

Traci's story is, essentially, the saga of a poor little rich girl who had to learn to love herself. She had been overweight and tried to slim down by forcing herself not to eat. She developed a nearly fatal case of bulimia.

When Beth decided to lose weight, her sensible course of action (eating properly and exercising) was adopted by Traci as well. Week after week, viewers saw an actual weigh-in; whatever Beth lost, Traci lost.

Traci's relationship with her former husband, Brad, is formally over, but they are linked by their daughter and by those lingering ties between them.

Philip Moon: Keemo Volien Abbott. Keemo's mother, Luan Volien, came to Genoa City with her daughter, Maia, to open a restaurant. She spoke often of Keemo, the son she had to leave in Vietnam. Chris Blair and Paul Williams helped locate him and persuaded him to return to the United States with them.

Keemo was filled with rage in his first days in the United States. He raged against the American father he never knew; against his Vietnamese neighbors who taunted him for being half-American; and against anyone else who made the mistake of getting him riled up.

In time, Keemo allowed himself to have romantic feelings for Chris (although she didn't reciprocate); he eventually accepted the fact that Jack Abbott was his real father, and that Jack and his mother would marry. It helped that his grandfather, John Abbott, rushed to acknowledge him, while his aunts Ashley and Traci did likewise.

Shemar Moore: Malcolm Winters took advantage of his beautiful sister-in-law, Dru, when she was under medication that made her drowsy: Thinking he was her husband Neil, she invited him into bed. Malcolm slept with her. When she became pregnant, she learned about the medication and realized that since she and Neil used protection, Malcolm had to be the father.

Malcolm vowed to keep their secret. But can Dru depend on him not making a claim, someday, for the beautiful daughter she gave birth to? Promises are sometimes meant to be broken...

Victoria Rowell: Drucilla Barbara Winters (Dru), a former ballet student, was a difficult teenager who grew into a lovely young woman and a successful model. She is married to one of Jabot's important executives, Neil Winters, and is the mother of their daughter, born May, 1995.

However, she knows the baby's real father could be Neil's brother, Malcolm, a photographer's assistant. When Dru had the flu, her sister, Dr. Olivia Barber Hastings, gave her medication that left her in a mental haze. She imagined Neil had returned early from a business trip and invited him to come into bed as soon as he could. Malcolm, the recipient of her invitation, didn't bother to set her straight.

Although Dru almost aborted the child when she learned that Malcolm might have fathered it, her sister persuaded her to keep the baby. Dru feels one day the truth will come out — and what will happen then?

Michelle Stafford: Phyllis Romalotti could be the most disliked woman in America. After all, she broke up the marriage of popular rock star Danny Romalotti and Christine Blair Romalotti by claiming he had fathered her son, Danny, Jr.

Phyllis had been involved with a man named Brian when she set her cap for Danny while he was starring in a Broadway production. They made love just once. But as Phyllis said, once was enough to start them both on

Victoria Rowell, Kristoff St. John, and Tonya Lee Williams in a "family portrait."

the road to parenthood. (She even managed to get paternity tests to prove Danny was the father. But on a soap, that's easy enough to do if you have a friend at the lab — as Phyllis did.) Danny, of course, married her: It was the noble thing to do. But Phyllis always felt Christine would somehow persuade him to come back, so she tried to run Christine down with a rented car; instead she hit Christine's fiancé, Paul Williams. Paul canceled his wedding to Christine for the duration of his subsequent impotency.

Will Phyllis prove to be a liar, cheat, and manipulator? Maybe. But, as Michelle Stafford told the author, "...people say they may not like what Phyllis does, but they find the character interesting."

Kristoff St. John: Neil Winters is married to Drucilla Barber, a once aspiring ballet dancer who has become a model. She had resisted having a child until she felt more secure in her career. Much to Neil's surprise and delight, Dru became pregnant and delivered a baby girl. What Dru didn't tell him is that his brother, Malcolm, could be the father of the child, since he made love to her when she was under medication that led her to believe Neil was in bed with her.

Neil is a close friend of Ryan McNeil, a fellow Generation X-er and associate at Jabot.

Kristoff, who had previously been on *Generations,* described Neil once as a "Buppy; he's a black, upwardly mobile young professional who knows he's good at what he does, and is determined to prove it to everyone, including himself, over and over again."

Elizabeth Sung: Luan Volien Abbott was the woman Jack Abbott fell in love with when he served in Vietnam. He lost contact with her after being ordered to leave the country; later, despite searches, he was never able to find her again, although he always kept her photo in his safe deposit box.

In 1994, Luan came to Genoa City with her daughter, Maia, to open a restaurant. She had legal problems, which Christine helped straighten out, and confided to Christine that she had left behind a son in Vietnam. Chris helped find young Keemo and brought him back to America.

Jack came to realize that Luan was the woman he had loved and thought he had lost forever. When the two found each other again, she told him he was the father of Keemo, the sometimes angry young man who worked at Jabot.

Luan married Jack. Her story line reveals that she may be chronically ill, but chose not to tell anyone — above all Jack. However, her rival for Jack, Mari Jo Mason, knows something's wrong.

Michael Tylo:

Alex "Blade" Bladeson, a photographer, is married to Ashley Abbott, who never learned that she had shared her bed with Blade's twin brother while her real husband was being kept prisoner by him.

Blade had previously been involved with Mari Jo, whose hold on him resulted from her knowledge that he had let his brother drown after the two had a fight. Of course, that proved to be a lie, and Mari Jo left town with Blade's brother. Later, she returned alone.

Tonya Lee Williams:

Dr. Olivia Barber Hastings is the sister of Drucilla Winters and the wife of Nathan Hastings. Her aunt is Mamie Johnson, housekeeper for the Abbott family. She is a dedicated doctor and a woman of great personal courage. Although she was diagnosed with cancer, she insisted on giving birth to the baby she was carrying. She also risked her marriage to care for her increasingly demanding mother, the late Lily Belle.

Bibliography

Eileen Fulton with Brett Bolton. *How My World Turns*. New York: Warner Books, 1970.

Eileen Fulton with Desmond Atholl and Michael Cherkinian. *As My World Still Turns, The Uncensored Memoirs of America's Soap Opera Queen*. New York: Birch Lane Press, 1995.

Harding Lemay. *Eight Years In Another World*. New York: Atheneum, 1981.

Thomas O'Neil. *Emmys — Star Wars, Showdowns, and the Supreme Test of TV's Best*. Penguin Books (A Wexford Press Book).

Christopher Schemering. *Guiding Light: A 50th Anniversary Celebration*. New York: Ballantine, 1987.

Christopher Schemering. *The Soap Opera Encyclopedia*. New York: Ballantine, 1987.

Raymond William Stedman. *The Serials: Suspense and Drama by the Installment*. Norman, Oklahoma: University of Oklahoma Press, 1977.

Mary Stuart. *Both of Me*. New York: Doubleday, 1977.

Gary Warner. *All My Children Complete Fan Scrapbook*. Santa Monica, CA: General Publishing Group, 1994.

Ruth Warrick with Don Preston. *The Confessions of Phoebe Tyler*. Englewood Cliffs, New Jersey: Prentice-Hall, 1980.

Cast Lists

All My Children

ACTOR	CHARACTER
Grant Aleksander	Alec McIntyre
Kevin Alexander	Adam Chandler Jr.
Julia Barr	Brooke English
Olivia Birkelund	Arlene Vaughan
Teresa Blake	Gloria Marsh
Chris Bruno	Michael Delaney
John Callahan	Edmund Grey
David Canary	Adam/Stuart Chandler
William Christian	Derek Frye
Keith Hamilton Cobb	Noah Keefer
Marc Consuelos	Mateo Santos
Raul Davila	Hector Santos
Jim Fitzpatrick	Pierce Riley
Brian Gaskill	Bobby Warner
Gina Gallagher	Bianca Montgomery
Helen Gallagher	Nurse Harris
Sarah Michelle Gellar	Kendall Hart
Winsor Harmon	Del Henry
Kimberly Hawthorne	Belinda Keefer
Eileen Herlie	Myrtle Fargate
Cheryl Hulteen	Winifred
Steve Kanaly	Seabone Hunkle
James Kiberd	Trevor Dillon
Michael E. Knight	Tad Martin
Felicity La Fortune	Laurel Dillon
Jill Larson	Opal Cortlandt
Eva La Rue	Maria Santos Grey
Christopher Lawford	Charlie Brent
Susan Lucci	Erica Kane Marick
Ray MacDonnell	Joe Martin
Sean Marquette	Jamie Martin
Rudolf Martin	Anton Lang
Robin Mattson	Janet Green
Cady McClain	Dixie Martin
Shane McDermott	Scott Chandler
Anne Meara	Peggy Moody
Tommy J. Michaels	Tim Dillon
James Mitchell	Palmer Corlandt
Michael Nader	Dimitri Marick
Rosa Nevin	Cecily Davidson
Sydney Penny	Julia Santos
Kelly Ripa	Hayley Vaughan
Lauren Roman	Laura
Socorro Santiago	Isabella Santos
Richard Shoberg	Tom Cudahy
Kelli Taylor	Taylor Roxbury-Canon
Lynne Thigpen	Grace Keefer

403

Gillian Spencer . . . . . . .Daisy Cortlandt
Michelle Trachtenberg . . . . .Lily Benton
Ruth Warrick   .Phoebe Tyler Wallingford
Walt Willey . . . . . .Jackson Montgomery
Amir Jamal Williams   . . .Jamal Cudahy

Another World

ACTOR	CHARACTER
Joseph Barbara	.Joe Carlino
Alice Barrett	.Frankie Winthrop
Barbara Berjer	.Bridget Connell
Randy Brooks . . . . Marshall Lincoln Kramer III	
Kale Browne	.Michael Hudson
Jensen Buchanan	.Victoria Hudson
Amy Carlson	.Josie Watts
Robin Christopher	.Lorna Devon
Matt Crane	.Matthew Cory
Linda Dano	.Felicia Gallant
Tom Eplin	.Jake McKinnon
David Forsyth	.John Hudson
Timothy Gibbs	.Gary Sinclair
Eddie Earl Hatch	.Billy Cooper
Anna Holbrook	.Sharlene Hudson
Michelle Hurd	.Dana Kramer
Charles Keating	.Carl Hutchins
Judi Evans Luciano	.Paulina Cory McKinnon
Kevin McClatchy	.Nick Terry
Grayson McCouch . . .	.Morgan Winthrop
Tony Montero	.Eddie Carlino
Jodi Lyn O'Keefe	.Maggie Cory
Mark Pinter	.Grant Harrison
Peter Ratray	.Christophe Boudreau
Stephen Schnetzer	.Cass Winthrop
Hillary Scott	.Alli Fowler
Diego Serrano	.Tomas Rivera
Peg Small	.Clara Hudson
Anna Stuart	.Donna Hudson
Kim Sykes	.Judy Burrell
Christine Tucci	.Amanda Cory
Paul Michael Valley	.Ryan Harrison
Victoria Wyndham	.Rachel Cory Hutchins/Justine Kirkland Harrison

As the World Turns

ACTOR	CHARACTER
Brooke Alexander .	.Samantha Markham

ACTOR	CHARACTER
Claire Bloom	.Orlena Grimaldi
Jordana Brewster	.Nikki
Patricia Bruder	.Ellen Stewart
Larry Bryggman	.John Dixon
Martha Byrne	.Lily Grimaldi
Shawn Christian	.Mike Kasnoff
John Dauer	.Jeremy Wheeler
Scott DeFreitas	.Andy Dixon
Ellen Dolan	.Margo Hughes
Dan Frazer	.Dan "Mac" McCloskey
Ed Fry	.Larry McDermott
Christopher Fuller	.Jef Hamlin
Eileen Fulton	.Lisa Grimaldi
Michael Genet	.Lamar Griffin
Don Hastings	.Bob Hughes
Kathryn Hays	.Kim Hughes
Benjamin Hendrickson . . . .Hal Munson
Scott Holmes	.Tom Hughes
Elizabeth Hubbard . . . . .Lucinda Walsh
Rita Lloyd	.Edwina Cabot
Marie Masters . . . . . . .Susan McDermott
Kelley Menighan	.Emily Stewart
Jenny O'Hara	.Thelma Dailey
Yvonne Perry	.Rosanna Cabot
Colleen Zenk Pinter	.Barbara Ryan Munson
Margaret Reed	.Shannon O'Hara
JoAnna Rhinehart	.Jessica Griffin
Allyson Rice-Taylor	.Connor Walsh Stricklyn
Paolo Seganti	.Damian Grimaldi
Christian Seifert . . .Christopher Hughes
Susan Marie Snyder	.Julie Snyder
Michael Swan . . . . .Duncan McKechnie
Patrick Tovatt	.Cal Stricklyn
Robert Vaughan	.Rick Hamlin
Helen Wagner Nancy Hughes McCloskey	
Greg Watkins	.Evan Walsh
Doug Wert	.Scott Eldridge
Maura West	.Carly Tenney
Kathleen Widdoes	.Emma Snyder
Tom Wiggin	.Kirk Anderson
Ashley Williams . .Danielle Andropolous
Graham Winton	.Caleb Snyder

The Bold and the Beautiful

ACTOR	CHARACTER
Scott Thompson Baker . . .Connor Davis

Kabir Bedi . . . . .Prince Omar Rashid
Ian Buchanan . . . . .James Warwick
Darlene Conley . . . . .Sally Spectra
Barbara Crampton . . . .Maggie Forrester
Bobbie Eakes . . . . .Macy Alexander
Susan Flannery . . . . .Stephanie Forrester
Michael Fox . . . . .Saul Feinberg
Rita Gomez . . . . .Maria
Ken Hanes . . . . .Mike Guthrie
Schae Harrison . . . . .Darla Einstein
Steve Hartman . . . . . . .Eric Forrester Jr.
Brent Jasmer . . . . .Sly Donovan
Katherine Kelly Lang . . . . .Brooke
Logan Forrester
John McCook . . . . .Eric Forrester
Ronn Moss . . . . .Ridge Forrester
Dylan Neal . . . . .Dylan Shaw
Lindsay Price . . . . .Michael Lai
Michael Sabatino . . .Anthony Armando
Kyle Sabihy . . . .Clarke Garrison Jr. (C.J.)
Jeremy Snider . . . . . . .Eric Forrester Jr.
Jeff Trachta . . . . .Thorne Forrester
Jordan and Morgan Turner . . . . .Bridget
Forrester
Hunter Tylo . . . . .Taylor Hayes Forrester
Lark Voorhies . . . . .Jasmine
Maitland Ward . . . . . . .Jessica Forrester

Days of Our Lives

ACTOR **CHARACTER**
Kristian Alfonso . . . . .Gina Horton/
Hope Brady
John Aniston . . . . .Victor Kiriakis
Jaime Lyn Bauer . . . . .Laura Horton
Tanya Boyd . . . . .Celeste
Jason Brooks . . . . .Peter Blake
Eric Christmas . . . . .Father Francis
Christie Clark . . . . .Carrie Brady
John Clarke . . . . .Mickey Horton
Roark Critchlow . . . . . .Michael Horton
Bryan R. Dattilo . . . . . . .Lucas Roberts
Eileen Davidson . . . . . . .Kristen DiMera
Scott Groff . . . . .Shawn-Douglas Brady
Ivan G'Vera . . . . .Ivan Marais
Deidre Hall . . . . .Marlena Evans
Drake Hogestyn . . . . .John Black
Stan Ivar . . . . .Daniel Scott
Renee Jones . . . . .Lexie Carver

Thyme Lewis . . . . .Jonah Carver
Joseph Mascolo . . . . . .Stefano DiMera
Peggy McCay . . . . .Caroline Brady
Frank Parker . . . . .Shawn Brady
Miriam Parrish . . . . . . .Jaime Caldwell
Austin Peck . . . . .Austin Reed
Thaao Penghlis . . . . .Anthony DiMera
Peter Reckell . . . . .Bo Brady
Melissa Reeves . . . . . . .Jennifer Horton
Deveraux
Frances Reid . . . . .Alice Horton
James Reynolds . . . . .Abe Carver
Lisa Rinna . . . . .Billie Reed Brady
Suzanne Rogers . . . . . . .Maggie Horton
Louise Sorel . . . . .Vivian Alamain
Alison Sweeney . . . . .Sami Brady
Tammy Townsend . . . .Wendy Reardon
Mark Valley . . . . .Jack Deveraux

General Hospital

ACTOR **CHARACTER**
George Alvarez . . . . . . .Detective Garcia
Rachel Ames . . . . .Audrey Hardy
Senai Ashenafi . . . . .Keesha Ward
Matthew Ashford . . . . .Tom Hardy
Felecia Bell . . . . .Simone Hardy
Maurice Benard . . . . .Sonny Corinthos
John Beradino . . . . .Steve Hardy
Susan Brown . . . . .Gail Baldwin
Steve Burton . . . . .Jason Quartermaine
Lisa Canning . . . . .Meg Lawson
John Capodice . . . . . . .Carmine Cerullo
Rosalind Cash . . . . . . .Mary Mae Ward
Leslie Charleson . .Monica Quartermaine
Norma Connolly . . . . .Ruby Anderson
Stuart Damon . . . . . .Alan Quartermaine
Anita Dangler . . . . .Madame Maia
Zachary Ellington . . . . . .Tom Hardy Jr.
Mary Beth Evans . . . . . .Katherine Bell
Genie Francis . . . . .Laura Spencer
Anthony Geary . . . . .Luke Spencer
Ron Hale . . . . .Mike Corbin
Peter Hansen . . . . .Lee Baldwin
Glenn Walker Harris Jr. . . . . . .Sly Eckert
Lynn Herring . . . . .Lucy Coe
John Ingle . . . . .Edward Quartermaine
Jonathan Jackson . . . . . . .Lucky Spencer
Sean Kanan . . . . . . .A.J. Quartermaine

Stephen T. Kay . . . . . .Reginald Jennings
Shell Kepler . . . . .Amy Vining
Wallace Kurth . . . . .Ned Ashton
Anna Lee . . . . .Lila Quartermaine
Jon Lindstrom . . . . .Kevin Collins
Roger Lodge . . . . .James
Vanessa Marcil . . . . .Brenda Barrett
Ricky Martin . . . . .Miguel Morez
Brad Maule . . . . .Tony Jones
Leigh J. McCloskey . . . . .Damian Smith
Kimberly McCullough . . .Robin Scorpio
Lilly Melgar . . . . .Lily Rivera
Michael O'Connell . . . . . .Rick Johnson
Joseph C. Phillips . . . . . . .Justus Ward
Robyn Richards . . . . .Maxie Jones
Jay Sacane . . . . .Lucas Stansbury
Rena Sofer . . . . . . .Lois Cerullo Ashton
Michael Sutton . . . . .Stone Cates
Amber Tamblyn . . . . .Emily Bowen
Susan Tara . . . . .Remi
Ellen Travolta . . . . .Gloria Cerullo
Kristina Wagner . . . . .Felicia Jones
John J. York . . . . .Mac Scorpio
Jacklyn Zeman . . . . .Bobbie Jones

Guiding Light

ACTOR	CHARACTER
Frank Beaty	.Brent Lawrence
Kimberly J. Brown	.Marah Lewis
Lisa Brown	.Nola Reardon Chamberlain
Bryan Buffinton	.Bill Lewis
Gregory Burke	.Ben Reade
Jean Carol	.Nadine Cooper
Brett Cooper	.Shayne Lewis
Amy Cox	.Abigail Blume
Carey Cromelin	.Wanda Hite
Russell Curry	.David Grant
Justin Deas	.Buzz Cooper
Frank Dicopoulos	.Frank Cooper
Marj Dusay	.Alexandra Spaulding
Maureen Garrett	.Holly Lindsey
H.E. Greer	.Kirk
Charles Jay Hammer	.Fletcher Reade
Melissa Hayden	.Bridget Reardon
Rick Hearst	.Alan-Michael Spaulding
Scott Hoxby	.Patrick Cutter
Vincent Irizarry	.Nick Spaulding

Alison Janney . . . . .Ginger
Elizabeth Keifer . . . . . . .C. Blake Marler
Maeve Kinkead . . .Vanessa Chamberlain
Nina Landey . . . . .Cassie Lawrence
Tammy Lang . . . . .Donna
Graeme Malcolm . . . . .Viktor Pachinoff
Amelia Marshall . . . . .Gilly Grant
W.T. Martin . . . . .Sean Reardon
Kurt McKinney . . . . .Matt Reardon
Wendy Moniz . . . . .Dinah Marler
Kelly Neal . . . . .Sid Dickerson
Robert Newman . . . . .Josh Lewis
Michael O'Leary . . . . .Rick Bauer
Petronia Paley . . . . .Vivian Grant
Keith Pruitt . . . . .DA Robertson
Ron Raines . . . . .Alan Spaulding
William Roerick . . .Henry Chamberlain
Gil Rogers . . . . .Hawk Shayne
Jennifer Roszell . . . . .Eleni Cooper
Sonia Satra . . . . .Lucy Cooper
Peter Simon . . . . .Ed Bauer
Tina Sloan . . . . .Lillian Raines
Eugene Troobnick . . .Stavros Kouperakis
Jerry ver Dorn . . . . .Ross Marler
Marcy Walker . . . . .Tangie Hill
Stuart Ward . . . . .Levy
Cynthia Watros . . . . .Annie Dutton
Vince Williams . . . . . .Hampton Speakes
David Wolos-Fonteno . . . . . .Dr. Charles Grant
Michael Zaslow . . . . .Roger Thorpe
Kim Zimmer . . . . . . .Reva Shayne Lewis

Loving

ACTOR	CHARACTER
Nancy Addison Altman	.Deborah Brewster
Wesley Addy	.Cabot Alden
Alimi Ballard	.Frankie Hubbard
Philip Brown	.Buck Huston
Augusta Dabney	.Isabelle Alden
Geoffrey C. Ewsing	.Charles Harrison
Meta Golding	.Brianna Hawkins
Larry Haines	.Neal Warren
Amelia Heinle	.Stephanie Brewster
Catherine Hickland	.Tess Wilder
Hallee Hirsh	.Heather Forbes
T.W. King	.Danny Roberts

Jean LeClerc . . . . .Jeremy Hunter
Randolph Mantooth . . . . . .Alex Masters
Christopher Marcantel . . . .Curtis Alden
Debbi Morgan . . . . .Angie Hubbard
Ryan and Timothy Musick . . . . . . .Tyler Bowman
Christine Tudor Newman . . . .Gwyneth Alden
Corey Page . . . . .Richard Wilkins
George Palermo . . . . .Tony Soleito
Dennis Parlato . . . . .Clary Alden
Lisa Peluso . . . . . . .Ava Rescott Masters
Jacob Penn . . . . .Sandy Masters
Danny Roberts . . . . .T.W. King
Nada Rowand . . . . .Kate Slavinsky
Laura Sisk . . . . .Ally Bowman
Michael Spadafora . . . . . . .Christopher
Lauren-Marie Taylor . . .Stacey Donovan Forbes
Christine Tudor . . . . . . .Gwyneth Alden
Robert Tyler . . . . .Trucker McKenzie
Geoffrey Wigdor . . . . .J.J. Forbes
Darnell Williams . . . . . .Jacob Johnson

One Life to Live

ACTOR	CHARACTER
Jack Armstrong	Kevin Buchanan
Susan Batten	Luna Moody Holden
Laura Bonarrigo	Cassie Callison Carpenter
Philip Carey	Asa Buchanan
James DePaiva	Max Holden
Christopher Douglas	Dylan Moody
Patricia Elliott	Renee Buchanan
Nathan Fillion	Joey Buchanan
Jason Alexander Fischer	Al Holden
Margaret Hall	Elizabeth McNamara
Susan Haskell	Marty Saybrooke
Robert Hogan	Charlie Briggs
Roger Howarth	Todd Manning
Ken Kenitzer	Kevin Buchanan
Wortham Krimmer	Andrew Carpenter
Rene Lavan	Javier
John Loprieno	Cord Roberts
Yorlin Madera	Christian Vega
Patricia Mauceri	Carlotta Vega
Mari Morrow	Rachel Gannon

Tyler Noyes . . . . .C.J. Roberts
Peter Parros . . . . .Ben Price
Hayden Penettiere . . . . . . .Sarah Roberts
Wendee Pratt . . . . .Andy Harrison
Nathan Purdee . . . . .Hank Gannon
Kamar de los Reyes . . . . .Antonio Vega
Clint Ritchie . . . . .Clint Buchanan
Erika Slezak . . . . .Viki Carpenter
Hillary B. Smith . . . . . . .Nora Gannon
Timothy D. Stickney . . . . .R.J. Gannon
Robin Strasser . . . . .Dorian Lord Vickers
Krista Tesreau . . . . .Tina Roberts
Gina Tognoni . . . . .Kelly Cramer
Erin Torpey . . . . .Jessica Buchanan
Tonja Walker . . .Alex Olanov Buchanan
Tuc Watkins . . . . .David Vickers
Kassie Wesley . . . . .Blair Daimler Manning
Stephanie E. Williams . . . . . .Sheila Price Gannon
Robert S. Woods . . . . . . .Bo Buchanan

The Young and the Restless

ACTOR	CHARACTER
Tina Arning	Sasha
Diana Barton	Mari Jo Mason
Lauralee Bell	Christine Blair
Peter Bergman	Jack Abbott
Laura Bryan Birn	Lynne Bassett
Eric Braeden	Victor Newman
Tracey E. Bregman	Lauren Fenmore
Sharon Case	Sharon Collins
Tricia Cast	Nina McNeil
John Castellanos	John Silva
Eddie Cibrian	Matt Clark
Signy Coleman	Hope Adams Newman
Carolyn Conwell	Mary Williams
Jeanne Cooper	Katherine Chancellor Sterling
David Cowgill	Cliff Wilson
Steve Culp	Brian
Abby Dalton	Lydia Summers
Michael Damian	Danny Romalotti
Doug Davidson	Paul Williams
Don Diamont	Brad Carlton
Jerry Douglas	John Abbott
Brenda Epperson Doumani	Ashley Abbott Bladeson

407

Michael Evans . . . . .Douglas Austin
Sharon Farrell . . . . .Flo Webster
Kathleen Fitzgerald . . . . .Connie
Veronica Redd Forrest . . . . .Mamie
Johnson
Vivica A. Fox . . . . .Stephanie
Bennet Guillory . . . . .Walter Barber
Mark Harrison . . . . . . .Dr. Bernard Laski
Karen Hensel . . . . .Doris Collins
Adam Lazarre-White . . . . .Nathan
Hastings
Kate Linder . . . . .Esther Valentine
Beth Maitland . . . . .Traci Connelly
Christine McCall . . . . .Jeri Paulsen
Courtland R. Mead . . . . .Phillip
Chancellor III
Freeman Michaels . . . . . .Drake Belson
Philip Moon . . . . .Keemo Volien
Shemar Moore . . . . . .Malcolm Winters
Julianne Morris . . . . .Amy Wilson
Joshua Morrow . . . . .Nicholas Newman
J. Eddie Peck . . . . .Cole Howard

Anthony Pena . . . . . . .Miguel Rodriguez
Marianne Rees . . . . .Mai Volien
Scott Reeves . . . . .Ryan McNeil
Victoria Rowell . . . . . . .Drucilla Winters
Melody Thomas Scott . . . . .Nikki
Newman Abbott
Shane Siler . . . . .William "Billy" Abbott
Michelle Stafford . . . . .Phyllis Romalotti
Kristoff St. John . . . . .Neil Winters
Robert Stoekle . . . . .Dr. Campbell
Elizabeth Sung . . . . .Luan Volien Abbott
Christoher Templeton . . . . .Carol
Robbins-Evans
Heather Tom . . . . .Victoria
Newman Howard
Michael Tylo . . . . .Blade
Jess Walton . . . . .Jill Abbott
Patty Weaver . . . . .Gina Roma Radison
Tonya Lee Williams . . . . . .Olivia Barber
Hastings
William Wintersole . .Mitchell Sherman
Greg Wrangler . . . . . . .Steve Connelly

Fan Clubs

SOAP OPERA FRIENDS
c/o Patricia Foote
PO Box 36524
Grosse Pointe, MI 48236

    Founded in 1989, this 1,000 member group includes fans of all 10 daytime television soap operas as well as prime time "soaps." The group's goal is promoting correspondence and communication among members interested in particular programs; requests for information will be answered if accompanied by self-addressed stamped envelope. A reference library is maintained with holdings of clippings, periodicals, and photographs. Membership Dues: $2.

All My Children

ALL MY CHILDREN FAN CLUB
c/o Carol Dickson
1218 N. Main St.
Glassboro, NJ 08028

JULIA BARR FAN CLUB

JOHN CALLAHAN FAN CLUB

JILL LARSON FAN CLUB

WALT WILLEY FAN CLUB
c/o St. Laurent & Associates, Inc.
PO Box 20191
Cherokee Station, NY 10028-9991

JAMES KIBERD FAN CLUB
c/o ABC-TV — All My Children
77 W. 66th St.
New York, NY 10023

ROBIN MATTSON FAN CLUB
c/o ABC-TV — All My Children
320 W. 66 St.
New York, NY 10023

Another World

ANOTHER WORLD FAN CLUB
c/o Mindi Schulman
34 Davison Ave.
East Rockaway, NY 11518

As the World Turns

AS THE WORLD TURNS FAN CLUB
c/o Deanne Turco
212 Oriole Dr.
Montgomery, NY 12549

The Bold and the Beautiful

THE BOLD AND THE BEAUTIFUL FAN
    CLUB
7800 Beverly Blvd., Suite 3371
Los Angeles, CA 90036

Days of Our Lives

NATIONAL DAYS FAN CLUB
424A Johnson St.
Sausalito, CA 94965
(415) 332-1819

THE OFFICIAL DAYS OF OUR LIVES FAN
    CLUB
PO Box 11508
Burbank, CA 91510-1508

DEIDRE HALL FAN CLUB
c/o Evelyn Reynolds
9570 Apricot
Alta Loma, CA 91737
(714) 980-8654

General Hospital

FANS OF GENERAL HOSPITAL
c/o Sue Corbett
PO Box 8023
West Chester, OH 45069

LESLIE CHARLESON FAN CLUB
c/o Kay Marrs
349D Circuit Lane
Newport News, VA 23602

JONATHAN JACKSON FAN CLUB

SEAN KANAN FAN CLUB

JON LINDSTROM FAN CLUB

BRAD MAULE FAN CLUB

MICHAEL SUTTON FAN CLUB
ABC-TV — General Hospital
4151 Prospect Ave.
Hollywood, CA 90027

WALLY [KURTH]'S FRIENDS
PO Box 640
Merrick, NY 11566-0640

ANNA LEE FAN CLUB
868 West Knoll Dr.
Los Angeles, CA 90069

ROGER LODGE FAN CLUB
c/o Erin M. Kohler
3119 Andrea Ct.
Woodridge, IL 60517

VANESSA MARCIL FAN CLUB
PO Box 1578
LaQuinto, CA 92253

LEIGH MCCLOSKEY FAN CLUB
c/o Laura Luxtrum
PO Box 1342
Gig Harbor, WA 98335-0123

JOHN REILLY FAN CLUB
c/o Debbie Morris
13518 Louisville St.
Houston, TX 77015

KRISTINA WAGNER FAN CLUB
PO Box 22625
Indianapolis, IN 46224-0625

SHARON WYATT FAN CLUB
8949 Falling Creek Court
Annadale, VA 22003

JOHN J. YORK FAN CLUB
4755 White Oak Place
Encino, CA 91316

Guiding Light

GUIDING LIGHT FAN CLUB
c/o Sharon Kearns
104 St. George Dr.
Camillus, NY 13031
(315) 488-6544

Loving

LOVING FAN CLUB

JEAN LECLERC FAN CLUB

ROBERT TYLER FAN CLUB
c/o Carol Dickson
1218 N. Main St.
Glassboro, NJ 08028

NANCY ADDISON ALTMAN FAN CLUB
c/o ABC-TV— Loving
320 W. 66th St.
New York, NY 10023

LISA PELUSO FAN CLUB
c/o Shauna Sickenger
PO Box 301
Ramona, CA 92065

LAUREN-MARIE TAYLOR FAN CLUB
c/o St. Laurent & Associates, Inc.
PO Box 20191
Cherokee Station, NY 10028-9991

One Life to Live

ONE LIFE TO LIVE FAN CLUB
c/o Carol Dickson
1218 N. Main St.
Glassboro, NJ 08028

LAURA BONARRIGO FAN CLUB
c/o Life With Laura
PO Box 9624
New Haven, CT 06535-9624

JAMES DEPAIVA FAN CLUB

PATRICIA ELLIOTT FAN CLUB
c/o St. Laurent & Associates, Inc.
PO Box 20191
Cherokee Station, NY 10028-9991

JOHN LOPRIENO FAN CLUB
c/o Debbie Morris
13518 Louisville St.
Houston, TX 77015

CLINT RITCHIE FAN CLUB
c/o Nadine Shanfeld
140 Alexander Ave.
Staten Island, NY 10312

ERIKA SLEZAK FAN CLUB
c/o Walter Miller, Jr.

64 Presidential Drive, #5
Quincy, MA 02169

TIMOTHY STICKNEY FAN CLUB
c/o Laurel Dusenberry
1012 NW 51st St.
Vancouver, WA 98663

TONJA WALKER AND U
c/o One Life To Live
56 W. 66th St.
New York, NY 10023

The Young and the Restless

THE YOUNG AND THE RESTLESS FAN
    CLUB

LAURALEE BELL FAN CLUB

ERIC BRAEDEN FAN CLUB

OFFICIAL KATE LINDER FAN CLUB
c/o CBS-TV — The Young and the Restless
7800 Beverly Blvd., Ste. 3305
Los Angeles, CA 90036
(213) 852-2527

Daytime Emmy Awards

And the Winner Is....

Those four little words were not heard for at least 25 years after NBC went on the air with *The First 100 Years,* the first televised soap that wasn't a test airing. The Academy of Television Arts and Sciences, the organization that awards the Emmys, largely ignored the daytime genre, with one exception: In 1962, Mary Stuart, the star of *Search for Tomorrow,* was nominated for Outstanding Continued Performance by an Actress in a Series. She was one of several actresses up for the award, all of whom (except Mary) were from prime-time shows.

In 1966, the Academy decided to add a category, Outstanding Achievement in Daytime Programming, to cover both individuals and shows. Joan Bennett and Macdonald Carey won Outstanding Achievement Awards in 1967–68; Ms. Bennett for her work in the gothic soap *Dark Shadows,* and Mr. Carey for his work in *Days of Our Lives.* The buzz was that the two veteran actors were chosen not so much for their daytime performances, but because the Academy had strong ties to the old Hollywood gang whence these two came.

The categories grew from just one for 1971–1972, to two the following year, and have continued to evolve and change. The listings that follow indicate best or outstanding actors and actressses in their categories (supporting, younger, juvenile, etc.) and the best show of that year.

1971–1972

Outstanding Acheivement in Daytime Drama . . . .*The Doctors,* NBC

1972–73

Outstanding Program Achievement in Daytime Drama . . . .*The Edge of Night,* CBS

Outstanding Achievement by an Individual in Daytime Drama . . . .**Mary Fickett**
(Ruth Brent, *All My Children*), ABC

1973–74

Outstanding Daytime Drama Series . . . .*The Doctors,* NBC

Best Actor in a Daytime Drama Series . . . .**Macdonald Carey**
(Tom Horton, *Days of Our Lives*), NBC

Best Actress in a Daytime Drama Series . . . .**Elizabeth Hubbard**
(Althea Davis, *The Doctors*), NBC

1974–75

Outstanding Daytime Drama Series . . . .*The Young and the Restless,* CBS

Outstanding Actor in a Daytime Drama Series . . . .**Macdonald Carey**
(Tom Horton, *Days of Our Lives*), NBC

Outstanding Actress in a Daytime Drama Series . . . .**Susan Flannery**
(Dr. Laura Horton, *Days of Our Lives*), NBC

1975–76

Outstanding Daytime Drama Series . . . .*Another World,* NBC

Outstanding Actor in a Daytime Drama Series . . . .**Larry Haines**
(Stu Bergman, *Search for Tomorrow*), CBS

Outstanding Actress in a Daytime Drama Series . . . .**Helen Gallagher**
(Maeve Ryan, *Ryan's Hope*), ABC

1976–1977

Outstanding Daytime Drama Series . . . .*Ryan's Hope,* ABC

Outstanding Actor in a Daytime Drama Series . . . .**Val Dufour**
(John Wyatt, *Search for Tomorrow*), CBS

Outstanding Actress in a Daytime Drama Series . . . .**Helen Gallagher,**
(Maeve Ryan, *Ryan's Hope*), ABC

1977–78

Outstanding Daytime Drama Series . . . .*Days of Our Lives,* NBC

Outstanding Actor in a Daytime Drama Series . . . .**James Pritchett**
(Dr. Matt Powers, *The Doctors*), NBC

Outstanding Actress in a Daytime Drama Series . . . .**Laurie Heineman**
(Sharlene Frame, *Another World*), NBC

1978–79

Outstanding Daytime Drama Series . . . .*Ryan's Hope,* ABC

Outstanding Actor in a Daytime Drama Series . . . .**Al Freeman, Jr.**
(Captain Ed Hall, *One Life to Live*), ABC

Outstanding Actress in a Daytime Drama Series . . . .**Irene Dailey**
(Liz Matthews, *Another World*), NBC

Outstanding Supporting Actor in a Daytime Drama Series . . . .**Peter Hansen**
(Lee Baldwin, *General Hospital*), ABC

Outstanding Supporting Actress in a Daytime Drama Series . . . .**Suzanne Rogers**
(Maggie Horton, *Days of Our Lives*), NBC

1979–1980

Outstanding Daytime Drama Series . . . .*Guiding Light,* CBS

Outstanding Actor in a Daytime Drama Series . . . .**Douglass Watson**
(Mackenzie Cory, *Another World*), NBC

Outstanding Actress in a Daytime Drama Series . . . .**Judith Light**
(Karen Wolek, *One Life to Live*), ABC

Outstanding Supporting Actor in a Daytime Drama Series . . . .**Warren Burton**
(Eddie Dorance, *All My Children*), ABC

Outstanding Supporting Actress in a Daytime Drama Series . . . .**Francesca James**
(Kelly Cole, *All My Children*), ABC

Outstanding Cameo Appearance in a Daytime Series . . . .**Hugh McPhillips**
(Hugh Pearson, *Days of Our Lives*), NBC

1980–81

Outstanding Daytime Drama Series . . . .*General Hospital,* ABC

Outstanding Actor in a Daytime Drama Series . . . .**Douglass Watson**
(Mackenzie Cory, *Another World*), NBC

Outstanding Actress in a Daytime Drama Series . . . .**Judith Light**
(Karen Wolek, *One Life to Live*), ABC

Outstanding Supporting Actor in a Daytime Drama Series . . . .**Larry Haines**
(Stu Bergman, *Search for Tomorrow*), CBS

Outstanding Supporting Actress in a Daytime Drama Series . . . .**Jane Elliott**
(Tracy Quartermaine, *General Hospital*), ABC

Trustees Award for Special Achievement in Television . . . .**Agnes Nixon**, creator of
All My Children, One Life to Live,
co-creator of *As the World Turns,*
Search for Tomorrow.

1981–82

Outstanding Daytime Drama Series . . . .*Guiding Light,* CBS

Outstanding Actor in a Daytime Drama Series . . . .**Anthony Geary**
(Lucas Lorenzo Spencer, *General Hospital*), ABC

Outstanding Actress in a Daytime Drama Series . . . .**Robin Strasser**
(Dorian Lord Callison, *One Life to Live*), ABC

Outstanding Supporting Actor in a Daytime Drama Series . . . .**David Lewis**
(Edward Quartermaine, *General Hospital*), ABC

Outstanding Supporting Actress in a Daytime Drama Series . . . .**Dorothy Lyman**
(Opal Gardner, *All My Children*), ABC

1982–83

Outstanding Daytime Drama Series . . . .*The Young and the Restless,* CBS

Outstanding Actor in a Daytime Drama Series . . . .**Robert S. Woods**
(Bo Buchanan, *One Live to Live*), ABC

Outstanding Actress in a Daytime Drama Series . . . .**Dorothy Lyman**
(Opal Gardner, *Search for Tomorrow*), ABC

Outstanding Supporting Actor in a Daytime Drama Series . . . .**Darnell Williams**
(Jesse Hubbard, *All My Children*), ABC

Outstanding Supporting Actress in a Daytime Drama Series . . . .**Louise Shaffer**
(Rae Woodard, *Ryan's Hope*), ABC

Trustees' Award for Continued Distinguished Service in Television . . . .**Robert E. Short,**
Procter & Gamble production executive

1983–84

Outstanding Daytime Drama Series . . . .*General Hospital,* ABC

Outstanding Actor in a Daytime Drama Series . . . .**Larry Bryggman**
(Dr. John Dixon, *As the World Turns*), CBS

Outstanding Actress in a Daytime Drama Series . . . .**Erika Slezak**
(Victoria Lord Buchanan, *One Life to Live*), ABC

Outstanding Supporting Actor in a Daytime Drama Series . . . .**Justin Deas**
(Tom Hughes, *As the World Turns*), CBS

Outstanding Supporting Actress in a Daytime Drama Series . . . .**Judi Evans**
(Beth Raines, *Guiding Light*), CBS

1984–85

Outstanding Daytime Drama Series . . . .*The Young and the Restless,* CBS

Outstanding Lead Actor in a Daytime Drama Series . . . .**Darnell Williams**
(Jesse Hubbard, *All My Children*), ABC

Outstanding Lead Actress in a Daytime Drama Series . . . .**Kim Zimmer**
(Reva Shayne Lewis, *Guiding Light*), CBS

Outstanding Supporting Actor in a Daytime Drama Series . . . .**Larry Gates**
(H.B. Lewis, *Guiding Light*), CBS

Outstanding Supporting Actress in a Daytime Drama Series . . . .**Beth Maitland**
(Traci Abbott Romalotti, *The Young and the Restless*), CBS

Outstanding Juvenile/Young Man in a Daytime Drama Series . . . .**Brian Bloom**
(Dustin Donovan, *As the World Turns*), CBS

Outstanding Ingenue in a Daytime Drama Series . . . .**Tracey E. Bregman**
(Lauren Fenmore Williams, *The Young and the Restless*)CBS

Trusteees Award for Distinguished Service to Daytime Television . . . .**Charita Bauer**
(Bert Bauer, *Guiding Light*), CBS

Trusteees Award for Distinguished Service to Daytime Television . . . .**Larry Haines**
(Stu Bergman, *Search for Tomorrow*), NBC

Trusteees Award for Distinguished Service to Daytime Television . . . .**Mary Stuart**
(Jo, *Search for Tomorrow*), NBC

Note: *Search for Tomorrow* was on CBS from September 3, 1951 to March 26, 1982, and
moved to NBC on March 29, 1982, where it remained until cancelled on December 26, 1986

1985–86

Outstanding Daytime Drama Series . . . .*The Young and the Restless,* CBS

Outstanding Lead Actor in a Daytime Drama Series . . . .**David Canary**
(Adam / Stuart Chandler, *All My Children*), ABC

Outstanding Lead Actress in a Daytime Drama Series . . . .**Erika Slezak**
(Victoria Lord Buchanan, *One Life to Live*), ABC

Outstanding Supporting Actor in a Daytime Drama Series . . . .**John Wesley Shipp**
(Douglas Cummings, *As the World Turns*), CBS

Outstanding Supporting Actress in a Daytime Drama Series . . . .**Leann Hunley**
(Anne DiMera, *Days of Our Lives*), NBC

Outstanding Younger Leading Man in a Daytime Drama Series . . . . . .**Michael Knight**
(Tad Gardner Martin, *All My Children*), ABC

Outstanding Ingenue in a Daytime Drama Series . . . .**Ellen Wheeler**
(Marley/Victoria Love, *Another World*), NBC

1986–87

Outstanding Daytime Drama Series . . . .*As the World Turns,* CBS

Outstanding Lead Actor in a Daytime Drama Series . . . .**Larry Bryggman**
(John Dixon, *As the World Turns*), CBS

Outstanding Lead Actress in a Daytime Drama Series . . . .**Kim Zimmer**
(Reva Shayne, *Guiding Light*), CBS

Outstanding Supporting Actor in a Daytime Drama Series . . . .**Gregg Marx**
(Tom Hughes, *Search for Tomorrow*), CBS

Outstanding Supporting Actress in a Daytime Drama Series . . . .**Kathleen Noone**
(Ellen Chandler, *All My Children*), ABC

Outstanding Younger Leading Man in a Daytime Drama Series . . . . . .**Michael Knight**
(Tad Gardner Martin, *All My Children*), ABC

Outstanding Ingenue in a Daytime Drama Series . . . .**Martha Byrne**
(Lily Walsh, *As the World Turns*), CBS

Outstanding Guest Performer in a Daytime Drama Series . . . .**John Wesley Shipp**
(*Santa Barbara*), NBC

1987–88

Outstanding Drama Series . . . .*Santa Barbara,* NBC

Outstanding Lead Actor in a Daytime Drama Series . . . .**David Canary**
(Adam/Stuart Chandler, *All My Children*), ABC

Outstanding Lead Actress in a Daytime Drama Series . . . .**Helen Gallagher**
(Maeve Ryan, *Ryan's Hope*), ABC

Outstanding Supporting Actor in a Daytime Drama Series . . . .**Justin Deas**
(Keith Timmons, *Santa Barbara*), NBC

Outstanding Supporting Actress in a Daytime Drama Series . . . .**Ellen Wheeler**
(Cindy Parker Chandler, *All My Children*), ABC

Outstanding Younger Leading Man in a Daytime Drama Series . . . .**Billy Warlock**
(Frankie Brady, *Days of Our Lives*), NBC

Outstanding Ingenue in a Daytime Drama Series . . . .**Julianne Moore**
(Frannie and Sabrina Hughes,*As the World Turns*), CBS

1988–89

Outstanding Drama Series . . . .*Santa Barbara,* NBC

Outstanding Lead Actor in a Drama Series . . . .**David Canary**
(Adam/Stuart Chandler, *All My Children*), ABC

Outstanding Lead Actress in a Drama Series . . . .**Marcy Walker**
(Eden Capwell Castillo, *Santa Barbara*), NBC

Outstanding Supporting Actor in a Drama Series . . . .**Justin Deas**
(Keith Timmons, *Santa Barbara*), NBC

Outstanding Supporting Actress in a Drama Series . . . . .TIE

Debbi Morgan
(Dr. Angie Hubbard, *All My Children*), ABC

Nancy Lee Grahn
(Julia Wainwright, *Santa Barbara*), NBC

Outstanding Juvenile Male in a Drama Series . . . .**Justin Gocke**
(Brandon Capwell, *Santa Barbara*), NBC

Outstanding Juvenile Female in a Drama Series . . . .**Kimberly McCullough**
(Robin Scorpio, *General Hospital*), ABC

1989–90

Outstanding Drama Series . . . .*Santa Barbara,* NBC

Outstanding Lead Actor in a Drama Series . . . .**A Martinez**
(Cruz Castillo, *Santa Barbara*), NBC

Outstanding Lead Actress in a Drama Series . . . .**Kim Zimmer**
(Reva Shayne Lewis, *Guiding Light*), CBS

Outstanding Supporting Actor in a Drama Series . . . .**Henry Darrow**
(Rafael Castillo, *Santa Barbara*), NBC

Outstanding Supporting Actress in a Drama Series . . . .**Julia Barr**
(Brooke English, *All My Children*), ABC

Outstanding Juvenile Male in a Drama Series . . . .**Andrew Kavovit**
(Paul Stenbeck, *As the World Turns*), CBS

Outstanding Juvenile Female in a Drama Series . . . .**Cady McClain**
(Dixie Martin, *All My Children*), ABC

1990–91

Outstanding Drama Series . . . .*As the World Turns,* CBS

Outstanding Lead Actor in a Drama Series . . . .**Peter Bergman**
(Jack Abbott, *The Young and the Restless*), CBS

Outstanding Lead Actress in a Drama Series . . . .**Finola Hughes**
(Anna Lavery, *General Hospital*), ABC

Outstanding Supporting Actor in a Drama Series . . . .**Bernard Barrow**
(Louie Slavinsky, *Loving*), ABC

Outstanding Supporting Actress in a Drama Series . . . .**Jess Walton**
(Jill Foster Abbott, *The Young and the Restless*), CBS

Outstanding Younger Actor in a Drama Series . . . .**Rick Hearst**
(Alan-Michael Spaulding, *Guiding Light*), CBS

Outstanding Younger Actress in a Drama Series . . . .**Anne Heche**
(Victoria Hudson/Marley McKinnon, *Another World*), NBC

1991–92

Outstanding Drama Series . . . .*All My Children,* ABC

Outstanding Lead Actor in a Drama Series . . . .**Peter Bergman**
(Jack Abbott, *The Young and the Restless*), CBS

Outstanding Lead Actress in a Drama Series . . . .**Erika Slezak**
(Victoria Lord Buchanan, *One Life to Live*), ABC

Outstanding Supporting Actor in a Drama Series . . . .**Thom Christopher**
(Carlo Hesser, *One Life to Live*), ABC

Outstanding Supporting Actress in a Drama Series . . . .**Maeve Kinkead**
(Vanessa Chamberlain Lewis, *Guiding Light*), CBS

Outstanding Younger Actor in a Drama Series . . . .**Kristoff St. John**
(Neil Winters, *The Young and the Restless*), CBS

Outstanding Younger Actress in a Drama Series . . . .**Tricia Cast**
(Nina Chancellor, *The Young and the Restless*), CBS

1992–93

Outstanding Drama Series . . . .*The Young and the Restless,* CBS

Outstanding lead Actor in a Drama Series . . . .**David Canary**
(Adam/Stuart Chandler, *All My Children*), ABC

Outstanding Lead Actress in a Drama Series . . . .**Linda Dano**
(Felicia Gallant, *Another World*), NBC

Outstanding Supporting Actor in a Drama Series . . . .**Gerald Anthony**
(Marco Dane, *General Hospital*), ABC

Outstanding Supporting Actress in a Drama Series . . . .**Ellen Parker**
(Maureen Bauer, *Guiding Light)* CBS

Outstanding Younger Actor in a Drama Series . . . .**Monti Sharp**
(David Grant, *Guiding Light*), CBS

Outstanding Younger Actress in a Drama Series . . . .**Heather Tom**
(Victoria Newman, *The Young and the Restless*), CBS

Lifetime Achievement Emmy Award . . . .**Douglas Marland**

1993–94

Outstanding Drama Series . . . .*All My Children,* ABC

Outstanding Lead Actor in a Drama Series . . . .**Michael Zaslow**
(Roger Thorpe, *Guiding Light*), CBS

Outstanding Lead Actress in a Drama Series . . . .**Hillary B. Smith**
(Nora Gannon, *One Life to Live*), ABC

Outstanding Supporting Actor in a Drama Series . . . .**Justin Deas**
("Buzz" Cooper, *Guiding Light*), CBS

Outstanding Supporting Actress in a Drama Series . . . .**Susan Haskell**
(Marty Saybrooke, *One Life to Live*), ABC

Outstanding Younger Actor in a Drama Series . . . .**Roger Howarth**
(Todd Manning, *One Life to Live*), ABC

Outstanding Younger Actress in a Drama Series . . . .**Melissa Hayden**
(Bridget Reardon, *Guiding Light*), CBS

1994–95

Outstanding Drama Series . . . .*General Hospital,* ABC

Outstanding Lead Actor in a Drama Series . . . .**Justin Deas**
("Buzz" Cooper, *Guiding Light*), CBS

Outstanding Lead Actress in a Drama Series . . . .**Erika Slezak**
(Victoria Lord Carpenter, *One Life to Live*), ABC

Outstanding Supporting Actor in a Drama Series . . . .**Jerry ver Dorn**
(Ross Marler, *Guiding Light*), CBS

Outstanding Supporting Actress in a Drama Series . . . .**Rena Sofer**
(Lois Cerullo, *General Hospital*), ABC

Outstanding Younger Actor in a Drama Series . . . .**Jonathan Jackson**
(Lucky Spencer, *General Hospital*), ABC

Outstanding Younger Actress in a Drama Series . . . .**Sarah Michelle Gellar**
(Kendall Hart, *All My Children*), ABC

Lifetime Achievement Emmy Award . . . .**Ted and Betty Corday**
(presented posthumously)

Soap Opera Digest Awards

1984 — First Annual Awards

DAYTIME

Outstanding Daytime Soap . . . . *Days Of Our Lives*
Outstanding Lead Actor . . . . .Peter Reckell
Outstanding Lead Actress . . . . .Deidre Hall
Outstanding Supporting Actor . . . . John de Lancie
Outstanding Supporting Actress . . . . .Lisa Trusel
Exciting Male Newcomer . . . . .Michael Leon
Exciting Female Newcomer . . . . .Kristian Alfonso
Outstanding Actor in a Mature Role . . . . .Macdonald Carey
Outstanding Actress in a Mature Role . . . . .Frances Reid
Outstanding Villain . . . . .Joseph Mascolo
Outstanding Villainess . . . . .Nancy Frangione
Outstanding Juvenile Actor . . . . .David Mendenhall
Outstanding Juvenile Actress . . . . .Andrea Barber

PRIME TIME

Outstanding Prime Time Soap . . . . *Dynasty*
Outstanding Lead Actor . . . . .John Forsythe
Outstanding Lead Actress . . . . .Linda Evans
Outstanding Supporting Actor . . . . .Steve Kanaly
Outstanding Supporting Actress . . . . .Lisa Hartman
Exciting Male Newcomer . . . . .Doug Sheehan
Exciting Female Newcomer . . . . .Priscilla Presley

Outstanding Actor in a Mature Role . . . . .John Forsythe
Outstanding Actress in a Mature Role . . . . .Barbara Bel Geddes
Outstanding Villain . . . . .Larry Hagman
Outstanding Villainess . . . . .Joan Collins
Outstanding Juvenile Actor . . . . .Omri Katz
Outstanding Juvenile Actress . . . . .Shalane McCall

1985

DAYTIME

Outstanding Daytime Soap . . . .*Days of Our Lives*
Outstanding Lead Actor . . . . .Peter Reckell
Outstanding Lead Actress . . . . .Deidre Hall
Outstanding Supporting Actor . . . . .John de Lancie
Outstanding Supporting Actress . . . . .Arleen Sorkin
Outstanding Male Newcomer . . . . .Charles Shaughnessy
Outstanding Female Newcomer . . . . .Arleeen Sorkin
Outstanding Actor in a Mature Role . . . . .Macdonald Carey
Outstanding Actress in a Mature Role . . . . .Frances Reid
Outstanding Villain . . . . .Joseph Mascolo
Outstanding Villainess . . . . .Cheryl-Ann Wilson
Outstanding Juvenile Actor . . . . .Brian Autenrieth
Outstanding Juvenile Actress . . . . .Andrea Barber

PRIME TIME

Outstanding Prime Time Soap . . . .*Dynasty*
Outstanding Lead Actor . . . . .Patrick Duffy
Outstanding Lead Actress . . . . .Linda Evans
Outstanding Supporting Actor . . . . .Steve Kanaly
Outstanding Supporting Actress . . . . .Catherine Oxenberg
Outstanding Male Newcomer . . . . .Alec Baldwin
Outstanding Female Newcomer . . . . .Catherine Oxenberg
Outstanding Villain . . . . .Larry Hagman
Outstanding Villainess . . . . .Joan Collins

1986

DAYTIME

Outstanding Daytime Soap . . . .*Days of Our Lives*
Outstanding Lead Actor . . . . .John Aniston
Outstanding Lead Actress . . . . .Patsy Pease
Outstanding Supporting Actor . . . . .Stephen Nichols
Outstanding Supporting Actress . . . . .Harley Jane Kozack
Outstanding Young Leading Actor . . . . .Peter Reckell
Outstanding Young Leading Actress . . . . .Ellen Wheeler
Outstanding Villain . . . . .John Aniston
Outstanding Villainess . . . . .Linda Gibboney

Outstanding Comic Relief . . . . .Arleen Sorkin
Outstanding Juvenile . . . . .Kimberly McCullough
Outstanding Super Couple . . . . .Charles Shaughnessy and Patsy Pease

PRIME TIME
Outstanding Prime Time Soap . . . .*Knots Landing*
Outstanding Lead Actor . . . . .Larry Hagman
Outstanding Lead Actress . . . . .Joan van Ark
Outstanding Supporting Actor . . . . .Doug Sheehan
Outstanding Supporting Actress . . . . .Susan Howard
Outstanding Villain . . . . .Larry Hagman
Outstanding Villainess . . . . .Donna Mills
Outstanding Comic Relief . . . . .Margaret Ladd
Outstanding Super Couple .Kevin Dobson and Michele Lee

1987 — no awards given

1988

DAYTIME
Outstanding Daytime Soap . . . .*Days of Our Lives*
Outstanding Lead Actor . . . . .Stephen Nichols
Outstanding Lead Actress . . . . .Kim Zimmer
Outstanding Hero . . . . .A Martinez
Outstanding Heroine . . . . .Robin Wright
Outstanding Supporting Actor . . . . .Nicolas Coster
Outstanding Supporting Actress . . . . .Anna Lee
Outstanding Villain . . . . .Justin Deas
Outstanding Villainess . . . . .Brenda Dickson
Outstanding Comic Actor . . . . .Michael T. Weiss
Outstanding Comic Actress . . . . .Arleen Sorkin
Outstanding Newcomer . . . . .Ian Buchanan
Favorite Super Couple . . . . .Charles Shaughnessy and Patsy Pease

PRIME TIME
Outstanding Prime Time Soap . . . .*Knots Landing*
Outstanding Lead Actor . . . . .Kevin Dobson
Outstanding Lead Actress . . . . .Michele Lee
Outstanding Supporting Actor . . . . .Steve Kanaly
Outstanding Supporting Actress . . . . .Tonya Crowe
Outstanding Villain . . . . .Larry Hagman
Outstanding Villainess . . . . .Donna Mills
Favorite Super Couple .Kevin Dobson and Michele Lee

1989

DAYTIME
Outstanding Daytime Soap . . . .*Days of Our Lives*
Outstanding Lead Actor . . . . .Eric Braeden

Outstanding Lead Actress . . . . .Jeanne Cooper

Outstanding Hero . . . . .Stephen Nichols

Outstanding Heroine . . . . .Marcy Walker

Outstanding Supporting Actor . . . . .Quinn Redecker

Outstanding Supporting Actress . . . . Joy Garrett

Outstanding Male Newcomer . . . . .Scott Thompson Baker

Outstanding Female Newcomer . . . . .Anne Heche

Outstanding Villain . . . . .Matthew Arnold

Outstanding Villainess . . . . .Lynn Herring

Outstanding Comic Actor . . . . .Stephen Schnetzer

Outstanding Comic Actress . . . . .Robin Mattson

Favorite Super Couple . . . . .Stephen Nichols and Mary Beth Evans

PRIME TIME

Outstanding Prime Time Soap . . . .*Knots Landing*

Outstanding Lead Actor . . . . .David Selby

Outstanding Lead Actress . . . . Joan van Ark

Outstanding Supporting Actor . . . . .William Devane

Outstanding Supporting Actress . . . . .Tonya Crowe

Outstanding Villain . . . . .Larry Hagman

Outstanding Villainess . . . . .Donna Mills

1990

DAYTIME

Outstanding Daytime Soap . . . .*Santa Barbara*

Outstanding Lead Actor . . . . .A Martinez

Outstanding Lead Actress . . . . .Marcy Walker

Outstanding Hero . . . . .Doug Davidson

Outstanding Heroine . . . . .Finola Hughes

Outstanding Supporting Actor . . . . .Robert Gentry

Outstanding Supporting Actress . . . . Jane Rogers

Outstanding Male Newcomer . . . . .Kurt Robin McKinney

Outstanding Female Newcomer . . . . .Jean Carol

Outstanding Villain . . . . .David Canary

Outstanding Villainess . . . . .Jane Elliot

Outstanding Comic Actor . . . . Joe Marinelli

Outstanding Comic Actress . . . . .Robin Mattson

Outstanding Story Line .Eden's Rape, *Santa Barbara*

Outstanding Super Couple .A Martinez and Marcy Walker

PRIME TIME

Outstanding Prime Time Soap . . . .*Knots Landing*

Outstanding Prime Time Actor . . . . .William Devane

Outstanding Prime Time Actress . . . . .Nicollette Sheridan

Outstanding Supporting Actor . . . . .Ken Kercheval

Outstanding Supporting Actress . . . . .Tonya Crowe

Outstanding Villain . . . . .Teri Austin

Outstanding Story Line . . . . .Jill's Descent into Madness

1992

DAYTIME

Outstanding Daytime Soap	*Days of Our Lives*
Outstanding Lead Actor	David Canary
Outstanding Lead Actress	Anne Heche
Outstanding Supporting Actor	Doug Davidson
Outstanding Supporting Actress	Jane Elliot
Outstanding Villain	Michael Zaslow
Outstanding Villainess	Lynn Herring
Outstanding Male Newcomer	Paul Michael Valley
Outstanding Female Newcomer	Alla Korot
Outstanding Younger Leading Actor	Ricky Paull Goldin
Outstanding Younger Leading Actress	Tricia Cast
Best Wedding	Jennifer and Jack, *Days of Our Lives*
Best Love Story	Jennifer and Jack, *Days of Our Lives*
Best Death Scene	Marcy Walker
Outstanding Comic Performance	Robert Mailhouse

PRIME TIME

Outstanding Show	Knots Landing
Outstanding Prime Time Actor	Kevin Dobson
Outstanding Prime Time Actress	Michele Lee
Best Death Scene	Shee J. Wilison
Soap Opera Digest Editors Award for Outstanding Contribution to the Industry	*The Bold and the Beautiful* and *The Young and the Restless*

1993

DAYTIME

Favorite Show	*Days of Our Lives*
Outstanding Lead Actor	Peter Bergman
Outstanding Lead Actress	Susan Lucci
Outstanding Supporting Actor	Richard Biggs
Outstanding Supporting Actress	Ellen Dolan
Outstanding Male Newcomer	Monti Sharp
Outstanding Female Newcomer	Yvonne Perry
Outstanding Villainess	Kimberlin Brown
Outstanding Comic Performance	Matthew Ashford
Outstanding Younger Leading Actor	Matt Borlenghi
Outstanding Younger Leading Actress	Alicia Coppola
Outstanding Child Actor	Kimberly McCullough
Outstanding Social Issue Story Line	Margo's Rape, *As the World Turns*
Hottest Male Star	Mark Derwin
Hottest Female Star	Crystal Chappell
Favorite Song	One Dream, *Days of Our Lives*

1994

DAYTIME

Favorite Show . . . .*Days of Our Lives*
Outstanding Lead Actor . . . . .Robert Kelker-Kelly
Outstanding Lead Actress . . . . .Jess Walton
Outstanding Supporting Actor . . . . .Justin Deas
Outstanding Supporting Actress . . . . .Deborah Adair
Outstanding Male Newcomer . . . . .Patrick Muldoon
Outstanding Female Newcomer . . . . .Lisa Rinna
Scene Stealer . . . . .Victoria Rowell
Outstanding Child Actor . . . . .Scott Groff
Outstanding Younger Leading Actor . . . . .Scott Reeves
Outstanding Younger Leading Actress . . . . .Melissa Hayden
Hottest Male Star . . . . .Drake Hogestyn
Hottest Female Star . . . . .Melissa Reeves
Musical Achievement . . . .*Days of Our Lives*
Outstanding Villain/Villainess . . . . .Louise Sorel
Favorite Story Line . . . .**Who fathered Marlena's baby?** *Days of Our Lives*

1995

DAYTIME

Favorite Show . . . .*Days of Our Lives*
Outstanding Lead Actor . . . . .Tom Eplin
Outstanding Lead Actress . . . . .Deidre Hall
Outstanding Supporting Actor . . . . .Brad Maule
Outstanding Supporting Actress . . . . .Signy Coleman
Outstanding Male Newcomer . . . . .Keith Hamilton Cobb
Outstanding Female Newcomer . . . . .Brooke Alexander
Outstanding Villainess . . . . .Kimberlin Brown
Outstanding Villain . . . . .Jason Brooks
Outstanding Younger Leading Actor . . . . .Roger Howarth
Outstanding Younger Leading Actress . . . . .Rena Sofer
Outstanding Child Actor . . . . .Jonathan Jackson
Hottest Male Star . . . . .Drake Hogestyn
Hottest Female Star . . . . .Kristina Wagner
Outstanding Male Scene Stealer . . . . .Michael E. Knight
Outstanding Female Scene Stealer . . . . .Louise Sorel
Hottest Soap Couple . . . . .Lisa Rinna and Robert Kelker-Kelly

Photo Credits

Photographs appearing in *The Ultimate Soap Opera Guide* were received from the following sources:

AP/Wide World Photos: **pp. 36, 39, 42, 47, 62, 71, 73, 113, 155, 159, 166, 213, 214, 238, 257, 273, 290, 295 (bottom), 327, 339, 341, 346, 349, 350, 351, 355;** Tony Rizzo: **pp. 44, 46, 58, 75, 83, 91 (top and bottom), 112, 118, 120, 123, 125, 129, 139, 147, 149, 151, 152, 156, 157, 158, 161 (bottom), 162, 177, 178, 181, 185, 187, 192, 193, 196, 198, 201 (top and bottom), 216, 230, 232, 234, 241, 245, 249, 279, 291, 293, 302, 308, 311, 316, 317, 333, 353, 354, 361, 363, 367, 370, 371, 373, 374, 376, 377, 379, 381, 383, 387, 398;** NBC: **pp. 68, 86,** 87, 93, 99, 102, 103, 104, 105, 191; Globe Photos: **pp. 89, 96, 171, 174, 195 (top and bottom), 210, 212, 217, 218, 255, 300;** CBS: **pp. 117, 119, 121, 131, 132, 133, 135, 141, 153, 161 (top), 277, 287, 289, 295 (top), 301, 366, 378, 385 (top and bottom), 388, 390, 395, 397 (top and bottom);** Doreen Stone/Alliapoulos & Associates: **p. 244;** Photo Trends: **p. 263;** Imagination Photos: **p. 271;** Ed Geller/Globe Photos: **pp. 280, 282;** Bridget Petrella: **p. 297;** Lesley Bohm/CBS: **p. 399.**

Index

A

Abe Carver 205
Ace, Goodman 3
Adair, Deborah 357
Adam Chandler 40, 41, 42–3, 47, 55, 57, 60
Adam Chandler, Jr. 42, 55
Adam Hughes 128, 130, 131
Adam Thorpe 320
Adams, Lynne 268
Adams, Maria 150
Adams, Mary Kay 288
Addie Horton Olson Williams 165, 166, 169, 170, 176, 185, 187, 335
Addison-Altman, Nancy 310
Addy, Wesley 305, 310
A.J. (Alan, Jr.) Quartermaine 223, 225, 233, 235, 237, 243, 255
Al Weeks 207
Alan Quartermaine 211, 214, 216, 217, 219, 222, 225, 226, 233, 235, 236
Alan Spaulding 271, 272, 273, 274, 276, 277, 278, 279, 281, 282–3, 291, 295, 296, 302
Alan-Michael Spaulding 272, 277, 279, 280, 282–3, 290–2, 296, 297

Albee, Denny 326
Alda, Robert 185
Alec McIntyre 39, 40, 51, 60
Aleksander, Grant 39–40, 272
Alessandro Coronal 330
Alex "Blade" Bladeson 384, 399
Alex Crown 330
Alex Hunter 314
Alex Marshall 168, 174
Alex Masters 308, 314, 315, 316
Alex Olanov Hesser Buchanan 344, 352
Alexander, Brooke 115–6
Alexander, Denise 166, 208
Alexander, Millette 266
Alexandra Quartermaine 212
Alexandra Spaulding von Halkein 274, 278, 279, 288, 289, 291, 292
Alfonso, Kristian 176, 189, 190
Alford, Bobby 107, 114
Alice Horton 165, 166, 179, 186–7, 189
Alice Matthews Frame Gordon Frame 64, 67, 68, 71, 72, 78, 79, 200, 324, 338
Alison Bancroft 361
Alison, Jone 283

All My Children 9, 14, 17, 22, 24, 25, 27, 29–65

All My Children "Family Tree" 31

Allan, Jed 174

Allen, Vera 67, 78

Allison "Alli" Fowler 73, 99

Allison, Jone 259

Allison Rescott Slavinsky Bowman 317

Amanda Cory Fowler 72, 73, 75, 99

Amanda Dillon 55

Amanda Wexler Spaulding 272, 273, 296

Ames, Rachel 208, 229

Amos 'n' Andy 2

Amy Tyler 30, 37

Amy Vining 225

Anderson, Richard Dean 210, 230, 234

Andrew Carpenter 333, 343, 347

Andrews, Tina 172

Andy Dixon 119, 121–2, 127

Andy Richards 365

"Angel" 174

Angela Corelli 98, 102

"Angelique" 174

Angelique Marick 58

Angie Hubbard 309, 312, 315, 317

Aniston, John 169, 190–1

Ann Alden Forbes 305, 306

Anna Brady 176

Anna Devane 215, 216–7, 255, 257

Anna Wolek Craig 319, 322, 340, 341

Anne Tyler Davis Martin 30, 35, 37

Annie Dutton 281, 282, 295, 299

Annie Stewart-Ward 112, 118

Another Life 19

Another World 7, 13, 14, 16, 25, 26, 27, 30, 64, 66–105, 265, 318, 324, 327

Another World "Family Tree" 69

Another World: Somerset see Somerset

Anthony Armando 150, 157, 158

Anthony, Gerald 319, 326

Anton Cunningham 115

Anton Lang 45, 54, 59

Antony Dimera 198–9

Aprea, John 86

April Stevens 363, 365, 378

Arielle Ashton 217

Arlene Vaughan 43, 60

Arlt, Lewis 96

Arnold, Tom 223

As the World Turns 7, 10, 12, 13, 26, 64, 66, 106–142, 164, 264, 318

As the World Turns "Family Tree" 109

Asa Buchanan 70, 319, 328, 330, 332, 334, 344, 348, 352

Ashe, Jennifer 305

Ashenafi, Senait 229–30

Ashford, Matthew 181, 204, 208, 218, 230, 329

Ashley Abbott 368, 370, 383–5, 387, 391, 397, 399

Audrey March Baldwin Hardy 208

Augusta McLeod 210

Austin Reed 180, 194, 195, 202–3

Ava Rescott Alden Masters 308, 314, 316, 317

B

Bachelor's Children 6

Backstage Wife 5

Bacon, Kevin 270

Badler, Jane 323

Bailey, David 79

Bailey, Ruth 259

Baker, Scott Thompson 216

Baldwin, Judith 144, 150

Ballard, Alimi 311

Balley, Paul Michael 104

Balsam, Martin 165

Barbara Jean "B.J." Jones 216, 225, 240, 250

Barbara, Joe 76, 81

Barbara Ryan Stenbeck Munson 110, 114, 128, 135, 141–2

Barbara Vining 210

Barcroft, Judith 37

Barr, Julia 39–40

Barrett, Alice 87, 100

Barrow, Bernard 309, 317

Barry, Patricia 187

Bartholomew, Fred 115

Barton, Peter 366

Bauer, Charita 259, 260, 284

Bauer, Jaime Lyn 168, 188, 191–2, 357, 358

Bay City 67

Bea Reardon 271

Beal, John 67, 78

Becky Lee Abbott 332, 344

Bedi, Kabir 153

Behar, Phyllis 322, 340

Behrens, Sam 214, 240

Belack, Doris 340

Bell, Bill *see* Bell, William J.

Bell, Lauralee 358, 366, 376

Bell, Lee Phillip 15, 17, 27, 143, 356, 357

Bell, William J. 3, 8, 14, 15, 17, 27, 30, 66, 143, 165, 168–9, 356, 357, 360

Ben Howard 324
Ben Jerrod: Attorney at Law 13, 206
Ben Olson 165, 166, 170
Ben Scott 266
Benard, Maurice 223, 231, 248, 251
Benedict, Nick 32, 369
Benesch, Lynn 336
Benet, Brenda 175, 185
Benish, Lynn 319
Bennett, Meg 369
Benoit, Patricia 110
Beradino, John 206, 207, 208, 227, 231–2
Berenger, Tom 324
Berg, Gertrude 5
Bergman, Peter 367, 391
Berjer, Barbara 268, 281
Bernau, Christopher 271, 296
Bersell, Michael 30, 34
Bert Bauer 265, 266, 268, 269, 270, 275, 283
Bertha "Bert" Miller 260, 264, 284
Best Seller 11
Beth Logan 144–5, 147, 150
Beth Martin 35, 37
Beth Raines 274, 276, 277, 303
Betsy Stewart 108, 111, 127
Betts, Jack 326
Betty and Bob 2, 3
Betty Stewart 110, 117
Between Heaven and Hell see One Life to Live
Beulah Garrick 273
Bielack, Doris 319
Bierdz, Thom 372
Big Sister 6, 11
Bill Bauer 260, 262, 263, 264, 265, 266, 267, 270, 285
Bill Brady 330
Bill Eckert 220, 221
Bill Foster 363, 364, 365
Bill Horton 166, 168, 169, 170, 171, 174–5, 185, 187, 188
Bill Lewis, Jr. 302
Bill Matthews 67, 80
Bill Moray 270
Bill Spencer 146, 151
Billie Reed 180, 182, 195, 200, 201
Billy Bristow 305
Billy Lewis 267, 274, 275, 276, 277, 278, 286, 290, 293
Bishop, Loanne 215
Blair Daimler Manning 334, 335, 336, 345, 355
Blair, Pamela 305
Blake, Teresa 40–1

Blake (Cristina) Thorpe Lindsey Spaulding Marler 268, 269, 276, 277, 278, 281, 289, 291, 292, 294, 300
Blanchard, Susan 35
Blanks, Lynn 112
Blanks, Mary Lynn 34
Bloom, Brian 119, 121, 128
Bloom, Claire 111, 116, 138
Bo Brady 176, 178, 179, 180, 182, 185, 186, 189, 191, 193, 199–201, 203
Bo Buchanan 70, 319, 328, 329, 330, 332, 344, 351
Bob Anderson 170, 172, 175
Bob Hughes 107, 111, 112, 114, 119, 124, 126, 127, 130, 134, 140
"Bobbie" Barbara Jean Spencer Meyer Brock Jones 211, 212, 214, 215, 216, 218–21, 225, 236, 240, 250
Bobby Martin 30, 34
Bold and the Beautiful, The 17, 24, 66, 143–63, 358
Bold and the Beautiful, The "Family Tree" 145
Bolger, John 272
Bonarrigo, Laura 342
Bond, Steve 213
Borgeson, Linda 72, 79
Boruff, John 266
Boyd, Tanya 192
Brad Carlton 362, 379, 384, 388–9, 392, 396
Brad Eliot 325, 326, 328, 341, 358
Brad Vernon 326
Bradley Ward 222, 233, 242, 246, 253
Braeden, Eric 368–9, 390, 391
Brandon "Lujack" Luvonaczek Spaulding 274, 276, 278, 288, 291
Braxton, Stephanie 34
Breen, Joseph 308
Bregman, Tracey *see* Recht, Tracey E. Bregman
Brenda Barrett 223–4, 231, 248, 254
Brennan, Melissa *see* Reeves, Melissa (Brennan)
Brent Davis 383
Breslin, Patricia 226
Brian McColl 108, 112
Bridget Reardon 278, 280–1, 286, 290, 293
Bright Horizon 9
Brighter Day, The 10, 12
Brock Reynolds 360, 374–5, 393

Brooke English 39–40, 41, 42, 47, 55, 62
Brooke Hamilton 172, 175
Brooke Logan Forrester Forrester 143–4, 146, 150, 164–5, 389
Brooks, Jason 169, 180, 193
Brooks, Randy 82
Brothers, Joyce 337
Brown, Gail 72
Brown, Kale 73, 83
Brown, Kimberlin 153–4
Brown, Lisa 120, 129, 270, 301–2
Brown, Philip 310–1
Brown, Tom 207
Bruce Banning 284
Bruce Elliott 124
Bruce Henderson 362
Bruder, Patricia 117
Bryce, Ed 267, 285
Bryce, Scott 111, 129
Bryggman, Larry 112, 118–9
Buchanan, Ian 144, 154, 162, 216
Buchanan, Jensen 84, 99, 302, 332
Buck Huston 309, 310, 311
Buffinton, Bryan 302
Bundy, Brooke 172–3, 185
Bunny Eberhart 75
Burch, Shelly 329
Burnett, Carol 62
Burnett, Nancy 150
Burr, Ann 107, 113
Burton, Robert 326
Burton, Steve 232–3
Buzz Cooper 279–81, 286–7
Byrne, Martha 111, 117, 120, 128
Byron, Jeffrey 35

C

Cabot Alden 305–6, 308, 310–2
Cal Stricklyn 140
Caleb Snyder 129
Call, Anthony 329, 342
Callahan, John 41
Cameron Faulkner 210
Cameron, Lisa 78
Campbell, Kay 33
Canary, David 42, 72, 79
Capitol 16, 17
Carey, Macdonald 165–6, 186
Carey, Phil 70, 319, 343–4
Carl Hutchins 70, 74, 76–7, 91, 93–4, 96, 103–105
Carl Williams 378
Carla Bernari 323
Carla Gray 319

Carla Hall 327
Carlson, Amy 86
Carlson, Gail Rae 233
Carly Manning 179–80, 200, 202
Carol Demming 130–131
Carol, Jean 278, 286
Carol Robbins Evans 365
Caroline Brady 177, 191, 193, 205
Caroline Spencer Forrester Forrester 144, 146, 150–1, 162
Caroline Stafford 101
Carr, Paul 188
Carrie Brady 194–5, 202–3
Carrington, Elaine 6, 10
Carroll, James 309
Case, Sharon 370–1
Casey Bowman 313, 317
Casey Reed 360, 362, 364, 370, 387
Cash, Rosalind 218, 222, 233
Cass Winthrop 71, 87, 89, 96, 98, 100–3
Cassie Callison (Reynolds) Carpenter 329–30, 333–4, 341–3, 347
Cast, Tricia 371, 391
Cate, Holly 122
Cathy Craig 322, 324, 338, 341
Cecile de Poulignac 70, 89, 96, 101
Celeste 182–3, 193
Celia Quartermaine 213–5
Central City 9
Chapman, Liza 67, 78
Charita Bauer 275
Charity Gatlin 236
Charles Harrison 309, 312, 315, 317
Charles Tyler 30, 35–6, 38, 62
Charleson, Leslie 210, 234
Charlie Brent 51, 60
Charlie Winthrop 100–1
Charlotte Waring 266, 267, 283
Charney, Jordan 340
Chase, Allan 14, 164–5
Cheatham, Marie 166, 188
Chelsea Reardon 276
Cheryl Stansbury 218, 219, 250
Chris Blair 396
Chris Brooks 358, 361 363, 364
Chris Hughes 107, 108, 114, 124, 130
Chris Kositchek 184
Chris, Marilyn 322
Christian, William 43
Christina Karras 35
Christine "Cricket" Blair Romalotti 358, 366–7, 368, 372, 376, 377, 378, 379, 381, 382, 389, 397, 398
Christopher, Robin 86
Chuck Shea 131

Chuck Tyler 30, 33, 34
Chuck Wilson 328
Cibrian, Eddie 371
Cindy Clark 80
Cindy Parker 382
C.J. Buchanan 331, 339
Claire Lowell 107, 113
Claire Ramsey 275
Clare, Lu 'n' Em 2
Clark, Christie 176, 194
Clark, Marsha 264, 269, 270
Clarke, Brian Patrick 150, 213
Clarke Garrison 147, 157
Clarke, John 188, 194
Clarke, Jordan 274
Clarke, Robert 207
Clary, Robert 173, 184, 358
Clay Alden 308, 309, 310, 311, 312,
    313, 314, 315, 316
Cliff Wilson 373
Clint Buchanan 319, 322, 328, 329,
    330, 331, 332, 333, 334, 337,
    338, 342, 346, 348, 349
Cobb, Keith Hamilton 44
Colbert, Robert 358, 362
Cole Howard 370, 379, 386, 391, 392
Coleman, Jack 175, 184
Coleman, Signy 370, 372–3
Colla, Dick 165
Collins, Kate 57
Collins, Kevin Quartermaine 247
Colton Shore 216, 217, 240
Conboy, John 16, 20, 23, 28, 356–7
Conley, Darlene 147, 157, 372
Connolly, Norma 215
Connor Davis 152
Cook, Jennifer 270
Cooper Alden 310, 313
Cooper, Jeanne 372, 373–4
Corbett, Michael 372
Cord Roberts 331, 332, 334, 339, 348
Corday, Betty 165
Corday, Ken 165
Corday, Ted 14, 164–5
Corinth, Pennsylvania 306
Coster, Nicholas 68, 110, 111, 117,
    119, 138
Court, Geraldine 270
Courtney Baxter 122
Courtney, Jacqueline 64, 67, 72, 79,
    324, 338
Cowgil, David 373
Craig, Carolyn 207
Craig Merrill 165
Craig Montgomery 111, 127, 129,
    132, 135
Cram, Cusi 342

Crampton, Barbara 156, 370
Crane, Matt 87–8
Crane Tolliver 213
Cranston, Brian 305
Crawford, Christine 206
Crawford, Joan 206
Crawford, Lee 358
Cristina Blake Thorpe *see* Blake
    (Cristina) Thorpe Lindsey
        Spaulding Marler
Critchlow, Roark 188, 194–5
Cullen, Kathleen 296
Cunningham, John 305
Cunningham, Sarah 67, 78
Curtis Alden 305, 309, 314, 315, 316
Curtis, Craig 207
Curtis Reed 180, 195
Cynthia Allison 207
Cynthia Preston 57

D

Dabney, Augusta 268, 305, 312
Dailey, Irene 78
Damian Grimaldi 111, 117, 128, 132,
    138, 139
Damian, Michael 367, 375, 376
Damian Smith 223, 225, 231, 237,
    240–1, 243, 250, 251
Damon, Les 107, 113
Damon, Stuart 235–6
Dan Rooney 228
Dan Stewart 108, 110, 117, 127, 134,
    135
Dane Hammond 306, 308, 310, 315
Danny Fargo 80–1
Danny Romalotti 367, 375, 376–7,
    378, 389, 396, 397
Danny Romalotti, Jr. 397
Danny Wolek 320, 332, 337, 341
Dano, Linda 70, 77, 87, 88–9, 101
Danson, Ted 68
Dark Shadows 13, 14, 30, 318
Datillo, Bryan 180, 195
Dave Reed 144, 152
David Banning 170, 172, 173, 184,
    185
David Gray 213
David Hamilton 210, 211
David Harum 6
David Kimble 372
David Martin 166–7, 169
David Reynolds 330, 341, 342
David Rinaldi 330, 342
David Siegel 319, 322
David Stewart 110, 117, 118, 119

David Thatcher 96
David Vickers 334, 335, 339, 342, 346, 355
Davidson, Doug 367, 377, 378
Davidson, Eileen 169, 180, 193, 195–6
Davies, Lane 185
Davies, Peter 305
Dawn "Dee" Stewart Dixon 112, 118, 119, 131
Dawson, Mark 30, 32
Days of Our Lives 3, 9, 14, 22, 23, 66, 164–205, 329
Days of Our Lives "Family Tree" 167
de Lancie, John 184
De Paiva, James 319, 331, 344, 345
Dean Frame 98
Deanda, Peter 319
Deas, Justin 279, 286
Deborah Brewster Alden 310, 313, 316
Decker Moss 217
Dee, Ruby 283
Deerfield, Lynn 268
DeFreitas, Scott 121–2
Del Henry 50, 56
Delilah Ralston 329, 330, 332
Dengel, Roni 78
Denniston, Leslie 112, 275
DePriest, Maggie 175
Derek Frye 43
Derek Mason 111, 120
Derek Thurston 375, 393
Detective Cutter 280, 286
deVegh, Diana 30, 37
Diamont, Don 379, 392
Diana Taylor 210
Diane Ballard 272
Diane Colville 178
Dick Grant 263
Dicopoulos, Frank 280, 287, 289
Diller, Phyllis 163
Dillon Albert Quartermaine Hornsby 220, 244–5
Dimitri Marick 54, 58–9, 63
Dina Abbott Mergeron 381, 383, 394
Dinah Chamberlain Marler 276, 281, 292, 293, 294
Dion, Colleen 98, 150
Dixie Cooney Chandler Martin 42, 47, 48, 55, 55
D.L. Brock 214, 215
Dobson, Bridget 17
Dobson, Jerome 17
Doctors, The 13, 20, 26
Doherty, Carla 165
Dolan, Ellen 122
Dominique Baldwin 221, 237
Domino 217, 219

Don Craig 174
Don Hughes 114, 124
Don Stewart 127
Donna Beck 33, 34, 57
Donna Logan 144, 147, 151
Donna Love Hudson 73, 77, 83, 84, 88, 96, 98, 103–5
Doohan, James 155
Dorian Cramer Lord Callison Vickers 319, 323, 324, 325, 326, 329, 330, 334, 335, 336, 337, 339, 343, 347, 355
Dorian, Joanne 337
Doris Collins 371, 395
Dottie Thornton 48
Doug Williams 166, 169, 170, 172, 173, 174, 175, 176, 185, 187, 200
Dougie LeClair 173, 185
Douglas Austin 370
Douglas, Burt 165
Douglas Donovan 305
Douglas, Jerry 358, 380, 382
Douglas Marland 112, 302
Douglas, Susan 259, 263, 284
Dragon, The 176, 189, 200
Dreams Come True 4
Drew Ralston 329, 332
Drew, Wendy 107, 117
Drucilla Barbara Winters 397, 398, 399
Duke Kramer 122, 129, 132, 134
Duke Lavery 216–7
Dumont, Paul 30, 37
Duncan, Carmen 96
Duncan McKechnie 120, 136, 137
Dusay, Marj 274, 287–9
Dustin "Dusty" Donovan 119, 121, 128
Dwyer, Virginia 67, 79
Dylan Shayne Lewis 275, 277, 290

E

Eakes, Bobbie 147, 158
Earl Bancroft 361
Earl Mitchell 125
Earley, Candice 57
Easy Aces 3
Echo di Savoy 328–30
Ed Bauer 265, 266, 268, 269, 273, 275, 277, 282, 283, 296, 298, 300
Ed Hall 319, 323, 327
Eddie Maine 244, 254
Eddie Weeks 207
Edge of Night, The 10, 13, 106, 107, 108
Edith Hughes 107, 110, 115

Edmund Grey 41, 50, 58
Edna Thornton 48
Edson, Hilary 216, 250, 282
Eduardo Grimaldi 110, 111, 117, 119, 123, 125, 132, 138
Edward Bauer 260, 265, 283
Edward Quartermaine 213, 215–6, 218, 219, 222, 225, 230, 233, 236, 242, 244, 246, 253
Edwina Lewis 326
Egg and I, The 11
Eileen Riley Siegel 319, 322, 324, 342
Elena de Poulignac 70, 71
Eleni Cooper 280, 286, 287
Elg, Taina 328
Elizabeth Saunders 332
Elizabeth Spaulding 271, 272, 296
Elizabeth Talbot Stewart 108, 134
Ellen Lowell Stewart 110, 113, 117–18
Ellie Snyder 135
Elliot, Jane 57, 211, 244, 273
Elliott, Patricia 319, 332, 353–4
Elsie May Krumholtz *see* Tiffany Hill
Emhardt, Robert 71
Emily Stewart 108, 111, 129, 134, 135–6
Emma Snyder 129, 140
Eplin, Tom 71, 75, 90
Epperson, Brenda 382–3, 391
Eric Forrester 144, 146, 148, 149, 176, 179, 389
Eric Forrester, Jr. 146
Eric Garrison 383
Eric Kane 37
Erica Kane 30, 32, 33, 35, 37, 38, 42, 52–3, 58, 63, 64
Espy, William Grey 358, 364
Esther Valentine 375, 396
Eubanks, Shannon 305
Eugene Bradford 184
Eva Guthrie 298
Evan Frame 74
Evan Walsh 141
Evan Whyland 185
Evans, Andrea 338
Evans, Judi *see* Luciano, Judi Evans
Evans, Mary Beth 220, 237
Eve Guthrie 282
Eve Howard 370, 391, 392
Everly, Patricia 362
Ewing, Geoffrey 312

F

Fairchild, Morgan 305
Faith Kipling 326

Faith Roberts 151–2
Falken-Smith Pat 172, 175
Farrell, Sharon 395
Felicia Cummings Jones 215, 216, 217, 221–2, 225, 250, 252, 257
Felicia Forrester 143, 147, 150
Felicia Gallant 76, 77, 83, 86, 88, 101
Ferrell, Kristi 275
Fibber McGee and Molly 1
Fickett, Mary 30, 34, 43–4
Fillion, Nathan 345
First Hundred Years, The 11
Fishburne, Laurence 319
Flaks, Niki 319
Flame in the Wind 164
Flannery, Susan 144, 149, 158, 325
Fletcher Reade 275, 279, 281, 288, 289, 292
Fletchworth, Eileen 35
Flip Malone 267
Florence Webster 395
Floyd Parker 270, 271
For Richer, For Poorer 16, 70
Ford, Steven 365
Forrest Alamain 180
Forrest, Veronica Redd 395
Forsyth, David 71, 76, 83, 92, 103
Forsyth, Henderson 110, 117
Fowkes, Connard 114, 124
Francis, Genie 176, 178, 207, 210, 238
Frangione, Nancy 34, 70, 101
Frank, Charles 35
Frank Cooper *see* Buzz Cooper
Frank Cooper, Jr. 287
Frank Smith 211, 215, 223, 224, 231, 237, 240, 251
Frankie Brady 178, 191
Frankie Frame Winthrop *see* Mary Francis "Frankie" Frame Winthrop
Frankie Hubbard 311, 312, 315
Franklin, Hugh 30, 36
Freeman, Al, Jr. 319, 323
Frisco Jones 215, 216, 217, 219, 221–2, 225, 249, 257
Front Page Farrell 9
Fry, Ed 119
Fulton, Eileen 110, 114, 117, 119, 123, 130, 140

G

Gabet, Sharon 323
Gabrielle Medina 331, 332, 345
Gabrielle Pascal 178
Gagnier, Holly 342

453

Gallison, Joe 67, 80, 188, 197, 319, 320
Garrett, Maureen 268, 288
Garth Slater 305
Geary, Anthony 176, 207, 220, 238–9
General Hospital 12, 13, 17, 22, 26, 28, 30, 166, 175, 176, 206–57, 270, 318, 329
General Hospital "Family Tree" 209
Generations 18, 22
Genesse, Brian 144, 152
Genoa City 360
Gentry, Robert 57, 328
George, Anthony 325
George Curtis 362
Georgie Jones 221, 257
Gerald Anthony 327
Gibson, John 365
Gibson, Thomas 111
Giles Morgan 328
Gillis, Gwyn 37
Gilly Grant 302, 303
Gina Roma 375, 376
Girl Alone 6
Gloria Marsh Chandler 40–1, 43, 60
Goetz, Theo 259, 284
Goldbergs, The 5
Goldin, Ricky Paul 98
Golding, Meta 312
Goodwin, James 276
Gorney, Karen 30, 34
Goulet, Nicolette 276
Grandma Matthews 67, 78
Grandpa Hughes 107, 113
Granger, Farley 325
Grant Andrews 213, 214
Grant, Bernard 266, 322
Grant Colman 114, 124
Grant Harrison 71, 75, 76, 85, 93, 96, 98, 99–100, 104, 112
Grant Putnam 213
Graves, Ernest 336
Gray, Charles 364
Green, Dorothy 358, 362
Greg Foster 358, 360, 363–4, 370, 378, 387
Gregory, Michael 210
Griggs, Robyn 98, 101
Groh, David 214
Guiding Light, The 7–8, 9, 10, 12, 20, 25, 64, 67, 106, 164, 206, 258–303, 318, 330
Guiding Light, The "Family Tree" 261
Gumps, The 5
Guthrie, Richard 172
G'Vera, Ivan 179, 204
Gwen Parrish 79
Gwyneth Alden 308–9, 314, 315, 316

H

Haddad, Ava 342
Haines, Larry 309, 312, 317
Hal Munson 128, 131, 135, 141
Hall, Deidre 172, 175, 196
Hall-Lovell, Andrea 174
Hallick, Tom 358
Hamilton, Margaret 164
Hamilton, Neil 207
Hammer, Jay 288, 289
Hank Eliot 112
Hank Gannon 351, 354
Hansen, Peter 230
Harlan Barrett 248
Harley Davidson Cooper 277, 290
Harmon, Jennifer 322
Harney, Susan 79
Harper Deveraux 178, 189, 204
Harrington, Kate 33
Harrison Davis 217–8
Harry O'Neill 330
Haskell, Susan 333, 339, 347, 354
Hasselhoff, David 364
Hastings, Don 112, 114, 119, 125–6, 130, 140
Hatch, Richard 30, 32
Hauser, Wings 363
Hawk Shayne 276
Hawkins Falls 11
Hayden, Melissa 289–90
Hayes, Allison 207
Hayes, Bill 166, 170, 184–5
Hayes, Susan Seaforth 166, 175, 184, 188
Hayley Vaughan 39, 41, 43, 51, 60–1
Haynes, Hilda 30
Hays, Kathryn 114, 119, 126, 268
H.B. Lewis 275
Hearst, Rick 290
Heather Grant 234
Heaven and Hell see One Life to Live
Hedison, David 71, 85, 93, 104
Heen, Gladys 259
Heflin, Fra 30, 37, 38, 65
Heinle, Amelia 313
Helena Cassadine 212, 214, 215
Hendrickson, Benjamin 127–9
Henry Chamberlain 273, 293, 303
Hensel, Karen 395
Hensley, Jon 111, 128
Herb Callison 329, 330, 342
Herlie, Eileen 45
Herrera, Anthony 110, 306
Herring, Lynn 216, 239–40
Hickland, Catherine 309, 313
Higgins, Michael 268

Hill Top House 6–7
Hillary Kincaid 264, 269, 270
Hillary Wilson 48
Hirson, Alice 322
Hodiak, John 259
Hogestyn, Drake 166, 178, 193, 196
Holbrook, Anna 94, 95
Holden Snyder 111, 121, 128–9, 132, 135, 138
Holly, Ellen 319, 323
Holly Norris Bauer Marler Thorpe Lindsey Reade 268, 270, 276, 277, 278, 279, 281, 288–9, 300
Holly Sutton 213, 214, 215, 216, 220–1
Holmes, Scott 116, 130
Home of the Brave 9
Home Sweet Home 4
Hope Adams Newman 370, 373, 388, 390
Hope Bauer 265, 272, 273, 277, 296
Hope Williams Brady 176, 177, 182, 185, 187, 189, 193, 200
Hopkins, Kaitlin 74
Houghton, James 358, 363
Howarth, Roger 333, 339, 346
Hoxby, Scott 280, 302
Hubbard, Elizabeth 110, 116, 119, 131
Hughes, Finola 215
Hummert, Anne 1, 6
Hummert, Frank 1, 6
Hunley, Leann 176
Hursley, Doris 17
Hursley, Frank 17
Huston, Pat 165, 187
Hutchison, Fiona 280, 287, 331

I

Ian Rain 74
India von Halkein 274, 288
Ingle, John 241
Ingram, Michael 340
Irene Manning Clayton 330, 334, 338, 339, 355
Iris Cory Carrington Delaney Bancroft 70, 71, 72, 73, 78, 80, 83, 91, 96
Iris Fairchild 226
Irizarry, Vincent 278, 288, 291
Isabella "Belle" Toscano Kiriakis Black 169, 179, 191, 204
Isabelle Alden 305, 311, 312
Iva Snyder 120, 129
Ivan Kipling 326
Ivan Marais 179, 202, 204

J

Jack Abbott 357, 362, 368, 370, 377, 381, 382, 384, 387, 388, 391, 394, 397, 398
Jack Boland 233, 253
Jack Deveraux 173, 178, 181, 193, 204
Jack Forbes 305, 306, 315
Jack Hamilton 163
Jack Hammond 310
Jackie Marler 272
Jackie Templeton 213
Jackson, Jonathan 222, 242
Jackson Montgomery 48, 63
Jacob Johnson 309, 312, 315, 317
"Jagger" (John) Cates 215, 223, 249–50
Jake Kositchek 175, 184
Jake MacLaine 148, 151
Jake McKinnon 71, 73, 74, 75, 76, 82, 84, 91, 92
Jake Meyer 214–5, 216, 240
James Lowell 113
James Matthews 78
James Stenbeck 110, 129, 131, 135, 141
James T. Lowell 107
James Warwick 144, 154, 155–6, 162, 163, 389
Jamie Caldwell 205
Jamie Frame 72, 73, 77, 84, 89, 88, 103
Jamie Gardner 40, 47
Jane Cox 48, 55
Jane Marie Stafford 272
Jane Quartermaine 215
Janet Banning 169
Janet Green 46, 48, 49, 55, 56, 58
Janet Mason 266, 268, 269
Janet Matthews 67, 78
Janice Frame Cory 71, 87
Janice Maxwell 122
Janney, Leon 78
Jarred Carpenter 140
Jason Frame 89, 101
Jason Maxwell 38
Jason Quartermaine 214, 223, 225, 230, 232–3, 235, 236, 255
Jay Stalling 130–1
"Jean" 335, 337, 346
Jed Andrews 357, 388, 394
Jeff Baker 115
Jeff Hartman 309
Jeff Martin 30, 33, 35, 38
Jeff Ward 112
Jeff Webber 210, 230, 234
Jenna Bradshaw 280, 287

Jennifer Brooks 358, 362, 365
Jennifer Horton 204
Jennifer Richards 270, 272, 273, 296
Jennifer Rose Horton Devereaux 172, 181, 188, 189, 193
Jennifer Ryan 114, 126, 127
Jennifer Smith 211, 215, 223
Jenny Eckert 220, 244
Jenny Vernon 319
Jenny Wolek Siegel Reynolds 324–5, 326, 328, 330, 340, 341
Jeremy Hunter 308, 314, 315
Jerry "Cash" Cashman 365, 375
Jesse Hubbard 309, 312, 315, 317
Jessica Abbott Grainger 366, 368, 381, 382
Jessica Blake 174
Jessica Buchanan 335, 337, 346
Jessica Forrester 156
Jessica Griffin McKechnie 119, 132, 136–7
Jessie Brewer 207, 208, 210, 227–8
Jill Foster Reynolds Chancellor Brooks Abbott 357, 360, 363, 364, 368, 372, 374, 375, 379, 381, 384, 388, 393–5
Jim Craig 320, 323
Jim Fisk 165
Jim Frazier 283
Jim Grainger 366, 367, 381, 382
Jim Jefferson 35
Jim Lowell, Jr. 107, 113
Jim Matthews 67, 68
Jim Vochek 305, 306, 308, 309
Jimmie Lee Holt 213, 214, 236, 246
Joann Curtis 364
Joe Carlino 76, 81, 82, 91
Joe Martin 33, 53
Joe Riley 319, 320, 322, 324, 326, 327, 331, 332, 337, 338, 341–2
Joe Roberts 284, 285
Joe Robertshim 263
Joey Martin 35
Joey Riley Buchanan 327, 334, 335, 337, 338, 341, 346
John Abbott 358, 361, 363, 367, 368, 372, 379, 380–2, 384, 393, 394, 395, 397
John Black 166, 178–83, 191, 193, 197, 198, 204
John Cates see "Jagger" (John) Cates
John Dixon 112, 114, 118, 119, 123, 125, 126, 127, 129, 132, 134, 137, 140
John Eldridge 110, 124, 140
John Hudson 71, 73, 74, 76, 80, 83, 92, 95, 103

John Matthews 73
John Randolph 80
John Walker 343
John's Other Wife 6
Johnny Bauer 276
Johnny Fletcher 266, 267
Johnson, Joanna 144, 146, 151–2
Johnson, Raymond Edward 259
Johnstone, William 107, 113
Jonah Carver 205
Jones, James Earl 283
Jones, Renee 183, 193, 205
Jones, Tommy Lee 319, 322
Joseph Martin 30, 32
Josh Lewis 273, 275, 278, 279, 281, 282, 295, 299
Joshua Hall 319
Josie Watts 74–6, 80, 86, 87, 95
Joyce Colman 114, 124
Judith McConnell 210
Julia Barrett 248
Julia Medina 349
Julia Santos 45, 50, 54, 59–60
Julian Jerome 218
Julie Conrad 265, 290
Julie Olson Banning Anderson Williams Williams 165, 166, 169, 170, 172, 174, 185, 188
Julie Siegel 322, 324
June Slater 305, 306
Just Plain Bill 3
Justin Marler 272, 274
Justine Kirkland Harrison 76, 85, 93–94, 96, 104–5
Justus Ward 218, 222, 230, 233, 242, 246, 253

K

Kalember, Patricia 305
Kanan, Sean 225, 243
Karen Forrester 152
Karen, James 37
Karen Martin 319, 325–6, 327, 328, 340
Karen Peters 112, 119
Karen Spencer 151–2
Karen Wexler 223
Karen Wolek 319, 341
Kasdorf, Lenore 269
Kate Baker 76, 93, 95, 102
Kate Martin 30, 33
Kate Rescott 309, 313, 317, 331
Kate Roberts Kiriakis 181, 185, 191, 202
Kate Saunders 345

Katherine "Kay" Chancellor 360, 364, 365, 368, 372, 374–5, 377, 384, 386, 393, 394, 396
Katherine Bell 220, 237, 240, 243, 251, 254, 257
Kathleen McKinnon 101
Kathy Roberts Lang Grant Holden 263–4, 265, 267, 284
Katie Logan 144, 147, 151
Katrina Karr 326
Kayla Brady 178, 179, 189, 191, 204
Keane, Teri 305, 325
Keating, Charles 70, 76–7, 95
Keemo Volien Abbott 367, 368, 377, 396, 398
Keesha Ward 223, 230, 233
Keifer, Elizabeth 292
Keith, Larry 30, 35
Keith, Susan 70, 101, 325
Kelker-Kelly, Robert 200
Kelly Nelson 270, 273
Ken Baxter 67, 81
Ken Martin 207
Kendall Hart 38, 54, 59
Kennedy, H. Wesley 175
Kepler, Shel 225
Kerwin, Brian 363
Kevin Bancroft 361, 370, 387, 390
Kevin Buchanan 325, 333, 341
Kevin Chamberlain 240
Kevin Collins 221, 224
Kevin Riley 337, 338
Kiberd, James 45–6, 305, 306
Kim Reynolds Stewart Dixon Andropoulous Hughes 114, 119, 126–7, 134
Kimberly Brady 176, 177, 178, 186, 189, 191
King, T.W. 313
King's Row 10
Kingston, Lenore 207
Kinkead, Maeve 292
Kirk Anderson 116, 140
Kirkland Harrison 75, 85, 99, 100
Kirkwood, James 164–5
Knapp, Robert 165
Knight, Michael E. 46–7
Koslow, Lauren 144, 147, 152
Krimmer, Wortham 343, 346
Kristen Blake 169, 179, 180, 181–3, 193, 198, 199
Kristen Forrester 143, 144, 147, 150
Krystal Lake 102
Kurt Corday 275, 276
Kurth, Wallace 243
Kyle Sampson 275–6, 295

Labine, Claire 15, 227, 255
Lafortune, Felicity 48
Lando, Joe 332
Lang, Katherine Kelly 143, 144, 150, 159–60
Langley Wallingford 45, 62
Larry Ewing 73
Larry McDermott 119, 134
Larry Wolek 320, 323, 325, 326, 327, 328, 332, 337, 340–1
Larson, Jill 49, 57
LaRue, Eva 50
Laura Cudahy 40
Laura Grant 270, 285
Laura Spencer Horton 168, 169–72, 174–5, 176, 181, 188, 189, 193, 200, 202, 204
Laura Templeton 213
Laura Williams Vining Baldwin Spencer Cassadine Spencer Spencer 207, 210–4, 215, 220, 221, 222, 223–4, 230, 231, 235, 253
Lauralee Brooks 168, 357, 358, 360, 362, 363, 369, 383, 387
Laurel Banning Montgomery 46, 48–9, 63
Lauren Fenmore Grainger 377, 378, 379, 389–90
Lauren-Marie Taylor 305
Lawford, Christopher 50–1
Lawrence Alamain 179, 180, 189, 200, 204
Lawson, Lee 271
Leanna Love 370, 383
LeBlanc, Christian 358
LeClerc, Jean 308, 314
Lee, Anna 211, 245
Lee Baldwin 208, 210, 230
Lee Dumonde 174, 175, 185
Leighton, Roberta 370
Lemay, Harding 71–2, 79
Lenny Wlasuk 45, 62
Leo Burnell 309
Lesley Lu Spencer 222
Lesley Williams Webber 208, 210, 211, 214, 234–5
Leslie Bauer 265, 268, 269, 271–2, 283
Leslie Brooks 358, 362
Lester, Terry 116, 133, 357
Lewis, Judy 210
Lewis, Thyme 205
Lexi Carver 183, 193, 205
Lien Truong Hughes 122
Life of Mary Sothern 5

Light, Judith 319, 325, 341
Light of the World 3
Ligon, Tom 305
Lila Quartermaine 211, 213, 219, 225, 246
Lillian Raines 274, 276, 303
Lily Rivera 224, 231, 249, 254
Lily Slater 305, 306
Lily Snyder 138
Lily Walsh Mason Snyder Grimaldi 111, 117, 120–1, 128, 129, 132, 133
Lincoln Tyler 30, 37
Linder, Kate 375, 396
Lindley, Audra 78
Lindsey Wells 368
Lindstrom, Jon 221, 246–7
Linn, Teri Ann 144, 150
Lipton, James 67, 259, 263, 266, 284
Lipton, Robert 112
Lisa Miller Hughes Eldridge Shea Colman McColl Mitchell Grimaldi 110, 114, 117, 119, 123–5, 127, 130, 132, 137, 139, 140
Liz Chancellor 364
Liz Chandler 175, 197
Liz Foster 358, 363, 364, 365, 394
Liz Matthews 67, 78, 80
Liza Colby 48
Lois Cerullo Ashton 220, 224, 237, 244, 254
Lois Sloane 30
Lonely Women 9
LoPinto, Dorian 325
Loprieno, John 331, 347–48
Lord Ashton 217
Loring, Gloria 175, 197
Lorna Devon 76, 86, 88, 89, 100
Lorna Forbes 305
Lottie Chandler 57
Love Is A Many Splendored Thing 21, 318
Love of Life 10, 11–12, 25, 260, 262
Love Song 6
Lovers and Friends 16
Lovers and Other Friends 70
Loving 17, 20, 22, 24–5, 304–317
Loving "Family Tree" 307
Lowell, Ellen 107
Luan Volien Abbott 368, 396, 398
Lucas Jones 219
Lucas Roberts 180, 188, 194, 195
Lucci, Susan 30, 38, 51–2, 64
Lucia, Chip 338
Luciano, Judi Evans 91
Lucinda Walsh Dixon 110, 116, 119, 120, 125, 128, 132–3, 134, 136

Lucky Spencer 222, 243
Lucy Coe Jones 216, 219, 221, 224, 236, 237, 240–1, 247, 250, 251
Lucy Cooper 280, 287, 291, 297
Lujack Spaulding *see* Brandon "Lujack" Luvonaczek Spaulding
Luke Spencer 176, 200, 207, 211–4, 215, 220, 221, 222, 223–4, 231, 237, 253, 270, 339
Luna Moody 345
Lupton, Tom 187
Lyla Montgomery 111, 119, 131
Lyman, Dorothy 36
Lynd, Janice 358, 362
Lynn Topping 358

M

Ma Perkins 4
Mac Scorpio 221, 222, 237, 252, 255, 256
MacDonnell, Ray 30, 33, 53
Mackenzie Cory 70, 71, 73, 78, 79, 80, 87, 91, 96, 98, 99
MacLaughlin, Don 107, 108, 114
Macrae, Elizabeth 226
Macy Alexander Forrester 147, 150, 151, 157, 158
Madame Mergeron 383
Maeve Stoddard 275–6
Maggie Cory 89, 97, 98, 102
Maggie Forrester 156–7
Maggie Scott 266
Maggie Simmons Horton 171, 185, 205
Maguire, Kathleen 340
Maia 396, 398
Maitland, Beth 376, 396
Malcolm Winters 397
Malis, Claire 323
Mallory, Ed 175
Mallory, Paul 188
Mallory, Victoria 362
Malloy, Larkin 275
Malone, Laura 72
Mamie Johnson 382, 394, 395, 399
Mantooth, Randolph 308, 314
Manza, Ralph 207
Marah Lewis 276, 278, 295, 327
Marcantel, Chris 270, 305, 314
Marcil, Vanessa 223, 247–48
Marco Dane 319, 326
Marcoux, Ted 330
Margo Flax 35
Margo Horton 173, 175
Margo Hughes 125, 128, 135, 141

Margo Lynley 144, 152
Margo Montgomery Hughes 111, 112, 119, 122, 130
Margo Spencer 147
Maria Santos Grey 41, 50, 59
Marianne Randolph 80
Marie Horton 166, 174, 187, 188
Marie, The Little French Princess 3
Marie Wallace 285
Mario Corelli 319, 326
Marion Colby 48
Mark Brooks 168, 187, 188
Mark Dalton 38
Mark, Flip 165
Mark Holden 263, 284, 285
Mark Toland 319, 322, 323–4
Marland, Douglas 17, 25–6, 28, 112, 270
Marlena Evans Craig Brady 172, 173, 174, 175–6, 178–84, 197, 198, 200
Marley Love Hudson McKinnon 75, 83, 84, 88, 91
Marlowe, Hugh 78
Marshall, Amelia 302
Marshall Lincoln Kramer III 76, 83, 90
Martha Frazier 283
Martin, Ricky 248, 249
Martin, Rudolf 54
Marty Dillman 267
Marty Hansen 171
Marty Saybrooke 333, 334, 339, 347
Marx, Gregg 184
Mary Frances "Frankie" Frame Winthrop 82, 85, 87, 89, 100, 101
Mary Kennicott 35
Mary Mae Ward 218, 222, 230, 233, 242, 246, 253
Mary Matthews 67, 68, 79
Mascolo, Joseph 166, 197
Masquerade 10
Masters, Marie 112, 133
Matt Clark 371, 385
Matt Cory 72, 75, 77, 79, 83, 87, 103
Matt Reardon 278, 281, 293–4
Mattson, Robin 54–5, 234
Mauceri, Patricia 335, 354
Maule, Brad 215, 236, 249
Maureen Reardon Bauer 273, 275
Max Holden 319, 331, 334, 335–6, 343, 345
Maxie Jones 221, 225
Maxwell, Frank 228
Mayer, Paul Avila 15
McCambridge, Mercedes 259

McCarthy, Julianna 358, 364
McCay, Peggy 177, 193, 205, 226
McClain, Cady 55–6
McClatchy, Kevin 97–8
McCloskey, Leigh J. 223, 237, 250–1
McCook, John 144, 149, 160
McCouch, Grayson 97
McCullough, Kimberly 215, 251–2
McCullough, Linda 269
McGuire, Maeve 70
McHale, Philip 338
McIntyre, Marilyn 305
McKee, Todd 148
McKinney, Kurt 293
McKinsey, Beverlee 70, 71, 274
McLaughlin, Emily 207, 208, 227, 228
McLean, Dick 165
McMahon, Julian 74
McVicar, Daniel 147
Meadows, Kristen 328
Meeker, Ken 330
Meg Baldwin 208, 210, 226
Meg Bennett 370
Megan Gordon 324, 332, 338, 341, 345
Melgar, Lilly 231
Melinda Cramer 323, 326, 335
Melissa "Missy" Palmer Matthews 67, 80–1
Menighan, Kelly 135
Meredith "Merri" Lord Wolek 319, 320, 322, 326, 336–7, 340, 341
Meredith Reade 276
Merrill Vochek 306
Meta Bauer Roberts Banning Banning 262–3, 283, 285
Michael Baldwin 358, 367
Michael Cates *see* "Stone" (Michael) Cates
Michael Horton 170–1, 173, 181, 188–9
Michael Hudson 71, 73, 83, 84, 88, 98, 102, 103, 104
Michael Randolph 80
Michael Scott 365, 369
Michael Shea 112, 124
Mickey Horton 166, 168, 169, 170–1, 181, 188
Miguel Morez 224, 248–9, 254
Mike Bauer 67, 80, 260, 265, 266, 267, 269, 270, 271, 272
Mike Costello 207
Mike Donovan 300, 305, 306, 308
Mikkos Cassadine 212
Miles, Joanna 37
Milgrim, Lynn 78
Miller, Allan 319, 322
Milli, Robert 268, 320

Mimi King 328
Mindy (Melinda Sue) Lewis 274, 275,
      276, 277, 291–2
Miranda Marlowe 111
Miss Susan 11
Mitch Blake 73, 79, 86, 87, 89
Mitch Williams 211
Mitchell, James 56–7
Mitchum, Carrie 145, 146, 149, 153
Modern Cinderella 6
Moment of Truth 14, 164
Mona Kane 30, 36, 37–38, 62
Monica Bard Webber Quartermaine
      210, 211, 215, 217, 219, 225–6,
      233, 234–5, 236, 244, 246
Moniz, Wendy 294
Montgomery, Julie 325
Monty, Gloria 12, 17
Moon, Philip 367, 377, 396
Mooney, William 35
Moore, Demi 213
Moore, Shemar 397
Moreland, Douglas 304
Morgan, Debbi 309, 312, 315
Morgan Richards 270, 271, 273
Morgan Winthrop 76, 77, 87, 97, 101
Morning Star 14, 164
Morris, Phil 365
Morrow, Joshua 371, 384–5
Moss, Ronn 143, 144, 149, 161
Mr. Big 111
Mrs. Wiggs of the Cabbage Patch 5
Muldoon, Patrick 180
Muniestieri, Mary Ryan 15
Murray, Mary Gordon 329, 344
Myrt and Marge 2, 6
Myrtle Lum Fargate 45

N

Nader, Michael 58
Nadine Cooper Lewis Cooper 278,
      279–80, 286, 287, 290
Nancy Davis 81–82
Nancy Hughes McClosky 107, 108,
      113–4, 124
Natalie Bannon 131
Natalie Dillon 48
Natalie Hunter 46, 55, 57, 58, 314
Nathan Hastings 399
Neal Alcott 116, 133, 140
Neal, Dylan 156
Neal, Kelly 303
Ned Ashton 211, 217, 219, 220, 222,
      223, 224, 225, 235, 237, 244–5,
      254

Neil Curtis 188, 197
Neil Wade 115
Neil Winters 397, 398
Nelson, Herb 259, 285
Never Too Young 164
Newman, Christine Tudor 315
Newman, Robert 273, 294–5
Nicholas Alamain 179, 180, 200, 202
Nicholas Newman 371, 385, 390, 395
Nicholas Reed 385, 386
Nicholas Van Buren 219
Nichols, Stephen 178, 184
Nick Andropoulos 127
Nick Davis 30, 33, 35, 37, 38
Nick McHenry Spaulding 278, 282,
      288, 291–2
Nick Terry 83, 97, 98, 102, 104
Nicole Love 89, 101, 103
Nielsen, Tom 270
"Niki Smith" 320, 330, 337
Nikki Reed Foster Bancroft Newman
      Abbott Abbott 357, 360, 362,
      363, 366, 368, 370, 373, 378,
      379, 383, 384, 386–88, 390, 391
Nina Webster Chancellor Kimble
      McNeil 371–2, 386, 391, 395
Nixon, Agnes 3, 8, 13, 14, 17, 20, 24,
      27, 29, 32, 63–5, 68, 172, 264,
      283, 304, 318
Noah Drake 212
Noah Keefer 45, 59, 61
Nola Reardon Chamberlain 270, 271,
      273, 301
Nora Gannon Buchanan 335, 344,
      351
Norcross, Clayton 144, 150
Noreen Vochek 305, 306
Northrop, Wayne 175, 179
Nouri, Michael 68
Nurses, The 164

O

O'Hurley, John 366
O'Keefe, Jody 97, 98
O'Leary, Michael 266, 281, 295–6
O'Rourke, Tom 336
O'Sullivan, James 35
Oakdale, Illinois 108
Olivia Barber Hastings 397, 399
Olympia Buchanan 328
Omar Rashid 153, 162, 163
One Life to Live 13, 17, 19–20, 21, 24,
      28, 68, 72, 172, 318–355
One Life to Live "Family Tree" 321
One Man's Family 12

Opal Gardner Purdy Cortlandt 36, 47, 49–50, 57
Orlena Grimaldi 111, 117, 121, 138, 139
Ortega, Santos 107, 113
Our Gal Sunday 7
Our Private World 68

P

Painted Dreams 3
Palermo, George 315
Palmer Cortlandt 42, 47, 49, 50, 55, 57–58
Paolo Seganti 138
Papa Bauer 262, 264, 284
Paradise Bay 14, 164
Parker, Frank 205
Parker, Jameson 68, 325
Parlato, Dennis 308, 315–6
Parrish, Miriam 205
Pat Ashley Kendall Lord 324, 328, 338
Pat Matthews Randolph 67, 77, 80, 265
"Patch" Johnson *see* Steve "Patch" Johnson
Patric London 332
Patrick Cutter 302
Patterson, Lee 319, 320, 341
Patty Williams 377
Paul Fletcher 266, 267, 283
Paul Hornsby 220, 244
Paul Kendall 325
Paul Martin 35–6, 37
Paul Slavinsky 308
Paul Stenbeck 135–6
Paul Stewart 108, 110, 117, 134, 141
Paul Williams 365, 367, 377, 378–9, 389, 396, 398
Paulina Cantrell Cory 72, 74, 76, 82, 91
Pearcy, Patricia 323
Pease, Patsy 189
Peck, J. Eddie 370, 372
Peg English 40
Peggy Brooks 358, 362, 394
Peggy Scott Dillman Fletcher 266, 267, 269
Peluso, Lisa 308, 316
Penberthy, Beverly 67, 77, 80
Penghlis, Thaao 169, 180, 197–198, 199
Pennock, Christopher 211
Penny Hughes 110, 115
Penny, Sydney 59
Pentecost, George 101

Pepper Young's Family 6
Perrault, Robert 35
Peter Blake 169, 180, 181, 189, 195, 204
Peter Cooney 57
Peter Jansen 326
Peter Lewis 278, 286, 290, 293
Peter Taylor 210
Peters, Pamela 358, 362
Peterson, Arthur 259
Petty Mercer 207
Peyton Place 10
Pfenning, Wesley Ann 79
Philip Mercer 207
Phillip Brent 30, 32–3, 34
Phillip Brewer 207, 208, 210, 228
Phillip Chancellor 360, 372, 375, 393, 394
Phillip Chancellor, III 386
Phillip Charles Tyler 34
Phillip Kiriakis 185, 191
Phillip Spaulding 272, 274, 276, 277
Phillips, Irna 3, 7, 9, 10, 11, 12, 13, 14, 20, 27, 29–30, 66, 106, 107, 108, 109, 143, 164–5, 258, 260, 262, 263–4, 265, 318, 360
Phillips, Joseph C. 218, 252–3
Phoebe English Tyler Wallingford 35, 36–7, 38, 45, 62–3, 115
Phyllis Romalotti 367, 376, 377, 378, 397
Pickles, Christina 70
Pierre Boulland 358
Pilon, Daniel 271, 296
Pine Valley 32
Pinkerton, Nancy 323
Pinter, Colleen Zenk 110, 112, 141
Pinter, Mark 71, 99, 104, 108, 112
Polen, Nat 320
Pomerantz, Jeffrey David 326
Ponzini, Anthony 320, 340
Port Charles, New York 208
Porter, Rick 73
Portia Faces Life 9, 12
Powers, Hunt 207
Prentiss, Ed 259
Price Trainor 319, 323
Prince Nicholas 176
Prince, William 67, 81
"Princess" 335, 337
Princi, Elaine 111, 323
Prinz, Rosemary 30, 110, 115
Priscilla Longworth 207
Pryor, Nicholas 37, 67, 81
Purdee, Nathan 354

Q

Quinton McCord Chamberlain 271, 273

R

Rabat, Ken 35
Rabin, Al 175
Rachel Davis Matthews Frame Cory 68, 70, 71, 72, 73, 74, 76–7, 78, 79, 80, 81, 84, 85, 87, 89, 91, 92, 95, 96, 99, 103
Rachel Gannon 351
Rafe Garrison 330
Raines, Ron 271, 296
Rapaleye, Mary Lyn 326
Ray Gordon 79
Reagan, Michael 365
Rebecca "Becky" Lee Abbott Abbott 329
Rebecca LeClair 172, 173, 185, 185
Recht, Tracey E. Bregman 153, 377, 388–9
Reckell, Peter 189, 199
Redeker, Quinn 168, 377, 386
Reed, Margaret 136
Reeves, Melissa (Brennan) 172, 189, 201
Reeves, Scott 385
Reginald Love 96, 103
Reid, Frances 165, 166, 186
Reinholt, George 64, 68, 72, 79, 324, 338
Renee Divine Buchanan 319, 332, 353
Renee Dumonde 169
Return to Peyton Place 15
Reva Shayne Lewis Lewis Lewis 274, 275, 276, 277, 278, 281, 290, 293, 295, 296, 299
Reverend Rutledge 260
Rex Allingham 101
Rex Sterling 375, 377, 384, 386, 394
Reynolds, James 205
Rhinehart, Joanna 136
Rich Man's Darling 6
Richard Grant 284
Richard Martin 168
Riche, Wendy 227
Rick Bauer 266, 268, 274, 276, 282, 295, 298, 299
Rick Webber 210, 211, 214, 235–6, 236
Ridge Forrester 143, 144, 146, 149–50, 162, 163, 389
Right to Happiness 9
Riley, John 215
Rinna, Lisa 180

Ripa, Kelly 60
Rita Mae Bristow 305
Rita Stapleton 269, 296, 300
Ritchie, Clint 70, 319, 348–9
R.J. Glover 351, 354
Road of Life, The 7, 12
Road to Reality, The 13, 206
Rob Coronal 330
Robert "Bob" Hughes 113–4
Robert LeClair 173, 175, 184, 186
Robert Scorpio 212, 213, 214, 215, 216, 218, 220–1, 252, 256–7
Robin Holden 265
Robin Jacobs 188
Robin Scorpio 215, 216, 221, 226–7, 252, 255, 257
Robinson, Chris 234
Rocco Carner 144, 152
Rodell, Barbara 268
Roerick, William 293, 303
Roger Forbes 305, 306
Roger Gordon 332, 338
Roger Thorpe 266, 268, 269, 276, 278, 279, 281, 288–9, 290, 293, 294, 299, 300–1, 330
Rogers, Ingrid 61
Rogers, Suzanne 185, 205
Rogers, Tristan 212, 214
Roman Brady 175–6, 178, 179, 191, 197, 200
Romance of Helen Trent, The 4
Rose DeVille 372
Rose Donovan 305
Rose Kelly 215
Roseanne 223
Rosemary 10
Rosemary Kramer 119
Ross Chandler 42, 57
Ross Lewis 276, 292
Ross Marler 273, 281, 292, 293, 294, 299
Roszell, Jennifer 297
Roux, Carol 67, 80
Rowand, Nada 309, 316–7
Rowell, Victoria 397
Roxie Shayne 275
Roy Lansing 207
Roy McGuire 115
Royce Keller 116, 133, 136
Roylance, Pamela 188
Ruby Anderson 215
Ruby Bright 332
Russ Frame 79
Russ Matthews 67, 68, 73, 74, 79–80, 92, 95
Rusty Shayne 276, 277
Ruth Brent Martin 30, 34, 37, 44

Ryan Chamberlain 221, 224, 247
Ryan Harrison 71, 74, 75, 76, 85, 94, 96, 99, 100, 104–5
Ryan McNeil 372, 385–6, 391, 398
Ryan, Meg 111
Ryan, Michael M. 80
Ryan's Hope 15–16

S

Sabatino, Michael 157, 179
Sabato, Antonio, Jr. 223
Sadie Gray 323
St. John, Kristoff 398
Salem, Massachusetts 165–7
Sally Frame 72
Sally McGuire 358, 364
Sally Spectra 147, 150, 157–8, 372
Sally Spencer 79
Sam 'n' Henry 2
Sam Fowler 73
Samantha "Sami" Brady 174, 176, 179, 194, 202–3
Samantha Markham 116, 125, 133, 136, 140
Samantha Vernon 325, 328, 330
Samms, Emma 213, 214, 220, 221
Sampler, Philece 169
Sandy Alexander Cory 72, 73, 89, 96, 98
Sandy, Gary 68
Sandy Horton 168, 187, 188
Sandy Wilson 114
Santa Barbara 17–18, 23
Sara McIntyre 266, 267
Sarah Gordon 332, 339
Satra, Sonia 280, 297
Saunders, Lanna 188
Schnetzer, Stephen 71, 98, 100, 101
Schultz, Jacqueline 112
Scott Banning 169, 170
Scott Eldridge 110, 116, 124, 125, 131, 140–1
Scott Grainger 366, 381, 389
Scott, Melody Thomas 357, 370, 386, 390, 391
Scott Parker 42
Scotty Baldwin 208, 210, 211, 212, 214, 216, 221, 223, 230, 237
Seaforth, Susan *see* Hayes, Susan Seaforth
Sean Donely 215, 216
Sean Reardon 290
Search for Tomorrow 10, 11–12, 19, 64, 166, 260, 262, 318

Secret Storm, The 12, 206
Seganti, Paolo 111, 117, 121, 137
Selleck, Tom 357
Serena Baldwin 221
Serrano, Diego 97, 102
Shackleford, Ted 79
Shana Sloane 306, 308, 309, 311
Shane Donovan 176, 177, 178, 186, 189, 191
Shannon O'Hara 136, 137
Sharlene Frame Matthews Watts Hudson 73, 74, 76, 80, 87, 92, 94, 102
Sharon Collins 371, 385, 395
Sharon, Fran 78
Shaughnessy, Charles 176, 189
Shaw, Irwin 5
Shawn Brady 191, 205
Shawn-Douglas Brady 177, 179, 185–6, 200
Shayne, Carl 223
Shearin, John 305
Sheila Carter Grainger Rashid Forrester 150, 154, 155, 389
Shepherd, Ann 260
Shipp, John Wesley 270
Shortridge, Stephen 144, 153
Shriner, Kin 211
Shuman, Roy 112
Sid Dickerson 282, 302, 303
Siegel, Eileen Riley 342
Silver Dalton 38
Simon, Peter 297–298
Simone Hardy 217–18, 230, 231, 270
Sisk, Laura 313, 317
Slate, Jeremy 328
Slezak, Erika 319, 337, 349–50
Sloan Carpenter 333, 337–8, 343, 346, 347, 349
Sloan, Nancy 144, 147, 151
Sloan, Tina 303
Smith Family, The 1, 2
Smith, Hillary B. 335, 344, 350
Smith, Melanie 111
"Snapper" Foster *see* William "Snapper" Foster
Snyder, Nancy 326
Sofer, Rena 220, 253
Somerset 14, 68
Song of the City 4
Sonny Corinthos 223–4, 231, 248, 251, 254
Sorel, Louise 179, 200, 201, 202
Spencer, Gillian 57, 337
Spencer Harrison 71, 74, 76, 85, 93–4, 96, 104–5

Springfield 260
Springfield, Rick 212
Staab, Leonard 290
Stacey Donovan Forbes 305, 311, 313, 315
Stafford, Jane Marie 296
Stafford, Michelle 376, 398
Stanley Norris 268
Starcher, Brian 112
Stauffer, Jack 30
Stavros Cassadine 214
Stefano DiMera 166, 169, 176, 177, 178, 180, 181, 183, 193, 197, 198, 200, 203, 204
Stella Dallas 9
Stephanie "Steffi" Brewster 309, 310, 313, 315, 316
Stephanie Forrester 144, 146, 148, 149, 157
Stephen Logan, Jr. see "Storm" (Stephen, Jr.) Logan
Stephens, Perry 305
Stepmother 9
Steve "Patch" Johnson 178, 184, 189, 204
Steve Andropoulos 108
Steve Burke 322, 328, 331, 332, 341
Steve Connelly 379, 396
Steve Frame 64, 68, 71, 72, 73, 77, 79, 85, 87, 95, 103, 324, 338
Steve Hardy 207, 208, 217, 227
Steve Holden 332
Steve Jackson 265, 269
Steve Logan 147
Steve Olson 165
Steven Lars 234
Steven Lassiter 370, 383
Stevens, K.T. 207
Stevenson, Robert J. 165
Stewart, Catherine Mary 178
Stewart, Don 67, 80, 265
Stewart, Trish 358, 361
Stickney, Timothy D. 354–5
"Stone" (Michael) Cates 223, 226–7, 231, 252, 255, 257
"Storm" (Stephen, Jr.) Logan 143, 144, 147, 150–1
Storm, James 340, 345
Storm, Jim 144, 146, 151
Storm, Michael 340, 341, 345
Story of Mary Marlin, The 5
Strange Paradise 71
Strasser, Robin 35, 64, 68, 71, 319, 323, 351
Street, Roberta 366
Strudwick, Shepperd 78, 319, 336
Stuart, Anna 83, 102

Stuart Brooks 358, 362–3, 364, 394
Stuart Chandler 40, 41, 42–3, 382
Sudro, Lyle 259, 285
Sung, Elizabeth 398
Susan Burke Stewart McDermott 108, 112, 114, 122, 127, 134, 135
Susan Martin 166–7, 169, 170
Susan Matthews 78
Susan Moore 213, 214, 233, 235, 236
Sutton, Michael 223, 226, 252, 254
Swan, Michael 120
Sward, Anne 111, 119
Sweeney, Alison 202

T

Tad Gardner Martin 40, 44, 47–48, 56, 57
Talbot Huddleston 325–6
Tangie Hill 279, 282, 295
Tanya Roskov Jones 216, 240, 250
Tara Martin 30, 32, 33, 34–5
Taylor, Elizabeth 206, 207, 214, 215
Taylor Hamilton Hayes Forrester 146, 150, 153, 155, 162–3
Taylor, Holland 68
Taylor, Josh 184
Taylor, Lauren–Marie 305
Taylor Roxbury Cannon 45, 61
Ted Brent 30, 32
Ted Clark 80
Ted Clayton 328, 338, 340
Ted Holmes 240
Ted Orsini 47, 56
Ted White 283, 284
Templeton, Christopher 365
Terri Brock 215
Terry Regan: Attorney at Law 8
Tesreau, Krista 274, 338, 351–2
Tess Wilder 309, 313, 314
Texas 15, 16, 70, 327
Thayer, Brynn 319, 324
Thinnes, Roy 207, 208, 228, 330, 333, 343
Thomas, Christine 30, 33
Thorne Forrester 143, 144, 146, 148, 150, 151
Thorson, Linda 349
Tiffany Hill 215–6, 218, 219, 250
Tim "T.J." Werner 270, 271
Tim Siegel 324–5, 340
Times for Us, A 164
Timothy Hunter Dillon 314
Tina Clayton Lord Roberts 326, 328, 330, 331, 332, 334, 336, 338–9, 345, 348

Today's Children 9
Todd Manning 333–4, 336, 339
Todd Tori 335, 336
Tognani, Gina 335
Tom Baldwin, Jr. *see* Tom Hardy
Tom Baxter 67, 80, 81
Tom Cudahy 40
Tom Dennison 331, 342
Tom Edwards 319, 320
Tom Hardy 208, 217–8, 230–1
Tom, Heather 370, 372, 390
Tom Horton 165, 166, 168, 169, 186
Tom Horton, Jr. 166, 168, 187, 188
Tom Hughes 111, 112, 114, 116, 123, 124, 128, 130–1, 135
Tomas Rivera 97, 98, 102
"Tommy" 335, 337
Tommy Horton *see* Tom Horton, Jr.
Tonio Reyes 129, 135
Tony Cassadine 212
Tony DiMera 169, 180, 181, 183, 193, 197
Tony Jones 215, 216, 219, 221, 225, 236, 240, 249–50
Tony Merrill 165
Tony Randolph Lord 324, 325, 330, 336, 338
Tony the Tuna 99–100
Topping, Lynn 361
"Tori" 337
Trachta, Jeff 143, 150, 161
Traci Abbott Romalotti Carlton Connelly 365, 376, 379, 384, 389, 396, 397
Tracy Delmar 266, 267
Tracy Quartermaine 211, 217, 219, 220, 235, 236, 244
Travis Montgomery 38, 63
Tremayne, Les 336
Trent, Joey 67, 79
Trevor Dillon 46, 48, 55
Trish Clayton 173
Trish Lewis 273, 274
Trisha Alden 308, 309, 311, 315
Trucker McKenzie 308–9, 310, 311, 313
Trudy Bauer 262–3
Trustman, Susan 67, 80
Tuck, Jessica 332
Tulley, Paul 340
Turner, Janine 213
Tylo, Hunter 146, 161–2
Tylo, Michael 271, 273, 399
Tyrone Jackson 365
Tyson, Cicely 283

V

Valerie Grant 172
Valley, Mark 181, 203–4
Valley, Paul Michael 71, 96, 104
van Devere, Trish 336
Vanessa Chamberlain Lewis 273, 274, 275, 276, 278, 281, 290, 292, 293, 294
Vaughn, Robert 142
ver Dorn, Jerry 273, 298
Verla Grubbs 62
Vic and Sade 2
Victor Cassadine 212
Victor Kiriakis 169, 177, 179, 181, 185, 186, 191, 202, 204
Victor Lord 319, 320, 322, 324, 330, 332, 334, 335, 336, 337, 338, 339, 343, 346, 355
Victor Newman 360, 361, 362, 365, 366, 368, 369–70, 373, 382, 383, 384, 385, 386, 387, 388, 390, 391, 392, 393, 395
Victor Newman, Jr. 373, 385, 388, 390
Victoria "Viki" Lord Gordon Riley Burke Riley Buchanan Buchanan Buchanan Carpenter 320, 322, 324, 325, 327, 329, 330, 331, 332, 333, 334, 335, 337–8, 346, 347, 348, 349
Victoria Love Frame Harrison Hudson 73, 74, 75, 83, 84–5, 88, 91, 94, 99, 100, 103, 104
Victoria Newman McNeil Howard 370, 372, 379, 386, 387, 390–2
Vigard, Kristen 270
Vinnie Wolek 320, 322, 323, 325, 328, 340, 341
Vivian Alamain 179, 181, 185, 191, 200, 202

W

Wagner, Helen 107, 108, 114, 138
Wagner, Jack 215
Wagner, Kristina 215, 256
Walker, Marcie 295, 279
Walker, Nicholas 345
Walker, Tonja 344, 352
Walters, Alexander 139
Walters, Susan 305
Walton, Jess 392
Wanda Webb 322
Ward, Maitland 156
Warrick, Lee 322

Warrick, Ruth 35, 36, 61–2, 107, 110, 115
Watkins, Tuc 334, 342, 355
Watros, Cynthia 281, 282, 299
Watson, Douglass 70, 71, 73
Wayne, Ethan 143, 144, 150
Weatherly, Michael 310
Weaver, Patty 375, 376
Weaver, Sigourney 68
Wedgeworth, Ann 68
Weiss, Michael 188
Wells, Sarajane 259
Wendy Warren (Girl Reporter) 10
Wert, Douglas 140
Wesley, Kassie 334, 355
When a Girl Marries 9
Whit McColl 124
White, Peter 37
Wickwire, Nancy 78
Widdoes, Kathleen 129, 139
Will Cooney 48, 55, 56
Will Jeffries 276, 277
Will Vernon 325, 326, 330
Willey, Walt 63
William "Snapper" Foster, Jr. 358, 360, 361, 363, 364
William Edward Bauer, Jr. *see* Ed Bauer
William Foster Abbott 364, 368, 382, 394
William Matthews 78
William Spencer 144
Williams, Ann 305
Williams, Billy Dee 283
Williams, Darnell 309, 317
Williams, JoBeth 68

Williams, Tonya Lee 399
Willis Frame 79
Wines, Christopher 30, 35
Winsor, Roy 318
Witter, Karen 338
Wolters, Sherilyn 213
Woman in White 9
Woman of America 10
Woman to Remember, A 11
Woods, Robert S. 70, 319, 344, 353
Wyndham, Victoria 64, 71, 77, 96, 105

Y

York, John J. 221, 237, 252, 256
Young and the Restless, The 14, 15, 16, 17, 20, 22, 23, 26, 66, 165, 168, 169, 172, 356–399
Young and the Restless, The "Family Tree" 359
Young Dr. Malone 9
Young, John M. 9
Young Marrieds, The 13
Your Family and Mine 9
Yourman, Alice 259, 285

Z

Zaslow, Michael 268, 300, 330, 342
Zeman, Jacklyn 211, 236, 257, 325
Zenk, Colleen *see* Pinter, Colleen Zenk
Zimmer, Kim 295, 301, 328